The 9 Competencies and 31 Component Behaviors (EPAS, 2015):	Chapter(s) Where Referenced:
Competency 5 Engage in Policy Practice:	
a. Identify social policy at the local, state, and federal level that impacts well-being, service delivery, and access to social services.	4, 7, 8, 9, 12, 13, 14, 15
b. Assess how social welfare and economic policies impact the delivery of and access to social services.	14
c. Apply critical thinking to analyze, formulate, and advocate for policies that advance human rights and social, economic, and environmental justice.	1, 2, 4, 5, 6, 7, 8, 9, 10, 11, 12, 13, 14, 15
Competency 6 Engage with Individuals, Families, Groups, Organizations, and Communities:	
a. Apply knowledge of human behavior and the social environment, person-in-environment, and other multidisciplinary theoretical frameworks to engage with clients and constituencies.	
b. Use empathy, reflection, and interpersonal skills to effectively engage diverse clients and constituencies.	3
Competency 7 Assess Individuals, Families, Groups, Organizations, and Communities:	
a. Collect and organize data, and apply critical thinking to interpret information from clients and constituencies.	
b. Apply knowledge of human behavior and the social environment, person-in-environment, and other multidisciplinary theoretical frameworks in the analysis of assessment data from clients and constituencies.	
c. Develop mutually agreed-on intervention goals and objectives based on the critical assessment of strengths, needs, and challenges within clients and constituencies.	
d. Select appropriate intervention strategies based on the assessment, research knowledge, and values and preferences of clients and constituencies.	
Competency 8 Intervene with Individuals, Families, Groups, Organizations, and Communities:	
a. Critically choose and implement interventions to achieve practice goals and enhance capacities of clients and constituencies.	
b. Apply knowledge of human behavior and the social environment, person-in-environment, and other multidisciplinary theoretical frameworks in interventions with clients and constituencies.	
c. Use inter-professional collaboration as appropriate to achieve beneficial practice.	
d. Negotiate, mediate, and advocate with and on behalf of diverse clients and constituencies.	1, 2, 3, 5, 6, 7, 8, 10, 11
e. Facilitate effective transitions and endings that advance mutually agreed-on goals.	
Competency 9 Evaluate Practice with Individuals, Families, Groups, Organizations, and Communities:	
a. Select and use appropriate methods for evaluation of outcomes.	
b. Apply knowledge of human behavior and the social environment, person-in-environment, and other multidisciplinary theoretical frameworks in the evaluation of outcomes.	
c. Critically analyze, monitor, and evaluate intervention and program processes and outcomes.	
d. Apply evaluation findings to improve practice effectiveness at the micro, mezzo, and macro levels.	

empowerment series

Foundations of Social Policy
Social Justice in Human Perspective

Sixth Edition

Amanda Smith Barusch

University of Otago, New Zealand and
University of Utah, U.S.A

Australia • Brazil • Canada • Mexico • Singapore • United Kingdom • United States

Empowerment Series: Foundations of Social Policy: Social Justice in Human Perspective, Sixth Edition
Amanda Smith Barusch

Product Director: Marta Lee-Perriard

Product Manager: Julie Martinez

Content Developer: Alexander J Hancock

Product Assistant: Allison Balchunas

Marketing Manager: Zina Craft

Art and Cover Direction, Production Management, and Composition: Lumina Datamatics, Inc.

Manufacturing Planner: Karen Hunt

Cover Image: carterdayne/E+/Getty Images

Unless otherwise noted all items © Cengage Learning®

For product information and technology assistance, contact us at
Cengage Customer & Sales Support, 1-800-354-9706.
For permission to use material from this text or product, submit all requests online at **cengage.com/permissions.** Further permissions questions can be e-mailed to **permissionrequest@cengage.com.**

Library of Congress Control Number: 2016963459

ISBN: 978-1-305-94324-7

Cengage
200 Pier 4 Boulevard
Boston, MA 02210
USA

Cengage is a leading provider of customized learning solutions with employees residing in nearly 40 different countries and sales in more than 125 countries around the world. Find your local representative at **www.cengage.com**.

To learn more about Cengage platforms and services, register or access your online learning solution, or purchase materials for your course, visit **www.cengage.com**.

Printed in Mexico
Print Number: 09   Print Year: 2022

Dedicated to my beloved, Lawrence Roos Barusch

Preface

Social workers promote social justice. . . .
—**PREAMBLE TO THE NASW CODE OF ETHICS (1996)**

Social justice is central to the mission of social work and the focus of intense debate throughout the world. Social work professionals contribute to these debates, providing a personal and deeply empathetic understanding of the consequences of injustice for the vulnerable populations we serve.

Like most people, social workers (and social work students) understand justice less in an abstract sense and more in the ways events and conditions affect individual lives. This text takes a human perspective on social justice, focusing on the ways individuals shape policy as well as the ways policy touches our lives. Most chapters begin with human examples that help focus our analysis and critique. Content also includes biographical material on policy leaders and the direct experiences of social advocates. At the same time, the book takes a global look at social policy. Together, the international content and the human perspective prepare students to work effectively in policy arenas that extend beyond the traditional turf of social work and equip them to advocate for vulnerable people in the United States and throughout the world.

About the Book

This book is designed for use in foundation social policy courses and is organized in three parts. Part I introduces U.S. social policy and policy practice, Part II addresses social problems that have been (or are becoming) targets for collective action, and Part III focuses on vulnerable populations. A brief conclusion addresses global social policy concerns. Discussion topics, web-based exercises, suggested readings, and relevant websites are included at the end of each chapter.

Theoretical content is interspersed throughout. Social justice theory is addressed in detail in Chapter 1. The introduction to Part II offers a framework for understanding when and why certain problems become the targets of collective action. The introduction to Part III considers discrimination and oppression from a theoretical perspective and introduces the concepts of **intersectionality** and **implicit bias**. Finally, theories of liberation are discussed in the Conclusion.

Part I includes Chapters 1 through 3. Chapter 1 discusses social justice from theoretical and philosophical perspectives, tying these viewpoints to contemporary U.S. social policy. The role of government in promoting social justice is the focus of Chapter 2, which links philosophical perspectives to contemporary politics and describes the structure and function of the U.S. government and provides an introduction to U.S. tax policy. Chapter 3 begins with a case study in advocacy and then presents policy analysis frameworks and techniques before addressing philosophical and tactical considerations in policy practice.

Part II introduces a framework for determining when a group or a nation will develop collective responses to social problems. Chapters in this part of the book examine problems that have been approached through collective action in the United States: Social Security (Chapter 4), poverty and inequality (Chapter 5), physical illness (Chapter 6), mental illness (Chapter 7), disability (Chapter 8), and criminal justice (Chapter 9). Each chapter opens with a human perspective. These brief case studies are based on interviews with people chosen because their experiences illustrate key issues related to the chapter's topic. Following the case study, we explore the development of policies and services, as well as contemporary policy issues and debates. These chapters provide background material necessary for students to apply the policy analysis frameworks introduced in Chapter 3.

Part III introduces the concepts of discrimination, oppression, implicit bias, and intersectionality. Each chapter explores a population that has experienced oppression in the United States: people of color (Chapter 10); gay, lesbian, bisexual, and transgendered individuals (Chapter 11); children (Chapter 12); women (Chapter 13); the elderly (Chapter 14); and working Americans (Chapter 15). The structure of these chapters mirrors Part II, with the addition of major social/demographic trends affecting each population.

The book closes with a glance toward the future of our profession within a global context. Following an introduction to theories of liberation, the Conclusion revisits the philosophical perspectives presented in Chapter 1 and considers the implications of globalization, rising inequality, and environmental justice for the social welfare state and the social work profession.

What's New in the Sixth Edition

When I began working on the first edition of this book, I never imagined it would extend to a sixth edition. Each revision has brought the tantalizing fantasy of absolute perfection, and each has delivered the slightly less tantalizing reality of steady improvement. Those familiar with previous editions of the book will find some changes. I have, of course, updated demographic figures and policy content, as well as the web-based exercises. In addition, I continue to revise in the hope of making the book more engaging and readable.

This edition reflects major sea changes in U.S. social policy. It has a new chapter on crime and criminal justice, not because the risk of crime is any more widespread than it was when the first edition came out, but because the risk of incarceration bears down so heavily on people of color and vulnerable communities. Another sea change: marriage equality and its ripple effects are celebrated in this edition. The election of Donald Trump is addressed, though its policy implications remain unclear as we go to press. The new edition also reflects changes more accurately characterized as "shifts" in policy and its context. It includes:

- Expanded treatment of inequality (trends, causes, and consequences) (Chapter 5)
- Introduction to "social impact bonding," a new incarnation of privatization also known as "Pay for Success" (Chapter 4)
- Expanded content on trafficking as a labor issue (Chapter 15)
- Discussion of legalization of marijuana (Chapter 9)
- Consideration of the impact of the Affordable Care Act (Chapter 6)
- Introduction of the concept of "implicit bias" (Introduction to Part II)
- Discussion of the decline in U.S. manufacturing that set the stage for the election of Donald Trump (Chapter 15)

Additional new content is outlined below:

- Chapter 1 introduces new content on social class and upward .
- Chapter 2 introduces social impact bonding and discusses tax preparation for vulnerable taxpayers.
- Chapter 4 includes updates from the 2016 OASDI Trustee Report.
- Chapter 5 examines the global decline in poverty and, consistent with its new title, provides expanded content on inequality.
- Chapter 6 offers new content on the ACA, looking at its impact as well as the controversy over the requirement that insurance cover contraceptive care and the Supreme Court decisions in *Burwell v. Hobby Lobby Stores* and *King v. Burwell*.
- Chapter 7 has a new box on the prevention of home-grown terrorism, as well as an introduction to the 21st Century Cures Act.
- Chapter 8 includes new content on the disproportionate representation of children of color in special education programs.
- Chapter 9 examines the history of criminal and juvenile justice, locating the roots of mass incarceration of Americans in the failed wars on crime and drugs. It considers the ripple effects of this phenomenon and the disproportionate representation of people of color in all components of the U.S. **carceral state**. The chapter also introduces the concept of restorative justice as an alternative paradigm.
- Chapter 11 discusses the *Obergefell v. Hodges* case, which established marriage equality in the United States, and explores policies that affect GLBTQ individuals.
- Chapter 12 includes an expanded discussion of trauma, referencing the Adverse Childhood Experiences (ACE) studies.
- Chapter 14 discusses recent expansions in access to assisted suicide through state legislation and referendums.
- Chapter 15 examines the causes and consequences of the decline in U.S. manufacturing.

About the Educational Policy and Accreditations Standards (EPAS)

Established in 1952, the Council on Social Work Education is charged with ensuring that social work programs throughout the United States meet certain standards.[1] In 2015, these standards were revised to refine the 2008 focus on competency-based education. Following a consultative process, nine core competencies were identified by the Commission on Accreditation. Each social work program must now demonstrate how it delivers and assesses these core competencies, most of which relate to some aspect of policy analysis or policy practice. Table P.1 inside the front cover summarizes the EPAS competencies and indicates where they are addressed in this text.

Instructor Supplements

The **Online Instructor's Manual** contains information to assist the instructor in designing the course, including assignment rubrics, discussion questions, teaching and learning activities, learning objectives, and additional online resources.

The **Online Test Bank** includes true/false, multiple-choice, and essay questions for each chapter. Each question is tied to learning objectives and EPAS standards.

---

[1] Although global standards have been approved by the International Association of Schools of Social Work in cooperation with the International Federation of Social Workers (Sewpaul & Jones, 2004), there is no international accrediting authority for the profession: each nation operates a separate process.

Online PowerPoint Slides are available to assist instructors with their lecture by providing concept coverage using images, figures, and tables directly from the textbook.

An **Online Curriculum Quick Guide** provides instructors with a table to correlate the core text and available test bank questions with updated EPAS standards.

MindTap

MindTap®, a digital teaching and learning solution, helps students be more successful and confident in the course — and in their work with clients. MindTap guides students through the course by combining the complete textbook with interactive multimedia, activities, assessments, and learning tools. Readings and activities engage students in learning core concepts, practicing needed skills, reflecting on their attitudes and opinions, and applying what they learn. Videos of client sessions illustrate skills and concepts in action, while case studies ask students to make decisions and think critically about the types of situations they'll encounter on the job. Helper Studio activities put students in the role of the helper, allowing them to build and practice skills in a non-threatening environment by responding via video to a virtual client. Instructors can rearrange and add content to personalize their MindTap course and easily track students' progress with real-time analytics. Finally, MindTap integrates seamlessly with any learning management system.

An Invitation

Since the first edition of this book was published, I have received phone calls, e-mails, and visits from readers offering suggestions, corrections, and compliments. This input is terrifically valuable each time I update the book. Whether you are an instructor or a student, I would love to hear from you! Let me know what works and (more important, really) what doesn't work in this new edition. Please send your comments to Amanda.Barusch@socwk.utah.edu, with "foundations text" in the subject line, or write me at the College of Social Work, 395 South 1500 East, University of Utah, Salt Lake City, UT 84112. I look forward to hearing from you.

Acknowledgments

Each edition of this book benefited from the talents and energies of my students, colleagues, and friends at the University of Utah and the University of Otago, my home away from home in New Zealand.

The sixth edition of this book reflects the creative efforts of many. Janet Tilden served as copy editor. Her careful attention to detail and commitment to excellence is evident in every page. Cengage Content Developer Alexander Hancock kept me going while he lined up images and managed endless details for Cengage. He shepherded the publication process with great élan. Sharib Asrar, Associate Program Manager at Lumina Datamatics, saw the manuscript through production.

People from various walks of life shared their experiences with me to contribute to the education of professional social workers. The stories they told enrich every chapter. Although I can't name them here, I will always be grateful for the time we spent together.

My family is at the center of everything. My husband Larry tolerated my absence and distraction with infinite patience and served as my resident expert on taxation and homelessness. Our children are a constant source of amazement and inspiration. Nathan questions the habits and assumptions of medical practice even as he delivers psychiatric care to those with mental illness. Meanwhile, in her legal practice, Ariana fights every day to protect the rights of vulnerable families and individuals.

Brief Contents

Contents

Policy Analysis: Frameworks and Tools

© Neil Orloff. Courtesy Art Access Gallery, Salt Lake City, Utah

Solidarity and justice go hand in hand.

Social justice is central to social work practice. But what is it? This is the focus of Part I, which moves from a broad theoretical consideration of social justice, through the role of government as a vehicle for promoting social justice, to the application of a social justice framework in policy practice. Chapter 1 reviews **modern** and **postmodern** approaches to defining this surprisingly elusive concept. Processes and components of justice are considered, and the link between justice and **human rights** is introduced. The chapter then examines three philosophical conceptions of social justice. Understanding these divergent perspectives will strengthen your analytic skills, enabling you to recognize the assumptions underlying other people's arguments and to frame your own arguments in terms more likely to persuade. Following a brief discussion of inequality, the chapter explores the role of social work in America's pursuit of social justice and introduces Bertha Capen Reynolds, a 20th-century policy practitioner. Government is an important vehicle for defining and promoting social justice. Chapter 2 examines the philosophical perspectives of political parties and offers a general description of the structure and processes of the U.S. government and an introduction to **privatization**. Chapter 2 provides a brief introduction to the nation's tax system that considers not only the mechanics but also the philosophical assumptions that drive the system. For some readers, this chapter will be a review, but for most it offers new insights and useful reference material. Chapter 3 turns to policy practice skills, focusing on analysis and advocacy strategies. The chapter presents a brief definition of policy practice followed by an extensive discussion of policy analysis that addresses advocacy and empowerment, drawing upon advice and experiences of advocates throughout the country. Chapter 3 closes with the ethical issues and legal considerations that influence policy practice.

Social Justice and Social Workers

No, no, we are not satisfied, and we will not be satisfied until justice rolls down like waters and righteousness like a mighty stream.

MARTIN LUTHER KING JR.

Learning Objectives

This chapter will help prepare students to:

LO 1-1   Develop a well-informed definition of social justice

LO 1-2   Understand the processes by which social justice is achieved

LO 1-3   Identify the components of social justice

LO 1-4   Discuss the philosophical underpinnings of capitalism and its alternatives

LO 1-5   Discuss the relevance of social justice for micro and macro practice

LO 1-6   Describe the role of the social work profession in promoting social justice

LO 1-1   Develop a Well-Informed Definition of Social Justice

EP 2
EP 3a

"Social workers promote social justice," according to the preamble to the National Association of Social Workers Code of Ethics (NASW, n.d.). This simple statement raises a slew of questions, beginning with definitions. What is social justice? Here, we consider two approaches to this question that stem from contrasting views on the nature of reality: the "modern" and the "postmodern." The modern view treats justice as an objective, achievable end, or goal. Social workers often take this perspective, setting forth the characteristics of a just society. The postmodern view rejects the idea of an objective standard and holds that justice is socially constructed. This approach shifts our attention to the process by which groups and societies decide what is just.[1]

---

[1]The terms "social justice," "social and economic justice," and "distributive justice" are often used interchangeably. In this book, I use the term "social justice" to be consistent with our professional literature.

A HUMAN PERSPECTIVE   Melissa Williams

On a hot day in June, 150 people, mostly women, met in a hotel to discuss welfare and domestic violence. The program was led by a social worker and attended by state legislators, social workers, welfare administrators, academics, advocates, and religious leaders. In the context of a national debate about welfare reform, this session was designed to raise awareness of the importance of welfare as a resource for women leaving abusive homes. One such woman was Melissa Williams. During the luncheon, she and three other women told their stories.

Melissa is an attractive young woman with flowing blond hair and a gentle, reflective way of speaking. Clearly intimidated by the size of the group and the lectern in front of her, she spoke haltingly of her experiences with welfare and domestic violence.

Melissa grew up in a working-class family. Her father worked for a mining company and had little interest in children, let alone female children. Her mother was a silent woman, struggling to raise a large family on a miner's salary. Neither parent was physically abusive, but both reminded the children repeatedly that they were "worth less than nothing." For Melissa this emotional abuse intensified during puberty. Miserable in her own family, Melissa saw marriage to her boyfriend, Will, as a way out.

Will was strong, energetic, and determined. He seemed to have the world by the tail and promised the protection and appreciation that Melissa had never enjoyed. At 16, she married him. She laughed, recalling that "everyone thought we had to get married, but I wasn't even pregnant!"

Melissa did get pregnant immediately and left high school. Her husband finished high school and found a "good job"—one with health benefits. They rented an apartment and settled in. Three children were born in rapid succession. Will's job began to feel more and more like a dead end, and he took to hanging out in bars with old high school friends. He'd come home drunk and take out his anger on Melissa. Her medical records show three visits to the emergency room with facial bruising, lacerations, and a broken arm.

Suffering from a debilitating depression, Melissa was not roused to action until Will attacked one of the children. It was just a slap, but it was enough to send Melissa back to her parents' home, where her depression worsened. Her parents encouraged Melissa to stay away from her husband, but they could not afford to support Melissa and her three children. So, one day, Melissa and her mother took the bus to the welfare office. Melissa was enrolled in the "self-sufficiency program" and awarded emergency housing assistance. Depression was identified as a barrier to employment, and her caseworker arranged for counseling and medication. She also introduced Melissa to a women's advocacy group called JEDI Women (Justice, Economic Dignity, and Independence for Women).

At the time of the conference, Melissa was living independently with her children. She had divorced her husband and did not expect to remarry. Antidepressants and a support group were critical to her ongoing success. Her children had residual health and behavioral problems from witnessing domestic violence.

Deeply moved by Melissa's experience, her audience resolved to ensure that welfare reform in their state would not eliminate a key resource for women leaving abusive relationships. A few weeks later, President Clinton signed an executive order establishing a national hotline for victims of domestic abuse. Today, the state exempts victims of domestic violence from lifetime limits on public assistance.

This commitment to devote public resources to protect abused women represents a public decision about what constitutes social justice in today's society. It reveals a belief that the suffering caused by domestic violence is not a cost that women should bear alone but a social problem that demands a collective response. As we review diverse approaches to defining social justice, consider the implications of each approach for Melissa and women like her.

DEFINING JUSTICE: A MODERN APPROACH

Lee Ann Bell offers a modern vision of a just society. For her, it is one "in which the distribution of resources is equitable and all members are physically and psychologically safe and secure. We envision a society in which individuals are both self-determining (able to develop their full capacities), and interdependent (capable of interacting democratically with others)" (Bell, 1997, p. 3).

Social work writings often define a just society by the absence of injustice. So, for example, in their description of "emancipatory learning," Van Soest and Garcia (2003, p. vii) suggest that "[u]ltimately, the goal is to prepare social workers and other helping professionals to transform oppressive and unjust systems into non-oppressive and just alternatives." Similarly, van Wormer (2004) defined injustice as the result of inequality and oppression, urging social workers to devote themselves to eliminating these conditions through a commitment to restorative justice.

Thoughtful consideration of this issue is found in **David Gil**'s work, *Confronting Injustice and Oppression* (1998). A social work professor at Brandeis University, Gil locates the inspiration for this work in his experiences during the 1938 German occupation of Austria, which left him committed to reversing cycles of injustice and **oppression**. Gil defines justice as the opposite of injustice and oppression and directs social workers' attention to five key institutions of social life:

1. **Stewardship** (care of natural and human-created resources)
2. Organization of work and production
3. Exchange and distribution of goods, rights, and responsibilities
4. **Governance**
5. Biological reproduction, socialization, and social control

He argues that just societies treat people as equals, with equal rights and responsibilities in each of these five institutions.

Gil explicitly states two assumptions shared by all four of these social work authors: oppression is not inevitable, and a just society is achievable. Indeed, it would be hard to imagine anyone who did not share this belief pursuing a career in social work. Our moments of despair come when events challenge this cherished belief. Like Engels (*The Origin of the Family, Private Property, and the State,* 1884/1972), Gil (1998) argues that perfectly just human societies are possible and that they existed before technological and social change allowed for a stable economic surplus.

Of course, social workers are not the only ones to take a modern perspective on justice. Others, from **Plato** to **Ayn Rand**, have done so as well. Where Rand's philosophy of **Objectivism** promotes "rational selfishness" as the key to a just society, Plato's *Republic* offers a utopian vision in which rulers do not own private property, which allows them to concentrate on pursuing the common good. His "best-ordered state" has a communitarian feel: "[W]hen any one of the citizens experiences any good or evil, the whole state will make his case their own" (Edman, 1956, p. 416).

Plato argues that utopian visions need not necessarily be achievable. He rejects the claims of critics charging that his ideal city-state never existed, saying, "We were enquiring into the nature of absolute justice and the perfectly unjust, that we might have an ideal... would a painter be any the worse because, after having delineated with consummate art an ideal of a perfectly beautiful man, he was unable to show that any such man could ever have existed?" (Edman, 1956, p. 430). Justice is a virtue, and a just society is an ideal. The modern approach articulates that ideal and energizes social workers by focusing our efforts on pursuing an inspiring goal.

DEFINING JUSTICE: A POSTMODERN APPROACH

A postmodern approach to defining justice shifts our focus from the *end* (justice) to the *process* involved as people strive for justice.

The postmodern approach is not limited to contemporary scholars. In ancient Greece, Aristotle wrote, "[F]ire burns both in Greece and in Persia; *but conceptions of justice shift and change"* (Barker, 1962, p. 365, italics added). More than two thousand years later, in 1863, John Stuart Mill made a similar observation:

> The entire history of social improvement has been a series of transitions by which one custom or institution after another, from being a supposed primary necessity of social existence, has passed into the rank of a universally stigmatized injustice and tyranny. So it has been with the distinctions of slaves and freemen, nobles and serfs, patricians and plebeians; and so it will be, and in part already is, with the aristocracies of color, race, and sex. (Sterba, 1980, p. 104)

The accelerated pace of change in recent years has brought this observation into focus. For many, the "postmodern" era has brought a rejection of "objective" or "absolute" truth and a dawning recognition that truth may be socially constructed. Thus, conceptions of justice vary from group to group and change throughout the history of societies, families, and individuals. *Absolute* justice is a misnomer. Groups of all sizes strive to achieve an acceptable state of *relative* justice.

The social justice framework in this book relies on a postmodern definition: *Justice is fair allocation of the costs and rewards of group membership.*[2]

Costs of group membership range from the taxes paid by residents in a nation-state to the chores completed by the members of a family. Benefits may be labeled as such (**Social Security** *benefits*), or they may be more subtle (a sense of personal security). As we will see in Chapter 3, costs and benefits may be experienced immediately (like taxes or welfare checks), or they may accrue over a long period of time (like cancer risk or privilege).

The costs and benefits of group membership are allocated through *social justice processes.* Mundane decisions about who gets to use the family car reflect fundamental beliefs about what is a "just" or "fair" distribution of this benefit. In the United States, the benefits of citizenship include entitlements such as Social Security, tax deductions for home mortgage interest, and Medicaid.

Debates about social justice come up in groups of any size. They arise in families, for example, when new parents struggle to decide how to divide the responsibilities of rearing their baby. They come up in societies as well, as when members of the U.S. Congress debate tax reform proposals. Disputes about how many diapers a father should change or how much tax a corporation should pay are fundamentally social justice debates.

LO 1-2   Understand the Processes by Which Social Justice Is Achieved

EP 2a
EP 5c

Social justice process refers to the way a group of any size allocates the costs and benefits of membership. Sometimes, as with the formal development of social policy, these processes are open and public (and laborious!). Other times, **allocation rules** are implicit and assumed, noticed only when they are breached. **Critical theory** and related perspectives in the social sciences have taught us to question these rules even though it may take a social movement to change them.

Good process does not guarantee a fair outcome. Yet wars have been fought and tears shed over unfair processes that are virtually guaranteed to produce an outcome that is not perceived as just. Fair process is necessary but not sufficient for achieving just outcomes.

---

[2]While doing research for the second edition of this book, I discovered the work of David Miller, a fellow at Oxford College. Miller's definition of justice is similar: "[T]he subject-matter of justice is the manner in which benefits and burdens are distributed among men whose qualities and relationships can be investigated" (1976, p. 19).

The nature of the decision determines what we consider a fair process, with some types of decisions made by a single authority and others subject to democratic processes. For instance, the president of the United States can accomplish some changes through executive orders, but changes in the Constitution require ratification by Congress and state legislatures.

Groups and cultures differ in what they consider a fair process. Generally, if the allocation rules used by the group are considered fair by members of that group, then the group has achieved a measure of social justice. **Culturally competent practice** calls on social workers to understand and respect the processes by which diverse cultures seek to achieve justice.

Justice in process involves three key concepts: **membership**, **voice**, and the **rule of law**. *Membership* refers to the group's boundaries for distinguishing between "us" and "them." These boundaries often work to exclude what Bruce Jansson (2002) calls "out groups." People who differ from the majority of group members are vulnerable to being labeled "other" and denied membership. As a result, they may be deprived of group benefits and excluded from debate on matters that affect them. For example, a family may question its obligation to provide care to an elderly grandmother on the grounds that she is not "really" a member of the immediate family. A nation may question the provision of cash benefits to immigrants who are not "really" citizens. As we will see in later chapters, most of the history of the United States has been marked by progress toward extension of political and civil rights to those once considered undeserving. Women's suffrage and the civil rights movement are examples of a society redefining the terms of membership.

Fair Process Principle #1: Individuals should be treated as political equals.

Western democratic traditions have reached general agreement about what is and is not fair in decision making. These are summarized in three *fair process principles*. The first of these principles, a belief in **political equality**, is central to liberal philosophy and democratic thought. Although some people are privileged by birth and others by wealth, these privileges should not extend to the political sphere. To the extent that they do, this principle is violated.

Fair Process Principle #2: All parties affected by a decision should have a voice in the decision.

Voice refers to a person's ability to influence decision making within the group. At all levels of social organization, an individual's voice will be determined by the extent to which others hear and attend to that person's concerns. Americans have a strong preference for giving voice to people who are affected by decisions. Thus, our second fair process principle holds that all parties affected by a decision should have a voice in the decision. Violation of this principle was the stated cause of the Boston Tea Party. In elementary school, Americans are taught that wild-eyed colonists dressed up as Indians and threw bags of British tea into Boston Bay, shouting, "No taxation without representation!"

Fair Process Principle #3: Formal rules should apply equally to all similarly situated parties.

The rule of law is a third important component of just process. When formal rules are not universally and consistently applied, we cry "foul." In our country, we expect the law to apply equally to everyone. The notion of equal protection is embedded in the U.S. Constitution. But legislators cannot anticipate every eventuality, and individuals may disagree on what is a "similarly situated" party. This ambiguity keeps judges and lawyers occupied but should not detract from our general belief that no one is above the law.

But if a policy is legal, is it necessarily just? Does **majority rule** make for fair decisions? Like most of us, Aristotle answered "not necessarily." **Aristotle** distinguished between equity and justice, arguing that although they are made of the same stuff, equity is more universal and more natural than justice. For him, **equity** is akin to **natural justice**, which is broader than legal justice. Legal justice establishes rules that, even if perfectly followed, can lead to inequitable results. "The same thing, then, is just and equitable, and while both are good the equitable is superior" (Bostock, 2000, p. 133).

LO 1-3   Identify the Components of Social Justice

EP 5c

Miller (1976, 1999) identifies four components of social justice: desert, need, rights, and equality. The first three can be illustrated using a simple hypothetical situation adapted from Miller (1976). Suppose I hire three children to clean my windows, and I promise to pay them one dollar each for their efforts. Throughout the day I watch them work, and I observe that one child (the first child) is industriously cleaning. This child does more than her fair share of the work and does it very well. The other two dawdle along. One of them (the second child) looks ill. When I ask what's wrong, he tells me that he hasn't eaten for two days because his family has no money for food. The third child has no explanation for her sloughing but looks forward to receiving her dollar at the end of the day.

The first child represents *desert*. An outcome is considered just when each person involved gets what he or she deserves. In America, we believe that someone who works hard and does a good job deserves to be rewarded.

The second child represents *need*. Just outcomes take into account each person's need. In our hypothetical example, this child clearly needed money more than the other two.

The third child represents *rights*. From a contractual perspective, a right is an outcome to which we are entitled, based on a prior agreement or contract. Apart from whether she deserves or needs the money, the third child reminds me that under our contractual agreement she has the right to receive a dollar. We will consider rights in greater detail in the next section.

My task, as the all-powerful policy maker in pursuit of justice, is to balance the deserts, needs, and rights of these three children to achieve a just distribution of the reward. This task is illustrated in Figure 1.1. Similarly, analysis of the impact of policy on social justice should consider each of these components, particularly as they relate to vulnerable populations. For example, analysis of a proposal to provide public clinics for people who do not have health insurance might consider first whether these people deserve health care; second, whether they need such care; and finally, whether their rights as citizens are violated if the care is not provided. Equality is the fourth component of justice, and a policy's impact on inequality merits careful consideration. Now let us turn to more detailed consideration of two components of social justice: human rights and equality.

FIGURE 1.1 Balancing the Components of Social Justice

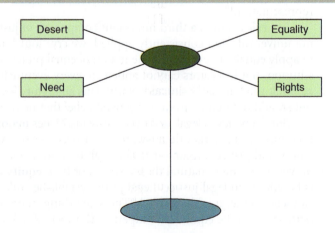

HUMAN RIGHTS

Most Americans can recite from the Declaration of Independence, "We hold these truths to be self-evident, that all men are created equal, that they are endowed by their Creator with certain unalienable Rights, that among these are Life, Liberty and the pursuit of Happiness." When Thomas Jefferson penned these words, he was part of a tradition that began in ancient civilizations and was reflected in documents written as early as two thousand years before the birth of Jesus, including the Code of Hammurabi (Mesopotamia), the Cyrus cylinder (Persia), and the edicts of Ashoka (ancient India) (Robertson & Merrills, 1996). Each of these documents treats human rights as universal and inalienable. Thus, rights are possessed by all people, and they cannot be (as my grandmother would say) "begged, borrowed, or sold."

The horrors of the Holocaust inspired members of the United Nations (U.N.) General Assembly to adopt the Universal Declaration of Human Rights in 1948. Although the declaration is not legally binding, it sets forth principles toward which many nations strive. **President Franklin D. Roosevelt** characterized it as an "international Magna Carta of all men everywhere" (in his address to the United Nations, December 9, 1948, Paris), but other U.S. politicians have been less enthusiastic. For instance, **Jeane Kirkpatrick**, U.S. Ambassador to the United Nations during the Reagan administration, reportedly described the declaration as "a letter to Santa Claus" (WordIQ.com, n.d.).

Nonetheless, the declaration was promptly ratified by the United States Senate in a process consistent with constitutional provisions governing international treaties. Although the president of the United States has authority to sign U.N. declarations, conventions, and treaties, ratification requires Senate approval. As a result, there can be a lengthy gap between the president's signature and Senate ratification.

Notably, the United States and Somalia are the only nations that have not ratified the Convention on the Rights of the Child, and we join Sudan, Somalia, and Iran in refusing to ratify the Convention on the Elimination of All Forms of Discrimination Against Women. President Obama signed the Convention on the Rights of Persons with Disabilities in 2009, but the Senate has so far been unable to achieve the two-thirds majority needed to ratify the treaty. The status of the United States with respect to other U.N. conventions affecting human rights (as of this writing) is summarized in Table 1.1.

Civil and political rights enjoyed by Americans are spelled out in the first ten amendments to the Constitution—the Bill of Rights—and in legislation ranging from the Civil Rights Act of 1960 to the Americans with Disabilities Act of 1990. While there is a strong tradition of protection for civil rights in the United States, this nation does not recognize economic, social, and cultural rights, or solidarity rights, some of which are identified in the Universal Declaration of Human Rights (Vasak & Alston, 1982).

Human Rights Violations and Restorative Justice

The world has seen a litany of **human rights violations** by governments. Here we will briefly consider South Africa's system of **apartheid** and the ongoing efforts at healing that followed.

The land we now know as South Africa has long been home to diverse ethnic groups. Its colonial history began in the 1400s with the arrival of Portuguese explorers, but most people date the period to the arrival of Dutch and British forces in the 17th century. These European powers fought over territory during the Boer Wars of the end of the 19th century before settling into an uneasy power-sharing arrangement. The Union of South Africa was formed in 1910, and the Afrikaner National Party rose to ascendency in the 1940s. Apartheid laws date to 1948, when the Population Registration Act required that all

TABLE 1.1 United Nations Conventions on Human Rights*

Title	Effective Year (requires 20 signatures)	U.S. Status
Universal Declaration of Human Rights	1948	Signed by President Truman, ratified by the Senate
Convention on the Prevention and Punishment of the Crime of Genocide	1951	Signed by President Reagan in 1988, ratified by the Senate with the proviso that America was immune from prosecution without its consent
International Covenant on Civil and Political Rights	1976	Signed by President Carter in 1977, ratified by the Senate in 1992 with reservations
Convention on the Elimination of All Forms of Racial Discrimination	1969	Signed by President Johnson in 1966, ratified by the Senate in 1994
Convention on the Elimination of All Forms of Discrimination Against Women	1981	Signed by President Carter, not ratified by the Senate
Convention Against Torture	1987	Signed by President G.H.W. Bush in 1988, ratified by the Senate in 1994 with stipulations
Convention Against Apartheid in Sports	1988	United States voted against the Convention
Convention on the Rights of the Child	1990	Signed by Madeleine Albright (under President Clinton) in 1995, not ratified by the Senate (like Somalia and South Sudan)
Convention on the Protection of the Rights of All Migrant Workers and Members of Their Families	2003	United States (along with other migrant-receiving states) has not signed
Convention on the Rights of Persons with Disabilities	2008	Signed by President Obama in 2009, not ratified by the Senate

*Please see the United Nations Treaty Collection for updated information on conventions and treaties (http://treaties.un.org/Home.aspx?lang=en).

South Africans be classified as white, black, or colored. The majority black population was confined to reserves known as "homelands" and required to carry "pass books" to enter non-black areas. Their voting rights were limited to homelands, which meant the South African parliament was elected by the minority non-black population.

Protests in the 1960s signaled the beginning of the **Anti-Apartheid Movement**. The government responded with violent repression, and the killing of 69 unarmed protesters in Sharpeville resulted in international calls for the economic isolation of South Africa. The following year (1961), South Africa was ejected from the Commonwealth, and in 1962 the United Nations General Assembly passed a non-binding resolution that established a Special Committee against Apartheid and called on member states to participate in a trade embargo against the nation. In 1970, South Africa was expelled from the Olympics. Finally, in 1990 President F. W. de Klerk entered into negotiations to end apartheid, and in 1994 the **African National Congress** won in the nation's first multiracial election. Nelson Mandela became president of South Africa.

The post-apartheid government established the world's first **Truth and Reconciliation Commission** (TRC). The TRC applied the principles of restorative justice to enable both victims and offenders to participate in the new democracy. While there is no universal agreement on the impact of this process, it is widely seen as a success. Truth and Reconciliation Commissions have been established in more than 19 countries in response to human rights violations (Chapman & van der Merwe, 2008).

Unlike the adversarial retributive justice system to which we are accustomed, restorative justice processes focus on repairing harm through a process of dialogue that involves both offenders and victims. In this context, crimes are seen as wrongs done to individuals and communities rather than to the nation-state (Van Ness, 1996). The focus of proceedings is on repairing harm that has been done and restoring social bonds. Restorative justice principles have also been applied in criminal justice contexts (see Chapter 9) as well as child protective services (see Chapter 12) (Morris & Maxwell, 1998; Vos et al., 2003).

The South African experience is instructive on many levels: first, human rights violations were rooted in a colonial system of economic exploitation and flourished in conditions of extreme inequality; second, proponents of apartheid used arbitrary racial categories to shore up the power of a minority; and third, apartheid was successfully dismantled only after decades of organized efforts within South Africa that were supported by an international solidarity movement.

Albert John Luthuli (1898–1967), president of the African National Congress (1952–1967) and winner of the 1960 Nobel Peace Prize

Terence Spencer/The LIFE Images Collection/Getty Images

Human Trafficking

Where apartheid involved government-sponsored exploitation of an entire race, human trafficking involves the market-based exploitation of vulnerable individuals. The U.N. Trafficking Protocol that went into effect in 2003 (and which the United States signed in 2005) provides the only widely agreed-upon definition of trafficking in persons:

a. … the recruitment, transportation, transfer, harbouring, or receipt of persons, by means of the threat or use of force or other forms of coercion, of abduction, of fraud, of deception, of the abuse of power, or of a position of vulnerability or of the giving or receiving of payments or benefits to achieve the consent of a person having control over another person for the purpose of exploitation. Exploitation shall include, at a minimum, the exploitation of the prostitution of others or other forms of sexual exploitation, forced labour or services, slavery or practices similar to slavery, servitude or the removal of organs;

b. The consent of a victim of trafficking in persons to the intended exploitation set forth in subparagraph (a) of this article shall be irrelevant where any of the means set forth in subparagraph (s) have been used;

c. The recruitment, transportation, transfer, harbouring, or receipt of a child for the purpose of exploitation shall be considered "trafficking in persons" even if this does not involve any of the means set forth in subparagraph (a) of this article (United Nations, 2000).

Reliable estimates of the number of people who have been trafficked are impossible to obtain, and the profits from this business are incalculable. Policies designed to address trafficking take three approaches: prosecution of traffickers, prevention of trafficking, and protection of trafficking victims. An "anti-trafficking policy index" has been used to rank national efforts in this area, and in 2013 the United States was not among nations with the strongest anti-trafficking policies due to its failure to provide amnesty to trafficking victims (Cho, 2014).

Of course, there is no simple remedy for human trafficking. Corruption complicates the task of prosecution. Raids on brothels risk re-victimizing victims, even as protective measures struggle to establish who is and who is not a bona fide trafficking victim. At the same time, the conditions that support trafficking are direct concerns for macro social work practice: extreme poverty, social norms and values that marginalize women and people of color, and a market that allows some to profit from the slave labor and prostitution of others. So scholars like Martha Nussbaum argue for measures to increase the capabilities of victims and potential victims: education for women and children, microcredit and employment options for the poor, labor unions for low-wage workers, and social networks that reduce isolation (Cavalieri, 2011). Measures that promote equality also help to restore human rights.

EQUALITY

We can identify three types of equality: social, political, and economic. **Social equality** exists to the extent that community esteem for individuals is not based on a hierarchy. This is seldom the case because informal hierarchies govern most of our social interactions; however, the lack of social equality is seldom a matter for policy intervention. Social policies more often target political and economic inequality. As we have seen, **political equality** is a fundamental value in democracy, personified by the notion of "one person, one vote." To the extent that a political system deviates from this value it is considered unjust. Finally, **economic equality**—the equitable distribution of income and wealth—is an important component of social justice. Few Americans believe that income and wealth should be equally distributed, but most endorse the concept of equal opportunity, and the American Dream of continually rising affluence remains an important part of the nation's psyche (ACLU, 2010). Yet, for decades, economic inequality has risen in the United States and in other developed nations. Its causes and destructive impacts are discussed in Chapter 5. As we will see, policies that govern our safety net, social security, and tax systems play an important role in determining the level of economic inequality in U.S. society.

Most philosophical conceptions of justice stem from or elaborate upon Aristotle's views. Aristotle saw distributive justice as the equal distribution of shares among people who are equal, and unequal distribution among people who are unequal. His concept of **proportional rewards** offers a rationale for unequal distribution of benefits. For Aristotle, justice, merit, and proportion are closely aligned. A just distribution of rewards is based on "merit" and is proportional. So an individual's rightful share is proportionate to the person's merit (Bostock, 2000, pp. 112–133). Aristotle acknowledges that people may define merit differently: "democrats identify it with the status of freeman, supporters of oligarchy with wealth (or with noble birth), and supporters of aristocracy with excellence" (p. 113).

Contemporary definitions of merit may hinge on skill in performing tasks, dedication or sacrifice, or personal characteristics. In our daily lives, most of us operate across settings that define merit in different ways.

Equality might be achieved by balancing disparate claims. In the *Ethics,* Aristotle argues that in the exchange of goods justice is the intermediate point between two unjust extremes. So a just price for a good lies between two prices that would be unjust (too low a price is unjust to the producer, and too high is unjust to the consumer): "[T]he virtuous man tends to take less than his share" (p. 130). In *Politics,* Aristotle suggests that a just state rewards individuals according to their contributions to the goals of the state, and the goals of a just state include a good quality of life.

As we have seen, equality is complex. The principle is easy to articulate, but the devil is in the details. Policy makers, family members, and philosophers struggle to determine the extent to which inequality should be tolerated (or encouraged). We will revisit this controversial topic during our discussion of economic fundamentals.

LO 1-4   Discuss the Philosophical Underpinnings of Capitalism and Its Alternatives

EP 5c

Capitalism refers to an economic system (sometimes called the "free enterprise system") based on trade among private individuals and corporations, in which the means of production are privately owned. Although the United States is commonly viewed as a "capitalist" nation, in reality it is a "mixed" economy with regulated markets and government ownership of some major industries (e.g., public utilities). Indeed, "**laissez-faire capitalism,**" in which markets operate with no government intervention, has probably never existed (Buder, 2009).

Adam Smith was an early defender of capitalism, and his seminal work, *An Inquiry in the Nature and Causes of the Wealth of Nations* (sometimes shortened to *The Wealth of Nations*) offers a persuasive argument that society as a whole benefits when individuals pursue their selfish interests in the marketplace. He coined the term "**invisible hand**" to describe how the forces of supply and demand direct human behavior.

Capitalist theory, as articulated by Smith and by 20th-century proponents of rational choice theory, introduces "**economic man**" or "Homo economicus," a being who seeks to possess as much wealth as he or she can accumulate with a minimum of labor or sacrifice. According to this view, humans rationally seek to maximize their own happiness or, as economists would say, "optimize their **utility**."

Unlike some modern economists, **Adam Smith** did not believe that all or even most of human nature was encapsulated in *Homo economicus.* In his less-renowned work, *The Theory of Moral Sentiments,* he observed that "However selfish soever man may be supposed, there are evidently some principles in his nature, which interest him in the fortune of others, and render their happiness necessary to him, though he derives nothing from it, except the pleasure of seeing it." Likewise, economic anthropologists like **Karl Polanyi** emphasized behaviors that reflect more communal motivations, such as redistribution of resources and reciprocal gift-giving in traditional societies (e.g., the Native American potlatch) (Dalton, 1968).

Several philosophical perspectives contribute to our understanding of capitalism and of the relationship between government and the marketplace. Here, we will consider three: **libertarianism**, **liberalism**, and **socialism**.[3] A summary of these perspectives is presented in Table 1.2.

---

[3]Summaries of the philosophical approaches are provided in Sterba (1980).

TABLE 1.2 Summary of Philosophical Approaches to Social Justice

Philosophical Perspective	Distributive Principle	Approach to Melissa
Libertarian philosophy	"From each according to his choice; to each according to his product."	Melissa chose to marry Will. Will chose his job. Tax funds that are taken coercively from others should not be used to intervene in their lives.
Liberal philosophy	"Economic liberty and political equality for all."	Intervention to bring Melissa above a social minimum is in order. Relief of her suffering will enhance community well-being.
Socialist philosophy	"From each according to his ability; to each according to his need."	Melissa's abuse is the natural result of capitalism and its oppression of laborers. Intervention should educate her about the societal roots of her suffering.

LIBERTARIAN PHILOSOPHY

With an abiding commitment to personal freedom, libertarian philosophy emphasizes the benefits of the free market over an economic system regulated by the government, arguing that a free-market society enjoys greater productivity among its workers and greater incentive to accumulate capital and pass it on to the next generation. A byproduct of this capital accumulation is lower interest rates. Furthermore, the free market encourages innovation and risk taking by offering high rewards for success in uncertain ventures such as speculative investment. Finally, proponents of this view argue that the free market is preferable to government coercion in the allocation of resources because it does not interfere with individual liberty. Ayn Rand, a strong proponent of libertarian philosophy, extolled individual liberty in *The Fountainhead,* published in 1943.

Libertarians argue that inequality is acceptable and promotes social well-being. **Oliver Wendell Holmes** exemplified this view when he said, "I have no respect for the passion for equality, which seems to me merely idealizing envy" (Hayek, 1960, cited in Sterba, 1980, p. 126). **Friedrich Hayek** argued that the only form of equality that did not interfere with liberty was equality before the law. With respect to the role of government, a libertarian view would hold that there is no justification for the state to treat people differently. "Before the law … people should be treated alike in spite of the fact that they are different" (p. 127).

Without specific policies to redistribute wealth, equal treatment under the law inevitably supports the unequal distribution of resources. Libertarians oppose policies such as progressive taxation or affirmative action that are designed to reduce inequality. For them, the pursuit of equality is not an appropriate policy goal; inequality is a small price to pay for freedom. Thus, libertarians typically view taxes as the coercive taking of private property. For example, Hayek argues that "economic inequality is not one of the evils which justify our resorting to discriminatory coercion or privilege as a remedy" (p. 128).

Robert Nozick's 1974 work, *Anarchy, State, and Utopia,* exemplifies the libertarian perspective. Nozick argues that inequality is not necessarily an indication of injustice if it results from a process that treats people fairly and equally. The fact that a free market results in disparate incomes is not cause for government intervention. Nozick disputes the notion of shared responsibility for vulnerable populations, offering a parable of 10 Robinson Crusoes on 10 separate islands. If these men have different levels of well-being, the differences result from variation in their abilities or in the natural resources available on their islands. In Nozick's view, because no Crusoe is responsible for any other Crusoe's disadvantages, none would be justified in demanding that the others transfer resources to him.

In a similar vein, **Milton Friedman**, one of President Ronald Reagan's economic advisors, argued that failure to allocate resources on the basis of productivity undermines prosperity. He suggested that the appropriate ethical principle for distribution of income in a free society is "[t]o each according to what he and the instruments he owns produces" (Wood & Woods, 1990, p. 366). Under this view, wealth and high incomes come to those who are fortunate (e.g., through inheritance) and who take risks (e.g., through speculation). The community as a whole benefits from the presence of the wealthy, in part because they provide "independent foci of power to offset the centralization of political power" (Friedman, 1962, cited in Sterba, 1980, p. 145) and in part because they become "patrons" of experimentation, novel ideas, and the arts.

It should be apparent that libertarians oppose government regulation of markets. But this viewpoint also has direct implications for welfare policy. With its general opposition to taxation, a libertarian perspective on social justice would clearly oppose the use of public funds to redistribute income toward the poor. The value placed on a free-market economy would suggest that welfare, as an alternative to paid work, should be made available only as a last resort. Finally, the emphasis on personal freedom, when extended to welfare recipients, would oppose coercion as a means of social control.

A libertarian perspective would emphasize Melissa's free choice in marrying Will and having children. Libertarians would note that Will chose his job. While acknowledging the problems that resulted from these choices, the libertarian would probably not condone the use of tax funds to help Melissa improve her situation.

LIBERAL PHILOSOPHY

Central to most liberal philosophies is an attempt to combine liberty and equality, specifically economic liberty and political equality. Liberal thinkers have taken two approaches to defining justice: the contractual and the utilitarian. The contractual tradition holds that the just state is based on an unwritten contract between free and independent citizens. In contrast, the utilitarian tradition rejects the centrality of a social contract, defining justice as that which optimizes the total well-being (or "utility") of society. **John Rawls** is widely cited for his contractual approach, whereas John Stuart Mill's work exemplifies the **utilitarian** tradition.[4]

A Contractual Approach (John Rawls)

John Rawls developed what he termed "a procedural interpretation" of Immanuel Kant's theories in his classic book, *A Theory of Justice*. According to Rawls, justice is the result of the rational choice a person would make behind a "veil of ignorance." This veil of ignorance represents a hypothetical position in which individuals are unaware of their social position, because "no one knows his place in society, his class position or social status; nor does he know his fortune in the distribution of natural assets and abilities, his intelligence and strength and the like" (Rawls, 1971, p. 137).

---

[4]See Locke's *Second Treatise of Government*, Rousseau's *The Social Contract*, and Kant's *The Foundations of Metaphysics* for examples of the contractual tradition. For the utilitarian tradition, see John Stuart Mill's *Utilitarianism*.

Rawls reasons that behind this veil people would minimize their risk of suffering. That is, they would choose distributive rules based on a "**maximin**" strategy—rules that would maximize the welfare of the least well-off. This conservative strategy, Rawls argues, would naturally be adopted if individuals did not know whether they would be among the least well-off.

For Rawls, distributive justice includes the fair distribution of not only economic goods and services but also nonmaterial "social goods," including opportunity, power, and the social bases of self-respect. He argues that a "social minimum" in all of these should be established, below which citizens of a state would not be allowed to fall. One general rule for determining the social minimum is that it be set as high as possible consistent with maintaining an efficient economic system (this condition being essential to the long-term well-being of the least advantaged).

Also central to Rawls's conception is the "just savings principle." Arguing that the veil of ignorance would deprive people of knowledge about the generation or cohort to which they belonged, Rawls suggests that "the just savings principle applies to what a society is to save as a matter of justice" (p. 288) to ensure the economic and cultural well-being of successive generations. This ensures against one generation spending all of society's resources and leaving subsequent generations impoverished.

Rawls formulated two principles of justice that he believed would be derived under these circumstances:

1. "Each person is to have an equal right to the most extensive total system of equal basic liberties compatible with a similar system of liberties for all."
2. "Social and economic inequalities are to be arranged so that they are both
   a. to the greatest benefit of the least advantaged, consistent with the just savings principle, and
   b. attached to offices and positions open to all under conditions of fair equality of opportunity."

The first principle establishes an absolute right to equal liberties, such as those spelled out in the U.S. Bill of Rights. Under the second principle, *all* **social goods**—liberty and opportunity, income and wealth, and the bases of self-respect—are to be distributed equally unless an unequal distribution of any or all of these goods is to the advantage of the least favored.

Suggesting that Rawls is "perhaps the most instrumental [writer] in widening the scope of the concept of distributive justice," Wakefield has applied Rawls's concepts to the practice of psychotherapy by social workers (1988, p. 193). His conclusions are discussed near the end of this chapter in the section on social work and social justice.

Rawls's concept of social justice contrasts sharply with the libertarian view in its treatment of the disadvantaged. Under his general conception of justice, inequality is tolerable only when it benefits the least-advantaged members of society. For Rawls, the welfare

BOX 1.1   John Rawls and the American Dream

What would John Rawls have to say about the American Dream—the notion that anyone can achieve wealth and prosperity if they work hard enough; the deep-rooted belief that progress is inevitable, and our children will be even better off than we are? If we don't succeed, we hope that our children or grandchildren will grab the brass ring and move into the upper 1 percent. American confidence in **upward mobility** may be misplaced. Research places the United States at the bottom of the 13 western democratic nations of the OECD in regard to income and occupational mobility (Corak, 2013a; Isaacs, n.d.).

problem would be turned on its head. Welfare mothers themselves would not be seen as "the problem." Instead, concern would focus on the presence of extreme wealth that does not contribute to the well-being of the poor.

A Utilitarian Approach (John Stuart Mill)

Mill sought to describe justice in his essay "On the Connection Between Justice and Utility" (1863). He begins with the premise that humans have a natural "feeling of justice"—that we intuitively recognize and respond negatively to injustice. That feeling of justice stems from the desire for social well-being. Mill argues that justice must be understood as that which is most "useful" to society as a whole or, to use his terms, that which generates the highest "utility"—the greatest good or well-being—for the greatest number.

Members of a subgroup of utilitarian liberals called *egalitarians* argue that the highest utility is achieved through equal distribution of wealth and income. This conclusion is based on a "diminishing returns" argument, which holds that the satisfaction we derive from possessing a good diminishes as that good becomes less scarce. Stated more concretely, a poor person will value an additional $50 per month more highly than a rich one. So, as Dalton argues, "unequal distribution of a given amount of purchasing power among a given number of people is ... likely to be a wasteful distribution from the point of view of economic welfare" (1925, p. 84). In other words, giving an additional $50 to the rich produces less overall well-being than giving it to the poor.

Central to the utilitarian argument is the principle that the happiness of each person is valued equally. For Mill, this "involves an equal claim to all the means of happiness except insofar as the inevitable conditions of human *life and the general interest in which that of every individual is included set limits to the maxim*" (Sterba, 1980, p. 103, italics added). Unlike Rawls, who holds that inequality must favor the least-advantaged members of society, Mill argues that unequal access to "the means of happiness" is justified only when it is in the interest of society as a whole.

Although both contractual and utilitarian approaches would place limits on inequality in a just society, utilitarians might tolerate inequality if it produced greater good for society, regardless of its implications for the poor. Nonetheless, both perspectives place a high value on providing benefits to the disadvantaged.

In Melissa's case, both liberal approaches (contractual and utilitarian) would support intervention. From the viewpoint of a contractual liberal such as Rawls, Melissa's depression and abuse would place her below an acceptable social minimum. His philosophy would support the use of community resources to bring her above that minimum. A utilitarian liberal would emphasize Mill's concept of an intuitive feeling of justice. Within this perspective, our abhorrence of domestic violence is a clear indication that it constitutes injustice. Furthermore, since a utilitarian liberal perspective values the happiness of each individual equally, relief of Melissa's suffering would merit the use of community resources.

SOCIALIST PHILOSOPHY

Describing his vision of a communist **Utopia**, **Karl Marx** writes, "In place of the old bourgeois society, with its classes and class antagonisms, we shall have an association, in which the free development of each is the condition for the free development of all" (Marx, 1888, cited in Sterba, 1980, p. 195). Under socialism, justice would consist of individuals contributing to communal well-being to the extent of their ability. ("From each according to his ability; to each according to his need.") Free from the alienation imposed by a capitalist system, labor would become not a means, but an end—an activity done for its own sake.

In its ultimate form, justice under socialism would involve distribution "to each according to his need," but this goal would be reached only after generations of workers had been raised in a cooperative society. For Marx, communist society "emerges from capitalist society" and thus is "still stamped with the birthmarks of the old society from whose womb it emerges" (p. 197). During the early phases of socialism, distributive justice would consist of returning to each individual according to that person's contribution. Several costs would first be subtracted from the "total social product," including (1) replacement of the means of production as needed; (2) costs of expansion of production; (3) a reserve or insurance fund to provide against "misadventures, disturbances through natural events, etc."; (4) costs of administration not belonging to production; (5) costs of meeting communal needs, such as schools and health services; and (6) funds for those unable to work.

The remainder, called the "diminished proceeds of labor," would be distributed to workers according to their work effort. Marx acknowledges that this would be an unequal distribution. Workers with greater strength or natural abilities contribute more work effort than those less fortunate. Also, workers who were supporting families would receive less per capita. But in Marx's view, "these defects are inevitable in the first phase of communist society. Right can never be higher than the economic structure of society and the cultural development thereby determined" (p. 198).

A Marxist perspective would hold that the current status of the poor in America is the result of the oppression of laborers by those who own the means of production. In this view, welfare is simply a method for controlling the disadvantaged while maintaining the labor pool at a subsistence level. Debates regarding the welfare system are irrelevant because this stage of societal development will inevitably yield to a higher one in which welfare will be obsolete.

Marxist analysis of Melissa's situation might see her abuse as the natural result of the oppression of laborers. Growing up in a working-class setting, Melissa was systematically taught to devalue herself, just as a capitalist society devalues laborers. Similarly, Will's violence can be seen as a response to alienating work and limited opportunities. Indeed, this violence may be seen as a harbinger of revolution. Intervention simply to alleviate the suffering would only perpetuate oppression. A Marxist viewpoint would support intervention that would teach Melissa and Will to view their situation as part of a broader socioeconomic context.

LO 1-5   Discuss the Relevance of Social Justice for Micro and Macro Practice

EP 5c
EP 8d

Social workers often assume that working for justice is the exclusive province of "macro" or "policy" practice. Yet social justice is a vital concern for "micro" or "clinical" practice as well. This is illustrated in three themes examined in this section with reference to Melissa's case: (1) social justice is personal and political, (2) families teach social justice, and (3) injustice undermines social bonds and nation-states.

SOCIAL JUSTICE IS PERSONAL AND POLITICAL

In response to cultural and historical pressures, some social workers "psychologize" human misery and ignore the political and economic dimensions of their clients' pain. They provide opportunities for introspection and personal change but fail to offer transformative insights rooted in understanding of broader social forces (Saleebey, 1990; Specht & Courtney, 1994). A therapist working in this vein might lead Melissa to see how her selection of a spouse was conditioned by childhood experiences or encourage her to view her tolerance of abuse as a symptom of low self-esteem.

Yet, as Saleebey notes, "Even the most private problems of relationship and consciousness have political and social dimensions" (1990, p. 38). A social worker might empower Melissa to seek transformative change by encouraging her to participate in an advocacy group such as JEDI Women. Participation in the group could increase Melissa's awareness of the social and political forces that contributed to her abuse, and she could begin to experience herself as a capable agent of change. Failure to acknowledge the social and political roots of individual misery can leave professionals as well as their clients in what Jacoby (1975) terms "the isolation that damns the individual to scrape along in a private world" (p. 44).

The diverse social, economic, and political forces that have influenced Melissa's life are elaborated throughout this text. Some are introduced below:

1. She was born into a society that does not provide universal family-planning services. Melissa's parents had a large family. Melissa, herself, bore three children she could ill afford. Nor does the United States offer direct financial support to parents. Nations such as Germany and Sweden offer limited financial support to all parents in the form of children's allowances. This is a "**universal**" approach to the income maintenance needs of children. In contrast, the United States has adopted a "**residual**" approach, providing public assistance only for the most needy.
2. Melissa's decision to leave high school during her first pregnancy may reflect a lack of support for education of pregnant teens. Programs for teenage mothers remain limited to major metropolitan areas where they serve only a small proportion of those who could benefit.
3. Will's "good job" provided health benefits but did not offer *career* mobility. Lack of universal access to health care often traps workers in unrewarding jobs. The resulting tension may have contributed to Will's abuse of Melissa and the children.
4. Although depression often goes untreated, Melissa was fortunate that her state's welfare program supported the identification and treatment of barriers to employment. With antidepressant medication and counseling, Melissa can remain in transitional employment. Her ability to support her family will depend on continuing income supplementation through her state's welfare program. Mandates at either the state or the federal level might cut off that support by imposing time limits on welfare.
5. Entering the labor market as an unskilled worker, Melissa may find employers who pay her 70 cents for work of "comparable worth" to that done by a man for a dollar. Or she may be unable to care for her children when they are ill because federal legislation exempts small companies from the Family and Medical Leave Act requirement to provide medical leave.

Clearly, social policies significantly influence the lives of Melissa and her family. Conversely, Melissa herself has affected public policy. By sharing her experiences, she helped mobilize key stakeholders to support the welfare program in her state. She has also become active in a women's organization, thereby joining an emerging grassroots effort to give voice to the concerns of vulnerable women like herself. For Melissa, this involvement triggered a transformation—she began to see herself not as a victim but as an agent of change.

FAMILIES TEACH SOCIAL JUSTICE

In her feminist critique of major political theories of justice, Susan Okin argued that (with the rare exception of John Stuart Mill) philosophers from Aristotle to Marx have confined their discussions to the public sphere, from which women historically have been excluded. Yet, as Okin, Rousseau, Mill, and others have observed, the moral development of children takes place in families, not in courts or legislatures. It is primarily in families that we "learn to be just" (Okin, 1989, p. 297). Politicians and developmental psychologists alike have linked the structure and operation of families to the broader structure and operation of the nations in which they exist.

Clearly, social justice is a significant concern within families, just as it is in the workplace and in national policy. Social workers in clinical practice promote social justice when they help families grapple to achieve a fair allocation of costs and benefits. This work may have as much impact on the nation's well-being as practice that focuses on legislative advocacy.

INJUSTICE UNDERMINES SOCIAL BONDS AND NATION-STATES

People often disagree on what is just. Like children, adults find it difficult to transcend self-interest and consider the well-being of the group as a whole. Central to this task is long-term commitment to the group. This commitment stems first from receiving the benefits of group membership, then from recognizing them as such, and later from observing that the benefits and costs of membership are fairly allocated. On a personal level, the thrill of newfound intimacy brings two individuals into a committed couple relationship, and that relationship is sustained by the partners' belief that costs and benefits are fairly allocated (i.e., that the relationship is just).

Injustice is also destabilizing at a more macro level. Governments do not endure if a significant number of their citizens view them as unjust. The long history of revolution emphasizes the role of perceived injustice as a trigger. Examples include the French, American, Russian, and Chinese revolutions, the overthrow of the Marcos reign in the Philippines, and the dissolution of the Soviet regime. By promoting social justice, social workers enhance the long-term stability of families, groups, and nations.

LO 1-6   Describe the Role of the Social Work Profession in Promoting Social Justice

EP 8d

Bertha Capen Reynolds (1885–1978) was instrumental in promoting social justice both within and outside her profession. After examining Reynolds's contributions, we will discuss how social work professionals continue to support her mission of building a more just society.

BERTHA CAPEN REYNOLDS: A PROFILE

The Bertha Reynolds Society was established in 1985 to honor a singular figure in the social work profession. Bertha Capen Reynolds was one of the nation's first professionally trained social workers, with experience spanning the first half of the 20th century. Her autobiography (Reynolds, 1963) chronicles the personal development of an inquiring and sensitive practitioner who entered the profession determined to master the psychiatric techniques she and her peers believed were the key to unlocking human potential. After graduating from Smith College in 1908, Reynolds spent most of her career as associate director of the school's social work program. But her practice ranged from academic pursuits to serving and residing in residential facilities for the mentally ill, supervising social workers providing relief during the Depression, and serving the seamen's union during World War II.

During the Depression, Reynolds joined the rank-and-file social workers of her time in their call for a new social order. Dissatisfied with the passivity she observed among caseworkers, Reynolds began to call for a professional commitment to community development. She noted that "the community is always involved in any professional relationship"

BOX 1.2   Charity or Justice?

Conservative commentators like Glenn Beck and Bill O'Reilly sometimes use the word "entitlement" as if it were pejorative. In this view, rather than demanding their right to assistance, vulnerable people should ask (or beg) for charitable support. This is compatible with a libertarian understanding of social justice, as it preserves the freedom of donors to deny aid—a liberty not enjoyed by taxpayers who are coerced into paying for entitlements. Charity also substitutes the warm glow of beneficence and personal gratitude for the cold bureaucratic exchange and the stigma associated with public assistance. Rather than demanding their rights, recipients of charity ask for help—behavior that the donors view as much more appropriate from the lower classes.

Public entitlements, on the other hand, confer rights—rights that society is obliged to defend. Recipients of assistance emerge, not as sympathetic individuals humbly seeking relief, but as members of an interest group using the politics of protest and the tools of jurisprudence to enforce public obligations. Bertha Reynolds and others have suggested that justice confers greater dignity than charity on the recipient of assistance. For example, she noted that during the Depression, social workers were surprised to find that "[t]hey [clients] did not seem to feel the 'stigma' which social workers attached to assistance, and some, indeed, came to prefer public aid … to which they felt they were entitled, to private 'charity'" (Reynolds, 1963, p. 140).

(Reynolds, 1963, p. 147) and argued that "the future of social work is bound up with the coming of a sounder social order… the members of this profession have not only the obligation to work for justice which good citizenship applies, but the professional duty" (p. 141).

Reynolds saw Marxism as the key to establishment of a better social order. At a student's suggestion she read the works of Marx and Engels and was persuaded that their theory of dialectical materialism accurately reflected the inevitable progress of society. She watched the development of the Union of Soviet Socialist Republics (USSR) with interest. Unfortunately, she did not live to observe its dissolution. Her interpretation of these events undoubtedly would have enriched the profession.

With her own brand of "brilliant common sense," Reynolds observed a parallel between the psychodynamic theory of her early training and the Marxism she discovered later in life. Both saw conflict as a necessary prerequisite to growth, and both relied on the clash of opposites (id-ego and capitalist-proletariat) to produce a synthesis that represented a higher order of development.

Reynolds never married. She cultivated and treasured her close relationships, in some cases carrying on lengthy correspondence with people she had never met. She understood **positionality** before the term became popular: "If one word is needed, then, to begin to sum up what fifty years of living have taught me, that word is *relatedness* … many people do not know that they stand in any particular place in society, and so they judge their viewpoint to be the only one possible for anybody. I believe it indispensable to a sound relatedness to others to know where one is to start with, for what biases and blind spots to make allowance, and to know that there exist other and quite different viewpoints" (Reynolds, 1963, pp. 314–315).

Social Work and Social Justice

Bertha Reynolds saw social justice as the hallmark of the profession and argued that social work techniques are authentic only to the extent that they serve this mission. She suggested that activities that focus exclusively on what she called the "mental hygiene" of the client should not be considered social work. For Reynolds, the proper clients for social work were the needy. She offered principles for social work practice during the Depression, saying, " . . . social work exists to serve people in need. If it serves other classes who have other purposes it becomes too dishonest to be capable of either theoretical or practical development" (Reynolds, 1963, p. 173).

Jerome Wakefield pursued the same line of reasoning to arrive at a more elaborate conclusion. He agreed that distributive justice is the "organizing value" of the profession and that "the purpose of social work is to see to it that anyone falling below the social minimum in any of the social primary goods is brought above that level in as many respects as possible" (Wakefield, 1988, p. 205).

But, as Wakefield notes, "for better or worse, social work has become one of the mental health professions" (1988, p. 187). Mental health practice is the most common social work activity, with 37 percent of licensed social workers reporting this as their primary practice area in a 2004 survey conducted by the National Association of Social Workers. Furthermore, the growth of private practice is one of the most significant trends in the recent history of the profession. Private practice is the single most common employment setting for social workers in mental health, and the most highly paid employment sector in the profession (NASW, 2006).

Wakefield sought to integrate these trends with the overall mission of the profession by specifying the conditions under which psychotherapy promotes social justice. Relying on Rawls's conceptualization, Wakefield argues: "It is the focus on minimal distributive justice that differentiates clinical social work from traditional psychotherapy" (1988, p. 206). Social workers focus on clients who are deprived or who fall below a basic social minimum. So, for example, a professional woman whose fear of flying interferes with her advancement is not an appropriate target for social work intervention. Even with the fear of flying, she enjoys social benefits well above any social minimum.

But as numerous authors (e.g., Leighninger, 1990) have noted, the status and credibility of a profession are largely determined by the power and affluence of the people it serves. Social workers who focus on the concerns of the middle and professional classes enjoy a measure of security and stature. This is the case for social workers in private practice and those who work in employee assistance programs (EAPs).

Social workers in these settings often struggle to integrate their professional mission of service to the needy with their day-to-day activities. Social workers in EAPs must regularly confront the reality that their paychecks depend on their ability to satisfy the members of the managerial ranks. Similarly, social workers in managed care environments face conflict between achieving cost-containment goals and meeting the care and treatment needs of patients. The ethical practice of social work requires that the client—not the employer or health-care provider—remain the focus of professional concern.

Closing Reflections

We began this chapter by contrasting modern and postmodern approaches to the definition of social justice. Although modern approaches are popular and offer satisfying definitions of what is and is not just, I believe a postmodern approach leads us to a more nuanced and humanizing definition of this elusive concept. We also examined philosophical perspectives on capitalism and social justice, suggesting that familiarity with these approaches can help us analyze the basic assumptions underlying most social policies. We then turned to micro practice, arguing that social justice is an important consideration in this arena and identifying three themes in support of this perspective: social justice issues are personal and political, families teach social justice, and failure to correct injustice can break up families and topple governments. Finally, using Bertha Reynolds as an example, we explored the role of social work and social workers in the pursuit of social justice.

The pursuit of social justice resembles the quest for the Holy Grail. It is time consuming and hazardous, its goal is ephemeral at best, and yet it is an integral part of the human experience. Policy practice, with its alternating victories and setbacks, brings social workers into this quest. Effective policy practice requires a clear vision of social justice and the ability to operate within existing social, economic, and political frameworks to promote that vision. Government is one such framework. In Chapter 2 we will explore the role of government in the search for social justice.

Think About It

1. Are the three fair process principles introduced in this chapter universal, or are they relevant only to Western cultures?

2. For Aristotle, justice consisted of equal treatment for people of similar merit. How is merit defined in your classroom? In your family? In your practicum site? Which setting do you find the most rewarding on a personal level?

3. Which of the philosophical approaches discussed in this chapter is most congruent with your worldview? Do your classmates differ in this regard? Are some conceptions not represented among them?

4. Describe a personal conflict or negotiation that involved the allocation of costs and/ or rewards of group membership. How was this conflict resolved? Did the process adhere to the "fair process principles" outlined in this chapter?

5. Suppose that the members of a group agree that a practice (such as genital mutilation of young girls) is acceptable, but an outside observer finds it abhorrent. Is the practice just? Does the outsider, a social work professional, have the responsibility to intervene if no one who is involved objects to the practice? What about the young girls? Do they have a voice?

Web-Based Exercises

For direct links to all the sites mentioned in these exercises, visit the *Foundations of Social Policy* Companion Site at www.cengagebrain.com and select the resources for Chapter 1.

1. Go to the website of the Foundation for Critical Thinking at http://www.criticalthinking.org. First, explore the site and develop your own concise definition of critical thinking. Click on "Begin Here" and explore the resources available to college and university students. Scroll down to the link for the article on "Universal Intellectual Standards." Print it out and carry it around for a week to see the extent to which your classmates and teachers apply these standards. Compare your findings with those of a friend or colleague.

2. Go to the United Nations website at http://www.un.org/en/universal-declaration-human-rights/index.html. Review the provisions of the Universal Declaration of Human Rights. Which articles are consistent with U.S. law? Which are not?

Competency Notes

As mentioned in the preface to this text, the Council on Social Work Education has designated nine core competencies and related practice behaviors that must be addressed by accredited social work programs. In these notes, I will specify the way chapter content addresses these competencies and behaviors. (This information is designed to assist with the accreditation process.) Please refer to the "helping hands" icons for the locations of specific content in this chapter. Here you will find a brief explanation of how the accompanying content relates to the specified competency or practice behaviors.

The following list indicates where EPAS competencies and practice behaviors are addressed in this chapter.

EP 2   **Engage Diversity and Difference in Practice.** The chapter describes philosophical and structural forces that sustain injustice.

EP 2a   **Apply and communicate understanding of the importance of diversity and difference in shaping life experiences in practice at the micro, mezzo and macro levels.** The chapter notes the role of cultural diversity in defining social justice and the importance of cultural competence in practice.

EP 3a   **Apply understanding of social, economic, and environmental justice to advocate for human rights at the individual and system levels.** The chapter addresses diverse understandings of justice to prepare students to engage in advocacy.

EP 5c   **Apply critical thinking to analyze, formulate, and advocate for policies that advance human rights and social, economic, and environmental justice.** The chapter discusses the philosophical and structural forces that sustain injustice, as well as diverse understandings of justice to prepare students to advocate with people of different philosophical and political leanings.

EP 8d   **Negotiate, mediate, and advocate with and on the behalf of diverse clients and constituencies.** The chapter notes that advocacy can take place in the context of micro practice; and argues that advocacy strengthens practice at all levels.

Suggested Resources

Bostock, D. (2000). *Aristotle's Ethics*. New York: Oxford University Press.

Finn, J. L., & Jacobson, M. (2016). *Just Practice: A Social Justice Approach to Social Work* (2nd ed). Peosta, IA: Eddie Bowers Publishing.

Goffman, A. (2014). *On the Run: Fugitive Life in an American City*. Chicago: University of Chicago Press.

Hobbs, J. (2014). *The Short and Tragic Life of Robert Peace*. New York: Scribner.

Mill, J. S. (1863). On the Connection Between Justice and Utility, in *Utilitarianism*. Chapter 1. (Originally published by London: Parker, Son, and Bourn.) Available at: http://www.utilitarianism.com/ mill1.htm.

Reynolds, B. C. (1963). *An Uncharted Journey: Fifty Years of Growth in Social Work*. New York: Citadel Press.

The Government's Role

All I want is the same thing you want. To have a nation with a government that is as good and honest and decent and competent and compassionate and as filled with love as are the American people.
JIMMY CARTER, 1976

Learning Objectives

This chapter will help prepare students to:

LO 2-1 Understand the philosophical perspectives of contemporary political parties and political labels

LO 2-2 Describe the workings and interactions of federal, state, and local levels of government

LO 2-3 Describe the workings of the legislative, executive, and judicial branches of government

LO 2-4 Understand privatization and its theoretical and practical limits

LO 2-5 Understand the structure and philosophical underpinnings of the U.S. tax system

Democracy, or "rule of the people," comes in various forms. Sometimes, as in town meetings or community councils, members of the public directly participate in governance. More often, we participate through our elected representatives. A nation that uses this system is known as a **republic**. During the 20th century, the number of democracies increased significantly, and by the 21st century approximately half of the world's population lived under democratic rule (Karatanycky, 2000). This trend may continue in the aftermath of the Arab Spring.

As anyone who stays up to watch election returns knows, the U.S. president is not directly elected. Instead, each state sends electors to the "**Electoral College**," where they are (in 48 of the 50 states) directed to vote for the candidate who received a plurality in that state. This is known as a **winner-take-all** system and can result in the election of a candidate who receives fewer popular votes than his rival (as was the case in the 2000 election of George W. Bush). Likewise, our congressional elections are based on a "winner-take-all" system rather than the **proportional representation** system used in many other countries.

For all its idiosyncrasies, the U.S. system of democracy is among the most stable and effective in the world. Key to its effectiveness are the **Bill of Rights**, which ensures against tyranny of the majority; other constitutional guarantees, such as **checks and balances** to ensure that no single branch of government accumulates too much power; and the orderly transfer of power through frequent, fair elections.

LO 2-1   Understand the Philosophical Perspectives of Contemporary Political Parties and Political Labels

EP 5c

Some readers may have skimmed the discussion of philosophical perspectives in Chapter 1, thinking, "This ancient stuff is no longer relevant." On the contrary, these philosophies are directly relevant to contemporary politics in the United States, where libertarian and liberal perspectives are both well represented. Socialist philosophy is seldom evident in mainstream U.S. politics, which leads some conservatives to crow that "the left is dead." Rather than debate this issue, let us consider political parties and political labels.

POLITICAL PARTIES

A political party is an association of like-minded individuals organized to accomplish shared goals. In most states we have the opportunity to declare a party preference when we register to vote. Voter registration rolls are available to the public, and parties use them to organize their *Get Out the Vote* campaigns. Candidates wishing to run under a party banner must have the official sanction of the party to be on the ballot. Although the United States operates on a two-party system, third parties have been established and at times exercise considerable influence through the **spoiler effect**.[1] This arises when a spoiler candidate draws votes away from a mainstream candidate with similar views.

The Republican Party (also known as the Grand Old Party, or GOP) emerged in opposition to the compromise of 1850 (the Fugitive Slave Act). Antislavery activists joined advocates for free distribution of western lands, protective tariffs, and a transcontinental railroad. The party has a strong foundation in libertarian philosophy. Its first presidential nominee, John C. Fremont, ran under the banner, "Free soil, free labor, free speech, free men, Fremont!" Abraham Lincoln ran for president as a Republican, as did Theodore Roosevelt, Ronald Reagan, George H. W. Bush, George W. Bush, and others.

The libertarian beliefs in John C. Fremont's campaign slogan were echoed in later Republican rhetoric. For example, Barry Goldwater ran for president in 1964 as a "classical conservative." He focused "on three general freedoms—economic, social, and political," saying that "the conservative movement is founded on the simple tenet that people have the right to live life as they please, as long as they don't hurt anyone else in the process" (Karger & Stoesz, 2002, p. 15).

Lately, the Republican Party has become home to **neoconservatives**, and its commitment to liberty has morphed into opposition to government in general and "big" government in particular. Consistent with these views, Republicans tend to portray government as an obstacle to personal achievement and economic growth. This position has found eager support among business interests that chafe at government regulation. As the champion for business, the party sometimes abandons its opposition to government

---

[1]Other third parties include the American Reform Party, the Libertarian Party, the Personal Choice Party, the Constitution Party, the U.S. Pacifist Party, the Socialist Workers Party, the Prohibition Party, Communist Party USA, the American Nazi Party, the U.S. Marijuana Party, and the Objectivist Party.

intervention, as when businesses seek, and Republicans deliver, government protection from foreign competition (e.g., protective steel tariffs) or government relief from business losses (e.g., Troubled Asset Relief Program). In these cases Republican opposition to government intervention is set aside in favor of business interests.

The 2004 election was a victory for the **social conservative** element of the Republican Party. Social conservatives find changing gender roles and family forms abhorrent and do not hesitate to use the government to enforce their moral code. This election signaled an end to, or at least a pause in, what Piven and Cloward called **electoral economism** (1997)—that is, the tendency of elections to revolve around economic issues. The slogan of the 1992 Clinton campaign was "It's the economy, stupid!" But in 2004 most Americans did not vote their pocketbooks. The Republican victory was widely attributed to the ascendance of "moral values" over economic considerations in the minds of American voters. Piven and Cloward were prescient when, in 1997, they wrote that "fundamentalism is flourishing in American politics" (p. 77).

The **Tea Party movement** has had a significant influence on Republican politics since 2009, when CNBC commentator Rick Santelli proposed that Chicago hold a Tea Party to protest President Obama's mortgage relief plan. A clip of his comments went viral on the Internet, and soon conservative commentators like Glenn Beck and Republican politicians Sarah Palin, Jim DeMint, and Dick Armey were providing encouragement and support to protests around the country. Tea Party candidates like Marco Rubio, Paul Ryan, and Ted Cruz were elected to office and became a force for the **Republican establishment** to reckon with. In 2013, Tea Party Republicans fostered a three-week shutdown of the federal government in their campaign against the Patient Protection and Affordable Care Act (also known as "Obamacare"). Support for the Tea Party's agenda was largely fueled by conservative dissatisfaction with President Obama, and Tea Party adherents included many "birthers" who suggested he was born outside the United States and therefore not eligible to be president, among them President Donald Trump.

Although there is no centralized Tea Party platform, adherents generally espouse libertarian principals and reference the constitution to advance their goal of limited government. Some chapters and individuals weigh in on social issues such as gun control, immigration, and abortion. Some argue that the rise of the Tea Party set the stage for Trump's candidacy; however, some of his views (including support for abortion and gay rights) were anathema to the movement.

The Democratic Party traces its roots to 1792, when the "Democratic Republican" Party was organized by Thomas Jefferson to support the Bill of Rights. It was known as "the party of the common man" when Jefferson was elected president in 1800. In the 1820s the party was transformed by Andrew Jackson. Jacksonians eliminated the property requirement for voting (which expanded suffrage for white males), reduced government control over national banking, and instituted a "spoils system." Democrats organized immigrants under city "bosses," and during the Polk administration they achieved America's "manifest destiny," seizing one-third of Mexico and extending the U.S. border to the Pacific Ocean.

Emphasis on equality characterizes many of the positions supported by the modern Democratic Party and is reflected in its composition. Some have described the party as "a big tent" that welcomes working-class Americans, people of color, immigrants, gays and lesbians, and other traditionally disenfranchised groups. Unlike Republicans, Democrats do not necessarily view government as a social ill. For example, both President Kennedy and President Johnson promised to use the power of government to eliminate social ills caused by poverty and discrimination.

In 1992 Bill Clinton ran as a "new Democrat" and embraced some positions traditionally associated with Republicans. His administration helped eliminate Aid to Families with Dependent Children (AFDC) and created "reinventing government" initiatives that reduced the size of the federal government (see Chapter 5).

In 2008 Americans elected our first black president, Democrat Barack Obama. In announcing the results, the *New York Times* proclaimed, "Mr. Obama's election amounted to a national catharsis—a repudiation of a historically unpopular Republican president and his economic and foreign policies and an embrace of Mr. Obama's call for change" (Nagourney, 2008). The election had an unusually high voter turnout, particularly among African Americans and young voters, which produced favorable results for Democratic candidates to Congress as well. With net gains of 21 seats in the House of Representatives and eight in the Senate, the party expanded its majorities in Congress. But Democratic preeminence would be short-lived. In 2010 they lost their majority in the House, leaving Obama with a divided Congress for the duration of his presidency.

2012 saw the first election after the Supreme Court's 2010 "Citizens United" decision to lift restrictions on political spending. Campaign costs skyrocketed accordingly, with over $6 billion spent by "super PACs." A sharply divided electorate was subjected to what the *New York Times* called "an unprecedented torrent of advertising," much of it negative, and pundits speculated about the role of money in U.S. politics (Zeleny & Rutenberg, 2012). In the end, the Latino vote proved to be a decisive factor in President Obama's reelection, reflecting the nation's changing demographics (see Chapter 10).

Demographic fundamentals were also in evidence in 2016. Bernie Sanders and Hillary Clinton squared off in a grueling contest for the Democratic nomination. Some point to her proposal to expand Medicare to those 50 and over as evidence that Sanders's progressive agenda pulled Clinton toward the left (see Rappeport & Sanger-Katz, 2016). There is no question that Sanders mobilized millions of (mostly young) voters, and brought inequality and social justice to the fore in the 2016 electoral discourse. But Sanders's appeal rested largely with white voters, and Clinton became the first woman in U.S. history to secure the presidential nomination of a major political party.

POLITICAL LABELS

In American politics the words **conservative** and **liberal** have assumed connotations beyond their strict definitions. But let's begin with definitions. *Webster's Dictionary* defines "conservative" as "Tending or disposed to maintain existing institutions; opposed to change or innovation." "Liberal" is defined as the converse, referring to "a person who favors a political philosophy of progress and reform and the protection of civil liberties" (Webster's Dictionary, n.d.).

Although these definitions may hold true in a broad sense, the terms *conservative* and *liberal* take on different meanings when they become political bywords. For example, the conservative movement in the United States emphasizes personal liberty and argues against government involvement in the economy. Indeed, conservatives tend to favor a laissez-faire economic approach characterized by minimal government regulation. But the conservative movement is a coalition of groups and individuals whose agendas do not always agree. Social conservatives favor government regulation of personal and familial decisions in areas such as reproductive rights and marriage. Fiscal conservatives seek to minimize government spending and regulation. Some argue that the contradictions within the conservative movement threaten to break up the coalition that kept President George W. Bush in office (Micklethwaite & Wooldridge, 2004).

Conservatives and neoconservatives tend to differ when it comes to foreign policy. Except when confronted with the global threat of **communism**, conservatives were generally isolationist. Neoconservatives, on the other hand, show aspirations to global American hegemony—an idea with roots reaching back to William McKinley's acquisition of foreign lands.

The terms *liberal* and *progressive* have also taken on political connotations beyond their strict definitions. Historically, liberals have looked to government as a tool for social change, supporting legislation such as the New Deal, Johnson's **Great Society** antipoverty programs, the civil rights legislation of the 1960s, and the Clean Air Act. Oddly enough, once these legislative reforms are in place, roles become confused. Conservatives advocate for radical reform in Social Security (see Chapter 4) and liberals fight to maintain the program. Yet essential features of liberal and progressive politicians continue to be (1) their willingness to embrace (or at least accept) broad social changes, (2) their view of government as a tool for social improvement, and (3) their defense of civil liberties.

But liberals are not libertarians. They value freedom *and* equality. By freedom they generally mean civil liberties, as opposed to property rights. So when environmental preservation steps on the toes of property owners, self-identified liberals tend to value community well-being over personal property.

In this section we have explored the philosophical underpinnings of contemporary political debates. Often these debates are fundamentally about the role of government in American society, a topic we will return to later when we examine the **privatization** of government functions. But first a basic understanding of the structure and operation of government is in order. (Those who have recently completed a civics course may choose to skim these sections.)

LO 2-2   Describe the Workings and Interactions of Federal, State, and Local Levels of Government

EP 3a

The United States government operates at three levels: federal, state, and local. At the federal level, Congress is vested by the Constitution with the power to tax, provide for the common defense and general welfare, borrow money, regulate interstate commerce, manage immigration and naturalization, regulate bankruptcies, coin money, set standards for weights and measures, establish post offices, issue patents and copyrights, establish courts, declare war, raise and support military forces, and protect civil rights. Under the Tenth Amendment, powers that are not specifically delegated to the federal government are reserved for the states or the people.

State government structures mirror those of the federal government. Like the federal legislative branch, nearly all states have bicameral legislatures (that is, legislatures made up of two houses, such as a senate and a house of representatives).[2] Similarly, the federal courts have parallel entities in the various state judicial systems. Finally, at both federal and state levels, the executive branch consists of a head of state (the president or governor), an appointed cabinet, and a cadre of civil servants who implement policy. Governments at county and city levels typically consist of two branches: legislative entities, such as county commissions or city councils, and an executive branch headed by a mayor or city manager who directs employees of various city or county agencies.

Overlapping areas of authority among the various levels of government can create confusion about which entity is responsible for addressing a given problem. A recurring theme in U.S. history has been the struggle to determine the nexus of authority for social policy. The federal government enjoys no authority over state governments except that

---

[2]At the time of this writing, Nebraska is the only state with a unicameral legislature.

which pertains to constitutional violations. (As we will see in Chapter 10, the civil rights movement called on federal authority to overturn discriminatory policies endorsed by southern states.)

The federal government extends its capacity to pursue a social agenda through categorical and block grants to the states. These grants, sometimes known as "grants-in-aid," provide federal funds to states for specific purposes, allowing the federal government to deliver programs that might arguably extend beyond its constitutional authority. In the case of categorical grants (like Medicaid, Head Start, and SNAP), federal regulations are quite specific, and sometimes state governments find that these requirements represent unmanageable demands. In this case states might enter into negotiations with federal authorities to secure a "waiver" of certain regulations. Such waivers have become commonplace in relation to Medicaid, and four types of waivers are specifically authorized by the Social Security Act: Research and Demonstration Projects (Section 1115); Managed Care Waivers (Section 1915b); Home and Community Based Services Waivers (Section 1915c); and Concurrent Waivers (1915b and 1915c). Under the 2010 Patient Protection and Affordable Care Act, states had the opportunity to apply for grants to establish health insurance exchanges or to provide health insurance consumer assistance. As we will see in Chapter 4, some governors have refused to participate in these categorical grant programs.

State officials seldom object to block grants, which differ from categorical grants in imposing relatively few requirements or restrictions on the states. In a process known as "devolution," block grants are often used to transfer responsibility for social programs from the federal to the state level of government. Such was the case in 1996, for example, when the federal entitlement known as Aid to Families with Dependent Children (AFDC) was converted to a block grant known as Temporary Assistance to Needy Families (TANF). State-level discretion over the program increased, and the federal financial contribution was capped. The same thing happened in 1981 when Title XX was converted to the Social Services Block Grant. Typically, the rationale for devolution is that officials at the state level, who are closer to program clients, can better respond to their needs. Critics argue that devolution creates a problem known as "race to the bottom," in which states try to ensure that their social services and benefits are no more attractive than those of neighboring states to avoid migration by potential welfare recipients.

Just as there is tension between levels of government, there is also dispute about the proper roles of the legislative, executive, and judicial branches of government in social

BOX 2.1   Democracy in Action: The Electoral Process

Donald Trump became president in 2016 without securing a majority of the popular vote. How could this happen? Simply put, American presidents are not elected by the American people. They are chosen by the Electoral College. The College was not developed simply because the founding fathers thought members of the general public were not qualified to choose a leader. It stemmed from their commitment to states' rights and their concern that citizens in isolated rural areas might be disenfranchised in a popular election. As it turned out, the Electoral College does support states' rights. It also gives voice to rural voters and sustains the major political parties. Each state has a number of electors equal to its two senators plus its representatives. So, urban states have more electors, but not exactly in proportion to their greater populations. States develop the rules that determine how electors vote, and all but two states call for a "winner-take-all" system in which the candidate with a majority of popular votes gets support from all of the state's electors. The two exceptions are Nebraska and Maine. As a result, President Bush was able to win the election without winning a majority of the popular votes. For more information on the Electoral College, visit the website of the Federal Election Commission at http://www.fec.gov/.

policy. For example, some argue that decisions like the 1973 *Roe v. Wade* decision that established a woman's right to abortion moved the Supreme Court into an "activist" role in which it created social policy rather than simply interpreting the laws. The 1954 Supreme Court ruling against segregation in *Brown v. Board of Education* has also been cited as an example of judicial activism, as was its 2010 ruling in *Citizens United v. Federal Election Commission* that overturned a law limiting corporate political contributions.

LO 2-3   Describe the Workings of the Legislative, Executive, and Judicial Branches of Government

EP 3a
EP 5c
EP 8d

Social workers—indeed, anyone interested in influencing policy—must be conversant with how the branches of government operate because each of these entities plays a role in social policy. Put simply, the legislative branch passes the laws. The executive branch issues regulations and executive orders that determine how laws will be implemented and, in many cases, directly implements social policy. The judicial branch issues opinions that interpret laws and creates a body of case law in the process of resolving disputes. Thus, a comprehensive understanding of social policy should address the contributions of all three branches of government: legislation passed by the legislative branch, regulations promulgated by the executive branch, and opinions issued by the judicial branch.

THE LEGISLATIVE BRANCH

> *All Legislative Powers herein granted shall be vested in a Congress of the United States, which shall consist of a Senate and House of Representatives.*
>
> —ARTICLE I, SECTION 1, UNITED STATES CONSTITUTION

The U.S. Congress consists of the Senate and the House of Representatives. The Senate has 100 members, 2 from each state. Members of the Senate serve six-year terms. The House of Representatives has 435 members, with each state's representation being proportionate to the size of its population. At the time of this writing, the most populous state is California, which has 53 members in the House. The smallest delegations come from the states of Alaska, Delaware, Montana, North Dakota, South Dakota, Vermont, and Wyoming, which have one representative apiece. Members of the House serve two-year terms. The primary functions of the U.S. Congress are legislation (creation of laws) and budgeting (collection and allocation of public funds).

Legislation

Legislation begins with a proposal in the form of a bill or a resolution.[3] (See Figure 2.1.) A bill is used for most legislation. Bills originating in the House of Representatives are designated by the letters "H.R.," while those originating in the Senate begin with "S." These letters are followed by a number that the bill retains until it is enacted into law. Students interested in tracking the status or history of legislation will find an excellent source of information in the "Thomas" website maintained by the Library of Congress located at http://thomas.loc.gov.

Any House member may introduce a bill at any time while the House is in session. Traditionally, a receptacle known as the "hopper" (next to the clerk's desk in the House

---

[3]Most of the information presented in this section is found in a congressional document called *How Our Laws Are Made*, available through the U.S. House of Representatives: http://www.senate.gov/reference/resources/pdf/howourlawsaremade.pdf (accessed October 4, 2016).

FIGURE 2.1 How Our Laws Are Made

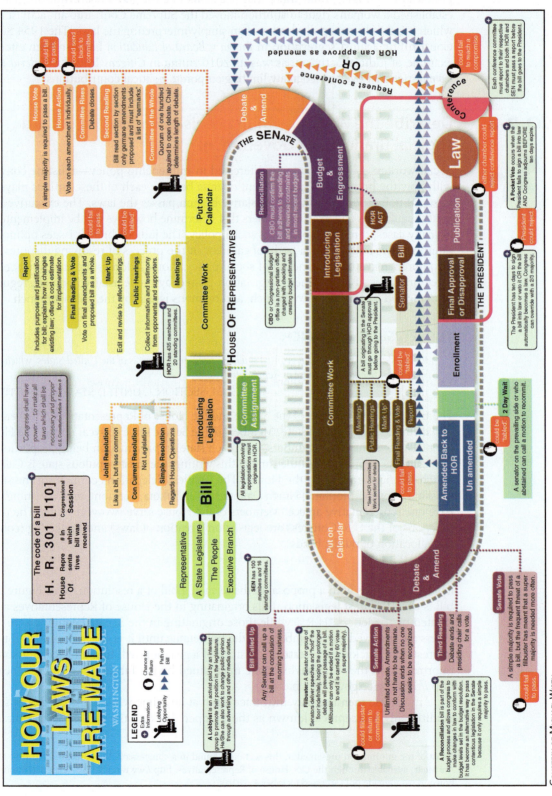

COURTESY OF MICHAEL WIRTH

chamber) was provided for this purpose; hence the expression "putting it in the hopper" refers to introducing an idea or proposal. The sponsor's signature must appear on the bill. A bill may have an unlimited number of cosponsors. It is assigned a number by the clerk and referred to the appropriate committee by the Speaker of the House.

The Speaker of the House enjoys some discretion in deciding which committee will receive a bill and thus can greatly influence its fate. For example, the Speaker can slow a bill's progress by forwarding it to a committee that is hostile to its intent. Consideration by committees is an important phase of the legislative process. It is the time when the public has an opportunity to be heard. Usually the first step in this process is a public hearing in which committee members hear testimony from witnesses representing diverse viewpoints. Each committee publicly announces the date, place, and subject of any hearing it conducts. A transcript of testimony taken at the hearing is frequently printed and distributed by the committee. These are available through the "Thomas" website (thomas. loc.gov) or federal depository libraries.

After hearings are completed, the bill is reviewed in what is popularly known as a "mark-up" session. Here members of the committee study the bill and review the testimony. Amendments may be offered, and committee members vote to accept or reject these changes.

When the committee has finished its deliberations, a vote is taken to determine what action to take on the bill. The bill may be reported, with or without amendment, or tabled, which means the bill has "died in committee." If the committee has approved extensive amendments, it may decide to report a new bill. This is known as a "clean bill," which will have a new number. If the committee votes to report a bill, the report is written by a committee staff member. It describes the measure and reasons for approval. Committee reports are excellent sources of information for those interested in congressional intent.

Although consideration of a bill generally occurs only after it is reported out of committee, sometimes the Speaker brings measures directly to the floor. Consideration of a bill may be governed by a resolution that sets out the debate procedures for the specific measure. Certain aspects, such as the amount of time allowed for debate and whether amendments can be offered, may be determined at this time. Debate time for a measure is usually divided between proponents and opponents. Each side yields time to members who wish to speak on the bill. When amendments are offered, these are also debated and voted upon. After the debate is concluded and amendments are determined, the House votes on final passage. In some cases, a vote to "recommit" the bill to committee is requested. This is usually an effort by opponents to change or table the measure. If a vote to recommit fails, a final vote is ordered.

The standing rules of the Senate differ from those of the House. They permit senators to debate at length in a process known as the "filibuster." A filibuster cannot be ended by a simple majority, but can be ended only if "cloture" is invoked by three-fifths of all senators. Senators also enjoy the right to propose floor amendments that are not germane to the matter under consideration. Thus, individual senators can raise issues and subject them to vote even if they have not been reviewed by a standing committee.[4]

The filibuster is traditionally reserved for issues on which senators hold strong opinions, although it has become a popular delaying tactic for the Senate minority. Republican senators used filibusters extensively during President Obama's first term. Several initiatives met with filibusters or threatened filibusters, including the 2009 stimulus package and the

---

[4]I am grateful to Stanley Bach, senior specialist in the legislative process, government division, for his discussion of the rights of senators and his introduction to Senate processes.

2010 health-care reform bill. Indeed, President Obama considered using a process known as "reconciliation" to ensure that the Affordable Care Act would not be subject to filibuster. Instead, the bill passed the Senate on a vote of 60-39. Several proposals have been advanced to reform the filibuster, and a voting procedure known as the "**nuclear option**" was used in 2013 to approve a measure that prohibited filibuster of executive branch and some judicial nominees.

After a measure passes in its originating chamber (either the House or the Senate), it goes to the other chamber. It must pass both bodies in the same form before it can be presented to the president for signature. If either chamber changes the measure, it must return to the originating chamber for concurrence or additional changes. This negotiation may occur on the floor of the House or Senate. Often a conference committee will be appointed with both House and Senate members. This group will resolve differences and report identical versions to both sides for a vote. Conference committees also issue reports outlining the final version of the bill.

After a bill has passed both the House and Senate, it is considered "enrolled" and is sent to the president, who may (1) sign the measure into law; (2) veto it and return it to Congress (where a two-thirds vote is required to override the veto); (3) let it become law without out signature; or (4) give it a "pocket veto" if the bill arrives at the end of a session; that is, if Congress has adjourned and the president does not sign a bill, it is automatically vetoed.

Resolutions

Generally speaking, a resolution differs from a bill in that it does not become law but is either an expression of the opinion of Congress or an administrative act governing the operation of Congress. Resolutions may originate in either the House of Representatives or the Senate. Like bills, resolutions are numbered sequentially, with a brief designation that reflects their origins. Those introduced in the House of Representatives are numbered with the designation "HRES," which stands for "House resolution." Those originating in the Senate are designated "SRES" for "Senate resolution." Joint resolutions (designated "HJRES" or "SJRES") are enacted in the same manner as bills. The only exceptions to this rule are joint resolutions proposing an amendment to the Constitution. Upon approval of such a resolution by two-thirds of both House and Senate, it is sent not to the president but to the administrator of general services for submission to the individual states for ratification. Such was the case with the Equal Rights Amendment (discussed in Chapter 13).

Budgeting

Budgeting is a gargantuan task in the United States, involving executive and legislative branches.[5] The calendar complicates public understanding of the process. The federal budget year, or fiscal year, extends from October 1 of each year through September 30 of the following year (see Table 2.1). The president is required by law to submit a proposed federal budget for the next fiscal year to Congress by the first Monday in February. This proposed budget is prepared by the White House Office of Management and Budget (OMB) under the president's direction and with consultation from cabinet members and other senior officials. The president's budget typically consists of several volumes, covering thousands of pages. But it is only a proposal and is subject to congressional approval.

Congress first passes a "budget resolution" that outlines the framework for budget decisions. It includes total spending, revenue projections, deficit figures, and targets for

---

[5]Much of the content in this section is drawn from *A Citizen's Guide to the Federal Budget*, which is available through the Office of Management and Budget.

TABLE 2.1 Major Steps in the Federal Budget Process

Budget Step	Budget Activities	Time Frame
1. President formulates budget for fiscal year (Oct. 1–Sept. 30).	Agencies in executive branch develop budget requests for submission to Office of Management and Budget (OMB). President reviews, requests, and develops budget.	February–December (Year 1)
2. Budget is transmitted.	Budget documents are prepared and sent to Congress by OMB.	December (Year 1); February/March (Year 2)
3. Congress reviews and approves budget.	Congress reviews the president's proposals, passes its "budget resolution," holds hearings, and approves annual appropriations bills.	March–September (Year 2)
4. The fiscal year begins.		October 1 (Year 2)
5. The budget is implemented.	Under supervision of the OMB and Government Accountability Office (GAO), agencies use the funds appropriated.	October 1 (Year 2)– September 30 (Year 3)
6. Actual spending and receipts are tabulated.	Agencies and OMB prepare reports on outlays and receipts.	October–November (Year 3)

two types of spending: discretionary and mandatory (Office of Management and Budget, 2001). *Discretionary spending* represents about a third of all federal spending, the portion that the president and Congress may spend through 13 annual appropriations bills. *Mandatory spending,* roughly two-thirds of federal spending, is authorized by permanent laws. It includes entitlements such as Social Security, Medicare, veterans' benefits, and SNAP. It also includes interest on the national debt. Changes in mandatory spending cannot be made without revising the laws that govern these programs.

Congressional examination of the president's budget consists of hearings and meetings by scores of committees and subcommittees. It is important to remember that despite a plethora of technical details, budgeting is a political process characterized by negotiation. Budget negotiations are carried out under time pressure, and failure to reach compromise can produce massive disruption. Such was the case in 2013 when federal agencies closed temporarily due to the lack of an approved budget.

BOX 2.2   The Budget Control Act of 2011

In 2011 the country's debt once again reached the ceiling approved by Congress. Ordinarily, a vote to raise the debt ceiling would be a simple formality, since it just authorizes the Treasury to borrow funds to cover expenses Congress has already approved. Facing the threat of a national default, Congress overcame bitter partisan divisions and the Budget Control Act of 2011 was passed.

The law created a Congressional Committee on Deficit Reduction (also called "the super committee") charged with negotiating agreement on measures to balance the budget. In the event the committee was unable to reach agreement or its agreement was not approved by Congress by the end of 2012, the law called for budget sequestration (across-the-board budget cuts) in all discretionary spending and some mandatory spending categories.

After the president and Congress approve a budget, it is monitored by agency managers and budget officials, the OMB, congressional committees, and the Government Accountability Office (an auditing arm of Congress).

Where the Money Goes   Government revenues may be placed in one of four types of funds. The "General Fund" is the largest. It is used to account for all revenues that are not required by law to be placed in a separate fund. "Special Funds" are used for revenues that must be applied to specific functions or activities, such as nuclear waste disposal. "Revolving Funds" are used when revenues from the sale of products or services are used to fund the operation. The Postal Service uses a revolving fund. Finally, "Trust Funds" are used for revenues that are dedicated to specific purposes such as Social Security, Medicare, and unemployment insurance (Office of Management and Budget, 2013). The federal budget presents spending across all four types of funds.

The country's budget reveals its priorities, and the lion's share of the U.S. budget is devoted to **mandatory** spending that is dictated by law. Sometimes this is called "entitlement" spending. Once the largest item in the entire budget, Social Security spending has been outstripped by security (which includes national defense and homeland security) since 2008. Still, the largest mandatory spending item is Social Security. The next-largest item, "other mandatory," includes SNAP, Temporary Assistance for Needy Families, Supplemental Security Income, Child Nutrition, the Earned Income Tax Credit, and veterans' pensions. Medicare comes next, followed by Medicaid. In the wake of the Great Recession, the Troubled Asset Relief Program (TARP) was added as a mandatory item. Categories of federal spending in 2017 are shown in Figure 2.2.

FIGURE 2.2 Estimated Federal Spending, Fiscal Year 2013

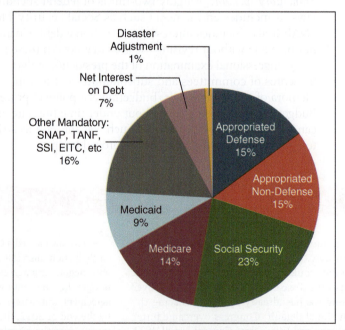

Source: Table S-5, Proposed Budget by Category, Summary Tables, Budget of the United States Government, Fiscal Year 2017, Office of Management and Budget (http://www.whitehouse.gov/sites/default/files/omb/budget/fy2017/assets/tables.pdf).

Discretionary or "appropriated" spending is divided between two categories: "defense" and "non-defense." Defense spending includes funding for the Department of Defense, as well as Homeland Security. Defense spending has declined since its most recent peak in 2011; however, the U.S. still spends more on defense than any other nation. Indeed, the country's mammoth defense budget is roughly equal to the combined defense spending of the next 14 highest countries (International Institute for Strategic Studies, 2015). Non-defense discretionary funding supports a wide array of programs, including education, training, science, technology, housing, transportation, and foreign aid.

Interest on the national debt is treated as a separate line item. After Hurricane Katrina an "adjustment for disaster costs" was added as a budget line. This represents the likelihood that federal outlays (either in the form of tax relief or direct expenditures) will be called for in case of disaster. It came just in time for the British Petroleum oil spill and Hurricane Sandy.

Trends in Federal Spending   Figure 2.3 illustrates broad trends in federal spending from 1940 to 2015, based on data provided by the Office of Management and Budget (OMB). The figure presents the proportion of federal outlays devoted to five broad functions: security (national defense), human resources, physical resources, net interest, and other functions.

Whereas National Defense is self-evident, the other categories deserve some explanation. Human Resources includes education and social services, health care, income security, Social Security, and veterans' benefits and services. Physical Resources includes energy, natural resources and the environment, commerce and housing credits, transportation, and community and regional development. Net Interest is payment on the debt. Finally, Other Functions includes international affairs, general science, space and technology, agriculture, administration of justice, and general government.

The dramatic growth in human resource spending is largely due to Social Security expenditures. In 1940 the largest human resource expenditure category was education, training, employment, and social services. That year, the (inflation-adjusted) $28 million spent on Social Security represented 6.8 percent of human resource outlays, which combined took up a trivial fraction (4.3 percent) of the nation's gross domestic product (GDP). By 2020, Social Security expenditures are projected to exceed $1.1 trillion and account for

FIGURE 2.3 Trends in Federal Spending

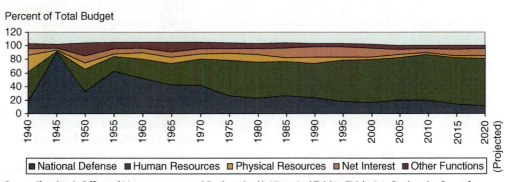

Percent of Total Budget

■ National Defense ■ Human Resources □ Physical Resources ■ Net Interest ■ Other Functions

Source (for data): Office of Management and Budget (n.d.), Historical Tables, Table 3.1: Outlays by Superfunction and Function: 1940–2021 (http://www.whitehouse.gov/omb/budget/Historicals).

over a third (34 percent) of human resource expenditures, which combined will make up . 15.8 percent of GDP (Office of Management and Budget, n.d.a)

By contrast, defense expenditures reached an all-time high of 90 percent of the federal budget in 1945 at the height of World War II, and by September 11, 2001, they had declined to an all-time low of 16 percent of the 2001 budget. These figures might have given defense contractors a moment's pause. Of course, they do not represent a decline in the absolute dollars devoted to defense. In 1945 defense expenditures were $82.9 billion in today's dollars. Even at its 2001 low, defense spending had grown to over $304 billion (in constant dollars). The Bush years were good for defense contractors and Obama's budgets only slightly reversed this trend. As of this writing it is unclear how President Trump's defense budget will stack up.

THE EXECUTIVE BRANCH

The executive power shall be vested in a President of the United States of America.
—ARTICLE II, SECTION I, UNITED STATES CONSTITUTION

Headed by the chief executive (the president), the executive branch is organized into 15 departments, each represented by a member of the president's cabinet. Although social workers are most familiar with the Department of Health and Human Services (HHS), most cabinet-level departments provide some kind of health or social services.

Within HHS, agencies range from the Administration for Children, Youth and Families (ACYF) to the Administration on Aging (AOA). There are also agencies charged with health and mental health, such as the Centers for Disease Control and Prevention (CDC), Food and Drug Administration (FDA), National Institutes of Health (NIH), National Institute of Mental Health (NIMH), and National Library of Medicine (NLM).

BOX 2.3   Understanding the Federal Budget Deficit

The federal budget deficit, which is computed annually, represents the difference between revenues and expenditures in the General Fund. It differs from the national debt, which is money borrowed to cover the accumulated deficits. For each year in which expenditures exceed revenues, more money is borrowed, which increases the national debt.

During World War I, the notion of a "debt ceiling" was introduced to enable the Treasury to borrow money without going to Congress for approval. From time to time Congress has been called upon to raise the debt ceiling. After the Republicans won a majority of the house in 2010, they refused to support raising the debt ceiling. Finally, in a last-minute compromise that involved significant (but delayed) cuts in discretionary spending, legislation was passed and signed to increase the ceiling.

Government borrowing is much like personal borrowing in that it is affected by the prevailing interest rate, which is determined by the Federal Reserve. Where individuals go to banks for loans, the U.S. Treasury borrows money from individuals when it issues notes and bonds.

Knowing the exact amount of the debt is less useful for analytic purposes than knowing its size relative to the Gross Domestic Product. Thus, debt is often reported as "percent of GDP." Although many politicians justify austerity measures by arguing that our debt is too high, no one really knows how much debt the U.S. economy can sustain without ill effects. Most agree, though, that a debt ratio that continually rises (in good times and in bad) is not sustainable. Indeed, the possibility of unlimited debt tends to undermine fiscal discipline just as the presence of easy money can lure consumers into bankruptcy. The challenge for our leaders is to ensure that we borrow only to make investments that will improve the nation's economic well-being. When debt is incurred for purposes that do not contribute to future prosperity, it becomes a drain on future generations. [Please see Kogan (2013) for a discussion of the national debt.]

The Supplemental Nutrition Assistance Program (SNAP, formerly known as Food Stamps) is a bit of an anomaly since it is administered by the Department of Agriculture—more commonly associated with farm subsidies, commodities distribution, and food price supports. SNAP does help stabilize demand for agricultural products, and as a benefit for low-income Americans it counteracts the regressive impacts of agricultural price supports.

Military and social spending are often considered polar opposites. (A once-popular bumper sticker read: "Won't it be nice when schools have plenty of money and the Army has to hold a bake sale to build a bomber?") This dichotomy is a bit misleading, however, because the Department of Defense provides a wide range of social and health services to military personnel and their families and is a major employer of professional social workers. Likewise, social workers deliver a wide range of services in the Department of Veterans Affairs.

Even the Department of Commerce has some bearing on social policy because it houses the Census Bureau. Decisions about the census provide the very information on which social policy is based. For example, sampling techniques may underrepresent marginalized groups such as same-sex couples. Likewise, the census treatment of people of mixed ethnicity in the United States changed in 2000 to reflect new understanding of culture and identity.

The Department of Housing and Urban Development (HUD) has a mandate to address issues related to community planning and development and fair housing, but it increasingly finds itself addressing social policy issues that affect residents of public housing. Programs under HUD are described in detail in Chapter 5.

The Department of the Interior is involved in the direct provision of social services and health care through the Bureau of Indian Affairs (BIA), which is addressed in more depth in Chapter 10.

The executive branch is by far the largest employer in the federal system. In 2010 more than 2.7 million people worked as civilian employees of the federal executive branch. The Department of Defense was the largest employer, with a civilian workforce of over 772,000, followed by the Postal Service, with about 643,000. Health and Human Services paled by comparison, with about 69,800 on its 2010 payroll. Also modest are the other two branches, with the judicial branch employing 33,800 people and the legislative, 30,600 (U.S. Census Bureau, 2012d).

The Regulatory Process

In high school we were taught that "Congress makes the laws and the executive branch carries them out." As with many such lessons, this one oversimplifies the situation. The executive branch does create policy through the regulatory process by which it translates legislation into services, resources, and daily decisions. Furthermore, the rules and regulations promulgated by executive agencies do have the force of law.

Agencies don't make rules and regulations in a vacuum. Federal rulemaking is governed by the Administrative Procedures Act (APA), which has several provisions for public participation.[6] Usually rulemaking is initiated in response to legislative action, but the APA does allow for the public to petition an agency to begin rulemaking. Once the process begins, the APA requires that departments keep a record that reflects both public participation and the factual conclusions on which the rule is based. Rulemaking must begin with a reasonable period of "notice and comment" (usually 60 days). Agencies provide public

---

[6]States have their own laws that govern rulemaking by state agencies. These laws are also typically called Administrative Procedures Acts.

notice of their intent to begin rulemaking by publishing a statement in the *Federal Register.* Often this statement is accompanied by press releases as well as targeted electronic notices. At the end of the comment period, the agency prepares a summary of comments received and its response. This summary is followed either by a new round of notice and comments or by publication of the rule (Lubbers, 1998).

Since 1990, a procedure known as negotiated rulemaking (or "neg reg") has enabled agencies to bring interested parties into the process at an early stage and involve them in drafting rules. Agencies that anticipate controversy might use neg reg to reach a compromise among key players before the period of public comment begins.

As an advocate for your clients, you have three potential avenues for participation in rulemaking. First, you might petition an agency to begin rulemaking. Second, during the notice and comment period, you can comment on a proposed rule and offer revisions. Finally, you can ask to be identified as an interested party and then participate in negotiated rulemaking. Social work advocates naturally pay close attention to the legislative process, but if they fail to participate in the rulemaking process their advocacy efforts may be ineffective.

THE JUDICIAL BRANCH[7]

The Judicial Power of the United States shall be vested in one Supreme Court, and in such inferior courts as the Congress may from time to time ordain and establish.

—ARTICLE III, UNITED STATES CONSTITUTION

There are two judicial systems in the United States: the federal court system created by Congress under the Constitution and the state and local courts established by state laws.

Under the Constitution, only the **Supreme Court** is indispensable. Congress has established and abolished other federal courts over time. The current federal system includes the Supreme Court, 13 U.S. courts of appeals, and 94 U.S. district courts and specialized courts. The U.S. courts of appeals serve 12 regions (in addition to the 12 regional courts, there is a federal court of appeals), and for historical reasons they are often referred to as circuit courts. During the 19th century, judges in courts of appeals rode the circuit on horseback.

Most controversies are decided in the state courts because the power of federal courts is restricted. Under Article III of the Constitution, federal courts may decide *"[c]ontroversies between two or more states; between a State and Citizens of another State; between Citizens of different States; [or] between Citizens of the same State claiming Lands under Grants of different States."* Federal courts also hear cases in which the U.S. government or one of its officers is suing someone or being sued, as well as cases for which state courts might be biased or inappropriate.

Federal cases originate in district courts and may be reviewed by courts of appeals upon the request of one party. The final appeal in a few cases is heard in the Supreme Court. For example, the case of *Roe v. Wade* involved a class action suit challenging criminal abortion laws in Texas. A three-judge district court from the Northern District of Texas declared the state's abortion statutes void. The case was argued in 1971 before the Supreme Court, which also declared the Texas statutes unconstitutional. This case is discussed in more detail in Chapter 13.

---

[7]Much of the material in this section is drawn from *About Federal Courts*, available online at http://www.uscourts.gov/about-federal-courts (as of October 2016).

The Supreme Court of the United States consists of nine justices appointed for life by the president with advice and consent of the Senate. In the nation's history, all but 27 Supreme Court justices nominated by a president have secured Senate confirmation. Each justice is assigned to one of the district courts of appeals for emergency responses (urgent appeals that cannot wait until the full court is in session), and the chief justice assumes additional administrative responsibilities. The Supreme Court convenes each year on the first Monday in October and usually remains in session until the end of June. During this period, the Court reviews about 5,000 cases annually. In most, a brief decision is offered, indicating that the case is not of sufficient importance to warrant review. Each year the court reviews about 150 cases of national importance.

While officers of the Supreme Court are called justices, those presiding over courts of appeals, district courts, and other courts are called judges. All federal judges are appointed by the president with the advice and consent of the Senate. Most judicial appointments are for life or, in the language of the Constitution, they *"hold their Offices during good Behavior."* These judges may be removed from office against their will only through *"impeachment for, and conviction of Treason, Bribery, or other high Crimes and Misdemeanors."* Between 1789 and 1992, 2,627 men and women served as federal judges. Of those, 184 (7 percent) resigned for reasons other than health or age. In the last 200 years, Congress has removed 7 federal judges following contested impeachment proceedings. Furthermore, between 1818 and 1980, at least 22 judges resigned or retired following allegations of misbehavior (Van Tassel, Wirtz, & Wonders, 1993).

The judicial system, like the executive branch, plays an important role in social policy development. In the nation's history several programs and laws have been challenged in federal courts. These include the Child Labor Act, which was twice declared unconstitutional, and the Social Security Act, which was successfully defended against a constitutional challenge. Disputes over federal entitlements such as Supplemental Security Income have also been heard in federal courts. Indeed, some opponents of federal entitlements have argued that they clog the federal courts with disputes between citizens and states.

In this section we have examined the basic structure of the U.S. government in terms of both levels and branches. It takes only a basic level of understanding of human behavior to see that there are inevitable tensions among these levels and branches. The authors of the Constitution understood and anticipated these tensions and crafted "checks and balances" to prevent the concentration of power in any single individual or entity. As we saw in Chapter 1, some libertarian thinkers have argued that powerful private interests also serve as checks on the power of government. In the following section we will briefly examine privatization and explore its implications for the evolving role of government in the United States.

LO 2-4   Understand Privatization and Its Theoretical and Practical Limits

EP 5c

Privatization refers to the private financing, production, development, and/or distribution of public assets or services: all practices that have been justified on the basis of **neoliberal** ideology, which holds close to the tenets of **laissez-faire capitalism**. Since the 1980s, the term "neoliberal" has generally been used by critics to describe economic policies, such as deregulation and fiscal austerity, that are designed to expand markets and minimize the role of government. (For in-depth consideration of neoliberalism and its impact on social work practice, please see Gray et al., 2015).

When the privatization of Social Security is discussed (as in Chapter 4) it refers to the transfer of retirement savings from government trust funds to private brokerage accounts. Privatization of services generally involves a contract between a government entity and a private company, as when the City of Atlanta outsourced its water system to United Water, now a subsidiary of the French company Suez Lyonnaise des Eaux (Cotchett, 2004); or when a state employs a private firm like Corrections Corporation of America to manage its prisons. At the local level, privatization may be used to arrange for a company to deliver basic city services such as garbage collection or ambulance services. The term *private-public partnership* is sometimes used to describe the practice of hiring private providers to deliver public services.

Privatization of human services is not a new concept. State and local governments have employed private-sector organizations to deliver child welfare services since the early 1800s (Rosenthal, 2000); but privatization received a major boost in the 1980s from the Reagan administration. Vowing to end "the era of big government," President Reagan introduced privatization, arguing that it would increase the efficiency of public services and make them more responsive to local needs and concerns. Indeed, the 1988 report of the Presidential Commission on Privatization argued that the strategy would reverse the government expansion that began with the Progressive movement of the late 19th and early 20th centuries (Karger & Stoesz, 2002).

The 1991 dissolution of the Soviet Union, seen by many as a victory for capitalism, gave further impetus to privatization. American enthusiasm for the free market seemed boundless, leading Nancy Jurik (then president of the Society for the Study of Social Problems) to observe, "We now live in a society characterized by a hyper-privatization that is reconstructing everything from non-profits and government, to community, family, and individual life—all in the image of the market" (2004, p. 1). Jurik invoked the term "new privatization" to describe the impetus to reinvent social institutions according to market principles.

The result has been an explosion in revenue for human service corporations and what Frumkin and Andre-Clark (1999) termed "the rise of the corporate social worker." In 2008, NASW reported that nearly a third (28 percent) of its members were employed in for-profit settings (Whitaker & Arrington, 2008). Human services such as child welfare, child support enforcement, employment services, and TANF are increasingly carried out by for-profit corporations. A 2015 review indicated that there was no evidence that private management of TANF resulted in greater efficiency or improved client outcomes, though there was some indication that nonprofit management was associated with better employment outcomes (Butz, 2015).

Construction and management of prisons has been another growth area for private for-profit corporations. In 2016, the Department of Justice announced that it was discontinuing its use of private prisons, in response to a report indicating that they were associated with more violence and higher recidivism rates (Zapotsky & Harlan, 2016). The federal action only affects about 22,000 prisoners, as most people who are incarcerated in the U.S. are in state prisons. In 2013, an estimated 133,044 prisoners (8 percent of the prison population) were incarcerated in private facilities. The two largest private prison management companies, Corrections Corporation of America and the GEO group, which control about 75 percent of this "market," reporting revenues of $2.8 billion, and profits that were roughly double the rate of average private firms in the United States. One key to the profitability of this industry has been "guaranteed occupancy" provisions in contracts, under which the state agrees to pay for beds up to a certain occupancy rate (often 90 percent) whether they are used or not. Prison contracting processes are typically influenced by political relationships, often greased by lobbying and campaign contributions. (Tylek, 2015)

Pay for Success, also known as **Social Investment Bonding** (SIB) is a financing mechanism that seeks to attract private investment to public services. Through carefully structured contracts, investors such as Goldman Sachs provide funding to operate a program in exchange for a healthy return if an independent evaluator determines that the effort has achieved carefully defined goals. While some claim that SIB programs "do not cost taxpayer money," (i.e., Porter, 2015) they do require substantial public subsidies, including federal start-up money provided through the "Social Innovation Fund" in the form of grants for technical assistance provided by third-party organizations like the Harvard Kennedy School Social Impact Bond Lab and Third Sector Capitol Partners. They also involve local philanthropies (for example, Bloomberg Philanthropies or United Way) in guaranteeing at least part of the investment. In addition, should a program prove successful, the government pays investors not only the cost of the program, but also a healthy return on their investment.

SIBs are not used to finance innovative or experimental programs, but are applied only to interventions that demonstrably reduce costs (Cohen, 2014). Still, the first social impact bond in the United States (a project designed to provide cognitive behavioral therapy to youth incarcerated at Rikers Island) was discontinued because it failed to deliver on its promise of reduced recidivism. Nonetheless, as of this writing, eleven Pay for Success Projects are underway in major cities throughout the United States (Nonprofit Finance Fund, n.d.); millions of dollars have been made available as seed money for Pay for Success projects through the "Social Innovation Fund" of the Corporation for National and Community Service (a federal agency); and in 2015 Representatives. Young (Indianna) and Rep. Delaney (Maryland) introduced the Social Impact Bond Act (HR 5170) to provide federal funding and allow state and local educational funds to be diverted to Pay for Success initiatives. The bill was passed unanimously in June, 2016, by the House of Representatives, and as of this writing was pending in the Senate. Like other privatization initiatives, Pay for Success taps into the American enthusiasm for private-sector solutions to public problems. It may not work for every problem, and it may not be the most efficient approach; but, as one politician explained to me, "If it increases the funding available for effective programs, I'm all for it."

Of course, the privatization trend is not a one-way street. As some services are contracted out to the private sector, others are brought back under the auspices of government in a process known as **reverse contracting** (Hefetz & Warner, 2004). The most well-known recent example of reverse contracting is seen in airports. Prior to the 9/11 attacks, private companies were charged with airport security. Despite clear documentation of its ineffectiveness, this system remained in place, with devastating results. Amid public outcry the Transportation Security Administration (TSA) was established, and airport security officials are now employees of the federal government.

LIMITS OF PRIVATIZATION

Supporters of privatization usually emphasize a perceived need to reduce the size of government. They exploit the popular stereotype of government workers as unresponsive and inefficient and invoke the notion that private-sector employees are all motivated and nimble. Unfortunately, decisions to privatize are typically based on sweeping political and ideological arguments rather than practical or theoretical considerations (Hefetz & Warner, 2004; Nicholson-Crotty, 2004). On a practical level, privatization initiatives may not be the most efficient way to deliver public services, as when the American passion for market-based solutions results in a diversion of public funds into private profits.

Economic theory suggests distinct roles for the private market and public agencies, with government stepping in when the market "fails."[8] The private market fails when the conditions that support competition are not met. These include access to diverse providers, informed and able consumers, and a product that can be compared with others.

Access to Diverse Providers

Competition is the hallmark of a free market. To obtain market efficiencies there must be multiple providers competing for a government contract or a consumer's business. Without competition (i.e., in a monopoly situation) there is no incentive to optimize cost-effectiveness or to maintain high standards. Without diverse providers, the market fails to deliver an efficient outcome.

Practically speaking, it is difficult to identify multiple providers in many rural and inner-city locations. The unwritten history of privatization includes tales of public managers who have worked for months to prepare elaborate requests for proposals, only to find that just one firm is interested in delivering the product or service.

BOX 2.4   Managing the Economy

The Great Recession can be seen as an inevitable part of the U.S. business cycle. Like the Great Depression, it triggered calls for government intervention. Faced with massive job losses and the evaporation of their wealth, Americans looked to our newly elected president to halt the decline, and President Obama's response was based on Keynesian economics.

J. Maynard Keynes (1883-1946) has been credited with saving capitalism with his radical idea that in times of contraction governments should spend money—even money they don't have. His views stood in sharp contrast to the "neoclassical" economic paradigm advanced by Milton Friedman (economic adviser to President Reagan). Friedman and his colleagues from the "Chicago School" (of economics) argue that government can't regulate the business cycle and that if private markets are left alone long enough they will self-correct. Of course, as Keynes pointed out in his criticism of neoclassical economics, "In the long run we are all dead."

President Obama had two tools to deal with the recession: fiscal policy and monetary policy. Fiscal policy requires congressional action to lower taxes and increase government spending. The "stimulus package" is an example of fiscal policy, which is designed to jump-start demand for goods and services. Other examples of fiscal policy are the progressive income tax (which can put a lid on demand by drawing off part of rising incomes) and the welfare system (which sets a floor under demand by providing income during economic downturns).

Monetary policy involves controlling the supply of money. It is implemented by our national bank, known as the Federal Reserve. We see the Federal Reserve reducing interest rates during downturns and raising them during periods of economic expansion (when inflation becomes a concern).

---

[8]For a more detailed discussion of the conditions necessary for market competition, see Lewis and Widerquist (2002).

Informed and Able Consumers

Consumers must have the information and resources necessary to make intelligent choices among multiple providers. Consumers who are not competent to make their own choices, either because of limited capacity or because they are in state custody, cannot optimize their well-being. In this situation the market tends to favor the provider who can deliver the greatest cost savings, irrespective of quality considerations.

Vulnerable populations are vulnerable consumers—unwilling or unable to distinguish among providers—so contracts for services to children, prisoners, the poor, and the mentally ill may be awarded to the lowest bidder, and it can be years before quality failures come to the attention of decision makers. For instance, prison privatization began in the U.S. in 1983, and it was over 30 years before quality concerns led the federal government to *begin* the process of reverse contracting described above.

Comparable Products

To determine the value or the quality of a product or service, it must be comparable—subject to objective assessment. Intangible aspects of a service (such as empathy or relationship) are difficult if not impossible to objectively evaluate. If these intangibles are important, it is difficult to select among possible providers or to determine the effectiveness of a contract with a private provider.

Petr and Johnson (1999) provided an example that illustrates the difficulty in assessing human services. They reported on the privatization of foster care services in Kansas. Contracts with private contractors stipulated that 90 percent of children in foster care would experience three or fewer moves. Contractors met this requirement by redefining a move to exclude "emergency" placements that lasted less than 30 days. If the term "moves" is subject to interpretation, imagine the difficulties involved in defining a concept like "care."

As we have seen, the absence of conditions that support competition should (theoretically) mitigate against privatization. Richard Titmuss offered another critique of privatization. He was one of the first to view privatization as part of a broad, dehumanizing trend. In his 1971 work, *The Gift Relationship,* Titmuss examined the privatization of America's blood banks. Comparing the commercial system in the United States with the voluntary system in England, he argues not only that the quality of the blood suffered but, perhaps more importantly, treating blood as a commodity undermined human bonds that were established through charitable giving.

Under the right conditions privatization can improve the delivery of goods and services. When the market offers a competitive supply of contractors, when the consumer or recipient of the service is able to make choices and provide feedback, and when the product can be standardized, the private market can be an excellent allocation mechanism. For example, it is perfectly reasonable for the military to purchase food and even sophisticated weapons on the private market. Roads, electricity, and phone service are good examples of products that can be standardized and effectively delivered through privatization. The political and ideological climate of our times favors privatization. As a result, most professional social workers will be touched in some way by this trend. Yet, as we will see in later chapters, the privatization of human services such as child care, welfare, health care, and prisons has seldom lived up to the promises of its proponents.

LO 2-5   Understand the Structure and Philosophical Underpinnings of the U.S. Tax System

EP 3a
EP 5c

Benjamin Franklin is quoted as saying that only two things are inevitable: death and taxes. The two are sometimes approached with equal dread! No one likes to pay taxes.[9] Indeed, public polls have revealed that a majority of Americans have cheated on their tax returns. Some of us spend more money on tax-avoidance schemes than the schemes ever save us in taxes. There is something intrinsically satisfying about avoiding taxes. Throughout the nation's history, policy makers have tapped into this mindset, using it to advance social agendas through the judicious use of tax credits and deductions. In this section we will first examine the U.S. tax system and then describe the use of taxation to accomplish social goals.

STRUCTURAL AND PHILOSOPHICAL CONSIDERATIONS

Americans pay taxes to each level of government. As with legislative processes, taxes at lower levels generally mirror those at the federal level. Sales taxes and property taxes are exceptions to this general rule as they are not applied at the federal level. Occasionally, proposals for a national sales tax or "value added" tax have surfaced, but to date none has been established in the United States.

There are few constitutional limits on the taxation authority of the federal government. Congress has the power to *"lay and collect Taxes, Duties, imposts and excises, to pay the Debts and provide for the common Defence and general Welfare of the United States"* (Article I, Section 8, Clause 1). Nonetheless, both income and Social Security taxes have been subjected to constitutional challenges. The Sixteenth Amendment, passed in 1913, affirmed the authority of the federal government to levy income taxes. Two Supreme Court cases upheld the constitutionality of the Social Security tax (see Chapter 4).

The utilitarian liberal philosophical perspective introduced in Chapter 1 emphasizes the distinction between regressive and progressive taxes. A regressive tax is one that falls most heavily on the poor. For example, a head tax exacts the same amount from each person. Since poor people have less money, the tax represents a greater proportion of a poor person's resources. The rate of a progressive tax increases as a person's affluence increases, and so the amount of tax paid is greater for the wealthy. Simply put, progressive taxes are based on the taxpayer's ability to pay. The federal income tax is a progressive tax, while sales and payroll taxes (described later in this chapter) are regressive.

The rationale for progressive taxation stems directly from a utilitarian liberal tradition. Under this philosophy, the goal of policy is to optimize well-being, or (since we're talking about taxes here) to minimize distress. For those individuals who are at, or very close to, a social minimum, taking 30 percent of their income will place them at a significant disadvantage. But for individuals who are well above a social minimum, taking 30 percent of their income will create much less distress. Or, to put it more simply, if you have $2 and I take $1, you will be unable to buy a half-gallon of milk. But if you have $200 and I take $100 or even $125, you will be able to buy much more than a half-gallon of milk. Under this view (which dominates federal, and to a lesser extent, state income tax structures), the community as a whole experiences less distress with a progressive tax than with a regressive one.

---

[9]This section draws heavily from the third edition of a law text by Michael J. Graetz and Deborah Schenk, *Federal Income Taxation Principles and Policies,* and the advice of a singular tax attorney, Lawrence Barusch.

A HUMAN PERSPECTIVE   Advocacy: Broad Coalition Proposes a Tax Increase

Contributed by Connie Ginsberg, Family Connection of South Carolina, Incorporated (retired executive director) and Leon Ginsberg, Appalachian State University, Boone, North Carolina

Confronted with severe Medicaid cuts in 2001, a coalition of organizations in South Carolina proposed to increase the state cigarette excise tax—then the lowest in the nation—and use the revenue to meet the health-care needs of low-income families and children. Connie Ginsberg was a leader in the coalition. She served on the steering committee, joined health providers in meeting with newspaper editorial boards throughout the state to explain the need for additional revenue, and organized a grassroots effort among families with children who had chronic illnesses or disabilities. The coalition, which included nonprofit organizations serving families and children, health organizations (including physician specialty groups, lawyers' organizations, and educators), and health insurance companies such as Blue Cross and Blue Shield, pressed its case in the state legislature and in public forums, including editorial boards of South Carolina's major daily newspapers, press conferences, and a rally on the grounds of the State House.

After months of work, the legislation to increase the cigarette tax failed in the South Carolina House of Representatives by five votes. The incumbent governor, a Democrat who was facing a tough reelection campaign in 2002, which he ultimately lost, lobbied against the tax increase in the critical hours leading to the vote. Coming

so close to success, however, was a major victory in this tobacco state.

In 2002 a new governor, this time a Republican, pledged to reduce taxes. Although an attempt was made to reintroduce the cigarette tax increase in his first years of office, for four years the cigarette tax proposal was dormant.

The issue came up again in 2007 when the South Carolina House of Representatives set forth a plan to increase the cigarette tax. Raising health-care coverage for low-income children was proposed as another item in the budget, not tied to the cigarette tax increase. This time, the governor supported a tobacco tax increase in his executive budget, but only as a basis for reducing other taxes.

The increased cigarette tax did not pass the state legislature in 2007. The Senate did not consider it, and South Carolina's cigarette tax remained the lowest in the nation. However, improving health-care coverage for children became a goal of the legislature, and state funds were dedicated to increasing children's Medicaid coverage in the 2008 fiscal year budget. The governor vetoed the increase, but a 100 percent vote of the legislature overrode his veto. So the main objective of the process was achieved without a cigarette tax increase.

From a political science viewpoint, the ultimate outcome of this effort was not surprising. Legislatures frequently resist dedicated taxes and prefer, instead, to appropriate funds overall, from whatever sources of revenue are available. Children's health services are popular, but a cigarette tax increase was controversial.

John Rawls's concept of a social minimum offers another argument in favor of progressive taxation. Under this view, a regressive tax would put a larger proportion of the population below an acceptable minimum standard of living than would a progressive tax.

Federal Income Tax

The individual income tax is the largest single source of revenue to the federal government, projected to equal 49 percent of total revenues in 2017 (compared with corporate income taxes, which are estimated at just 11 percent of 2017 revenues). The federal income tax is a progressive tax. For wages, the tax rate increases as a taxpayer's income rises. (This is not true of dividend and interest income, which is taxed at a lower flat rate, currently 15 to 20 percent.)

To compute their tax obligations, Americans first determine their **gross income**. Then certain exclusions (e.g., employer payments for health insurance or qualified retirement plans) and deductions (e.g., alimony, business expenses, retirement contributions) are subtracted to arrive at the taxpayer's **adjusted gross income** (AGI). The AGI is used for some purposes. Then the taxpayer may take itemized deductions (e.g., interest on home mortgage). Instead of taking itemized deductions, the taxpayer can subtract a **standard deduction**. She can then subtract **personal exemptions** for herself and her dependents. The result is **taxable income**.

Each person's tax is then assessed by applying the appropriate rates to the portions of income in each of the tax code's steps or **brackets**. Federal income tax brackets are adjusted annually for inflation. From time to time they are also changed through tax legislation. By the time you read this chapter, the brackets for federal income tax will no doubt be different. Nonetheless, these figures should help you understand the general concepts. The 2016 Tax Rate Schedule for individuals included seven brackets. The results for seven hypothetical taxpayers are presented in Table 2.2.

Here is a simplified illustration: Consider three taxpayers from our table. Pam (Taxpayer A) works part-time for a cleaning company, Sandra (Taxpayer C) is a social worker, and Veronica (Taxpayer G) is a neurosurgeon. In 2016, Pam had $6,000 in taxable income, Sandra had $50,000, and Veronica had $600,000. Assuming that Veronica's income was all from wages, she would pay not only the highest absolute dollar amount but also a higher proportion of her income.

In 2016, Pam would have paid 10 percent on all of her taxable income ($600 in taxes), Sandra would pay the same rate as Pam on her taxable income up to $9,275 ($927.50 in taxes). On income in the next bracket, Sandra would pay the next higher rate, 15 percent. Here, Sandra would owe $4,256.10 (15 percent of $28,374, which is $37,650 minus $9,276). Finally, Sandra would have some income in the third, 25 percent bracket: $50,000 minus $37,650 equals $12,350. Twenty-five percent of this would equal $3,087.25. Sandra's total tax bill would equal $8,270.85 ($927.50 + $4,256.10 + $3,087.25). Sandra's effective tax rate would be 16.5 percent ($8,270.50/$50,000. Veronica would pay the most tax and the highest rate. Her tax is computed using all seven of the income brackets listed in Table 2.2: $927.50 (10 percent of $9,275) plus $4,256.10 (15 percent of $27,325) plus $13,374.75 (25 percent of $53,499) plus $27,719.72 (28 percent of $98,999) plus $73,655/67 (33 percent of $223,199) plus $594.65 (35 percent of $1,699) plus $73,239.80 which is 39.6 percent of the remaining income

TABLE 2.2   Computing Federal Income Tax (2016 Rates)

Taxable Income Rates for Single Filers	Hypothetical Taxpayer (Taxable Income)*						
	A ($6,000)	B ($25,000)	C ($50,000)	D ($100,000)	E ($200,000)	F ($400,000)	G ($600,000)
$415,051 and up (39.6%)							$73,239.80
$413,351-415,050 (35%)							$594.65
$190,151-$413,350 (33%)					$3,250.17	$69,250.17	$73,655.67
$91,151-$190,150 (28%)				$2,477.72	$27,719.72	$27,719.72	$27,719.72
$37,651-91,150 (25%)			$3,087.25	$13,374.75	$13,374.75	$13,374.75	$13,374.75
$9,276-$37,650 (15%)		$2,358.60	$4,256.10	$4,256.10	$4,256.10	$4,256.10	$4,256.10
0–$9, 275 (10%)	$927.50	$927.50	$927.50	$927.50	$927.50	$927.50	$927.50
Tax Owed	$927.50	$3,286.10	$8,270.85	$21,036.07	$49,528.24	$115,528.20	$193,768.20
Effective Tax Rate	10%	13.1%	16.5%	21%	24.8%	28.8%	32.3%

*Figures under each taxpayer indicate the amount of tax owed in each income bracket.

over $415,051. Veronica's total tax bill would amount to $195,364, which yields an effective tax rate of 33 percent. Her *marginal* rate would be 39.6 percent. In a progressive tax, the marginal rate (highest rate paid on the last taxable dollar) is higher than the effective rate (average rate paid on all taxable dollars).

Of course, in the real world, Veronica would probably take advantage of various opportunities to reduce her taxes. Some kinds of income, such as the interest on certain municipal bonds, are not taxed at all. As mentioned above, dividends, interest, and long-term capital gains from sale of stock are taxed at a maximum rate of only 20 percent. Often tax can be deferred, which effectively reduces it as inflation erodes the value of the dollar. For example, high-ranking executives may receive **incentive stock options** that allow them to purchase company stock at a price much lower than the market value at the time of purchase (already an economic gain). They then defer paying any tax until they sell the stock.

Personal Exemptions

In 2016 the personal exemption for an individual taxpayer was $4,050, and the standard deduction was $6,300. So a single taxpayer with income below $10,350 was not required to file a return that year. (Of course, he or she might have chosen to do so in order to receive a refund on taxes that were withheld.) A dependent exemption for the same amount can also be claimed for those who meet certain criteria. These exemptions are phased out for taxpayers with incomes over about $259,400 (in 2016).

Tax Preparation

As you can see, the process of filing tax returns gets complicated quickly. The Volunteer Income Tax Assistance (VITA) program provides help for low-income taxpayers, people with disabilities, and those with limited English proficiency. In addition, the Tax Counseling for the Elderly (TCE) program provides free help to those aged 60 and over. A tool for locating programs within your zip code can be found at this site: https://www.irs.gov/individuals/free-tax-return-preparation-for-you-by-volunteers.

Unfortunately, only a small fraction of low-income taxpayers report accessing free tax preparation services. Over half report that they pay a professional to prepare their returns, often using a **Refund Anticipation Check** to cover the cost (Maag, 2005; Tax Policy Center, n.d.).

Social Security Tax

The 1935 passage of the Social Security Act financed the nation's retirement, disability, and unemployment insurance systems through a tax on wages. This tax was originally set at 1 percent of wages and was expected to increase to 5 percent as the program grew. The payroll tax was equally divided between employees and employers. It was immediately subjected to a constitutional challenge, and the Supreme Court upheld the payroll tax (*Chas. C. Steward Machine Co. v. Davis*). Today the payroll tax amounts to 15 percent of the nation's wages, up to a limit called a "cap." Income above this amount is not subject to the payroll tax. In 2016, the wage cap was $118,500. Half of the tax is taken directly from workers' paychecks, and half is paid quarterly by employers. The tax is usually listed on pay stubs as the **FICA contribution**, with FICA standing for Federal Insurance Contribution Act. In addition to the FICA tax, wages are taxed at 2.9 percent (again split between employer and employee) to finance Medicare's hospital insurance program. There is no wage cap on this Medicare tax, and high income earners pay an additional Medicare tax of 0.9 percent.

Until 2013, income from investments did not support Social Security or Medicare. Some advocates argued that applying Social Security taxes to investment income would go a long way toward eliminating threats to the solvency of these programs, and as part of the Affordable Care Act, Americans with adjusted gross incomes over $200,000 (individuals) or $450,000 (couples) are subject to a 3.8 percent unearned income tax that supports Medicare.

State Taxes

Most state revenues are drawn from state income taxes, property taxes, and sales taxes. Among these, state income taxes are the most progressive. They generally mirror those at the federal level, except that state tax rates are lower. Property taxes are considered moderately progressive to the extent that those with the most valuable property pay the highest amounts. Sales taxes are the most regressive of the state tax alternatives. They are collected by vendors at the point of sale and usually range from about 3 percent to 10 percent. Some states try to reduce the regressivity of their sales taxes by exempting essential items, such as food or medicine. Nonetheless, as the Institute on Taxation and Economic Policy (ITEP) argues, states tend to rely heavily on sales tax revenues and consequently they tax lower- and middle-income Americans more heavily than affluent Americans (Institute on Taxation and Economic Policy, 2013).

The notion of a "race to the bottom" certainly applies to state income and sales taxes, as state officials worry that if their rates are higher than those of neighboring states, their more affluent residents (and corporations) will relocate or purchase big-ticket items elsewhere.

The Great Recession hit state budgets hard, reducing revenues from income tax and increasing demand for health and social programs. In addition to spending cuts, most states responded with tax increases. So-called "sin" taxes on alcohol and tobacco were easy targets, but states also raised rates on income, sales, and business taxes, as well as motor vehicle registrations and other fees (Johnson, Nicholas, & Pennington, 2009).

Local Taxes

Traditionally, local governments have collected the bulk of their revenues through property taxes. Tax rates on real property (e.g., land and some personal property, such as cars) can vary tremendously within a state and from state to state. The tax is based on a formal appraisal of value. The timing of this appraisal can vary. Jurisdictions experiencing rapid changes in property values may conduct appraisals on a regular basis, such as three- to five-year intervals. In other areas property is appraised only when it is sold. The proportion of local revenues drawn from property taxes declined from 90 percent in 1960 to 74 percent in 1984 (Graetz & Schenk, 1995). The property tax is the primary source of funding for most public schools.

As Piven and Cloward (1997) noted, state and local governments are vulnerable to pressure from large businesses seeking tax reductions. Existing businesses threaten to relocate unless states exempt them from taxes—generally property taxes. Under the guise of "economic development," many cities spend public money trying to lure new businesses, often with promises of **tax abatements**. In this case, big businesses are generally the winners and public services are the losers. In some cases, businesses have taken tax breaks from local governments, only to renege on their promises. For example, officials in Galesburg, Illinois, gave Maytag Corp. over $2 million in tax breaks, only to have the company move its factory to Mexico. Maytag claims it paid all taxes that were due, but city representatives feel they were deceived (Egan, 2004).

With declining revenues from property taxes, local governments often rely on sales taxes for revenue. Local sales tax rates can vary from 1 to 3 percent. Local sales tax revenues may be used to finance specific services, such as parks or cultural activities, or may fund local government activities.

Tax Revolts

The sources of government revenues have shifted over the years. At the federal level, a growing proportion has been drawn from payroll taxes. The contribution of individual income taxes has remained steady, and that of corporate income taxes has diminished. At the local level, we have seen a diminished contribution from property taxes, coupled with increased reliance on sales taxes. Most of these trends reflect the influence of a popular movement known as the tax revolt.

While corporate lobbyists have worked quietly to reduce the corporate income tax burden, citizens' groups have publicly focused on reducing their property tax obligations (Dworak, 1980). California has led the nation in tax protests. After nearly a decade of dramatic increases in property values (and property taxes), in June 1978 the state's residents voted to support Proposition 13, a constitutional amendment that dramatically altered the state's tax system and set the stage for a new era of citizen involvement. Proposition 13 limited residential property taxes to 1 percent of value and required a two-thirds legislative majority to pass tax increases. As a result, local revenues diminished by nearly a third, and the state's educational and municipal institutions suffered.

Other states followed California's lead, and during the late 1970s property tax limitation measures passed in Idaho, Nevada, Oregon, Michigan, Alabama, Massachusetts, and Missouri (Dworak, 1980). President George H. W. Bush took the tax revolt nationwide in his 1988 campaign when he issued the disastrous statement, "Read my lips: no new taxes!" Since then, few politicians have dared to advocate for tax increases. Anti-tax organizations, such as the National Taxpayers Union, are quick to oppose any measure that might raise taxes.

The irony of tax revolt in the United States is not lost on our trading partners. U.S. citizens pay less in taxes than our competitors in the global market. In 2010 U.S. tax revenues were about 25 percent of GDP. The average for countries in the Organisation for Economic Co-operation and Development (OECD) was 34 percent. Comparable figures for similar nations that year were as follows: Canada (31), France (43), Germany (36), Italy (43), Japan (28), and the United Kingdom (35) (Organisation for Economic Co-operation and Development, n.d.).

Still, as Rubin (1998) pointed out, tax revolts are not about relative levels of taxation but about *the consent of the governed*. In the face of increasing government spending, citizens resist taxation. Uncontrollable economic events, such as inflation, also contribute to tax revolts. Finally, and perhaps most significantly, government spending on ineffective or unpopular programs can trigger popular resistance. Thus, the challenge in a democracy is to maintain a level of consensus, both about the fairness of the tax system and about the social goals that it advances.

A BRIEF HISTORY OF FEDERAL TAXES

The United States has not always had a federal income tax. George Washington and his Secretary of the Treasury, Alexander Hamilton, imposed the nation's first taxes on "distilled spirits and carriages." Money from this whiskey tax was needed to pay debts from the Revolutionary War. But, more importantly, Washington felt the tax was needed to establish the power of the new government. Like many of its successors, the nation's first sin tax met with protests. In 1794, protestors in Washington County, Pennsylvania, burned a tax collector's home, leading the president to send 13,000 troops into the area. This action suppressed the rebellion and secured the taxation power of the federal government.

The first federal income tax was proposed in 1862 by Abraham Lincoln to finance the Civil War. The tax affected relatively few Americans. It applied only to those with annual incomes over $600. Up to $10,000, these incomes were taxed at a rate of 3 percent. Income over $10,000 was taxed at 5 percent. The tax was subjected to a constitutional challenge and was upheld in 1880 by the Supreme Court (*Springer v. United States*, 102 U.S. 586). In subsequent years, the tax was raised and lowered, eliminated and reinstated. In 1895, the Supreme Court reversed its earlier decision and declared the income tax unconstitutional (*Pollock v. Farmers' Loan and Trust Co.*, 158 U.S. 601). This led to the adoption of the Sixteenth Amendment, which allows Congress to tax income. Still, it was not until the World War II era that income taxes were applied to most Americans. The tax rates peaked at a marginal rate (not an effective rate) of 94 percent during this period, as funds were needed to cover wartime expenses. Historic trends in federal income tax rates are illustrated in Figure 2.4.

Since the 1950s, individual income taxes have provided about half of the revenues collected by the federal government. In 1953 individual income taxes accounted for

FIGURE 2.4 Federal Income Tax Rates, 1944–2016

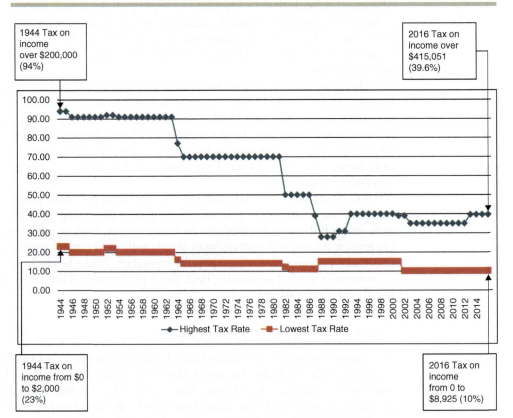

Source (for data): http://www.taxfoundation.org/publications/printer/151.html

42.8 percent of federal revenues. That figure ranged from 44.1 to 48.1 percent between 1983 and 1993. In contrast, the contribution of corporate income taxes diminished during the same period, from 30.5 percent in 1953 to about 10 percent (Graetz & Schenk, 1995).

The Bush Tax Cuts

The second half of the 20th century saw significant federal tax cuts, which affected 21st century revenues. Here we will focus on the 2001 and 2003 "Bush tax cuts" as they affected federal income tax brackets, treatment of capital gains and dividends, and the estate tax. These tax cuts shifted much of the nation's tax burden from the rich toward the middle class, increased the federal budget deficit, and reduced funding available for public programs.

First, the federal income tax saw the addition of a new 10 percent bracket and a one-to two-point across-the-board reduction in the other brackets. The top bracket declined from nearly 40 percent to 35 percent.

Second, tax rates for dividends and capital gains were reduced. Capital gains tax is paid on the sale of capital assets (stocks, real estate, bonds) that have been held for at least a year. Dividends are sometimes paid to stockholders as a way of distributing a corporation's income. In 2000, capital gains and dividends were treated as regular income, subject to a maximum tax of 39.6 percent. The maximum tax rate on capital gains dropped to 15 percent in 2008.

Third, estate tax rates were reduced. In 2000 the first $675,000 in estate value was exempt from federal tax. The maximum rate of 55 percent was paid by estates valued above $20 million. With the Bush tax cuts, the exemption rose to $3.5 million in 2009. The maximum rate dropped to 45 percent.

The estate tax was established in 1916 to prevent the accumulation of massive fortunes and maintain the stability of our democracy. Many believed that inheritance encouraged sloth and that the estate tax would encourage charitable giving. But eliminating the estate tax, or as opponents call it, the "death tax," was a cause célèbre for the Republican Party. The public relations campaign for this policy goal emphasized potential savings to family-owned small businesses and farms. Yet in 2000 the vast majority of family farms and small businesses were already exempt from the federal estate tax because their values were below the $675,000 exemption limit. The estate tax is probably the most progressive tax in America, drawing most of its revenues from estates valued in excess of $10 million.

The net effect of the Bush tax cuts was to dramatically reduce taxes paid on "passive" or investment income. In 2004, the Institute on Taxation and Economic Policy (ITEP) reported that federal taxes on earnings averaged 23.4 percent while the tax rate for investment income was 9.6 percent. Taxes on earnings include Social Security and Medicare taxes, which, at an average of 12.7 percent, exceeded the average federal income tax of 9.1 percent paid in 2010 (Tax Policy Center, 2012).

The "Fiscal Cliff Deal"

When the Bush tax cuts expired in 2011 the nation was still in the throes of the Great Recession, so Congress passed and President Obama signed a measure to extend the cuts for two years. In addition to this temporary extension, Congress reduced the payroll tax by 2 percent for one year and extended unemployment insurance benefits.

As the extension came to an end, President Obama was up for reelection. He signaled that he would not support renewing the cuts for high-income taxpayers (defined as individuals with incomes of $200,000 or higher and couples with incomes above $250,000). Obama said, "We cannot afford $1 trillion worth of tax cuts for every millionaire and billionaire in our society. We can't afford it. And I refuse to renew them again" (Jackson, 2011).

Meanwhile, with the expiration of the Bush tax cuts and a series of across-the-board spending cuts dictated by the Budget Control Act of 2011, the national budget was approaching what some termed a "fiscal cliff."

The fiscal cliff deal (formally the 2013 American Tax Relief Act) was a compromise that made no one happy. Most of the Bush tax cuts were made permanent, except that the marginal rate on those with incomes over $400,000 ($450,000 for couples) increased to 39.6 percent, and deductions were capped for individuals with incomes above $250,000 ($300,000 for couples). The payroll tax cut was eliminated, unemployment benefits were extended, and the sequestration budget cuts were postponed for two months.

The Trump Agenda

As of this writing, it is unclear what tax changes the Trump administration will promote. During the campaign, President Trump offered a series of proposals to cut taxes at all income levels, with the highest benefits going to high income taxpayers. These included:

- reduction of marginal tax rages and increase in standard deductions;
- repeal of alternate minimum taxes, as well as estate and gift taxes;
- taxation of profits of foreign subsidiaries of U.S. companies in the year they are earned; and
- reduction of the corporate tax rate to 15 percent

The Tax Policy Center estimated that the plan presented by the Trump campaign would significantly reduce federal revenues. Unless accompanied by sizable spending cuts, it could dramatically increase the national debt. The Center acknowledged that the plan could increase incentives to work, save, and invest if interest rates do not rise (Nunns, Burman, Rohaly, & Rosenberg, 2015).

Taxation as Social Policy

Taxes have long been used to influence social trends in the United States. As Graetz and Schenk (1995, p. 1) observed:

> Today's income tax provisions, for example, favor new development of natural resources over recycling, tell people it is far better to own their own homes than to rent, give a break to families that have one spouse who stays at home rather than those that have both husband and wife in the job market, and make it cheaper for some people to marry, cheaper for others to divorce or remain unmarried. Federal alcohol taxes favor wine drinkers over beer drinkers, and both over those who prefer whiskey. Shortly after his inauguration, President Clinton proposed a new energy tax that would have given economic force to fathers' eternal admonitions to their children to turn off the lights, but Congress refused to enact it.

In addition, corporate income tax provisions favor companies that provide pension and health coverage to employees.

Tax policy attempts to influence social behavior through the imposition or the withdrawal of tax obligations. We are most familiar with the imposition of taxes to discourage or limit certain kinds of behavior. Thus, for example, we impose "sin" taxes on purchases of tobacco, alcohol, and gasoline. On the flip side, desirable behavior can reduce a person's tax liability through tax deductions or exemptions. Home ownership is encouraged by laws that provide for a home mortgage interest deduction. More recently, tax deductions have been used to encourage home care of the elderly. The medical expenses associated with such care can be deducted from one's income.

To encourage some kinds of investment, income from these sources can be declared tax exempt. For example, a state may declare that interest paid on municipal bonds will be exempt from state income tax.

Deductions and exemptions represent "forgone revenue" to the federal government and should be considered with the same deliberation as proposals for new expenditures. To encourage this view, the president is required to submit an annual **Tax Expenditure Budget** to Congress. Also known as "The Green Book," this budget is a useful document for policy analysts interested in the use of taxes for social policy.

Oddly enough, Americans seldom subject tax expenditures to the level of scrutiny that they apply to revenue expenditures. Tax exemptions and deductions are popular because Americans hate taxes. However, these exemptions and deductions favor the wealthy and do little or no good for the poor because they operate by reducing a person's income tax obligation. Given the progressive nature of the federal income tax, this reduction has the greatest value to those with the greatest tax obligation—the affluent (see Barusch, 1995).

This problem does not hold for tax credits, which can result not only in reduced taxes but in a refund from the Internal Revenue Service (IRS). A refund that is the result of a tax credit is not the same as a refund that comes because you have overpaid your taxes. The refund most people are familiar with is not based on their deductions per se, but on the fact that they have had more money withheld than they owed. A tax credit actually changes the amount that the taxpayer owes. For that reason, the Earned Income Tax Credit (EITC) provides significant benefits to the nation's working poor. The EITC, discussed in Chapter 15, provides a refund to low-income workers with children. In essence, it is an antipoverty measure embedded in the U.S. tax code.

Few of us make personal decisions on the basis of tax consequences. Taxes operate in the background, punishing and rewarding behavior in ways that may influence us without our awareness. But the U.S. tax system is an important tool for achieving social justice. It allocates billions of dollars every year and plays a significant role in distributing the costs and benefits of citizenship.

Closing Reflections

John Rawls said, "Justice is the first virtue of social institutions, as truth is of systems of thought. A theory, however elegant and economical, must be rejected if it is untrue. Likewise laws and institutions no matter how efficient and well-arranged must be reformed or abolished if they are unjust" (Rawls, 1971, p. 3). Here we have considered the role of the U.S. government in promoting social justice.

First, we examined the philosophical perspectives outlined in Chapter 1, linking them to contemporary American politics and offering a working description of political parties and labels and examining diverse views on the proper role of government. Government in the United States has levels (federal, state, and local) as well as branches (legislative, executive, and judicial). Each plays an important role in the creation and implementation of social policy. We examined the movement to privatize government functions and offered an approach for determining whether privatization of human services is appropriate. Finally, we discussed the U.S. tax system and its role in social policy.

It is easy to become overwhelmed by the complexity of government; but by achieving a basic understanding of its structure, and remembering that the mission of a democratic government is to carry out the will of the people, social workers can engage in effective policy practice on behalf of their clients. Policy practice is the focus of Chapter 3.

Think About It

1. List three arguments in favor of having the states, not the federal government, operate a major social program such as Social Security. Now list three arguments opposing state management. We are all familiar with constitutional limits on the federal government. Does the Constitution limit the powers of the states?

2. What is the largest tax expenditure in the current Tax Expenditure Budget? What social goals does it serve?

3. Has your community used tax exemptions to attract business in the past year? What were the terms of those exemptions? Who benefited?

4. Can you think of an example of a third-party candidate who influenced a presidential election in the US? Would proportional voting eliminate this effect?

Web-Based Exercises

For direct links to all the sites in these exercises, visit the *Foundations of Social Policy* Companion Site at www.cengagebrain.com and select the resources for Chapter 2.

1. Is the U.S. Government for sale? Let's learn more about campaign financing with help from the Center for Responsive Politics. Go to their website at www.opensecrets.org and consider the summary of candidates' monthly reports to the Federal Election Commission. Under "Politicians & Elections" find the presidential race and look at the candidate summaries for Hillary Clinton and Donald Trump. Scroll down to see (1) who raised the most money; (2) who relied most heavily on contributions from Political Action Committees (PACs); and (3) who received a greater proportion of small, individual contributions. Now look at the most recent congressional races in your state. (Under "Politicians & Elections" choose "Congressional Elections" and then select your state from the menu.) Did the winners always raise the most cash?

2. The judiciary has played a vital role in shaping social policy. Go to http://www.law.cornell.edu/supct/cases/topic.htm to view "Historic Supreme Court Decisions – by topic," sponsored by the Legal Information Institute (LII). Then search for one of more of the following Supreme Court cases:

Social Security
Steward Machine Co. v. Collector of Internal Revenue
Helvering v. Dams

Segregation
Plessy v. Ferguson
Brown v. Board of Education

Abortion
Roe v. Wade

Sterilization
Skinner v. Oklahoma

Marriage
Loving v. Virginia

Welfare Benefits
Saenz v. Roe

Read the Court's opinion in each case and describe (a) the facts of the case, (b) the Court's conclusion, and (c) the effect of this case on contemporary U.S. social policy. Was a dissent filed in the case? If so, what argument was made?

3. Go to: https://www.whitehouse.gov/omb/budget/Overview to see the president's proposed budget for the most recent fiscal year available. Open "The Budget" and scroll down to the Summary Tables section, where you'll find a table titled "Proposed Budget by Category." There, you can compare outlays and receipts for major programs. Check out the "Agency Fact Sheet" for HHS to compare expenditures for social programs (like TANF) with expenditures for health programs (like Medicaid).

4. Visit www.fairvote.org to learn how proportional representation could change electoral politics in the United States (look under "innovations"). Along the way, check to see whether your congressional district is one of the few that's expected to be competitive in the upcoming election.

Competency Notes

As mentioned in the preface to this text, the Council on Social Work Education has designated nine core competencies and related practice behaviors that must be addressed by accredited social work programs. In these notes, I will specify the way chapter content addresses these competencies and behaviors. (This is designed to assist with the accreditation process.) Please refer to the "helping hands" icons for the locations of specific content in this chapter. Here you will find a brief explanation of how the accompanying content relates to the specified competency or practice behaviors.

The following list indicates where EPAS competencies and practice behaviors are addressed in this chapter.

EP 3a   **Apply their understanding of social, economic, and environmental justice to advocate for human rights at the individual and system levels.** The chapter discusses the roles of values, philosophies, and government structures in sustaining privilege.

EP 5c   **Apply critical thinking to analyze, formulate, and advocate for policies that advance human rights and social, economic, and environmental justice.** The chapter examines the development and roles of conservative and liberal ideologies and assists in the application of critical thinking skills in the context of policy analysis.

EP 8d   **Negotiate, mediate, and advocate with and on behalf of diverse clients and constituencies.** The chapter alerts students to the function and importance of rulemaking, as well as basic legislative and budgeting processes.

Suggested Resources

Hall, K., & Ely, J. W. (2009). *The Oxford Guide to United States Supreme Court Decisions* (2nd ed.). New York: Oxford University Press.

Piven, F. F., & Cloward, R. A. (1997). *The Breaking of the American Social Compact*. New York: New Press. This book, particularly Chapter 3, "Welfare and the Transformation of Electoral Politics," is a must-read for anyone struggling to understand American politics in the 21st century.

www.gao.gov. The Government Accountability Office (GAO) is "the investigative arm of Congress." This site provides access to GAO reports and testimony, legal decisions and opinions, and presentations by the Comptroller General on a "wide range of timely topics."

www.gpoaccess.gov. Maintained by the Government Printing Office, this site provides access to the huge array of government publications. And, best of all, their exhaustive Catalog of U.S. Government Publications is searchable. You can use it to locate the latest government publications on a subject of your choice.

www.thomas.loc.gov. This site is maintained by the Library of Congress "in the spirit of Thomas Jefferson." It provides a searchable database with the text and status of bills going back several years. It is an excellent source of up-to-date information on congressional proposals.

CHAPTER 3

Policy Analysis and Policy Practice

We must complain. Yes, plain, blunt complaint, ceaseless agitation, unfailing exposure of dishonesty and wrong—this is the ancient, unerring way to liberty, and we must follow it.
W. E. B. DUBOIS, 1905

Learning Objectives

This chapter will help prepare students to:

LO 3-1   Understand what constitutes policy practice

LO 3-2   Conduct an effective policy analysis

LO 3-3   Practice effective advocacy

LO 3-4   Understand the meaning and processes of empowerment

LO 3-5   Identify ethical issues in policy practice

LO 3-6   Understand legal considerations that affect policy practice

Some compare policy development to a ***marketplace of ideas*** where new concepts compete and only the best survive. Others emphasize struggle, treating policy debate as a boxing match where the mightiest fighters knock their opponents flat with left hooks. Some prefer to think of policy development as a rational process of identifying and solving problems in the steady march toward a better world. Still others would like to dismiss the whole business as "a tale told by an idiot, full of sound and fury, signifying nothing."[1] Each of these metaphors captures an element of policy practice, yet none captures the concept in its entirety. Here we will explore key skills and approaches that can help you operate effectively in this complex arena.

---

[1]From Shakespeare's *Macbeth*, Act 5.

A HUMAN PERSPECTIVE   Advocacy: Free Public Education

In 1895 when Utah became a state, its constitution guaranteed each citizen a "free" public education, at least until the end of the eighth grade. Initially, the practice of charging fees for "extras" provided by the public schools, such as uniforms and supplies for special art projects, seemed compatible with the constitutional mandate. In time enrolment grew and educational funding fell behind. Schools relied on fees to bridge the revenue gap.

By the early 1970s, the use of fees in Utah's public schools had extended to include not only the extras but also basic necessities such as books and educational supplies. Local advocates became aware that the fees were interfering with the educational opportunities available to children from low-income families. Over the next 20 years, advocates from a statewide organization called Utah Issues used a broad range of advocacy strategies to address the problem. Their efforts included careful analysis, individual advocacy, coalition building, research, and finally, litigation. The story of universal access to public education in Utah offers an instructive example of long-term advocacy.

Why are school fees a significant social justice issue? Irene Fisher, an advocate in the early stages of the effort, explained that the fees stigmatize children from poor families, emphasizing class differences. She explained, "When I grew up in South Dakota, no one knew we were poor. I was a cheerleader, and the school issued me a uniform just like everybody else. It may have been used in previous years, but so was everyone else's." In contrast, a low-income Utah parent wrote, "They threatened to withhold my daughter's grades and they always hounded her for money. I didn't have a job and we didn't have any money, but every couple of weeks they would pressure my daughter for the fees. She finally gave up and dropped out of school." Another parent explained that her son had been arrested for shoplifting. He had stolen art supplies. His teacher had a special box of "poor kids' supplies" for children whose parents could not afford to pay the art supply fee. The boy stole supplies rather than face the humiliation of using the supplies for poor kids.

At first, fees enabled schools to fund enhancements without additional legislative appropriations. But the practice got out of hand. Concerns surfaced as early as the 1930s when the state legislature passed a bill requiring that public schools be free. Two years later, a state court interpreted the law, ruling that no fees could be charged

for registration or tuition and that all necessary supplies and books must be provided to students through grade 8. Although the law was clear, its enforcement mechanism was not. Schools continued to charge fees—sometimes in ways that were clearly illegal.

During the 1970s, the staff of Utah Issues began working on the school fee issue. With a mandate to advocate for low-income residents, the organization helped parents battle illegal fees on a case-by-case basis. In time it became clear that individual advocacy efforts were insufficient, and the organization began holding workshops and conferences with affected parents, seeking support from other advocacy groups, and preparing reports that the state legislature routinely ignored. The state superintendent of public instruction was concerned about the issue, however, and issued a memo to local districts urging them to develop clear policies allowing for waiver of school fees depending on family circumstances. This memo and related documents became the state's policy on school fees.

At this point it became clear that three realities affected advocates' progress toward their goals. First, even though school fees were harmful and often illegal, decision makers believed they were necessary in view of the fiscal constraints facing education. Second, some policy makers felt that the availability of waivers effectively solved the problem. Third, those within the educational system who were most concerned about fees—the state superintendent of schools and the state board of education—were state, not local, officials. Utah's strong commitment to local autonomy limited state officials' authority over local decisions related to fees.

These circumstances strained the energies and resources of the Utah Issues staff. They had to operate not only at the state level but also in 40 individual school districts. Nonetheless, over the next several years advocates held workshops with affected parents, helped parents plead their cases with local school personnel, and documented examples of continued harm.

Textbook fees emerged as a major target. Advocates tried during four state legislative sessions to obtain supplemental funding to permit elimination of textbook fees before finally getting a $2 million appropriation for that purpose in 1975. But local districts continued to charge textbook fees, and the state board of education continued to resist pressure to intervene. In 1981 there was a major setback when the legislature passed a bill authorizing the sale and rental of textbooks to children in high school. A waiver provision was included in the law, but this was the first legislative sanction for fees involving basic educational expenses. Advocates continued their efforts, but success seemed out of reach.

Perhaps as a result of this setback, Utah Issues found itself in 1985 with fewer collaborators on the school fee issue. Finally, no one else showed up for a key strategy meeting. The staff of Utah Issues decided to involve its board of directors in deciding how to approach an issue that seemed to have lost its following. The board chair, who was an attorney, volunteered to work with the staff to investigate strategic options. Over the next year, the board chair and staff developed and implemented a new phase of the school fee advocacy effort. The goal was to obtain statutory protections to reduce the harm done to low-income children by imposition of fees.

A legislative interim study committee was persuaded to investigate the school fee issue, and low-income public school students gained a handful of well-educated, committed legislators "on their team" who managed during the 1986 session to pass three laws. The first required that waivers be made available to low-income children for any fees associated with school-sponsored activities. The second mandated parental notification regarding the availability of waivers and the application process. The third law provided for local school board review and approval of all fees in a public meeting. The state board of education was required to develop rules implementing the new laws, and a low-income advocate gained a seat on the board's school fee task force. The presence of advocates on the task force provided the opportunity for successful coalition building.

That same year also brought a number of less positive developments. The legislature passed a resolution to place a question on the ballot asking voters if they would approve of ending Utah's constitutional guarantee of free public education for children in grades 7 through 12. This would set the stage for greater reliance on fees. Fearful that extracurricular activities would be eliminated if fees were not charged, voters passed the ballot measure. Over the next seven years, some legislatures tried to remove free public education from the state's constitution entirely, but these efforts were defeated. Public policy advocates and other legislators worked together to convince a majority that elementary school children were too young to face the painful experiences their older brothers and sisters had endured.

The 1986 school fee law and resultant state board policy provided new tools for advocates, who forged strong working relationships with Utah State Office of Education staff charged with monitoring compliance over the next five years. Some parents reported success in securing fee waivers, but advocates continued to hear from parents that fees were not being waived and that inadequate or inaccurate information was presented. Children were still excluded from school activities and denied supplies.

In 1991 advocates launched a three-pronged research effort to quantify the extent of the problem. Committed to producing information that was both credible and reflective of the impact on children, they selected three approaches. First, a survey of low-income parents was conducted to assess their children's experiences with school fees and the fee waiver process. Second, all local district fee policies were systematically analyzed to gauge compliance with the 1986 laws and state board policy. Third, a history of the school fee issue was prepared to place the issue within a clearer context. The resulting report, *School Fees in Utah: The Law and the Practice,* contained the advocates' findings and recommendations. The report was released to a broad audience and left no question that the majority of local school districts had, even after five years, failed to meet the law's requirements. Children in low-income families still faced challenges and embarrassment over fees.

At the same time, a group of parents contacted Utah Legal Services, which had hired an attorney experienced in school law. As the attorney investigated these parents' circumstances, he approached the state superintendent of schools about the policies and practices of the individual school districts involved. After many discussions and further study, he concluded that the superintendent and state board were caught in a dilemma. State appropriations for education were inadequate, forcing local districts to rely on fees to cover programs and activities. Although the state board was aware of many violations, the philosophical principle of local governance was strong, the state board had no relief to offer to districts if they waived fees for their low-income students, and the state board believed it had done all it could since 1986 to force local districts to comply. When pressed, the superintendent admitted to the attorney that it would take a lawsuit to change the situation.

Thus, in July 1992, Utah Legal Services filed a class action lawsuit against the Utah State Board of Education, the Utah State Office of Education, and the state superintendent of schools in Third District Court (*Doe v. Utah State Board of Education*). The judge immediately granted a preliminary injunction requiring the state board to

(continued)

A HUMAN PERSPECTIVE   Advocacy: Free Public Education (*continued*)

enforce state fee waiver statutes. The board was ordered to withhold funds from schools and districts that were not in compliance.

The preliminary injunction increased pressure to resolve the issue. As the Utah State Office of Education's legal staff worked to bring local districts into compliance, local school boards struggled with their economic dilemma. They were suddenly faced with a choice between economic sanction for not complying with the law and a loss of revenue if they did comply. Some turned to their legislators, calling for long overdue appropriations. Other districts mounted efforts to evaluate the impact of fees and to ascertain their role in fulfilling the mission of the public schools. Some student groups pledged to raise funds to support low-income students' participation. In a few areas, teachers and students worried that their favorite activities might be eliminated and lashed out at low-income children.

Attention in the education community turned to resolving the funding problem behind school fees; low-income advocates, education administrators, parents, and teachers worked together on strategies to obtain legislative support during the 1994 general session. Backlash among some powerful legislators, resentful of the litigation and the assertive stance of the court, led to creation of a legislative school fee task force. Those selected for the task force were largely hostile to an appropriation to help districts cover fee waivers. The coalition of education advocates who supported waiver funding attended six months of difficult meetings with this hostile group of legislators. The task force was preparing legislation to water down the waiver laws before the judge's permanent injunction was finalized, but that injunction, which was stronger than the first order, was released in October 1994. The task force disbanded.

Although the outcome of *Doe v. Utah State Board of Education* was a tremendous leap forward for low-income children, in social advocacy few victories are permanent. The underlying cause of schools' reliance on fees—limited state funding for education—still has not been addressed. Until it is resolved, school districts under financial pressure remain highly motivated to ignore waiver policies and impose fees in ways that are damaging and painful to low-income children.

A SOCIAL WORK PERSPECTIVE

This advocacy effort illustrates several basic principles of policy practice:

Persistence Is Vital

Victories and setbacks must be understood in the context of a struggle that may extend beyond our lifetimes. When the state constitution was drafted, someone thought to include a guarantee of free public education. This provision suggests that the issue of educational equity had been around since statehood. Clearly those who hunger for a "quick fix" will be disappointed in the advocacy arena. This doesn't mean progress is not possible but that it may take a very long time.

Every Individual Counts

Despite—or perhaps because of—the magnitude of the struggle, each individual's efforts count. From the parents who called to complain and tell their stories to the lawyers who donated time to pursue a class action lawsuit, each contribution was important. Not all individual contributions receive public recognition, but all are vital to the success of an advocacy effort. Sometimes advocacy consists of "drops in the bucket."

The Issue Is Not "Us Versus Them"

There is seldom a clear enemy to fight. Local districts in this example operated under impossible funding constraints. The state board was hampered in its job by the overriding principle of local control of schools. The legislature struggled to stretch tax dollars as far as possible. At most, these entities can be accused of lack of consideration for vulnerable children, not of intentional harm. It is tempting, but counterproductive, to label an organization "them" and to dismiss its employees and volunteers as "the enemy."

Social Policy Is More Than Legislation

Just as social policy includes laws, court opinions, and regulations, social advocacy takes place in all of these arenas. Many people think of advocacy as lobbying for legislation or program budgets. These efforts represent only one piece of the advocacy pie. Every bit as influential as the high-profile individual who testifies before legislative bodies and files lawsuits is the detail-oriented person who monitors the drafting of regulations and gently, but firmly, suggests revisions on behalf of vulnerable individuals.

Source: This account is based on interviews with advocates involved in the effort, and it draws heavily from a booklet by Bill Crim entitled *Sometimes You Need a Hammer: An Unfinished Story of Social Advocacy and Equal Educational Opportunity in Utah* (Salt Lake City: Utah Issues, 1994).

LO 3-1   Understand What Constitutes Policy Practice

EP 3a
EP 8d

Just as "individual practice" seeks to change individuals, "policy practice" focuses on changing policy. As Bruce Jansson explained, "We define policy practice as efforts to change policies in legislative, agency EP 8d, and community settings, whether by establishing new policies, improving existing ones, or defeating the policy initiatives of other people" (1999, p. 10). But policy practice is only partly about advocacy. It also requires analysis. Social workers carry out policy practice when they strive to understand the laws and regulations governing the services they provide, or when they critically analyze the implications of a court opinion or a new bill. A policy practitioner who is engaged in advocacy might employ a wide range of tactics, from preparing an argument for expanded disability services to organizing a coalition of child welfare organizations. When community organizers teach residents in a low-income neighborhood about racial profiling, they are using policy practice for *empowerment*. In this chapter we will explore three elements of effective policy practice: policy analysis, advocacy, and empowerment.

LO 3-2   Conduct an Effective Policy Analysis

EP 3a

Policy analysis is the systematic examination of a discrete aspect of social policy. It is distinct from **social problem analysis**, which is discussed in the introduction to Part II.

As you study social policy, your approach to policy analysis will change. You will become aware of the widespread and complex impacts of social policies. Your knowledge of the history of social policy will give you a deeper understanding of its purposes and effects. Finally, your focus on social justice will allow you to assess the contribution of policy to a more just society. In its most advanced form, your approach to policy analysis will represent your personal view of the meaning of the policy enterprise and the proper role of government. It will reflect your perspective on what is just, as well as your awareness of the assumptions behind your views. While it is always important to get your facts straight, your analysis of social policy will be neither "right" nor "wrong." At best, it will be well informed and clearly reasoned, but it will always be subject to change as your personal and career development progresses.

Policy analysis might begin with selection of a framework, a set of questions or topics that directs the analyst's attention. Or it might begin with a question like "How was this policy developed?" or "How is this policy implemented?" or "What is the impact of the policy?" In the following sections we will consider three types of policy analysis frameworks introduced by social work scholars Mary O'Connor and Ellen Netting (2008). We will then consider approaches that examine three stages in the life of a social policy: the policy development process, the implementation of social programs, and the impact of a social policy.

CHOOSING A POLICY ANALYSIS FRAMEWORK

There is no single correct way to conduct policy analysis, as is evidenced by the many policy analysis frameworks that have been offered by social work scholars. Based on their underlying assumptions, O'Connor and Netting (2008) divide these frameworks into three categories: "rational," "interpretive," and "critical."

Rational Frameworks

Those who view the world as a logical, orderly place may be most comfortable with rational policy analysis frameworks. The assumptions of these frameworks match those of a "positivist" research tradition in assuming that social policy can be understood through a rational, linear approach modeled on the natural sciences (Lejano, 2006). Under this view, policy decisions are the result of reasoned (objective) analysis in which alternatives are selected based on clear (if not always universally accepted) criteria. Rational or "classical" policy analysis proceeds through a series of well-defined steps or questions to arrive at a single conclusion or recommendation. Perhaps the best-known of these is the six-step policy analysis framework developed by Bruce Jansson (2008), which can be summarized in these questions:

1. What is the social problem or issue under consideration?
2. What strategies can be identified to address it?
3. What are the costs and benefits of each of these options?
4. What specific policy proposal would support the most advantageous of these options?
5. How can support for this proposal be generated?
6. What information do advocates need to communicate to support the proposal?

Frameworks in this tradition tend not to grapple with questions of meaning or competing values, and they tend to focus on policy outcomes rather than policy development processes (O'Connor & Netting, 2011).

Interpretive Frameworks

Those who are comfortable with ambiguity and complexity may find interpretive or "constructivist" frameworks attractive. These frameworks emphasize the role of individual perspective (subjectivity). They accept multiple competing truths and acknowledge the possibility that one solution or policy proposal may not be "best." They emphasize the process of policy development and the role of power in policy decisions.

Rather than an established set of questions or steps that must be pursued in a particular order, interpretive approaches provide a range of questions or aspects to consider. The analyst may then adapt the approach, in an iterative (even circuitous) exploration that shifts its (hermeneutic) focus from detail to context. These approaches offer metaphors and images to direct the analyst's attention. So, for instance, an interpretive approach to policy analysis might ask about the "policy window" that opens from time to time to allow public consideration of an issue. It might use a fluid metaphor to explore how ideas bubble to the surface in policy debates. It might examine the language and assumptions used to describe social issues or define social problems. Interpretive approaches often consider the context—both immediate and historic—that shapes the policy development process, as well as the political dynamics that determine alternatives (O'Connor & Netting, 2011).

Deborah Stone (2002) offered an interpretive approach to understanding political decision making in her book, *Policy Paradox*. Noting that "Paradoxes are nothing but trouble … and political life is full of them" (p. 1) she directs the policy analyst's attention to multiple perspectives on a range of considerations, including: politics, goals, problems, and solutions. The questions she asks and the issues she raises are designed to unearth competing values and political dynamics that shape the process of policy development.

Critical Frameworks

Those who are eager to change the world may find critical policy analysis frameworks satisfying. As Raul Lejano (2006) explained, "Critique is a legitimate and often powerful mode of policy analysis with roots dating back to the earliest philosophers" (p. 115). Critical frameworks approach policy analysis with an anti-oppressive agenda that critiques existing social policy as serving the **status quo.** Under this view, the oppression of vulnerable and disenfranchised individuals calls for radical change in the social order, and policy analysis serves to bring about that change (O'Connor & Netting, 2011).

Where rational frameworks aim for an objective stance and interpretive frameworks emphasize the subjective, critical frameworks adopt a "critical realist" perspective. They accept certain policy realities as the object of critique, but their critique is informed by a subjective, value-laden posture, often relying on a strong theoretical perspective on social justice such as that derived from Marxist or feminist thought. Critical frameworks may use the data and methods of both rational and interpretive frameworks with the goal of accomplishing policy change. Thus, policy analysis becomes more than an intellectual exercise; it becomes part of a process designed to accomplish fundamental social change.

Oddly enough, critical frameworks are relatively uncommon in social work (O'Connor & Netting, 2008). The social justice framework introduced later in this chapter might be considered a critical framework. Another example is the "feminist policy analysis framework" introduced by Beverly McPhail (2003). This framework views policy through a gendered lens with the goal of "making women visible." It offers the analyst a series of questions about the extent to which policy is informed by feminist values; the involvement of women in policy development; and the impact of the policy on gender equity and women's rights.

CONDUCTING PROCESS, IMPLEMENTATION, OR IMPACT APPRAISAL

Approaches to policy analysis vary in the questions they address. *Process* techniques focus on the policy development process, with questions like "Is there a need for this policy or program?" or "What are the chances this policy change will be approved?" Need assessment and Prince Policy Appraisal are discussed here as examples of process techniques (Coplin & O'Leary, 1998).

Implementation (sometimes called "product") approaches to policy analysis ask about the social programs that are the products of policy. Perhaps the most well known of these product approaches is the framework described by Gilbert and Terrell (2002) that clearly articulates the dimensions of a social program.

Finally, **impact** assessments such as cost–benefit analysis consider the effect of a policy. The choice of question will, of course, depend on the purpose of the analysis. Any of these questions can be informed by a social justice perspective, which helps make explicit the underlying values and implications of policy.[2]

PROCESS APPROACHES

The approaches described in this section address two questions: "Is there a need for this policy?" and "What is the likelihood that this policy change will be approved?"

Need Assessment

In public policy, **need** is sometimes hard to define and measure. Rubin and Babbie (2001) distinguish between definitions that use a **normative** approach and those based on **demand**. [To define need using a normative approach, we would compare the situation

---

[2]This section will introduce you to some of the most interesting methods for the analysis of social policy. It offers a brief description that will enable you to use some of these methods but does not offer anywhere near the level of detail that is available elsewhere. Please see references throughout the section and suggested resources for books that can provide greater depth of information for any of these approaches.

of a target group to norms in its society or community. On the other hand, when need is defined based on demand, only needs that are voiced would be considered. This emphasis on demand shifts our focus to groups capable of perceiving and articulating their needs.

Normative Definition of Need   The normative approach reflects Rawls's notion of a social minimum (see Chapter 1). This social minimum varies across societies. In international research, poverty is commonly defined as an income of less than one dollar per day. But developed nations such as the United States generally define poverty as a threshold that allows for a person's **basic needs**. These are the physical and social goods necessary to sustain life. The human body requires air, water, food, safety, and shelter. Beyond this, infants cannot survive without affectionate contact. In the arena of basic needs, we distinguish between resources necessary to sustain life and those necessary to maintain health. Physical health requires, for example, that air, water, and food be free of damaging pollutants.

Most social work scholars (i.e., Gil, van Wormer, Van Soest, and Garcia) include psychological well-being among the basic needs. Maslow's hierarchy of needs is commonly used to suggest that opportunities for belonging and self-actualization are necessary for survival in complex societies. Erik Erikson's concept of meaningful engagement has also been treated as a basic need in our professional discourse. Any list of basic psychological needs should include intellectual development, since education is necessary for effective social participation.

Indeed, the presence of a large national program constitutes public recognition of a basic need. As we see in Table 3.1, it is not difficult to identify major programmatic efforts to address basic needs.

Gil (1992) argues, "When the realization of basic needs is thwarted consistently, beyond a level of tolerance, by a society's way of life and social policies, constructive developmental energy tends to be blocked and transformed into destructive energy" (p. 19). Similarly, Piven and Cloward (1971) argued that a central role of our profession is ensuring that basic needs are minimally met to prevent social decay and violence. Thus, we might argue that a healthy society is one in which everyone is able to meet his or her basic needs.

Demand-Based Definition of Need   When we define need based on demand, the discourse becomes more political. Under this definition, need must be both perceived and expressed. Basic needs that are not expressed don't count. So if homeless people in the United States do not express their need for decent, affordable housing, that need does not come under consideration. By contrast, if the chamber of commerce expresses a need for sales tax relief, this need would be considered.

Some people question the legitimacy of expressed needs that are not basic needs. David Gil suggested that expressed or *perceived* needs can substitute for basic psychological needs that people believe cannot be fulfilled. So, for example, the perceived need to

TABLE 3.1 Social Policy and Basic Human Needs

Policy Goal	Basic Need	Programmatic Examples
Survival	Air, water, food, safety, shelter	Food stamps, public housing
Physical health	Clean environment, health care	EPA Superfund, Medicaid, Medicare
Psychological well-being	Belonging, self-actualization, meaningful engagement, intellectual development	Public education system, mental health system, volunteer opportunities

accumulate personal wealth might substitute for the basic need for belonging. You can see why some people would become staunch advocates of policies that support their need to accumulate wealth. Highly sophisticated marketing efforts are sometimes used to generate perceived needs.

While it may lack veracity, the demand-based approach to need reflects the realities of policy development (and family life!). Unless someone expresses a need, it may go unmet. In policy practice, social workers can empower disenfranchised groups to express their basic needs in ways that can be understood by the majority or the powerful. And sometimes social workers must express needs on behalf of those who are unable to do this for themselves. As we will see, the legitimacy conferred by the basic needs of clients can be a source of power for social work advocates.

Prince Policy Appraisal

Niccolo Machiavelli wrote his best-known political treatise, *The Prince,* during the 16th century.[3] Schooled in the political intrigues of Florence, he focused on the effective use of political power. Aptly named for Machiavelli's work, the technique of Prince Policy Appraisal can be used to gauge the power dynamics that determine political support for a new policy initiative, offering a systematic approach to understanding political processes that might otherwise seem mysterious (Coplin & O'Leary, 1998). This technique consists of five steps:

1. Identify the **players** who are likely to affect the decision.
2. Determine a **position** for each player.
3. Estimate the **power** that each player brings to the issue.
4. Estimate the **priority** of the issue for each player.
5. Calculate the **likelihood** that the policy will be implemented

▶ Rally to change US gun policies.

---

[3]I am indebted to Emma Gross who introduced me to Prince Policy Appraisal and to generations of Utah students who have implemented and refined this approach.

Prince Policy Appraisal begins with a clear description of a policy proposal. It is important that the object of the analysis be a specific proposal, such as "to increase child care provisions for TANF recipients," rather than a broad policy goal such as "to decrease poverty." Once the proposal has been outlined, analysis proceeds through each of the five steps outlined above (see Coplin and O'Leary, 1998, for more detail on how to conduct and apply this method).

Apart from providing an informed guess about the likelihood of implementation, Prince Policy Appraisal offers insight into the power dynamics behind the political process that can be used to inform advocacy. By directing attention to these dynamics, the method can help advocates set their intervention priorities for greatest impact. Results of Prince Policy Appraisal remind us, for instance, that it is more effective to change the position of a powerful player than that of a less influential one or that sometimes the most effective way to accomplish policy change is to increase the priority or salience of an issue for its less enthusiastic supporters.

IMPLEMENTATION APPRAISAL

Implementation appraisal is a detailed description of public programs that are the **products** of social policy. This approach considers five key aspects of a program: the goal or the social problem it addresses, the basis for entitlement (or eligibility), the nature of the benefit or service provided, the administrative structure used to deliver the program, and the program's financing mechanism. (Chambers, 2000, and Gilbert & Terrell, 2002, provide more detailed presentations of this approach.)

Goal or Social Problem

Analysis begins with specification of the program goal and the problem it addresses. We then turn to the best scientific evidence available to describe the affected population and the causes of the problem.

Public values and beliefs about the problem and about its relationship to other social problems can affect attitudes toward the program. The war on drugs reflects a widespread belief that people who buy illegal drugs are, first and foremost, criminals. This dictates a much different approach from that generated by the belief that people who purchase drugs are addicts. So, in addition to empirically based knowledge of the problem's causes, our assessment of goals must take popular beliefs into account.

Some programs that were originally designed to address one problem have evolved over the years to focus on a different concern. Social Security is a good example. During the Depression unemployment was a primary concern. The retirement program established by the Social Security Act of 1935 addressed this problem by requiring that those receiving benefits exit the workforce. A **retirement test** was instituted to encourage older workers to leave and make way for others. As we will see in Chapter 4, the problem of unemployment receded and the cost of the program mushroomed, which eventually led to elimination of the retirement test.

Basis for Entitlement

Knowledge of eligibility criteria is central to understanding a program's intent and operations. Eligibility might be based on membership in a group assumed to be needy (e.g., people with HIV/AIDS, the blind, or the elderly). It might be based on a carefully assessed need (e.g., disability, poverty). Or it may be limited to those who work (e.g., Earned Income Tax Credit) or those who don't work (e.g., unemployment compensation). Finally, it may be related to prior social contributions such as military service or to payroll tax deductions.

Gilbert and Terrell (2002) examined the distinction between eligibility and access, noting that people who are eligible for a program do not necessarily receive benefits. Barriers to access, both formal and informal, can make eligibility little more than a joke. The presence of such barriers is indicated when a program is "underutilized." As we will see in Chapter 4, only a fraction of older adults eligible for Supplemental Security Income participate in the program. In mental health services, underutilization by people of color is common. Although program staff may be inclined to blame non-utilizers for their failure to take advantage of society's offerings, a more productive stance might be to ask what features of the program constitute barriers to participation. The list of possible barriers is long and includes lack of minority personnel, publication of program documents in English only, lack of outreach to inform people about the program's existence, location of the program in areas that are not accessible to some groups, complex and stigmatizing eligibility procedures, and paltry benefits. Some argue that privatization exacerbates access problems, as providers create barriers that keep out difficult or unprofitable clients. This process is known as *creaming* (as in selecting the "cream of the crop").

Nature of the Benefit

Public programs offer four types of benefits: services, goods, vouchers, and cash. Of course, some provide a combination of these. Benefits vary in the degree of choice (or power) afforded to the recipient. Services and goods provide the least choice. Social workers like to believe that our professional services empower the needy. But how many of the needy would choose to receive them? Even the way we deliver services can disempower recipients, since we usually make ourselves available from 9 to 5, a schedule that is convenient for the professional but not for the low-income working adult. We sometimes apply punitive measures to force clients to use services. In the TANF program, for instance, a client who chooses not to receive services may risk losing her grant.

Goods offer a little more choice because clients can usually "take it or leave it." Distribution of food commodities is characteristic. In one community, low-income adults stand in line at 6:00 in the morning waiting for the "cheese truck" to arrive at the community center. Large slabs of cheese are passed out to eager recipients, along with a dose of humiliation.

Vouchers limit choice to a range of products. Still, recipients can usually select when and where they will receive the goods. SNAP is a classic example. The products that can be purchased under this program are restricted, but shoppers can choose the store and shop at their convenience using an EBT (electronic benefits transfer) card.

Cash provides the greatest choice and flexibility to the recipient. It can be used anywhere, at any time, to purchase anything. As a result, programs that deliver cash are subject to criticism that their recipients are incapable of making rational decisions about money management.

Administrative Structure

We can describe the administrative structure of a public program with reference to four aspects: centralization, staff characteristics, citizen participation, and appeal procedures.

The principles of efficiency and access compete in decisions about the centralization of public programs. Highly centralized programs have few offices and benefit from economies of scale. They are efficient but hard to access. By contrast, satellite offices cost more but allow convenient access. Sometimes the degree of centralization is an inverse function of the political power of program beneficiaries. Neighborhoods and groups with power advocate for convenient access to the public programs they use. Compare the number of fire stations in a middle-class neighborhood with the number of welfare offices in low-income neighborhoods.

The faces of staff speak volumes about the program. Lack of bicultural and bilingual staff in a program serving people of color represents a *de facto* barrier to access. Extensive reliance on paraprofessionals may reflect budget shortages or limited interest on the part of professional staff. However, some programs employ former clients as a way to reach out to their target populations.

Echoes of the citizen participation movement of the 1960s and 1970s recur in some public programs. Rather than reserve important decisions for the experts, these programs refer them to advisory groups or clients, former clients, or community members. Of course, some citizen advisory groups and councils, like those described by Alexis in Chapter 8, are for appearances only. Nonetheless, these token groups still have the potential for citizen participation. You never know when they will erupt and demand meaningful engagement!

Some public programs have established appeal or complaint procedures. These range from informal review processes to full-fledged administrative hearings. The presence and operation of these procedures are important factors to consider when describing a program. If all appeals are denied, the analyst has an inkling that administrators may not be fair and impartial in resolving conflicts. On the other hand, if all appeals are granted, we might infer that mistakes are common and we might wonder what happens to clients who don't have the nerve or the resources to launch an appeal.

Financing Mechanism

To understand a program, we would do well to "follow the money." Once we understand where the money comes from, we know a great deal about the program. Methods of financing vary from coercive to voluntary along a continuum based on the experience of the giver. They also vary in the degree of separation between giver and client.

No one voluntarily pays taxes, so programs that are funded using tax dollars are at the extreme end of the coercion continuum. Taxes weigh more heavily on some citizens than others, and some programs are financed through regressive taxes that weigh most heavily on the working poor and the middle class. So (as we saw in Chapter 2) it is not enough to know that a program receives tax funding; we must also know what kind of tax provides the funds.

In a coercion-free world, all programs would be financed through voluntary contributions. Charity is an important source of program funding, particularly in the social services. Unfortunately, charity is unreliable. Donor preferences as well as their ability to give can shift without notice, so for vital social functions charity falls short. We saw this in the wake of the Great Recession. Facing increased needs, two-thirds of public charities saw reduced donations in 2008 (see American City Bureau, 2009).

Programs also differ in the nature of the relationship between donor and recipient. In some cases there is no relationship. In others, participants are donors, as partial funding comes from the user fees they pay.

Today, many social service programs draw funding from an array of financing mechanisms. For instance, a meal program for older adults might be supported primarily through county taxes and funds authorized under the Older Americans Act, with a short-term federal grant providing supplemental funding and user fees covering the balance.

IMPACT APPRAISAL

This section turns to the use of cost–benefit analysis to assess program impact. Then we describe a social justice framework for analyzing impact and other aspects of social policy. Whereas cost–benefit analysis can be predominantly technical, the social justice perspective offers a value-based approach to policy analysis.

Cost–benefit Analysis

What we call "cost–benefit analysis" actually includes two techniques. The first technique involves estimating the monetary values of costs and benefits, actual **cost–benefit analysis**. The second technique, called **cost–effectiveness analysis**, does not assign a dollar value, focusing instead on clearly describing costs and benefits. Social workers are generally more comfortable with the latter approach, although the precision of monetary estimates is sometimes worthwhile.

Costs and benefits may be immediate or long term, and they may be either direct or indirect results of the policy under consideration. Sometimes costs and benefits—especially indirect or long-term ones—are open to dispute. Deriving the best possible estimates can be a challenge. Table 3.2 offers examples of the possible costs and benefits of a hypothetical proposal to make Medicaid coverage available to all low-income workers with financing through a payroll tax.

Costs and benefits are sometimes probabilistic—they are not always sure bets. This is especially true when they are long-term or indirect. In this example we might ask how likely it is that this program will result in higher prices for health care. Simple economics of supply and demand would predict that increased demand would raise the price of care. We would consult an economist (or the General Accounting Office, if we were in Congress) to answer a question of this kind. Similarly, a public health expert might address the program's potential impact on the risk of contagious disease. The end result may be a consensus view that predicts little to no impact on pricing and a 15 percent drop in disease risk.

Cost–benefit analysis can be a useful way to organize and understand public debate about a policy proposal. The cost–benefit grid presented in Table 3.2 can be used in public meetings to generate lists of potential costs and benefits in each category. It can also help students to understand public policy debates. Emotionally charged rhetoric can be distilled into beliefs regarding possible benefits or costs. Laid bare, some beliefs can be dismissed as irrational and others may be seen to contain a germ of truth.

Like any evaluation method, cost–benefit analysis has advantages and disadvantages. One advantage stems from its focus on *logos*. It directs attention away from emotionality and partisan politics and toward the practical consequences of a proposal. It can be a splendid tool for organizing ideas and debunking speculation. It is, however, only a tool. Cost–benefit analysis says little about the morality of a proposal (Nussbaum, 2001). From the perspective of this method, all policy proposals are morally equal. Yet, as we saw in the last chapter, perfectly "rational" decisions that violate human rights are unjustified regardless of their potential benefits.

TABLE 3.2 Costs and Benefits of a Proposal to Expand Medicaid Coverage

	COSTS		BENEFITS	
	Immediate vs. Long Term		Immediate vs. Long Term	
Direct	Increased tax on wages	Higher proportion of federal budget devoted to health care	Access to affordable health care	Lower incidence of preventable illness among low-income workers
Indirect	Drop in new hires	Greater demand and funding for health care raises cost of care	Less use of emergency room for primary care	Lower population risk of contagious disease

Social Justice Framework for Policy Analysis

When justice is the goal of social policy, fairness becomes the target of analysis. So, for example, a need assessment that is conducted using a social justice framework would not pretend to be value-free or "objective." In the advocacy example at the opening of this chapter, advocates for social justice developed a careful description of the problem to help make the case for legislation to protect low-income students' educational rights. Even the most technically sophisticated cost–benefit analysis is informed by a basic understanding of what is just or beneficial. In this way social justice pervades policy analysis as a philosophy, a mission, and a goal.

Our understanding of social justice as the fair allocation of rewards and benefits of group membership generates a distinctive approach to policy analysis that has been called the **social justice perspective**. When this perspective is employed, we consider both the process of policy development and the impact of the policy itself. The steps of this approach are summarized as follows:

1. Assess the fairness of the policy development process.
2. Describe the allocation rules embodied in the policy.
3. Determine the net effect of the policy on vulnerable populations.
4. Reach a conclusion regarding the policy's impact on social justice.

Assessing the Process   The fair process principles introduced in Chapter 1 can be used to assess policy-making processes. The first question to consider is whether the parties involved have operated according to established rules. Whether the process takes place in the halls of Congress or the chambers of a city council, it should proceed according to rules. Careful scrutiny sometimes leads to the conclusion that rules were not followed or were stretched. Decisions that should have been made in open meetings are made in closed caucuses, proper notice of a vote is not provided, people who are not qualified are allowed to vote, or (as in Florida's 2000 electoral process) legitimate voters are turned away. Sometimes these deviations are just mistakes, but they can reflect an attempt to derail democracy in favor of an individual or group.

Fair policy process not only follows the rules but also includes the affected parties. Voice and access are pivotal to effective democracy. But sometimes people whose lives will be changed by a policy do not have a voice in policy development. When the voices of affected parties are silenced, the likelihood of an unjust result is high. If someone is treated as "other" and denied access to policy debates, basic principles of fairness are violated. Usually, there is a rationale for declaring a person "other." He or she may be an undocumented immigrant about to be deprived of health care, a "union agitator" seeking a representation vote in a nonunion shop, or an "enemy combatant" seen as a threat to national security. In any case, the label "other" is used to exclude people from decisions that affect them.

The principle of "one person, one vote" is also vital to a working democracy. Yet this principle is violated when access to policy development is lopsided. At present the campaign-financing system used in the United States guarantees wealthy people and organizations better access to policy makers. Social workers can strive to restore balance by pointing out the problem and amplifying the voices of vulnerable groups.

Describing the Allocation Rules

The first step in describing the allocation rules embodied in a policy is asking, "What are the costs and/or benefits under consideration?" As we have seen, costs and benefits can be either immediate or long-term and either the direct or the indirect result of social policy. In this stage, the social justice perspective uses the tools of cost–benefit analysis. But this approach goes beyond cost–benefit analysis in its focus on the people involved. Here we ask **who** bears the costs, **who** receives the benefits, and what justification there is for this

TABLE 3.3 Who Bears the Costs and Benefits of a Proposal to Expand Medicaid Coverage?

	COSTS		BENEFITS	
	Immediate vs. Long Term		**Immediate vs. Long Term**	
Direct	Increased tax on wages (paid by all workers and employers)	Higher proportion of federal budget devoted to health care (Congress/executive have less discretion in funding)	Access to affordable health care (for low-income workers/families)	Lower incidence of preventable illness (among low-income workers/families)
Indirect	Drop in new hires as employers absorb increased payroll costs (fewer jobs for unemployed and new job hunters)	Greater demand and funding for health care raises cost of care (for general population)	Less use of emergency room (ER) for primary care frees ER for patients with real emergencies, reduces budget needs for ER	Lower population risk of contagious disease (enjoyed by general population)

allocation. With this information we can derive the allocation rules, both informal and formal, that govern who receives and who pays. By understanding and articulating the allocation rules, we can reveal the philosophical underpinnings of a policy or policy proposal and illuminate its potential impact on social justice. Table 3.3 takes the hypothetical example already discussed and outlines its human dimension.

In social justice analysis we can examine the allocation pattern in each type of cost or benefit. In the preceding example, the results would be as follows:

- Immediate/direct—A tax paid by all workers and employers funds health-care coverage for low-income workers and their families.
- Long-term/direct—Congress and the executive branch have less discretion in funding decisions so that low-income workers and their families can have fewer preventable illnesses.
- Immediate/indirect—Fewer jobs for the unemployed and new job hunters are the cost of lower use of emergency room services.
- Long-term/indirect—The price of health care for the general population rises, and the population has lower risk of contagious disease.

This analysis illuminates some of the underlying dynamics in the policy. Immediate costs are borne by workers, employers, and the unemployed, while immediate benefits go to low-income workers in the form of greater access to care and less pressure to use emergency rooms for primary health care. Here the general working population pays for the care of its more vulnerable members. Over the long term, the discretion of federal budget makers is reduced and the health of low-income workers is improved. The population as a whole may experience rising health-care fees even as it enjoys less disease. Most of the costs we have identified are borne by broad segments of the population and groups who will not be unduly burdened. The only exception here is the cost borne by those who are not hired when employers tighten their belts to cover their share of the payroll tax. The benefits focus on low-income workers, a relatively needy group, as well as the general population.

Determining the Effect on Vulnerable Populations (Desert, Need, Rights, and Equality)   A social justice perspective in social work demands special attention to the potential impact of policy on vulnerable populations. These are people living with economic insecurity and groups who have historically been oppressed or underrepresented. Too often benefits to one such group come at a cost to another.

In Chapter 1 we examined the primary components of social justice as described by David Miller: desert, need, rights, and equality. We can return to these to develop a conclusion regarding the social justice impact of a proposal. Here, we consider: (1) the extent to which people will receive what we (and they) feel is deserved, (2) whether a human need is being met (or ignored) in this proposal, (3) whether the proposed change violates anyone's rights, and (4) the potential impact of the proposal on equality. The importance of each component will depend on the focus of the policy; nonetheless, each component has special relevance for vulnerable populations, and the social work profession has a mandate to ensure that these aspects are addressed in policy debates.

Taking these components into account adds a new dimension to the appraisal of costs and benefits in our example. Our proposed Medicaid expansion would help meet the health *needs* of low-income workers and their families. The costs would be borne by all workers and employers, who probably believe the increased tax deprives them of wages they *deserve*. The *needs* of unemployed workers and young people entering the labor force may be jeopardized if employers hire fewer workers. And, of course, in the United States, citizens do not enjoy a *right* to health care, even though some advocates argue that we should. If we focus on vulnerable populations, then to assess this proposal we must balance the health-care needs of low-income workers against the deserts of all workers and the needs of the potentially unemployed.

Reaching a Conclusion   Aristotle said the outcome of a just act is a social world that is more just. The outcome of a just policy is the same. Those of us who are not omniscient will be hard-pressed to anticipate the full impact of a policy (or, as chaos theory would have us believe, a butterfly's flight). So we do the best we can, keeping in mind our philosophical perspectives and personal biases.

Given any set of facts, diverse philosophical perspectives dictate various conclusions about the social justice impact of a given policy. By the time the analysis has reached this stage most people have reached a tentative conclusion about this impact. (Indeed, they may have *begun* with a conclusion.) The final challenge of social justice analysis is to present a conclusion and articulate its philosophical foundations. The perspectives we reviewed in Chapter 1 can prove helpful in this regard.

In our hypothetical example we may begin analysis with the belief that it is good to provide health care to people in need. This stems from our (contractual liberal) belief that health care is a social good that should be available to all. A utilitarian liberal perspective would support the redistributive aspect of this proposal, based on the belief that the well-being of society is enhanced when those who have more resources give to those who have less. Because this intervention does little to reorder the dynamics of our capitalist society, staunch socialists may find it uninspired. Still, the notion of meeting a need as basic as that for health care would be appealing to the socialist viewpoint. By contrast, libertarians and those who support oligarchy might view the proposal more critically. A libertarian perspective would weigh the imposition of a tax heavily, viewing redistribution or care of the needy as less important. An adherent of oligarchy might oppose any change in allocation as a threat to established order.

Policy analysis is fundamentally an intellectual process. The approaches outlined here can be used individually or in combination to improve our understanding of policy development, public programs, and the impacts of social policy. They can also be used to inform advocacy efforts—moving from thought to action. In the following section we turn to advocacy, drawing from the experiences of policy practitioners, as well as from communication theory and research on persuasion.

LO 3-3   Practice Effective Advocacy

EP 1a
EP 8d

Mark Ezell (2001) offered a useful definition of **advocacy** when he argued that it "consists of those purposive efforts to change specific existing or proposed policies or practices on behalf of or with a specific client or group of clients" (p. 23). That is where we social workers come in. We ensure that the voices of vulnerable groups are heard, and to do this, we must persuade. In *Rhetoric,* Aristotle described three components of effective persuasion: *logos,* reason based on content and logic; *pathos,* reason based on passion and emotions; and *ethos,* reason based on the merits and character of the speaker. Today, advocacy is still informed by Aristotle's views. We rely heavily on the three components of persuasion, and any advocate would do well to use all three when making an argument. We also rely on a healthy dose of chutzpah, as *we question the invincible and challenge the inevitable.* Drawing on assessment and analysis, advocates use a variety of tactics to accomplish their goals. Four key advocacy areas are examined here: arguments, compromise, relationship, and coalitions. Aristotle's three components of persuasion can help in each of these areas.

PREPARING, COMPOSING, AND DELIVERING ARGUMENTS

Persuasion, or argument, is central to advocacy. Arguments must be based on careful reasoning and solid research (*logos*). They must be presented in a way that engages the audience's passions (*pathos*). Finally, advocates must preserve their professionalism and credibility (*ethos*). Here, we discuss three steps: preparation, composition, and delivery.

Preparation: Speak to the Audience

"Speaking to the audience" sounds simple but actually requires considerable analysis, empathy, and skill. Communication specialists describe the process as "constructing a receiver profile" (Johnston, 1994). Advertising firms spend millions of dollars constructing profiles of their targets. As social advocates, we can increase our effectiveness by learning about our audience (the "target" of our persuasion).

Constructing a receiver profile is complicated by the strong likelihood that an argument will be presented to multiple audiences. Several of these audiences, such as those charged with making a decision, are of primary importance, while others, such as fellow advocates, may be less important. Nonetheless, effective arguments speak to as much of the audience as possible.

In a way, this is an exercise in perspective taking. O'Keefe and Shepherd (1987) identified four developmental levels in perspective taking. At the first level, no attempt is made to determine the target's needs or interests; at the second, the advocate's needs are communicated without regard to those of the target; at the third level, the advocate is familiar with the target's position and has prepared counterarguments designed to change the target's mind; at the fourth level, the advocate focuses on the target and elaborates on the advantages to the target of taking the desired action (Johnston, 1994). When you finish this course, you should be operating at the fourth level.

Operating at the fourth and highest level of perspective taking begins with knowledge of audience demographics. As my grandmother (and others) said, "You never get a second chance to make a first impression!" Appearances speak volumes, so if your audience is an all-male legislative committee, consider including at least one man among the presenters. Or if you are speaking to a group of welfare recipients, think twice before putting on that dress-for-success suit. Beyond appearances, consider the audience's beliefs, attitudes, and values.

Advocates can establish connection with U.S. audiences by tapping into core American values. Steele and Redding (1962) conducted a study of these values. Their results, which were remarkably similar to those identified in a 1940 study, are still relevant today. The following list summarizes these core values.[4]

Core American Values

- *Puritan and pioneer morality:* Hard work, honesty, self-discipline, and cooperation
- *Individuality:* Personal integrity, the value of the life of even one person, personal rights
- *Achievement and success:* Personal success, money, self-made achievement, social status
- *Change and progress:* "New and improved," future and present always better than past, change for better
- *Ethical equality:* All equal before God; one person, one vote
- *Effort and optimism:* No problem too big
- *Efficiency, practicality, and pragmatism:* Getting things done
- *Rejection of authority:* Power of individual; freedom and rights over duties and obligations
- *Science and secular rationality:* Reason, control, prediction
- *Sociality:* Networking
- *Material comfort:* Happiness can be bought
- *Quantification:* Bigger, faster, more, longer, quantity over quality
- *External conformity:* Popularity, social status
- *Humor:* Leveling influence
- *Generosity and consideration:* Welfare, benevolence
- *Patriotism:* Loyalty to America and its values over loyalty to nation of origin

By appealing to these values, you can generate agreement and identification in a wide range of target audiences. Of course, for a given argument, only some values might apply, and audiences vary in the degree to which they embrace each value. Advocates should identify the audience's most important core values. An advocate speaking before a group of social workers, for example, might focus on generosity and consideration. Someone appearing before the chamber of commerce might emphasize achievement and success. Of course, patriotism is popular across a wide range of audiences.

Your appeal to values should be carefully calibrated. Any audience will be offended by manipulation or pandering. Condescension or an underlying message that the audience is ignorant or unfeeling is an immediate turnoff. Moral outrage can alienate anyone who does not share the same fervor.

Last, but certainly not least, comes self-interest—what the audience wants. Politicians have rather predictable needs. They want to be reelected. Suppose, for example, that you are writing a report on the effect of school fees on low-income families. Several groups— the media, school board authorities, state legislators, the families themselves, and other advocates—will read the report, but your goal is to pass legislation that will provide fee waivers to children from low-income families. The report must speak credibly to the interests of all these groups, but its primary target is state legislators. Naturally, your report will be impeccably accurate, giving a concise but well-supported argument, without moralizing or assigning blame. It will present a clear solution to the problem. But this is not enough, because it does not address the legislator's self-interest. To do this, the report should acknowledge the constraints that legislators face, perhaps noting that "no one wants to increase taxes, but we all want to support schools, and no one wants to see

---

[4]From D. Johnston, *The Art and Science of Persuasion*, p. 227. ©1994. Reprinted with permission of the McGraw-Hill Companies.

children stigmatized or left out." It might include a list of leading members in the community who have endorsed your bill (perhaps even the head of the chamber of commerce). With this report you'll have their attention!

Composing the Argument

Here, we will consider three strategies for composing strong arguments: anticipating opposing arguments, using authority, and combining analytic material (facts and figures) and anecdotal material (stories and illustrations).

Anticipating the Opposition   As a general rule, advocates should anticipate and address arguments that will be made by the opposition. In the field of communication, this is referred to as a "two-sided" argument. When you use a two-sided argument, you present your case and rebut the case you expect from the opposition. These are contrasted with "one-sided" arguments, in which you present only your case.

Some advocates believe it is simpler to offer one-sided arguments, noting that if you present a two-sided argument you work against yourself by presenting the opposing case. But most summaries of communication research on this issue suggest that one-sided arguments should be used only under limited circumstances, such as when the audience is already in favor of your position, is easily confused on the issue, or is not aware that there are opposing views (Johnston, 1994; O'Keefe, 1992). The final case, in which the audience is unaware of opposition, should be treated with care. If you present a one-sided argument and the audience becomes aware of the opposing point of view, you can lose both credibility and the argument.

Generally, it is best to anticipate the opposition and present a two-sided argument or, at a minimum, to acknowledge opposing views. Communication scholars recommend this approach when the audience is sophisticated, aware of contradictory positions, and not already in agreement with your position (Johnston, 1994). Effective arguments not only anticipate opposing arguments but present counterarguments that will inoculate the audience against the opposing side. In the school fees example, advocates anticipated the argument that some parents would misuse the program and defused it by suggesting a simple process under which children eligible for free school lunches were automatically eligible for fee waivers.

Using Authority   Advocates rely on authority to persuade. Their authority might stem from the care and accuracy of their observations (*logos*) or their personal credibility (*ethos*). Personal or professional experiences and academic credentials both contribute to authority. Sometimes one can borrow from other sources, such as scientific, moral, or political authorities. Community leaders also contribute authority to an argument.

BOX 3.1   An Approach to Avoid When Composing Arguments

We have all heard "slippery slope" arguments. When we were young, our teachers may have told us, "If I do this for you, I'll have to do it for *all* of the children." More sophisticated forms of this argument surface in contemporary debates such as the controversy over assisted suicide. Opponents argue that permitting assisted suicide for the terminally ill will lead to euthanasia of the disabled or even the unattractive. Slippery slope arguments have what my grandmother used to call "ear appeal." They sound good. They make sense at first blush. But upon careful consideration they are seldom persuasive. Indeed, a good debater can undermine an opponent's credibility by pointing out that the person has used a slippery slope argument.

The audience should be taken into account, as some authorities can be perceived as alienating. A group of secular humanists is likely to be more susceptible to the authority of definitive research than to religious authority. Your colleagues might be impressed by the use of professional experience. State legislators in the Bible Belt might be persuaded by a well-chosen biblical passage.

Combining Analytic and Anecdotal Material   A corollary to the observation that most arguments are presented before multiple audiences is the requirement that arguments speak to people using multiple approaches. Some members of an audience will be intrigued and impressed by the *logos* of an argument—the facts and figures. But others will find them dull or incomprehensible. Those who are either bored or intimidated by careful statistical analysis may perk right up when *pathos* is brought in through a strong, illustrative example.

Communications research underscores the importance of examples or stories. O'Keefe's (1992) review of research on the topic suggested that examples are generally more effective with all but the most sophisticated audiences. This is consistent with Douglass's (1997) analysis of the nearly effective antihomosexual campaign of the Oregon Citizens Alliance (OCA) in 1993. Douglass wondered how such an unsophisticated campaign could have led to the near passage of Measure 9, an effort to amend Oregon's constitution to define homosexuality as "abnormal, wrong, unnatural and perverse." After careful study, he concluded that the OCA's effective use of narrative (even without compelling analytic arguments) was the key to their success in securing a 47 percent "yes" vote on Measure 9. (See also Fisher, 1987.)

The value of illustrations, such as graphics, should not be ignored. An effective presentation incorporates multiple approaches to communication: facts and figures, illustrative examples, and symbols. This multifaceted approach will engage a diverse audience and employ both logos and pathos for effective persuasion.

Successful Delivery

I once had paralyzing stage fright that was especially acute when I faced a microphone. You can image what this did for my ability to testify before legislative committees! Of course, I was not alone. Many social workers struggle with fear and awkwardness when they are confronted with microphones and cameras. Self-help books can be useful in dealing with stage fright. I especially like the book called *I Can See You Naked* (Hoff, 1988).

While imaging and breathing exercises can also help, I think the essence of effective speaking is *intent*—knowing why you are there and keeping your *energy* and your presentation focused on your message. Everything else is peripheral. I like to develop

---

BOX 3.2   Another Approach to Avoid When Composing Arguments

Policy makers, representatives of the media, and the public at large have grown impatient with what I call "Ain't it awful?" arguments. These arguments outline, in exquisite detail, the horrible conditions an advocate has discovered—and they stop at that point. Although such a presentation can reflect a tremendous amount of effort and study, it leaves an audience feeling frustrated and impotent. Advocacy presentations should generally close with at least one specific recommendation that is likely to address the problem. At a minimum, the person presenting the complaint should recommend further study of the problem that has been identified. Beyond this, discussion of possible solutions— particularly those that have proven effective in different settings or with similar problems—is always advisable.

presentations with three to five points and use the time prior to delivery to breathe deeply and review those points.

When organizing a presentation, keep in mind that people remember what is said first and what is said last. They tend to forget what happened in the middle. I like to use my first few sentences to make a connection with the audience, tell them who I am and why I am there in a way that relates to them and their values. And I like to close with a recommendation or a plea that tells them what I want them to do. Another simple rule of organization is "Tell them what you will say. Say it. Then tell them what you said."

A written script should be used only as a last resort. If you are going to be in front of television cameras or hundreds of people, and severe stage fright is likely, a script can be a useful tool. But a script can leave you with a lifeless presentation. Ordinarily, an outline with key points and evidence should suffice.

Any contact that acknowledges the audience's nonverbal communication enlivens your presentation. If the audience laughs or looks skeptical, a speaker should acknowledge their reaction and incorporate it into the presentation. This responsiveness will involve the audience and make the presentation more like a dialogue than a lecture.

Of course, speeches (and reports) should be organized and concise. All policy reports should include a one to two-page executive summary for use by members of the press who have little time and need quotable material. The executive summary will also help legislators who are pressed for time and unable to read every report they receive. Policy makers invariably appreciate a summary of key policies in the area, objective facts and figures, and clear recommendations. All audiences appreciate a table of contents and clear, jargon-free language.

Thus far, our discussion has focused on the more formal aspects of advocacy. But negotiation and compromise often take place behind closed doors. In the following section we will consider this aspect of policy practice.

NEGOTIATION AND COMPROMISE

Politics has been called "the art of compromise." Effective compromises give each party something highly valued while asking that each give up something of lesser value. The net result (for the utilitarian liberal) is an increase in overall satisfaction. Negotiation is the process used to reach a compromise. Before entering into negotiations, advocates must understand their own positions.

Tedeschi and Rosenfeld (1980) offered a useful approach to analyzing positions in negotiation. They suggest that all parties have a **status quo point**, a **resistance point**, and a **level of aspiration**. The status quo point is the place at which negotiations begin. If the negotiations fail, both parties will be at their status quo point. The resistance point is the minimum result necessary to reach an agreement. The level of aspiration is what each party hopes will come from the negotiation. Both will be satisfied if they come close to this level. The distance between the resistance point and the level of aspiration is called the **bargaining range**. This is the crux of the negotiation, where the skill and power of the negotiators come into play. Before entering into negotiation, advocates should clearly articulate their own priorities, possibly in terms of their status quo, resistance point, and level of aspiration. Then it will be time to consider the other party.

Unless an advocate has become familiar with the opposition, either through repeated exposure or through inside information, it will be difficult to anticipate their priorities. Therefore, a first stage in the process of negotiation is usually an exchange of information concerning goals and priorities. This exchange may not be framed as such, but a proposed "informational meeting" might have, as its hidden agenda, the opportunity to initiate negotiation toward a compromise.

USE OF RELATIONSHIP

Social workers have long understood the importance of relationship. As the advocacy experience described at the beginning of this chapter illustrated, advocacy is not about allies and enemies. It is about people, and today's opponent may be tomorrow's ally. While it is tempting, and sometimes emotionally gratifying, to cast the opposition as evil demons, in the end this is counterproductive. Any dispute, debate, or disagreement is an opportunity to build a relationship with the opposition. Social advocates seldom have the financial resources to influence policy with money, but our capacity to establish and maintain relationships can be as effective as the perks served up by corporate lobbyists.

Social exchange theory offers a useful perspective for understanding relationships in the policy arena. Within this framework, reciprocity (simple give-and-take) is the glue that holds society together. It is our sense that a favor creates an obligation to reciprocate. Social workers are frequently given opportunities to do favors, as when a policy maker asks for information or advice, a candidate asks for a contribution or an endorsement, a colleague asks for moral support, or an administrator asks for supportive testimony. These requests are opportunities to build relationships.

Over the course of their professional careers, social workers give and receive assistance to the point where they forget who owes whom. Some exchange theorists argue that friendship is simply a reciprocal relationship that has reached this point. Both parties feel vaguely indebted to the other, and each would help the other without hesitation—partly to fulfill a sense of obligation but partly because "that's what friends do."

In addition to this kind of exchange-based relationship, advocates enjoy the opportunity to build alliances based on mutual interests and shared respect. A long-term commitment to building supportive relationships will enhance an advocate's effectiveness. Sometimes this commitment requires separating the messenger from the message—acknowledging that although you disagree with another's views, you are fond of each other as people. I have seen state legislators debate vigorously, almost to the point (I thought) of coming to blows. After the debate, in quieter quarters, the combatants checked in with each other, apologized for their excesses, and affirmed their friendship. This capacity to sustain relationship through controversy is vital to effective advocacy.

BUILDING AND MAINTAINING COALITIONS

In a pluralistic democracy, coalitions can be powerful. The challenge for advocates is to identify potential coalition partners and then to establish clear guidelines for maintaining the coalition.

Potential coalition partners are groups and individuals who share an advocate's goal. A coalition is not a marriage—these groups need not necessarily be personally or philosophically compatible. My first job taught me about unlikely partners in coalition. I worked for the Oregon Environmental Council, organizing a coalition of diverse groups, all interested in maintaining stream flows (keeping water in rivers). Our first task was to identify parties who shared our interest in keeping water in rivers. The coalition eventually included Native Americans, commercial fishermen, sports fishermen, and environmentalists. These groups were on opposite sides of the fence on other issues, but when it came to minimum stream flows they came together to form a remarkably effective coalition. On a much grander scale, the civil rights movement involved a powerful coalition of religious and labor leaders from white and African American communities who demonstrated that they could transcend their differences and work together for a common cause.

Common goals are essential. But a shared purpose does not guarantee a smoothly functioning coalition. Coalition building can become an intensely personal business. People who disrespect or loathe each other make difficult coalition partners. An organization known for its confrontational tactics and extreme positions may not be able to find willing partners. An advocate known for alienating or embarrassing the opposition will have similar problems. Coalitions are built and maintained by moderates whose positions and tactics are palatable to most partners—people who get along well with others. This does not mean that the more extreme personalities or groups cannot instigate a coalition, only that they may have a harder time facilitating ongoing operations or recruiting potential partners.

Coalitions require care and tending. Roles must be carefully defined. Partners must agree about how they will make decisions, what types of issues they will (and will not) address, how partners will be informed about developments, and who is (and is not) empowered to speak on behalf of the coalition. A general rule of coalition maintenance is "When in doubt, talk it out." Particularly in the early stages of development, coalitions need both routine ways to communicate (e.g., monthly meetings) and emergency routes of conversation (e.g., e-mail, phone trees). The emergency routes are useful when a partner identifies the need for immediate action and needs feedback and agreement before committing the coalition to a course of action.

Sometimes, in the heat of an advocacy effort, a decision maker will approach one member of the coalition and offer a deal. The advocate is asked, on behalf of the coalition, to agree to a compromise. An advocate once told me, "This goes with the territory." But making a commitment without consulting with coalition partners has put many an advocate in hot water. That's why it is important that everyone agree on who is empowered to negotiate on behalf of the coalition. Agreement on this point should be among the first items on any coalition's agenda.

LO 3-4   Understand the Meaning and Processes of Empowerment

EP 6b
EP 8d

Empowerment is a central goal of policy practice. When we speak on behalf of others we are generally less effective than when we empower others to speak on their own behalf. This is true in part because our motives can be suspect when we claim to represent the interests of clients. Opponents argue, for instance, that when we advocate for increased program budgets or support for the poor, we are actually trying to enhance our professional stature and line our pockets.

When clients speak for themselves, they enjoy special credibility. As Pat Powers and others have noted (Hardcastle, Wenocur, & Powers, 1996), an advocate's credibility is greatest when the policy under consideration has directly affected either the advocate or a member of the advocate's family. A former welfare mother or the sister of a person with a disability brings personal credibility to an advocacy effort. This credibility can be more influential than professional experience and degrees, moral and legal authority, and good science put together. Unfortunately, the same forces that generate personal credibility with regard to social problems (poverty, disability, prejudice, and discrimination) work against effective involvement in the policy arena.

We can empower people by helping them secure the knowledge, skills, resources, and opportunities to advocate for themselves. When Utah Issues held workshops to inform parents about the school fee issue and waiver regulations, it empowered parents by providing knowledge. When a social worker coaches a welfare mother through testimony before the state legislature, the client is empowered by acquiring new skills. When an activist hunts down a bus to transport children from low-income families to a march on the capital, he is empowering people by securing resources. When a bureaucrat suggests that clients be represented on an advisory committee, she empowers clients by securing an opportunity for them to speak for themselves.

While direct advocacy places social workers on the firing line, empowerment interventions enable us to work in the background. Sometimes organizations and individuals who find the confrontational aspects of social advocacy unpleasant or abhorrent find empowerment efforts more acceptable. For instance, a foundation that would never fund lobbying may be willing to support client education. Similarly, a public official who would oppose expansion of welfare benefits may support a program to enhance the communication skills of welfare recipients.

LO 3-5   Identify Ethical Issues in Policy Practice

EP 1a
EP 6b
EP 8d

Some people think politics and policy practice are sordid activities. This perspective is sometimes used to justify deviating from ethical standards. In his now-classic work *Rules for Radicals,* Saul Alinsky (1972) offered another rationale for deviation. Alinsky argued that in social activism, as in war, the ends justify the means. He felt that the power differential between social advocates and policy makers was so huge that advocates were justified in suspending the rules of ethical conduct to achieve important policy victories.

It is important to keep in mind, however, that Alinsky was writing for activists who were excluded from the realm of policy decisions. Unlike most of Alinsky's street-level activists, social work advocates are professionals. We have colleagues in most state legislatures, and to a great extent we are insiders in the policy arena. The power differential between social work advocates and some policy makers may be substantial, but it is never big enough to justify deviating from the rules of ethical communication. We will consider ethics in greater detail in the next section.

IS ADVOCACY AN ETHICAL OBLIGATION?

Mark Ezell (2001) observed that the National Association of Social Workers (NASW) Code of Ethics includes several statements that may support an ethical obligation to do advocacy:

- Social workers *should* advocate for living conditions conducive to the fulfillment of basic human needs and should promote social, economic, political, and cultural values and institutions that are compatible with the realization of social justice (Ethical Standard 6.01).
- Social workers *should* engage in social and political action that seeks to ensure that all people have equal access to the resources, employment, services, and opportunities they require to meet their basic human needs and to develop fully (Ethical Standard 6.04 [a]).
- Social workers *should* act to prevent and eliminate domination of, exploitation of, and discrimination against any person, group, or class on the basis of race, ethnicity, national origin, color, sex, sexual orientation, age, marital status, political belief, religion, or mental or physical disability (Ethical Standard 6.04[d]).

The use of the word "should" suggests that social workers are strongly encouraged, but not required, to undertake these activities and goals. Had that word been replaced with "must" or "will," the code could have been interpreted differently. Nonetheless, policy practice remains central to the professional mission of promoting social justice and human well-being.

SHARPENING THE MESSAGE

The practice of sharpening the message or "getting to the gist" is common in storytelling (Gilovich, 1991). We weed out extraneous details, narrowing our presentation to include only those facts that convey our message in the most efficient way possible. Dorothea Dix used this approach in her many presentations on the treatment of the mentally ill. She "sharpened" her message, and as a result was (perhaps rightly) accused of exaggeration and outright lies.

Modern advocates often do the same thing, seeking and presenting information that supports their case while ignoring contradictory facts. This common practice has both ethical and practical ramifications for social work professionals. Social workers have a clear ethical prohibition against deceit. The NASW Code of Ethics includes several statements that emphasize the importance of truthfulness. Integrity is identified as a core value of the profession, and the code requires that "social workers behave in a trustworthy manner."

Does this prohibition against deceit require us to present facts that do not support our position? The line between "sharpening the message" and deceit may be fuzzy, but both practices threaten the credibility of social advocates. In the advocacy arena, social workers have little to offer but professional and personal credibility. We do not give big campaign contributions. We seldom control committee assignments or votes. Instead, we strive to represent the disenfranchised and the vulnerable in a way that is credible, balanced, and persuasive. As professionals, social workers should emphasize balance and accuracy in our advocacy efforts, even at the risk of delivering a message that is less focused or dramatic than we might like.

USING CLIENTS

Involving clients in advocacy also brings social work practitioners into delicate ethical territory. For some clients, like Annie Boone (Chapter 13), advocacy is empowering and transformative. For others, though, it may be terrifying, humiliating, and damaging.

How can a practitioner determine whether it is ethical (as opposed to advisable) to involve a client in an advocacy effort? The concept of self-determination, a core social work value, provides some direction here. When a client chooses to enter into an advocacy effort with full knowledge of what this effort is expected to entail, that client is exercising the right to self-determination. The social worker's obligation is not to protect the client from discomfort or to promise immediate results but to inform the client—insofar as possible—what to expect.

Consider the ethics of client involvement. Martin Buber suggests that we can hold two distinct attitudes toward other people: an "I–thou" attitude or an "I–it" attitude. An "I–thou" attitude recognizes the individuality of the other and treats the person as worthy of respect. An "I–it" attitude treats the other as an object designed to serve the communicator's selfish needs (Friedman, 1960). Ethical client involvement requires that clients be treated with respect and that communication be characterized by honesty and directness, without the use of power or subordination. Clients must never be treated as a means to an end. The advocacy effort must not "use" clients but "engage" them in a mutual effort to achieve a shared goal.

A practitioner cannot always predict how the client will respond to advocacy experiences but must be sure the client is informed about what to expect. A social worker who worries about "using" a client should consider whether the client was able to make an independent decision about involvement and whether the client fully understands, based on the social worker's explanation, what to expect, both of the advocacy experience itself and of its potential results.

KEEPING CONFIDENCES

Advocacy is a public act, in a public arena in which one should assume that "there are no secrets." This may seem strange, since we know on its face the assumption is probably not true. Nevertheless, it is a useful assumption to live by. Whenever an advocate begins to think that "no one will ever find out about it," he or she is taking a risk that could jeopardize a relationship, or worse. In policy practice it is best to assume that every word one utters and every act one commits will become public knowledge. Advocates live in fishbowls, and the more controversial the cause, the more transparent the bowl.

A corollary to "there are no secrets" is the danger of receiving confidences. When you are engaged in policy practice, people may offer to share confidences with you. They may offer secrets so tantalizing and interesting that it is hard to resist hearing them. Resist you must as a simple act of personal protection. Consider this: If this person is willing to tell you this secret, how many other people have been told? And even if you are not the one who reveals it, how can you ensure that no one else will? How do you know you won't be blamed? Unless you have a strong relationship with someone in the political arena, it is best to avoid these "dangerous confidences."

Obviously, if you do accept someone's confidence, you must guard it carefully. Sometimes it is unclear that something is said "in confidence." Most of us have had the painful experience of inadvertently revealing a confidence we thought was common knowledge. When someone tells us something that seems sensitive or newsworthy, it is important to ask that person, "Am I free to pass this on and give you as the source? Or would you prefer that I hold it in confidence?" This will let you know where you stand, even as it builds trust in the relationship.

CHARACTERISTICS OF ETHICAL PERSUASION

In the marketplace of ideas, ethical persuasion is a two-way process, with expectations for both advocate and listener. Johnston (1994) offered a summary of the expectations of both communicators in an ethical exchange:[5]

Ethical Communication Guidelines

1. Persuaders are clear, direct, and honest about their intentions.
2. Communicators promote mutual respect and mutual satisfaction of goals, rather than self-interests.
3. Communicators use strategies that confirm others and preserve the dignity of others.
4. Communicators seek input and elaboration from each other.
5. Persuaders avoid the use of active deception and the withholding of relevant information, except when the truth may cause significant harm to others.
6. Communicators listen and critically process each other's messages.
7. Communicators welcome and explore dissent.
8. Communicators analyze their own and others' biases without defending or threatening their own or others' egos.
9. All participants in the persuasion process share the ethical responsibility of persuasive outcomes and respond to each other with resoluteness and openness.
10. Communicators weigh opinions equally, rather than on the basis of individual power or status.

---

[5]From D. Johnston, *The Art and Science of Persuasion*, p. 72. ©1994. Reprinted with permission of the McGraw-Hill Companies.

11. Communicators assess probable consequences of their message on others.
12. Communicators employ persuasion to celebrate the human qualities of diversity, personality, intelligence, passion for beliefs, humor, and reasoning.
13. Communicators encourage social discussion and social contact.
14. Communicators critically challenge claims of certainty and truth.
15. Decisions are subject to revision over time.
16. The relative power of the persuader and the receiver determines the degree of ethical responsibility.
17. Communicators maintain free speech, but the probability of harmful consequences guides the ethical decision to produce a persuasive message.

In an advocacy exchange, both advocate and listener are responsible for ensuring that the debate about social issues results in the best possible decision. Both parties share an obligation to ensure civil, fair-minded interaction.

Clearly, advocates cannot control the behavior of their audiences—and audiences sometimes misbehave. It takes only a short time in the advocacy trenches to encounter a listener who is more intent on humiliating the advocate than on hearing a new perspective. Indeed, most experienced advocates can tell horror stories of public attacks by elected officials.

It is difficult not to take attacks personally, but that is exactly what an advocate must do. I believe it is helpful for beginning advocates who are under attack to ask themselves why the official is behaving in this way. The person may be grandstanding or playing to a constituency that is hostile to your position. He or she may be threatened by your effectiveness or may just be in a bad mood. It also helps to recall that public attack is a violation of the "rules of engagement," and the attacker's colleagues probably view it that way. They may be embarrassed by the attack. Indeed, the sympathy generated by a virulent attack may advance your cause![6]

LO 3-6   Understand Legal Considerations That Affect Policy Practice

EP 8d

Some readers of this book may be independently wealthy and engage in social work as philanthropy. The rest of us will be using other people's money. Such use imposes legal obligations. Technical rules are often difficult to understand, remember, and apply. You will find it useful to remind yourself, from time to time, who is providing the funds for your activity and what those persons expect of you. Social advocates often find themselves working for the government or for public charities. Some of the limitations on these groups are discussed in the following sections.

THE HATCH ACT

The Hatch Act is a federal statute passed in 1939 to regulate the political activity of civil servants. Its primary purpose was to ensure that federal employees did not use the power or resources of their offices to promote political candidates. The act was amended in 1993 to allow some political involvement by federal employees. The Hatch Act also applies to employees of private, state, and local organizations whose activities are financed by federal

---

[6]Sometimes a beginning advocate may feel under attack when legislators or officials are asking questions the advocate cannot answer. In such situations, it is best to admit ignorance and offer to find the answer and provide it to the questioner later.

loans or grants (e.g., Head Start employees). Most states have adopted provisions similar to the Hatch Act for state employees.

Employees who are covered by the Hatch Act are not permitted to do any of the following:

- Use their official authority or influence to affect an election
- Solicit or discourage political activity of anyone with business before their agency
- Solicit or receive political contributions
- Be candidates for public office in **partisan** elections
- Engage in political activity while on duty, in a government office, wearing an official uniform, or using a government vehicle
- Wear partisan political buttons while on duty

The key to Hatch Act compliance is avoiding misuse of the power or authority of government office. The act certainly does not rule out all political involvement by government employees. They can, for example, run as candidates in **nonpartisan** elections (e.g., school board), register and vote as they choose, contribute money to political organizations, attend fundraising functions, be active and hold office in a political party or club, and campaign for or against candidates in partisan elections on their own time.

PRESERVING TAX-EXEMPT STATUS

Groups that rely on public support usually seek to qualify for tax-deductible contributions. Such groups are described in Section 501(c)(3) of the Internal Revenue Code and are therefore often referred to as "501(c)(3)'s" or "501(c)(3) organizations." Donors can usually make contributions to such organizations free of estate and gift tax as well as federal and state income tax.

These attributes "stretch" the donor's dollars. Suppose Mr. A is willing to part with $100 of his personal wealth to support your organization. If he makes a gift of $150 and receives a tax deduction of the same amount, he may "save" $50 in taxes; thus, he is out of pocket only $100 while your organization receives $150 in revenue. Special provisions in the tax code can help stretch contributions in a variety of ways. These include special treatment for appreciated property, private foundations, charitable remainder and charitable lead trusts (including trusts established during life and by will), charitable annuities, and "endowment funds" (usually mutual funds) permitting current deductions for future contributions. If you become involved with the "development" (fundraising) side of your organization, you may need to learn more about these provisions.

The extra $50 from Mr. A comes from the government in the form of taxes not collected. Naturally there are "strings attached." A few organizations are unwilling to accept the strings. They may still be nonprofit entities and often are tax-exempt—that is, they do not pay income tax per Internal Revenue Code Sections 501(c)(4) to 501(c)(22). However, unless the rules of Section 501(c)(3) are followed, there will be no deductions available to donors—no "stretching" of the donor dollar.

Perhaps the most famous example of a nonprofit organization that decided to forgo 501(c)(3) status is the Sierra Club. This group was formed for summer treks in the mountains and preservation of the lands visited. In the mid-1960s the Sierra Club found itself fighting to preserve the Grand Canyon from dams. The organization lobbied Congress to oppose reclamation projects proposed by state and local governments. Using government funds to influence legislation, particularly legislation supported by other governments, raises serious issues. The Sierra Club decided, in effect, to stop taking government handouts. It gave up its 501(c)(3) status and continued its advocacy efforts.

Social advocates are likely to find themselves in a similar position. You may be trying to persuade legislators or other policy makers to take actions opposed by other parts of government. Here are some of the rules that apply.

A 501(c)(3) organization is one in which "no substantial part of the activities … is carrying on propaganda or otherwise attempting to influence legislation … and which does not participate in, or intervene in (including the publishing or distributing of statements) any political campaign on behalf of (or in opposition to) any candidate for public office."[7] For public charities that wish to engage in limited political activities, Congress has provided what is known as a "**Conable election**,"[8] or "**safe harbor**"[9] that may offer greater ability to act with less risk of challenge. The Conable election may be selected by filing a form with the IRS.[10]

Under the safe harbor (or Conable election) clause, certain activities are explicitly permitted without the need to report them as lobbying. The following activities are included:

- Making available results of nonpartisan analysis, study, or research
- Providing technical advice or assistance to a political body in response to a written request from such body
- Appearances before or communications to legislative bodies that affect the existence of the organization, its powers and duties, or its tax exemption
- Communication between an organization and its members with respect to legislation of interest to the members, other than efforts to encourage members or others to attempt to influence legislation

Under the Conable election, any communication with a government official or employee who is not a member of the legislative body considering action (e.g., a staff member or executive) is permitted as long as it is not intended to influence legislation.

Influencing legislation (lobbying) includes attempts to influence the opinion of the general public or any segment of the public or any legislative body. It includes matters before local government bodies and extends to any initiative, referendum, constitutional amendment, motion, resolution, or bill.

Under the Conable election, the amount of "influencing legislation" that can be done is clear, relatively easy to calculate, and once determined, allows the organization to make informed choices about its activities. The 501(c)(3) knows that when it is really critical to lobby (or influence legislation) it can do so without fear of jeopardizing its tax status. The amount that can be spent to influence legislation is based on an organization's total budget, not including fundraising expenses, and may not exceed $1,000,000 per year regardless of the budget. The amount of permitted expenditure for an organization is called its "lobbying nontaxable amount." If the limits on this amount are "normally" exceeded by 150 percent, the organization will lose its 501(c)(3) status.

The preceding discussion is a summary of current law, which may change. Details have been omitted. You may wish to consult Internal Revenue Service Publication 557, *Tax Exempt Status for Your Organization*. The Alliance for Justice, located in Washington, DC, also helps nonprofits understand laws governing their advocacy efforts. There are

---

[7]Internal Revenue Code §501(c)(3).

[8]The Conable election, which is found in §501(h) of the Internal Revenue Code, is named after Barber Benjamin Conable Jr., a congressional representative for the state of New York from 1965 to 1985.

[9]Code §§503(h) and 4911.

[10]Currently made by filing Treasury Form 5768.

also separate laws in many states that govern these activities and require reporting by any entity that engages in lobbying.

You should be aware of these laws, but don't let them distract you from your mission. Laws are the rules of a game. To some extent they may control how you advocate, but they need not and should not determine your long-term goals.

Closing Reflections

David Gil (1998) criticized most frameworks for policy analysis, arguing "that major aspects of prevailing institutional and cultural realities tend to be treated as 'constants' rather than as variables" (pp. 117–118). Gil urges social workers to question contextual factors that most people take for granted. Today, these might include the "right" of corporations to make a profit or the inevitability of zero-sum budgeting.[11] Too often, social advocates are stymied by opponents who argue that their proposals would "cost too much money." Keeping their values in sight, social workers can question these constants, noting that failure to solve a social problem may ultimately prove to be more costly than taking action or arguing that the amount spent on humanitarian values is dwarfed (as it is in most community budgets) by the amount committed to economic development or even transportation infrastructure.

This chapter offered several approaches to policy analysis. Each directs attention to a different aspect of social policy. The process-based approaches (need assessment and Prince Policy Appraisal) can be used to assess policy development. Implementation analysis can be used to systematically describe the program itself. Performance-based methods such as cost–benefit analysis enable us to describe the impact of a social policy. Finally, the social justice perspective focuses our attention on the basic fairness of a policy. This approach is new, and you may find it unsatisfying. We all want formulas and simple answers. But in a complex world, simple answers are usually incomplete. By addressing the questions in the social justice framework, you will develop a deep, nuanced perspective on social policy. Informed by your personal philosophy, this perspective will represent your professional assessment of the impact a policy will have on social justice.

Of course, this chapter can only begin to prepare you for policy practice. Here is a reminder of some important themes:

- *The struggle is long.* Social advocates usually set high goals such as "the elimination of injustice." These won't be reached immediately. To shore up our patience we must celebrate the victories and acknowledge the setbacks without losing sight of our long-term objectives.
- Every *individual counts.* Each contribution to an advocacy effort is important and deserves acknowledgment. As my grandma would say, "Write your thank you notes!" That way you can be the agent of acknowledgment.

---

[11]Zero-sum budgeting assumes that increased funding in one human service area must be offset by reduced funding in another area. In some settings (such as personal budgeting), this approach is appropriate and necessary, but in the complex arena of federal (or even state) budgeting, it can artificially restrict the range of options available for advocates. Along these lines, it was astonishing to witness how quickly after September 11, 2001, Congress found billions of dollars to bail out the airline industry and mount a military response. Prior to the terrorist attacks, a budget request of such magnitude would have faced stiff opposition.

- *"Us vs. them"* does not apply here. There is no evil conspiracy to deprive vulnerable Americans of the means to live. Sometimes people take opposing positions, but that does not mean they are enemies. The better you understand the reasons for their positions, the more effectively you will be able to change their minds.
- Social policy is more than legislation. It is easy for advocates to focus on getting a bill passed and forget about the regulations that will be created by the executive branch, or budgets that will be generated, or judicial opinions that may alter the bill's impact. Effective advocacy is ongoing in all three branches of government.

Beyond these themes, this chapter introduced the notion that policy practice is participation in a marketplace of ideas. We discussed Aristotle's suggestion that effective persuasion incorporates *logos, pathos,* and *ethos,* offering specific tactics for advocacy, coalition building, and client empowerment. We addressed ethical issues in policy practice and argued that responsibility for effective debate is shared by the advocate and the audience. The chapter closed with a brief review of major legal considerations governing policy practice by social workers and with an exhortation to *question the inevitable and challenge the invincible.*

Think About It

1. You are the director of a small antipoverty organization, and you have been invited to join a well-established welfare-rights coalition. After agreeing to join, you find the coalition's tactics are so confrontational that your continued participation risks alienating some of the organizations that have given your organization money. What should you do?

2. The homeless shelter in your town has hired you to do a study of "repeaters"—that is, people who come back to the shelter over and over but don't seem to change their lives. The shelter director sees these people as a problem and wants to identify them early and keep them out of the shelter. Your results suggest that these "repeaters" tend to have intractable problems such as substance abuse and mental illness. When you submit your report, the director calls and withdraws his previous invitation for you to present it before the board of directors. What, if anything, should you do?

3. The band director from an inner-city school asks for your advice. The band has been invited to compete in a prestigious contest. The director has enough money to buy new instruments. The band's current instruments are old and dented and cannot produce good music. However, she does not have funds to purchase new uniforms for everyone. She is thinking about asking students to purchase their own uniforms, except for those who cannot afford them. What are her alternatives? What factors should she consider in making her decision?

4. Consider these possible explanations for violence: (1) humans are naturally violent, and without proper constraint (either internal or external) they will commit violent acts; (2) humans who resort to violence are aberrant and unable to control their deviant impulses; (3) individuals who commit violent acts have been deprived of basic needs and see no other way to meet them; and (4) those who commit violent acts are incapable of seeing their victims as humans. Using the Palestinian intifada as an example, consider the implications of each explanation. What kind of intervention would it justify?

Web-Based Exercises

For direct links to all the sites in these exercises, visit the *Foundations of Social Policy* Companion Site at www.cengagebrain.com and select the resources for Chapter 3.

1. Go to the NASW website (www.socialworkers.org) and click on Advocacy in the menu at the top. Under "issues," you will find NASW positions on key policy issues for social workers. Explore this site to see what resources NASW provides for advocates.

2. Go to www.iscvt.org and subscribe to the newsletter of the Institute for Sustainable Communities. It's easy to unsubscribe whenever you no longer want to receive the newsletter, and the publication will give you news about the activities of social justice advocates around the world.

Competency Notes

As mentioned in the preface to this text, the Council on Social Work Education has designated nine core competencies and related practice behaviors that must be addressed by accredited social work programs. In these notes, I will specify the way chapter content addresses these competencies and behaviors. (This is designed to assist with the accreditation process.) Please refer to the "helping hands" icons for the locations of specific content in this chapter. Here you will find a brief explanation of how the accompanying content relates to the specified competency or practice behaviors.

The following list indicates where EPAS competencies and practice behaviors are addressed in this chapter.

EP 1a   **Make ethical decisions by applying the standards of the NASW Code of Ethics, relevant laws, models for ethical decision-making, ethical conduct of research, and additional codes of ethics as appropriate to context.** Ethical issues in policy practice are addressed in this chapter and linked to the NASW Code, and the chapter provides tools and perspectives for ethical decision making in policy practice.

EP 3a   **Apply their understanding of social, economic, and environmental justice to advocate for human rights at the individual and system levels.** Use of appropriate advocacy and negotiation strategies is discussed in depth.

EP 6b   **Use empathy, self-regulation, and interpersonal skills to effectively engage diverse clients and constituencies.** The chapter encourages perspective taking and effective use of self in policy practice.

EP 8d   **Negotiate, mediate, and advocate with and on behalf of diverse clients and constituencies.** The chapter notes that vulnerable groups may be unable to voice their needs or advocate for themselves and addresses the role of popular beliefs and stigma in social policy.

Suggested Resources

Cohen, D., de la Vega, R., & Watson, G. (2001). *Advocacy for Social Justice: A Global Action and Reflection Guide.* Bloomfield, CT: Kumarian Press.

Cole, D. (2016). *Engines of Liberty: The Power of Citizen Activists to Make Constitutional Law.* New York: Basic Books.

Hick, S. F., & McNutt, J. G. (Eds.). (2002). *Advocacy, Activism and the Internet.* West Brookfield, MA: Lyceum.

Hoefer, R. (2011). *Advocacy Practice for Social Justice* (2nd ed.). Brookfield, MA: Lyceum.

NASW. (2015). *Social Work Speaks: NASW Policy Statements* (10th ed.). Washington, DC: NASW Press.

Ronson, J. (2003). *Them: Adventures with Extremists.* New York: Simon & Schuster.

VeneKlasen, L., & Miller, V. (2007). *A New Weave of Power, People, and Politics: The Action Guide for Advocacy and Citizen Participation.* Rugby, UK: Practical Action.

www.afj.org. The Alliance for Justice strives to "strengthen the public interest community's ability to influence public policy and foster the next generation of advocates." Their website offers information about IRS regulations and laws governing nonprofits, access to their publications, advocacy alerts, and job announcements.

www.iscvt.org. Maintained by the Institute for Sustainable Communities, this site provides resources and networking opportunities for social justice advocates throughout the world.

www.osc.gov. This is the official site of the Office of Special Counsel, an excellent source for information about compliance with the Hatch Act (Reference 5 U S C chapter 73, Sub-chapter III, as amended, 5 CFR part 734, PL 103-359 Section 501 [k]).

www.statepolicy.org. This site is part of Influencing State Policy, an initiative designed to help social work faculty and students become more involved in state policy. It includes a link to stateline.org, which provides policy-relevant news for each state, as well as inspiring descriptions of advocacy initiatives that have received awards.

PART II

Collective Responses to Social Problems

© Neil Orloff, Courtesy Art Access Gallery, Salt Lake City

▶ Must we face problems alone?

Problems come in many forms. In the early stages of intellectual development, our problems are intensely personal and we have a limited ability to empathize with other people's troubles. As we mature, we develop the capacity to view adversity from diverse perspectives and to empathize with others.

In this section, we will consider two approaches to understanding social problems. The first, developed by Abram de Swaan, a professor of social sciences at the University of Amsterdam, examines the conditions necessary for personal problems to be treated as social problems (de Swaan, 1988). Once this happens, policy serves as a vehicle for organizing collective action. The point here is not to evaluate policy but to determine when it might be mobilized to address a particular problem.

BOX II.1   John Snow's Map

In 1854, London's Soho neighborhood was subject to a sudden outbreak of cholera. At the time, many believed the disease was caused by "miasma" in the air. John Snow, now a hero to epidemiologists (and Londoners), painstakingly developed a map that showed the residences of people who suffered (and usually died) from cholera. This map has been recreated by Robin Wilson at Southampton University, and it clearly shows cases clustered around a water pump on Broad Street. Further research revealed the pump was contaminated by a cesspool where a cholera-infested diaper had been dumped. Snow's accomplishment is commemorated in true London style, with a pub named after him on the site where the pump used to be.

Courtesy of the John Snow Society

The second approach, **social problem analysis**, begins where the first leaves off. It examines the values and beliefs that shape our understanding of social problems. One of the best examples of this approach was developed by Donald Chambers, a social work professor at the University of Kansas (Chambers, 2000). His method offers a great way to understand the underlying rationale for social policies.

Predicting Collective Action

During the Paleolithic era, humans banded together to hunt mammoths. In the 20th century, they paid Social Security taxes. Since the dawn of our species, humans have used collective action to meet personal needs, but no human society responds collectively to every personal problem. How can we determine whether a problem can or should be addressed collectively?

Abram de Swaan (1988) identified three conditions that facilitate collective solutions to personal adversity. First, the **external effects** of the adversity must be recognized. One person's suffering must affect another, and the "other" must recognize that effect. Second, **individual remedies** must be of limited effectiveness. Attempts by individuals to escape the external effects or to avoid the problem must prove ineffective. Finally, when adversity and/or its external effects can strike at any time with unpredictable magnitude (**uncertainty of moment and magnitude**), collective responses are more likely. The development of modern plumbing serves as an excellent example.[1]

In the 19th century, cholera epidemics devastated many European cities. The 1832 wave of cholera took 18,000 victims in England and a comparable number in Paris. Nineteenth-century scientists quickly linked the infection to lack of fresh water and inadequate sewage removal. Those who could apply individual solutions (the rich) removed themselves to healthier (usually higher) quarters; but the disease was rampant among the poor and began to invade the quarters of the rich. As de Swaan notes, "Mass epidemics provided a striking image of interdependency between fellow city-dwellers, poor and rich, established and newcomers, ignorant and cultivated alike" (p. 124). As the failure of individual solutions became evident, there was widespread agreement that a collective approach was in order.

Experts decided that citywide sanitation systems were the best solution, although they would be disruptive and expensive. Initially, sewer lines were installed in wealthy neighborhoods and financed through what we now call user or connection fees. As soon as wealthy neighborhoods were saturated with pipes, the "venous-arterial system" of sanitation networks was extended throughout the city—a "public good" supported by compulsory taxes and fees. Sanitation departments were established to collect fees and maintain the systems.

Thus, modern plumbing, the collective approach to supplying fresh water and removing sewage, developed because of the external effects of the adversity experienced by the poor (the wealthy were exposed to cholera), the failure of individual remedies (moving to higher ground did not protect against the disease), and uncertainty regarding the moment and magnitude of adversity (one never knew whether, when, or how badly one might be affected by the disease).

The problems discussed in Part II are shared, to various degrees, by all Americans. Each meets de Swaan's three criteria for collective action (external effects are recognized, individual remedies are of limited effectiveness, and there is uncertainty of moment and magnitude), and each of these problems has mobilized governmental action to allocate benefits and resources. As a result, progress toward social justice has been achieved through collective action in the form of government policies and programs.

Social Problem Analysis

Social problem analysis helps us understand the nature of collective responses to problems. It has four key components: problem definition, causal analysis, identification of ideology and values, and consideration of winners and losers. Here, we will use the example of unemployment to clarify these concepts.[2]

---

[1]De Swaan's book *In Care of the State* serves as the basis for much of this discussion. Drawing from two distinct intellectual traditions, welfare economics and historical sociology, de Swaan asks, "How and why did people develop collective, nationwide and compulsory arrangements to cope with deficiencies and adversities that appeared to affect them separately and to call for individual remedies?" The result is a compelling work.

[2]The interested reader will find a terrific discussion of problem analysis in Chambers (2000), from which I have drawn heavily to prepare this section.

Problem definition begins with the premise that social problems are important problems. Their importance may be a function of two things: the status of the people experiencing or observing the problem and the sheer number of individuals affected by the problem. Often social workers begin to define a problem by describing the affected population. We might go further and consider their demographic features and historic trends.

In the case of unemployment, we might begin with a description of who, exactly, we will consider unemployed. Because the Department of Labor regularly monitors the number of people who fit its definition of "unemployed," it is relatively easy to say whether the problem is increasing or decreasing. As you might expect, when the number of people experiencing a problem is increasing, it is easier to identify it as an important social problem. A concern for social justice might lead us to focus on groups, such as youth, older adults, and people of color, who are more vulnerable to unemployment than others.

In the United States, people who are not actively looking for work are not officially considered unemployed. Some dispute the government's definition, arguing that workers who have become too discouraged to search for a job should be counted among the unemployed. Generally, these people seek to make the case that unemployment is important—possibly more important than the government would have us believe.

Causal analysis in social policy differs from research designed to identify causes. In social policy analysis, we are less interested in objective reality than in public perceptions. The question is not "What causes this problem?" but "What do key participants in policy development believe causes the problem?" Of course, good research should never be disregarded. Responsible policy makers should be aware of research into the causes of a social problem. But *social policy analysis must acknowledge pervasive beliefs that lack scientific foundation.* Beliefs about causes influence the design of social policies and programs to address problems. In fact, it is sometimes interesting to go backward in this analysis by looking at the specifics of a policy or program and deciphering what they imply about the perceived causes of the problem.

Identifying ideology and values embedded in popular definitions of social problems is an interesting exercise in itself. In Part I, we saw how values can influence social policies. As professionals, our challenge is to bring these hidden assumptions into the open for public examination and dialog. It is sometimes hard to distinguish what we know from what we believe. Values that serve as the basis for social policies generally reflect judgments about how people should or should not behave. So the official definition of unemployment reflects the core American belief that hard work and persistence will result in success. From this perspective, someone who gives up on finding a job must be deficient and unworthy of consideration. An advocate might challenge this belief by documenting and sharing the experiences of workers who have become discouraged and given up the job hunt.

As Chambers (2000) noted, some people benefit from social problems, and these "winners" can become obstacles when social workers try to ameliorate the problem. Returning to our case example, major employers might appreciate a large pool of potential workers. It strengthens their ability to negotiate wage cuts and reduces the cost of discharging an employee. *Consideration of both winners and losers* enhances problem analysis. Beyond this, our description of losers should expand beyond those directly affected by the problem. Clearly, unemployment affects the unemployed workers and their families. But the risk of unemployment can also affect working conditions for those who are employed. It might also affect the tax base of local communities, limiting resources available for services.

About Parts II and III

It may be helpful to clarify the organizational structure of this book. Part II focuses on social problems that have been addressed through collective action, while Part III turns to vulnerable populations. Some may ask, "Aren't people living in poverty, experiencing mental illness, or suffering from physical illness *vulnerable*?" and "Don't the vulnerable populations discussed in Part III have *problems*?" Apart from that, don't these problems and vulnerabilities intersect? Certainly. But there is also an underlying rationale.

The problems addressed in Part II are risks that most Americans share. With some qualifications, *anyone* could experience poverty, mental illness, physical sickness, disability, or crime. By contrast, the populations discussed in Part III are vulnerable because of personal characteristics that are not shared throughout the population. Their vulnerability is typically the direct result of oppression and discrimination. These constructs are introduced in greater depth in the introduction to Part III, as is the concept of intersectionality.

With some exceptions, the policy approach to broadly distributed risks examined in Part II differs from that used to protect the vulnerable populations discussed in Part III. Social insurance programs are typically designed to distribute shared risks among members of society, while corrective policies such as civil rights laws or affirmative action are usually designed to eliminate the oppression of vulnerable populations.

Part II Content

Part II begins by exploring the framework that defines our nation's collective response to many social problems: the **Social Security Act**. This is the focus of Chapter 4. Then, we will trace the development of policies and programs to address four social problems: poverty (Chapter 5), physical illness (Chapter 6), mental illness (Chapter 7), disability (Chapter 8), and crime (Chapter 9). In each case, society's collective response can be traced to the conditions that de Swaan identified: external effects, failure of individual remedies, and uncertainty of the moment and magnitude of adversity. And in each case, our understanding is informed by the four analytic components that Chambers described: problem definition, causal analysis, identification of ideology and values, and consideration of winners and losers. Each chapter will focus on a specific type of problem, beginning from a human perspective with a case study and then examining definitional issues, the history of policies and services, and emerging policy issues. Each chapter includes the background material necessary for students to apply the policy frameworks presented in Part I to emerging issues in the field.

The Social Security Act

We are moving forward to greater freedom, to greater security for the average man than he has ever known before in the history of America.

FRANKLIN DELANO ROOSEVELT, FIRESIDE CHAT, SEPTEMBER 30, 1935

Learning Objectives

This chapter will help prepare students to:

LO 4-1 Discuss the historical foundations of social insurance in Western Europe and the United States

LO 4-2 Become familiar with the history and current structure of key social insurance programs authorized under the Social Security Act

LO 4-3 Understand contemporary debates and proposals to address the **solvency** of Old Age and Survivors Insurance

LO 4-4 Become familiar with the history and basic structure of means-tested programs authorized under the Social Security Act

LO 4-5 Become familiar with health and social service programs authorized under the Social Security Act

LO 4-6 Understand the philosophical foundations of Social Security in the United States

Most Americans think of Social Security as a retirement program for older adults. In fact, as this chapter will reveal, three types of programs are authorized under the Social Security Act: social insurance, public assistance, and health and social services that serve Americans of all ages and income levels.

A HUMAN PERSPECTIVE   Glenn and Grace Collins

Glenn and Grace Collins married in 1939, two years before the United States entered World War II. The country was in a terrible depression, but Glenn made good money as a welder for Standard Oil of California. Their future looked promising, but they decided to postpone having children until they could afford to buy their own home. They rented a little apartment in Long Beach and settled in. Grace took to homemaking easily, and Glenn was a calm influence.

Then, the Japanese attacked Pearl Harbor and everything changed. Glenn went straight to the recruiting station to volunteer and learned he had a heart murmur. "I'd never been sick a day in my life!" he recalled later. But it disqualified him for military service, a humiliation that would rankle for decades. Still, the country needed skilled workers for the war effort, and Glenn left his stable job at Standard Oil to take a new job building Liberty ships in Los Angeles. Grace didn't like the hustle and bustle of the city, but Glenn appreciated the sense of purpose that hummed through the shipyard. He was glad to be part of the war effort, and Grace was proud of him. He put in long days and sometimes worked weekends, and the years flew by. They celebrated VJ day with other shipyard families who saw it as a new beginning.

But VJ day meant the end of Glenn's job. With the second war to end all wars over, the nation wouldn't be needing Liberty ships anymore. The focus turned to welcoming home the GIs and building the little houses they'd settle in to raise their families. Beginning a family was on Grace's mind as well. She was pushing 30, but it was starting to look like they'd never be able to own a home in Los Angeles since real estate prices were going through the ceiling.

The couple moved to Oregon, living in an aluminum trailer while Glenn built a small home in a small town on the Rogue River. It was a peaceful place but there were no welding jobs available, so Glenn worked stocking shelves in the local market. He didn't make much money, but Grace took up gardening and canning, so they never went hungry. Children didn't come. During summers, she and Glenn took in their nephew Gilbert, a sweet little guy with curly blond hair. The child brought them great joy, and they were as proud as parents when he joined the Merchant Marines.

Glenn's back eventually gave out. It couldn't take lifting and hauling on the cement floor of the market. So he retired early at 62 and began receiving Social Security benefits. It meant less money, but Glenn felt lucky. He remembered how awful it had been when his grandmother lived with his family in her final years. Instead of burdening Gilbert, his wife, and children with live-in relatives, he and Grace could host them during summers at their home on the river. They spent long hot evenings playing Yahtzee with Gilbert's children on the lawn.

My dad's uncle Glenn said he voted for FDR, "and I'd do it again even though he's dead!" He and Aunt Grace credited FDR for their comfortable old age. They lived hand-to-mouth on nothing but Social Security for the last two decades they had together. Grace went first, and when Glenn passed away we were surprised to learn that he'd left their little house to me and my brother. With some regret we sold it and used the money to pay for college.

A SOCIAL WORK PERSPECTIVE

Glenn worked for over 30 years, first as a skilled craftsman and then as a manual laborer, and with each paycheck he contributed to Social Security. He and Grace had to spend every penny they earned just to live modestly. Thanks to Social Security's generous replacement rate for low earnings they enjoyed a secure old age. They didn't worry about inflation because of the COLA (cost-of-living adjustment). They didn't worry about health care because the new Medicare program took care of their expenses. They looked back at what earlier generations had experienced and felt "downright lucky!"

Today's retirees may not enjoy the security that Glenn and Grace did. Policy changes have increased the penalty for early retirement, and proposed changes could decrease the value of the COLA. Older adults spend much more money on health care now. If they were alive today, Glenn might have applied for disability, which he'd have found humiliating. I wonder whether he and Grace would have been able to afford their little place in Oregon.

LO 4-1   Discuss the Historical Foundations of Social Insurance in Western Europe and the United States

EP 3a
EP 5a
EP 5c

The retirement program known as Old-Age Insurance (OAI) was part of the original Social Security Act, along with unemployment insurance, public assistance programs for the aged, the blind, and dependent children, and health services for mothers and children. Subsequent amendments added survivors' insurance, disability insurance, medical insurance for the aged, and two means-tested programs: Medicaid and Supplemental Security Income (SSI). Other less well-known programs administered under the Social Security Act include the Maternal and Child Health Services Block Grant, the Social Services Block Grant, and the State Children's Health Insurance Program. Table 4.1 compares the titles of the 1935 act with the current titles.

SOCIAL INSURANCE IN WESTERN EUROPE

Early social insurance schemes in Western Europe addressed the "three fears" of industrial workers: poverty in old age, illness, and unemployment. As several historians have pointed out, the social insurance programs established during the 19th century were adopted by authoritarian, rather than democratic, regimes (Flora, 1983; Flora & Heidenheimer, 1981; Rimlinger, 1971).[1] An important motivation was undoubtedly the need to secure loyalty from the growing number of industrial wage earners.

The regime of Otto von Bismarck in Germany is credited with establishing Europe's first social insurance program through a series of acts passed in the 1880s. Popular myth holds that Bismarck's motivation for establishing this program was to force his political foes into retirement. A more likely explanation is that the social insurance program (*Sozialversicherung*) was established as part of an effort to strengthen the German state by securing the allegiance of the industrial working class. *Sozialversicherung* was successful in this regard. It offered workers a stake in the political order and gained enough popular support to survive two world wars, National Socialism, and foreign occupation and still remain a central feature of the German welfare state (de Swaan, 1988).

Oddly enough, leaders of the German labor movement opposed the establishment of *Sozialversicherung*. Drawing on Marxist doctrine, labor leaders believed that workers should have global allegiance to other members of the proletariat rather than to a nation-state. Leaders of workers' parties may also have seen the program as another tactic in the government's ongoing repression of their organizing efforts. Despite their initial opposition, labor leaders were effectively co-opted by the program. As de Swaan (1988) notes, union leaders and Socialist Party officials were quickly "integrated into the state's fabric as executives of the national insurance system" (p. 188).

In England, the elaborate system for relief created by the Elizabethan Poor Law (see Chapter 5) was a barrier to the development of social insurance. Leaders of charity organization societies that provided aid to the indigent were adamant in their belief that poverty was the result of personal failings and that efforts to relieve it should focus on moral reform of individuals. But as industrialization advanced, local authorities were overwhelmed by the needs of older workers. With the 1906 election of a Liberal government, Lloyd George and Winston Churchill formed an activist regime that, with the support of organized labor, passed the Pension Act of 1908, establishing social insurance for retirement income.

---

[1]Germany, Austria, Finland, Sweden, and Italy had established compulsory social insurance programs for workers by the end of the 19th century (de Swaan, 1988).

The French social insurance system was established in 1930. Small property owners had successfully opposed social insurance for several decades. These members of the "petite bourgeoisie" feared that government control of the large sums of capital accumulated in national insurance funds would increase government control of the capital market, disrupting their businesses. They also argued that social security taxes would undermine workers' ability to accumulate personal savings. The establishment of the French program has been attributed to the erosion of the bourgeois power base and the support of moderate labor organizations (de Swaan, 1988).

France's position on social insurance was unusual, since most European nations had mandatory old-age insurance programs in place prior to World War I (1914–1918). Throughout the continent, these new programs served a state-building function, converting wages into accumulated capital through a mandatory system operated by a public administrative apparatus. The programs enhanced workers' loyalty to the state by giving laborers a stake in the government.

SOCIAL SECURITY IN THE UNITED STATES

Like the French, Americans established social insurance for workers later than most European nations. Despite growing recognition of old-age dependency as a social problem, the widespread belief that poverty was caused by personal inadequacies effectively precluded comprehensive federal legislation. Workers were expected to set aside personal savings for their retirement.

Many workers bought private insurance against accidents and illness. In 1910, roughly half of the workforce had such insurance (Achenbaum, 1986). These workers typically filed disability claims if old age forced them to retire. Those who failed to provide for their old age were left to the mercies of their families or to the limited public and charitable assistance that was available.

After the 1920s, several large companies (public utilities, railroads, and manufacturing firms) established private pension plans for their employees. Retirement insurance was made available to federal employees in 1920 through the establishment of the Federal Employees Retirement Program. By 1931, 18 states had established compulsory old-age insurance programs for workers (Piven & Cloward, 1971). By 1933, 21 states and the territories of Alaska and Hawaii were operating relief programs for dependent elderly people (Achenbaum, 1986).

In this context, proposals to establish a national social insurance program for old-age dependency were unsuccessful. They surfaced periodically during the Progressive Era, promoted by advocates such as Abraham Epstein and I. M. Rubinow. Epstein founded the American Association for Old-Age Security in 1927 to advance his social insurance scheme. But for the most part, these proposals did not have the support of workers or federal politicians, and there was widespread belief that a mandatory social insurance program would be declared unconstitutional by the Supreme Court (Kingson & Berkowitz, 1993).

The Great Depression was not the first major economic upheaval in the United States, but its duration and intensity were overwhelming. Achenbaum (1986, p. 16) described the economic impact:

> Between October 1929 and June 1932, the common-stock price index dropped from 260 to 90. The nation's real GNP, which had risen 22 percent between 1923 and 1929, fell 30.4 percent over the next four years. Nearly 5,000 banks, with deposits exceeding $3.2 billion, became insolvent; 90,000 businesses failed. Aggregate wages and salaries in 1933 totaled only 57.5 percent of their 1929 value. The gross income realized by farmers was cut nearly in

BOX 4.1   Frances Perkins: An Architect of Social Security

Born in 1882, Perkins was the first woman appointed to a cabinet position in the United States. She served for 12 years as Roosevelt's Secretary of Labor and was one of the key architects of Social Security. Perkins was an unforgettable figure in the Roosevelt administration. Arthur Schlesinger described her by saying, "She had a pungency of character, a dry wit, an inner gaiety, an instinct for practicality, a profound vein of religious feeling, and a compulsion to instruct." She remained in federal service until the death of her husband in 1952 and continued to lecture until her death in 1965. (For more information, see http://www.ssa.gov/ history/fperkins. html.)

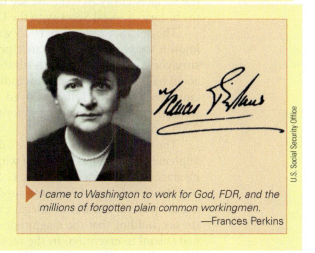

U.S. Social Security Office

I came to Washington to work for God, FDR, and the millions of forgotten plain common workingmen.
—Frances Perkins

half; the farm-product index took a dive from 105 to 51 between 1928 and 1932. More than a thousand local governments defaulted on their bonds.... Insecurity pervaded the land.

The Depression overwhelmed local and state relief programs, and widespread insecurity undermined the popular belief that poverty was the result of personal irresponsibility. No longer could middle-class Americans feel confident that hard work would insulate them from poverty. Job loss and destitution, once seen as individual problems, now seemed to call for collective action. The external impacts of insecurity were evident in the domino effects of bank and business closures. Individual remedies, from personal initiative to private insurance, had little effect. Finally, no one really knew who would be singled out for unemployment.

A wide range of reform proposals came to the fore. Most involved the use of taxes to fund guaranteed incomes in old age. Francis E. Townsend, a retired doctor from California, organized "Townsend Clubs" to support his proposal that everyone over 60 who was unemployed[2] be given $200 a month on the condition that they spend the amount within 30 days. The program was to be funded through a tax on business transactions. Others, including Upton Sinclair and Senator Huey P. Long, advanced similar ideas.

President Hoover argued that the market should be left alone to correct itself. His 1932 defeat brought Franklin Delano Roosevelt into office with a clear mandate to "do something." Roosevelt and his colleagues supported the establishment of a government insurance program to protect the unemployed and the aged. Roosevelt established the cabinet-level Committee on Economic Security (CES), under the direction of Edwin E. Witte, to draft proposals for New Deal programs in collaboration with Frances Perkins, a social worker who was appointed Secretary of Labor. In January 1935, Roosevelt presented Congress with "the most comprehensive social welfare bill that any president had

[2]The requirement that Social Security recipients be unemployed was an integral part of the act. Some have argued that this "retirement test" evolved in an effort to reduce unemployment. It effectively moved the elderly out of the labor force to make jobs available to younger workers.

ever asked Congress to consider" (Kingson & Berkowitz, 1993, p. 35). It combined programs for the unemployed, children, and the elderly within a single piece of legislation, the Social Security Act. (Please see http://www.ssa.gov/history for interesting material on the history of Social Security in the United States.)

The act that passed in 1935 was only a skeleton of the Social Security Act as we know it today. Old-age insurance provided benefits only to retired workers, not to their survivors or to workers with disabilities. Further, the original program only covered about half of the labor force, excluding many farm and domestic workers, state and local employees, and the self-employed. This led the NAACP to protest that the act was "a sieve with holes just big enough for the majority of Negroes to fall through" (Katznelson, 2005, pp. 43–48).

The Social Security Act was subjected to two constitutional challenges before the Supreme Court in 1937, both of which focused on its only compulsory element, old-age insurance. In the first case (*Chas. C. Steward Machine Co. v. Davis*), the Charles C. Steward Machine Company of Alabama sued to recover its share of Social Security taxes, claiming the **payroll tax** was an illegal **excise tax**. The Court upheld the constitutionality of the tax, holding that the magnitude of the emergency presented by the Depression justified federal intervention. In the second case (*Helvering et al. v. Davis*), a shareholder with Edison Electric Illuminating Company of Boston argued that deducting Social Security taxes from wages would produce unrest among employees and "would be followed by demands of increases in wages and that corporations and shareholders would suffer irreparable loss" (Supreme Court, 1937). In rejecting this argument, the Court relied on the concept of **general welfare**:

> Congress may spend money in aid of the general welfare.... The purge of nation-wide calamity that began in 1929 has taught us many lessons. Not the least is the solidarity of interests that may once have seemed to be divided. Unemployment spreads from state to state, the hinterland now settled that in pioneer days gave an avenue of escape.... *The hope behind this statute is to save men and women from the rigors of the poorhouse as well as from the haunting fear that such a lot awaits them when journey's end is near.* (Supreme Court, 1937, p. 640, italics added)

Despite these challenges, the program was put in place. Retirement benefits were financed by employer and employee contributions of 1 percent each on a wage base of $3,000, with a maximum contribution of $30 per year. Benefits were paid out at age 65 and amounted to about $22 per month for single workers and $36 per month for couples. To allow a reserve to accumulate, no benefits were paid until 1940. The first benefit paid was $22 per month to Miss Ida Fuller, a retired secretary. Miss Fuller lived to be over 100. She paid less than $100 in Social Security taxes and collected about $21,000 in benefits (Schulz, 1995). As we will see later in this chapter, other women have fared less well under Social Security.

LO 4-2   Become Familiar with the History and Current Structure of Key Social Insurance Programs Authorized Under the Social Security Act

EP 3a
EP 5a

Old-age insurance was not the only program established through the Social Security Act of 1935. The act included 11 titles (see Table 4.1). In the following sections, we will trace the history and current structure of the key programs authorized through the Social Security Act of 1935 and its later amendments.

TABLE 4.1 Contents of the Social Security Act: 1935 and Today

Preamble: An act to provide for the general welfare by establishing a system of Federal old-age benefits, and by enabling the several States to make more adequate provision for aged persons, blind persons, dependent and crippled children, maternal and child welfare, public health, and the administration of their unemployment compensation laws; to establish a Social Security Board; to raise revenue; and for other purposes.

Titles in 1935 Social Security Act	Titles in Current Social Security Act
Title I Grants to States for Old-Age Assistance	Title I (replaced in 1974 with SSI)
Title II Federal Old-Age Benefits	Title II Old-Age, Survivors, and Disability Insurance Benefits (commonly called "Social Security")
Title III Grants to States for Unemployment Compensation Administration	Title III Grants to States for Unemployment Compensation
Title IV Grants to States for Aid to Dependent Children	Title IV replaced with Temporary Assistance to Needy Families in 1996 and Child Welfare Services
Title V Grants to States for Maternal and Child Welfare	Title V Maternal and Child Health Services Block Grant
Title VI Public Health Work	Repealed
Title VII Social Security Board	Title VII Administration of the Social Security Act
Title VIII Taxes with Respect to Employment	Title VIII Employment Taxes (superseded by IRS Code)
Title IX Tax on Employers of Eight or More	Title IX Miscellaneous Provisions Related to Employment Taxes
Title X Grants to States for Aid to the Blind	Title X replaced with Supplemental Security Income (Title XVI)
Title XI General Provisions	Title XI General Provisions
	Title XII Advances to State Unemployment Funds
	Title XIII Special Benefits for Certain World War II Veterans (expired)
	Title XIV Grants to States for Aid to the Permanently and Totally Disabled (replaced with Supplemental Security Income, Title XVI)
	Title XV Unemployment Compensation for Federal Employees (added in 1954; repealed in 1966)
	Title XVI Supplemental Security Income for the Aged, Blind and Disabled (SSI)
	Title XVII Grants for Planning Comprehensive Action to Combat Mental Retardation (inactive)
	Title XVIII Health Insurance for the Aged and Disabled (Medicare)
	Title XIX Grants to States for Medical Assistance Programs (Medicaid)
	Title XX Block Grants to States for Social Services
	Title XXI State Children's Health Insurance Program

OLD-AGE AND SURVIVORS INSURANCE

In 1936, Franklin Roosevelt won a second term, soundly defeating Alf Landon, the Republican challenger. The Roosevelt administration set out to expand protections under the Social Security Act, spearheading the 1939 amendments to add coverage for workers' survivors and dependents. Widows of both active and retired workers received a portion of the benefits to which the workers were entitled, as did other dependents.

The next three and a half decades were marked by expanded coverage. In 1950, domestic laborers, nonprofit workers, and the self-employed were added. In 1954, agricultural workers, state and local employees, and other groups were brought in, expanding the program to cover about 90 percent of the labor force. Disability coverage was added. Provisions for retiring at age 62 were added for women in 1956 and for men in 1961.

The 1970s brought double-digit inflation that eroded the value of benefits and prior earnings. In 1972, the cost-of-living adjustment (COLA) was established to protect the value of Old-Age, Survivors, and Disability Insurance (OASDI) by *indexing* annual increases to the Consumer Price Index (CPI). In 1977, new benefit computations were put in place to adjust each year's income for inflation. This resulted in more generous treatment of earnings from the early years of a worker's career.

The 1980s marked the beginning of a retrenchment period for Social Security. By this time, program expansions had eroded reserves, and the OASDI trust fund seemed to be on the verge of bankruptcy. Anticipating the demands that would be presented by the baby boomer cohort, in 1981 President Reagan appointed a bipartisan commission, the National Commission on Social Security Reform, chaired by Alan Greenspan, to recommend measures to restore the program's solvency. The following measures were implemented in 1983:

1. *Revisions in the COLA.* These included a one-time delay of the COLA and a "stabilizer" on future COLAs. If the trust fund falls below certain measures, the COLA will be indexed, not to the CPI but to the average increase in wages (if it is lower). This provision has not been applied to date.
2. *Taxation of benefits.* Up to half of benefits were made subject to federal income tax.
3. *Increased retirement ages.* Starting in 2003, the age for receipt of full retirement benefits was set to rise gradually. By 2027, the retirement age for full benefits would be 67.
4. *Work incentives.* Early retirement would bring 70 percent rather than 80 percent of the regular benefits, and the delayed retirement credit for workers who postpone retirement up to age 70 was increased to 8 percent per year for those turning 65 after 2007. Provisions also increased the amount beneficiaries could earn through employment before their Social Security benefits were reduced and eliminated the reduction of benefits altogether for workers over 70.

The Commission's work was pivotal in two ways. First, its recommendations improved the program's solvency; and second, the process of reform undertaken by the Commission reduced the influence of partisan politics and enhanced the quality of technical information that was used in the Social Security debate. These reforms also represented fundamental shifts in the program's approach. First, by subjecting Social Security benefits to income tax, the reforms introduced another progressive element into the program. As discussed in Chapter 2, the income tax draws a higher proportion from affluent Americans than it does from the poor. Second, the introduction of work incentives represented a significant departure from earlier policies under which retirement was a condition for receiving benefits. (See http://www.ssa.gov/history/1983amend.html for details of the 1983 amendments.)

Clearly the 1935 policy goal of removing older workers from the labor force has become less compelling. In 2000, in rare unanimous votes in both houses, Congress eliminated the Social Security retirement test altogether. Under PC 106-182, the Senior Citizens' Freedom to Work Act, beneficiaries at full retirement age can continue to work with no reduction in benefits. Beneficiaries under their full retirement age are still subject to reductions in benefits for earnings above the exempt amount. In 2017, this amount was $16,920 per year (for details and updates, please see "How Work Affects Your Benefits" at http://www.ssa.gov/pubs/10069.html).

HOW OASI OPERATES: THE NUTS AND BOLTS

In 1999, the Social Security Administration launched what it called "the largest custom-ized mailing ever undertaken by a federal agency" (Social Security Administration, 1999). Over 125 million workers received annual statements titled "What Social Security Means to You" reporting their earnings records and predicting their estimated benefits. These statements are powerful tools not only for individual retirement planning but also for raising public awareness of how the program operates. You should receive yours about three months before your birthday each year, or you can request it at the agency website www.ssa.gov.[3] Here, we will consider the ideas and mechanics behind the numbers.

OASI is a carefully crafted compromise between two objectives, offering "welfare" to low-income seniors, "investment" to the middle and upper classes, and a measure of security for all. The program integrates the principles of **equity** and **adequacy**. Equity is achieved when benefits drawn are based on contributions paid—in other words, when individuals receive a return that is proportional to their investment in the program. Under the principle of adequacy, benefits should be sufficient to maintain a decent standard of living, regardless of individual contributions.

To achieve equity, benefits are computed on the basis of contributions. Benefits are based on a person's "average indexed monthly earnings" (**AIME**). Earnings between ages 21 and 62 that were subject to the payroll tax (as of 2017, this included earnings up to the wage cap: $127,200) are adjusted for inflation. Then, the five years with lowest earnings are dropped. The resulting total is averaged to produce the AIME. To be eligible to draw Social Security benefits, an individual must have worked in covered employment for at least 40 quarters (i.e., 10 years).

Adequacy is the guarantee of a modest income in old age. The **replacement rate** is the proportion of earnings that you receive in retirement. To provide adequacy, OASI benefit computations replace lower earnings more generously than high earnings. To put it tech-nically, the *Primary Insurance Amount has two bend points.* These are adjusted annually for inflation. So in 2017, the first bend point came at $885. The AIME up to that amount had a replacement rate of 90 percent. Above that amount, earnings up to $5,336 per month (the second bend point) were replaced at the rate of 32 percent; and earnings between $5,336 and the wage cap ($10,600 per month in 2017) were replaced at 15 percent (see http://www.ssa .gov/OACT/COLA/piaformula.html). Of course, income above the wage cap is not replaced at all, so in 2017 the maximum benefit for a worker retiring at full retirement age was about $3,010 per month. Because of these bend points, workers with low earnings enjoy greater replacement than those with high earnings. This does not mean their Social Security checks are larger but that the difference between their working income and their Social Security benefit is smaller than it would be for someone with high earnings. (Consider, for instance, the difference between Discovery Communications CEO David Zaslov's monthly 2016 salary of $13,006,493 and the maximum Social Security benefit he might receive.)

OASDI is financed through a payroll tax authorized under the Federal Insurance Contributions Act (FICA). Originally, this was set at 1 percent of earnings up to $3,000 (a maximum contribution of $30 per year). In 2017, this tax was 15.30 percent of wages up to a cap. As you will recall, in 2017 the wage cap was set at $127,200 per year. Half of the tax is paid by the employer and half by the worker. The largest portion of these combined contributions (12.4 percent of wages) is allocated to OASDI. The remainder (2.9 percent of wages) goes to finance Medicare. The Medicare portion is not subject to a wage cap.

---

[3]The SSA provides a "Retirement Estimator." Based on your earnings history, it will estimate benefits you would receive under current law. The program also estimates benefits based on "what if" scenarios. It is currently available at http://www.socialsecurity.gov/estimator/.

In 2011, employees' 6.2 percent contributions to the payroll tax were reduced by two points under the Middle Class Tax Relief Act of 2010; later, this payroll tax cut was extended to the end of 2012. The funds lost to Social Security trust funds due to this temporary tax reduction were replaced by general fund revenues.

High-income workers pay more tax, and low-income workers receive more generous replacement income. This is the redistributive feature of the Social Security program and the reason it serves to reduce inequality.

The "minimum monthly benefit," another redistributive feature, is now a historic relic. At the program's inception, the minimum benefit was set at $10 per month (Achenbaum, 1986). Through the 1972 amendments, Congress indexed the minimum benefit to inflation. By 1981, it had increased to $170.31 per month for a worker retiring at age 65. Faced with rising Social Security costs, Joseph A. Califano, then Secretary of Health, Education, and Welfare, proposed repealing the minimum benefit. The primary argument for repeal was that the establishment of Supplemental Security Income (SSI) in 1974 eliminated the need for a minimum benefit. In 1981, the Reagan administration repealed the minimum benefit. The next year it was reinstated, but today the Social Security Administration reports that there is no minimum benefit provided under the program.

A quick look at the sources of Social Security revenues and expenditures gives greater understanding of the program's operation. First of all, in 2014 OASDI revenues exceeded expenses by $55.2 billion, increasing reserves to $2.7 trillion. The payroll tax accounted for 84 percent of the revenue. Roughly 12 percent was investment income: interest paid on the reserves at an annual rate of 3.6 percent. (This interest rate will surface again when we look at approaches to the solvency issue.) Another 4 percent of OASDI revenue came from federal income taxes collected on Social Security benefits. Nearly all (99 percent) of OASDI expenditures paid retirement, survivor, and disability benefits, with small fractions allocated to railroad retirement programs and administrative expenses (Social Security Administration, 2015d). This is illustrated in Figure 4.1.

FIGURE 4.1 Social Security Revenues and Expenditures, 2014

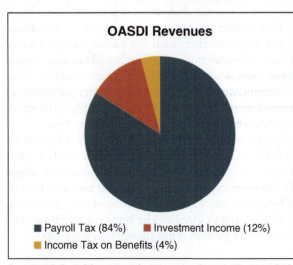

OASDI Revenues

- Payroll Tax (84%)
- Investment Income (12%)
- Income Tax on Benefits (4%)

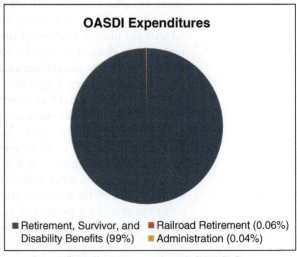

OASDI Expenditures

- Retirement, Survivor, and Disability Benefits (99%)
- Railroad Retirement (0.06%)
- Administration (0.04%)

Source: U.S. Social Security Administration (2015). *The 2015 OASDI Trustees Report.* (http://www.ssa.gov/oact/tr/2015/II_B_cyoper. html#96807).

UNEMPLOYMENT INSURANCE

When the Social Security Act passed in 1935, unemployment was the overriding concern. About 15 million workers were unemployed, and the pressure on relief programs was staggering. A few states, most notably Massachusetts and New York, had tried to pass unemployment insurance legislation prior to the Depression. But these bills had consistently failed in state legislatures (Altmeyer, 1963).

Unemployment insurance (UI) was an integral part of the Social Security Act of 1935. It was one of the two social insurance programs the president and his advisers felt should be enacted immediately (the other was an old-age insurance). After some debate, UI was established as a federal–state partnership rather than a strictly federal program like OAI. The role of the federal government was limited to making grants available to states interested in administration of UI. Funds for these grants were provided through a federal payroll tax paid by employers. A tax credit was made available to employers whose states met federal guidelines for UI. Within two years, UI programs were established in all states. Originally, the program only applied to workers in firms with eight or more employees. Later, coverage was extended to those in firms with at least four employees. With the exception of employers of agricultural employees, who are now required to pay UI taxes if they have 10 or more employees during 20 calendar weeks, employers are subject to UI taxes if they have at least one employee during 20 weeks of the year (U.S. Department of Labor, n.d.b).

Financing for the UI program is provided through state and federal payroll taxes paid by employers. The federal unemployment tax covers the administrative costs of state UI and job service programs, as well as half the cost of extended unemployment benefits. It also funds a pool from which states can borrow if needed to cover benefits. The federal tax is 6 percent of the first $7,000 of covered employee wages. Some of these funds can be applied to offset state unemployment tax (U.S. Department of Labor, n.d.b).

State unemployment insurance taxes are used only to pay benefits. State unemployment tax rates vary depending on each firm's use of unemployment compensation during previous years. This is known as **experience rating**. Firms that have had high rates of unemployment pay higher payroll taxes than those with lower rates. The use of experience rating was designed to reduce unemployment by giving employers an incentive to stabilize their workforce. This reflects a social justice interest in allocating the cost of unemployment benefits more heavily on companies that are most likely to produce the problem (Altmeyer, 1963).

UI was designed to provide temporary replacement of lost wages for workers who had strong attachment to the labor force. As a result, eligibility is based on three factors: the worker's earnings history, the reason for unemployment, and the worker's availability for work. Within these categories, specific requirements vary from state to state. Most states require that a worker be in covered employment for the first four of the last five calendar quarters prior to filing a claim. Earnings must be above a minimum that is set by the state. Second, the job loss must be due to factors beyond the worker's control. Workers who choose to leave their jobs are not eligible for unemployment benefits. Finally, recipients of unemployment benefits must actively seek employment and must accept suitable employment if it is offered. Most states also require that workers be unemployed for at least one week before filing for UI benefits.

Like eligibility requirements, benefit levels vary from state to state. Most states provide half of a worker's salary for up to 26 weeks. Congress may extend this period to 39 weeks during economic recessions. Most states have maximum benefits, and some have argued that inflation erodes the value of unemployment compensation (Altmeyer, 1963; McMurrer & Chasanov, 1995). Another concern has been the disparity of benefits

BOX 4.2   Unemployment and the Great Recession

The Great Recession threatened the solvency of unemployment insurance (UI) trust funds. In December 2007, the United States entered the longest and deepest recession since the 1930s. From a low of 4 percent, unemployment rose to peak at 10.2 percent in October 2008. It would stay in that range for months. Unemployment, it seems, is a "lagging indicator" of changing economic conditions. With the sluggish economic growth of recent years, jobs have been slow to return. Congress

responded with a stimulus bill and other extensions of UI that amounted to nearly 99 weeks of unemployment benefits. Facing depletion of the UI trust fund, Congress passed legislation in 2009 to allow the fund to draw down money from general revenues in what is essentially a low-interest loan. Most states also were given loans to restore their depleted accounts. The experience raised broad questions about the solvency and effectiveness of the unemployment insurance program.

paid from state to state. Since state unemployment taxes are based on benefits paid, firms in states with high benefit rates suffer from a competitive disadvantage. This situation can lead to a "race for the bottom," in which states compete for the lowest unemployment tax rates. One way to succeed in this race is to keep benefits as low as possible.

Since UI's inception, the role of the federal government has expanded. In 1970, the Extended Unemployment Compensation Act was passed to allow the use of federal funds to provide benefits beyond state time limits during periods of high unemployment. Further, the Emergency Unemployment Compensation program was established in 1991 to supplement state coverage during times of high unemployment (McMurrer & Chasanov, 1995). The federal government finances all of the costs of this program through general revenues.

Nearly all U.S. workers are covered by unemployment insurance. In 2000, the Department of Labor reported that 97 percent of employees were covered (OMB, n.d.). Only workers on small farms and the self-employed are not.

Despite near-universal coverage, only a fraction of unemployed workers actually receive UI benefits. During the Great Recession only about a third (36 percent) of the unemployed received UI benefits (Stone, Greenstein, & Coven, 2007). This figure rose somewhat in 2010, mainly due to multiple extensions of federal benefits and the unprecedented length of unemployment for many American workers. But with the end of federal extensions and changes in state policies, the proportion of unemployed who actually receive benefits has reached record lows (below 24 percent) since 2011 (Gould-Werth & Shaefer, 2012; McHugh & Kimball, 2015).

Low rates may also be due to unemployed workers themselves, among whom the proportion submitting applications varies from 30 to 50 percent. The most common reason for not applying seems to be that workers do not know they are eligible for benefits. Notably, less educated workers and those from racial and ethnic minority groups are both less likely to apply and less likely to receive UI benefits (Gould-Werth & Shaefer, 2012).

DISABILITY INSURANCE

The Social Security Act of 1935 did not provide for disability insurance (DI). Although some in the Roosevelt administration were concerned about workers who lost earnings due to disability, the dominant view was that a DI program might encourage malingering. As one member of the Social Security advisory council put it, "You will have workers like those in the dust bowl area, people who have migrated to California and elsewhere … who will imagine they are disabled" (Berkowitz, 2000).

It was not until 1956 that the Social Security Act was amended to provide monthly benefits to "permanently and totally disabled" workers aged 50 to 64 and to adult disabled children of deceased or retired workers. With this addition, OASI came to be known as OASDI, with DI funded through a portion of the payroll tax.

Congress passed DI by "the barest of margins" (Berkowitz, 2000) despite opposition from the American Medical Association (AMA), private insurance companies, and employers' organizations. Even the Eisenhower administration opposed disability coverage (Altmeyer, 1963). Opposition stemmed from fear that it would reduce the incentive to work. Reflecting this concern, coverage was limited to workers who were "permanently and totally disabled," and disability determination requirements were strict.

In 1958, DI benefits were extended to disabled workers of all ages and to dependents of disabled workers; however, to be eligible a worker had to have completed at least 10 years in covered employment. The DI share of the payroll tax was increased to accommodate these program expansions.

In 1994, the trustees declared that DI faced "imminent insolvency." Congress changed the allocation of payroll taxes to increase the proportion that went to the DI fund from 1.2 to 1.8 percent of total payroll (Social Security Administration, 2005). Congress also passed the Ticket to Work and Work Incentives Improvement Act of 1999, which required the Social Security Administration to offer recipients of DI (and SSI) the opportunity to participate in rehabilitative services to enhance their ability to be self-supporting. While beneficiaries who went to work would lose their cash payments, they would retain Medicare or Medicaid coverage and be assured that their cash assistance could be reinstated if their effort to work did not succeed.

Recent years have also seen changes in the program's treatment of people who suffer from addiction. Prior to 1996, severe drug addiction or alcoholism was considered an appropriate basis for receiving disability benefits under DI (or SSI). As the number of individuals whose disability stemmed from drug addiction or alcoholism increased, there was rising concern that they were abusing federal disability programs. As we will see in Chapter 8, the result was a series of initiatives that ultimately resulted in denial of benefits to anyone who is disabled primarily as the result of addiction.

Despite these efforts, the number of DI beneficiaries continued to grow, and in 2015 the trustees issued a warning: "Social Security's Disability Insurance (DI) Trust Fund now faces an urgent threat of reserve depletion, requiring prompt corrective action by lawmakers if sudden reductions or interruptions in benefit payments are to be avoided." Reserves in the DI Trust Fund were projected for depletion in the latter part of 2016, which would have triggered an automatic 19 percent reduction in benefits. (So the program's revenue would equal its expenditures.)

Of course, DI benefits were barely above the poverty level, so any reduction would impose serious hardship. In 2015, for example, the average disabled worker received $1,166 per month (119 percent of the federal poverty threshold); and the average benefit paid to a disabled worker with a spouse and child was $1,839 per month (109 percent of the poverty threshold) (Social Security Administration, 2015b).

So, at the end of 2015, Congress voted to direct funds from OASI revenues to cover the deficit in DI—a strategy that was also applied in 1994. DI is relatively small compared to OASI. Where OASI served nearly 50 million Americans in 2015, just over 11 million people received DI benefits (Social Security Administration, 2015a). Combining the two funds has a relatively minor impact on that program's solvency, though it fails to address the underlying problems with DI. We will reexamine the solvency issue later in this chapter and revisit issues related to disability in Chapter 8.

MEDICAL INSURANCE

With the exception of the United States, all developed countries provide some form of national health insurance. In our country (as of this writing), only the elderly and the poor have access to public health insurance. The elderly are served by Medicare (Title XVIII of the Social Security Act) and the poor by Medicaid (Title XIX).

The Development of National Health Insurance in Europe

Medical insurance originated with "sickness insurance" provided to craftsmen in 16th- and 17th-century Europe. The craft guilds collected dues from members to establish funds to help sick and disabled colleagues. With industrialization, sickness insurance extended to factory workers. Industrial laborers in Germany joined *Krankenkassen,* or sickness insurance societies, often operated under the auspices of their unions. In 1854, Prussian legislators made sickness insurance compulsory for low-wage workers.[4]

Otto von Bismarck became chancellor of the German Empire in 1871. He saw sickness insurance, like pension insurance, as a vehicle for cementing workers' loyalty to the German state. From 1881 to 1883, Bismarck spearheaded the passage of a law that required low-wage workers in certain occupations to join sickness insurance funds. Two-thirds of the cost of premiums were paid by the worker, with one-third contributed by the employer. As Roemer (1993) observed, "It is noteworthy that physicians raised no objections to this legislation; it ensured payment for their services to low-income patients; more affluent middle-class patients remained in the private market" (p. 92). Passage of this law set the stage for the expansion of national health insurance throughout Germany and the rest of Europe.

In Britain, the National Health Insurance Act passed in 1911 under Prime Minister Lloyd George. Based on the German model, this legislation established compulsory health insurance coverage for low-wage workers. "Friendly societies" were the British equivalent of Germany's sickness insurance funds. They covered prescription drugs and general practitioner services, since hospital and specialist care were offered through public and charitable hospitals. After World War II, the British Labour Party passed the National Health Service (NHS) Act of 1946, establishing the program of national health insurance that currently operates in Great Britain. Rather than simply covering drugs and general practitioner care, the NHS offered broad medical coverage to all British residents. Financed through general revenues, it served as a model for post–World War II health insurance reform in other European nations.

France was the last major European nation to establish national medical insurance for industrial workers. As in most nations, private sickness insurance societies had proliferated. French physicians were politically powerful, and they insisted that insurance operate on an "indemnity" basis, under which the patient pays the doctor's fee and then seeks reimbursement from the insurance provider. For patients who were undergoing economic hardships, physicians agreed to use a negotiated fee schedule (Roemer, 1993).

Medical Insurance in the United States

Discussion of national health insurance in the United States began as early as 1912 with a proposal from Theodore Roosevelt's Bull Moose Party. In 1935, the designers of the Social Security Act were concerned about medical costs, but most believed that unemployment and old age were more immediate risks to workers than inability to pay for medical care. There was also the threat that physicians would oppose national health insurance.

---

[4]Prussia was one of the 30 German states at the time.

In the 1940s, President Truman made national health insurance a legislative priority. But he was less effective than Roosevelt at working with Congress, and the American Medical Association (AMA) derailed his proposal. In addition, the post–World War II expansion in employee benefits meant that a growing number of workers were covered by private health insurance through their unions or employers. Consequently, Medicare was not enacted until 1964.

Pressure for Medicare came in part from the recognition by Social Security officials and others that the elderly had been left behind during the expansion of private health insurance. Retired workers were usually unable to obtain group insurance through a former employer, and insurance companies were reluctant to insure them as individuals, viewing the aged as bad risks. As President Johnson put it, "Many of our older citizens are still defenseless against the heavy medical costs of severe illness."

Robert Ball (commissioner of Social Security under Presidents Kennedy, Johnson, and Nixon) explained that advocates for Medicare saw it as "a first step toward universal national health insurance" (Ball, 1996). The American Medical Association (AMA) had favored national health insurance in 1916, but by the time Medicare came up for debate, the AMA vigorously opposed any government-sponsored health insurance. Most business groups, especially those in the insurance industry, joined the opposition to Medicare (Ball, 1996). Medicare's strongest advocates were leaders of the labor movement, who supported enactment in 1957 and made a final push during the expansion of Lyndon Johnson's Great Society programs.

As initially conceived, Medicare was limited to hospital insurance. This was intended to defuse AMA opposition by limiting federal involvement in the patient–physician relationship. But the original legislation was amended in Congress to include doctors' services. The resulting program offered both hospital insurance (Part A) and optional coverage for physician services (Part B). Those who do not enroll for Medicare Parts A and B when they become eligible are subject to "late enrollment penalties." Medicare operates in the same way as private indemnity insurance, paying "reasonable fees" for all covered services.

Today, Part A coverage is provided at no charge to recipients and covers most of the cost (subject to deductibles and copayments) of many services provided in hospitals and brief stays in nursing homes, as well as home health services and some hospice care.

Part B covers a wide range of services related to physician care, including doctors themselves, therapists, ambulance transportation, and diagnostic services as well as prostheses, medical equipment, and certain other medical services and supplies. Part B is purchased through a monthly premium which, since 2003, has been subject to a means test. So Part B premiums are greater for high-income beneficiaries. As with Part A, the program has deductibles and copayments, so beneficiaries are responsible for a significant (and growing) proportion of the costs of care.

Two additional parts have been added to Medicare since its inception. Part C, now known as Medicare Advantage, was authorized by the Balanced Budget Act of 1997. It allows beneficiaries to enroll in managed care plans. Part D, established under the Medicare Modernization Act of 2003, provides coverage for prescription medications. Premiums and benefits under Parts C and D vary depending on the plan chosen by the beneficiary. As with Parts A and B, late enrollment penalties apply to Medicare Part D.

The Patient Protection and Affordable Care Act (also known as Obamacare) made some important changes in Medicare. Beneficiaries save money on prescription drugs, but perhaps more importantly, the law slowed the annual growth in per-enrollee expenditures. As the Kaiser Family Foundation reported, "Annual growth in total Medicare spending averaged 4.1 percent between 2010 and 2014, compared to 9.0 percent between 2000 and 2010… despite growth in the number of beneficiaries and increases in health costs over these years" (Kaiser Family Foundation, 2015). In the long term, this substantially improves Medicare's solvency, leading the White House to crow in 2014: "In 2009, the Trustees projected the Hospital Insurance Trust Fund would not be able to pay its bills in 2017. Today's new date is 2030, *13 years later than that projection.*" (White House, 2014, italics added). The 2016 Trustees' report estimated depletion of the Hospital Insurance Trust Fund in 2028 (Social Security Administration, 2016b). Medicare is discussed in greater detail in Chapter 6.

LO 4-3   Understand Contemporary Debates and Proposals to Address the Solvency of Old Age and Survivors Insurance

EP 3a
EP 5c

The Old Age and Survivors Insurance program (OASI) covers 94 percent of workers in the United States and is an income source for nine out of ten older Americans, many of whom would live in poverty without it. In 2015, benefits to retired workers and their dependents and survivors totaled $870 billion (Social Security Administration, 2015). Its size and importance dictate that any major changes be undertaken with great care. Still, changes (not all of them major) are needed, both to sustain the program and to enable it to respond to socio-demographic changes. In this section, we will consider proposals that address fiscal sustainability of the program, ranging from privatization to revising the COLA computation. We will also address proposals designed to bring the program up to date with the way Americans live today, including caregiver credits and earnings sharing.

THE SOLVENCY ISSUE

The word **solvency** refers to one's ability to pay legitimate debts. The question of Social Security solvency focuses on operations of the trust funds. Further, a central theme in the debate over Social Security is the legitimacy of the debt that is owed, particularly to older adults who are not financially needy.

Social Security is a **pay as you go** program. That is, most of the revenue goes to pay for the benefits of current recipients. The remainder goes into four separate reserve funds: Old Age and Survivors Insurance (OASI), Disability Insurance (DI), Hospital Insurance for Medicare Part A (HI), and Supplementary Medical Insurance for Medicare Part B (SMI). Until the early 1980s, revenue matched benefits paid, at approximately $200 billion per year. Since the passage of the 1983 amendments, the OASI trust fund has been accumulating reserves to pay for the retirement of the baby boom generation. In 2015, for example, these reserves increased by $51 billion, for a total reserve in excess of $ 2.78 trillion (Social Security Administration, 2016b). By law, these funds can only be invested in U.S. Treasury notes where they earn a fairly low rate of return.[5]

With such massive reserves, it is hard to imagine that Social Security might become insolvent. Indeed, it may not. Each year, the trustees of the Social Security and Medicare trust funds issue a report that provides their "best guess" of program solvency under various scenarios. Their financial projections include what they call "key dates." These are adjusted to reflect the economic realities of the time and should never be taken (as the press tends to do) as reliable predictions. Still, they can tell us a bit about the relative status of the programs. Key dates from the 2016 report are provided in Table 4.2. Let's begin

---

[5]The return after inflation has been estimated at 2.7 to 2.8 percent (Century Foundation, 2005; Reischauer, 1999).

TABLE 4.2 Key Dates from 2016 Trustees' "Intermediate" Estimates

	OASI	DI	HI
Year of peak trust fund ratio	2011	2003	2003
First year outgo exceeds income excluding interest	2010	2019	2015
First year outgo exceeds income including interest	2022	2019	2021
Year trust funds are exhausted	2035	2023	2028

Source: https://www.ssa.gov/OACT/TRSUM/index.html.

with the OASI trust fund here. We will save further discussion of the Medicare funds (HI and SMI) for Chapter 6 and the disability (DI) fund for Chapter 8.

In 1996, the trustees estimated that OASI reserves would be exhausted in 2031 (see http://www.ssa.gov/history/reports/trust/1996/overview.htm). In 2007 (just before the Great Recession), they projected exhaustion of OASI reserves in 2042; in 2011, the date was 2035, where it remained in 2016. Keep in mind that it is difficult to predict economic conditions decades in advance—imagine predicting today's economy on the basis of 1979 conditions. Nonetheless, the trustees' best guess is the best we have to go on, and policy makers rely heavily on these estimates.

Depletion of the trust fund reserves does not mean OASI would be unable to pay beneficiaries. The trustees project that under current tax rates, the fund will be able to pay about three-fourths of its costs from revenues, even with no reserves. Absent changes in the financing of OASI, the remainder could be funded through annual transfers from the general fund. As we have seen, a transfer of this kind was made in 2011 for the stimulus package. Such transfers are relatively common in other countries but tend to be controversial in the United States. Some argue that they undermine the social insurance rationale for the program, and others question the stability of the transfers in light of other pressures on the budget (Reischauer, 1999).

Extensive (and sometimes misleading) discussions of Social Security solvency issues threaten to undermine public confidence in the program. Challenges to the system reached the level of absurdity in 1995, when a group calling itself Third Millennium reported that more people aged 18 to 35 believed in UFOs than believed they would ever collect Social Security benefits.[6] More credible challenges have come from economic conservatives who advocate an "ownership society" or "personal responsibility," both code for replacing social insurance with personal risk (please see Marmor & Mashaw, 2006, for an excellent discussion of this topic).

"REFORMING" SOCIAL SECURITY

During the Clinton and Bush administrations, privatization proposals dominated the solvency debate. Other alternatives include raising payroll taxes, eliminating the wage cap, investing the trust fund for greater return, increasing the retirement age, and reducing benefits.

---

[6]Third Millennium was a group with about 1,700 members that claimed to represent the interests of younger workers, also known as "Generation X." In the early 1990s, this group organized a poll, conducted by Frank Luntz, reporting that more young Americans believe in flying saucers than in the future of Social Security. Although the results of the poll have been widely disseminated, its methodology has been questioned (see McLeod, 1995).

Privatization

Solvency issues affecting social insurance programs around the world have presented an opportunity to those who seek a radical "reform" of the programs, known as privatization (Orenstein, 2008; Svihula & Estes, 2008). Under privatized systems, individual retirement accounts are established for investment of all, or part, of workers' retirement savings. These accounts are then invested in private equities. Advocates of market-based reforms have been successful at promoting the partial privatization of social insurance in nations as diverse as Chile, Great Britain, and Sweden.

Chile was first in the line of nations that experimented with privatization. In 1981, the Pinochet regime, under the direction of José Piñera, then labor minister, oversaw the privatization of the oldest social insurance program in the Americas. Under the new system of individual retirement funds (Administradores de Fondos de Pensiones, or AFP), workers were required to contribute 10 percent of their salary to these accounts. The program was beset with difficulties. The return on individual accounts was volatile, producing losses in some years; administrative expenses were high, ranging from 15 to 20 percent of annual contributions; many workers underreported their wages to avoid paying into their accounts; and finally, by all estimates, the program would not provide sufficient retirement income to keep low-wage workers out of poverty (Century Foundation, 2005).

The British experience with privatization has been described as "a bloody mess" (Cohen, 2005). In 1984, the Thatcher government swept into its second term with a scheme to privatize the nation's old-age pension program known as the State Earnings-Related Pension Scheme, or SERPS. Under the British **carve out system**, workers were encouraged to divert their retirement funds away from SERPS and invest in private plans called Approved Personal Pension (APP). The government funded a huge marketing scheme to encourage workers to "contract out" of the public system and into the private plans. Indeed, between marketing costs and incentives to contract out, the government spent considerably more than it saved through reduced benefit payments (Turner, 2005). The government then reversed course, encouraging workers to "contract in" and return to SERPS. Over the next few years, the government changed the rules governing APPs repeatedly. Plagued by high administrative costs and volatile returns, the APPs left many workers worse off than they would have been under SERPS.

BOX 4.3 Raiding the Trust Funds?

Highly charged political rhetoric about Social Security erodes public confidence in the system. To stop Congress from "raiding the trust funds," candidates promise to "put Social Security funds in a lock box." These arguments have little bearing on the realities of Social Security financing and a lot to do with the politics of fear.

Money paid into the Social Security trust funds, like money put in a bank, is not kept there. Just as the bank invests money, the money in the trust funds is invested as well. The safest investment in this country is U.S. Treasury notes. They do not provide high returns, but payment is guaranteed by the federal government. As we have seen, the national debt consists of outstanding Treasury notes. So when the Social Security trust funds invest in Treasury notes, they are "for accounting purposes" reducing the deficit. This accounting approach has been in place since the 1970s and is known as the "unified budget." In other words, the budget takes the trust fund resources into account. Fundamental to the success of this system (and of the nation) is the federal government's commitment to honor its contractual obligations by paying off Treasury notes and paying Social Security benefits. The unified budget does not, in itself, jeopardize Social Security, but large deficits can reduce the government's financial stability. Thus, the problem is not the unified budget itself but use of Social Security funds to mask irresponsible federal spending.

The Swedish approach to privatization has been characterized as "pro choice" (Cronqvist & Thaler, 2004). Workers must contribute 18.5 percent of their income to retirement, with 16 percent going into a publicly managed plan. The remaining 2.5 percent is used as an *add-on* to fund individual retirement accounts. Then workers are allowed to choose from over 700 pension funds or to allow their funds to be invested in the "default fund." The vast majority of new participants choose the default fund, which is managed by the government and invested largely in equities. A single agency collects all contributions to individual accounts, and the government distributes all annuities. Retirees are guaranteed a minimum rate of return of 2.7 percent on their annuities.

Privatization is the transfer of risk from the collective to the individual. It has had mixed results, depending on how it is implemented. The introduction of individual accounts inevitably raises administrative costs, which must be weighed against the possibility of greater returns. The transition from traditional systems to privatized systems imposes costs as well, because revenue that would otherwise fund public retirement benefits is diverted to private accounts. This cost can be minimized in a Swedish-style add-on system but is particularly high when funds are carved out of the public system as in Britain. Of course, the volatility of the stock market is a significant factor, so retirement income from individual accounts may depend on when an individual begins to draw. This introduces an element of insecurity as workers are less able to predict the level of their retirement benefits. Further insecurity is introduced as governments change the rules to adjust to changing conditions.

In the wake of the Great Recession, privatization appeals to only the most ardent free-market proponents. It has not been seriously proposed in the United States since the Bush administration. During his candidacy, President Trump did not mention privatization, but Paul Ryan and members of the Trump transition team have supported this approach in the past.

Other Approaches to the Solvency Issue

In May 2010, the Senate Committee on Aging issued a report titled "Social Security Modernization: Options to Address Solvency and Benefit Adequacy."[7] Setting the stage for subsequent policy debates, the report outlined several strategies to address the OASI solvency problem. These include raising payroll taxes, eliminating the wage cap, investing the trust fund for greater return, increasing the retirement age, and reducing benefits.

In 2009, the trustees reported that Social Security could be brought into "actuarial balance" for the next 75 years through an immediate increase in the OASI portion of the payroll tax from 12.4 to 14.4 percent. As noted in the Senate report, an increase of this kind might be phased in over a 20-year period to ease the impacts on workers (and politicians!). Drawbacks to this simple solution are the regressive nature of the tax and the American antipathy for tax increases. Still, even at 14.4 percent, the U.S. tax rate would be lower than the average among the world's developed nations, as indicated in Figure 4.2.

Less regressive than an increased payroll tax would be elimination of the wage cap. The Senate report proposed that the additional contributions then not be included in benefit calculations. This would sacrifice the program's equity, which, as you recall, demands that larger contributions result in higher benefits. On the other hand, the costs would fall on the affluent, who can bear them more easily. Both of these changes in financing could produce the greatest financial impact on the program, but they do present serious political risks.

---

[7]Available at http://aging.senate.gov/ss/ssreport2010.pdf.

FIGURE 4.2 Taxation of Labor*

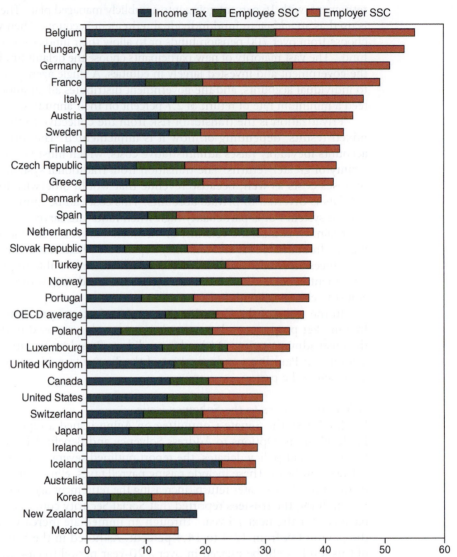

*Note: SSC stands for Social Security Contribution.
Source: OECD Taxing Wages - Main Trends, http://www.oecd.org/ctp/tax-policy/taxingwages-tax-burden-trends-latest-year.htm.

Diversifying investment of trust fund assets to increase the rate of return may prove less controversial. In 1935, the framers of Social Security were understandably leery of stock market investment. Thus, the act required that assets be invested in the safest possible instrument: U.S. Treasury notes. The Senate report included a proposal to gradually invest a fraction (15–40 percent) of assets in equities, a measure that has been taken in other countries to increase revenue. Of course, this would expose the funds to risk during economic downturns.

Building on the effectiveness of the 1983 amendments, the Senate committee also considered increasing the age for receipt of full benefits to either 68 or 70 years. Neither scenario would eliminate the shortfall. Increasing the retirement age to 70 was expected to reduce it by just under a third. Increases in retirement age have been relatively uncontroversial in the United States and other countries, but they pose serious disadvantages to workers who are forced to retire early for health reasons. During his campaign, President Trump did not weigh in on raising the retirement age.

Among the various benefit cuts considered, the most effective at forestalling the revenue shortfall is lowering the cost-of-living adjustment (COLA). Recall that the 1983 amendments included a one-time delay in the COLA. Reduction by 1 percent each year is projected to reduce the shortfall by 78 percent; however, this would cause steady erosion in the purchasing power of retirees, with the greatest impact on the very old.

The Obama administration evidently had these considerations in mind when crafting the president's 2014 budget proposal. In it, the president proposed changing the way the COLA was calculated for entitlement programs, including Social Security. Instead of using the CPI, the "chained CPI" would be used as a measure of inflation. This takes into account alternative goods that people can purchase to avoid paying for those with rapidly rising costs. The chained CPI would reduce COLA increases over the years, effectively reducing benefits by slowing their increase. The initial impact would be small, but over the years it would add up. To address this problem, the president offered to provide supplemental payments to those aged 76 to 85 years and to exempt SSI from the switch (Office of Management and Budget, n.d.a). Nonetheless, proposals to reduce the COLA remain very unpopular.

Each of these reform proposals generates winners and losers. To the extent that revisions to OASI are dictated by political considerations, we can predict outcomes by weighing the political clout of the winners against that of the losers. In this balancing act, social workers must put our thumbs on the metaphorical scale to insure that the needs of vulnerable populations are taken into consideration.

REFORM PROPOSALS FOR WOMEN

Social Security provides lower retirement incomes for women. In 2014, the average monthly retirement benefit paid to retired men was $1,488 compared with a mean of $1,167 for women (Social Security Administration, 2015c). Yet, women are more likely than men to rely on Social Security as their sole or primary source of income. In 2015, 30 percent of older women received over 90 percent of their income from Social Security; compared with 23 percent of older men (Older Women's League, 2015). Recognizing the program's importance for women, organizations such as the Older Women's League (OWL) and the Institute for Women's Policy Research have become active participants in the Social Security reform debates. To understand these debates, you need to be familiar with provisions that affect older women as dependents, as widows, and as divorcees.

Today, most women receive benefits based on their own work histories, but married women who have not been in the workforce are entitled to 50 percent of their husbands' retirement benefits. A woman cannot receive benefits as *both* dependent *and* retired worker. Upon retirement, she receives benefits as a dependent unless those based on her own work history would be higher.

In 2015, 4.1 percent of Social Security beneficiaries (most of them women) received *only* the spousal benefit (Social Security Administration, n.d.a). This means they were residing with their spouse, and either had no work experience or had earnings substantially below those of their spouse.[8] These married couples receive 150 percent of the workers' benefits (100 percent for him and 50 percent for her). In 2015, 7 percent of Social Security beneficiaries were widows and parents of deceased workers. Upon the worker's death, the surviving spouse is entitled to 100 percent of the worker's benefit. So the survivor (usually a woman) experiences a one-third drop in household income and a concomitant increase in her risk of poverty.[9]

With rising divorce rates of the latter half of the 20th century it became clear that provisions for dependents and widows left out a growing category of women: divorcees who had been dependent on their husbands for support. Therefore, in 1965 spousal benefits were made available to those who had been married for at least 20 years. In 1977, that period was decreased to 10 years. So a woman who was married to a worker for at least 10 years is eligible to receive spousal benefits.

Proposals addressed in the 2010 Senate report include provisions that would reduce the duration of marriage required for spousal benefits, increase the amount of survivor benefits, and provide for a minimum benefit. These measures would reduce the financial vulnerability of spouses (mostly women) with little or no earnings; caregiver credits would also.

Caregiver Credits

To accommodate their caregiving responsibilities, women often leave work or reduce their work commitment, which can reduce their retirement benefits. Proposals to award social security credits for caregiving address this concern.

The 2010 Senate report included discussion of caregiver credits. Three options were considered. One would allow a certain number of caregiving years (3–4) to count as covered employment at the average wage rate. Another would exclude some caregiving years from computation of benefits, effectively raising the AIME for caregivers. The final option would be an income-tested supplement for retired workers with children.

Caregiver credits aim to provide retirement income to people (still primarily women) who leave work to care for children and older adults. They have some appeal as measures to recognize women's unpaid labor and to reduce older and leave them vulnerable to poverty in later life. Failure to address their needs undermines the adequacy of Social Security. Caregiver credits would address this concern. Women's risk of poverty. But they do have drawbacks. The first two options provide no benefits to those who take on double duty, meeting family care responsibilities without leaving the workforce. Administrative complications arise as well, as workers have to demonstrate that they provided care. The simplest way to document caregiving may be a child's birth certificate, but there may be no straightforward way to document elder care. Finally, caregiver credits would impose an additional cost on the already overburdened program.

REFORM PROPOSALS FOR DUAL-EARNER COUPLES

Early debate about the Social Security Act referred to "men and women" workers, lending an impression of gender neutrality. But in its original form, Social Security reflected the

---

[8]Considerably more women used the spousal benefit to augment their worker benefit, essentially topping up their benefit amounts (Iams, Reznik, & Tamborini, 2010).

[9]While this may seem (and is intended to be) fairly generous treatment of widows, in essence it means they are expected to live on two-thirds of the amount they had been receiving while they were part of a married couple. For low- and moderate-income couples, this reduction often leaves the widow in poverty.

TABLE 4.3 Differential Treatment of Dual-Earning Couples

	Couple A	Couple B	Couple C
Monthly earnings 1	$6,000	$5,000	$3,000
Monthly earnings 2	0	1	3,000
Monthly OASI tax (12.4%)	744	744	744
Benefit base 1	6,000	5,000	3,000
Benefit base 2	3,000	2,500	3,000
Combined base	9,000	7,500	6,000

dominant family structure of the day, in which nearly all women were financially dependent on men. The program still favors this family form.

Table 4.3 provides a simplified illustration of the effects on couples in three different situations. Each couple earns the same total monthly income. For Couple A, one partner earns a monthly salary of $6,000 and the other partner is not employed. The wage earner's retirement benefits are based on 100 percent of earnings, and the spouse's benefits are based on 50 percent of the same earnings. Thus, the couple's combined retirement income is based on 150 percent of the wages earned, or a combined wage base of $9,000.

Dual-earner couples fare less well. In Couple B, both spouses are employed. The first earner makes $5,000 per month and the second makes $1,000 per month. The first earner is entitled to benefits based on $5,000. The second earner will draw retirement benefits based on 50 percent of the wages of the higher-earning partner. Thus, Couple B receives benefits based on a combined wage base of $7,500, even though their total income was the same as Couple A's.

Couple C includes two earners with equal monthly salaries. Each partner earns $3,000 per month. Their retirement benefits are based on 100 percent of each person's wages, or $6,000, the lowest wage base of the three couples in our comparison.[10]

Social Security treatment of dual-earner couples undermines the equity of the program. As we have seen, single-earner couples receive proportionately greater benefits for their payroll taxes. Or, to put it another way, because women typically earn less than men, the payroll taxes paid by working women, whether they are married or not, yield less benefits than those paid by working men with dependent spouses.

This equity problem is exacerbated upon the death of a spouse. When a member of the one-earner couple (Couple A) dies, the surviving spouse will receive about two-thirds of what both had received as a couple. In the dual-earner couple (Couple C, for instance), the remaining spouse receives about half what they had received as a couple. So the bereaved spouse in Couple C gets no benefit from the additional payroll taxes he or she paid. Measures to provide adequate benefits for the dependent widow in Couple A exacerbate the inequity experienced by the working spouse in Couple C.[11]

Earnings Sharing

Proposals for **earnings sharing** address the problems of dual-earner couples. Under this approach, spousal benefits would be eliminated. The earnings of a married couple would be combined, with half credited to each partner for each year of the marriage. Retirees would receive benefits based on their accumulated earnings.

---

[10]For another explanation of this phenomenon, with benefit computations, see Schulz (1995).

[11]I leave to you the question of what happens with the death of either spouse in Couple B.

Earnings sharing would eliminate the inequities experienced by dual-career couples. It would also benefit people who divorce after less than ten years of marriage, giving them credit for half of their spouses' earnings. Thus, earnings sharing could improve the equity of Social Security; however, there is some concern about its impact on the program's adequacy. Under most versions of earnings sharing, the gains experienced by these two groups must be balanced against the losses to single-earner couples. Further, several studies suggest that earnings sharing might exacerbate the financial vulnerability of low-income widows and couples, as well as women aged 90 and older (for example, Iams, Reznik, & Tamborini, 2010).

LO 4-4   Become Familiar with the History and Basic Structure of Means-tested Programs Authorized Under the Social Security Act

EP 3a
EP 5a

The Social Security Act authorizes three public assistance programs: Temporary Assistance to Needy Families (TANF), Supplemental Security Income (SSI), and Medicaid. Here, we will provide an overview of their history and basic structure, reserving more detailed consideration for later chapters. While the social insurance programs are administered by the federal government, these public assistance programs operate as federal–state partnerships. Most of their funding comes from the general fund at the federal level, but states do contribute and, particularly in the case of Medicaid, those contributions make up ever-increasing shares of state budgets.

TEMPORARY ASSISTANCE TO NEEDY FAMILIES (TANF)

Title IV of the Social Security Act of 1935 authorized federal grants to states that chose to provide Aid to Dependent Children (ADC). In 1955, Nevada was the last state to join the program. By that time, provisions of the Social Security Act of 1950 had taken effect. These allowed grants under the program to take into account not only the needs of dependent children but also those of their caregivers, usually their mothers.

In 1962, the Kennedy administration proposed several revisions to ADC. Most noticeably, the program was renamed Aid to Families with Dependent Children (AFDC) in an effort to emphasize the family context. The same year, amendments to the Social Security Act called for the delivery of social services to AFDC recipients. This was the last major expansion of public assistance to dependent children under the Social Security Act.

During the 1970s and 1980s, growth in the welfare rolls exceeded population growth. At the same time, real wages eroded and public support for welfare deteriorated. In 1982, newly elected president Ronald Reagan popularized the call to "end welfare as we know it." Responding to this call, Congress and the president enacted the Family Support Act of 1988, which added a work requirement to AFDC. Harshly criticized as "work-fare" by advocates for the poor, this measure was only a hint of what was to follow.

The 1996 Personal Responsibility and Work Opportunity Reconciliation Act (PRWORA) effectively dismantled the New Deal guarantee of a minimum income for needy children. The act abolished the AFDC entitlement, substituting a block grant to the states. Federal guidelines required states to enforce work participation requirements and established a five-year lifetime limit for assistance under the new program, called Temporary Assistance to Needy Families (TANF).

The transition from AFDC to TANF was fraught with controversy and ambiguity. Welfare advocates were horrified at the prospect of families being abruptly cut off from public assistance. Program recipients were often unaware of provisions that affected them, such as the measure that exempts victims of domestic violence from the requirement that they assist officials in collecting child support if doing so would present "undue hardship" or the 20 percent exemption that allows some recipients to continue receiving assistance after they have passed the lifetime limit. Further, the work participation requirements have been interpreted either broadly (to include a wide range of activities such as participating in mental health or substance abuse treatment) or narrowly (to include only paid employment). The use of sanctions also varies.

As is typical of federal block grants, states enjoy considerable discretion in the operation of TANF. Thus, decisions made at the state level have greater impact on recipients' lives under TANF than was the case under AFDC. Under the maintenance of effort provision (MOE), states must contribute funds to the program. State and federal funds may be spent to address four goals set forth in PRWORA: "(1) provide assistance to needy families so that children may be cared for in their own homes or in the homes of relatives; (2) end the dependence of needy parents on government benefits by promoting job preparation, work, and marriage; (3) prevent and reduce the incidence of out of wedlock pregnancies and establish annual numerical goals for preventing and reducing the incidence of these pregnancies; and (4) encourage the formation and maintenance of two parent families." Notably absent from these goals is any intent to reduce poverty or ease hardship among needy families in the United States and, as we will see in Chapter 5, the TANF program does considerably less than AFDC in this regard.

SUPPLEMENTAL SECURITY INCOME (SSI)

Sometimes described as a "program of last resort," Supplemental Security Income (SSI) was authorized by the Social Security Act Amendments of 1972 (and implemented in 1974) to provide a minimum guaranteed income for elderly, blind, or disabled persons (Ball, 1973; Elder & Powers, 2006). SSI combined three state-administered, categorical programs (Aid to the Blind, Aid to the Disabled, and Old-Age Assistance) into a single entity. It is administered as a federal–state partnership in which state agencies manage eligibility determination and may supplement SSI payments while the Social Security Administration manages federal contributions and regulations.

Eligibility is based on categorical status (recipients must be aged, blind, or disabled) and financial hardship. Since its inception, SSI enrollment has more than doubled, from 3.9 million in 1974 to 8.3 million in 2014. (During the same period the U.S. population grew by less than 50 percent.) Over the years, SSI beneficiaries have come to include more adults under 64, more children, and fewer older adults.

As Figure 4.3 illustrates, program enrollment for people 64 and younger increased dramatically between 1990 and 1996. The number of children on SSI tripled, and the number of adults under 64 nearly doubled.

The increase in children is attributed to the Supreme Court decision in the *Zebley* case. Advocates for children with disabilities successfully argued that their eligibility should

FIGURE 4.3 SSI Beneficiaries, 1974–2014

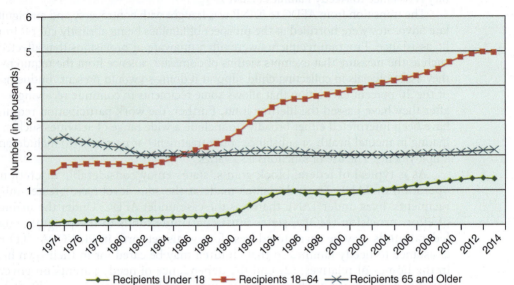

SOURCE (for data): SSI Annual Statistical Report, 2011, Table 4, Recipients by age, December 1974–2014 (http ://www.ssa.gov/ policy/docs/statcomps/ssi_asr/2014/ssi_asr14.pdf, accessed April 26, 2013).

take into account age-appropriate behavior. Consequently, the number of children on SSI who had mental illness and behavior disorders such as attention deficit/hyperactivity disorder (ADHD) increased.

SSI enrollment of older adults has declined since the 1970s despite population aging. In 1974, 2.4 million older adults constituted 61 percent of SSI participants. By 2001, their participation had bottomed out at 1.9 million, 30 percent of recipients (Social Security Administration, 2015d). Many low-income older adults do not participate in SSI, and this problem has persisted since the program's inception. Only about half of the aged who are eligible for SSI benefits participate in the program (Davies et al., 2002; Zedlewski & Meyer, 1987). Some attribute this to the steady erosion of SSI benefits to inflation, while others point to the difficulty of eligibility determination, which falls more heavily on those with functional limitations. Elder and Powers (2006) noted that increases in retirement age for Social Security are likely to increase the need for income supplements among low-income seniors, which lends greater urgency to the problem of nonparticipation in SSI.

SSI was revised, along with AFDC, food stamps, and Medicaid, through the 1996 Personal Responsibility and Work Opportunity Reconciliation Act (PRWORA). Under this welfare reform legislation, legal immigrants lost access to SSI and food stamps unless they or their spouses had worked for 10 years and had not received benefits previously. Following implementation of the 1996 reforms, an estimated 500,000 immigrants (more than half of them elderly) became ineligible for SSI. Another 935,000 immigrants (many of them elderly) lost their eligibility for food stamps.[12] SSI benefits for most of these "pre-enactment" immigrants were restored by the Balanced Budget Act of 1997; however, this act did not restore benefits for "post-enactment" immigrants who arrived in the United States after August 1996 (Fix & Passel, 2002). PRWORA also tightened eligibility standards for children.

---

[12]Although states were allowed to prohibit legal immigrants from participating in Medicaid, most have consented to continue to provide Medicaid benefits to immigrants who were on the program before welfare reform as well as to new immigrants after five years of U.S. residency.

Also contributing to slower growth in adult enrollment was legislation that prohibited eligibility on the basis of drug or alcohol addiction. In 1996, Congress passed the Contract with America Advancement Act (PL 104-121), which ended SSI benefits for Americans who were disabled because of drug addiction and/or alcoholism.

As we will see in Chapter 5, the minimum guaranteed income provided by SSI often does not lift recipients out of poverty. The role of SSI as a source of income for people with disabilities is discussed in Chapter 8.

MEDICAL CARE FOR THE INDIGENT: MEDICAID

As the nation's third-largest source of health insurance (after employer coverage and Medicare), Medicaid funds health care for millions of Americans (U.S. Department of Health and Human Services, 2005). It is a major source of funding for long-term care of older adults, as well as for prenatal care and delivery. In 2010, Medicaid covered 41 percent of long-term care in the United States (Center for Health Care Strategies, 2010). Further, the program pays for over one-third of births in the United States (Kaiser Family Foundation, n.d.). As further evidence of its central role in U.S. social policy, we will return to Medicaid in Chapters 5, 6, and 13. For now, let's consider a brief overview of the program's history.

In 1950, the first federal program of medical care for indigent Americans was established as a grant-in-aid program. Authorized under Social Security Act amendments, it offered a federal match to states wishing to provide medical care to participants in public assistance programs; however, some states did not elect to participate. Along with Medicare, Medicaid was supported by the Johnson administration and it was established in 1965. But in many ways the history of Medicaid more closely parallels that of SSI.

Medicaid was authorized under Title XIX of the Social Security Act to operate as a federal–state partnership with most of the cost borne by the federal government and most of the administrative responsibilities borne by the states. Medicaid was more generous than the program it replaced, funding health care for low-income women, children, elderly people, and people with disabilities. Nonetheless, it took 17 years for all 50 states to establish their Medicaid programs. (Arizona did not sign on until 1982.) We still see a certain ambivalence in many states' approaches to Medicaid.

Steady enrollment growth marked the program's early years, and the outreach associated with SSI implementation in the early 1970s brought Medicaid coverage to more people with disabilities. The late 1970s saw high inflation in medical costs, and program expenditures increased as well. Cost containment became a Medicaid theme in the 1980s as managed care came on the scene. The 1990s saw important policy changes that extended eligibility to cover more pregnant women, infants, and children, as well as the *Zebley* decision, which brought Medicaid coverage to more people with disabilities (Klemm, 2000).

Exponential increases in enrollment were associated with exponential increases in federal and state costs and increasing pressure to restrict access to Medicaid. In the mid-1990s, the Republican Party's Contract with America made reference to eliminating the Medicaid entitlement and replacing it with a block grant, but this was not to be. Nonetheless, Medicaid enrollment began to fall in 1996, possibly due to the passage of PRWORA. This trend reversed during the Great Recession when, like SSI, Medicaid enrollment began to climb.

The 2010 Patient Protection and Affordable Care Act was designed to expand Medicaid eligibility by effectively requiring states to extend eligibility to most low-income Americans under age 65, with nearly all of the costs borne by the federal government. Actually, the federal government was authorized to withhold all Medicaid funds from states that did not expand Medicaid eligibility. But in 2012, the Supreme Court ruled that the threat of withholding Medicaid funds was coercive and therefore unconstitutional (see *National Federation of Independent Business (NFIB) v. Sebelius*). So the proposed Medicaid expansion was rolled out unevenly as states grappled with their newfound freedom to decide whether or not to participate. We will examine the politics of Medicaid expansion in greater detail in Chapter 5.

LO 4-5 Become Familiar with Health and Social Service Programs Authorized Under the Social Security Act

EP 5a

In addition to social insurance and public assistance, the Social Security Act authorizes the use of federal funds to provide some health and social services. Four of the act's titles authorize services: Title IV allows for child welfare services, Title V establishes maternal and child health services, Title XX authorizes social services, and Title XXI creates the State Children's Health Insurance Program. Although federal staff are employed under these titles, they do not provide direct services because doing so is generally considered incompatible with constitutional limitations on the power of the federal government. Instead, federal staff members administer grants to the states. States then deliver services or arrange for their delivery in ways that are compatible with the federal regulations governing each program.

CHILD WELFARE SERVICES (TITLE IV)

Title IV of the 1935 Social Security Act established a program of grants-in-aid for states to set up their ADC programs. The title also allowed for child welfare services, allocating $1.5 million for that purpose (Social Security Administration, n.d.c). An initial focus was on the development of child welfare services in rural areas, although states had flexibility in using their child welfare allocations. Katharine Lenroot, director of the Children's Bureau in 1935, explained that

> [t]he basic principle followed in planning programs, especially in child welfare, was that of taking each state where it was, and encouraging initiative and flexibility, with great emphasis on local responsibility.... The term "child welfare service" was seen for the first time, in many states, as extending far beyond institutional care, or foster home care, or protective services, or cooperation with juvenile courts, to include a variety of measures, such as casework service, homemaker service and day care to strengthen and supplement the child's own home so that he could remain in it. (Social Security Administration, n.d.c, p. 2)

Just as the 1950s were a time of expansion for other Social Security Act programs, child welfare experienced tremendous growth and increased federal appropriations. With the shift from a rural to an urban emphasis, child welfare services reflected the broad social transition of the United States into an urban, industrialized nation.

Today, child welfare services under Title IV include federal payments for foster care and adoption assistance, preventive services designed to keep children in their homes, services to develop alternative placements for children for whom foster care or adoption are not feasible, and family reunification services. Family preservation services are authorized under Title IV to provide intensive support to maintain children in their homes. Funds are also provided for training of child welfare professionals and research in methods for improving services in the field. States receive fixed allocations under these statutes, although some must meet matching requirements. Child welfare services are discussed further in Chapter 12.

MATERNAL AND CHILD HEALTH SERVICES (TITLE V)

Title V of the 1935 Social Security Act allowed for grants to states in support of maternal and child health services. This program enabled the U.S. Children's Bureau to continue the work it had begun in establishing clinics for mothers and children throughout the nation. Grants for maternal and child health did not require states to provide matching funds, but the program's regulations did stipulate that states had to use funds to extend or improve upon existing services (not to replace them) and that states were required to focus on needy, typically rural, areas and groups with the severest hardships.

Today, these services are provided in each state under the Maternal and Child Health Services Block Grant. With a focus on low-income mothers and those in rural areas, these block grant funds are used to meet the health objectives established under the Public Health Service Act of 2000. States have latitude in allocating these funds. Typical services provided include immunizations, visiting nurse activities, rehabilitative services for blind and disabled children, and case management for children with special health-care needs. In addition to the state allocations, federal funds are available under Title V for training health personnel and conducting research on health-care delivery, genetic testing and counseling, hemophilia, and early interventions.

SOCIAL SERVICES BLOCK GRANT (TITLE XX)

Title XX of the Social Security Act was passed in 1975 to provide social services to vulnerable Americans. A funding cap of $2.5 billion was established, making the program a "capped entitlement." It was converted to the Social Services Block Grant (SSBG) through the Omnibus Budget Reconciliation Act of 1981. The SSBG provides funds to states for social services directed toward achieving economic self-sufficiency; preventing or remedying neglect, abuse, or exploitation of children or adults; preventing or reducing inappropriate institutionalization; and securing referrals for institutional care. Within these broad goals, states have flexibility to decide what services they will provide. SSBG funds are typically used to provide day care for children, home-based services for the elderly or disabled, and protective services. Each state's allocation is based on its population. The SSBG does not have a state matching requirement.

CHILDREN'S HEALTH INSURANCE PROGRAM (TITLE XXI)

CHIP was established after the 1993 failure of comprehensive health care reform during the Bill Clinton administration. In 1995, an estimated 10 million children, 13.8 percent of Americans under the age of 18, were not covered by medical insurance (Weil, 1997). Concern for these children led to the creation, through the 1997 Balanced Budget Act, of the State Children's Health Insurance Program, known as SCHIP, or simply as CHIP. The program authorizes funding for states to provide health coverage to uninsured, low-income children. It targets children in families with incomes between 100 and 200 percent of the federal poverty threshold, who are not eligible for Medicaid but generally cannot afford private insurance. States enjoyed flexibility in designing their CHIP programs and could either expand their existing Medicaid coverage or establish separate programs. The CHIP program limits enrollees' costs by prohibiting deductibles and limiting copayments above nominal amounts. Usually, premiums are not allowed.

CHIP detractors have argued that families are using it instead of private coverage, an argument that received support from a 2007 report by the Congressional Budget Office (CBO). The CBO concluded that somewhere between one-quarter and one-half of the

8 million children covered in 2007 were in families that had dropped private insurance (CBO, 2007). This was clearly on President Bush's mind in 2007 when he vetoed the Children's Health Insurance Program Reauthorization Act. With a price tag of $35 billion, the bill would have raised income eligibility to 300 percent of the poverty level, extending coverage to an additional 4 million children. The expansion would be funded through an increase in the excise tax on tobacco. The bill passed the House and Senate with bipartisan support. However, President Bush argued that it "would move health care in this country in the wrong direction," citing his concern that greater numbers of families would drop their private health insurance coverage to get their children enrolled in CHIP (Silva, 2007).

Under the Patient Protection and Affordable Care Act, CHIP eligibility and enrollment are coordinated with Medicaid and the Affordable Insurance Exchanges. CHIP eligibility levels vary from state to state, with about half covering children in families with incomes up to 400 percent of the federal poverty threshold through subsidies on the exchanges (in the form of tax credits) (Kaiser Commission on Medicaid and the Uninsured, 2013b).

Although the benefits of CHIP would seem self-evident, the program has not been without its critics. Some, like Bush, argue that the private insurance industry suffers as the result of subsidized coverage for children. Others suggest that the program is too expensive or that it could be a lure for "illegal" immigrants. An intriguing study could provide a response to the economic complaint. In 2015, researchers from the National Bureau of Economic Research conducted a massive analysis of national datasets from the IRS and other sources and concluded that children in families who were eligible for CHIP paid more in federal taxes by the age of 28, thus partially offsetting the cost of their coverage (see Brown, Kowalski, & Luri, 2015).

LO 4-6   Understand the Philosophical Foundations of Social Security in the United States

EP 5c

The Social Security Act is the foundation of America's safety net and a central vehicle for promoting social justice. It is pivotal for allocating the costs and benefits of U.S. citizenship. Perhaps the most controversial of the act's provisions stem from the costs it has imposed on citizens, as in the constitutional challenges to the compulsory payroll tax. The payroll tax has risen from 2 percent of wages and a $3,000 cap to more than 15 percent of wages and a (2013) cap of $113,700. Thus, OAI absorbs a significant proportion of the incomes of low- and middle-income workers. Proposals to increase the payroll tax continue to fuel the controversy over this cost of citizenship.

Other costs imposed by the Social Security Act are tied less directly to the act itself but are every bit as controversial as the payroll tax. The public assistance and service programs funded under Social Security are financed through general revenues at both federal and state levels. As we saw in Chapter 2, these revenues are generated through individual and corporate income taxes. Since these taxes are progressive, Social Security's public assistance and service programs represent a significant redistribution of income from the affluent to the needy.

In a reversal of Robin Hood's strategy, movements to dismantle these programs (for example, PRWORA) and reduce the tax burden of affluent Americans (for example, Bush tax cuts) redistribute the nation's resources from the poor to the rich. Thus, we see strong pushback from the political right, often presented under the guise of reform.

As a distinctly American approach to vulnerability and social justice, Social Security reflects the two philosophical perspectives on social justice most compatible with American political and economic thought: libertarianism and liberalism. It was carefully crafted to minimize libertarian objections. The imposition of compulsory taxes was minimized, as was the role of the federal government in delivery of assistance and services.

The increasing use of block grants to fund Social Security Act programs is part of a trend toward devolution, or moving decision making as close as possible to the individual level. This movement is an indirect outgrowth of the libertarian emphasis on personal freedom. The Social Security Act defers to the private market in several areas, as when it establishes benefit levels that are well below the poverty threshold. No able-bodied worker would be motivated to forgo employment with the promise of such minimal assistance. This unwillingness to provide an alternative to private employment illustrates the principle of **less eligibility**, which will be discussed in Chapter 5.

The contribution of liberal philosophies to Social Security in the United States is readily apparent. The act established a social minimum for income, below which the **deserving poor** should not fall. Thus, the SSI program delivers a minimum income for the aged, blind, and disabled. The public assistance and health and social service programs under Social Security can also be viewed through a utilitarian lens as optimizing social well-being. Financed through progressive taxes, they use income from those who can afford it most easily to enhance the well-being of those who are most in need of assistance.

Closing Reflections

This chapter has examined the programs established through the Social Security Act of 1935 and its amendments. From a historical perspective, Social Security is not simply a tool for improving well-being but also a political vehicle for securing worker loyalty to the state. Even as it secures worker loyalty, it presents tremendous administrative demands, requiring the development of an elaborate government administrative apparatus. In essence, Social Security offers a compelling rationale for the existence of government with its promise of strengthening national cohesion and enhancing the well-being of vulnerable Americans. And yet, like our democracy, the programs authorized under the Social Security Act are works in progress. Their periodic modifications impose shifts in the costs and benefits of citizenship, which enable us to trace our nation's evolving understanding of social justice.

Think About It

1. The Social Security Act of 1935 was carefully crafted to comply with constitutional provisions restricting the role of the federal government. Compare the act's insurance programs with its means-tested programs. Do they differ in the roles assigned to the states? How and why?

2. On June 26, 2015, the Supreme Court held that same-sex married couples were entitled to the same recognition afforded to heterosexual couples. How do you think marriage equality in the United States has affected the Social Security system? What about Medicare and Medicaid?

3. Proposals to subject Social Security benefits to a means test surface from time to time. In 2010, for instance, House Republican leader John Boehner argued for cutting or eliminating benefits for retirees with substantial other income. Supporters question why Social Security benefits should go to people who don't really need them when the system is in financial difficulty. Do you support or oppose this approach to Social Security reform? Why?

4. Since its inception, the Social Security Act has aimed to provide a safety net for the unemployed. How well has it done? What are your state's eligibility requirements for receipt of UI benefits?

Web-Based Exercises

For direct links to all the sites in these exercises, visit the *Foundations of Social Policy* Companion Site at www.cengagebrain.com and select the resources for Chapter 4.

1. Go to the Social Security Administration website at http://www.ssa.gov/planners /benefitcalculators.html. Use the quick calculator to estimate your retirement benefits based on the earnings you anticipate as a professional social worker. Now double your earnings estimate. What difference does that make in your estimated benefits? Investigate your "breakeven date." Do you expect to live longer than this? If so, would you be better off retiring at 62, your full retirement age, or 70 years of age? Which has a greater impact: early retirement or low wages? Go to http://www.ssa.gov/OACT/TR to view the current report of the Social Security Trustees. Have the projected dates of trust fund depletion changed in the past few years? Can you explain these changes? How do the trustees explain the situation? Do you find their explanation compelling?

2. Go to http://socialsecuritygame.actuary.org/ and play "The Social Security Game" designed by the American Academy of Actuaries to give you first-hand experience of what policy-makers go through as they evaluate various options to reform the program.

Competency Notes

As mentioned in the preface to this text, the Council on Social Work Education has designated nine core competencies and related practice behaviors that must be addressed by accredited social work programs. In these notes, I will specify the way chapter content addresses these competencies and behaviors. (This is designed to assist with the accreditation process.) Please refer to the "helping hands" icons for the locations of specific content in this chapter. Here, you will find a brief explanation of how the accompanying content relates to the specified competency or practice behaviors.

The following list indicates where EPAS competencies and practice behaviors are addressed in this chapter.

EP 3a   **apply their understanding of social, economic, and environmental justice to advocate for human rights at the individual and social levels.** The chapter illuminates the role of wealth and self-interest in proposals to radically restructure Social Security programs and in objections to social insurance.

The chapter describes the advocacy involved in developing Social Security in the United States and abroad, including the roles of key social workers such as Frances Perkins.

EP 5a   **Identify social policy at the local, state, and federal level that impacts well-being, service delivery, and access to social services.** The chapter introduces social insurance programs that affect the well-being of the U.S. population, as well as more targeted service programs established under the social security act.

EP 5c   **Apply critical thinking to analyze, formulate, and advocate for policies that advance human rights and social, economic, and environmental justice.** The chapter suggests a degree of skepticism when confronted with "expert" opinions on the decline of Social Security programs and the need to cut programs. It also explains the eligibility requirements and benefits provided under these programs. It discusses the development of Social Security and the forces that opposed social insurance for workers. It also addresses discriminatory aspects of the original Social Security programs to enable students to critically analyze the economic and political dynamics behind social policies.

Suggested Resources

Achenbaum, W. A. (1986). *Social Security: Visions and Revisions*. Cambridge: Cambridge University Press.

Downey, K. (2009). *The Woman Behind the New Deal: The Life of Frances Perkins, FDR's Secretary of Labor and His Moral Conscience*. New York: Nan A. Talese/Doubleday.

Kingson, E. R., & Berkowitz, E. D. (1993). *Social Security and Medicare: A Policy Primer*. Westport, CT: Greenwood Publishing Group.

www.ssa.gov. Maintained by the Social Security Administration, this site offers outstanding historical material on the act as well as the opportunity to subscribe to a free e-mail newsletter that gives updates on news affecting Social Security.

CHAPTER

5

Poverty and Inequality

Poverty is the parent of revolution and crime.
ARISTOTLE

Learning Objectives

This chapter will help prepare students to:

LO 5-1   Discuss how poverty has been defined and understand the implications of various definitions

LO 5-2   Understand the values and beliefs that inform American policies toward the poor

LO 5-3   Become familiar with the history of poverty interventions in the United States

LO 5-4   Describe contemporary issues affecting key programs that serve America's poor

LO 5-5   Know who is most likely to be poor in the United States

LO 5-6   Understand the secondary risks associated with poverty

LO 5-7   Become aware of rising inequality, its causes, and its consequences

Americans often attribute poverty to individual flaws such as laziness, intemperance, or inability to defer gratification. This tendency to **blame the victim** is reflected in policies and interventions designed to redress poverty. Of course, it becomes less tenable when economic disasters demonstrate that the risk of poverty is widespread and unpredictable. The conditions for collective action discussed in the introduction to Part II were present during the Depression, and the New Deal was enacted. Social Security became the nation's most effective antipoverty program. But the Depression ended more than 70 years ago; despite reminders like the 2008–2010 recession, it is easy to forget the lessons of that difficult time. Consequently, Americans have allowed our safety net to erode. Our enthusiasm for market-based answers to social problems has at times further disadvantaged the poor, even as our tax policy has driven benefits to the affluent. The result is a level of inequality that we haven't seen since the "roaring '20s." In this chapter, we take a close look at poverty before considering the causes and implications of growing inequality.

A HUMAN PERSPECTIVE   Antonia Flores

Driving away from my meeting with Antonia, I had an angry lump in my stomach. It was hard to parse the feeling since Antonia herself was so cheerful and positive. In fact, the main advice she had for other women on TANF was "Stay positive. I know it's sometimes hard, but you have to stay positive." Besides, Antonia Flores does not fit the stereotype of a welfare mother. She is bright and articulate. Her home is immaculate. Her son and the niece she cares for are healthy and well-behaved.

Antonia lives with her mother, her brother, and her son in a modest three-bedroom home located in a working-class neighborhood within a stone's throw of the interstate highway. Walking up the drive, I saw tulips blooming in the flower bed of her tiny post-WWII bungalow. The neighborhood was well cared for, and I suspected that it had been a peaceful place to live until the interstate went in.

I rang the door and waited for a bit, noticing the lace curtains on Antonia's front window and the multiple locks on the front door. Antonia undid the locks one by one, then flung open the door and greeted me with a twinkling smile. At 34 years old, Antonia describes herself as square: "4 feet high and 4 feet wide." She is, in fact, less than 5 feet high and morbidly obese. The day we met, Antonia was dressed in a black tank top and slacks, with dark eye makeup and bare feet.

Antonia is the only member of her family who has ever received public assistance. Her father immigrated from Mexico and works as a mechanic. Her mother, who is of Irish descent, works as a registered nurse. Her siblings all work at "good" jobs. Antonia identifies as a Latina. She finished high school and got a good job with Discover Card, moving up through the ranks to become a senior account manager. Despite the impressive title, the job did not pay especially well; however, it did offer health insurance.

While working for Discover Card, Antonia met her husband, Ted. They married in 1999, and the man who had courted Antonia abruptly disappeared. In his place was the "new Ted," an addict who promptly lost his job at a fast-food outlet and became verbally abusive. By the time Antonia fully realized what her husband was like, she was pregnant with her son Christopher. When Chris was born, Antonia was the sole support of the family. Even when sober, Ted was not much of a companion, and when he was high, he could be downright abusive, calling Antonia names and criticizing her. One morning when Chris was 3 months old and she was late to work, Antonia made the mistake of asking Ted to change a diaper. When he blew his stack, she walked out on him for good.

That was five years ago. Antonia had a good job, and she moved in with her mother and brother. Family support provided a stable environment for her son, and life went smoothly until Antonia began to have health problems.

After weeks of nighttime stomach aches, she learned that her gall bladder had to be removed. When that was done, her knee gave out, and she had surgery to repair it. She developed asthma and missed work for occasional attacks. With all this going on, people at work were getting fired. There were rumors that Discover was weeding out longtime workers to replace them with new employees at lower wages. Antonia tried to avoid missing work, but when her knee was reinjured in a car accident, she had no choice. She went in for a repeat surgery, never imagining it would cost her the job she had held for 14 years.

As Antonia explains, Discover sent a letter demanding physician certification of her injury. The letter went out via UPS and was left at a back door. By the time she found it, the deadline for submitting verification had passed. Nonetheless, she rushed to the doctor's office and watched as they faxed the certification to Discover. Despite multiple requests, her employer never acknowledged receipt of the document, and Antonia was summarily terminated. Although she was eligible for unemployment benefits, the human resources people at Discover recommended that she go on TANF.

Although paperwork was a bizarre hassle at times, Antonia speaks highly of her experiences with TANF. The transition to Medicaid was smooth. All of her doctors agreed to accept Medicaid payments, and it was cheaper than COBRA benefits. Her caseworker was "great," as was the social worker. The program even gave her counseling to help her deal with "relationship issues." Her caseworker helped her apply for support from the WIC program, which she described as "great!" She applied for public housing but faced a waiting list a yard long. It would be years before Antonia and her son would be eligible.

Antonia felt that TANF benefits were insufficient to meet her needs. She received $640 per month, of which $300 went for child care and $250 went to her mother for rent. And the program had a 30-hour-per-week work requirement. The work was sometimes pointless, requiring Antonia to hang around the TANF office waiting for someone to give her a task. Day care was subsidized, but it was hard to find a provider willing to accept TANF rates.

But Antonia's greatest concern was the TANF limitations on schooling. She wanted to complete a college degree and learn to be either a counselor or a computer programmer. Given her people skills, Antonia thinks she could be a great counselor, but she thinks computer programming might be more marketable. Under TANF neither is possible. The program will support only approved Associate of Arts programs. And there seems to be a mismatch between available programs and Antonia's needs and abilities. For instance, on a list of approved programs was one that would train her to be a trucker. Antonia pointed out to her caseworker that this was "ludicrous." She couldn't even reach the pedals on a truck, and when would she get to see her son?

Antonia is not one to complain, but she was happy to offer recommendations on how TANF could be improved. In her state, Medicaid does not pay for dental care. So she and her son live without regular exams and routine cleanings. If a tooth becomes infected, Medicaid will pay for extraction but not repair. So one of the worries that keeps Antonia up at night is the fear that she will break a tooth and end up with an empty space in her mouth. Antonia recommends that Medicaid provide limited preventive care for dental needs— "maybe just once a year." She is also concerned about a mismatch between the training programs approved as work participation for TANF and the job market in her state. Despite great demand for computer professionals, no computer training is provided under TANF. Antonia sees this as a missed opportunity. She argues that fathers should be held accountable for their children's well-being. Her husband goes from job to job, quitting as soon as the state begins to garnish his wages for the back child support he owes.

After six months on TANF, Antonia decided that it wasn't worth it. She went off cash assistance, keeping her Food Stamps and Medicaid. I asked whether she did this because of the lifetime limit on cash assistance. Antonia said she had never heard of the lifetime limit. She asked for details with alarm, worrying that the deadline might apply to Food Stamps and Medicaid.

I asked Antonia about her worries, and she said they were all "American dream" worries: "Will I be able to own a home? Can I have a car? Will I be able to pay for my son to go to college? Will I ever be able to retire?" These and other concerns made sleep impossible until Antonia discovered Ambien. She takes the sleep medication every night, and it seems to make life easier. She takes six or seven other medications as well, and notes that Medicaid coverage is better than the insurance she had when she was working. Under private insurance those copayments really mounted up.

Antonia's dreams focus on her son. "He's a wonderful kid—sometimes sassy, but just great!" Since her state has just established a school voucher program, she would like to take Chris out of the local public school. Because it is under renovation, he takes a half-hour bus ride to a school with large classes where he has experienced some bullying. Antonia has talked with the local Catholic school, and they are willing to accept the voucher even though it won't cover all of his tuition. She will be allowed to work off the difference by providing assistance in the school office. With a good education, Chris will be able to live the American dream, even if Antonia won't.

Reflecting on poverty in America, Antonia acknowledges that her income is below the poverty threshold but says she does not consider herself poor. She thinks she is fortunate because her family is so supportive and her son so terrific. She thinks the main problem is low wages, reporting that when she worked for Discover she sometimes had to call in sick because she didn't have enough money for gas. Commenting on rising inequality and the high cost of housing, Antonia asks, "Is profit really that much more important than people?"

Antonia provides day care to her 2-year-old niece, and the child calls her "Mama." During our interview, she alternately nestled in Antonia's generous arms and romped around the bare living room, flirting with me and showing off her tricks. This child care provides the only source of cash for Antonia and her son. I had offered to pay her $20 for our interview, and when I gave her the money, she exclaimed, "Now we get to see Spider-Man 3!" The movie wouldn't be out for weeks, but she knew her son would love it.

A SOCIAL WORK PERSPECTIVE

Why did Antonia's experiences make me so angry? Antonia followed the rules. She finished high school, got a job, got married, had a child. Lacking major physical or mental disabilities, she should have had a good shot at the American dream. But this was not to be. Her employer had shifted into the 21st-century paradigm in which employees are highly dispensable. So when she began to have health problems after 14 years of low-paid employment, Antonia was "terminated." Evidently, it was no longer profitable to employ her. Discover passed the buck to TANF. Other major corporations such as Walmart and McDonald's use public assistance to fill gaps left by their inadequate pay and nonexistent health coverage. Then, through their politicians, they put the squeeze on recipients, labeling them the "welfare problem."

LO 5-1

EP 3a
EP 5c

Discuss How Poverty Has Been Defined and Understand the Implications of Various Definitions

Poverty can be defined in either absolute or relative terms. **Absolute poverty** is based on a fixed level of resources, or threshold. Someone whose resources fall below the threshold experiences absolute poverty. Eligibility requirements for public poverty programs such as TANF reflect the notion of absolute poverty. **Relative poverty** is based on comparison. Someone whose situation is disadvantaged compared with another person or time experiences relative poverty. Compared with her siblings, Antonia experiences relative poverty, but with her babysitting income and family support she is advantaged in comparison with other TANF recipients. Some have argued that relative measures of poverty are more informative than absolute measures because the self-images, experiences, and prospects of poor families are affected by the affluence they observe in the broader culture. Thus, as we will see, inequality exacerbates the destructive impacts of poverty.

The most common definition of poverty used in the United States, the **Federal Poverty Threshold**, is an absolute measure. The Census Bureau uses it to describe trends in poverty, and programs such as **Food Stamps**, **Supplemental Security Income**, **Medicaid**, and **Temporary Assistance for Needy Families (TANF)** use it to determine eligibility.[1]

The federal poverty threshold was developed in the 1960s by **Mollie Orshansky**, an economist who worked for the Social Security Administration. Charged by the Kennedy administration with developing an effective measure of poverty, Ms. Orshansky found that the only existing measure of family needs was the Economy (or "Thrifty") Food Plan that had been developed by the U.S. Department of Agriculture. The plan estimated the cost of food required to sustain nutritional adequacy during a temporary emergency or shortage of funds. Food costs were assumed to be one-third of a family's total costs, so the poverty threshold was set by multiplying the Economy Food Plan by three. Initially, the poverty threshold for farm families, female-headed households, and the elderly was lower than the standard amount. These differences were based on consumption studies conducted by the Department of Agriculture that revealed lower food expenditures among women and the elderly. Farm families were believed to have access to inexpensive garden produce, and nutritional studies suggested that the elderly had lower caloric requirements (Orshansky, 1965).

The poverty threshold has undergone two kinds of changes since it was created. Since 1969 it has been tied to the **Consumer Price Index** (CPI), so most years it rises with inflation. The Bureau of Labor Statistics has computed the CPI since 1914, and from time to time this arcane computation has become controversial. For instance, there were objections when a new index was created that left out food and energy prices, when the "hedonic quality adjustment" was introduced to take into account improved quality of goods, and when President Obama proposed to use a "chained" CPI for indexing Social Security benefits. (See Chapter 14 for more information on the chained CPI.)

At any rate, the general economic trend has been toward rising costs. Inflation reached double-digit growth during two eras: the run up to the **Great Depression** (from 1918 to 1922) and the energy crises of the mid- to late-1970s. The nation saw deflation (lower prices) during the Depression; briefly in 1955; and in 2009 (Bureau of Labor Statistics, 2012). In 2010, rather than lower the poverty threshold and disqualify people from receiving public assistance, Congress took the unprecedented step of retaining the 2009 poverty guidelines.

---

[1]Technically speaking, there is a difference between the poverty "threshold" and the poverty "guidelines." The guidelines are based on the threshold and are used to determine program eligibility, whereas the threshold is used for statistical purposes such as the measurement of poverty. The guidelines are issued by the Department of Health and Human Services, and the threshold is issued by the Census Bureau.

TABLE 5.1   2016 Poverty Guidelines

Persons in Family or Household	48 Contiguous States and DC	Alaska	Hawaii
1	$11,880	$14,840	$13,670
2	$16,020	$20,020	$18,430
3	$20,160	$25,200	$23,190
4	$24,300	$30,380	$27,950
5	$28,440	$35,560	$32,710
6	$32,580	$40,740	$37,470
7	$36,730	$45,920	$42,230
8	$40,890	$51,120	$47,010
For each additional person, add:	*$4,160*	*$5,200*	*$4,780*

Source: U.S. Department of Health and Human Services (2016). (https://aspe.hhs.gov/poverty-guidelines, July 5, 2016).

The second change to the poverty threshold came in 1981. In response to political pressure and technical arguments, the thresholds for farm families and female-headed households were raised to the standard level (Fisher, 1997). The threshold for those older than 65 is still 8 to 10 percent below other households. This difference does not affect their eligibility for public programs, but it is reflected in Census Bureau poverty estimates.

Each year, the Department of Health and Human Services publishes the latest poverty guidelines in the **Federal Register** and on its website (www.hhs.gov). The poverty guidelines for 2016 are listed in Table 5.1.

CRITIQUES OF THE POVERTY THRESHOLD

Some people think the federal poverty threshold overestimates the extent of poverty in the United States because it does not consider income to include **in-kind benefits** such as Food Stamps, housing assistance, and medical programs (Friedman & Friedman, 1979; Murray, 1994). According to this view, the in-kind benefits available to the poor should be counted as income, based on their market value. Charles Murray argued that these benefits made it "possible for almost anyone to place themselves [*sic*] above the official poverty level" (Murray, 1994, p. 64). Going even further with this argument, Gilder (1981) suggested that the poor receive benefits every bit as valuable as a middle-class job because they have more leisure time and they work "off the books." Others have argued that the poverty threshold should be revised to include assets as well as income because some poor people own their homes (see Oliver & Shapiro, 1990).

On the other hand, others think the federal poverty threshold underestimates financial hardship. Mollie Orshansky later suggested that the threshold she developed was at least 40 percent too low because the multiplier used to estimate total budget at three times food costs was too small (Chambers, 1982). Recent estimates suggest that low-income families in the United States spend roughly one quarter of their income on food, compared with a national average of about 12 percent. This would suggest a multiplier of 4 rather than 3 (see Ruggles, 1990).

Other critics of the poverty threshold focus on the Economy Food Plan itself. Some note that it was intended as a *temporary* budget and is inadequate for sustaining health over an extended period. The plan also places heavy demands on homemakers. It requires a shopper to buy the least expensive commodities; to transport and store large quantities of food; and to have the time, energy, and ability to prepare meals from basic staples (Chalfant, 1985; Wilson, 1987).

Another problem with the federal poverty threshold is its failure to take into account regional differences in the cost of living. A family of four would be hard pressed to live on $24,300 (the 2016 poverty threshold) in New York City, but they might find it easier in Mississippi.[2] The threshold also does not take into account other circumstances that might affect a family's needs, such as chronic illness or disability.

There are other ways to measure financial hardship. Apart from the United States, most developed countries are shifting to a focus on relative poverty. Countries in the European Union (EU), for instance, treat poverty as a proportion (50 or 60 percent) of median income. Some nations focus on the deficits caused by poverty, such as inability to purchase housing or education. In these countries, residents are surveyed about whether, for instance, they are able to afford home repairs or a winter coat. The United Nations Development Programme treats poverty as the inability to secure basic needs, such as food (United Nations, 2010). **The World Bank**, on the other hand, argues that global poverty should be measured on the basis of the "dollar-a-day" measure. Established in 1990, this measure set the poverty line at $1 per day which, it argued "was a typical line amongst low-income countries." (The World Bank, n.d.) World Bank researchers take the position that anyone with incomes below this amount is indisputably poor. More recently, the measure has been adjusted for inflation, such that it could now be referred to as the "$1.90 a day" measure of poverty. (The World Bank, 2010).

Using a different approach, U.S. researchers Holden and Smeeding (1990) focused on financial vulnerability. They noted five sources of vulnerability that affect the elderly: lack of health insurance, limited assets, Social Security benefits that preclude Medicaid eligibility, high housing costs, and chronic disability. Using these, they concluded that 35 percent of older people experienced financial vulnerability. Robert Binstock (1985) suggested that measures of poverty incorporate expenditure patterns as well as ability to cope with hardship.

BOX 5.1 Asset-Based Anti-Poverty Strategies

Definitions of poverty have historically been based on income, but a growing number of activists and scholars (most notably Michael Sherraden at Washington University) advocate for an asset-based approach to understanding and ameliorating financial deprivation. It is based on the simple observation that low-income Americans not only lack income but also lack assets. Indeed, over 8 percent of U.S. households do not have any relationship with banks or credit unions (Federal Deposit Insurance Corporation, 2012). These "unbanked" Americans rely on "alternative financial services" like money orders, non-bank check cashing, payday lenders, and refund anticipation loans, all of which entail significant fees, interest, and/or penalties that further disadvantage their vulnerable households.

An asset-based approach to fighting poverty generates interventions designed to enhance the financial capability of the disadvantaged by addressing both their ability and their opportunity to accumulate assets. These efforts range from micro-loan programs around the world to "matched savings accounts" and financial clinics here in the United States. Proponents of this approach target predatory loan practices and consumer fraud, and advocate for the redistribution of public asset subsidies (like tax-free IRAs or the mortgage interest deduction) toward those who are disadvantaged.

---

[2]This issue is at least partially addressed when the threshold distinguishes between Alaska and Hawaii and the 48 contiguous states. The poverty threshold for Alaska is 1.25 times that used in the 48 states, while that of Hawaii is 1.15 times the mainland threshold.

But these alternative measures would involve complex assessments. The federal poverty threshold, on the other hand, is easy to administer and its long-term use allows for historic comparisons. As a result, it will probably remain the dominant measure of financial hardship used in the United States.

LO 5-2   Understand the Values and Beliefs That Inform American Policies Toward the Poor

EP 3a

Accurate or not, public values and beliefs about poverty influence social policy. Some of these focus on how society ought to *respond* to poverty, such as religious teachings about charity, punitive responses to the poor, and the notion of poverty as motivation. Other perspectives focus on *explaining* poverty. These include "human capital" approaches, "culture of poverty" explanations, "restricted opportunity" explanations, and "pauperization" arguments. These ideas emerged in diverse historical contexts; each perspective represents a distinct outlook on the individual and structural factors that contribute to poverty, and each supports a different approach to intervention.

RELIGIOUS BELIEFS ABOUT CHARITY

Charity is central to the teachings of most world religions. Buddhism teaches that "emancipation of the heart through love and charity" is the most important form of righteousness. Islamic teachings view charity not as a "favor done by the giver" but as "spending for the cause of Allah … as a means to purify the soul of the giver and to … unite him with his poor brother" (Center for Muslim-Jewish Engagement, n.d.).

Ancient Jewish doctrines treated care of the poor as a matter of justice, teaching that not only did the well-off have a duty to give to charity, but the poor had a right (and even a duty) to receive it. The Talmud, a collection of biblical texts accompanied by rabbinical commentaries, prescribes in careful detail how relief is to be administered. Under Talmudic law, a poor man should receive "Sufficient for his needs in that which he wanteth … [if he is hungry] he should be fed; if he needs clothing, he should be clothed; if he lacks household utensils, they should be purchased for him" (Trattner, 1989, p. 3).

Christianity retained this emphasis on care of the poor. The New Testament emphasizes that the soul's entry into heaven depends on deeds of mercy and charity. Most telling in this regard is the description of Judgment Day in the Gospel of St. Matthew: "And the King shall answer and say unto them, Verily, I say unto you, Inasmuch as ye have done it unto one of the least of these my brethren, ye have done it unto me" (Matthew 25:40). In Christian teachings, care of the poor is a matter of both justice and charity. The needy have a right to assistance, and the spiritual well-being of the rich depends on charity. The Christian notion of salvation requires the faithful to care for the poor, not only for altruistic reasons but also for the benefit of their own souls.

As early as the sixth century A.D., care of the poor was an integral part of some Christian monastic traditions. Using income from land holdings and donations, monks cared for the needy who came to their doors, as well as those who lived in nearby communities. Medieval hospitals, many of which were attached to monasteries, also provided services to the disadvantaged.[3]

---

[3]This discussion draws heavily from Walter Trattner, *From Poor Law to Welfare State: A History of Social Welfare in America* (New York: Free Press, 1989).

Later, during the Middle Ages, the Catholic Church organized the first comprehensive system of relief in Europe. From the 12th through the 14th centuries, relief for the poor operated under the direction of the Medieval Poor Law, a set of policies developed by church leaders to specify relief measures for the indigent. Under this system, "a poor man was considered an honorable man, and the only test for aid was need" (Segalman & Basu, 1981, p. 60).

Thus, religious approaches to poverty do not attempt to explain why some people are poor and others are not. Poverty is treated as neither individual nor societal failure but an integral part of the human condition, offering the opportunity, requirement, or possibility of personal charity. This view stands in sharp contrast to approaches that treat poverty as a crime.

POVERTY AS CRIME

Punitive responses to poverty are based on the belief that the poor are lazy and intemperate and they need punishment to overcome their evil ways. Most obvious among these "undeserving" poor are individuals who are able-bodied but do not work. But their ranks also include alcoholics and spendthrifts.

In 1834, Benjamin Disraeli argued that England's new poor law, "announces to the world that in England poverty is a crime." (Himmelfarb, 1983, p. 182). But the new law reflected a tradition that extended back hundreds of years. During the 16th-century England assigned severe punishments to able-bodied beggars. As Trattner (1989) reported, "They were to be brought to the market place and 'there to be tyed to the end of a carte naked and be beten with whyppes throughe out … tyll [their bodies] be blody by reason of suche whypping'" (p. 7).

Modern approaches to the poor are seldom as harsh but are nonetheless punitive. The poor are no longer subjected to whipping but to shame and indifference. Lengthy waits are one form of punishment. In *Tyranny of Kindness,* Theresa Funiciello noted a sign in a New York welfare office that said, "NO MATTER WHAT TIME YOUR APPOINT-MENT IS, IF YOU ARE NOT HERE BY 8:30 A.M. YOU WILL NOT BE SEEN" (Funiciello, 1993, p. 3). Likewise, the enthusiasm in some state legislatures for administering drug tests to recipients of public benefits introduces additional humiliating procedures even as it delivers profits to private testing firms (American Civil Liberties Union, 2013). As we will see below, this punitive approach is consistent with the needs of a capitalist economy.

POVERTY AS MOTIVATION

Some have argued that in preindustrial nations there is no individual poverty. Families, communities, and even nations as a whole may experience deprivation, but individuals are not left to experience poverty alone, and the poor are not isolated as "other" or "different." Under this view, capitalist industrial economies require poverty because they need a large unemployed segment in their labor force. The hardship and embarrassment associated with unemployment are seen as necessary motivators that make workers willing to leave their homes and seek employment in industrial centers where they will labor for low wages in difficult conditions. Herbert Gans noted that poverty could be eliminated if the wealthy chose to do so. The fact that they have not done so indicates their need for a reliable source of cheap labor (Gans, 1971).

Regulation of charity in the interest of maintaining a labor force predates the industrial revolution. As we will see when we examine poverty interventions, the British parliament enacted the Statute of Labourers in 1348 to ensure that all able-bodied people were forced to work. Later, the **Elizabethan Poor Law** would require anyone capable of working to do so, if only to earn the right to receive assistance.

As Antonia noted, TANF benefits are quite limited. This illustrates the principle of "less eligibility" and reflects the belief that poverty is an important motivator. Under this principle, no one on relief should be as well-off as the lowest-paid laborer. Less eligibility is an integral part of U.S. poverty interventions. It is manifest in the low level of benefits provided by public assistance programs and by humiliating administrative practices such as those described above.

HUMAN CAPITAL EXPLANATIONS OF POVERTY

Some explanations of poverty focus on the skills, education, and experience or "human capital" that an individual brings to the marketplace. According to this view, the poor simply have inadequate or outdated skills and experience. Neither the individual nor the system is responsible for poverty, which is seen as the inevitable consequence of a dynamic economy. With rapidly changing technology, workers need to constantly develop new skills. If, for whatever reason, they do not bring the appropriate skills to the labor market, they will not secure the jobs necessary to keep them out of poverty. Further, workers in dead-end, low-paying jobs are those who did not receive the education or training necessary to get a better job.

The association between educational attainment and poverty offers empirical support for this perspective. Figure 5.1 illustrates that association. Clearly people with higher levels of education enjoy much lower risks of poverty.

Human capital explanations of poverty blame neither the individual nor the society, and they bring a (some would say simplistic) spirit of optimism to the task of reducing poverty.

FIGURE 5.1 Educational Attainment and Poverty

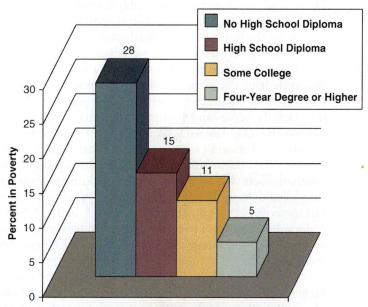

SOURCE: U.S. Census Bureau, Current Population Survey, 2014 American Community Survey, Subject Tables "Educational Attainment" (S1501) (https://www.census.gov/acs/www/data/data-tables-and-tools/subject-tables/) (http://www.census.gov/hhes/www/cpstables/032012/pov/toc.htm).

Interventions based on this outlook might incorporate job training and education for the poor. They might offer subsidized employment designed to improve job skills. Federal job training programs, such as those funded under the federal Workforce Investment Act (WIA) of 1998 are examples of this approach to alleviating poverty. The WIA funds job training for dislocated workers and low-income youth to enable them to succeed in the modern labor market. The Ticket to Work program described in Chapter 4 also reflects this perspective.

CULTURE OF POVERTY EXPLANATIONS

The term **culture of poverty** was coined by Oscar Lewis, an anthropologist who studied poor families in Mexico and Puerto Rico. In his words, "The culture of poverty is both an adaptation and a reaction of the poor to their marginal position in a class-stratified, highly individuated, capitalistic society. It represents an effort to cope with feelings of hopelessness and despair which develop from the realization of the improbability of achieving success in terms of the values and goals of the larger society" (Lewis, 1965, p. xliv).

The culture of poverty is a distinct set of values that arise in the context of hopeless disadvantage. These include a present-time orientation that seeks immediate gratification and precludes long-term planning or deferred reward. According to this view, people raised in poverty prefer the instant rush of intoxication to the sustained effort of education. They may be seen as improvident or lazy, when in fact they have learned that effort is not rewarded, life is short, and pleasures are rare. Their behavior represents an adaption to lifelong—even intergenerational—poverty. Drug addiction or teenage pregnancy can be understood as the natural consequence of growing up in poverty. Crime may be the logical reaction to repeated failure, and family breakup the inevitable result of a chaotic and unrestrained social milieu. Yet, as Segalman and Basu note, "The coping mechanisms by which the poor adjust to their state also serve to prevent them and their children from ever moving out of poverty" (1981, p. 13). An important component of this view holds that victims of poverty cannot make use of opportunities that present themselves later in life because they have been irreparably damaged by their culture.

Several authors have focused on describing the culture of poverty. Noting an inability to plan for the future or defer gratification among the poor, Edward Banfield of Harvard University argued that "extreme present-orientedness, not lack of income or wealth is the principal cause of poverty in the sense of the culture of poverty" (Banfield, 1970, 125–126). Acknowledging that some people become poor through accidents or misfortunes that are short-lived, he argued that others would be poor regardless of their circumstances because they lack the values and strengths necessary to succeed. Giving them money would be pointless because they would squander it on nonessentials.

Nicolas Lemann (1986) suggested that residents of black ghettos in inner cities inherited the values and traits of sharecroppers. Most of them, he noted, come from rural Southern roots, where sharecroppers could neither own property nor save money and thus failed to learn the values necessary to preserve family stability and accumulate financial reserves (see Segalman & Basu, 1981). In 1969, Senator Daniel Patrick Moynihan endorsed the culture of poverty argument in his controversial book *Maximum Feasible Misunderstanding,* which argued that poverty among African Americans reflected the failure of their family life.

Apart from the question of accuracy, culture of poverty explanations apply only to lifelong, intergenerational poverty. Interventions based on such explanations attempt to change the values of low-income adults or to teach their children a different set of values. Historically, the latter objective was used to justify removing children from their homes and placing them in middle-class settings where they were expected to learn the values of thrift, abstinence, and productivity. Two striking examples of this practice are found in the history of U.S. child welfare practices. During the 19th century, Charles Loring Brace of the Children's Aid Society removed children from urban tenements and placed them with middle-class farm families. Similarly, from the 19th well into the 20th century, Native American children were removed from their homes on reservations and lodged with middle-class white families. Other interventions based on this viewpoint simply exposed poor adults to middle-class role models (e.g., in settlement houses) in the hope that they would absorb new habits and values.

RESTRICTED OPPORTUNITY THEORIES OF POVERTY

Like culture of poverty explanations, **restricted opportunity** theories about poverty surfaced in the 20th century. But where the culture of poverty explanation attributes poverty to personal attributes, restricted opportunity explanations focus on structural barriers that prevent individuals from securing the education or jobs necessary for financial success. Noting that "the playing field is not level," proponents of this view hold that institutional discrimination on the basis of gender, race, or other characteristics restricts opportunities and increases a person's risk of poverty. They question the notion that America provides exceptional opportunities for upward mobility, noting the role of parental wealth in determining the life chances of children (see Pfeffer & Hallsten, 2012).

Proponents note that poverty is not randomly distributed in the U.S. population. Female-headed households are more vulnerable than those headed by men; people of color are more likely to be poor at any age than Caucasians; people with disabilities experience high rates of poverty; and children who grow up in impoverished conditions face the strong likelihood of spending their lives in poverty.

This greater risk of poverty can be explained with reference to discriminatory practices in education and the workplace. Some of the programs established under President Lyndon Johnson's War on Poverty during the 1960s reflected this perspective, trying to increase the educational, employment, and political opportunities available to the poor. Civil rights laws and affirmative action, designed to provide equal opportunities for women and people of color, also reflect the restricted opportunity explanation of poverty.

THE PAUPERIZATION ARGUMENT

In 1994, President Bill Clinton promised to "end welfare as we know it." He was certainly not the first U.S. policy maker to make this promise, which reflected a widespread belief that welfare did not *relieve* poverty but *caused* it by fostering dependence on a system that destroyed the incentive to work. Under this view, the welfare system created "paupers" (permanently poor people) from those who might otherwise have succeeded. If there were no welfare, the pauperization argument holds, those who receive public assistance would be motivated to find jobs and pull themselves out of poverty.

In itself, this idea was not unique to the 20th century. Nineteenth-century advocates of poorhouses raised the specter of pauperization to criticize the practice of **outdoor relief** (providing financial support to people in their homes, rather than requiring them to enter a poorhouse). Indeed, the pauperization argument has been used frequently to criticize systems of cash assistance for the poor.

The following section considers the development of poverty interventions in England and in America. The Eurocentric scope of the discussion does not imply that other parts of the world have nothing to contribute to our understanding of poverty, but it does reflect the historic realities that have shaped U.S. policies and programs.

LO 5-3 Become Familiar with the History of Poverty Interventions in the United States

EP 3a
EP 5c

Poverty interventions bring out deep-seated ambivalence, particularly in capitalist nations where we see a fundamental incompatibility between the allocation principle used in most assistance programs ("to each according to his need") and that of a capitalist economy ("to each according to his product"). What roles have poverty interventions played in these economies? Are they expressions of compassion? Expansions of human rights? Vehicles for "regulating the poor"? Or tools to manage the surplus labor pool? See what you think after reading this brief review of their history.

ENGLISH APPROACHES TO POVERTY

In 1348, an outbreak of bubonic plague decimated the populations of several European nations. In England a labor shortage led to the passage of the Statute of Labourers, which forbade giving charity to able-bodied beggars. The law also set maximum wages and imposed travel restrictions to ensure that laborers would stay within their home parishes and accept employment there, rather than traveling to pursue opportunities elsewhere. This law is a striking illustration of the use of poverty policies to control the labor force, based on the idea of poverty as a motivator. It also represents an early policy constraint on private relief efforts.

Two hundred years later, during the 16th century, England passed a series of laws to regulate begging. These laws established a clear distinction between the "deserving" and the "undeserving" poor. Severe punishment was meted out to able-bodied people who were not inclined to work, but those unable to work were assigned areas where they could beg. In 1536 the Act for the Punishment of Sturdy Vagabonds and Beggars elaborated both the punishments for undeserving beggars (which included branding, enslavement, and execution) and government relief for the deserving poor. The act directed local public officials to collect donations from the churches for poor relief. In this way, government poverty policy moved from the regulation of beggars to the administration of relief in partnership with the church. It provided for training of indigent youth and community service employment for unemployed adults, reflecting the human capital explanation of poverty.

Later in the 16th century, the parish system was unable to collect sufficient voluntary donations to meet the need for relief. A new statute called the Elizabethan Poor Law was passed to levy a tax for the care of the poor and create an administrative structure for the management of relief efforts. Also known as the Poor Law of 1601, this statute remained essentially unchanged for 250 years and served as the foundation of the measures European colonists put in place in the New World. Its basic principles included the following.

- *Family responsibility.* Parents were legally responsible for supporting their children and grandchildren, and conversely, children were responsible for their aged parents and grandparents.
- *Local responsibility.* Aid was managed through local units of government called parishes, and strict residency requirements discouraged vagrancy. Indigents who did not meet residency requirements were returned to their home parishes. Community relief efforts provided for needy neighbors, not for wandering strangers.
- *Differential treatment.* The law distinguished between the deserving and the undeserving poor. It recognized three types of deserving poor: children, the able-bodied

unemployed, and those incapacitated by disability or age (the "impotent"). The undeserving included those who were too lazy, shiftless, or drunk to support themselves.

- *Preference for work.* Public relief was not meant to be an alternative to employment. Those who could work were expected to do so. Children were employed in apprenticeships, the able-bodied unemployed were given jobs, and the undeserving were sent to workhouses to perform forced labor. Only the disabled were excused from the work requirement.
- *Public assistance through compulsory taxation.* Under the Poor Law, taxes were collected to finance the relief of poverty. Every household in a parish was taxed, and the money was collected by overseers of the poor. Those who did not pay the tax were threatened with imprisonment.

The Elizabethan Poor Law served as the foundation for later U.S. interventions to alleviate poverty and maintain social equilibrium. Echoes of its principles reverberate in the categorical eligibility requirements for SSI and Medicaid, the work preference manifest in TANF requirements, and the use of taxes to fund public assistance.

AMERICAN APPROACHES TO POVERTY

Relief in colonial times was a chancy affair—a person's care depended not only on the town in which he or she lived but also on good relationships with community leaders. Still, poverty could be managed on a case-by-case basis until the 19th century, when needs exceeded the capacity of local governments. Expanded poverty programs were accompanied by widespread intolerance for public relief and contempt for the poor. These attitudes would lead to the growth of poorhouses. Social work emerged in this period, with its contradictory approaches to poverty: the **Charity Organization Societies** and the **Settlement Movement**.

In time, the Great Depression would convince 20th-century Americans of the need for a federal system of relief, and a social worker (Frances Perkins) would champion the New Deal. Later in the 20th century it became difficult at times to separate rhetoric from reality and message from messenger. For example, President Lyndon Johnson declared an "unconditional war on poverty," yet his Great Society programs did little to expand relief for the poor. President Richard Nixon spoke ardently against welfare, yet his administration was marked by expanded benefits for the poor. Republican Presidents Ronald Reagan and George H. W. Bush were at the forefront of anti-welfare rhetoric, but it would take a Democrat (Bill Clinton) to dismantle the federal relief entitlement for children.

Poverty Interventions in Early America

America was not colonized as a refuge for the poor of Europe. Instead, the New World was a haven for adventurers and religious minorities. The first permanent settlement was established at Jamestown in 1607. The Virginia Company sent a group of adventurers to identify ways of exploiting the region's natural resources. Women joined the settlement in 1608. The pilgrims didn't come to New England until the English civil war was imminent. Refugees from that conflict, the pilgrims—craftsmen, small shopkeepers, and farmers— had limited means but were not destitute.[4] Later, colonists who could not pay for their passage financed their trips by selling their labor as indentured servants. Although

---

[4]During the 19th century the British shipped prisoners and beggars to Australia, but this practice was not widespread in North America. Nonetheless, it was a significant concern to the colonial leaders. In 1776, Benjamin Franklin was sent to England to protest the transportation of criminals to the colonies.

these servants entered the colonies without resources, the terms of their indenture were generous, and in at least one state (Pennsylvania) they received land grants at the end of their service.

During the early years of shared deprivation, government programs to alleviate poverty were a luxury the colonies could ill afford. Individual misfortune, such as disease or bereavement, met with neighborly kindness—or at least, assistance.[5] But the number of people living in poverty—including widows and orphans, those disabled by age or disease, and others—increased.

By the mid-17th century most of the colonies had initiated formal provisions that made local taxpayers responsible for supporting their poor neighbors. Modeled on the Elizabethan Poor Law, the measures reflected the principles of family and local responsibility. Care of the poor was provided by the town in which they lived, using one of three approaches. The most straightforward was to send the needy to live with their kin. The second involved placing the poor in homes of non-relatives at public expense. The fee was usually set at an auction where those in need were offered to the lowest bidders, with the fees paid by the town. A third approach was sometimes used when people needed only temporary aid. In this practice, called **outdoor assistance** or **outdoor relief**, money was given directly to the person in need.

Under the principle of local responsibility, people who were displaced or had left their homes of origin were not entitled to aid. Most towns discouraged needy strangers from staying. Some "warned away" visitors who might become a burden, prohibited the sale of land to strangers without official permission, and required residents who brought in servants to support them. Port towns, troubled by the arrival of needy immigrants, required captains of vessels to post bonds for each passenger they discharged. In some cases, the towns forced captains to return the destitute to their points of origin.

Despite these efforts, strangers kept arriving and ultimately, the "unsettled poor" proved the system's undoing. Wars and migration overwhelmed towns' ability to provide assistance, as refugees from Indian wars arrived with little more than the clothing on their backs. Eventually, towns asked colonial authorities for funds to provide relief for these strangers. Thus, the colonial treasury began to reimburse towns for the care of the unsettled poor and the principle of local responsibility began to erode.

Relief in the New Nation

The War of Independence left many widowed, orphaned, or disabled, and it disrupted economic ties to England and other European nations. Although private philanthropy supplemented public relief efforts, local relief organizations were overwhelmed by requests for assistance. Many of these came from people who did not meet local residency requirements. As a result, one of the first actions undertaken by the new states was to establish administrative structures for poor relief. New York was the first state to do so, setting up the Committee on Superintendence of the Poor.[6] At this stage, although the U.S. Constitution allowed for federal action to promote the general welfare, the federal government left poor relief to state and local governments.

---

[5]A possible exception to this neighborly assistance was the treatment of witches, who were usually single older women of limited means who violated community norms.

[6]The state of New York was at the forefront of poverty relief for several decades. New York is the only state that addresses relief of poverty in its constitution, and it led the nation in establishing relief during the Great Depression.

Relief in 19th-Century America

Demand for workers to fuel industrial expansion triggered new criticism of outdoor relief in the 19th century. Economists argued that relief interfered with the natural relationship between capital and labor by providing an alternative to factory work. Other critics suggested outdoor relief created dependency. Still others noted that the needy were embracing the notion of a right to relief. Coupled with the taxes that financed relief efforts, this ingratitude was seen as a barrier to private charity.

These arguments were effective in both England and the United States. In England, the Poor Law Reform Bill was passed to eliminate outdoor relief and relegate the disadvantaged to almshouses and workhouses. Unlike their counterparts across the Atlantic, American poverty officials did not completely dismantle the system of outdoor relief. But they did expand **indoor relief**, sending many of the nation's poor to institutions.

Most states assigned responsibility for poorhouses to the counties. For example, in 1824, New York enacted the County Poorhouse Act, calling for the construction of one

---

A HUMAN PERSPECTIVE   Advocacy: Historic Organization Continues Its Tradition of Advocacy and Support

Contributed by Saliwe M. Kawewe, Southern Illinois University at Carbondale, School of Social Work, and president, Delmo Housing Corp.

Sharecropping farm families in the 1930s had limited resources and few options, living in near-perpetual bondage to landowners. The Southern Tenant Farmers Union (STFU) was established in 1934 in Memphis, Tennessee, to seek better working conditions, freedom, and homeownership for the croppers in the Mississippi Delta. Leadership included Reverend Owen Whitfield, an African American sharecropper and lay preacher of socialist bent; H. L. Mitchell, a white man with links to New Deal agencies; and Thad Snow, a planter sympathetic to the cause. Over time, many leaders, organizations, and churches in St. Louis and beyond were appalled by the croppers' living conditions, including faculty and students from the George Warren Brown School of Social Work at Washington University, St. Louis.

The STFU used a variety of tactics, from demonstrations such as the Roadside Demonstration of 1939 to media campaigns and consultations with leading politicians. Their efforts produced results. Between 1940 and 1941, the Farm Security Administration (FSA) built low-income rental houses for tenants and croppers. Organized as "villages," the houses were located on ten plantations, with seven designated for whites and three for blacks.

When the FSA was phased out, planters hoped to take over the housing themselves and evict the tenants. Instead, in 1945 the Delmo Housing Corporation (DHC) was formed as a self-help project to help tenants purchase their homes. As a result of the DHC's intervention, the villages continue to provide housing for low-income farm families.

The situation of tenant farmers who were the early beneficiaries of DHC services has changed, but the organization has survived, adapting its operations in response to human need, availability of resources, and changing political environments. It has established credit unions in the villages and made small loans to support home-based enterprises. Today, the DHC operates a thrift shop and conducts voter education and leadership development programs. For those in need of more extensive medical care, clinics have been established and transportation is provided. The DHC has advocated for improvements in local educational systems to make them more responsive to the needs of tenants' children, and it has established day care centers and recreational facilities.

Despite pervasive racial tensions, the DHC maintains its tradition of racial diversity, with representatives from diverse origins serving on its board of directors and among its volunteers. It is organized as a tax-exempt entity.

Economic conditions in Missouri's "Bootheel" are stagnant, and the region experiences a brain drain similar to that reported in many Third World nations. Promising young people migrate north in pursuit of career advancement. The DHC is working to stem this tide, providing scholarships and leadership to shore up regional opportunities. The work of the DHC is as relevant today as it was when the organization was founded 60 years ago—a testament to its strong leadership and community support.

or more poorhouses in each county. These institutions proliferated. For most, they served as temporary shelters in times of need. Families might move into poorhouses during an especially harsh winter or stay there during periods of temporary unemployment. Over time, more and more elders spent their final months in poorhouses, so these facilities were precursors to today's nursing homes.

The end of the Civil War saw a new population in need of assistance—newly freed African Americans in Southern states. For several million formerly enslaved people, the abrupt change in status brought needs for education, employment, and assistance. To address these, a Bureau of Refugees, Freedmen, and Abandoned Lands was established in the U.S. War Department two months before the war ended. This agency, usually called the Freedmen's Bureau, took what today would be called a holistic approach. As Trattner (1989) pointed out,

> [The Freedmen's Bureau] served as a relief agency on an unprecedented scale, distributing twenty-two million rations to needy persons in the devastated South. It served as an employment agency … a settlement agency, leasing certain abandoned properties to black cultivators … it employed doctors and maintained hospitals … it encouraged the founding of black schools and then provided them with financial aid … it served as legal agency, maintaining courts in which both civil and criminal cases involving ex-slaves were dealt with in an informal and just manner. (p. 79)

In its second year of operation, the **Freedmen's Bureau** triggered controversy between President Andrew Johnson (a Southerner) and Congress.[7] Congress voted to extend the Bureau, but Johnson vetoed the measure, arguing that the Constitution did not permit a federal system of relief. Congress overrode his veto, and the Bureau continued to operate for six years. In 1876, the Freedmen's Bureau was closed. It had clearly demonstrated that the federal government could deliver comprehensive relief to those for whom states either could not or would not provide.

By the end of the 19th century, the United States had been transformed from a small local economy to a world-class manufacturer. This industrialization brought an explosion of jobs in settings that can only generously be described as sweatshops. Textile mills in the newly reconstructed South offered much-needed jobs to white and African American workers, but they were jobs with low pay and horrible working conditions. Rapid economic growth created huge fortunes, such as those enjoyed by William Henry Vanderbilt, John D. Rockefeller, and J. P. Morgan, while raising the general standard of living. Growth also brought rising demand for laborers willing to endure periodic unemployment and difficult working conditions. Public support for government relief efforts waned.

The dominant economic philosophy was social Darwinism. Under this view, people who did not flourish in the booming economy were inferior specimens. Public care for them not only undermined private charity but also weakened the human race by permitting the "unfit" to survive and reproduce. Members of the economic elite found in social Darwinism a philosophy that was closely aligned with their interests. In this intellectual climate, public relief efforts deteriorated.

The decline in public relief was not accompanied by a drop in poverty. The 19th century saw a series of financial crises at 10- to 20-year intervals that led John Kenneth Galbraith to remark later that the times between crises corresponded "roughly with the time it took people to forget the last disaster" (Strouse, 1998, p. 66). Panics disrupted the stock market and threw millions out of work. Private charities raced to respond, and the result was a chaotic proliferation of organizations, all serving the same indigents.

This disorganization horrified many charity workers, who argued that private relief efforts needed to be rationalized along "scientific" lines. So when the Reverend Stephen

---

[7]Johnson's ongoing battles with Congress eventually led to the nation's first presidential impeachment hearings.

Humphreys Gurteen proposed organizing charities into a charity organization society (COS) for Buffalo, New York, his suggestion met eager acceptance. In coming years, charity organization societies, with names like Society for Organizing Charity, Associated Charities, and Bureaus of Charities, proliferated.

Charity organization societies did not provide relief. Instead they conducted detailed investigations to distinguish the worthy from the unworthy poor and referred those deemed worthy to relief agencies. The goal was to raise the morals of the poor by exposing them to well-intentioned volunteers from middle- and upper-class backgrounds. Long before the term "culture of poverty" was coined, this intervention reflected the belief that upright role models could improve the values of the poor. Thus, "friendly visiting" was born. Mary Richmond's 1917 book, *Social Diagnosis,* widely considered the first systematic description of social casework, grew out of the experiences of COS visitors.

The movement was not without its critics. Jane Addams was one of the most vocal. She argued that charity organization societies were "cold and unemotional, too impersonal, and stingy ... pervaded by a negative pseudo-scientific spirit." Their vocabulary, she argued, was one of "don't give," "don't act," "don't do this or that"; "all they have for the poor is advice, and for that they probably send the Almighty a bill" (Trattner, 1989, p. 91).

Of course, Addams was committed to the settlement house movement, which differed in philosophy, approach, and goals. Under the COS philosophy, indigence was the result of individual moral failure. Members of the settlement movement viewed poverty within a broader social context. Whereas COS workers carefully investigated individual worthiness, settlement workers focused their equally systematic research efforts on the social conditions of urban poverty. Where the COS movement fostered social casework, the settlement house movement set the stage for community organization. The primary goal of COS intervention was to improve the morals of the worthy poor. Settlement interventions did not distinguish between worthy and unworthy, but aimed to reduce class divisions and improve living conditions in the slums. The testy relationship between COS workers and settlement workers reverberates today in the tensions between social workers committed to individual treatment and those who focus on social change.

At the end of the 19th century, the relief of poverty was largely a private affair, with social work pioneers in leading positions. Jane Addams founded Hull House in Chicago to reduce poverty through social change, while Richmond and her colleagues in charity organization societies conducted friendly visits to improve the morals of the poor. The public role was generally limited to care in poorhouses and other institutions for the "dependent, defective and delinquent" (Leiby, 1978). The role of government in poverty relief and amelioration would change dramatically in the next century.

Twentieth-Century Approaches to Poverty in America

At the beginning of the 20th century, huge personal fortunes were made through monopolies in oil and railroads. "Robber barons" such as John D. Rockefeller (Standard Oil), Andrew Carnegie (steel magnate), and Cornelius Vanderbilt (New York railroads) controlled government and industry. Inequality reached extremes that had not been possible in an agricultural economy. Care of the poor was left to private charities, and outdoor relief was minimal. In these conditions the Progressive movement was born.

The **Progressive era** spanned the first two decades of the 20th century and marked a sea change in the role of government. First on the reform agenda was eliminating government corruption. Legislative initiatives addressed civil service reforms and revised election procedures. Leaders of the Progressive movement also set out to ease the suffering of industrial laborers and the poor through child labor laws, health and safety laws, antitrust provisions, and establishment of the progressive income tax.

The notion that government should play a role in caring for the poor was accompanied by increased acceptance of outdoor relief. Some date the changing attitude to the 1909 White House Conference on Children, convened by President Theodore Roosevelt. Conference participants, 200 of the nation's elite, concluded that children should be cared for in their own homes, and that the "home should not be broken up for reasons of poverty" (Trattner, 1989, p. 200). Like their contemporaries, conference participants were opposed to public relief, but they recognized the problems that developed when families were forced into poorhouses. To keep families in their homes, they thought **widows' pensions** should be funded by private charities under the direction and supervision of the charity organization societies. In actual practice, however, many private agencies refused to give funds to women who were capable of working. Widows were forced to work, often for long hours at low wages, to support children they were unable to supervise.

Advocates of widows' or mothers' pensions argued that it was ultimately less costly, in both human and economic terms, to give public assistance to women with dependent children. This approach would preserve children from neglect, prevent juvenile delinquency, and protect the health of mothers. Proponents noted that the boom and bust nature of the industrial economy exposed workers' families to financial insecurity and jeopardized the well-being of children. They thought mothers were performing a valuable public service in caring for their children. Not only were they the best possible caregivers, but they did not belong in the workplace.

Dorothea Lange/Stringer/Archive Photos/Getty Images

▶ Dorothea Lange, who took this iconic photo, explained, "I did not ask her name or her history. She told me her age, that she was 32. She said they had been living on frozen vegetables from the surrounding fields and birds that the children killed. She had just sold the tires from her car to buy food." (Library of Congress, n.d.)

Many social workers—especially those employed by private charity organizations—opposed widows' pensions. They protested against transforming voluntary personal charity into an impersonal entitlement, arguing that entitlements would undermine the work ethic of the poor. Their arguments would prove unsuccessful.

In April 1911, Missouri became the first state to enact a widows' pension law that provided cash assistance to mothers with dependent children. By 1935, all but two states—South Carolina and Georgia—offered public assistance to widows with dependent children. Over time, these programs were extended to include other single mothers. A few recipients were single mothers with "illegitimate" children. Others were wives of men who were incapacitated, imprisoned, or otherwise unavailable to support their families. In what were termed "suitable home" provisions, mothers were required to maintain healthy and supportive environments for their children. These widows' pensions set the stage for Title IV of the 1935 Social Security Act, which would establish a grant-in-aid program known as Aid to Dependent Children.

The Depression and the New Deal

Prior to the Depression, only a few crusaders saw relief as a public responsibility. Some of these advocates sought a fundamental reorganization of the U.S. economy toward a socialist model. Others preferred mandatory social insurance to buffer the effects of capitalism. But these were minority views. It took economic calamity to shake the antipathy most Americans felt toward public assistance.

For President Herbert Hoover, it would take more than economic calamity. Despite his personal background in relief work,[8] Hoover was reluctant to intervene during the Depression. He felt the economy was basically sound, and as soon as confidence had been restored, prosperity would return. Thus, he repeatedly assured the public that "the worst is over." Hoover saw in federal relief the enslavement of the American people. Consistent with this philosophy, in December 1930 the president approved an appropriation of $45 million to feed the livestock of struggling Arkansas farmers but opposed an additional $25 million to feed the farmers and their families. While the president postponed federal action, private charities around the country folded.

State and local governments did their best to shore up the failing private relief effort. The most notable effort was undertaken in New York. Then-governor **Franklin D. Roosevelt** had commissioned studies of the situation by the state's charity organization societies. He called a special legislative session to discuss the crisis, and New York became the first state to provide unemployment relief. Millions of dollars were distributed to local governments to provide subsidized work opportunities and relief. Roosevelt appointed a New York City social worker, Harry Hopkins, to direct the effort as head of the new Temporary Emergency Relief Administration.

Roosevelt's philosophy stood in sharp contrast to President Hoover's. Roosevelt saw relief as a matter of public duty, not charity. With this viewpoint, he accepted the Democratic Party's nomination for president and defeated Hoover by a landslide in 1932.

The first order of business in Roosevelt's **New Deal** was emergency relief for the unemployed. The Federal Emergency Relief Act, signed into law in May 1933, established a series of grants-in-aid that were provided to the states through the Federal Emergency Relief Administration (FERA) under the direction of Harry Hopkins. Hopkins and Roosevelt agreed that all federal relief programs were to be operated by public agencies. They felt that provision of public subsidies to private agencies resulted in corruption and

---

[8]President Hoover had organized a flood relief effort in the Mississippi Valley and served as a relief administrator during World War I. As Secretary of Commerce in 1921, he organized a conference on unemployment relief. As a result of this background, he enjoyed widespread support from social workers in the 1928 election.

inefficiency. Thus, the relief and commodity distribution programs operated under FERA were administered by governmental units. Along with the FERA, a veritable alphabet soup of programs was created. Most emphasized work in exchange for relief, an approach that would prove popular with Americans.

In addition to emergency relief measures, Roosevelt sought to establish a system of social insurance for workers. In 1934, he created the Committee on Economic Security (CES) to develop a proposal. The committee included four cabinet members and Harry Hopkins. It was headed by the nation's first female cabinet official, Frances Perkins, Secretary of Labor. Edwin E. Witte, a professor from the University of Wisconsin, served as the CES executive director. In January 1935, after six months of intensive deliberation, the committee delivered its outline for a social security program to the president.

Public assistance programs established under the Social Security Act did not involve the federal government in the direct provision of relief. Instead, they established grant-in-aid programs under which revenue from the general fund was distributed to the states. The states then established relief programs that operated in accordance with regulations set at the federal level.

These grant-in-aid programs departed from the Poor Law principle of local responsibility in financing and authority, if not in distribution. Local authorities no longer used local funds to support local indigents. Financing came from federal revenues. Eligibility requirements and grant levels were determined by a federal agency. Local agencies were left to distribute relief under the direction of federal authorities.

New Deal relief efforts touched millions but did little to end the Great Depression. All of the federal relief programs (FERA, the Civil Works Administration [CWA], and Works Progress Administration [WPA]) ended before the hardships had passed. Even the establishment of Social Security did not stimulate economic recovery. It would take World War II to pull the United States out of its most devastating economic crisis.

World War II and the War on Poverty

World War II brought prosperity to a nation tired of hardship. To reduce discrimination in the defense industry, President Roosevelt issued the famous Executive Order 8802, forbidding "discrimination in the employment of workers in defense industries or Government because of race, creed, or national origin" (Trattner, 1989, p. 279). Employment opportunities expanded and personal incomes rose for all workers, including women and people of color. Rosie the Riveter became emblematic of the need for women to work in support of national defense.

BOX 5.2   Did World War II End the Depression?

Although economists and politicians debate over what ended the Great Depression, there is no question that it ended during World War II. Perhaps government spending on the war effort triggered recovery. As the war began, American factories started making war goods to sell to countries like Britain. This growth in exports created jobs. At the same time, millions of American men went into armed services, which freed up jobs. The war did bring full employment, but some feared that its end would bring a return to Depression-era conditions. Instead, the economy continued to grow. Construction jobs were created to provide housing to returning veterans, and the technological innovations of the war set the stage for new industries such as aerospace.[9]

---

[9]Please see http://eh.net/encyclopedia/article/tassava.WWII for discussion of this issue.

The war ended in 1945, and for many the postwar years proved unusually prosperous. There were recessions (1948–1949, 1953–1954, 1957–1958), but the postwar economic boom, with its increased demand for labor, led many to believe that poverty would simply wither away in a growing economy.

By the 1950s, John Kenneth Galbraith would argue that poverty had become insignificant in his 1958 book, *The Affluent Society*. Acknowledging the existence of poverty at the fringes, Galbraith and others contributed to the widespread perception that poverty in the land of plenty was the result of inadequate skills and faulty personal choices.

Meanwhile, the welfare rolls told a different story. Not only did the number of Americans on public assistance grow, but their composition changed. Prior to Social Security, the majority of public assistance recipients were elderly. After the New Deal, they were replaced by a new class of unemployed: former agricultural workers. Technological developments from 1940 to 1960 mechanized the nation's farms, increasing productivity and reducing the number of agricultural jobs. Most of these jobs had been located in the South, and African Americans were disproportionately represented among the newly unemployed.

Some public programs for the poor expanded during this era. In 1950, the Aid to Dependent Children (ADC) program (established with the 1935 Social Security Act) was amended to include "caretaker" grants for mothers of dependent children. Later, its name was changed to Aid to Families with Dependent Children (AFDC). Social services were added to AFDC, and the Department of Health, Education and Welfare was created. The Social Security Act was further amended to include a new categorical program, Aid to the Permanently and Totally Disabled.

With these expansions and the continued elimination of agricultural jobs, relief rolls continued to grow during the 1960s. Indeed, the number of people receiving public assistance more than doubled from 1960 to 1970, while the nation's population increased by only 12 percent. John F. Kennedy brought to his presidency a commitment to eliminate poverty, hunger, and unemployment. The young president inspired belief that these ancient problems could be eliminated through determined intervention. But this spirit of optimism, like the Kennedy administration itself, would be short-lived. Under his administration, the federal poverty threshold was established, enabling the nation to systematically monitor financial hardship. Figure 5.2 illustrates trends in poverty since the establishment of the threshold.

FIGURE 5.2 Number of Americans with Incomes Below Poverty, 1959–2015

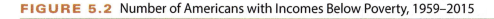

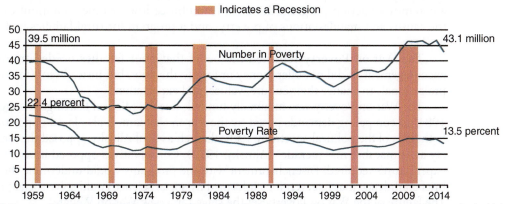

SOURCE: U.S. Bureau of the Census. Historical Poverty Tables from Current Population Survey and Income & Poverty in the United States Reports (2013 and 2014). (http://www.census.gov/hhes/www/poverty/data/historical/people.html; also https://www.census.gov/content/dam/Census/library/publications/2015/demo/p60-252.pdf).

When Kennedy took office in 1961, AFDC was expanded to include low-income, two-parent families headed by an unemployed member. This new program, called Aid to Families with Dependent Children—Unemployed Parent (AFDC-U), was designed to provide help to families who had been ineligible due to the presence of a "man in the home." AFDC-U was conceived as a temporary measure, and states were not required to participate.

The following year, the 1962 Public Welfare Amendments to the Social Security Act were signed into law. They provided federal support for state provision of social services (casework, job training, and other services) to AFDC recipients and echoed the belief of the COS movement that individual change was pivotal (perhaps even more important than material relief) in reducing poverty. Under the amendments, material relief and personal improvement were linked, and public assistance recipients found in their caseworker both an eligibility worker and a friendly visitor.

Public assistance was expanded through the 1964 passage of the Food Stamp Act, which provided for the distribution of vouchers to the needy for the purchase of food products. The Department of Agriculture was charged with administration of the program, seen by some as a way of reducing the impact of agricultural price supports on the poor.

During the mid-1960s, riots erupted in the slums of major cities. Unlike the antiwar riots that would follow, these protests targeted social conditions such as discrimination, unemployment, inadequate housing, and poverty. In 1966, welfare rights demonstrations broke out in cities across the nation. In their classic work *Regulating the Poor*, Piven and Cloward (1971) argued that the subsequent expansion of public relief programs was a response to social unrest, and hence the role of public programs (and the social workers who staffed them) was to maintain a status quo that relied on the oppression of the poor.

President Johnson established the Kerner Commission to investigate the causes of the riots and recommend ways to prevent future unrest. The commission recommended creation of a federal jobs program for the unemployed.

President Johnson had already declared an "unconditional war on poverty" in his 1964 State of the Union address, calling on Congress to support his **Great Society** programs designed to vanquish "the most ancient of mankind's enemies." These were established through the Economic Opportunity Act, which created a federal Office of Economic Opportunity. They included Volunteers in Service to America (VISTA), a domestic version of the popular Peace Corps; the Neighborhood Youth Corps, which provided jobs to unemployed teens; Operation Head Start, which offered preschool training to children; a community action program designed to mobilize low-income communities to fight the causes and manifestations of poverty; and a program for rural families and migrant workers.

The War on **Poverty** reflected the belief that poor families needed training and encouragement. It did not offer money or jobs to the poor, but instead sent (middle-class) professionals to change their culture, values, and expectations.

The War on Poverty was minimally funded, due (as Michael Harrington suggested in 1984) to competing demands posed by the war in Vietnam. It also faced opposition from both ends of the political spectrum. Radicals such as Saul Alinsky opposed the Great Society as "a macabre masquerade" (Alinsky, 1972). Conservatives opposed it because of the expenditures required. Disenchantment with the programs would undermine the nation's brief confidence that interventions informed by social science could solve social problems. The failure of the War on Poverty set the stage for a new War on Welfare.

The War on Welfare

In 1968, Richard Nixon won the presidential election by a wide margin. A staunch conservative, the new president saw in his election a mandate to dismantle the Great Society programs. A vocal critic of welfare recipients, the new president set out to do just that.

He proposed to replace the federal-state AFDC program with a single federal program called the Family Assistance Plan (FAP). The FAP would have created a federally guaranteed minimum annual income for families with children. It called for strict penalties and strong incentives to ensure that everyone who was able-bodied (including mothers of children over 3 years old) worked in paid employment.

While not generous in its benefits, the FAP would have increased the incomes of AFDC recipients in poor Southern states. It also represented a significant philosophical change because it assigned primary responsibility for public assistance to the federal government and promised a guaranteed minimum income to all Americans.

These ideas were also reflected in the "Negative Income Tax" experiments, designed to test the impact of a guaranteed minimum income in four U.S. locations between 1969 and 1978. Although the impact of the income guarantee on work effort was minimal, the experiments' findings were widely interpreted as an indictment of this approach.[10]

Many liberals, including social workers, opposed the FAP. In part, this reflected their distrust of Nixon, but in an era of high unemployment, the plan's work requirements (dubbed "workfare" by opponents) struck many as ludicrous. Welfare rights activists thought the guaranteed minimum was too low, and they were concerned that the plan would lower benefits to welfare recipients in more generous states. Conservatives were unhappy with the expanded federal role proposed under the FAP, and some objected to the notion of mothers with young children being forced to work. The president showed no commitment to the plan, and eventually it died in committee. (See Wadden, 1998, for an excellent comparison of FAP and PRWORA.)

Although Nixon struck the first blows in the War on Welfare, reforms proposed and enacted during his administration did more to enhance the status of the poor than all the Great Society programs combined. While AFDC remained unchanged, the Nixon era saw significant improvements in other public assistance programs. These included expansion of the Food Stamp Program, the establishment of cost-of-living adjustments (COLAs) for Social Security, the creation of an Earned Income Tax Credit (EITC), and the consolidation of three categorical assistance programs (Old-Age Assistance, Aid to the Blind, and Aid to the Permanently and Totally Disabled) into Supplemental Security Income (SSI). The Social Service Amendments (Title XX of the Social Security Act), which were also passed during this period, provided $2.5 billion to states to deliver social services to welfare recipients.[11] Notably, these expansions took place in an era of high unemployment (low demand for labor).

Following Nixon's resignation in 1974 in the wake of the Watergate scandal, Gerald Ford enjoyed a brief term as president. Best known for his unconditional pardon of Nixon, Ford presided over an era of "stagflation." Economic growth was stagnant, while unemployment climbed to its highest rate since 1941 (9 percent) and inflation was in double digits. The number of Americans living in poverty rose dramatically, and white American male-headed families emerged for the first time as a group at significant risk of poverty.

---

[10]For more information about the negative income tax, please see http://www.irp.wisc.edu/publications/focus/pdfs/foc232a.pdf.

[11]Title XX also marked the first time the federal government provided funding for social services to individuals with incomes above the poverty line. While welfare recipients received means-tested services, those with higher incomes could use Title XX services on a fee-for-service basis.

President Jimmy Carter contributed to the anti-welfare rhetoric of his day. In 1977, he proposed the Better Jobs and Income Program (BJIP), which would replace existing public assistance programs, such as AFDC, SSI, and Food Stamps, with a two-tiered system. For the able-bodied, the program would offer part-time subsidized jobs that paid the minimum wage or better. Those deemed unable to work included the aged, the blind, the disabled, and parents of children under 14 years old. They would receive a cash benefit more generous than that offered under existing public assistance programs. Unlike the FAP, Carter's proposal offered universal coverage (it was not restricted to families with children); benefits were more generous, and work exemptions extended to parents of children aged 3 to 14. But, perhaps most significantly, the BJIP proposed to guarantee jobs for those able to work. This work guarantee triggered opposition from conservatives. Industry representatives feared that publicly subsidized jobs would compete with those available in the private sector. Liberals opposed the work requirement, dubbing the plan yet another attempt to impose workfare on welfare recipients. After introducing his plan in Congress, the president encountered other challenges (such as the Iran hostage crisis) that undermined his ability to pursue significant domestic policy initiatives.

Ronald Reagan, a movie actor and former governor of California, swept into office with an overwhelming victory in the 1980 election. Reagan declared that the War on Poverty had been won, and he labeled welfare recipients "cheats" and "freeloaders." Reagan argued that the federal government should not be in the business of providing welfare, which he believed was best left to private charities in local communities. Thus began a 12-year period (two Reagan administrations, followed by one administration headed by Reagan's vice president, George H. W. Bush) marked by tax cuts for the wealthy, ever-expanding defense budgets, and reduced domestic spending.

Just before his reelection to a second term, President Reagan signed his "sweeping overhaul" of the nation's welfare system. The Family Welfare Reform Act, sponsored by Daniel Patrick Moynihan, had as its major provision the Job Opportunities and Basic Skills (JOBS) program. The program revised, but did not fundamentally alter, the conditions of public relief. Under JOBS, all welfare recipients had to secure jobs or enroll in job training or educational programs. Mothers of children under age 3 were exempted from the work requirement. Those who did go to work were to receive assistance with child care and transportation expenses and Medicaid for one year. The act required states to participate in the AFDC program for two-parent households, dubbed AFDC-Unemployed Parent (AFDC-U). It also included new procedures for collecting child support from noncustodial parents of children whose custodial parents received welfare assistance. The basic premise of JOBS was that welfare recipients needed little more than training and motivation to become self-sufficient, a view that would be repeated in subsequent welfare reform.

BOX 5.3   Legislating Morality

In the 1960s, states routinely cut off benefits for unmarried women who had men in their homes. Social workers who learned of these relationships were charged with terminating benefits, a role some found incompatible with their professional mission of service to the poor. "Man-in-the-house" regulations were based on the premise that these men were "substitute fathers" and should be responsible for the children's care. This premise was rejected by the Supreme Court in the 1968 case *King v. Smith,* and man-in-the-house rules became a thing of the past. But the impulse to use welfare to legislate the morals of poor people continues. TANF legislation expresses preference for married, two-parent families, and recent reauthorization attempts have evinced willingness to spend billions of dollars to promote this family form.

Ending Welfare as We Know It

Unlike his predecessors, President Bill Clinton presided over an era of relatively low unemployment. Like his predecessors, Clinton came into office promising to "end welfare as we know it." Unlike his predecessors, he did it. Clinton authorized the most sweeping welfare reform since the Great Depression: the **Personal Responsibility and Work Opportunity Reconciliation Act (PRWORA)** of 1996.

PRWORA was part of the "Contract with America" offered by Republican representatives to Congress in 1994. In the flush of victory, the new Republican majority took aim at a variety of federal entitlement programs, including Food Stamps, Medicaid, and AFDC, and proposed converting federal assistance into block grants. This conversion would allow for reduced federal allocations and greater state discretion over the programs. Although the **Food Stamp Program** and **Medicaid** survived as federal entitlements, AFDC did not. PRWORA converted AFDC to a state block grant known as **Temporary Assistance for Needy Families** (TANF). States were allowed to spend TANF funds on a wide range of activities, as long as they were consistent with TANF purposes (set forth in Chapter 4).

PRWORA was designed to reduce federal welfare expenditures. It converted the open-ended entitlement under AFDC to time-limited assistance with a mandatory work requirement. It also reduced Food Stamp and SSI benefits by

- prohibiting most legal immigrants from receiving either SSI or Food Stamps (a measure that accounted for much of the budget reductions),
- establishing more stringent eligibility requirements for children receiving SSI,
- reducing the level of Food Stamp benefits, and
- adding lifetime limits and work requirements for receipt of Food Stamps by able-bodied adults without children.

Reductions in SSI and Food Stamp participation no doubt contributed to the decline in federal spending in the wake of PRWORA (Winicki, 2003).[12]

Ending a 50-year-old entitlement for needy children and their families, PRWORA was the most far-reaching welfare reform legislation since the **New Deal**. It reflected several of the values and beliefs outlined at the opening of this chapter. PRWORA set lifetime limits on public assistance that could not exceed (but could be shorter than) five years. This reflected the belief that welfare promotes dependency (the pauperization argument). The legislation also established work requirements for welfare recipients, forcing them to develop job skills or enter the labor market. Although these requirements may have reflected a desire to increase human capital available to the poor, the act also included restrictions on the type and duration of job training. The work requirements seemed tailor-made to ensure that welfare would not serve as an alternative to employment in a growing economy with a high demand for laborers. PRWORA allowed states to exempt 20 percent of TANF recipients from lifetime limits, establishing a class of "deserving" poor and leaving the states to define that group. Most states incorporated physical disability into their exemptions, suggesting that these individuals continue to be the legitimate focus of relief. At the same time, the act established new categories of "undeserving" poor, including individuals with drug-related felonies, teenage parents who leave home, and legal immigrants.

---

[12]Able-bodied adults without children can receive Food Stamps for a maximum of three months in a three-year period, unless they meet certain work requirements.

PRWORA was amended by the Balanced Budget Act of 1997, which restored SSI benefits to most noncitizens, established a $24 billion program that allowed states to expand Medicaid eligibility or directly purchase health coverage for uninsured children, and set up a $3 billion welfare-to-work program for long-term welfare clients.

PRWORA was enacted through 2002 and operated under a series of continuing resolutions and extensions until it was reauthorized in the Deficit Reduction Act of 2005. The reauthorized program allowed states to use TANF funds to promote two-parent families. Indeed, the Deficit Reduction Act allocated $150 million per year for five years to promote "healthy marriage" and "responsible fatherhood," with activities such as marriage education and training, advertising campaigns, and values education in high schools (U.S. General Accountability Office, 2008).

Following passage of PRWORA, the nation's welfare rolls shrank by 59 percent, the greatest decline in American history. Over 4.4 million people lost benefits (U.S. Department of Health & Human Services, 2006). The decline in TANF caseloads continued, but as Liz Schott of the Center on Budget and Policy Priorities pointed out, "*Well over half* of the decline since the mid-1990s was not due to a decline in the number of *very poor families* with children that qualified for assistance, but rather a decline in the *share* of such families that actually receive income support from TANF" (Schott, 2009; emphasis added). Clearly, the 1996 reforms did end welfare as we knew it. They did not reduce poverty in the United States, but introduced tremendous variation in states' treatment of low-income parents (Bentele & Nicoli, 2012).

The pressing question is "What happened to the people who left the welfare program?" A growing body of research has ensued. Some entered employment, but it is unclear whether their job situations were stable or financially adequate. Many TANF "leavers" lost both Food Stamps and Medicaid. Medicaid enrollment, in particular, dropped following welfare reform (Ku & Garrett, 2000). There was wide variation in post-TANF incomes, with leavers in some locations reporting increased annual incomes. In 2007, the Urban Institute reported that about 20 percent of leavers were "disconnected." That means they were not working, did not have a working spouse, and had no public cash assistance (Acs & Loprest, 2007). There was some indication that the child welfare system saw greater demands associated with TANF leavers, and that some parents gave up custody of their children due to their inability to provide financial support (Taylor & Barusch, 2004).

During the Great Recession of 2008, TANF did not see the sharp enrollment increase that might have been expected. The American Recovery and Reinvestment Act provided for reimbursement to states that saw increased caseloads, but the increases did not materialize. Instead, caseloads grew by only 6.6 percent nationally by mid-2009. During the same period, the number of Food Stamp recipients grew by 27.4 percent, and unemployment rose by 80 percent (Women's Legal Defense and Education Fund, 2009). Especially telling were comments from Kay E. Brown, Director of Education, Workforce and Income Security Issues for the Government Accountability Office (GAO). In her 2012 testimony before the Senate Finance Committee, Brown reported on a survey of Americans who had exhausted their unemployment benefits during the recession: "While almost 40 percent of near-poor households with children that had exhausted UI received aid through the Supplemental Nutrition Assistance [Program] we estimated that less than 10 percent received TANF case assistance" (Senate Finance Committee, 2012). Trends in TANF and SNAP participation are illustrated in Figure 5.3.

FIGURE 5.3 Trends in Food Stamp and TANF Participation, 1969–2015

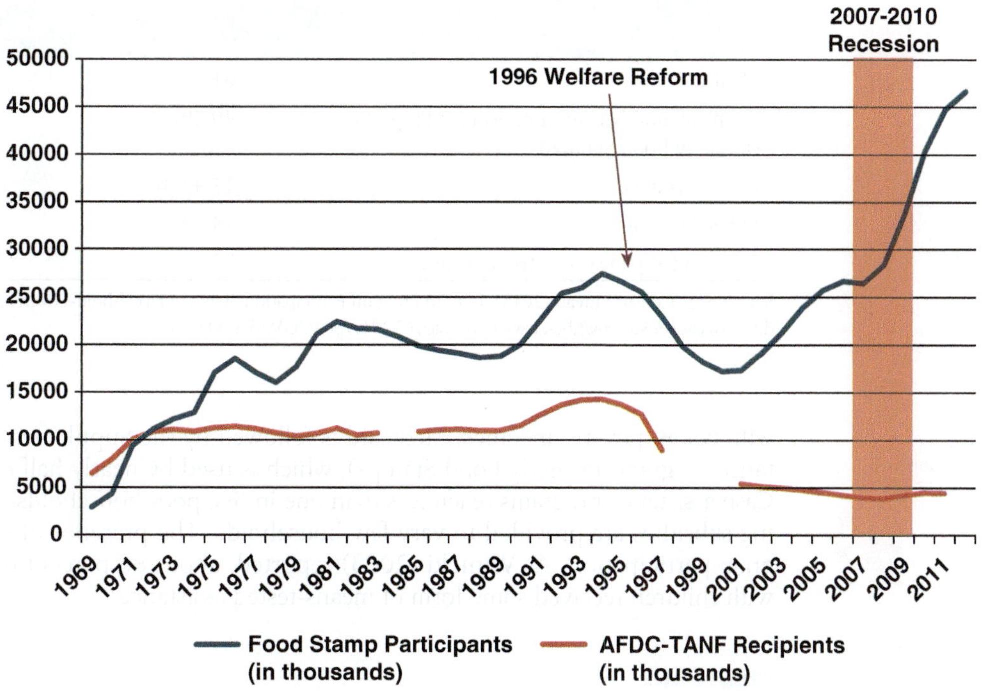

Food Stamp Participants (in thousands) — dark line; AFDC-TANF Recipients (in thousands) — red line. Annotations: "1996 Welfare Reform" and "2007-2010 Recession."

SOURCES: Food Stamps: USDA (2013). Supplemental Nutrition Assistance Program Participation and Costs (http://www.fns.usda.gov/sites/default/files/pd/SNAPsummary.pdf).
TANF: Administration for Children& Families, Caseload Data 1960-2008 (average for calendar year) (http://www.acf.hhs.gov/programs/ofa/data-reports/caseload/caseload_recent.html#2006)
2009-2011 FIGURES: http://www.acf.hhs.gov/programs/ofa/resource/2009-recipient-tan (also 2010-recipient-tan, 2011-recipient-tan).
2012-2016 FIGURES: "TANF: Total Number of Recipients (Averages for calendar year) https://www.acf.hhs.gov/sites/default/files/ofa/2012trec_tan.pdf?nocache=1358959977
Tables missing for some years.

LO 5-4 Describe Contemporary Issues Affecting Key Programs That Serve America's Poor

EP 3a
EP 5c
EP 8d

Here we will examine five programs that serve America's poor: Medicaid, the Supplemental Nutrition Assistance Program (SNAP), programs of case assistance (TANF and SSI), and Housing Assistance. As we will see, the contemporary issues affecting each program include notions about the proper role of government and the differences between deserving and undeserving poor, even as these at times seem to be overshadowed by widespread concern over government finances.

A simple list of means-tested programs in the United States could suggest that the needs of the poor are met by these government interventions. That might be true if everyone with incomes below the poverty threshold received assistance. But, as Table 5.2 illustrates, means-tested programs do not reach all of the nation's poor. These figures underscore the importance of Medicaid, the only program that reaches a majority of those

TABLE 5.2 Program Participation by the Nation's Poor, 2013

	Percent Below Poverty	Percent at All Income Levels
Medicaid	61.3%	26.7%
Supplemental Nutrition Assistance Program (formerly Food Stamps)	49.5%	13.0%
Cash assistance	17.4.8%	6.5%
Public housing	14.8%	3.7%
Receiving any means-tested assistance	73.8%	33.5%

Source: U.S. Census Bureau (2013). POV26 Program Participation Status of Household-Poverty Status of People 2013 (http://www.census.gov/hhes/www/cpstables/032012/pov/POV26_000.htm).

with below-poverty incomes. Medicaid is followed by the Supplemental Nutrition Assistance Program (formerly Food Stamps), which is used by nearly half of the nation's poor. Cash assistance programs reach less than one in five poor households, while public housing subsidies are provided to very few households. The presence of children raises program participation. As Winicki (2003) reported, about 86 percent of poor households with children received some form of means-tested assistance.

MEDICAID

Established under the 1965 Amendments to the Social Security Act, Medicaid provides health insurance to some low-income families and individuals. Direct administration is carried out by each state, with federal matching funds meeting from 50 to 80 percent of program costs. States vary in their eligibility requirements, although all cover recipients of TANF and SSI. States also vary in the services covered. Some services are required by federal law, including inpatient hospital services, outpatient hospital services, rural health clinic services, laboratory and X-ray services, skilled nursing facility (nursing home) services, and physician services. Optional services include prescription drugs, eyeglasses, dental care, diagnostic screening, and preventive care.

Most Medicaid recipients are mothers and children like Antonia and her son, but the bulk of the program's expenditures go to care for low-income elderly and people with disabilities because of their greater need for medical attention. As we will see in Chapter 6, Medicaid is an important source of funding for long-term care.

TANF recipients who leave the program for jobs can keep their Medicaid coverage for up to 12 months under a program called "transitional Medicaid." For some low-income Americans like Antonia, medical coverage is more vital than cash assistance. Of course, transitional Medicaid coverage is only a short-term solution for many low-income workers, given the erosion of employer-based coverage. This topic is discussed further in Chapter 15.

Most metropolitan areas require Medicaid recipients to enroll with a managed care provider. This is a cost-control measure that may also improve health-care access for the poor. On the other hand, the focus on cost control that is characteristic of managed care may introduce barriers that prevent the poor from accessing needed care.

Under the Affordable Care Act, Medicaid eligibility would have extended to those under 65 years with incomes below 133 percent of the federal poverty threshold in 2014, providing health coverage to an estimated 15.1 million uninsured Americans (Kenney et al., 2012). For the first time, low-income adults without children would have been eligible for Medicaid, and coverage to families with children would have been extended. However, as we learned in Chapter 4, in the 2012 case of *NFIB v. Sebelius* the Supreme Court ruled that the federal government could not require states to participate in this Medicaid expansion.

As they considered whether or not to participate, state leaders should have taken into account the fact that the federal government would cover the lion's share of the expense. For the first three years, 100 percent of costs associated with the expanded eligibility were to be borne at the federal level. After that, the federal contribution would drop to 90 percent. This stands in contrast to the federal share of coverage for the "traditionally eligible" groups, which averages about 60 percent (American Public Health Association, n.d.). Leaders in states that did not elect to participate in the Medicaid expansion expressed concern that austerity measures designed to reduce the deficit might jeopardize federal Medicaid contributions, though there is good reason to suspect that ideological differences between Democrats and Republicans played a role as well.

States' decisions tended to divide along party lines as Republican governors and legislators continued to resist. As of June 2016, 26 states (including the District of Columbia) had adopted Medicaid expansion. Nineteen had not, and six were expanding Medicaid along non-traditional lines (See www.statereforum.org for an update on state reform efforts).

SUPPLEMENTAL NUTRITION ASSISTANCE PROGRAM (FOOD STAMPS)

The Food Stamp Program, now called SNAP (Supplemental Nutrition Assistance Program), has operated nationwide since 1974, under the Food Stamp Act of 1964. It is administered by the Department of Agriculture (USDA) and provides vouchers for the purchase of food items that in 2012 were valued at $74.6 billion (U.S. Department of Agriculture, 2013). The USDA covers 100 percent of benefit costs and 50 percent of administrative costs. The remaining administrative costs are borne by the state and county agencies charged with managing the program.

Eligibility requirements are established at the federal level at approximately 130 percent of the federal poverty threshold. In 2016, the maximum net monthly income limit for an eligible family of four living in the 48 contiguous states was $2,628. People who are receiving TANF or SSI are automatically eligible for SNAP benefits. Households may have up to $2,250 in countable assets, such as a bank account. A person's home and one vehicle may not be considered countable assets. Households in which at least one person is over the age of 60 or is disabled may be eligible with up to $3,250 in assets (USDA, n.d.a,, n.d.b).

Able-bodied adults between the ages of 18 and 50 who have no children are required to participate in workfare or employment training if they do not have jobs. They are only permitted to receive SNAP benefits during three months out of every three years, though states may suspend the three-month limit in areas with high unemployment. During the Great Recession many did so; however, this suspension was terminated in most states in January 2016 (Center on Budget and Policy Priorities, 2015).

The SNAP Program has been criticized for providing inadequate benefits.[13] For a family of four, the **maximum monthly allotment** is $649. But all families are expected to spend 30 percent of their income on food, so this amount is subtracted from the maximum monthly allotment. In 2015, the average SNAP benefit per person was $127 per month (Center on Budget and Policy Priorities, 2015). Benefit cuts in 2013 brought this amount down by about six dollars. From time to time, politicians and other public figures attempt to draw attention to the problem of inadequate benefits (and to themselves) by living on the Food Stamp allotment.

---

[13]Benefits for Alaska, Hawaii, and the U.S. territories of Guam and the Virgin Islands are higher, reflecting higher food costs in these areas.

BOX 5.4   The Earned Income Tax Credit

The Earned Income Tax Credit (EITC) is one of the nation's most effective antipoverty initiatives. It provides low-income workers a refundable credit that increases considerably when children are present. Indeed, two-parent families with two children who rely on a full-time worker at the federal minimum wage cannot move above the poverty line without EITC and SNAP benefits. In 2011, the EITC lifted 6.1 million people (about half of them children) out of poverty (Center on Budget and Policy Priorities, 2013). We will return to the EITC in Chapter 15.

Many Americans who are eligible for SNAP benefits do not participate in the program. Some are not aware they are eligible. Others conclude that Food Stamps just aren't worth the time, effort, and humiliation involved. It can take hours to complete an initial application, and some states require recertification every three months. Since most welfare offices are open only during the workday, low-income parents with jobs must leave work to secure and maintain their Food Stamps (see Castner & Cody, 1999; Mathematica, 2000; Rosenbaum, 2000). Indeed, participation fell to a low of 45 percent in 2001 and 2002. As a result of the Great Recession, restoration of benefits for "legal non-citizens," and some modifications in eligibility determination, participation by eligible households has increased. (We saw this in Figure 5.3.) At the time, the Department of Agriculture undertook some fairly aggressive outreach measures. By 2012 an estimated 83 percent of those eligible for SNAP were enrolled (USDA, 2015).

Even as participation has increased, the proportion of SNAP households with earned income has risen steadily, from about 20 percent in 1990 to 30 percent in 2010 (USDA, 2012). Today, SNAP is increasingly serving those employed in low-wage jobs, which delivers an important subsidy to employers like Walmart (Americans for Tax Fairness, 2014).

TEMPORARY ASSISTANCE FOR NEEDY FAMILIES

Serving over 4 million Americans, TANF is delivered through a federal block grant to the states. The program allows states to establish eligibility criteria, provided that their treatment of recipients is "fair and equitable" and that people convicted of drug felonies are excluded from participating. Key characteristics of the program include:

- Work requirements
- Lifetime assistance limits
- Maintenance of effort requirements
- Financial rewards and penalties to states
- Special requirements for teen parents
- Paternity determination and child support enforcement

Work Requirements
Employment is a central focus of TANF. States are required to assess each recipient's skills and develop a "personal employability plan" that identifies barriers to employment and training needs. TANF recipients can be "sanctioned" if they do not participate in their plans, and this may involve being terminated from the program. Indeed, there is some evidence that more families have been discontinued due to failure to comply with work requirements than are kicked off the program for reaching the lifetime limits discussed below (Farrell, Rich, Turner, Seith, & Bloom, 2008).

Participation can include vocational education (limited to 12 months), secondary education, up to six weeks of job search, community service, subsidized employment, unsubsidized employment, and child care for a recipient engaged in community service. Recipients may also comply with work requirements if they are working to eliminate barriers to employment, such as addiction or mental illness. With some exceptions, TANF recipients must work as soon as they are "job ready," which must be no later than two years after they begin receiving assistance. This constraint limits the educational and training opportunities available to TANF participants.

Lifetime Assistance Limits

Under federal law, families that have received 60 months of TANF cash assistance are not eligible for further federally funded cash assistance. States may elect a shorter limit. They may also give "hardship extensions" to up to 20 percent of their TANF caseload from the limit. Recipients who have been on TANF for longer than 60 months may be supported with state funds. As might be expected, states vary in their approaches to the lifetime limits. Two of the nation's largest states, New York and California, do not terminate benefits after 60 months. California removes adults from the case but continues to provide assistance to children (effectively reducing, but not terminating the benefit). New York transitions families who reach the 60-month limit to state and local programs that provide similar benefits. Other states may extend benefits to recipients who comply with the program's requirements or who face barriers to employment, such as domestic violence or ill health (Farrell et al., 2008).

Maintenance of Effort Requirements

TANF includes a cost-sharing requirement known as "maintenance of effort" (MOE), which requires that states spend a minimum amount on TANF activities. This amount is based on whether the state has met its required work participation rate in a given year. States that have met their rate requirements must devote 75 percent of the amount they spent on AFDC in 1994 to TANF. Those that have not must spend 80 percent of their 1994 expenditures. (Of course, as we will see below, these figures are not adjusted for inflation.) A contingency fund is available to states experiencing severe economic problems.

Financial Rewards and Penalties to States

Special bonuses are provided to "high performance states" in which high proportions of TANF recipients exit the program for employment or in which rates of teen pregnancy go down. States are subject to financial penalties in a wide range of circumstances, including failure to meet work participation requirements, noncompliance with the five-year lifetime limit, failure to satisfy MOE requirements, neglecting to sanction recipients who do not meet participation requirements, failure to comply with requirements regarding paternity establishment and child support collection, not submitting required reports, and inappropriate use of funds.

Special Requirements for Teen Parents

Teen parents are required to participate in training or school and may not receive assistance unless they live at home or in an approved adult-supervised setting.

Paternity Determination and Child Support Enforcement

As was the case with AFDC, TANF recipients are required to assist in identifying and locating their children's fathers. Those able to document domestic violence (usually through a police report) are exempt from this requirement. Failure to cooperate can result in reduction or termination of benefits. The state agency charged with administration of TANF operates a child support collection operation, and funds collected are used by the state to offset its TANF budget. While they are on TANF, mother and children do not receive this child support until the state has recovered its payments to the family. Even after the family's benefit period ends, some states continue to collect money from the noncustodial parent until the state's TANF costs are recovered. (Please see Pirog & Ziol-Guest, 2006, for a discussion of the redistributive effects of federal child support enforcement measures.)

Under PRWORA, the TANF block grant was set at $16.5 billion per year. Lacking any provision for inflation adjustments, that amount has remained constant, eroding the real value of the federal contribution by an estimated 30 percent. Further, state maintenance of effort (MOE) requirements set the amount they are required to spend at 80 percent of their 1994 AFDC contributions. The value of this required contribution has eroded as well, to about half of the amount spent on AFDC (Schott, 2012). Further, as we saw in Chapter 4, the law allows for funds to be spent on efforts that do not deliver cash assistance to needy families. Specifically, marriage promotion and teen pregnancy prevention efforts can target those who are not financially vulnerable.

SUPPLEMENTAL SECURITY INCOME

SSI is an entitlement program, so anyone who is eligible has a right to receive assistance. The program has both categorical and means-based eligibility standards. To be categorically eligible an individual must be aged, blind, or disabled. As poverty levels among older adults have come down (and because only a fraction of eligible older adults receive SSI benefits) people with disabilities have come to make up a growing share of SSI beneficiaries.

Disability determination is managed by state Disability Determination Service (DDS) agencies. It can take persistence and expertise for potential recipients to receive benefits. About half of the claims submitted are denied upon the initial application. And some people stop there, unaware of the possibility of appeal. Initial appeals are reviewed by DDS personnel, and the resulting success rate is fairly low; however, those denied at this level can appeal to an administrative law judge, where most claims are successful (Bilder & Mechanic, 2003). As you can imagine, applicants who have professional support—for instance, from a "linkage worker" in a homeless shelter or from Legal Aid—fare better in this demanding and time-consuming application process.

In 2016, income limits for eligibility were $733 per month for individuals and $1,100 per month for couples, but those applying for SSI (and those advocating on their behalf) should be aware that SSI income guidelines are a bit complicated. In-kind income, including food, clothing, or shelter (or "something" that can be exchanged for food, clothing, or shelter), is considered when determining eligibility, as is **deemed income** from other people in the household. On the other hand, some income is excluded from eligibility determinations, including Food Stamps, housing or home energy assistance, $20 per month of unearned income, $65 per month of wages, and half of earned income over $65 per month (Social Security Administration, 2013c).

Resource limits for SSI were subject to a one-time adjustment in 1984. Current asset limits are $2,000 for individuals and $3,000 for couples. Homes, adjoining land, and automobiles are not counted as assets in determining SSI eligibility, but life insurance policies with cash values in excess of $1,500 per person are considered.

Although the federal monthly benefit is fixed at the eligibility standard, benefit levels vary from state to state. Even the maximum federal benefit does not raise recipients' incomes above poverty levels. In 2016 the monthly federal benefit was $733 for individuals and $1,100 for couples—amounts that represent 74 percent and 82 percent of the respective federal poverty thresholds. Because some recipients have other sources of income, they do not receive the maximum benefit. Indeed, the average federal benefit paid in May 2016 was $541 per month (Social Security Administration, 2016a. Some states supplement this amount with contributions that range from $10 to $200.

The SSI program is a vital safety net, preventing extreme poverty among the elderly and the disabled. As Bilder and Mechanic (2003) pointed out, the program seeks to balance conflicting goals: "meeting need, encouraging work, and containing public expenditures" (p. 75). Each of these goals is evident in the program's operation. Its very existence responds to the felt need to prevent extreme poverty among the elderly and disabled; its low benefits would hardly compete with low-wage employment; and its onerous disability determination process helps contain public expenditures. We will return to SSI in Chapter 8.

HOUSING ASSISTANCE

In the United States, housing is not an entitlement but a private commodity to be traded for profit in the real estate market. As a result, budget allocations for assistance programs consistently fail to meet the need for housing, and low-income Americans who seek housing assistance confront waiting lists and complex bureaucratic requirements. In Table 5.2 we saw that only a small fraction of low-income Americans receive housing assistance.

Federal housing assistance is provided through three programs that date back to the New Deal, when public housing was developed for low-income working families. The structure of current federal low-income housing programs was in place by the mid-1970s. In 2013, HUD programs provided assistance to 4.8 million Americans. The largest of these, which supported roughly half of those receiving assistance, is the Section 8 voucher program. Another 1.1 million subsidized renters live in public housing developments, and 1.6 million live in developments that are privately owned and publicly subsidized (Joint Center for Housing Studies of Harvard University, 2015).

The Housing Choice Voucher Program (Section 8)
The Housing and Community Development Act of 1974 included Section 8 to provide rent subsidies for low-income families. In part, the program was designed to enable low-income families to move away from ghettos into safer neighborhoods with better transportation and schools. Recipients are expected to pay 30 percent of their income toward rent, and they receive a voucher that covers the difference between this and "fair market rent." But in many areas, HUD's idea of fair market rent is not sufficient for rentals in better neighborhoods. And landlords can refuse to accept Section 8 vouchers. Many in middle-class and upper-income neighborhood do, complaining that the required safety inspections are "burdensome" (Semuels, 2015).

As Mulroy (1990) pointed out, Section 8 was frequently cited as "a great liberator," freeing low-income families from slum lords and public housing. It has long failed to fulfill this promise. In 1980 the OMB noted, "The Section 8 may be likened somewhat to a lottery in which only a few strike it big. For those families fortunate enough to get into the program, many can be expected to stay in it for a long time" (U.S. General Accounting Office, 1980, p. 12). By 2015 the program only served about 25 percent of eligible households and those who did receive vouchers often find the program's procedures and regulations complex and difficult (Semuels, 2015).

Public Housing

The National Industrial Recovery Act (NIRA) of 1933 provided federal funding for housing construction, but the focus of New Deal efforts was less on provision of housing for the poor than on creation of jobs for the unemployed. Public housing was made available to the working poor who lived in "intact" families. Unwed mothers were excluded from most housing units, and few (usually 10 percent) of the units were available to families on welfare.

World War II brought a serious housing shortage. The Federal Housing Administration (FHA) and GI home mortgage programs offered low-interest mortgages to middle-class Americans and veterans. Members of Congress and welfare authorities argued that public housing should be reserved for those in greatest need. As a result, new policies lowered income limits for eligibility and prohibited discrimination against welfare families and unwed mothers.

By the mid-1960s, much of public housing had become a "war zone," replete with drug dealing and violent crime. Mildred Hailey was one of several resident leaders who advocated for reform. Reasoning that federal indifference and resident apathy conspired to create hellish living conditions, Hailey and others argued for returning control (and even ownership) of public housing to the residents. She took over the project she lived in, Bromley Heath in Boston, and with an administrative board of fellow housing residents set out to manage and police the project. Since then, a growing number of public housing units have been purchased or managed by the residents themselves.

Private Developments (Section 202 and the Low-Income Housing Tax Credit)

Section 202 of the Housing Act of 1959 authorized HUD to provide low-interest construction loans known as "capital advances" to nonprofit sponsors (such as churches and civic organizations) who were interested in providing housing for the low-income elderly and disabled. Once constructed, a Section 202 housing development was operated by the nonprofit sponsor with federal oversight. Through "Project Rental Assistance Contracts" HUD made up the difference between what residents could afford to pay (30 percent of their income) and the operating expenses of the facility. Section 202 funding for new facilities ended in 2012; however, the Low-Income Housing Tax Credit (LIHTC) continues to be an important subsidy for the construction of affordable housing.

Established under the Tax Reform Act of 1986, the LIHTC has contributed to nearly all of the affordable housing that has been built since it went into effect. Like the Earned Income Tax Credit, it is remarkably popular and resilient (Joint Center for Housing Studies of Harvard University, 2010). The LIHTC provides a federal tax credit to private developers who build multi-family low-income housing. The program is administered at the federal level by the IRS and at the state level by state housing authorities. Depending on how a project is structured, it may return either 70 percent or 30 percent of eligible costs to the investor over a 10-year period, with the requirement that for 15 years an agreed-upon proportion (not less than 60 percent) of the units be reserved for those with incomes below 60 percent of the **area median income**.

SUMMARY OF ATTITUDES AND INTERVENTIONS

The values and beliefs discussed earlier in this chapter shape the interventions designed to prevent or alleviate poverty. When poverty is seen as an opportunity for the affluent to do good deeds, charity is given with an open hand and little concern for its impact. When poverty is seen as a crime, the response is to inflict punishment and humiliation on the poor. When poverty is seen as a lack of human capital, education and training are provided to the poor. When poverty is viewed as a culture, the values and beliefs of low-income children and adults become the intervention target. When poverty is seen as the result of limited opportunities, we strive to reduce discrimination. And finally, when poverty is seen as an incentive to work, we decide that welfare creates a class of comfortable paupers and set out to "end welfare as we know it."

On the other hand, poverty might be a risk we all share. In the following section we turn to the characteristics of the poor. This will shed light on how the risk of poverty is distributed in the United States.

LO 5-5   Know Who Is Most Likely to Be Poor in the United States

EP 4c
EP 5c

In 2015, over 46 million Americans had incomes below the federal poverty threshold. Some of them received income assistance through public programs, but most did not. As we will see in this section, the poor are a heterogeneous group, and the causes and consequences of their poverty are varied and complex.

CHARACTERISTICS OF AMERICA'S POOR

If poverty is one of the risks, or costs, of membership in American society, its distribution reflects an important allocation principle. If the risks of poverty were randomly distributed, one might fairly argue that poverty is the result of personal failure. John Rawls's "veil of ignorance" (discussed in Chapter 1) would then predict that the nation's policies would maximize the well-being of the poor. But Americans do not enter the world with equal risks of poverty. In some ways, one's risk of poverty is inversely related to one's likelihood of serving in Congress. Several factors determine both probabilities, among them race, gender, age, residence, immigration status, and employment.

Race
Although white Americans make up the largest single group with incomes below the poverty threshold, they are under-represented among the nation's poor. For example, in 2015, non-Hispanic white Americans represented 61 percent of the U.S. population and made up 41 percent of America's poor. As Table 5.3 indicates, the poverty rate for non-Hispanic white Americans was relatively low compared with rates for other races.

TABLE 5.3   Ethnicity and Poverty in the United States, Individuals: 2015
(Overall Poverty Rate: 13.5 Percent)

Race/Ethnicity	Percent Below Poverty*	Percent of Poverty Population*	Percent of General Population**
White, not Hispanic	9.1%	41.2%	61.4%
Asian	11.4%	5.7%	4.8%
Hispanic	21.4%	17.8%	28.1%
American Indian and Alaska Native*	28.4%	NA	0.9%
African American	24.1%	23.2%	13.1%

*Based on 2014 Current Population Survey.
Data Sources: U.S. Census Bureau, *Current Population Survey, Income and Poverty in the United States: 2015* (Report # P60-256) Table 3: People in Poverty by Selected Characteristics (http://www.census.gov/content/dam/Census/library/publications/2016/demo/p60-256.pdf).

TABLE 5.4 Gender and Poverty in the United States, People in Families: 2013
(Overall Poverty Rate: 14.5 Percent)

	Percent Below Poverty			
	Female-Headed Households	Male-Headed Households	Married Couple Families	All Households
All races	33.2%	17.1%	6.8%	12.4%
White, not Hispanic	29.2%	14.6%	6.2%	10.1%
Asian	13.7%	12.5%	6.5%	7.7%
Hispanic (any race)	41.6%	18.9%	15.5%	22.3%
African American	42.5%	24.8%	11.3%	25.8%

Source (for data): U.S. Census Bureau, Current Population Survey, 2013 Annual Social and Economic Supplement, POV02: People in Families by Family Structure, Age, and Sex (https://www.census.gov/hhes/www/cpstables/032014/pov/pov02_100.htm)

Gender

Households headed by women are more likely to be poor than those headed by men, hence the phrase "feminization of poverty." Even as it confirms this pervasive trend, Table 5.4 reveals other patterns in the distribution of poverty. For instance, we see that households headed by married couples consistently have the lowest poverty rates. This observation has served as justification for spending millions of TANF dollars on "marriage promotion." Under this view, simply moving women from column A (Female-Headed Households) to column C (Married Couple Families) will substantially lower their risk of poverty.

Age

In the United States, children face the highest risk of poverty. Whereas the overall poverty rate in 2015 was 14.8 percent, 19.7 percent of children under 18 lived in poverty, as did 21 percent of those under age 6. Nearly half 42.6 percent) of children in families headed by a single mother lived in poverty. This was more than four times the rate (9.8 percent) experienced by children who lived in families headed by a married couple (U.S. Census Bureau, 2016).

At 8.8 percent, the 2015 poverty rate for older adults—aged 65 and over—was less than half the rate for children under 18 (19.7 percent). This does not mean that all of the nation's elderly are well-off. First, as mentioned previously, the poverty threshold for the elderly is lower than for other age groups; second, another five percent of older adults live with incomes between 125 percent of poverty and the poverty threshold. Among older adults, the risk of poverty increases with age. Age also magnifies the accumulated disadvantages associated with gender and race, so in 2014, the highest risk of poverty among olders adults (26 percent) was experienced by African American women over 75 years old (U.S. Census Bureau, 2016 & 2015b).

Residence

Since 1994, the South and the West have had the nation's highest rates of poverty. In 2015, the South had the nation's highest poverty rate, at 15.3 percent, compared with 13.3 percent for the West. This compares to poverty rates of 12.4 percent for the Northeast and 11.7 percent for the Midwest (U.S. Census Bureau, 2016). These regional trends are mirrored in the state-level rates.

The poverty rate in rural America once exceeded that in the nation's cities. Today the situation has reversed. The nation's highest poverty rates are found in the inner cities.

In 2015, the poverty rate in principal cities was 16.8 percent, compared with a rate of 10.8 percent for those living in the suburbs of metropolitan areas. Rural poverty, measured as that "outside metropolitan areas," was 16.7 percent (U.S. Census Bureau, 2016).[14]

Immigration Status

American citizens who are foreign-born have a slightly lower risk of poverty than those who are native-born. The poverty rate for naturalized citizens was 11.2 percent in 2015, compared with 13.1 percent for native-born citizens. Foreign-born individuals who have not attained citizenship have a substantially higher poverty rate. In 2015, 21.3 percent of this group lived in poverty (U.S. Census Bureau, 2016).

Employment

As we will see in Chapter 15, having a job does not guarantee escape from poverty. Many Americans with incomes below the poverty level are employed. In 2015, a majority of poor families reported having at least one member who worked. There is a substantial difference between the poverty rate experienced by those with full-time, year-round employment (2.4 percent) and those with part-time or part-year employment (15.5 percent) (U.S. Census Bureau, 2016).

Clearly the risk of living in poverty is not shared equally among Americans. There are worlds of difference between the risk faced by a married white man of 55 to 59 years (5.5 percent in 2014) and that confronted by an African American child under 5 years old living without a father (60.4 percent) (U.S. Census Bureau, 2015b). Of course, we know which one is most likely to serve in Congress.

LO 5-6   Understand the Secondary Risks Associated with Poverty

EP 5c

America's poor are not just economically vulnerable. They are exposed to homelessness and violence to a greater degree than other residents of the United States. Further, they are charged with fraud, despite the relatively small economic impact of the fraudulent activities of a few. In the following section, we will examine these secondary risks that accompany poverty.

HOMELESSNESS

In the United States a house is a commodity, developed and traded for profit. A house can provide shelter and protection. A *home* provides continuity and a social context for individuals and families, and those who become homeless lose more than shelter. They lose connection with their past, friends, and schools, and their place in a community. Two developments in the U.S. housing market have increased the vulnerability of low-income people. The first is a diminishing supply of low-cost rental housing; the second is a reduced federal commitment to housing assistance.

As we saw in Table 5.2, the majority of low-income families do not receive federal housing assistance. They also fare poorly in the private housing market. Since the early 1970s, the supply of low-cost rental housing has been diminishing. Urban renewal efforts have cost the nation more than a million rooms in "single-room-occupancy" (SRO) hotels.

---

[14]It is worth noting that, until 1981, the poverty threshold for farm families was lower than for others. The rationale was that farm families had access to low-cost food.

Major cities such as New York have lost many of their SROs. Some buildings have simply been demolished. "Gentrification" has also reduced the supply of low-cost housing. In 1984, Harrington described gentrification as "the process whereby the middle class and the rich take over the physically sound and architecturally charming housing of the poor" (Harrington, 1984, p. 119). "Public subsidies, such as tax abatements for refurbishment, have often subsidized this process. But there has not been a commensurate subsidy to provide housing for the displaced" (p. 120).

The supply of low-income housing continues to diminish. As an inevitable result of declining supply, the cost of housing has increased. Until the latest recession, the Consumer Price Index for shelter increased faster than the general Consumer Price Index. This trend forced low- and middle-income Americans to devote an ever greater share of their income to housing.

Traditionally, federal housing interventions attempted to bridge the gap between the financial resources of low-income Americans and the cost of housing, but recent decades have seen erosion in all three programs. This erosion was especially marked during the Reagan administration, when funding for public housing was severely reduced. Allocated funds dropped from $32 billion in 1981 to $6 billion in 1989 (Burton, 1992). The number of Section 202 units dropped from a high of 39,381 in 1978 to 7,281 in 1990 (Sonnenberg, Budget Analyst, Department of Housing and Urban Development, personal communication, 1993). In a despairing note, C. Theodore Koebel complained in 1998 that "[t]he failure of government to directly provide decent housing for low-income families is now accepted as a given" (p. 3). Coupled with a tight housing market, government inattention to the housing needs of the poor contributes to increased homelessness.

During the Great Recession the prices of housing plunged, and America faced the specter of foreclosed houses sitting vacant while families became homeless (Sard, 2009). During the 2008–2009 schoolyear, the U.S. Department of Education reported a 20 percent rise in the number of homeless students (U.S. Interagency Council on Homelessness, 2010). Some families "doubled up," moving in with relatives to weather the storm (National Alliance to End Homelessness, 2010). At the same time, homeless shelters in many cities reported increased demand (U.S. Conference of Mayors, 2008).

In response, several advocacy groups (e.g., Poor People's Economic Human Rights Campaign in Minnesota, Women in Transition in Kentucky, and Take Back the Land in Florida) organized to help homeowners fight eviction and to move homeless families into vacant properties.

In 2009, President Obama signed several measures designed to address the housing problems that emerged during the Great Recession (please see U.S. Interagency Council on Homelessness, 2010, for details). Notably, the 2009 Recovery Act (also known as the "Stimulus Package") included a $5-billion TANF Emergency Fund to enable states to deliver housing assistance (Schott, 2010).

Who Are the Homeless?

Michael Harrington (1984) suggests that people without homes be called "uprooted" rather than "homeless." Harrington notes that major economic transformations often create "a floating population" of people whose role in the old economic order has disappeared.

It is hard to estimate precisely the number of Americans who are homeless. Two methods yield very different results. The "point-in-time" approach asks how many people are homeless on a particular day (or night). Estimates in January 2014 indicated 578,424 homeless people in the United States (U.S. Conference of Mayors, 2015). The "period-prevalence" approach asks how many people have experienced homelessness during a longer period. For instance, in one of the more authoritative studies, the National Law

Center on Homelessness and Poverty estimated that 3.5 million Americans, 1.35 of whom are children, experience homelessness in any given year (National Law Center on Homelessness and Poverty, 2007). Of course, any of these figures risks underestimating the extent of homelessness as some people stay in places that are difficult for researchers to locate.

There are three distinct groups among our nation's homeless: single adults (most of them men), families, and "unaccompanied youths." Each year, the U.S. Department of Housing and Urban Development conducts a one-night count of homeless people in cities and counties across the nation. In 2014, that count resulted in HUD estimating that 578,313 people were homeless in the United States. Among them, an estimated 63 percent were individuals and the remaining 37 percent were in families. Children and youth (among whom 24 percent were unaccompanied) represented about a third of homeless people. (U.S. Conference of Mayors, 2015).

The U.S. Conference of Mayors periodically surveys homelessness in 23 cities across the country. Their results indicated that in 2014 on average 28 percent of single adults who find themselves homeless suffered from severe mental illness. About 22 percent were physically disabled. Nearly one in five (18 percent) were employed; 15 percent were victims of domestic violence; 13 percent were veterans; and 3 percent were HIV positive (U.S. Conference of Mayors, 2015).

Tens of thousands of teenagers flee (or are kicked out of) their homes each year to live on the streets of major cities. Children who "age out" of foster care are also at significant risk of homelessness (Russell, 1998). The 2014 HUD estimates translate into a total of 46,632 such "unaccompanied youths." Only about half go to homeless shelters, leading Slesnick (2004) and others to identify two types of homeless youth: "shelter kids" and "street kids."

All homeless children are vulnerable to physical and sexual abuse, and many of their basic needs go unmet (Karabanow, 2004). The Runaway and Homeless Youth Act provides funding for outreach, supportive services, and shelters for runaway and "thrown-away" youth under the auspices of the Department of Health and Human Services, Family and Youth Services Bureau.

BOX 5.5   Preying on the Disadvantaged

Driving through low-income neighborhoods in America, it is easy to spot the payday lenders, often in a central location of the popular strip mall. They offer short-term loans at interest rates that can exceed 400 percent. Marketed as the answer to cash shortfalls, these loans trap consumers in an expensive cycle of interest and fees, while the lenders take millions of dollars in profits. These companies market aggressively, hiring local staff who foster personal relationships with potential clients and offering loans over the Internet (Consumer Financial Protection Bureau, 2013; Mangan, 2012). Community organizations like Earned Assets Resource Network (EARN) and some credit unions do offer short-term loans at reasonable interest rates, but they lack the resources to compete with the payday lenders.

Several policies to limit predatory lending practices are already in place, and the Consumer Financial Protection Bureau has begun to enforce these with considerable vigor. The Servicemembers Civil Relief Act gives significant protections to members of the armed services, including limits on interest rates. The Center for Responsible Lending (n.d.) reports that 17 states and the District of Columbia have set caps on allowable interest rates, and some states limit the loan amount and the length of the loan. Local communities have also stepped up to regulate these practices. (Dallas, TX has some of the strongest local laws.) Still, there is a clear need for advocacy to expand protections at the local, state, and federal levels.

Federal policy toward the homeless has been marked by reluctance. When the growth in homelessness first reached public awareness in the early 1980s, the Reagan administration took the position that it was not a problem that demanded federal intervention. During this period advocates struggled to document the number of homeless people, and political debates about the extent of the problem raged. In 1983, a federal task force on homelessness was created, and in 1986 the Homeless Persons' Survival Act, later renamed the McKinney Homeless Assistance Act, was passed. Funding, as well as the type of programs that can be funded under the act, increased until 1995, when the budget reached a peak of $1.49 billion (National Coalition for the Homeless, 1999). Programs funded under the act have provided "safe havens" for the mentally ill who are homeless, ensured public education for children in homeless families, offered health care to the homeless, and established emergency shelters and food programs.

In 1988, Los Angeles launched the nation's first **Housing First** program as an alternative to shelters for the chronically homeless, often men with addiction and mental health problems. Since then, with funding through the Department of Housing and Urban Development, many cities have adopted this model to deliver housing and case management with no preconditions. **Rapid Rehousing** programs have also been established to reduce homelessness among families. These models have both emerged as best practices in the field. Though neither has been subject to a national evaluation, smaller studies have demonstrated their effectiveness at providing stable housing (see Montgomery, Hill, Kane & Culhane, 2013).

VIOLENCE

Michael Harrington (1984) argued that "[c]ertain social and economic conditions—above all, the experience of becoming marginal, useless—create not a fate, but a greater likelihood that some (a minority) will turn to violent crime either as means to an end, a way of earning a living, or else as an act of sheer rage" (p. 189). Poverty leaves people especially vulnerable to aggression and victimization.[15] Indeed, consideration of broad trends in violence in the United States led Gurr (1989) to comment that increases in violence have typically been associated with "immigration, war and economic deprivation" (p. 12). This may also be the case in France and Germany, where higher rates of violence have been documented among marginalized groups of immigrants (Short, 1997).

Social dislocation and extreme poverty foster violence. There is also some evidence that inequality is associated with higher homicide rates (Blau & Blau, 1982). Violent crime is concentrated where marginalized groups are restricted to certain neighborhoods or communities, such as inner-city ghettos, and is often gang related. It is unclear why ghetto residents experience more violence. Possible explanations include lack of opportunity, few role models for success, higher residential mobility, family disruption, and cultural values that tolerate violence (Short, 1997).

According to the Department of Justice, more than 1.2 million violent crimes (aggravated assault, robbery, rape, and murder) were reported in 2011, continuing a long-term trend of decline in the rate of such crimes. Regional differences were observed, with the South and West reporting the highest rates of violent crime. Finally, the DOJ reported that firearms were used in 68 percent of murders, 41 percent of robberies, and 21 percent of aggravated assaults (U.S. Department of Justice, 2012).

---

[15]James F. Short (1997) argues, and I agree, that violent crime creates two victims: the perpetrator and the identified victim. Both lives are either ended or permanently disrupted by the experience.

Poverty and race interact to leave young African American men at tragically high risk for violence. During the 19th and 20th centuries, African American men were more likely than white American men both to be murdered and to commit murder (Short, 1997). In 2003, African American men aged 25 to 44 were more than 10 times as likely to die as the result of homicide as white men the same age (Kaiser Family Foundation, 2006b).

WELFARE FRAUD

A popular urban myth holds that Food Stamp recipients use their vouchers to buy guns and drugs, and hundreds of Americans have heard that "a friend of a friend" saw a woman drive to the welfare office in a Cadillac. In reality, welfare fraud is neither as prevalent nor as straightforward as many believe.

SNAP administrators have been especially aggressive in fraud detection and prevention. As we have seen, SNAP distributes more than $74 billion worth of food vouchers, of which less than 1 percent is lost due to fraud. It is dishonest retailers, not the poor, who profit from most SNAP fraud. In the most common form (known as "trafficking") the retailer purchases SNAP benefits for 65 to 85 percent of their face value and then seeks full reimbursement. Although this practice frees participants to spend the reduced amount on whatever they like, the profit accrues to the retailer. In one of the largest cases, a retailer in Toledo, Ohio, improperly redeemed $7.2 million in Food Stamps. This individual previously had been convicted of fraud but evidently never quit the lucrative practice (Cook, 1989). Of course, that was before electronic benefits transfer (EBT) cards were developed. Similar to bank debit cards, EBT cards have dramatically reduced the extent of fraud in this program (U.S. Department of Agriculture, n.d.b).

Public assistance seems designed to produce fraud. As we have seen, cash assistance fails to raise incomes above the poverty threshold. Even when in-kind assistance such as Food Stamps, Medicaid, and housing supports are included, parents find it difficult to raise children with so little money. Thus, mothers find other sources of income—a practice that (if unreported) constitutes welfare fraud (see Funiciello, 1993). Antonia's babysitting is one example of this widespread practice.

Of course, the economic impact of welfare fraud pales in comparison with garden variety middle-class fraud. Fraud against Medicare alone deprives taxpayers of an estimated $60 billion each year (National Health Care Anti-Fraud Association, 2008). Common forms of Medicare fraud include billing for services not furnished (known as "phantom billing"), misrepresenting the diagnosis to justify payment, soliciting, offering or receiving a kickback, and "up-coding" (billing for more costly services than those actually delivered).

Tax evasion also takes its toll. Based on IRS data, the GAO reported that taxpayers pay only about 87 percent of the taxes they owe. Groups vary in the extent of their tax evasion, with wage earners reporting 99 percent of their earnings, while self-employed workers report only 19 percent. The difference between taxes owed and those collected, called the "tax gap," has increased. In 1981, the tax gap amounted to $76 billion, or 1.6 percent of the nation's gross domestic product (GDP). By 1992, that figure had grown to $127 billion, or 2 percent of the GDP (U.S. General Accounting Office, 1994b), and in 2008–2010, the IRS estimated the nation's average annual tax gap at $458 billion (IRS, 2016).

America's energetic pursuit of welfare fraud can hardly be attributed to its draw on the public purse. Even when the amount seems large, it is a small fraction of the amount lost to health insurance fraud and tax evasion. Yet welfare fraud raises the public ire in a way that tax evasion never could. Why is that? Is it more corrupt for a welfare mother like

Antonia to be paid under the table for providing child care to her neighbors than it is for a business person to conceal income from the IRS? Or is the furor over welfare fraud just another vehicle for humiliating recipients of public assistance?

LO 5-7   Become Aware of Rising Inequality, Its Causes, and Its Consequences

EP 3a
EP 8d

Today we speak of three types of inequality: first, **income inequality** refers to the differential between income, regardless of its source; second, **earnings inequality** describes differences in the wages received by workers; finally, **wealth inequality** examines the disparity among asset holdings. Recent decades have seen all three of these rise in the United States and most other developed nations.

The '60s and early '70s were a period of shared prosperity in America. Between 1967 and 1973, income increased for most Americans, regardless of whether they were in the top income quintile (the fifth of the population with the highest incomes) or the bottom quintile (the fifth of the population with the lowest incomes). Indeed, family incomes in the lowest quintile grew more than those of the most affluent. The Congressional Budget Office reported that mean adjusted family income for those in the lowest quintile increased by 30 percent, while it grew by 21 percent for the highest quintile.

But things have changed. While incomes overall have by some accounts continued a slow, halting rise, the **income share** of the bottom quintile has declined, while that of the highest has risen. This growth in inequality slowed somewhat during the 1990s but it resumed in the 21st century, and the American income distribution now looks very much as it did in the 1920s (Bernstein et al., 2000; U.S. Census Bureau, 2009b). In 2008, the OECD reported that the richest 10 percent of Americans had the highest incomes in the OECD, while the poorest had incomes about 20 percent lower than the OECD average. This is illustrated in Figure 5.4.

FIGURE 5.4   Distribution of Income in the United States, 2014

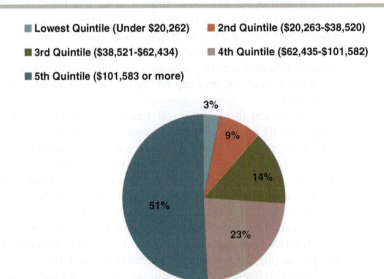

- ■ Lowest Quintile (Under $20,262)
- ■ 2nd Quintile ($20,263-$38,520)
- ■ 3rd Quintile ($38,521-$62,434)
- ■ 4th Quintile ($62,435-$101,582)
- ■ 5th Quintile ($101,583 or more)

3%
9%
14%
23%
51%

SOURCE: U.S. Census Bureau (2015) Income and Poverty in the United States: 2014, Table 2 (https://www.census.gov/content/dam/Census/library/publications/2015/demo/p60-252.pdf).

BOX 5.6   The American Dream

Americans tolerate inequality because we believe that a child raised in poverty can become rich. Sadly, this is seldom the case. Intergenerational social mobility of this kind is relatively low in the United States. Miles Corak (2013a, b) compared inequality and earnings mobility among the 13 OECD nations and found that the United States has unusually high inequality and relatively low economic mobility. Indeed, there is some evidence that rising inequality actually reduces social mobility. As the rungs on the social ladder grow further apart it gets harder to climb (Autor, 2014).

Following the Great Recession, the **Occupy Movement** brought inequality to public awareness with its slogan: "We are the 99%." Then, in his 2016 presidential campaign, Bernie Sanders mobilized millions to fight (or at least to protest) inequality. Today everyone knows that the incomes of average Americans have stagnated for decades, while the nation's most affluent have become even wealthier. Everyone knows that American CEOs take home hundreds of times the income of production workers. Some argue that Americans prefer inequality, that our social norms favor private wealth over public responsibility; that, thanks to the mythology around the American Dream, the poor expect that they or their children or grandchildren will eventually become rich.

Whether we prefer it or not, inequality has risen, and its causes and consequences are slowly coming into focus. In the United States, the "skill premium" associated with post-secondary education (a leading factor in earnings inequality) has doubled in the last three decades. In other words, the difference in earnings between high school and college graduates has grown due to declining wages among those without college degrees. As we will see in Chapter 15, the inflation-adjusted value of the minimum wage has diminished. America has also seen a sharp decline in "good" jobs—well-paying jobs that do not require college degrees. These range from clerical and administrative roles that have been replaced by automation to industrial jobs lost to international competition. So the skill premium enjoyed by college graduates is less due to *their* rising wages than it is to the *declining* wages of non-graduates. In other words, as most people are painfully aware, rising inequality is less the result of increased middle class incomes than of declining incomes among the less advantaged.

Public policies have contributed to this situation, even as they have failed to address it. As we saw in Chapter 2 (Figure 2.4), federal legislation has steadily reduced the marginal tax rates paid by the most affluent. Likewise, as of this writing, Congress had not raised the minimum wage since 2009. U.S. educational policies may also contribute. Princeton economist David Autor (2014) argues that "A central causal factor behind rising inequality in the United States has been the slowdown in the accumulation of skills by young adults almost thirty years ago." This points to the role of public policy in providing access to affordable college education. Unfortunately, as we will see in Chapter 12 (Children), the U.S. educational system does not serve as a "great equalizer" (to quote Horace Mann). It could be the most effective lever we have for reducing disparities. Instead, it reproduces broader inequalities.

The social consequences of inequality are difficult to measure; but Wolfson and colleagues (1999) used data from the National Longitudinal Mortality Survey to demonstrate that inequality has a direct, independent effect on mortality in this country. They compare it to a "miasma" or "air pollution." There is some support for the argument that inequality has an independent effect on public health. For instance, comparisons of U.S. states and cities also suggest higher mortality rates in regions with the greatest inequality (Deaton & Paxson, 2001; Deaton & Lubotsky, 2004). It has also been associated with higher crime rates and lower average educational achievements (Ferreira & Ravallion, 2008; United Nations Development Program, 2007).

Joseph Stiglitz (2012) attributes these social consequences to a decline in social cohesion, as the affluent withdraw from society. By moving into gated communities and sending their children to private schools they insulate themselves from social ills. No longer dependent on public systems that less-fortunate Americans must rely upon (police, health care, education), they call on Congress to reduce taxes they would otherwise pay to support those systems. Meanwhile, through segregation, voting restrictions, and related measures, the poor are excluded from the common weal.

Apart from these divisive social consequences, rising inequality may also have a negative impact on the economy. Based on his study of 30 years of OECD economic data, Federico Cingano (2014) concluded that "Income inequality has a negative and statistically significant impact on subsequent growth. . . what matters most is *the gap between low-income households and the rest of the population*." (Cingano, 2014, p. 6, italics added). His findings suggested that the lack of skill development among low-income households was a key factor, suppressing income growth in conditions of high inequality.

With this and similar studies, the long-term *economic* consequences of inequality come to the fore. In a surprising development, even researchers for the International Monetary Fund have acknowledged the adverse consequences of inequality. Ostry, Loungani, and Furceri described an "adverse feedback loop" that obtains when inequality suppresses growth, which fosters greater inequality (2016). They call for "increased spending on education and training, which expands equality of opportunity" and the use of taxation and government spending to redistribute income. They conclude that "*Fortunately, the fear that such policies will themselves necessarily hurt growth is unfounded*" (italics added). While President Trump drew support from those with limited education, his own affluence and strong ties to the wealthy suggest he may not share Bernie Sanders's commitment to fighting inequality.

Closing Reflections

This chapter began with the case of Antonia Flores, a bright, articulate woman struggling to ensure a better future for her son. Her success as a mother might in earlier eras have entitled her to public assistance. But under current welfare law, Antonia, along with millions of other welfare recipients, is encouraged to assume personal responsibility for her limited means.

The nation's collective responsibility for low-income families and their children is limited. Upon reaching their lifetime limits, former welfare recipients may retain Food Stamps, Medicaid, and housing assistance, but they will not have money to pay for other basic necessities such as utility bills or clothes.

Current welfare policies are based on the belief that for most people, work is the best antidote to poverty. This serves the needs of the capitalist economy, to which diminished work incentive represents a significant economic threat. Welfare reform reduces that threat, both by eliminating the choice between welfare and work, and by reducing the quality of life for those on welfare. Of course, as we will see in Chapter 15, many Americans like Antonia find that work does not provide the economic security they need for themselves and their families.

Walter Trattner (1989) ends his exhaustive survey of the history of the American welfare state by suggesting that "[p]erhaps a time will come anyway when most Americans will acknowledge—or be forced to acknowledge—what our colonial forebears simply took for granted, namely, that the poor will be with us, always, through no fault of their own, and that they, too, have a right to a healthy, happy, and secure life" (p. 342). Whether the poor will ever be able to live "a healthy, happy, and secure life" in the United States remains to be seen.

Think About It

1. Consider the three conditions that facilitate collective action to address individual problems, as outlined in the introduction to Part II. The events of the Great Depression led many Americans to see poverty as an individual problem with "uncertainty of moment and magnitude." Does this view still hold? Do any of these conditions play a role in contemporary debates about welfare reform? Should they? Does poverty in the United States have any "external effects"?

2. Which of the philosophical conceptions of social justice presented in Chapter 1 is most influential in the structure of the U.S. welfare effort?

3. How do these philosophical conceptions play out in the reactions of our politicians and pundits to economic inequality?

4. Why do you think the United States applies a residual approach to income maintenance (categorical assistance), rather than a universal one such as a guaranteed minimum income?

5. A college degree is more valuable today than ever before. Some politicians, like Bernie Sanders, advocate universal, free college access. What do you think of his proposal? Who would benefit? Who would lose?

Web-Based Exercises

For direct links to all the sites in these exercises, visit the *Foundations of Social Policy* Companion Site at www.cengagebrain.com and select the resources for Chapter 5.

1. Go to the poverty page maintained by the U.S. Census Bureau at http://www.census.gov/hhes/www/poverty/poverty.html. Click on "Small Area Income and Poverty Estimates," and then choose "State and County Data." Here you can compare the poverty rate in your state with that in other states and in the nation as a whole. Is your state's poverty rate higher or lower than the U.S. rate? How do you account for this finding?

2. Will a college education keep you out of poverty? Go to the Department of Census poverty site (http://www.census.gov/hhes/www/poverty/poverty.html) and find the latest release for "Income, Poverty and Health Insurance Coverage in the United States." There, under "Detailed Tables," find the section labeled "Years of School Completed by Poverty Status, Sex, Age, Nativity and Citizenship." After choosing "Below 100 percent of poverty," you can examine figures for those with and without college degrees of diverse race, age, and gender combinations. Does a college degree lower the risk of poverty the same amount for each combination? How do you explain your findings?

3. Go to the TANF website (http://www.acf.hhs.gov/programs/ofa/programs/tanf) and click on "Data and Reports" in the left menu. Scroll down to Reports and click on TANF Reports to Congress. Open the most recent report and see what the Administration for Children and Families has to say about the program. What issues are highlighted in the report? What are the characteristics of TANF families? Do you see any discussion of benefit levels? Is poverty mentioned?

4. If you are intrigued by the politics of welfare reform, go to http//www.Theatlantic .com/past/docs/issues/97mar/edelman/Edelman.htm and read "The Worst Thing Bill Clinton Has Done," a scathing critique of PRWORA, written by a leading welfare expert who worked for the Clinton administration.

Competency Notes

As mentioned in the preface to this volume, the Council on Social Work Education has designated nine core competencies and related practice behaviors that must be addressed by accredited social work programs. In these notes, I will specify the way chapter content addresses these competencies and behaviors. (This is designed to assist with the accreditation process.) Please refer to the "helping hands" icons for the locations of specific content in this chapter. Here you will find a brief explanation of how the accompanying content relates to the specified competency or practice behaviors.

The following list indicates where EPAS competencies and practice behaviors are addressed in this chapter.

EP 3a   **Apply their understanding of social, economic, and environmental justice to advocate for human rights at the individual and system levels.** This chapter considers the way beliefs about the poor and the policies that govern means-tested programs serve to maintain the status quo. It also examines factors associated with high risk of poverty, which can inform advocacy efforts.

EP 4c   **Use and translate research findings to inform and improve practice, policy, and service delivery.** This chapter illustrates how research on household expenditures has been used in policy practice to critique existing poverty measures. It also summarizes research on who is at risk of poverty.

EP 5c   **Apply critical thinking to analyze, formulate, and advocate for policies that advance human rights and social, economic, and environmental justice.** Here we examine the oppressive consequences of various approaches to poverty measurement and of poverty interventions through history to provide a solid base for critical analysis of contemporary proposals.

EP 8d   **Negotiate, mediate, and advocate with and on the behalf of diverse clients and constituencies.** Discussion of means-tested programs includes details regarding eligibility requirements and benefit levels, and discussion of Medicaid addresses negotiations with managed care providers on behalf of vulnerable groups. Further examination of inequality will sensitize students to its implications for marginalized populations.

Suggested Resources

Deparle, J. (2004). *American Dream: Three Women, Ten Kids, and a Nation's Drive to End Welfare.* New York: Viking Books.

Hanson, L. K. & Essenburg, T. J. (2014). *The New Faces of American Poverty: A Reference Guide to the Great Recession.* Santa Barbara, CA: ABC-CLIO.

Kilty, K. M., & Segal, E. A. (Eds.). (2006). *The Promise of Welfare Reform: Political Rhetoric and the Reality of Poverty in the Twenty-First Century.* New York: Haworth Press.

Rycroft, R. (Ed.) (2013). *The Economics of Inequality, Poverty, and Discrimination in the 21st Century.* New York: Praeger.

Silver, M. (2013). *Mary Coin*. Blue Rider Press.

www.census.gov/hhes/www/poverty.html. Maintained by the U.S. Census Bureau, this site is a good starting point for up-to-date information on poverty in the United States.

www.faireconomy.org. This site is operated by United for a Fair Economy (UFE), an organization devoted to policies that reduce inequality in the United States. UFE is grounded in the belief that our country "would be a far more democratic, prosperous, and caring community if we narrowed the vast gap between the very wealthy and everyone else." The UFE website offers an introduction to the organization and provides position papers on issues.

www.urban.org. Operated by the Urban Institute, a nonprofit organization, this site provides reports on social and economic problems.

The health of the people is really the foundation upon which all their happiness and all their powers as a state depend.

BENJAMIN DISRAELI, JULY 1877

Learning Objectives

This chapter will help prepare students to:

LO 6-1   Become familiar with the history of public health in the United States

LO 6-2   Understand the government's role in financing health care through Medicaid and Medicare

LO 6-3   Understand the role of the private market in financing and delivering health care

LO 6-4   Understand health disparities and sociodemographic factors that influence health outcomes in the United States

LO 6-5   Discuss how health expenditures and outcomes in the United States compare with those of other nations

LO 6-6   Become aware of global health inequities

LO 6-7   Know the history and current status of health-care reform in the United States

LO 6-8   Describe the role(s) social workers play in health policy

The role of government in health care has long been the subject of debate in the United States. Early public health reformers met vigorous opposition when they proposed what we now consider basic public health measures. With the debate over the **Affordable Care Act,** the role of government in financing and delivering health care is once again under dispute. At issue is the extent to which illness should be addressed through collective, as opposed to individual, action.

Allocation of health care is clearly a social justice issue, as is the extent to which a patient should be held responsible for the cost of treatment. America's reliance on private-market solutions to health problems has created a multibillion-dollar health-care industry designed to serve economically productive and affluent members of society.

Meanwhile, millions go without health insurance. Should health care be treated as a social good, with no one permitted to fall below a minimal standard? Is the private market the most efficient means of distributing medical care? Should individuals bear the risk (and the cost) of catastrophic illness? Should the public bear the cost of illnesses caused by personal behavior? These and related questions are considered throughout this chapter.

LO 6-1   Become Familiar with the History of Public Health in the United States

EP 3a
EP 5c
EP 8d

Most of us are familiar with the major medical breakthroughs of the 20th century: the development of antibiotics, immunizations, and advanced surgical techniques. Less familiar, but perhaps more significant, have been advances in public health. As we have seen, modern plumbing improved the health of populations around the world. In this section, we will focus on the development of public health interventions in the United States.

In some ways, the development of public health programs has paralleled the growth of the U.S. welfare state. Policy milestones include the 1912 creation of the Children's Bureau; the 1930 establishment of the Veterans Administration; the 1944 creation of the Public Health Service (PHS); the 1946 establishment of the Centers for Disease Control and Prevention (CDC); the 1953 creation of the Department of Health, Education, and Welfare; and the 1965 passage of Medicare and Medicaid.

Public health reformers in 19th-century America drew from the English approach to community health, seeing (perhaps more clearly than we do now) the close link between poverty and disease. Just as this nation imported major elements of the **Elizabethan Poor Law**, we also inherited the perspectives of Britain's "Sanitary Movement." Edwin Chadwick and other leaders of the movement advocated national oversight of sanitation in urban areas, government tracking of vital statistics, and local regulation of waste drainage and purification of drinking water. When they presented their suggestions to Parliament in 1844 and 1845, they met with shocked protest. Many saw the proposed measures as violations of private property rights and individual liberties. Nonetheless, a staunch group of reformers—mostly from privileged backgrounds—persisted, and in 1848 they won passage of the Public Health Act, which established local boards of health throughout the nation. Under the Act the establishment of a local board could be triggered either by petition of at least one-tenth of the taxpayers in the area or when mortality over a seven-year period exceeded 23 people per 1,000. Local boards dealt with water supply, sewage, management of cemeteries, control of "offensive trades" (such as prostitution), and investigation of conditions affecting community health.

Like the British model, the American approach to public health focused on local, as opposed to national, efforts. Local boards of health assumed responsibility for a wide range of public health tasks, from regulating and inspecting public eating establishments to maintaining vital statistics and managing quarantines. Fee and Porter (1991) described their work as "a kind of rearguard action against the filth and congestion created by anarchic economic and urban development" (pp. 20–21).

But there was a role for the federal government. In his classic history of the field, George Rosen (1993) dates the U.S. government's first involvement in public health to the Marine Hospital Service. Established by Congress in 1798, the service addressed the health-care needs of seamen. Crews of merchant vessels were integral to the commercial success of the nation, but they were not residents of any parish or town, so the system of local responsibility left them without care.

A HUMAN PERSPECTIVE   Tanya Johnson

At the age of 24, Tanya Johnson was considered uninsurable due to a preexisting condition. Tanya is HIV-positive. She sees herself as living with, not dying from, AIDS and refuses to view herself as a "victim" of the epidemic. Her situation illustrates some of the tensions experienced by people coping with chronic illness in the U.S. health-care system.

A bouncy, attractive woman with long, curly, auburn hair, Tanya describes herself as "perfectly healthy … I don't take medications, and I have good T cells, and I have a low viral load. I do have symptoms. My lymph nodes are swollen a lot and inflamed, and sometimes they ache. They don't hurt; they ache. And so I just take Motrin for it. I get fatigued very easily. I take Motrin for cramps, for chest pains, headaches. I'm a walking ibuprofen advertisement."

When she speaks to high school classes for the local AIDS foundation, she begins by saying, "My name is Tanya Johnson, and I've had HIV for four years that I contracted from a very lovely sociopathic IV drug user."

"He *was* [sociopathic]," she assured me. "He's in prison right now, as a matter of fact, so he's proven it." Tanya met her boyfriend at a party one night. "We'd gone to a party, and this guy was there, and he was friends with us," and so they started going out. "It just kind of happened. I'd go to his place and party sometimes, and it just happened one night. It wasn't like we dated or anything."

Tanya's boyfriend knew he had AIDS, but didn't tell her. "I'm not angry about this. 'Cause I'm not. It's my own fault, you know? I knew what I was doing, you know? And you have to take your own responsibility for yourself. I knew about safe sex and I knew about AIDS. I lost my virginity when I was 14, so I knew about all the precautions to take. I wasn't stupid. I was just crazy, I guess. I was immortal, and I was on top of the world, and nothing bad was ever going to happen to me. I was going to live forever—young, and beautiful, and thin."

After Tanya and her boyfriend broke up, she learned that he had AIDS. "So I went to go to get tested. I'd been tested before so I knew the drill. I waited past the 90 days 'cause I kind of really didn't want to know. I invented all the reasons in the world why it couldn't possibly be, and then all the reasons why it could possibly be, and I … you know? The flu-like symptoms that they tell

you about. I didn't feel good for a whole month. I called for my test results, and I was getting off at 3:30 p.m. I says, 'Are my test results in?' She says, 'Yes, they are.' I says, 'Great. I'll be in after work.' She says, 'No.' She says, 'Come in tomorrow.' I says, 'No, I can come in right now.' She says, 'No, come in tomorrow. How about 4:00?' And by now I'm panicked, 'cause I just know. And I says, 'What time do you open?' She says, '9 a.m.' I says, 'I will be there at 9 a.m.' I did not sleep that night. Did not have sex with my boyfriend that night, you know. And of course I hadn't told him about any of this. The next morning I go in. And you know when I go in, I have to sit and wait forever in the waiting room. And then I go in, and then … the lady that gave me the test took me into a room, and there was another lady sitting there. And I just started crying. They didn't even have to tell. And the lady that was in with her, she's a case manager for the state. And she's a wonderful lady. She says, 'What are you going to do when you leave here?' I says, 'I don't know … go home. She says, 'Call your mom right now. Make an appointment and meet her for lunch and tell her,' and I'm like, 'Okay.' She didn't want me to leave the office and have nowhere to go."

Tanya is an only child. She told her mother over lunch, and her mom responded, "So, do you want to live forever?" "I says, 'Well … yeah. I kind of would like to. You know? I'm 21 years old!' I couldn't tell Dad. She told Dad for me. I went home the next afternoon, and my dad came out of the bedroom, and my mom had told him, and he comes up to me and just gives me a big, huge hug, then went back to his bedroom. He couldn't stay with me because he was, you know, just too choked up. He says, 'I love you' and walked back in his bedroom. My family's been great. Except for my Uncle James, and he doesn't talk to me or won't come anywhere near me."

Tanya works as an office manager for a small firm with 10 employees. She likes her job. "The people are really nice, which is amazing, 'cause you know, usually at jobs, people are so cruel. And I like what I'm doing." The people at work don't know that Tanya is HIV-positive. It is important to her that her employers not know about her condition, because she was fired from her last job because of her HIV status.

When she was diagnosed, Tanya had worked as a computer operator for Homebase for four and a half years. She had health insurance and a 401(k). After careful

(continued)

deliberation she decided to tell the manager. "I thought he was a nice guy. I've never been a good judge of character. I thought maybe he could help me in case I needed some time off. I told him in confidence.

"He then has a staff meeting. Tells all the staff managers, my supervisor, his office staff."

Tanya describes the result as "nightmarish." After a year, she was fired for failing to come in for a scheduled shift. The manager had scheduled her for back-to-back closing and opening shifts. Because it was too draining, she had frequently asked not to be given this kind of shift and had been accommodated. "I requested, two weeks in advance, that the schedule be changed. I told the general manager, and he refused to change the schedule. 'Look,' I says, 'I'm not going to do this to myself. I know what will happen to my body if I do it…. It'll make me sick. Do you want me to be sick?' He told me I would just have to work it. Everybody worked back-to-backs. He says, 'You know, I get tired too. You don't see me calling in sick.' My God! He has no clue what tired means. And so I told him I wouldn't show up for the shift. So I worked the night shift, and in the morning I set my alarm and I called him, and I called in sick. 'Well, Tanya,' he says, we have a problem.' The next day I went to work and they suspended me. I knew they were going to fire me. Before I went in to work, they had taken my picture off the computer room door."

Tanya experienced a health crisis shortly after she was fired, and she talked to her doctor about the experience. Her doctor referred her to "an ACLU attorney," who found someone to take her case. After mediation and two hearings before the state industrial commission, Tanya had a ruling in her favor. The judge ruled that Homebase failed to provide the reasonable accommodation due to Tanya under the Americans with Disabilities Act. When Tanya received her notice in the mail, she was thrilled, not because of the money (back pay) she might receive, but because she had been vindicated. "They did something wrong and they hurt me, and so yeah, I'm fighting back … and if they'll do it to me, then they'll do it to someone else, you know? And I don't want someone else to go through what they put me through."

When she was fired, Tanya lost her health insurance. With her preexisting condition, getting new insurance was "a complete nightmare." In fact, she had no insurance coverage for four years. "I applied for it when my time came up. I filled out the paperwork and sent it in 'cause I wasn't going to give it to my employers. Well, at the same time my employer decided to change insurance companies. The gentleman that had sold us this insurance policy, I called him and I says, 'Norm, I'm gonna mail you my insurance application.' I says, 'When you get it, if there's a problem, call me. Not my supervisor.' He's all, 'Okay.' So about two days later he calls me. He goes, 'I got your application, and unfortunately we're gonna deny your entire group because of your application.'"

So Tanya's firm didn't include her in their group's applications. "'We're gonna do this,' he [her supervisor] says. 'If you can get insurance on your own, we'll pay 75 percent of the premium,' which he didn't do." Instead, Tanya went to the State Department of Health, which ran a Health Insurance Premium program for people with AIDS, funded under the Ryan White Act. To enroll in the program, Tanya needed to verify that the employer's insurance firm had reached its "cap." Under state law, health insurers are required to cover a certain proportion of "uninsurables" before they can begin denying coverage. But the insurance firm in this case had not reached its cap. As it turned out, "The insurance company just basically said, 'We're denying you,' but they hadn't really reached their cap." So the company was required to insure Tanya. "If I hadn't had to have verification, I never would have known, and I wouldn't have insurance."

Tanya had to wait a year for coverage of her preexisting condition. For care, she relied on the services provided under her state's Ryan White program, which she described in glowing terms. Her case manager was "absolutely amazing," her physician's assistant was "wonderful," and her physician walked on water. When we talked, her care needs were limited to biannual testing and periodic treatment of emerging symptoms.

Tanya taught HIV 101 to high school classes. Her new boyfriend accompanied her to one of these sessions. "The teacher, instead of putting Matt (that's my boyfriend) over on the side of the room—he was just gonna sort of sit and listen—he put his chair right next to me up front. So, Matt's sitting here, like okay, you know? And I go through my story and one of the kids asked, he says, 'Well, what does your boyfriend think about this?' And I said, 'I don't know. Matt, what do you think about this?' He's like, 'What?' And then they start asking him questions, and I think it was a really good thing to have him there. He came off with this just suave, smooth answer.... That's why I like him."

Matt moved in with Tanya, and they were talking about buying a house (or maybe a ranch) together and getting married. Tanya did not want children. "I did a talk, and a girl was very ... 'Well, can't you adopt?' I said, 'It takes a lot of energy to raise a child, and that's energy I need for myself if I'm going to stay healthy. My body works a lot harder than normal people's bodies, just at rest ... and I've never had a craving to have kids.'"

Tanya was exceptionally motivated, with a positive attitude toward life and toward coping with HIV. As she put it, "I don't understand depression. I don't get depressed. I get angry sometimes at people. I get pissy and whatever. But I don't get depressed." She made lifestyle changes to maintain her health: drinking distilled water, avoiding rare meat, reducing her alcohol intake, carefully washing fruits and vegetables, and avoiding overexertion. "I figure it's easier to change my lifestyle now, while I'm healthy, than later, when I'm sick. If I get sick, God forbid."

But Tanya knew people through the AIDS Foundation who didn't take care of themselves. "They don't enjoy their life. They still do drugs; they still drink. I have one friend who's not supposed to take his medication when he takes alcohol and drugs, so when he goes to parties, he doesn't take his medication." Tanya attributed her good health to lifestyle and attitude: "My basic frame of mind is to be happy."

When she was diagnosed, Tanya knew very little about what to expect from the disease. During the first few months she "wasn't thinking in terms of the future." She only thought she was going to die. But she has developed a new philosophy. "You know? It changes your whole outlook on life. I don't get upset about all the petty [things] ... [like] who squeezed the toothpaste on the wrong side of the tube. These things aren't important. My family and my friends, those are my priorities. Enjoying my life is my priority. Everyone's going to die. AIDS is not the only thing that people die from. People die from all sorts of cancers, and accidents ... natural disasters. Everyone is going to die. I'd kind of like to die with dignity."

A SOCIAL WORK PERSPECTIVE

Tanya's experience as an American with a chronic illness was influenced by several public policies, including Medicaid, the Ryan White Care Act, and the Americans with Disabilities Act (ADA) at the federal level, as well as state policies such as the regulation that required health insurance providers to serve the uninsurable. Unfortunately, she was diagnosed before passage of the **Patient Protection and Affordable Care Act** (PPACA, also known as "Obamacare"). Had she waited until 2010, Tanya might have had a simpler time purchasing insurance, since the Act prohibited denial of coverage for preexisting conditions. During his transition to the presidency Donald Trump pledged to retain this aspect of Obamacare.

In some respects, Tanya's experience paralleled that of anyone who seeks care in the U.S. health-care market. The care she received was determined by the political will of the nation. Had she become unable to care for herself, Tanya would have relied on family and friends as long as possible, hoping to avoid nursing home placement. But if she was forced into long-term nursing care, Tanya probably would have relied on Medicaid. Of course, she would have been required to "spend down" her personal resources to become eligible.

The stigma associated with AIDS still creates hysteria and discrimination. When Tanya was fired, she had access to legal remedies provided by the 1990 passage of the ADA. The ADA was not drafted with HIV/AIDS victims in mind. Nevertheless, disability policies such as the ADA and income supports such as Old Age, Survivors, and Disability Insurance (OASDI) and Supplemental Security Income (SSI) have become significant resources for this group, because HIV/AIDS is considered a disabling condition.

Tanya was distinctive in having access to effective drugs to mitigate the effects of HIV. She contracted AIDS after a tremendous burst of pharmacological research. She lived in an industrialized nation, which gave access to treatment that is unheard of in developing countries. But her treatment was expensive. At the time of our conversation, a three-drug regimen that included a protease inhibitor cost about $18,490 to $24,654 a year in today's dollars (Farmer, 1996, p. 264).

The United States is the only industrialized nation that does not offer universal health coverage. We depend on a private market to provide health care and health insurance. Perhaps as a result of the failures of that market, new laws are enacted each year to regulate the operations of insurers and providers. Even today, Tanya might be forced to depend on publicly subsidized care if she had lost her job.

The Marine Hospital Service provided medical and hospital care to sick and disabled seamen, financed through a monthly tax of 20 cents on each man's wages. The result was the world's first prepaid, comprehensive medical and hospital insurance plan. The Treasury Department collected the fees, and the service was placed under its jurisdiction. As a result, until 1935, most federal public health services operated under the Treasury Department.

Another federal health responsibility involved immigration. In the United States, as in Europe, human travel from infected areas was the primary vehicle for spreading epidemics. Immigrants were seen as sources of foreign contagion, which spread like wildfire through overcrowded urban slums. As a result, early attempts to control epidemics focused on immigrants. In 1878, the National Quarantine Act gave the Marine Hospital Service authority to inspect immigrants. At first, this screening was intended to bar "lunatics and others unable to care for themselves," but it later extended to "persons suffering from loathsome and contagious diseases." Federal involvement in public health continued to expand. In 1879, a National Board of Health was established to collect information, advise the federal government on public health issues, and devise a plan for quarantine procedures.

Meanwhile, the development of immunizations expanded the role of local health authorities. From 1880 to 1898, scientists in Europe identified specific organisms responsible for most of the infectious diseases of the time. Even before these organisms were identified, researchers observed that a mild case of disease could produce lifelong immunity. This observation was accompanied by experiments (often conducted on poor children) that attempted to produce immunity through injection of blood from an infected patient. Louis Pasteur is credited with developing the principle of prophylactic inoculation.

Public health scientists and officials in the United States observed these developments, and soon laboratories were added to local public health departments. Their staff performed diagnostic tests, conducted research, and distributed vaccinations to community physicians. As the efficacy of these measures became clear, the stage was set for widespread acceptance of government involvement in public health.

FEDERAL HEALTH AGENCIES

Three types of federal health agencies emerged in the United States during the 20th century (Hanlon & Pickett, 1979). These include:

- the PHS, the only national agency concerned with broad health issues
- agencies that serve specific groups, such as the Children's Bureau, the Women's Bureau, the Administration on Aging, the Bureau of Indian Affairs, and the Veterans Administration
- agencies that deal with specific problems or programs, such as the Office of Education, Food and Drug Administration, Department of Agriculture, and Bureau of Labor Statistics

We will briefly review the history of three of the largest federal health agencies: the PHS, the Children's Bureau, and the Veterans Administration. Together they provide an introduction to the evolving role of the federal government in the delivery of health care in the United States.

Public Health Service

Public health specialists generally consider the PHS the most important federal agency in the field. It grew out of the Marine Hospital Service. In 1902, Congress recognized the expanded responsibilities of the service by renaming it the Public Health and Marine Hospital Service and placing it under the direction of a surgeon general. In 1912, the agency was again renamed with the title it bears today: the U.S. **Public Health Service**. The 1935 passage of the Social Security Act charged the service with providing grants-in-aid to states and territories to assist in establishing health services and training health personnel. In 1953, the service moved from the Treasury Department into the newly established Department of Health, Education, and Welfare (HEW). In 1980, the Department of Education became a separate agency, and HEW was renamed the Department of Health and Human Services (HHS).

The service involved the federal government in direct provision of medical care. Originally, hospitals and clinics were established to serve those eligible for care (seamen, federal civilian employees who became ill in the line of duty, members of the Coast Guard, and anyone requiring immunization for yellow fever). Later, under the **Indian Health Service**, medical facilities for Native Americans and Eskimos were established. In time, however, direct operation of most hospitals and clinics was phased out.

Today the PHS supports direct care by providing grants to other organizations. Through its Health Resources and Services Administration (HRSA), the PHS finances the delivery of primary and preventive care to medically underserved residents in the United States and its territories. Services funded through these programs include black lung clinics for coal miners, prevention and primary care delivery at the U.S.-Mexico border, medical services to migrant farm workers, health care for native Hawaiians, comprehensive care for residents of public housing, and primary care and substance abuse services for the homeless. The PHS also delivers primary health care to people who are detained by the Immigration and Naturalization Service.[1]

Children's Bureau

Establishment of the **Children's Bureau** was debated for six years until Congress finally authorized it in 1912. With support from the National Consumers League, the National Child Labor Committee, and many women's organizations and church groups, the bureau was created to serve as a center of research and education. It was placed under the Department of Commerce and Labor, signaling an early focus on regulation of child labor. Under the direction of Julia Lathrop, the bureau was authorized only to investigate and report on health issues affecting children and their mothers.

But even this charge involved bureau staff in controversy. The bureau's research indicated serious maternal and child health problems in rural areas, lending momentum to an emerging movement to establish maternal and child welfare programs through federal grants-in-aid. Opponents of this effort included the American Medical Association, antisuffragists, the Sentinels of the Republic, and several other organizations who saw the bureau's proposals as a violation of personal, family, and states' rights and a step toward socialized medicine.

---

[1]For more information about HRSA programs, see http://www.hrsa.gov/index.html.

Nonetheless, in 1921 (the year Grace Abbott took over as director), the Sheppard-Towner Act was passed, authorizing the Children's Bureau to administer grants-in-aid to fund health and welfare programs for mothers and children. Abbott and her staff of reformers set out to establish programs throughout the states. They moved quickly and within the next two years set up programs in 15 states.

The original act included what we now call a **sunset clause,** which provided for review and extension of its programs after five years. This clause gave opponents another chance to attack the Bureau. As a result, a bill to extend Sheppard-Towner for seven years failed, and a two-year extension was passed. This signaled the end of the program. After the act expired, 35 states decreased appropriations for maternal and child welfare, and nine states eliminated this funding entirely (Hanlon & Pickett, 1979).

The hiatus in child and maternal health programming did not last long. In 1935, the Social Security Act not only restored the **Sheppard-Towner** programs but extended the Bureau's responsibilities to include child welfare services and services for crippled children, administered through grants-in-aid to the states.

Through subsequent decades, the Children's Bureau continued to pursue its original mandate to investigate and report on issues affecting children's welfare, and the programs and services under its auspices continued to expand. When wives and children of World War II servicemen were unable to pay for medical care, the Bureau alerted Congress to the situation and the Act for the Emergency Maternity and Infant Care for the Wives and Children of Servicemen was passed. In 1963, the Maternal and Child Health and Mental Retardation Planning Amendments (to the Social Security Act) gave federal support to state-run projects that offered comprehensive care for high-risk mothers and infants in low-income families. Two years later, the Social Security Act was again amended to authorize development of comprehensive health services for children and youth. Funds were allocated for clinics, hospital care, and health education for low-income families.

BOX 6.1   Grace Abbott on Washington Politics

"Sometimes when I get home at night in Washington I feel as though I had been in a great traffic jam…. In that traffic jam there are all kinds of vehicles moving up toward the Capitol … conveyances of the Army … limousines in which the Department of Commerce rides … it becomes more congested and more difficult, and then because the responsibility is mine and I must, I take a very firm hold on the handles of the baby carriage and I wheel it into traffic."

—Grace Abbott, Director, Children's Bureau, 1934

Library of Congress/Getty Images

▶ Grace Abbott (1878–1939).

The costs of the **Vietnam War** brought significant reductions in funding for these programs. Reorganization of the Department of Health, Education, and Welfare separated the health and social welfare functions of the Children's Bureau. Health functions, such as prenatal care for low-income mothers, primary health care for their infants and children, and disease prevention programs, were assigned to the newly created Maternal and Child Health Program that operates today in the PHS. The social welfare functions of the Bureau, including protective services and shelters for high-risk youth, child care for recipients of public assistance, and adoption services, are now lodged in the Administration on Children, Youth, and Families within the Department of Health and Human Services.

Department of Veterans Affairs

Government provision for veterans in the United States can be traced back to the Pilgrims. Following their war with the Pequot Indians, the Pilgrims passed a law providing that disabled veterans would be supported by the colony. Since then, expanded benefits for veterans have often been used as an inducement to join the military and as a reward for service. After the Civil War, many states established medical and convalescent facilities for veterans. Treatment was provided for all diseases and injuries, whether or not they were service-related. The first residential and medical facility for veterans was authorized by the federal government in 1811.

The current system of federal veterans benefits originated in 1917 when the United States entered World War I. Benefits included disability compensation, insurance, and vocational rehabilitation for the disabled. In the 1920s, these programs were administered by three different federal agencies: the Veterans Bureau, the Bureau of Pensions, and the National Home for Disabled Volunteer Soldiers. These agencies were combined to form a single **Veterans Administration (VA)** in 1930 "to consolidate and coordinate Government activities affecting war veterans." The status of the VA was enhanced in 1989, when it became a cabinet-level department. Upon creation of the new department, President George H. W. Bush said, "There is only one place for the veterans of America, in the Cabinet Room, at the table with the President of the United States of America" (U.S. Department of Veterans Affairs, n.d.).

In 1930, the VA had 54 hospitals. Today, according to the VA website, it "operates the nation's largest integrated health-care system, with more than 1,700 hospitals, clinics, community living centers, domiciliaries, readjustment counseling centers, and other facilities." With staff numbering over 300,000, these facilities provide a broad spectrum of mental health, medical, surgical, and rehabilitative care (U.S. Department of Veterans Affairs, n.d.)

Like most health-care programs, the VA medical system has seen dramatic cost increases in recent decades. Cost-containment attempts have included restrictions in medical coverage and in the population covered. For example, injuries and diseases that are not service-related are not always covered, and access to care may be subject to a means test. Thus, VA health care has transitioned from an entitlement for all veterans to a program that primarily serves low-income veterans. The transition has not been smooth, and in 1996 the General Accounting Office (GAO) and others called for "VA eligibility reform." The 1996 passage of the Veterans Health Care Eligibility Act was an attempt to clarify and simplify eligibility requirements for VA health care. Under this act, all veterans seeking health care can apply for enrollment in what the VA is calling a "Uniform Benefits Package." Health care will be allocated through enrollment priorities that are based on degree of disability and financial need.

The 2007 scandals at the Walter Reed VA hospital brought the system's weaknesses into sharp relief. More than 1.5 million Americans have served as volunteer soldiers in Iraq and Iran, and many of them returned with debilitating physical and mental wounds. In February 2007, a series of articles in the *Washington Post* exposed the appalling conditions in Walter Reed's Building 18. The problems of substandard housing and care had been raised in other venues for years, but this time the national outcry led to swift action by the Bush administration. Although he had been on the job for only six months, Major General George W. Weightman, commander of Walter Reed, was quickly and publicly relieved of duty. A bipartisan commission was formed to hold hearings and issue recommendations.

LO 6-2   Understand the Government's Role in Financing Health Care Through Medicaid and Medicare

EP 3a
EP 8d

While the PHS, the Children's Bureau, and the VA have all been involved in delivering health care, the federal role extends to health-care financing as well. Through Medicaid and Medicare, federal funding pays for care that is delivered by non-governmental providers. Medicaid finances care for low-income Americans, and Medicare provides coverage for those who are elderly or disabled. In the following sections we will briefly consider the history of Medicaid and Medicare, which will shed light on the role of government in financing health care in the United States. As you read this material, please keep in mind that through these programs the government either finances or delivers care to about a third of the U.S. population.

Health insurance coverage was not widespread in the early years of the 20th century. Most Americans simply purchased their care. As late as 1963, for example, only 56 percent of the elderly had hospital insurance (U.S. House of Representatives, Select Committee on Aging, 1990). Those who lacked coverage and financial resources either received no treatment or used community health clinics and charity hospitals, which were few and far between. Some states provided limited support to meet the health-care needs of public assistance recipients and others deemed "medically needy" or "medically indigent."

Early reform efforts date to the Progressive era, a period of economic prosperity and social reform lasting from roughly 1890 to the 1920s, when the American Association for Labor Legislation (AALL) campaigned for "sickness insurance" to cover workers and their dependents (Skocpol, 1995). The reformers' efforts were opposed by the American Medical Association (AMA) and business interests. Ultimately, the campaign and the organization itself were defeated. Theodore Roosevelt's Bull Moose Party proposed a national health insurance program in 1912, but more than 50 years went by before any form of national health insurance was established in the United States. The 1965 passage of Titles XVIII and XIX of the Social Security Act established Medicare and Medicaid, despite the objections of the **American Medical Association**.[2]

There is some irony to AMA objections, because the passage of **Medicare** and **Medicaid** established reliable financing for many of the services provided by its members. Both programs provided "indemnity" coverage, also known as fee-for-service insurance.

---

[2]The American Medical Association did not always oppose national health insurance. Indeed, the organization supported early efforts in this area.

Under this model, providers were reimbursed for all medically necessary services delivered to beneficiaries. Although there were some restrictions on fees, both Medicare and Medicaid have become major sources of revenue for health and allied-health providers, setting the stage for huge increases in public health-care expenditures. The establishment of Medicare and Medicaid financed tremendous growth in the health-care industry, even as the programs improved access to care for the poor, the aged, and the disabled.

MEDICAID

When Medicaid was established, the federal government had limited involvement in health care for the poor. Nonetheless, there was some precedent for federal intervention. The Hill-Burton Act of 1946 allocated federal funding for hospital construction and required that hospitals receiving these funds provide care to the indigent. Further, the 1950 amendments to the Social Security Act provided for some federal participation in meeting the medical needs of public assistance recipients.

Through Medicaid, "the poor were promised that they would soon have access to mainstream medical care and that health care was a basic right" (U.S. House of Representatives, Select Committee on Aging, 1990, p. 7). The program was established as a federal-state partnership, primarily funded through federal money, with a matching requirement for the states. Administration was carried out by the states, with federal regulation and oversight. Medicaid does not provide health care directly; instead it reimburses providers for the care of low-income patients.

During Medicaid's first 30 years, the population covered by the program expanded. Initially, eligibility was restricted to recipients of public assistance. Later, states were required to cover all pregnant women and infants living in households with incomes up to 185 percent of the poverty line, as well as low-income persons with disabilities. The Centers for Medicare & Medicaid Services reported that 20.1 percent of the U.S. population was enrolled in Medicaid at some point during 2006 (U.S. Department of Health and Human Services, 2009). This number is expected to increase with eligibility expansions under the Patient Protection and Affordable Care Act of 2010.

Partially as a result of the expanded beneficiary pool, the costs associated with Medicaid increased dramatically. Total expenditures more than doubled from 1988 to 1992, and they are still going up. In 2011, Medicaid spent $381.5 billion to provide health care to an estimated 53.9 million people. With this growth, matching funds for Medicaid consumed a greater share of state budgets; but Medicaid spending growth was not entirely due to increased enrollment. As the Center on Budget and Policy Priorities (2003) argued, only about one-third of the growth in cost was due to enrollment increases. The remainder was the result of rising health-care costs, particularly for enrollees who were aged or disabled.

Medicaid Cost Containment

Concern about rising Medicaid costs has fueled efforts at cost containment. The past two decades have seen draconian attempts to reduce costs. These include:

- adoption of a prospective payment system
- reductions in provider payments
- eligibility restrictions adopted through 1996 welfare reform legislation
- expanded use of managed care

Prospective Payment System In 1983, the Hospital Prospective Payment System was developed to reduce Medicaid costs. Instead of reimbursing hospitals for all reasonable costs, this system provides payment at a set rate for **diagnosis-related groups (DRGs).** Under prospective payment, a hospital receives the same amount for every patient with a certain diagnosis, regardless of the services provided. Designed to promote greater efficiency, the use of DRGs has led to earlier hospital discharges. Advocates and service providers agree that the prospective payment system has led hospitals to discharge patients "quicker and sicker" (Fischer & Eustis, 1989). In 1989, the principle of prospective payment was extended to include physician payments as well as hospital bills.

Provider Cuts Cost-containment pressure has led to reductions and freezes in provider payments under Medicaid. By 1990, Medicaid payments to physicians averaged 50 percent of their charges and 60 percent of the Medicare rate (Physician Payment Review Commission, 1991). The result of provider cuts was a drop in the number of physicians who were willing to serve Medicaid patients (Derlet & Kinser, 1994).

Welfare Reform On August 22, 1996, President Clinton signed the Personal Responsibility and Work Opportunity Reconciliation Act (PRWORA). In addition to replacing **Aid to Families with Dependent Children** (AFDC) with TANF, the act had significant implications for Medicaid. TANF beneficiaries who lost aid because they refused to work could also lose Medicaid coverage. Further, states were no longer required to cover pregnant women and children with household incomes between 133 percent and 185 percent of the federal poverty level. Finally, nonemergency care for legal immigrants was substantially reduced. States were required to provide Medicaid coverage to legal immigrants who had entered the country before January 1, 1997, as well as those who were veterans or on active military duty, refugees and some people who had been granted asylum, and those with a 10-year work history. But legal immigrants who had entered the United States after January 1, 1997, were banned from Medicaid coverage for five years.

The mid-1990s saw three years of Medicaid enrollment drops (1996–1998) (Klemm, 2000). Some of this was due to provisions limiting coverage for immigrants. As Kaushal and Kaestner (2005) pointed out, "Many observers believe that PRWORA created an atmosphere of fear and confusion among immigrants." But immigrant restrictions alone would not account for the magnitude of these drops. The strong economy that the nation enjoyed during these years may also have reduced the need for Medicaid coverage.

These measures did slow the growth in Medicaid expenditures. Indeed, the Center for Budget and Policy Priorities (CBPP) reported that in 2002 the growth in health-care costs per Medicaid enrollee was lower than the growth observed in private insurance plans (Ku & Broaddus, 2003). This trend was attributed to expanded use of managed care.

The Great Recession In the wake of the **Great Recession** Medicaid enrollment grew from 42.3 million in 2007 to 52.6 million in 2011. By 2011 about one in six Americans (17 percent) were enrolled in Medicaid. During the same period, Medicaid spending on medical services (not including administration) rose from $292.7 billion in 2007 to $381.5 billion in 2011 (Kaiser Commission on Medicaid and the Uninsured, 2013a). This growth, largely attributed to increased enrollment, brought Medicaid (once again) into the political crosshairs, as we will see later when we consider the Affordable Care Act of 2010.

Managed Care   Medicaid beneficiaries were familiar with **managed care** long before it became a household word. In 1981, the Omnibus Budget Reconciliation Act permitted state-level experimentation with Medicaid managed care. Arizona was the first state to require Medicaid clients to enroll in managed care through its Health Care Cost Containment System. Other states followed, and by 1996, 40.1 percent of Medicaid enrollees were in managed care programs (Zuckerman, Evans, & Holahan, 1997). These were primarily AFDC clients.

Today all states except Alaska, New Hampshire, and Wyoming have some Medicaid recipients enrolled with managed care organizations. Over half require managed care enrollment for at least some recipients, while others offer voluntary enrollment (Kaiser Family Foundation, 2010a). The growth in Medicaid managed care has not had a widespread effect on the program's elderly and disabled clients. Of course, the elderly and disabled have more complex health-care needs than other clients and may be less profitable for managed care organizations.

In the most common approach to Medicaid managed care, the state contracts with a managed care organization (MCO) to provide care for Medicaid clients on a "capitated" basis. Under capitation, the MCO receives a fixed amount for each Medicaid enrollee, regardless of the services provided.[3] Although Medicaid beneficiaries must enroll in managed care, the Freedom of Choice regulations of the Centers for Medicare and Medicaid Services (CMS) require states to allow enrollees to choose among contracted managed care providers.

The key to an effective system of Medicaid managed care lies in negotiation and monitoring of each state's contract with providers. The central role of state health departments represents an opportunity for social work practitioners to ensure that the needs of consumers are addressed in these processes (see Perloff, 1996). As advocates and employees, social workers can ensure that the service mix, the provider choices, and the contract monitoring procedures address the needs of Medicaid clients (see Rosenbaum et al., 1988). Further, social workers can amplify the voice of Medicaid recipients in decisions related to managed care. As Perkins, Olson, and Rivera (1996) observed, "Recipients have tended to take a back seat when it comes to consumer involvement with the Medicaid program and its services" (p. 3). Mechanisms for increasing the influence of Medicaid recipients include consumer surveys, grievance procedures, hotlines, and consumer representation on advisory boards. A few states have established Medicaid managed care ombudsman programs, which may encourage consumer involvement.

The impact of managed care on Medicaid clients seems to be mixed. Critics suggest that quality of care is sacrificed; but for some, managed care may improve access because providers under contract with state Medicaid programs are not allowed to refuse enrollment to an eligible client (Rowland & Salganicoff, 1994). For instance, a study in California reported improved access to ambulatory care and lower hospitalization rates (Bindman et al., 2005). A few studies have assessed Medicaid clients' satisfaction with managed care. In general, clients in MCOs reported higher satisfaction with their care

---

[3]Many MCOs are organized as health maintenance organizations or HMOs. The term HMO was coined by analysts for the Nixon administration and initially stood for "health management organization." A last-minute change, solely for public relations purposes, created the more user-friendly "health maintenance organization." The Nixon administration promoted the concept, which led to passage of the Health Maintenance Organization Act of 1973 (Petchey, 1987).

than those in traditional fee-for-service arrangements (Sisk et al., 1996; Temkin-Greener & Winchell, 1991).

Long-Term Care   Medicaid pays for roughly half of the nation's **long-term care** expenditures. During the 1980s and 1990s, two trends converged to increase the demand for nursing home care: the growth in the elderly population and increased life spans for people with disabilities. This period saw dramatic increases in the number of older adults who lived in nursing homes, and the rising demand for long-term care changed the role of Medicaid (Jonas & Kovner, 2002). Medicare offers only limited coverage for long-term care, so many turned to Medicaid for payment, making it the nation's *de facto* long-term care insurance program.

The widespread use and high cost of nursing home care led many to advocate for the expansion of intermediate alternatives (Estes, Swan, & Associates, 1993). This push for alternatives reflected the observation that many nursing home residents did not require the intense level of medical care provided by a nursing home. Indeed, most people with disabilities prefer to be cared for in their own homes.

Today, long-term care alternatives include residential care as well as other arrangements, such as in-home care and assisted living. Both Medicaid and Medicare offer limited funding for care provided in a patient's home, and many states fund community-based care using Medicaid's **Home and Community-Based Waivers**. We have also seen increased public recognition of the role played by family members in caring for people with disabilities.

Perhaps as a result of these developments, use of nursing home facilities (which peaked in the late 1990s) appears to have stabilized or even gone down slightly (U.S. Department of Health and Human Services, 2005; Jonas & Kovner, 2002). This is especially noteworthy given that the number of older adults in the U.S. population has increased. As we will see at the close of this chapter, the Patient Protection and Affordable Care Act of 2010 (ACA) included a national long-term care insurance program that never went into effect.

MEDICARE

The Medicare program differs fundamentally from Medicaid. It is not means tested, and it provides health coverage to workers who are at least 65 years old or disabled and who are eligible for Social Security benefits. It is not operated as a federal-state partnership but is managed exclusively by the federal government. Medicare is not welfare for the disadvantaged but an entitlement earned through participation in the workforce. Despite these differences, the history of Medicare parallels that of Medicaid in many ways.

For Medicare, the 1960s and 1970s saw expanded benefits and enhanced quality control. In 1972, Social Security Amendments added coverage for people with end-stage renal disease (ESRD). As Norman Levinsky explained, "In the 1960s and 1970s, when the cost of health care represented a much lower percentage of the gross national product than it does at present, the pressure not to deny lifesaving treatment to Americans solely because of expense was irresistible" (1993, p. 1395). These amendments also expanded coverage to people with disabilities and established professional standards review organizations (PSROs) as a vehicle for quality control. At the time, policy makers such as Robert

Ball, Commissioner for Social Security, and staff to congressional committees saw Medicare as the first step toward national health insurance (Levinsky, 1993; Social Security Administration, n.d.a).

Benefit expansion was also part of the 1982 amendments, which added hospice coverage. A subsequent effort to expand Medicare benefits was quickly repealed. In 1988, the Medicare Catastrophic Coverage Act (MCCA) provided for increased benefits (including prescription drug coverage) financed through a surtax on enrollees whose incomes were high enough that they owed federal income tax. Those who paid the surtax complained bitterly, arguing that they were being asked to do something that was required of no other segment of the population: pay for the care of others in their age group. Most MCCA provisions were repealed in 1989.

Recent decades have seen exponential increases in Medicare costs, coupled with repeated cost-containment efforts. The Hospital Prospective Payment System described earlier has been applied to Medicare as well as Medicaid. Diagnosis-related groups have successfully reduced Medicare's hospital costs, and the prospective payment system has been applied to services provided by physicians and other health-care providers (Prospective Payment Assessment Commission, 1995).

In the case of Medicare, cost-containment measures have extended beyond reductions and freezes in provider payments[4] to include increases in premiums and deductibles paid by beneficiaries. Despite these increases, the proportion of Medicare Part B costs covered by premiums has dropped. In 1967, the annual premium of $36 per enrollee covered roughly half of Part B costs. By 1991, premiums covered only a quarter of costs. In response, the Balanced Budget Act of 1997 required that premiums be set at levels that would cover 25 percent of costs. Under the Medicare Modernization Act, Part B, premiums vary on the basis of income. In 2013, individuals with annual incomes below $85,000 (or $170,000 for couples) paid the standard premium of $104.90 per month, whereas those with higher incomes paid an "income-related adjustment." The adjustment increased to a high of $335.70 per month for those with annual incomes in excess of $214,000 (see http://www.Medicare.gov). Even with this adjustment, the amount drawn from the general fund has grown and, with it, congressional opposition to the program (Rasell & Weller, 2001).

The late 1990s were marked by rising concern over the financial status of Medicare Part A as well. In 1996, the trustees predicted that unless radical changes were made, the **Hospital Insurance (HI) Trust Fund** (which funds Part A) would be depleted, and outlays would exceed revenue by 2001; so the Balanced Budget Act of 1997 included measures to reduce Part A costs. Savings from this measure, along with the economic growth of the late 1990s, led the trustees to revise their estimate. In 2001, the date of projected depletion was moved forward to 2029 (Rasell & Weller, 2001), but that was before the Great Recession. In 2009, the trustees projected that the HI trust fund would be depleted in 2017. Later, passage of the Affordable Care Act contributed to a more optimistic projection. The 2012 trustee estimate of HI depletion was 2026. These adjustments in the estimated depletion date reveal the impacts of major economic events (recessions) as well as public policy (the ACA) on the solvency of Medicare.

---

[4]Freezes and reductions in Medicare's provider fees have led to a growing number of physicians declining Medicare patients.

Medicare Advantage (Managed Care)

Some attribute Medicare's rising costs to unrestrained utilization by program beneficiaries. Managed care was widely perceived as an effective way to control utilization and reduce costs. So in 1995, the Medicare Risk Program, now called Part C or **Medicare Advantage**, was established to encourage beneficiaries to enroll in managed care organizations (MCOs). MCOs offer Medicare recipients lower out-of-pocket costs while using managed care techniques to control utilization.

Managed care is attractive to healthy elders, who take advantage of the preventive care offered and do not need much specialty care. The result is a phenomenon called **favorable selection**, which occurs when low-risk individuals seek insurance from a particular provider. It is favorable to the insurance company in that it reduces the financial risk to the company. A contrasting phenomenon, **adverse selection**, occurs when high-risk individuals seek insurance from a particular provider. These choices are adverse to the insurance company.

The experiment with managed care did not significantly improve the fiscal status of Medicare. Some argued that Medicare capitation rates paid to MCOs are too high for such a healthy subgroup of the elderly population (Butler, Lave, & Reuschauer, 1998). Others noted that the cost savings achieved through reduced utilization were less than the high overhead rates charged by MCOs, resulting in no net savings to Medicare (Brown et al., 1993). There was also concern that favorable selection results in a creaming effect, in which MCOs enroll the healthiest Medicare recipients, leaving high-risk elders in the fee-for-service system. Efforts to lower capitation rates to reflect the relative health of elders who enroll in MCOs have led growing numbers of providers to simply withdraw from the Medicare market. Indeed, by 2000 approximately 1 million Medicare beneficiaries had seen their HMO coverage canceled (Hoffman, 2000). By 2005, only 14 percent of Medicare beneficiaries were enrolled in managed care (U.S. Department of Health and Human Services, 2005). Reflecting these problems, the Patient Protection and Affordable Care Act of 2010 authorized cuts in Medicare Advantage that, ironically, are expected to reduce costs.

Medicare Prescription Coverage: A Case Study in the Politics of Reform

Since Medicare's inception, the practice of medicine has changed and prescription medications have emerged as an important tool with the potential to prevent or delay the onset of conditions that would be painful and costly to treat. The nation's seniors and their physicians recognized the efficacy of the new generation of prescription medications, and as a result their out-of-pocket expenses for drugs rose dramatically. Clearly, there was high demand for prescription coverage under Medicare.

Meanwhile the cost of prescription medications in the United States was rising. Pharmaceutical companies argued that these price increases were necessary to support the lengthy and complex research and development process required to bring new drugs to market. Critics attributed the price increases to advertising by drug companies. In addition to adding to the drug companies' expenditures, advertising triggered increased demand (and hence increased prices) for medications.

Unlike the United States, Canada regulates medication prices. As a result, Americans pay more for most medications than their northern neighbors do. Canadian pharmacies discovered a new market for their wares, and soon Americans were purchasing their drugs in Canada through online pharmacies and bus trips across the border. Legislation was passed to allow Americans to import prescription medications from Canada (since they were doing so anyway), but the George W. Bush administration stalled implementation.

BOX 6.2   Importing Prescription Drugs

The issue of importation remains contentious. In 2004, Vermont filed a lawsuit attempting to force the administration to act, but was unsuccessful. Importation legislation in both the Senate and the House in 2007 contained a "poison pill" provision requiring administration certification of safety—certification that both Clinton and Bush administrations refused to supply. Opponents of importation have raised the specter of terrorism, and—perhaps as a result— there have been reports of Homeland Security officials seizing prescription medications at the border. The issue came up again when Senators Dorgan and McCain introduced an amendment to the 2009 health-care reform bill that would have eased importation from Canada and Western Europe. The Senate rejected their proposal.

Regulations were never issued because the Department of Health and Human Services refused to certify that any drug bought in Canada was safe and effective—certification that was necessary to begin development of regulations.

The **pharmaceutical industry** is a major force in Washington. In 2001, the *New York Times* reported that the industry had 625 registered lobbyists and a $197 million budget for lobbying and campaign contributions—the largest of any U.S. industry (Wayne & Petersen, 2001). Further, according to Public Citizen (a public-interest group founded by Ralph Nader), pharmaceutical companies spent a record $108.6 million in 2003 on lobbying activities and employed an army of 824 lobbyists (Public Citizen, 2003). Of course, the American pharmaceutical industry has been extremely profitable, with the top 10 companies recording profits of $35.9 billion in 2002 (Public Citizen, 2003). In this context Congress set out to develop a Medicare prescription drug benefit in 2003.

During the 2002 election cycle, President Bush announced that reforming Medicare would be a priority for his administration. The Republican leadership began drafting legislation to add prescription coverage, with an estimated price tag of $400 billion over 10 years. Democrats criticized the legislation but offered little serious opposition. The Senate version of the bill passed with a narrow majority under the sponsorship of Bill Frist (R-TN), the Senate Republican leader, and four cosponsors. At the same time, a bill was working its way through the House under the sponsorship of Dennis Hastert (R-IL), Speaker of the House, and 20 cosponsors. By July 2003, bills had passed both houses, but negotiations to resolve the differences between House and Senate versions were lengthy and inconclusive. In November AARP endorsed the legislation and began a $4 million advertising campaign in support. With this pivotal endorsement, the conference agreement was approved and the Medicare Prescription Drug, Improvement, and Modernization Act was signed by the president on December 8, 2003.

Prescription coverage under the voluntary program began on January 1, 2006, offered through private insurance companies with government subsidies. Under the program, Medicare beneficiaries could purchase a Medicare discount card for medications. The program established a formulary, or list of approved drugs, for specific conditions. Drugs that were not on the formulary would not count toward deductibles. The legislation included a tax subsidy to ensure that firms providing prescription coverage to their retirees continue their coverage. It also included a little-known provision that prohibited private insurance companies from offering prescription drug coverage that competed with the Medicare program. Finally, the legislation prohibited Medicare officials from using the program's vast purchasing power to negotiate for lower drug prices.

Part D included an unintended consequence known as the "**Medicare donut hole**." This refers to the gap between the prescription drug coverage limit and the catastrophic coverage threshold. In 2009, it meant that after beneficiaries had reached a $295 deductible, Part D covered 75 percent of drug costs up to $2,700—none of drug costs between $2,700 and $6,154—and 95 percent of costs over $6,154. Seniors found the donut hole particularly galling, which led some insurance companies to offer gap coverage for an additional fee.

Reactions to the legislation were mixed, with some agreeing with Senator Ted Kennedy that prescription drug coverage could destroy the 40-year-old Medicare program. Many feared that Part D coverage would crowd out drug benefits provided by employers. Others worried that the prohibition on competing drug coverage and the use of a formulary would restrict seniors' choices. Finally, critics noted the act's failure to allow the Medicare program to negotiate for reduced drug prices. Meanwhile, fiscal conservatives objected to the program's price tag, arguing that the new program added to the nation's record debt. The Congressional Budget Office estimated 2006 program costs at $32 billion, with projected cumulative outlays of nearly $800 billion by 2015 (Lichtenberg & Sun, 2007). AARP was sharply criticized for its endorsement, with some noting that the organization derives nearly one-fourth of its income from the sale of health insurance to its members. Thus, some argue, AARP had a conflict of interest—on one hand charged with representing the interests of seniors and on the other drawing a profit from its insurance business.

LO 6-3   Understand the Role of the Private Market in Financing and Delivering Health Care

EP 3a

Since the passage of Medicare and Medicaid, the United States has seen a dramatic concentration of private capital in what has come to be called the "health industry." Before the 1970s, for-profit health companies were largely confined to the pharmaceutical sector. By the mid-1980s, hospitals had entered the for-profit sector, with profits exceeding those of drug companies. In 1987, for example, the largest for-profit hospital chains—Hospital Corporation of America, Humana, National Medical Enterprises, and American Medical International—each exceeded the sales of most pharmaceutical manufacturing firms (in excess of $3 billion). This growth was not confined to acute care. By 1990, 12 nursing home chains with total sales of $4.5 billion dominated the market, and 80 percent of nursing home facilities in the nation were proprietary.

The expansion of for-profit health-care facilities left a shrinking role for nonprofits, the traditional providers for the poor and underserved. Nonprofit hospitals have typically provided a fuller range of health services than for-profits and may be more responsive to community need. For example, most AIDS units are run by nonprofits, as are the vast majority of trauma units. Yet in the 1990s, nonprofits were rapidly taken over by for-profits who were "gaining market share by buying out competitors, reducing excess capacity in their markets" (Cerne, 1995, p. 44).

As J. Warren Salmon (1995) observed, "No other nation in the world has witnessed as absolute or rapid a growth in health expenditures as has the U.S., and no other nation has such a for-profit presence in its health sector" (p. 22). Even Wall Street analysts expressed concern with this trend. An analyst with Morgan Stanley suggested that "ultimately we're going to see the formation of oligopolies, where each market or state will have three or four major players, and that's it. We're heading toward a utility model by the end of the decade, and at that point the government will have to step in" (G. Wagner in Cerne, 1995, p. 42).

In the burgeoning for-profit health-care industry, the public policy goal of reducing tax expenditures for health care conflicts with the private sector's drive to increase profits. This conflict might explain the limited success of cost-containment measures in health-care programs. For example, when **Diagnosis Related Groups (DRGs)** were introduced, the Senate Finance Committee monitored their impact on hospitals and in 1985 reported that: (1) 81 percent of hospitals made a profit on their Medicare accounts; (2) the average profit margin was 14.12 percent, compared with 3.3 percent in the rest of the service sector; and (3) the return on capital averaged 24 percent (compared with 14 percent elsewhere in the service industry). The committee suggested that in one year alone Medicare contributed $5 billion to company profits. Perhaps because the private health-care industry is so well represented in Washington, much of its dramatic growth has been directly financed by Medicare and Medicaid in an elaborate process that converts beneficiary payments and federal and state tax dollars into corporate profits.

INSURANCE BASICS

Private insurance is a central element of the U.S. health-care system. Here we will briefly consider how it works and explain some jargon that will inform your understanding of health-care reform debates, including terms such as **moral hazard, community rating,** and **experience (or risk) rating.**

Fundamentally, insurance is a method for reducing the risks we face as individuals. It takes a bit of the fear out of our lives. We know that if we die our families will have some money; if our homes burn down we will be able to rebuild; and if we are hurt someone will take care of us. Insurance has taken three forms in the United States: mutual aid, government programs, and commercial insurance. In the mutual aid approach, we share (or "pool") risks with people like us. In the 18th and 19th centuries, organizations like the African Union Society or the East Baltimore Improvement Society provided their members with sickness and disability benefits as well as burial and survivor's insurance in exchange for membership fees (Harris, 1979). In government programs like Medicaid and Medicare we pool our risks with other Americans and share the cost through taxes, premiums, and copayments. In commercial insurance, we pay (or our employer pays on our behalf) a company to assume some of our risk.

Today's system of **private health insurance** is the result of innovations and public policies of the early to mid-20th century. At a time when European countries were adopting compulsory national health insurance, the United States pursued a system of private employer-based insurance. It began during the Depression, when hospitals saw troubling declines in revenue. Their solution was to sell prepaid hospital care, of which the most famous product was the first Blue Cross plan. In 1929 Baylor University Hospital agreed to provide coverage for 21 days of hospitalization to a group of Dallas teachers in exchange for an annual payment of $6.00. Prepaid hospital plans like Blue Cross proliferated during the Depression, but it was not until 1949 that the Blue Shield plans were established to provide prepaid physician care. Both Blue Cross and Blue Shield were (and still are) organized as nonprofit corporations, which exempted them from state insurance regulations (Thomasson, 2002).

Nonetheless, private insurers were reluctant to offer health insurance because of two problems: **adverse selection** and **moral hazard**. As we have seen, adverse selection occurs when those who are unhealthy purchase coverage. The Blue Cross and Blue Shield plans avoided this problem by marketing their products to groups of employees. They also achieved significant administrative efficiencies by having employers withhold premiums from workers' paychecks (Thomasson, 2002).

The **moral hazard** problem arises when having insurance against a bad outcome leads a person to engage in behaviors that increase the likelihood that the outcome will happen. For instance, a person who otherwise would not seek hospital care might do so because he or she has insurance to cover the cost. Moral hazard was considered endemic to health insurance, but not to life insurance and accident insurance. As one author put it, "… to collect on life insurance, the insured must be dead, to collect on accident insurance, he must have had an accident, while to collect on sickness insurance he must have a policy" (McCahan, 1956, p. 187). Later, innovations such as deductibles and copayments would be used to reduce the moral hazard associated with health insurance.

The expansion of Blue Cross and Blue Shield was facilitated by special enabling legislation passed in most states that allowed these companies to organize as nonprofit corporations with tax-exempt status and exempted them from insurance regulations. The success of these plans, as well as World War II policies that gave favorable tax treatment to employee benefits, encouraged other private companies to enter the health insurance market. As nonprofits, The Blues (as they are often called) were required to set premiums using "**community rating.**" That is, they charged the same premium to all members of a group regardless of the health status of individual members. For-profit insurers could use "**experience rating**" to set premiums for the sick higher than those charged to the healthy. This gave the for-profits a significant advantage. Nonetheless, Blue Cross/Blue Shield continues to dominate the field, now insuring over a third of the nation's population. As we will see later, the U.S. market for health insurance was considerably expanded by the provisions of the Affordable Care Act.

LO 6-4 Understand Health Disparities and Sociodemographic Factors that Influence Health Outcomes in the United States

EP 3a

In the distribution of health care, life itself becomes a social justice issue and survival becomes a function of privilege, as class, race, and gender influence the risk of becoming ill and the likelihood of receiving appropriate treatment in the United States.

POVERTY AND HEALTH DISPARITIES

Throughout the life span, income can determine the likelihood that one will contract a disease. Among children, poverty has long been associated with low birth weight, increased infant mortality, and nutritional deficits (Rice, 1991; Nkansah-Amankra, Dhawain, Hussey, & Luchok, 2010). Adults with poverty-level incomes have significantly higher risk of contracting AIDS and other infectious diseases. The effects of environmental insults and inadequate care compound in old age, when a history of exposure to health risks, environmental toxins, stress, poor nutrition, and limited care can undermine health. Income also affects mental health. The risk of depression, for example, has been linked to poverty (Gilman, Kawachi, Fitzmaurice & Buka, 2002; Joongbaeck, 2010; Joy & Hudes, 2010).

Poor health outcomes among low-income groups may result partially from the stresses associated with living in poverty, but reduced access to health care certainly compounds these difficulties (Barr, 2007; Himmelstein & Woolhandler, 1995). Those living in poverty have limited access to preventive care (Kelly et al., 1993), and a combination of financial barriers, limited transportation, and cultural differences militates against their receiving treatment (Williams, 1993). The net effect in the United States is poor health outcomes for those living in poverty.

THE UNINSURED

The United States is distinct among industrialized nations in the large number of residents without health insurance. In 2011, for example, 48.6 million Americans, or 15.7 percent of the population, had no private or public health insurance (U.S. Census Bureau, 2012e). Even more experienced sporadic lack of coverage. The Affordable Care Act reduced this figure considerably, and by the end of 2015, 28.5 Americans were uninsured (Kaiser Family Foundation, 2016). Among those who do not have coverage, some have incomes below poverty. As we saw in Chapter 5, only about 61 percent of Americans with incomes below the poverty threshold have access to Medicaid. The remaining 39 percent make up only part of the uninsured population. The others are people caught in the middle: working people, who are not eligible for Medicaid but who cannot afford to purchase health insurance. (Often I find that students in social work classes do not have health insurance.)

Without health insurance coverage, people may receive emergency treatment but do not have access to preventive care or routine treatment. Local health departments provide some preventive care, such as childhood immunizations, but preventive care for adults under the age of 65, such as mammograms, blood pressure screening, and cholesterol checks, is not widely available. The routine treatment that insured Americans seek through their primary care physicians is also not available to the uninsured. This lack of access to medical care contributes to the high cost of hospital care as hospital emergency rooms deliver primary care to uninsured persons and as neglected conditions deteriorate into costly illnesses (Hoffman & Paradise, 2008).

At a personal level, those who are uninsured tend to ignore symptoms and delay treatment, sometimes with lethal results. We see this in the cancer statistics, which reveal income **disparities** in diagnosis, treatment and, as a result, mortality rates. In recognition of this problem, the National Cancer Institute has established a "Center to Reduce Cancer Health Disparities," with a budget to establish community-based cancer programs (see www.cancer.gov).

RACE AND HEALTH DISPARITIES

The National Institutes of Health (NIH) define **health disparities** as "differences in the incidence, prevalence, mortality, and burden of diseases and other adverse health conditions that exist among specific population groups in the United States." These specific population groups are people of color. In the United States, people of color are more likely to fall ill than whites. Higher prevalence is evident in a wide range of diseases. For example, African Americans have higher rates of hypertension, cardiovascular disease, stroke, diabetes, some cancers, and end-stage renal disease than white Americans do (Johnson & Smith, 2002).

People of color are less likely than whites to have access to culturally appropriate, good-quality care (Yearby, 2011). As Johnson and Smith (2002) note, "The evidence of racial and ethnic disparities in health outcomes is overwhelming" (p. 30). This evidence is seen in cancer survival rates, where African Americans and Hispanic Americans have lower overall five-year cancer survival rates than whites (Johnson & Smith, 2002). It is also evident in infant death rates. As Figure 6.1 indicates, African American babies are twice as likely to die in the United States, primarily due to complications associated with low birth weight (see David & Collins, 2007).

Disparities are also evident in life expectancy, as Figure 6.2 reveals. Here we see the improvement between 1900, when an African American man's life expectancy at birth was only 32.5 years, to 2014, when an African American man could expect to live 72 years.

FIGURE 6.1 U.S. Infant Mortality by Mother's Race

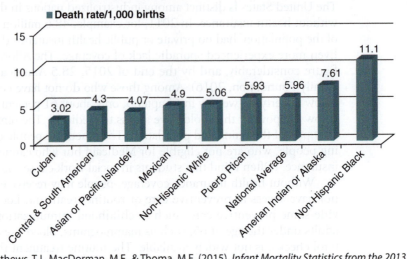

SOURCE: Mathews, T.J., MacDorman, M.F., & Thoma, M.E. (2015). *Infant Mortality Statistics from the 2013 Period Linked Birth/Infant Death Data Set*. National Vital Statistics Reports, U.S. Department of Health and Human Services (http://www.cdc.gov/nchs/data/nvsr/nvsr64/nvsr64_09.pdf).

FIGURE 6.2 Life Expectancy at Birth: 1900–2014

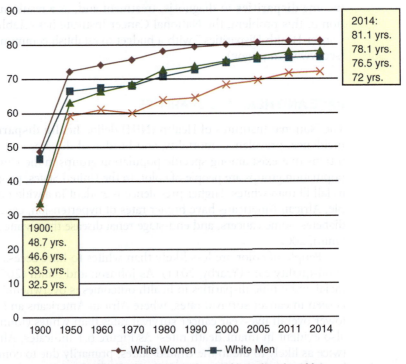

SOURCES: Centers for Disease Control (2008). Health, United States, 2008: With special feature on the health of young adults. Table 26. (http://www.cdc.gov/nchs/data/hus/hus08.pdf#026, July 12, 2010) 2011 figures: Centers for Disease Control (2013). Death in the United States, 2011. NCHS Data Brief #115 (http://www.cdc.gov/nchs/data/databriefs/db115.pdf, June 2, 2013). 2014 figures: Centers for Disease Control and Prevention (2016). Changes in Life Expectancy by Race and Hispanic Origin in the United States, 2013-2014. (http://www.cdc.gov/nchs/products/databriefs/db244.htm, August 30, 2016).

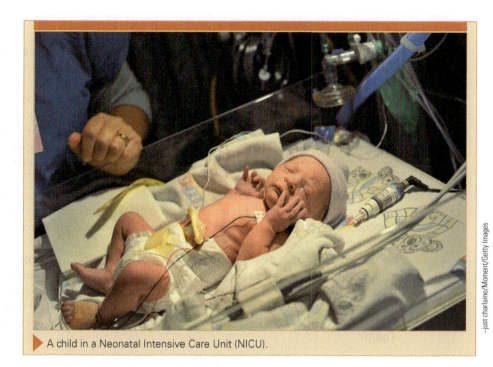

-just charlaine/Moment/Getty Images

▶ A child in a Neonatal Intensive Care Unit (NICU).

However, the racial disparity in life expectancy remains. In 2014, white men could expect to live four and a half years longer than African American men.

Infant Mortality in Harlem

Fidel Castro visited Harlem in October 1995 and bragged that Cuba's infant mortality rate (IMR) was not only the lowest in the Caribbean but was lower than that of Central Harlem. Castro and others argued that this difference demonstrated the failure of the U.S. economic system. Babies in Harlem, a low-income, primarily African American neighborhood in New York City, were at least three times as likely to die in their first year as those in the rest of the nation.

On August 11, 1998, the New York City Department of Health issued a press release reporting that infant mortality in the city had reached a "historic low." More specifically, the press release stated that "[i]n Central Harlem, the IMR plummeted by more than 56 percent, from 15.2 deaths per 1,000 live births in 1996 … to an IMR of 6.6 in 1997, below the Citywide average."

What could have produced this dramatic change? The mayor's office, along with advocates, social workers, and health-care professionals in Harlem attributed the change to a series of federally funded initiatives: new drop-in centers where pregnant women could receive health education, counseling, workshops, and case management from pregnancy through a child's first year of life; a program called Healthline that provided information and referrals; an Adolescent Parent Education program that trained young parents; Child Health Plus, a subsidized insurance program for children; and Healthy Start, an effort that began in 1991 and focused on decreasing mortality in high-risk neighborhoods. These initiatives paid off, and their impact reveals the power of sustained effort and reminds us that social and health indicators are amenable to intervention. Inequality in health care is not inevitable but is the direct result of allocation decisions made by professionals every day and policy choices made by elected officials.

GENDER AND HEALTH

As we saw in Figure 6.2, men have consistently shorter life expectancies than women do. This gender difference in mortality is worldwide and is expected to endure (Grambs, 1989).

Gender also influences the likelihood of becoming ill, known as "morbidity." In later years this translates into higher rates of acute illness among men and more chronic illness among women. For instance, arthritis is much more common among women, while coronary heart disease more often strikes men (Crimmins, Jung, & Sole-Auro, 2011; U.S. Senate Special Committee on Aging, 1988). Women develop late-onset diabetes at twice the rate of men (Dolger & Seeman, 1985; Gregg et al., 2002). Finally, women are more likely than men to suffer from urinary incontinence (Vaughan, Goode, Burgio, & Markland, 2011). Our health system more effectively meets the acute care needs more commonly experienced by men than it does the chronic care needs more often experienced by women (Estes, Swan, & Associates, 1993).

Gender differences have also been observed with respect to mental health conditions. Throughout life, women experience higher rates of mood and anxiety disorders than men, particularly depression (Kessler et al., 1994; McLaughlin, Xuan, Subramanian, & Koenen, 2011). Women's greater risk of depression has been linked to their increased risk of poverty (Belle, 1984; Ertel, Rich-Edwards, & Koenen, 2011; Feinson, 1991; Krause, 1986).

WHAT CAUSES THESE HEALTH DISPARITIES?

In the United States, it is hard to distinguish the effects of race or gender from those of class. Indeed, health policy analyst Vicente Navarro (1991) argued that in the United States, socioeconomic status is a more powerful determinant of health than race is (see also Fordyce, 1996). Observed differences among races in this country cannot be interpreted without reference to economic disparities and race-based oppression.

In some cases, race and class interact to produce higher risk of illness. The incidence of type 2 diabetes, particularly in later life, is strongly influenced by this interaction. The

---

BOX 6.3 The Obesity Epidemic: Are Americans Getting "Fat and Lazy"?

In 2005, S. Jay Olshansky and his colleagues published an article in the *New England Journal of Medicine* suggesting that the United States could face a significant drop in life expectancy due to increasing rates of obesity. Their review indicated that the prevalence of obesity had increased by about 50 percent per decade since 1980. Paul Terry, an epidemiologist at Emory University, offered a concise explanation for the epidemic: "The U.S. has the resources that allow people to get fat and lazy" (MacAskill, 2007).

But the distribution of obesity suggests that ample resources are hardly to blame. Obesity is most prevalent among low-income Americans and people of color. Seeking to contain the nation's obesity epidemic, analysts point to "lifestyle choices," suggesting that Americans need to be educated about nutrition and motivated to exercise. At the same time, an emerging body of research is identifying **neighborhood characteristics** that influence food choices and activity levels. Growing awareness of "**food ghettos**" where fresh produce is not available has led to a burgeoning urban garden movement in cities like Detroit, Milwaukee, and Los Angeles. Social workers interested in starting a community garden will find instructions through the American Community Gardening Association (http:// communitygarden.org/learn/starting-a-community-garden. php). Mobile farmers' markets also provide fresh produce to residents of food ghettos (see, for instance, http://fresh approach.org/mobile-farmers-market).

disease occurs more often among those with lower socioeconomic and educational levels (Kanjilal et al., 2006) and is concentrated among African Americans, Native Americans, and Hispanic Americans (CDC, n.d.a). In addition to inherited susceptibility, lifestyle considerations such as diet, lack of exercise, and limited access to preventive health care contribute to a person's risk of contracting diabetes.

Long-term oppression can undermine health as well. For example, Tay-Sachs disease is more common among the Ashkenazi Jews, whose ancestors originated in eastern Europe, than among other populations. This concentration has been attributed to the unique historical circumstances experienced by this group, including frequent migrations, numerous extermination attempts, dense concentration in urban ghettos, and periods of rapid population expansion and inbreeding (Fraikor, 1973). Tay-Sachs is an inherited condition, characterized by very early onset, which causes developmental retardation, paralysis, dementia, blindness, and death by age 3 or 4 (*Merck Manual*, 1992, p. 1051).

Oppression can also discourage members of minority groups from seeking treatment. Both culture and personal history come into play. For example, the Tuskegee syphilis experiments were conducted over a 40-year period from 1932 to 1972. Although the victims of these experiments have died, African Americans of all ages carry the memory of this extended period when black men with syphilis were told they were being treated when in fact researchers were just observing the progress of their disease. On a personal level, people of color commonly encounter health professionals who ridicule or disregard traditional health practices and treat them with disrespect and prejudice (Barr, 2007).

In 1998, President Clinton made a commitment to eliminate health disparities in six areas: infant mortality, cancer screening and management, cardiovascular disease, diabetes, HIV/AIDS, and immunizations. Since then, the NIH has assumed a central role in efforts to reduce health disparities. Research and educational efforts in this area have increased dramatically under this initiative, and health professionals are being trained to provide culturally appropriate care. Social workers in health-care settings frequently have the opportunity to contribute to this endeavor by serving as translators and mediators for people of color.

Although it is difficult to separate the effects of class, race, and gender on health outcomes, some generalizations can be made. Poverty brings increased risk of physical and mental health difficulties as well as diminished access to care. Oppression can make people more vulnerable to disease. Finally, in part because they live longer than men, women experience higher rates of chronic impairment and greater need for long-term care—an area long neglected by our health-care system.

HIV/AIDS AND HEALTH DISPARITIES

The World Health Organization estimates that 35 million people have died from HIV/AIDS since the epidemic began—about 1.1 million in 2015. Worldwide, 36.7 million are living with HIV/AIDS, among them over 1.2 million Americans (World Health Organization (n.d.a). The CDC estimates that one in eight infected Americans don't know they are carrying HIV (CDC, 2016).

The epidemic has hit African Americans and gay and bisexual men especially hard, as shown in Table 6.1 and Figure 6.3 (CDC, 2015). In 2014, African Americans, who represented about 12 percent of the U.S. population, comprised 44 percent of new AIDS diagnoses. Among new HIV diagnoses in 2014, African American men who were infected by having sex with men were the largest group (11,201), closely followed by white men who had sex with men (9,008) and Hispanic/Latino men who had sex with men (7,552).

TABLE 6.1 U.S. HIV/AIDS Cases Diagnosed by Ethnic Group (2014)

Ethnic Group	Diagnosed (New) Cases (per 100,000 population)
American Indian/Alaska Native	9.5
Asian	6.2
Black/African American	49.4
Hispanic/Latino	18.4
Native Hawaiian/Other Pacific Islander	10.6
White	6.1
Multiple Races	15.4

Source: CDC (2012). *HIV/AIDS Surveillance Report*, Diagnosis of HIV Infection in the United States and Dependent Areas, 2011. Vol. 23, Tables 1a & 11a.

FIGURE 6.3   Estimated New Diagnoses in the United States for the Most-Affected Subpopulations, 2016

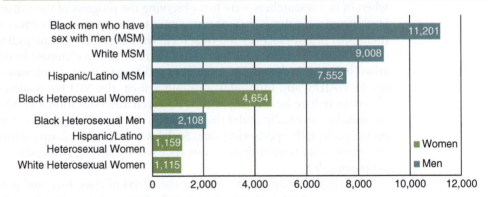

Source: http://www.cdc.gov/hiv/statistics/overview/ataglance.html.

Heterosexual contact accounts for about 24 percent of 2014 diagnoses. Among those infected through heterosexual contact, African American women were the largest group (4,654) followed by African American men (2,108), Hispanic/Latina women (1,159), and White women (1,115). White men who do not have sex with men are notably absent from the CDC's list of "Most-Affected Subpopulations." Only about 6 percent of 2014 diagnoses were due to injection drug use (CDC, 2016).

African Americans are not only the group most likely to be diagnosed with HIV/AIDS, but they also are less likely to enter care, to stay in care, to be prescribed **anti-retroviral treatment** (ART), and to experience **viral suppression**. The CDC reports that just over a third (37 percent) of African Americans living with AIDS in 2012 were receiving ART, and only 29 percent had reached viral suppression. Finally, over half (54 percent) of the deaths attributed to HIV/AIDS in 2013 were African Americans (CDC, 2016).

But epidemiological figures can obscure the social meaning of AIDS. As Peter Conrad (1986) explained, "AIDS is an illness with a triple stigma: it is connected to stigmatized

BOX 6.4   Appropriate Diagnosis Brings ADA Protections

Although Congress has refrained from listing conditions that make an individual eligible for disability benefits and protections available under the Americans with Disabilities Act (ADA), federal regulations and case law have clearly included AIDS as a legitimate disability (Stein, 1995). Therefore, appropriate diagnosis can provide protection against discrimination in employment and education, as well as income supports available under both Supplemental Security Income (SSI) and Social Security (OASDI). Yet complications in the diagnosis of AIDS can restrict patients' access to treatment and income supports. Symptoms of AIDS differ among affected subgroups. Children tend to display symptoms that resemble failure to thrive and developmental delays. Adults often develop rare cancers and infections. In women, AIDS may manifest as pelvic inflammatory disease, cervical dysplasia, and vaginal infections.

groups; … it is sexually transmitted; and, like cancer, it is a terminal wasting disease. It would be difficult to imagine a scenario for a more stigmatizing disease" (p. 53). In the early 1980s, the disease was associated with marginalized populations: homosexuals, drug users, Haitian immigrants, and Africans. Its early designation as "gay-related immune deficiency syndrome" reinforced the notion that AIDS was the product of a deviant lifestyle. So it was 10 years before we saw a significant federal response.

By 1990, the growing number of "blameless" victims (those who, as Kimberly Bergalis said in her 1991 congressional testimony, "didn't do anything wrong") moved U.S. policy makers to approve the primary legislative mechanism for funding prevention, treatment, and research on AIDS: the 1990 Ryan White Care Act, named after a teenage hemophiliac who died of the disease. Services provided by the states with these funds include health insurance programs that cover premiums for patients able to secure private coverage, drug programs that provide access to medication, and home-based health care. Recall that Tanya Johnson (whom we met at the beginning of this chapter) received health-care services and insurance funding through her state's Ryan White program.

Federal spending on HIV/AIDS has increased. The president's 2014 budget request included $29.7 billion in spending on domestic and global HIV/AIDS programs. In Medicare and Medicaid alone, spending for the care of people with HIV/AIDS was estimated at over $12.5 billion in 2014, while services provided through the Ryan White Care Programs cost an estimated $2.4 billion (Kaiser Family Foundation, 2013b).

Meanwhile, the epidemic raises questions of civil liberties as the nation debates mandatory testing, reporting, and partner notification. At present, AIDS testing is mandatory for blood and organ donors, some prison inmates, and military recruits and active duty personnel. Until 2010 it was required of immigrants and refugees as well (Kaiser Family Foundation, 2016). Mandatory partner notification has been debated, along with testing of all pregnant women or newborns. Partner notification laws have been passed in some states to require those who test positive for HIV to notify sex and/or needle-sharing partners. Failure to do so may result in felony prosecution. Some jurisdictions also require that inmates' HIV status be reported to public health authorities, parole officers, and spouses or sexual partners (AIDS.gov, n.d.). Other interesting policy questions will likely arise with the long-anticipated development of an HIV vaccine (DuBois et al., 2015).

As we have seen, health disparities are pervasive throughout the American health-care system. Yet some have continued to claim (as Sen. Jeff Sessions of Alabama did on

March 21, 2013) that this country has "the best health-care system the world has ever known." In the following sections we take an international perspective on health-care costs and outcomes to find out whether results support this claim.

We also need to keep in mind that the HIV/AIDS epidemic is also the result of social and economic inequalities that force young women into prostitution and create the ghettos that serve as breeding grounds for infection (Farmer, 1996). This argument certainly applies to the United States, where diagnoses of HIV/AIDS tend to be concentrated in low-income neighborhoods.

LO 6-5   Discuss How Health Expenditures and Outcomes in the United States Compare with Those of Other Nations

EP 3a

Although at least a third of the nation relies on the federal government to either finance or deliver its health care, some pundits and politicians and health industry advocates still claim that the free market is the best way to deliver health care in the United States. Does the private health-care market indeed operate with greater efficiency and effectiveness than national health-care programs in other industrialized nations? Let's look at the costs and services delivered by the U.S. health-care system from an international perspective.

HEALTH EXPENDITURES AND HEALTH OUTCOMES

The United States spends more on health care than any other nation in the world. To put it another way, we rank highest among the developed nations in health-care spending, both on a per capita basis and as a percentage of the GDP. America's 2015 per capita spending on health-care services was more than double that of other industrialized nations. That year, the United States spent $9,451 per person for health care, while the average for the 29 industrialized nations belonging to the Organisation for Economic Co-operation and Development (OECD) was less than half that amount at $3,740. Even France, widely recognized as having a generous national health-care program, spends about less than half the amount the United States does ($4,415 per capita) In 2015, U.S. health-care expenditures reached 16.9 percent of GDP, while the 55 nations in the OECD averaged 8.9 percent of GDP (OECD, 2016).] Figure 6.4 compares 1960 and 2015 health-care spending for selected nations in the OECD. Notice the change since 1960. What do we get for our money? Do these high expenditures translate to favorable outcomes in the population's health?

HEALTH OUTCOMES

As we have seen, the 20th century brought improvements in Americans' health status. Life expectancy, a key indicator of well-being, increased from 47.3 years in 1900 to 76.6 in 2000 (CDC, 2011). This was the direct result of improvements in public health and the decline of infectious diseases, improvements that have been especially helpful in reducing mortality among children under the age of 5. In 1900, child mortality accounted for nearly a third (30.4 percent) of all deaths. That rate had dropped to 1.4 percent by 1997 (CDC, 1999). Thus, in relation to both longevity and infant mortality, 20th-century trends suggest a substantial return on the nation's health expenditures. Compared with other developed nations, however, the U.S. result is less impressive.

FIGURE 6.4 Health Expenditures of Selected OECD Member Nations, 1960 and 2016

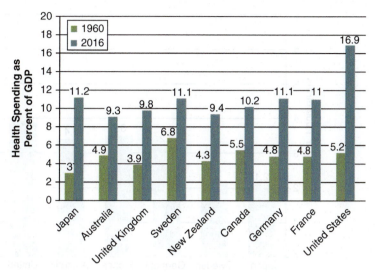

Source: OECD Health Statistics 2016: Frequently Requested Data (http://stats.oecd.org/index.aspx?Data SetCode=HEALTH_STAT) Sweden data for 1960 not available, 1970 figure presented instead.

The infant mortality rate, a widely accepted measure of community health, is usually measured as the number of infants who die before reaching one year of age per 1,000 live births. Data from the World Health Organization (WHO) permit international comparisons. Figure 6.5 compares infant mortality in the United States with that of eight other industrialized nations. Although the United States spends considerably more on health care, these expenditures have not translated into lower infant mortality rates. With six deaths per 1,000 live births in 2014, the United States ranked highest in infant mortality among these nations. Our rate was nearly three times the lowest rate of 2.1, reported by Japan.

A second measure of population health is life expectancy, which reflects how long, on average, an individual of a specified age (usually a newborn infant) can expect to live. Here, too, high U.S. expenditures don't seem to pay off. While the variations are small, America's 2014 life expectancy of 78.8 years was at the bottom of developed nations, considerably behind Japan, which enjoyed the OECD's highest life expectancy: 83.2 years.

This discrepancy between expenditures and health outcomes could lead to different conclusions. Thinking collectively, we might conclude that the U.S. healthcare system is due for a radical overhaul. But thinking personally, radical reform entails costs that many Americans are unwilling to bear. The United States has greater inequality and diversity than other industrialized nations. Our measures of population health are skewed downward by the poor health of those living in poverty or those who do not have access to culturally appropriate care.

When it comes to health care, we are a nation of "haves" and "have nots," and this poses a barrier to reform efforts. At times the "haves" seem to be talking at cross-purposes. On the one hand, no one wants Americans to suffer or die for lack of health care. On the other hand, no one wants to jeopardize his or her own health. As we will see, the politics

FIGURE 6.5 Infant Mortality in Selected OECD Member Nations, 2014

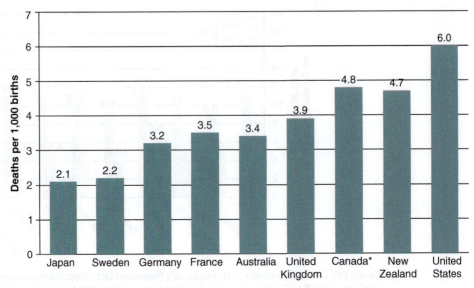

* Canada rate is for 2012 (most recent available)

SOURCE: OECD.Stat – Health Status: Maternal and Infant Mortality (http://stats.oecd.org/Index.aspx?DataSetCode=HEALTH_STAT).

of inequality have at times paralyzed efforts to achieve health-care reform in the United States. But first, let's take a quick look at global health inequities.

LO 6-6   Become Aware of Global Health Inequities

EP 3a

In the distribution of health care, life itself becomes a social justice issue. As we have seen in the United States, survival can be a function of privilege. This dynamic operates at a global level as well, and while U.S. health outcomes fare poorly in comparison with industrial nations of the OECD, they look pretty good compared to the third world. For instance, the 2014 U.S. infant mortality rate of six deaths per 1,000 births compares favorably to Sierra Leone, where 89 children per 1,000 live births died in their first year.

A baby girl born in the United States in 2015 had a life expectancy of 81 years. A girl born at the same time in Sierra Leone could expect to reach the age of 51. The same differential is seen in other sub-Saharan nations, including Cote d'Ivoire (54 years), Central African Republic (54), Chad (55), and Angola (54). Indeed, as we can see in Table 6.2, girls born in Africa in 2015 had an average life expectancy of 62 years, compared with average life expectancies of 80 years for girls in Europe and the Americas—a difference of nearly 20 years. This regional difference is largely the result of deaths from communicable diseases. The World Health Organization estimates that 69 percent of years lost to premature deaths in low-income nations are the result of communicable disease, compared with 8 percent in high-income nations (World Health Organization, 2010, 2012, 2016). Nonetheless, it is worth noting that life expectancy in all nations has increased

TABLE 6.2 Global Health Indicators

Region	2015 Infant Mortality Rate (probability of dying by age 1 per 1000 live births)	2015 Life Expectancy at Birth for Girls
Africa	55.4	61.8
The Americas	12.5	79.9
Southeast Asia	34.0	67.4
Europe	9.8	80.2
Eastern Mediterranean	40.5	70.3
Western Pacific	11.3	78.7

SOURCE: World Health Organization (2016). Global Health Observatory Data Repository (http://apps.who.int/gho/data/node.imr).

during the 21st century, with developing nations showing the greatest improvement (World Health Organization, 2016).

MODERN EPIDEMICS AND GLOBAL GOVERNANCE

During the 21st century epidemics have assumed greater ferocity and reach, bringing new meaning to the term "globalization" and new complications to international relations. As Beck (2004) noted, "Systems designed to enhance mobility of the factors of production facilitate the global spread of what decades ago would have been localized disease outbreaks." Lee and Dodgson (2000) expand on this idea, identifying the mechanisms through which globalization contributes to pandemics: "socioeconomic instability, intensified human interaction and mobility, environmental degradation, and inequalities within and across countries" (p. 11). In this section we examine the global HIV/AIDS epidemic and consider the weaknesses in global governance that were revealed by the 2002 SARS outbreak.

HIV/AIDS: A Global Epidemic

The global HIV/AIDS epidemic brings the social justice implications of disease into devastating focus. As mentioned above, over 35 million people around the globe have died of AIDS, and a comparable number are living with HIV/AIDS, most of them in sub-Saharan Africa (AVERT, n.d.).

The spread of this infection has been linked to sociopolitical conditions. As with most communicable diseases, poverty plays a key role.[5] Stillwagon (2000) reported that "HIV prevalence is highly correlated with falling calorie consumption, falling protein consumption, unequal distribution of income, and other variables conventionally associated with susceptibility to infectious disease" (p. 985). The deprivations of severe poverty result in a compromised immune system, leaving a person vulnerable to infectious disease.

But the relationship between economic status and HIV/AIDS is not simple. Sometimes forces associated with economic development, such as the breakdown of traditional social structures, can support the spread of HIV/AIDS. In Africa, for example, the role of truckers in spreading HIV is well documented (Whiteside, 2002). The spread of HIV has also been linked to U.S. colonial expansion. In both Puerto Rico (Baronov, 2003) and Honduras

---

[5]Poverty clearly facilitates the spread of infectious diseases. This is seen not only in the HIV/AIDS epidemic but also in the resurgence of tuberculosis.

(Altman, 1999), contact between local sex workers and U.S. military personnel has contributed to the spread of HIV/AIDS. Indeed, Altman (1999) argued that the spread of HIV in Southeast Asia and South America may be associated with the U.S. "war on drugs," which led to the substitution of injected drugs for smoked opium.

Among the millions of people living with HIV worldwide, most are in the developing world where access to antiretroviral drugs is limited (Gayle, 2000). Until recently, the drug combination necessary for keeping an HIV/AIDS victim alive cost $10,000 to $15,000 per year—an amount well beyond the reach of most people in developing nations. Very few of the HIV/AIDS patients in developing countries receive these life-saving medications.

Drug companies argue that these prices reflect the high cost of developing the new drugs. Patents give these companies the exclusive right to produce the drugs. In 1998, faced with the deaths of thousands of its citizens, the Brazilian government announced that it would disregard patents and produce generic versions of antiretroviral drugs. India and Thailand followed suit. By producing the drugs locally, they were able to reduce the cost of three key drugs to as little as $30 per month per patient.

Access to generic AIDS drugs has become an international controversy, pitting U.S. drug makers against world health authorities and AIDS organizations. Under U.S. law, funds allocated for international AIDS relief cannot be used to purchase generic drugs. U.S. officials argue that this stems from their concern for quality and that generic drugs are less effective. The William J. Clinton Presidential Foundation has been active in negotiating reduced prices for name-brand drugs through selected manufacturers. By contrast, the World Health Organization has promoted the use of generic drugs, arguing that they are effective and lifesaving. WHO operated a "three by five" campaign, with the goal of providing HIV/AIDS drugs to 3 million people by 2005. The campaign fell short, reaching only 1 million patients (World Health Organization, 2005).

Severe Acute Respiratory Syndrome (SARS)

"When a farmer sneezes in China, a fisherman goes bankrupt in Australia" (Beck, 2004, p. 64). The 2002 outbreak of severe acute respiratory syndrome (SARS) illustrated how interconnected our world has become. SARS is believed to have originated in live-animal food markets in Guangdong, China. The first case appeared in November 2002, and SARS quickly traveled around the world. As Beck (2004) reported, by May 2003 WHO had identified 6,234 cases of the disease. About 257 cases treated in Toronto hospitals were traced to a woman who had arrived from Hong Kong in February 2003. On April 22 WHO advised against nonessential travel to Toronto. The result was a significant loss in revenue, estimated by Ontario officials at $84 million (Canadian).

The 1918 flu epidemic killed more than half a million Americans and was followed by smaller outbreaks in 1957 and 1968. Given this history, it is not surprising that President Bush took action in 2005 following an overseas outbreak of avian flu. Bush requested billions of dollars to develop methods for detection and containment of the flu within the United States as well as funding to stockpile a limited supply of vaccinations and antiviral drugs.

Of course, tax dollars would be used to purchase the drugs from private companies. Then 2009 saw the emergence of H1N1, the "swine flu," in Mexico and the United States. The EU health commissioner advised Europeans to postpone nonessential travel to the United States or Mexico. Vaccinations were distributed, and measures for infection control were implemented in public settings such as schools. Deaths were few. What type of flu will come next?

Many analysts have argued that the spread of SARS was worsened by "deliberate obfuscation of information by the Chinese government" (Beck, 2004, p. 64). In February 2003, when international health organizations began posting information about the disease, Chinese officials claimed SARS had been contained. A CDC team sent to investigate was denied access to Guangdong for two months. When inspections were finally allowed, Chinese doctors reported that they had been told to hide SARS cases by packing people into ambulances while the inspectors were in their hospitals.

Global epidemics call for effective global governance, but existing systems and policies are rudimentary. "International Health Regulations" were developed in 1951 to reduce the threat of disease. These are periodically updated, and they outline procedures designed to limit transmission of infectious disease through shipping, aircraft, and other methods of transportation. They call on nations to report to WHO when certain diseases (cholera, plague, and yellow fever) appear within their territories. WHO's surveillance of infectious disease depends almost entirely on international goodwill, and the temptation to withhold information is great. Reporting an outbreak almost guarantees loss of tourism income and related revenues, and China is not the only country that has been reluctant to share such information with international authorities (Lee & Dodgson, 2000).

LO 6-7   Know the History and Current Status of Health-Care Reform in the United States

EP 3a
EP 8d

Two fundamental dilemmas mark contemporary debates about health care in America. The first, involving how risk should be allocated, is clearly a social justice question. The second—perhaps more fundamental—issue is the extent to which the private market can reliably and efficiently deliver health care. With respect to both questions, debate involves both ideological and pragmatic considerations.

ASSIGNING RISK

In the context of health insurance, a primary issue is the question of who bears the risk and who pays the cost of care. Under federally operated social insurance programs such as Medicare and Medicaid, the nation essentially self-insures. Those who pay taxes bear the risk. In Richard Titmuss's view (1971), these social entitlements establish a moral community in which assistance from strangers replaces the one-on-one assistance of earlier times. The state serves as an intermediary, collecting insurance premiums and allocating benefits.

When Medicaid recipients are required to enroll in managed care, the nation transfers risk to the health-care provider, typically a for-profit managed care organization or an HMO. Under capitation, Medicaid limits its risk to the amount allocated for each client under the capitation agreement. In the event of a health catastrophe, the MCO pays any additional cost, and if the enrollee does not use health care, the MCO reaps the benefit.

Some managed care entities pass the risk down the line to physicians through what is known as "physician incentive plans." In some cases, physicians are paid a capitated rate and required to cover any costs above the designated reimbursement. In other cases, physicians who provide or authorize high-cost care run the risk of salary reduction through penalties or loss of bonuses. When financial incentives or disincentives are used to regulate or influence physicians' decisions, the "fiduciary responsibility" of physicians is jeopardized. Fiduciary responsibility in this case refers to the doctor's obligation to put the patient's interests first. In 1998, editors of the *New England Journal of Medicine* argued that the financial risk borne by physicians should be limited to avoid potential conflicts of interest (Pearson, Sabin, & Emanuel, 1998). Although the CMS does require managed care organizations to report on their physician incentive plans, there are currently no regulations limiting physician risk under Medicare and Medicaid contracts.

In health care there are two types of risk: financial risks and health risks. Financial risks are borne by the entity that pays unanticipated expenses. Health risks, such as death or disability, are borne by the patient. Health insurance separates health risk from financial risk in a way that, some argue, leads to overutilization of health care. To minimize their health risks, some patients consume services without even thinking about cost. Co-payments and deductibles attempt to stem this tendency by assigning part of the financial risk to the patient. Allocating the financial risk of illness is clearly a social justice issue. Policy practitioners in this area must be prepared to effectively debate the fairness and desirability of assigning risk to the various entities involved: the patient, the physician, the MCO, the state, and the nation.

MARKET-BASED SOLUTIONS VERSUS PUBLIC PROVISION OF CARE

Fundamental to many debates about health care in the United States are assumptions about the extent to which health care is a commodity amenable to delivery through the private market. Some, like Siminoff (1986), have argued that health care can never conform to the ideal of the competitive market. We saw in Chapter 2 that in order for the market to operate efficiently, consumers must be able to make informed choices among various providers. In these circumstances the process of selection will favor those who provide the best care for the best price, and inefficient or ineffective providers will be weeded out. In the health-care market, however, purchase decisions are not made by individuals but by their employers. The values and priorities of employers do not mirror those of their employees. Another significant obstacle to rational consumer behavior is the difficulty of evaluating the quality of medical intervention. Few patients are able to consistently distinguish good from poor care. Finally, the life-and-death nature of health-care decisions complicates the process of choosing a provider.

Others argue that regulation of the private market can solve these problems. Because providers who fail to offer acceptable care are sanctioned by licensing and accrediting authorities, anyone offering medical care must meet minimal requirements. Since cost is a significant concern, the fact that employers may be more concerned about the cost of employee benefits than the quality of care may be an advantage. Several states have developed standardized "report cards" for MCOs and other managed-care providers to help consumers choose a provider that best meets their needs. Finally, public policy (through enforcement of antitrust laws) attempts to ensure that no single entity enjoys a monopoly in the health-care market.

Although a libertarian argument might hold that the private market, left unchecked, will efficiently provide health care for all Americans, experience has shown that this is not the case. Left unchecked, the market provides health care only for those with the means to pay for it. Further, even those with the means to pay for care may lack the technical expertise to shop for the best care. Failure of market-based solutions to provide health care equitably and efficiently is well established. The question is how to fix a system that is widely agreed to be broken. But before we consider health-care reform in the United States it may be instructive to take a historical perspective.

Prior to 2010, U.S. efforts at health-care reform were generally incremental, retaining the basic structure of the system but changing its components—for example, by regulating the insurance industry or encouraging the use of managed care. A few comprehensive proposals surfaced, most notably those that would rely on the government as the "single payer" for health care. Then in 2006, Massachusetts split the difference with a new law that could be characterized as a "comprehensive incremental" approach. At the federal level, the 2010 passage of the Patient Protection and Affordable Care Act brought a complex array of incremental reforms to the nation's health-care system. Before we turn to this landmark legislation, let's consider some earlier reform efforts.

INSURANCE REGULATION

In 1996, Congress passed and President Clinton signed the Health Insurance Portability and Accountability Act (PL 104-191), also known as "Kassebaum-Kennedy" for the bipartisan team who introduced the bill. The law's best-known provisions limited preexisting exclusions and improved the portability of health insurance. Under these provisions, insurers could impose only one 12-month exclusion period for any preexisting condition treated or diagnosed in the previous six months. This limitation was designed to ensure that employees who maintain continuous health coverage would only have one exclusion period in their lifetimes. The law introduced the notion of "creditable coverage," requiring that individuals be given credit for their prior coverage when applying for a new plan. This meant the new plan would be prohibited from enforcing a waiting period for coverage of preexisting conditions. Portability provisions allowed people, under certain conditions, to purchase health insurance if they left their jobs and sought coverage as individuals.

In a less familiar provision, the law provided for "guaranteed issue and renewability." If an insurer sold policies to small businesses, the law required the company to sell its products to any small business. It also required that insurers renew coverage for any group plan regardless of the health status of members of that group. This provision was important for people like Tanya Johnson. When her employer applied for coverage, the entire group's application was denied because of her HIV status. Under the Kassebaum-Kennedy legislation, insurers could neither terminate nor deny coverage in this way. This provision was implemented in response to small businesses, like Tanya's employer, that found their coverage canceled because of one high-cost employee.

Kassebaum-Kennedy also established a small demonstration program testing the use of medical savings accounts (MSAs). This controversial program allowed people to maintain special savings accounts analogous to individual retirement accounts (IRAs).

Contributions to MSAs could be made by workers or their employers and were tax deductible. Employees were required to purchase health insurance with high deductibles and could use their MSAs to cover routine health expenses. In 2004, the demonstration project ended, but as part of the Medicare Reform bill the tax benefits and basic structure of MSAs (also called health savings accounts, or HSAs) were continued. Opponents argue that these tax-free accounts only work for wealthy individuals who are in good health. The resulting adverse selection leaves sicker people to seek insurance through traditional providers at increased cost. Supporters argue that these accounts represent progress toward a more efficient, "consumer-driven" health-care system.

Kassebaum-Kennedy represented a significant departure from the traditional approach to insurance regulation in the United States. Historically, insurance had been regulated by the states. Each state has an insurance official (often called the insurance commissioner) charged with overseeing the solvency and market practices of companies doing business in the state. Observing the increase in insurer failures and the number of companies that do business in several states or even several countries, many questioned the capacity of the states to effectively regulate this enterprise. As we will see, the 2010 health-care reform included measures specifically targeting the insurance industry. But first, let's consider the role of managed care.

MANAGED CARE

Widely perceived as the solution to escalating health-care costs, managed care has been central to incremental health-care reform efforts.[6] Definitions of managed care abound. Most reflect the professional training of the author. For example, one economist (Wells, 1995) explains that managed care is designed to "provide comprehensive health care for a defined population within an available budget." A physician, writing in the *Journal of the American Medical Association* (Miller & Luft, 1994), says, "Physician practice is what is managed in managed care" (p. 1512) and argues that selection and management of physicians is the single most important distinguishing feature. A researcher (Eisenberg, 1995, p. 1670) describes managed care as "a natural experiment in health-care reform." Finally, Wall Street analysts view managed care as a promising investment option within the already profitable health-care industry.

Even as federal policy has expanded the use of managed care by Medicaid and Medicare beneficiaries, Congress and the president have found it necessary to regulate the medical practices of managed care providers. For example, in 1997 President Clinton signed an act prohibiting what he termed "drive-through deliveries." Under the provisions of this act, health-care providers are prohibited from discharging a new mother after a hospital stay of less than 48 hours. The 2001 Patients' Bill of Rights was yet another effort to rein in managed care.

SINGLE-PAYER PROPOSALS

Single-payer proposals advocate government provision of health care for all Americans. Supporters attribute the discrepancy between health expenditures and health outcomes to the fundamental inefficiency of the American health-care system. They argue that elimination of private health insurance providers would reduce this inefficiency by cutting administrative costs, reducing overhead, and eliminating profits.

---

[6]Terry Peak collaborated in the original research and drafting of the section on managed care.

As anyone who has used health insurance in recent years can testify, the administrative complexity of the U.S. health-care system is phenomenal. This led economist Gerald Friedman to conclude that conversion to a single-payer system could result in savings in excess of $500 billion dollars, primarily from the simplified administrative procedures of a single-payer system. The money saved would have been more than sufficient to provide health coverage to everyone in the United States who is currently uninsured (Friedman, 2013).

Representatives of the health insurance industry vigorously oppose single-payer proposals. The health insurance industry spends millions of dollars in campaign contributions to ensure access to the nation's policy makers, even as it conducts vigorous advertising campaigns to defeat reform proposals. These campaigns appeal to middle-class fears of losing access to high-quality care if the United States adopts a single-payer system. Despite evidence to the contrary, lobbyists suggest that a single-payer system would create a federal bureaucracy that would prove even less efficient than the current system. They argue that Canadians and Britons dislike their national health-care systems, offering examples of middle-class consumers who, frustrated with waiting lists in their nations, travel to the United States for complex procedures such as coronary bypass surgery and hip replacements.

Despite the efforts of these powerful financial interests, a movement to support the single-payer alternative has gained strength in the United States. Several grassroots organizations promote this reform, including Unions for Single Payer Health Care, HEALTH-CARE-NOW!, and the Universal Health Care Action Network (UHCAN).

Single-payer legislation has been introduced frequently in Congress, and Vermont senator Bernie Sanders argued for it during the 2016 presidential campaign when he advocated "Medicare for All." A quick search of the Library of Congress Thomas website (thomas.loc.gov) reveals that Senator Sanders, Rep. John Conyers, Rep. John Dingell, and other colleagues have introduced single-payer proposals under the "Medicare for All" and "American Health Security" names at least 18 times since 2003. Their terms vary, but most propose to phase in Medicare coverage to all who are citizens or "lawfully present" in the United States, over a period of 10 years. Rep. John Conyers (D-Michigan) has promised to introduce the provision every year until it become law. Notably, these measures do not call for public delivery of health care, instead proposing a universal, publicly financed, privately delivered system of care (like Medicare) that bypasses insurance companies.

HEALTH-CARE REFORM IN MASSACHUSETTS

In April 2006, Governor Mitt Romney signed the Massachusetts Health Care Reform Bill into law. The new law was described as a "comprehensive incremental" approach to health-care reform. Maintaining the basic structure of the health-care delivery system, the law included a series of initiatives focusing on a single objective: to ensure that nearly all of the state's residents would be covered by health insurance. The law combined mandates and subsidies, insurance market reforms, and redirection of health-care funds in a comprehensive approach that showed considerable promise. By June of 2007, nearly 80,000 adults were enrolled in the new Commonwealth Care Health Insurance Program (C-CHIP) for those with incomes below 300 percent of the federal poverty threshold (Kaiser Family Foundation, 2007b).

The new mandates applied to individuals and businesses. First, all adults in Massachusetts were required to obtain health insurance or be subject to tax penalties and fees. Premium subsidies were available on a sliding-scale basis to those with incomes below 300 percent of the poverty threshold. Second, businesses with more than 10 employees were required to contribute a "fair share" to employee health insurance premiums and implement Section 125 cafeteria plans that would allow workers to pay their health-care expenses with pretax dollars. Businesses that failed to meet these requirements paid penalties.

Insurance market reforms were an important aspect of the new law. Individuals and small businesses could purchase coverage through the new Commonwealth Health Insurance Connector, which collected premiums for the purchase of approved plans. These were limited to managed care providers who were already contracted to provide Medicaid care. The law did allow insurers to sell coverage exclusively designed for 19- to 26-year-olds, but it eliminated the costly "non-group" or individual insurance plans, merging them with "small group" plans, a move designed to reduce premiums for those who formerly had to purchase insurance on their own. The Connector Board was charged with establishing minimum coverage standards, although coverage requirements were not enforced until 2009. The board also determined affordability standards and premium amounts. As of March 2007, the board had eliminated premiums for those with incomes up to 150 percent of the poverty threshold and reduced them to $35 per month for those with incomes between 151 and 200 percent of the poverty threshold.

Benefits under the state's Medicaid program were expanded, and the total estimated cost of the measure for 2007–2008 was $1.725 billion. Most of this came from redirection of federal and state funds. Medicaid funds covered the bulk of the expenses. In addition, money in the state "Uncompensated Care Pool," which reimbursed providers for unpaid medical bills, was redirected into a Health Safety Net Trust Fund and used in part to subsidize coverage for low-income residents. The program was expected to draw an estimated $338 million in new monies from state General Funds in fiscal year 2007–2008.

The Massachusetts Health Care Reform Bill was a carefully crafted bipartisan compromise. Without fundamentally revising the delivery of health care, it called for significant expansion of the government's role in financing and regulating the health-care market. Several of its provisions would be included in the president's health-care reform proposal.

PATIENT PROTECTION AND AFFORDABLE CARE ACT OF 2010 (ACA)

Barack Obama ran for president with a plan to make health care in the United States affordable and accessible. His landslide election in 2008 signaled Americans' desire for change on several fronts, but it turned out that health-care reform was not on everyone's agenda.

Work on health-care reform began shortly after the new president took office, and by November 2009 the Affordable Health Care for America Act had passed the House. Nicknamed the "House bill," it included a government health insurance plan known as the "public option." The PPACA popularly known as the "Senate bill" did not include this provision, seen by some as a first step down a slippery slope to a single-payer system and by others as a serious threat to the health insurance industry (Geyman, 2010). The bill passed the Senate in December 2009 despite the opposition of every Republican.

For a few weeks, the nation seemed poised on the verge of significant reform. Ted Kennedy, a long-time proponent of health-care reform, had died of a brain tumor three months earlier. In January 2010 Kennedy's seat went to Republican Scott Brown. This deprived the Democrats of their filibuster-proof supermajority in the Senate. Like his Republican colleagues, Brown had signaled opposition to health-care reform. When he took his seat, Democratic leadership of the House decided to pass the Senate bill (PPACA), and the public option was abandoned. Later, a third bill called the Health Care and Education Reconciliation Act amended PPACA. It was passed by a simple majority through a reconciliation process that limited debate in the Senate, thereby precluding filibuster.

The resulting legislation, a compromise that satisfied no one completely, was unpopular with a skeptical American public. Shortly before and after its passage, polls showed a nation divided, with roughly half reacting negatively. Peter Brown summed up the public response: "The Democrats said the American people will grow to love this. We'll find out. At this point, they're not exactly jumping up and down" (Gerstein, 2010). The individual mandate requiring all Americans to purchase health insurance by 2014 or pay a penalty to the IRS was especially unpopular, and some state officials opposed the expansion of Medicaid. The 2010 mid-term elections gave Republicans a majority in the House of Representatives and six additional votes in the Senate.

Meanwhile, attorneys general from 26 states filed lawsuits challenging the constitutionality of what came to be called "Obamacare." In June 2012, in the middle of a hotly contested presidential election, the Supreme Court heard arguments in the case of *National Federation of Independent Business (NFIB) v. Sebelius*. After some entertaining discussion about the federal government requiring people to purchase broccoli (because it's good for them), the court upheld the Affordable Care Act with the exception of one provision. The Act called on states to make an "all or nothing" decision about Medicaid expansion. They could either extend coverage to those with incomes up to 135 percent of the poverty threshold or risk losing all federal participation in their Medicaid programs. Deciding that this requirement was unduly coercive, the court allowed states that did not elect to expand Medicaid to retain their existing programs. As we saw in Chapter 5, a number of states chose not to participate in the Medicaid expansion.

Key Provisions

By the time you read this, the ACA may have been repealed. But as of this writing, its key provisions remain in effect. Key provisions of the ACA[7] are summarized in Table 6.3. The **individual mandate** is among its more controversial measures. Most Americans are required to maintain health insurance or pay a penalty of $95 or 1 percent of their income, whichever is greater. Individuals can be exempted due to financial hardship or religious beliefs, or if they are Native Americans (Galewitz, 2010).

Insurance exchanges are central to the ACA reform. ACA called for each state to set up an exchange through which small businesses and individuals who do not have coverage through their work can purchase insurance. The federal government provided start-up funding and even runs the exchanges in states that elected not to set them up. The exchanges monitor plans to ensure that they comply with federal requirements. They strengthen the power of consumers in the health insurance market and enhance transparency and oversight of suppliers (Grier, 2010). By 2016, an estimated 12.7 million Americans had purchased coverage through these marketplaces.

The ACA includes requirements and incentives for employers to offer health insurance. Requirements target large businesses. Employers that have 50 employees or more and do not offer health coverage pay a fee of up to $2,000 per full-time worker if any of their workers purchases coverage through the insurance exchanges. Small businesses receive tax credits if they provide health coverage. Credits started at 35 percent of the cost

---

[7]The term "PPACA" is used here to refer to provisions of both the original act and amendments made under the Health Care and Education Reconciliation Act.

TABLE 6.3 The Patient Protection and Affordable Care Act of 2010: Key Provisions

Measure	Implementation Date
Individual mandate: Requires most people to have health insurance—those who don't will pay a penalty, with exceptions for financial hardship and religious objections.	2014
Insurance exchanges: Provides federal start-up funds to help states establish insurance exchanges for small business and individuals who lack coverage at work.	2014
Employer requirements: Assigns penalties to employers whose employees purchase coverage through the exchange (exemption for small business).	2014
Employer incentives: • Gives tax credits to small businesses that provide health insurance. • Under the Early Retiree Reinsurance Program, allows companies that provide benefits for retirees aged 55–64 to participate in a program to reduce premium costs.	2010 2010
Insurance reform: • Prohibits companies from denying coverage for preexisting conditions and from charging higher premiums based on preexisting conditions, health status, or gender. • Requires plans to provide comprehensive coverage with a minimum set of services, including preventive care. • Allows young adults to retain coverage under their parents' health insurance plans to age 26. • Requires insurers to spend 85 percent of large-group and 80 percent of small-group plan premiums on health care or return difference to customer as rebate. • Restricts annual spending caps and eliminates lifetime limits.	Phased in by 2014 2010 2010 2011 Phased in by 2014
Medicaid expansion: Extends eligibility to all persons under age 65 with incomes below 133 percent of poverty threshold (undocumented immigrants remain ineligible).	2014
Community health centers: Provides $11 billion in additional funding to community health centers and National Health Service Corps.	2011
CLASS Act provision: Creates a voluntary long-term care insurance program operated under the Secretary of Health and Human Services.	Premiums began in 2011, 5-year vesting requirement
Revenue measures: • Cuts spending and coverage in Medicare Advantage (managed care). • Extends Medicare payroll tax to include unearned income for high-income individuals and families. • Places an excise tax on "Cadillac" insurance plans. • Places excise taxes on pharmaceutical companies, insurance firms, and manufacturers of medical devices. • Places a tax on tanning salons. • Adds a range of fees and penalties, including annual fees paid by health insurance and pharmaceutical companies, excise taxes on "Cadillac" plans, taxes on medical devices and indoor tanning services, and penalties for individuals without coverage.	Not implemented 2014 2018 2010 2014 2014 and later

of premiums and increased to 50 percent in 2014. Another incentive is available to all employers: the Early Retiree Reinsurance Program reimburses companies for the costs of premiums they pay for retirees aged 55 to 64, as long as the insurance plan conforms to federal requirements. The program also reimburses employee costs, such as copayments and deductibles (Seyfarth Shaw LLP, 2010).

Members of the public who have wrestled with insurance companies can take a measure of satisfaction from ACA's insurance reform provisions. Central among them is the coverage requirement. As of 2014, companies are prohibited from denying coverage or raising premiums on the basis of preexisting conditions. In the interim, people with preexisting conditions may purchase insurance through a temporary high-risk pool. Insurance companies may no longer charge higher premiums on the basis of health status or gender; but higher premiums may be based on tobacco use, geographic area, or age (Blumberg, 2010). Beginning in 2014, plans were required to offer a comprehensive package that includes preventive care. Beginning in 2010, plans were required to allow dependent children under 26 years old to stay on their parents' plans. A provision limiting the amount companies could spend on administrative costs or distribute in profits has been phased in. Under this measure the "loss ratio," or proportion of total income spent on health care, must be 85 percent for large-group coverage and 80 percent for small-group plans. Finally, ACA aimed to eliminate lifetime coverage limits and restrict annual limits by 2014.

Medicaid expansions are the centerpiece of the act's access reforms. Effective in 2014, coverage was extended to everyone with incomes below 133 percent of the poverty threshold, including adults without dependent children. Some states already provide coverage up to this income level, but in other states that elected to participate this measure could effectively double Medicaid caseloads. Federal funding was available during the first two years to help states manage the expansion (Diamond, 2010).

The ACA authorized a funding increase of $11 billion for community health centers. Originally established as neighborhood health centers during the 1965 War on Poverty, these centers provide health care and social services to medically underserved communities. Located in all 50 states, they deliver primary care to the homeless, refugees, low-income families, and others who are not served by mainstream health providers (Taylor, 2004).

The CLASS Act was one of the more obscure programs set up by the ACA, but it could have had significant impacts on long-term care. CLASS stood for Community Living Assistance Services and Support. Under this measure, a voluntary government program of long-term care insurance would have been funded through automatic payroll deductions. Premiums, set by the Secretary of the Department of Health and Human Services, would be adjusted to maintain the actuarial soundness of the program. No tax dollars would have been used to finance the program, and benefits would have been provided to people who had paid premiums for five years if they developed multiple functional limitations or cognitive impairment. The Congressional Budget Office (CBO) estimated that this measure would reduce the federal deficit by $70.2 billion over 10 years (Kaiser Family Foundation, 2010c). But in fall 2012 Kathleen Sebelius, Secretary of Health and Human Services, shelved the program citing concerns that (in part due to adverse selection) it could not be actuarially sound. The program was formally repealed by Congress in the American Taxpayer Relief Act of 2012.

ACA Cost Savings

The ACA expanded coverage to millions of uninsured Americans, bringing the uninsured rate down from 16 percent in 2010 to 9 percent in 2015 (Congressional Budget Office, 2010, Obama, 2016. This, along with other measures, entailed significant costs. Yet the CBO expects the act to reduce the deficit by $124 billion by 2019. Where will the money come from? The single biggest items expected to produce savings are changes designed to improve productivity and other adjustments that affect providers, and cuts to Medicare Advantage plans. The Centers for Medicare and Medicaid Services outlined these measures in a recent report. They include the following changes:

1. Improving the quality of care, which is projected to generate savings by reducing readmissions and hospital-acquired conditions, bundling payments, and improving the quality of reporting
2. Reforming the delivery system through Accountable Care Organizations and Independent Payment Advisory Boards, which is expected to produce substantial cost savings
3. Reducing payments to Medicare Advantage plans and improving productivity, which is expected to account for the lion's share of ACA Medicare savings
4. Fighting waste, fraud, and abuse which, while uncontroversial, is expected to provide a drop in the bucket (CMS, n.d.)

The act also includes measures that generate revenue. First, the Medicare payroll tax applies to dividends, interest, and unearned income for individuals with incomes above $200,000 and couples with incomes greater than $250,000. The act also imposes an excise tax on high-cost insurance and a 10 percent tax on tanning salons (Kaiser Family Foundation, 2010b).

The ACA is a complex series of incremental measures, phased in over several years. It did not reject the market-based system of health-care delivery but was designed to improve access and reduce costs within that framework. Detailed analysis of its costs and potential benefits is hampered by the act's complexity and its attenuated implementation schedule. Two themes are clear: the act includes benefits for a wide range of groups, but it focuses federal (and to some extent state) resources on the poor and medically underserved; likewise, the revenue measures in the act distribute costs widely, but they focus on the affluent.

In 2016, several large insurers, including Aetna, United Health Group, Blue Cross Blue Shield, and others announced they were pulling out of the individual health insurance exchanges. They explained that they were losing money on the individual

---

BOX 6.7   Little Sisters of the Poor Challenge the ACA

The Affordable Care Act required health insurers to include preventive care in their coverage without an out-of-pocket charge. During rule making, the Department of Health and Human Services included FDA-approved contraceptives as preventive care, a measure that has long been advocated by women's health advocates. The rules carved out a religious exemption for churches and parochial schools, but this did not include church-affiliated organizations such as universities, hospitals, and charities. Nor did it exempt private companies from the contraceptive requirement. A for-profit arts and crafts company called Hobby Lobby, owned by an evangelical Christian named David Green, won its Supreme Court suit for exemption based on religious grounds (*Burwell v. Hobby Lobby*), but this ruling did not apply to nonprofit organizations. Meanwhile, several Catholic organizations, including the Little Sisters of the Poor (an order of nuns who operate several nursing homes) sued to be exempt from the requirement on the grounds that provision of contraceptives violated their right to religious freedom. After multiple lawsuits and decisions in favor of both the government and the plaintiffs, a compromise was hammered out that was designed to balance women's needs for preventive care with their employer's right to religious freedom. New rules were issued that exempt some religious employers altogether, and allow others to avoid providing free contraceptive coverage by arranging for their employees to seek coverage (often at no charge) from a third-party insurer.

exchanges, despite double-digit premium increases in some states, because patients were sicker than they had anticipated. These companies reported significant overall profits at the same time (Goozner, 2016). Concerned that many of the exchanges could have little or no competition, President Obama argued for revisiting the public option (a "Medicare for all" provision that was initially included in the Affordable Care Act), possibly by making the public option available to those who live in regions with exchanges that lack competitive providers (Obama, 2016; Wolfgang, 2016). Of course, this proposal was unlikely to find support in the Trump administration.

Prior to his inauguration, the President pledged to repeal the Affordable Care Act with the exception of two popular measures: the requirement that up to age 26 children be allowed coverage under their parents' plans and the prohibition on exclusions due to preexisting conditions.

LO 6-8   Describe the Role(s) Social Workers Play in Health Policy

Although social work in health care has been termed "a neglected area of practice" (DeCoster, 2001), social workers have long been involved in U.S. health-care policy as advocates, administrators, and practitioners. As director of the Children's Bureau, Grace Abbott took part in establishing programs for child and maternal health. Advocates in organizations such as Families USA work to ensure that the needs of the poor are taken into account in health-care reform. On a daily basis, discharge planners struggle to find appropriate care arrangements for people leaving hospitals.

Today's health-care system presents new challenges and opportunities for advocates, administrators, and practitioners. In a variety of settings and a variety of roles, social workers strive to ensure that vulnerable populations receive the care they need. At the state level, social workers battle against benefit cuts and monitor Medicaid managed care contracts. In clinics, hospitals, and other settings, social workers inform patients and their families of their rights and responsibilities and serve as intermediaries between members of minority groups and health-care institutions. In community agencies they work with nurses to educate low-income and immigrant families in the use of new and established medical technology. In Congress and state legislatures, social workers continue in the tradition of the Children's Bureau, investigating and reporting the needs and concerns of vulnerable Americans. Finally, social work professionals continue to find excellent opportunities for advocacy and community organization in the grassroots movement to promote justice in health-care policy.

Closing Reflections

This chapter began with the story of Tanya Johnson, a young woman living with HIV infection. Tanya's experiences were influenced by several federal policies. She received services through the Ryan White Care Act. When she was fired from her job, she sued her employer for not complying with the requirements of the Americans with Disabilities Act. Insurance regulations at the state level helped her secure coverage, and the Affordable Care Act was designed to ensure that others did not face the difficulties she experienced in seeking private health insurance.

We have traced the development of the U.S. health-care system, viewing it as a hybrid and noting that over a third of the population receives health care that is either financed or delivered by the government. We examined the development of public-sector interventions as well as the growth of the private health-care industry, observing the contribution of public financing to the growth of this private industry and the tension between the public sector's need for cost containment and the private sector's drive for profits. We considered health disparities in the United States, as well as the experiences of uninsured Americans. We discussed the nation's investment in health care, comparing it to health expenditures and outcomes in developed and developing nations. Then we addressed two fundamental dilemmas in U.S. health-care policy: the problem of assigning risk and implications of market-based delivery of health care. We briefly considered health-care reform and the role of social workers in health care.

The United States is the only industrialized nation in which health care is not viewed as a right. Here, health insurance is associated with employment, with public health care grudgingly provided to the needy. The resulting hybrid system has resulted in inefficiencies that increasingly affect not only the poor but the middle class as well. Rather than pursue an increased public presence in delivering health care, the United States has opted to expand access to private health insurance.

Health-care reform is a continuous (if unsteady) process in the United States. With a general understanding of the structure of our health-care system and a clear commitment to social justice, social work professionals can influence health-care debates. By adding the profession's voice and supporting our clients' voices on health-care issues, social workers can make a direct contribution to the social justice of our health-care system.

Think About It

1. The effectiveness of the immunizations developed and distributed by public agencies advanced public acceptance of government provision of health care. This technological advance enhanced the stature of public health tremendously. Has there been any comparable development in the field of social welfare?

2. What roles do social workers play in health care? How does the Affordable Care Act affect social workers?

3. What do you think of the individual mandate to purchase health insurance? Why was it put into place? Did you know that Japan's health-care system depends heavily on private insurance? (See T. R. Reid's book under Suggested Resources for interesting material on Japan's system and individual mandates.)

4. If you had a choice, how would you assign risk among these entities: a Medicaid client (think of someone with whom you are familiar), a physician, an HMO, your state, and the federal government? Who should bear the greatest risk? Why? Should the client bear any risk? Why or why not?

5. How would Tanya's experiences seeking health insurance have been different after the passage of the ACA?

6. In the case of SARS, lack of information hindered early response to the epidemic. What is more important: a patient's right to privacy or the public's need to be protected from disease? Use a case example to support your choice.

7. Review the discussion of conditions necessary for the free market to efficiently deliver goods and services (Chapter 2). Are these conditions present in the delivery of health care? What conclusions do you reach regarding the use of the market to deliver health care?

8. What social and economic factors do you think contribute to rising obesity in the United States?

9. Key policy makers expected Medicare to be followed by the establishment of national health insurance. Why didn't this happen? Do you think the United States will ever have national health insurance?

10. What kinds of health insurance do the people in your policy class have? Do you think you and your classmates are representative of the general U.S. population?

Web-Based Exercises

For direct links to all the sites in these exercises, visit the *Foundations of Social Policy* Companion Site at www.cengagebrain.com and select the resources for Chapter 6.

1. Go to http://www.who.int/publications/almaata_declaration_en.pdf to help you answer the following questions about the Alma-Ata Declaration on Primary Health Care.
   a. When was the declaration established?
   b. What are the basic provisions of this declaration?
   c. Are these consistent with U.S. health policy?
   d. What changes does WHO discuss in the years since the declaration was issued? (Please see the Director-General's Message in *World Health Report 2008: Primary Health Care, Now More than Ever.*)

2. Go to the CMS website on state health insurance marketplaces (http://www.cms.gov/CCIIO/Resources/Fact-Sheets-and-FAQs/state-marketplaces.html) and see what is happening in your state. Then go to a list of employers participating in the Early Retiree Reinsurance Program (http://www.cms.gov/CCIIO/Resources/Fact-Sheets-and-FAQs/state-marketplaces.html) and see whether your university is there. Do you recognize any of the employers listed?

Competency Notes

As mentioned in the preface to this volume, the Council on Social Work Education has designated ninecore competencies and related practice behaviors that must be addressed by accredited social work programs. In these notes, I will specify the way chapter content addresses these competencies and behaviors. (This is designed to assist with the accreditation process.) Please refer to the "helping hands" icons for the locations of specific content in this chapter. Here you will find a brief explanation of how the accompanying content relates to the specified competency or practice behaviors.

The following list indicates where EPAS competencies and practice behaviors are addressed in this chapter.

EP 3a   **Apply their understanding of social, economic, and environmental justice to advocate for human rights at the individual and system levels**. This chapter argues that the distribution of health risk and access to health care in the United States have oppressive consequences for vulnerable groups. It includes

EP 5c   **Apply critical thinking to analyze, formulate, and advocate for policies that advance human rights and social, economic, and environmental justice.** The history of public health illustrates the contribution of technology to policy development. The discussion also addresses the role of social and economic trends in the history of U.S. health policy.

EP 8d   **Negotiate, mediate, and advocate with and on the behalf of diverse clients and constituencies**. The chapter familiarizes students with the range of health programs they might help clients access.

Suggested Resources

Barr, D. A. (2007). *Health Disparities in the United States: Social Class, Race, Ethnicity, and Health*. Baltimore: The Johns Hopkins University Press.

Estes, C., Chapman, S., Dodd, C., Hollister, B, & Harrington, C. (2013). *Health Policy: Crisis and Reform*. Burlington, MA: Jones & Bartlett Learning.

Garrett, L. (2000). *Betrayal of Trust: The Collapse of Global Public Health*. New York: Hyperion Press.

Navarro, V. (Ed.). (2002). *The Political Economy of Social Inequalities: Consequences for Health and Quality of Life*. Amityville, NY: Baywood Publishing.

Reid, T. R. (2009). *The Healing of America: A Global Quest for Better, Cheaper, and Fairer Health Care*. New York: Penguin.

www.cms.hhs.gov. This is the site for the Centers for Medicare and Medicaid Services. Here you will find general information about these programs as well as statistics and material on current policy developments.

www.commonwealthfund.org. This site is maintained by the Commonwealth Fund, a foundation interested in health-care issues. It offers some excellent reports on current policy issues.

www.kff.org. The site of the Henry J. Kaiser Family Foundation is an excellent source of information about current issues in health-care policy and health-care delivery.

www.who.int. Maintained by the World Health Organization, this site is a good starting point for international comparisons.

Mental Health

Insanity is often the logic of an accurate mind overtaxed.
—**OLIVER WENDELL HOLMES**

Learning Objectives

This chapter will help prepare students to:

LO 7-1   Understand the social construction of mental illness and the role the DSM has played in this process

LO 7-2   Reflect on the values and beliefs that influence mental health policy in the United States

LO 7-3   Become familiar with the history of mental health interventions in the United States

LO 7-4   Describe factors that influence contemporary approaches to mental illness

LO 7-5   Describe the structure and financing of mental health services in the United States

LO 7-6   Become familiar with the role of social workers in the U.S. mental health system

LO 7-7   Understand emerging policy issues related to mental health

Americans often seem to have an insatiable appetite for anything that promises to enhance our mental health, from meditation retreats to self-help videos (McGee, 2007). This is hardly a new development. In colonial times, the pursuit of mental well-being led many to purchase monographs and newspaper advice columns written by "agony aunts" (Gudelunas, 2008). Then, early in the 20th century, the **mental hygiene movement** offered new and improved methods that focused on the family's role in "the production of mental adjustment, 'social efficiency' and responsible citizenship" (Toms, 2010, p. 18). Now, many social workers have joined the enterprise, engaging in private mental health practice with the worried well. Yet, with the possible exception of California, which once adopted mental hygiene as a public policy goal, government is seldom involved in the pursuit of mental health. Instead, public resources and policies generally focus on the care of those with serious mental illness.

There are important parallels between mental illness and physical illness. But widespread misunderstanding about the causes of serious mental illness and discomfort with its behavioral manifestations often result in stigma that is not commonly associated with physical illness. Until we are either directly or indirectly affected, many Americans still view mental illness as a personal problem for which collective action is not required. This perception will be a recurring theme throughout this chapter.

A HUMAN PERSPECTIVE   Rachel Sanders

Rachel Sanders is a dynamic woman of 50-something. She works for her state's mental health authority, coordinating consumer advocacy efforts under a federal grant. Rachel describes her job as "fantastic," and she clearly excels at her work. Yet, as Rachel points out, had she lived in the 17th century, she probably would have been "burned at the stake" during an episode of her illness. Rachel suffers from "atypical bipolar disorder and panic disorder," which has presented as bouts of severe depression alternating with severe paranoia, mania, and acute anxiety attacks.

Rachel is the oldest of eight children. Her parents were devoutly religious, and family life revolved around her father's academic career, the children's artistic pursuits, and the family's religious activities. From the outside looking in, she said, theirs was a model family. But privately, the children struggled to withstand their father's violent rages. Rachel was the primary target of his brutal verbal and physical attacks. Rachel's mother didn't stop the abuse, possibly because she drew satisfaction from being the family comforter. When Rachel was 19, the family spent two years in South America, where Rachel taught English as a second language to adults in a large international center. The family lived luxuriously, with many servants. This lifestyle gave the siblings time to socialize and become closer emotionally. Then Rachel's mother developed cancer. Rachel nursed her mother around the clock for the last four months of her life, and she was the only child present at her mother's death.

After a six-month stint traveling in Europe as a companion to a wealthy French woman, Rachel reentered college as a fine arts major. She was an award-winning writer and painter, a concert pianist, and a National Merit scholar. During college, she experienced long episodes of depression during which she would "hide and sleep" rather than attend classes. While still in college, she met and married a high-profile, good-looking entrepreneur from California, and the couple moved to Los Angeles. With the profits from their business they enjoyed first-class, round-the-world travel and an opulent lifestyle in Marina del Rey. They kept two foreign sports cars,

two private planes, and a 40-foot sailboat. In a spirit of adventure, Rachel took flying lessons and learned to pilot the boat. When the couple's ten-year marriage ended in divorce, Rachel went into real estate. During this period she began to experience panic attacks.

The first attack, which occurred when she was 32 years old, started on a Sunday afternoon and lasted for eight hours. Rachel called 911, screaming, "I'm dying! "I'm dying!" She thought she was having a stroke or a heart attack. Shorter attacks continued daily, and Rachel's circle of activities began to shrink. Although she took Valium as prescribed, Rachel couldn't safely drive on the freeway, and eventually she could barely leave the house.

During this period she married an extremely kind, sensitive older man of independent means, but this marriage ended amicably after less than three years. Faced with daily panic attacks, Rachel returned to her hometown and the emotional support of her siblings.

There, her life revolved around visits to the emergency room. She found an entry-level job at a hospital and was on Valium for two and a half years. Then she learned about Xanax and found that it more effectively controlled her panic attacks. Later, she returned to California and, as she put it, "got very grandiose." Rachel set up a corporation for international arts festivals and, as she said, "went through over a quarter of a million dollars of other people's money in less than 18 months."

Hoping to control her rising anxiety, she increased her Xanax intake until she began to develop psychotic symptoms. She had never heard of psychosis and firmly believed that people were trying to kill her. Finally, Rachel called a sister in Alabama and cried, "They're coming to get me." Within hours, her sister flew to California and, with a brother, committed Rachel to Long Beach General Hospital with severe depressive paranoid psychosis. She hadn't eaten or bathed in days. Rachel was put in restraints and spent five days on a locked ward. She recalls her hospitalization as a negative experience, remembering the crowded facility and aides who joked about her condition. She was put on Stelazine, and when that started to pull her out of the psychosis, she was transferred to a halfway house in Inglewood.

In retrospect, Rachel feels she was released to the halfway house too soon. There, she cowered in her room all night, peering out the window at people she thought were coming to kill her. For days, she refused medications, thinking they were poisoned. Finally, she said, a "big, boisterous black woman," who terrified Rachel, bullied her into taking her medication. What a difference it made! Soon Rachel was whistling in the halls and she was transferred to a residential care center in Watts, where she stayed for six weeks. Rachel enjoyed the center, which had a grand piano in the recreation room that she played for hours on end. Nonetheless, she was eager to leave. She took her medication regularly and convinced her sympathetic second ex-husband to let her stay with him. This arrangement didn't work well. She was heavily medicated and severely depressed, not capable of much more than long walks by the ocean all day while her ex-husband was away. Finally, one of her brothers invited her to visit for Christmas. She ended up living with him and his extraordinarily supportive wife and children for a year and a half, working in a medical setting and learning to cope with her frequent bouts of paranoid ideation.

Rachel eventually moved into an apartment of her own and found a stable position as a patient advocate in a clinic. She worked at the clinic for six years before recurrent panic attacks forced her to resign. She lived on her savings for a year and a half, caught in a downward spiral that she attributes to losing the validation and structure of work. This crisis led to her second hospitalization, which lasted five days.

When her health insurance ran out, Rachel asked to be referred to a public clinic. There, her new therapist helped her apply for Medicaid and recommended that Rachel join a local mental health clubhouse program. After a successful volunteer experience, Rachel entered a transitional employment program. She found a job as a receptionist with the state mental health authority. When a new administrative support position became available, Rachel moved into consumer programs, which set the stage for her current administrative job.

Rachel sees her therapist regularly at a community mental health center. After much adjustment of medication types and dosages, she takes what her therapist calls "a sprinkle" of Xanax daily as a prophylactic to ward off panic attacks, along with a small dose of antipsychotic medication and Prozac. Rachel has become confident, both in her therapist and in her pharmaceutical regimen, and describes her therapist, a nurse/MSW, as "extraordinarily deft." Her therapist is gifted with deep empathy, and Rachel thinks it helps that she is a woman of about her own age. With this level of care, Rachel is comfortable and happy. In fact, she describes this as "by far, the happiest time of my life."

Rachel occasionally has minor attacks of paranoia, but she's able to recognize them as such. After each one recedes, she experiences a warm feeling, "like you're coming back from a cold hell into a warm reality."

Rachel says, "You even learn to love your disease, as strange as that may sound. It forces you to develop compassion and is a marvelous lesson." She is grateful for these lessons and feels she wouldn't have been able to learn them any other way. The main problem she has encountered is the public's lack of knowledge about mental illness. She feels fortunate that she can remember every detail of her past psychotic episodes. Most consumers she works with don't have that degree of recall. For them, each episode is a new and terrifying experience.

As a leader among mental health consumers, Rachel has had the opportunity to discuss issues of concern at the state and national levels. She believes that in the consumer community she works with, there is support for forced medication. Some of the mental health consumers she encounters have expressed reservations about side effects and the impact of mandatory medication on self-determination, but they feel the benefits of psychotropic medications override these considerations. Rachel is confident that the coming years will see even more sophisticated medications for mental illness. Her state's consumers are also interested in gun control and housing. At least half of the people Rachel works with are upset about proposed restrictions on their ability to purchase guns. Arguing that they are statistically less violent than the general population, they believe such restrictions violate their rights. Those living on Supplemental Security Income (SSI) and Social Security Disability Insurance (DI) have trouble finding affordable housing and struggle to get by on meager benefits: "They want us to pay for the sin of having a mental illness." Mental health insurance parity is another big concern, which Rachel sees as a state issue.

A SOCIAL WORK PERSPECTIVE

Given the timing, it is tempting to attribute Rachel's first bout with depression to the loss of her mother. While this may have been a precipitating factor, Rachel explains her illness with reference to a combination of genetic and situational factors. She notes that depression and bipolar disorder are found on both sides of her family and that child abuse probably had an impact on her mental well-being. Her youngest brother was diagnosed with paranoid schizophrenia when he was 17 and tried to commit suicide. He is now in his early forties, living on DI and contributions from his siblings. Unlike Rachel, he has consistently resisted treatment.

(continued)

Despite her struggles, Rachel feels fortunate. At times she has lost most of her possessions, but she has never been homeless. She attributes this to the generosity of her siblings. Indeed, Rachel feels that she would not have survived without her family's enlightened support. Rachel has achieved an astonishing reconciliation with the father who traumatized her so badly in childhood. She feels they probably will never be emotionally close, but they now have a peaceful and supportive relationship.

It is interesting to speculate on what might have happened if her childhood abuse had come to the attention of public authorities. Would Rachel have been removed from her parental home? Would the foster care system have provided the kind of supports that have sustained Rachel through her episodes of illness? Would an experience with child welfare authorities have mitigated or exacerbated the impact of mental illness on her life? Without family supports, would Rachel have joined the ranks of the homeless mentally ill who now haunt the nation's towns and cities?

"Oh, worse than that!" Rachel sums it up emphatically. "I'm certain that without my artfully gifted professional treatment and enlightened support of my family and friends, I'd have been dead long ago!"

LO 7-1   Understand the Social Construction of Mental Illness and the Role the DSM Has Played in This Process

EP 4b
EP 5c

Perhaps the nation's first effort to define and gauge the impact of mental illness came in 1840 when the U.S. Census Office set out to count the number of Americans who were mentally ill. Since then there have been various efforts at counting, including a series of **Epidemiological Catchment Areas** (ECA) studies funded by the **National Institute of Mental Health.**

Of course, counting relies on definition, and definitions of mental illness have been notoriously hard to pin down. They vary, for instance, in their emphasis. Some underscore biology, defining mental illness on the basis of genetic configurations, neurological activity, or brain chemistry. Others emphasize behavior, treating mental illness as a failure of personality or personal development. During the 1960s and 1970s, R. D. Laing argued that mental illness was essentially a failure to conform. Likewise, Thomas Szasz argued that mental illness was a "myth" and that we label a person "crazy" or "mentally ill" as punishment for violating social norms (Szasz, 1960).

In 1952, the **American Psychiatric Association** released the first edition of the **Diagnostic and Statistical Manual**, now in its fifth edition (the *DSM-V*). This authoritative text reflects an ongoing effort to standardize psychiatric terminology that began during the 1920s. It defines mental illnesses in intricate detail, based on cognitive, emotional, and behavioral indicators. Many agree that the *DSM* is based more on pragmatics and politics than on science. Nonetheless, it plays a central role in the social construction of mental illness, not only in the United States but in Europe and Asia as well (Kawa & Giordano, 2012). Released in 1952, its first edition reflected a psychodynamic approach to mental illness. Mental disorders were classified on the basis of their presumed causes: organic brain dysfunction versus socioenvironmental stressors (from "psychoses" to "psycho-neuroses"). The *DSM-II*, issued in 1968, focused on describing psychiatric diseases, and its authors distanced themselves from the notion that mental illness was a "reaction" and focused instead on more fine-grained categorization of conditions (for example, "acute; chronic; not psychotic; mild; moderate; severe; in remission") (quote from Kawa & Giordano, 2012).

Described as a "turning point" in psychiatry, the *DSM-III* was issued in 1980. It rejected psychodynamic interpretations (eliminating the term "neurosis") and provided a scientifically based medical model of mental illness. New disorders were listed for the first time, including "Post-Traumatic Stress Disorder," "Attention-Deficit Disorder," "Psycho-sexual Dysfunctions," and "Disorders of Impulse Control Not Elsewhere Classified" (such as gambling). The *DSM-III* introduced a "multi-axial" system of diagnosis and provided detailed guidelines to facilitate differential diagnosis of disorders that might present similarly.

Later versions of the *DSM* still largely reflect the medical model, with growing emphasis on results of neuroimaging, neurochemical, and genetic research (Kawa & Giordano, 2012). They elaborate upon the classification schemes developed in the *DSM-III* and seldom mention the causes of mental illness (LaBruzza & Mendez-Villarrubia, 1994). One exception to this is the elimination of the "bereavement exclusion" from Major Depressive Disorder (MDD) in the *DSM-V* (issued in 2013). Prior to this edition, clinicians were advised not to diagnose MDD within the first two months of a major bereavement. This exclusion was eliminated to avoid giving the impression that grief should be resolved within two months and in recognition that bereavement is only one of several stressors that can trigger a depressive episode. Other notable revisions in the *DSM-V* include elimination of Asperger Syndrome, inclusion of a new approach to gender identity issues, and the introduction of "Gambling Disorder" (American Psychiatric Association, n.d.).

Addiction disorders pose a definitional challenge in the field of mental health, even as they illustrate the boundaries of the *DSM*'s influence. Addiction to alcohol or illegal drugs, per the *DSM*, is considered a mental illness. Further, advocates for those who suffer from addiction emphasize its biological component, framing the problem as a disease. Nonetheless, the general public and many policy makers view addiction not as a disease but as a moral failure. As we will see in Chapter 8, this view is reflected in a range of U.S. policies.

The *DSM*'s role in the social construction of mental illness has been described as "diagnosis by consensus" (LaBruzza & Mendez-Villarrubia, 1994, p. 38). The manual's treatment of homosexuality is illustrative. Homosexuality was listed as a mental illness in the first two editions of the *DSM*. During the 1960s and 1970s, gay rights groups opposed this designation, arguing that the difficulties experienced by homosexuals were caused by society, not by underlying mental pathology. In 1973, the American Psychiatric Association's board of trustees voted to delete homosexuality from the *DSM*. This revision was made in the 1973 printing of the *DSM-II* and made permanent with publication of the *DSM-III*. This led LaBruzza and Mendez-Villarrubia to comment in 1994 that "With a single vote the APA cured millions of gay men and women in America of the 'mental illness' of homosexuality" (p. 21).

The irony in this observation is not lost on other critics of the *DSM*. Noting the American Psychiatric Association's ties to the drug industry and the manual's tremendous impact, Gary Greenberg (2013) wonders why the APA "owns the naming rights to our pain." Smith and Grant (2016) echo his concern, noting that contributors to the *DSM-V* "all apparently had financial ties to the pharmaceutical industry" (p. 22) and concluding that it is all part of "the corporate construction of psychosis."

The *DSM* remains quite popular. Many social work programs teach courses on it. Apart from that, as Greenberg pointed out, it still "determines which conditions insurers will cover, which drugs regulators will approve, which children will receive special education services, and which criminal defendants will be able to stand trial..." Nonetheless, criticism is mounting, which led Edward Shorter (Oxford University Press Blogger and author of *How Everyone Became Depressed*) to suggest that "there probably will not be a *DSM-VI*" (Shorter, 2013).

LO 7-2

EP 5a
EP 5c

Reflect on the Values and Beliefs That Influence Mental Health Policy in the United States

As definitions of mental illness have evolved, so have attitudes toward people with psychiatric disorders. In this section, we will examine several perspectives on mental illness, suggesting that Americans have viewed it alternatively as eccentricity, sin, disease, and disability. As you read these sections, consider how policies and interventions for the mentally ill have been shaped by these beliefs.

MENTAL ILLNESS AS ECCENTRICITY

In some contexts, mental illness is viewed as a sign of eccentricity or uniqueness. In artists, this eccentricity may be seen as tolerable—even a sign of creativity. This attitude is most evident in the public response to artists who have mental diagnoses. Several of the nation's most creative artists have been diagnosed with depression or schizophrenia. (Please see Jamison, 1993, for a discussion of the relationship between creativity and insanity.)

In politics, however, eccentricity is less readily accepted. At its extreme, a negative approach to eccentricity among politicians is seen when insanity is used by authoritarian regimes to silence political opposition. Thus, for example, political activists in China and other nations have been imprisoned, not as criminals, but as victims of mental illness, with their political views presented as evidence of insanity. The United States has limited tolerance for mental illness among its politicians. News of Thomas Eagleton's psychiatric treatment led to his replacement as McGovern's running mate in the 1972 presidential election. Thus, it was courageous of Representative Lynn Rivers (D-MI) to publicly acknowledge her struggles with bipolar depression in 1998. The National Mental Health Association recognized her with its Legislator of the Year award.

MENTAL ILLNESS AS SIN

During the early 18th century, mental illness was more often attributed to supernatural causes than to biological or social conditions. Cotton Mather, a Puritan minister, wrote on both mental and physical illnesses. As was typical at the time, he saw madness as a consequence of sin (Grob, 1994). Treatment took the form of prayer, repentance, and exorcism.

In this respect mental illness differs from physical illness. Physical illness is seldom attributed to sin, while mental illness has often been linked to moral, personal, or familial failure. (Consider the concept of the "**schizophrenogenic** mother," for example.) When one is physically ill, treatment is provided as a matter of course, and (except in the case of severe contagion) incarceration is not even considered. But, as we will see, severe mental illness, with its problematic behavioral component, can lead to incarceration rather than treatment.

MENTAL ILLNESS AS DISEASE

Recent years have seen growing focus on the biological component of psychiatric disorder and with it, a widespread view that mental illness is disease. Schizophrenia, for instance, is widely considered a single illness despite the fact that its presentation, course, and response to treatment varies widely. Since 1965, researchers have sought biological biomarkers for the condition but found no conclusive results (Weickert et al., 2013), leading some, like Edward Shorter (2013) to conclude that it cannot be a single illness.

The distinction between disease and sin may depend on context. David Mechanic (1962) examined the definition of behavior as "sick" or "bad" and argued that "if the behavior appears to be peculiar and at odds with the actor's self-interests or with expectations of the way a reasonable person is motivated, the evaluator is more likely to characterize such behavior in terms of the sickness dimension" (Mechanic, 1999, p. 38). But if the behavior is in some way self-serving, it is more likely to be evaluated as "bad." Thus, a rich person who steals a loaf of bread is likely to be labeled "sick" or "crazy," while a poor person who does so will be labeled "bad."

MENTAL ILLNESS AS DISABILITY

As we will see in Chapter 8, the notion of mental illness as a disability is significant to social policy because it determines eligibility for programs and income supports. These entitlements include income maintenance as well as housing and rehabilitative services. Those whose mental illness renders them "unable to engage in any substantial gainful activity" (Social Security Administration, 2004) are eligible for monthly benefits through Supplemental Security Income (SSI) and Disability Insurance (DI). Like Rachel, they also have access to medical coverage under Medicaid, and those who are on DI for 24 months become eligible for Medicare coverage. Disability also may entitle a person with mental illness to receive food stamps.

The label "disabled" cuts two ways. A mental patient who can persuade authorities that she is "permanently and totally disabled" will receive income support, in-kind benefits, and medical coverage. In order to secure rehabilitative services, however, she may need to demonstrate that she can be rehabilitated. That is, she may be "totally" but not "permanently" disabled. Thus, an individual with severe mental illness faces a quandary: Is it better to give up hope of rehabilitation and gain a secure income or to cling to hope and thereby gain access to rehabilitation? This decision may be complicated by the fragmentation of the network of mental health interventions that have developed in the United States. The development of this network is described in the next section.

LO 7-3   Become Familiar with the History of Mental Health Interventions in the United States

EP 3a
EP 5c

In this section, we will trace the development of public interventions for people with mental illness in the United States.[1] As we will discover, support for these interventions seems to ebb and flow, reflecting the fluctuating enthusiasm for available treatment methods. We will also trace the changing role of social workers in the mental health service delivery system.

CARE OF PEOPLE WITH MENTAL ILLNESS IN COLONIAL AMERICA

Living in close proximity, American colonists were quick to recognize the external effects of mental illness. The impact of mental illness went beyond the victim's suffering, as Cotton Mather pointed out:

These melancholicks do sufficiently Afflict themselves, and are Enough their own Tormentors. As if this present Evil World, would not Really afford Sad Things Enough, they create a World

---

[1]Much of the material in this section is based on Gerald Grob's 1994 book, *The Mad Among Us,* and David Rochefort's 1997 work, *From Poorhouses to Homelessness.*

of Imaginary Ones, and by Medicating terror, they make themselves as Miserable, as they could be from the most Real miseries.

But this is not all; *They Afflict others as well as Themselves, and often make themselves In-suportable Burdens to all about them.*

In this Case, we must bear one anothers Burdens. (Jones, 1972, pp. 129–137, emphasis added)

The unpredictability of mental illness was also readily apparent. One never knew who might be the next victim. Thus, in 1651, when Roger Williams exhorted his fellow citizens of Providence, Rhode Island, to care for a widow who was "distracted," he reminded them that "we know not how soon our wives may be widowes and our children Orphans, yea and our selves be deprived of all or most of our Reason, before we go from hence, except mercy from the God of Mercies prevent it" (Grob, 1994, p. 13).

In colonial America, mental illness became a public concern when it interfered with community safety or jeopardized personal survival. Indeed, one of the first laws governing care of the insane ordered the selectmen of Massachusetts to care for them "in order that they do not Damnify others" (Grob, 1994, p. 7).

Public care of people with mental illness focused on meeting survival needs, but treatment was sometimes available. Therapies were eclectic, reflecting practitioners' varied notions about causes. Insanity was attributed to sin as readily as to extreme misfortune or digestive disturbances.

Richard Napier, an astrological physician of the era, treated thousands of patients for madness during his career. Treatments might include bleeding and purging, but Napier also used exorcism if he believed a patient was possessed and environmental manipulation if he thought the trouble came from that source (Grob, 1994).

Depression was identified early in the nation's history, and its causes and treatments were outlined in Robert Burton's famous 1621 work, ***Anatomy of Melancholy***. Burton, himself a frequent victim of melancholy, advised a range of treatments, including social contacts (avoiding solitude), music, prayer, and medicines. The latter might consist of "a decapitated head of ram … boiled with cinnamon, ginger, nutmeg, mace and cloves," or "living swallows, cut in two and laid reeking hott onto the shaved Head," and "blood of an ass drawn from behind his ear" (Grob, 1994, pp. 9–10).

These treatments, while often effective, were seldom part of public interventions. They were provided to those who could afford them, or in individual cases where charity dictated relief of suffering. The notion of a **right to treatment** was not part of the dialogue about public responsibility for people with mental illness.

THE PROMISE OF THE ASYLUM

By the mid-18th century, American understanding of mental illness focused more on personal and environmental influences and less on spiritual causes. During the age of enlightenment, belief in the potential for perfecting human beings—or at least improving their situations—raised general interest in curing mental illness.

With the growth of cities came the establishment of institutional settings for people with mental illness. Hospitals were available for those who could afford them, and almshouses were provided to the indigent. These almshouses initially sheltered the aged, young, infirm, and insane. Over time, however, efforts were made to separate the "distracted" from the rest of the population.

The nation's first public hospital designed exclusively for the insane, the Virginia Eastern Asylum, was established in Williamsburg in 1769. Rationale for its establishment included both the need for early intervention and recognition of the external effects of madness. The act that allocated funds for the hospital stated in its opening clause that "several persons of insane and disordered minds have been frequently found wandering in different parts of this colony" and noted that "no certain provision" had "yet [been] made either towards effecting a cure of those whose cases are not become quite desperate, nor for restraining others who may be dangerous to society" (Hening, 1809–1823, pp. 378–381).

During the latter part of the 18th century, public hospitals for people with mental illness proliferated, with a corresponding improvement in care. American institutions reflected a strong European influence. A Frenchman, Philippe Pinel, contributed to the expansion of the asylum by developing a new treatment approach. Based on exhaustive observations, he argued that bleeding and other practices generally were not effective. Pinel established what he called *a traitement moral* (moral treatment). Contrary to its name, Pinel's approach did not emphasize moral judgments or values. Instead, it offered a carefully structured environmental regimen in which the physician held complete authority. The goal was an institution in which physical abuse and neglect of patients were unheard of, and the environment was carefully structured to accomplish individual cures.

In England, William Tuke, a **Quaker** and merchant, applied Pinel's methods at the York Retreat. The Retreat was established by Quakers in 1792 to serve people with mental illness. Its well-considered regimen was remarkably effective. The success of the Retreat contributed to a widespread belief that hospitals for people with mental illness could accomplish cures. This optimism set the stage for expansion of mental institutions throughout England and the United States.

Of course, high-quality care was costly, and private institutions were forced to serve an affluent clientele in order to generate sufficient operating funds. Indigents were referred to public institutions where they would receive custodial care but not the most sophisticated treatment.[2] The result was a class-based system of care in which the affluent were not forced to mix with members of the lower or immigrant classes.

DOROTHEA DIX, "APOSTLE TO THE INSANE"

Enter Dorothea Dix (1802–1887), who has been called the "apostle to the insane." Ms. Dix was an educated woman from a middle-class family. Like many women of similar backgrounds, she found in social reform one of the few available outlets for her talents. Although she suffered illness and emotional trials, Dix was determined to contribute to society, observing that "life is not to be expended in vain regrets—self is not to be the object of contemplation—individual trials are not to be admitted to fill the mind to the exclusion of the sufferings of the *many*" (Brown, 1998, p. 76). When Dix was 39, she was invited to teach a Sunday school class at a jail outside of Boston. There, she found the insane housed with criminals in appalling conditions. Her outrage at this and similar situations fueled a career in social advocacy.

Dix developed an effective methodology for her crusade to establish asylums for people with mental illness. She would travel to a state, visit prisons and almshouses, and prepare a petition or report outlining her findings. Dix then met with policy elites and members of state legislatures to encourage establishment or expansion of the institutions in each state.

---

[2]Some public institutions did provide outstanding care. One of these was the Massachusetts State Hospital, established by Samuel B. Woodward, which served as a model of effective treatment under public auspices.

The National Library of Medicine, Prints and Photographs

© Library of Congress Prints and Photographs Division

▶ Dorothea Dix (1802–1887).

Like many advocates, she was not above exaggeration or hyperbole if it helped her cause. Some, like her fellow reformer Samuel Gridley Howe, saw her dramatic presentations as necessary to convey the urgency of her mission. Officials who ran the facilities raised strenuous objections, however. The administrators of the Danvers almshouse argued that Dix was in the facility for only five minutes and had then described "the high wrought fancies of [her] imagination, instead of the practical realities of life" (Brown, 1998, p. 95).

Howe linked the causes of insanity to the failings of social institutions, arguing that society caused insanity, so should be held responsible for care of its victims. Dix, on the other hand, held that the causes were irrelevant. A devout Unitarian, Dix argued for the moral necessity of protecting the insane from the "predatory forces of society" (Brown, 1998, p. 93).

The expansion of public hospitals for people with mental illness continued for more than a century. Through the course of her career (1840–1860), Dix was instrumental in founding or expanding 31 asylums for people with mental illness (Brown, 1998). Within these institutions, a new specialty called "**psychiatric social work**" was born. Paul Stuart (1997) traced the roots of psychiatric social work to 1907, when Massachusetts General Hospital assigned social worker Edith Burleigh to its neurological clinic. Burleigh served as a liaison between the hospital and the community, supporting treatment plans developed by a psychiatrist. Her work became a model for other hospitals, which began hiring social workers to assist in the care of people with mental illness. Within most mental asylums a rigid hierarchy prevailed in which psychiatrists enjoyed the highest status and the greatest decision-making authority. Second in status and authority were psychologists, with social workers a distant third.

The expansion of asylums peaked in 1955, when they housed more than half a million Americans diagnosed with mental illness. Ironically, this growth destroyed the very feature that inspired it: the promise of a cure for insanity. **Moral therapy** and similar approaches were costly and could not be sustained in overpopulated, underfunded institutions. The gap between the reality of life in asylums and the promise of effective treatment widened, even as institutional populations grew. Cures were not unheard of, but over time, intractable cases of chronic mental illness came to dominate the asylum population.

Thus began a vicious spiral. The growing proportion of chronically mentally ill living in institutions belied the promise that the environment could be used to effect a cure. Without that promise, patients with transient or acute problems did not seek treatment in the institutions. This increased the proportion of intractable cases, which included senile elderly patients as well as victims of syphilis. The asylum became a place of despair—a last resort for those with no other options.

COMMITMENT AS INCARCERATION

Even as Dorothea Dix was advocating for expansion of institutions, others argued that involuntary commitment of mental patients was incarceration without due process. The case of Elizabeth Packard provided a vivid example. As Gerald Grob tells it,

> Packard had been stricken at the age of nineteen with "brain fever" and spent six weeks … at the Worcester hospital in 1835. Four years later she married Theophilus Packard, a Protestant minister who was nineteen years her senior. An unhappy marriage was exacerbated by sharp religious differences. Elizabeth Packard adhered to a liberal theology, while her husband was a devout Calvinist who accepted the total depravity of humanity. When Packard refused to play the role of an obedient wife and expressed religious ideas bordering on mysticism, her husband had her committed in 1860 to the Illinois State Hospital for the Insane … where she remained for three years. After being released, she was confined by her husband in a locked room … a friend secured a writ of habeas corpus. In a trial that received national publicity, Packard was declared sane. She then spent nearly two decades campaigning for the passage of personal liberty laws that would protect individuals and particularly married women from wrongful commitment. (1994, p. 84)

Elizabeth Packard was instrumental in establishing the National Association for the Protection of the Insane and Prevention of Insanity in 1880. On behalf of people with mental illness, this group advocated stricter standards for involuntary commitment and protection of patients' rights within institutional settings. In 1908, Clifford W. Beers wrote *A Mind That Found Itself,* an autobiographical account that documented the indignities of institutional life and fueled the mental hygiene movement.

PREVENTING MENTAL ILLNESS: THE MENTAL HYGIENE MOVEMENT

Enthusiasm for **mental hygiene** flourished as the promise of the asylum faded. The mental hygiene movement treated mental illness as a problem of social and/or personal adjustment. Its rationale was similar to that of the public health movement of the same era, and its proponents shared a comparable zeal. They felt that improvements in family life and social conditions would prevent the occurrence of minor mental disturbances that, left untreated, could develop into incurable mental disorders (Richardson, 1989; Rose, 1996).

The National Committee for Mental Hygiene was founded in 1909 to foster the prevention of mental disorders, arguing that prevention is easier and less expensive than treatment. Leading philanthropic agencies such as the Rockefeller Foundation contributed to efforts to find the causes of mental illness. Childhood problems came to the fore, and the mental hygiene movement began to focus on promoting healthy child-rearing practices. By 1930, the precepts of mental hygiene were widely accepted. That year's White House Conference on Child Health and Protection declared childhood "the golden period for mental hygiene" (Richardson, 1989, p. 107).

Truancy and delinquency were seen as precursors of mental illness, and participants in the mental hygiene movement soon came to see the classroom as an ideal setting for preventive psychiatric work. Visiting teachers and psychiatric social workers served as on-site trainers and demonstrators in the public schools, "educating teaching staff into a different attitude toward children" (Richardson, 1989, p. 89). With funding from the **Commonwealth Fund**, child guidance clinics were established in eight U.S. cities to apply the principles of mental hygiene to the problems of childhood.

The most successful child guidance clinic funded by the Commonwealth Fund was in Los Angeles. Its focus was not on referrals from the courts or schools but on children brought in by their parents or other relatives because of adjustment problems. Children with mental retardation and established mental illness were referred elsewhere. Based on the popularity of the clinic, the state of California attempted to set up a statewide mental hygiene service (Richardson, 1989).

As mental health treatment moved out of the asylum, the roles of mental health professionals changed. The field of community psychiatry was born, bringing psychiatrists out of mental institutions and into schools, courts, and even private homes. In child guidance and community education programs, social workers enjoyed higher status than they had been accorded in the rigid hierarchy of mental institutions.

The mental hygiene movement promoted the idea that childhood experiences were relevant to public policy because they contributed to mental illness in adulthood. Unfortunately, little research had been conducted on the precursors of mental illness. As a result, much of the work done by mental hygiene proponents, such as the campaign to reduce "bad mental habits," had a propaganda-like feel. Popular wisdom was promoted as the solution to complex psychiatric problems. As the idea of heredity surfaced as a popular explanation for insanity, proponents of mental hygiene became advocates for "eugenic" policies such as sterilization of people with mental illness.

The basic premise of the eugenics movement was that human characteristics and behavior were determined by genetics; thus, sterilization was seen as the ultimate means of preventing mental illness. Indiana passed the first law requiring sterilization of people with mental illness. Many states followed suit, and by World War II, 30 had passed similar legislation. California was particularly active in pursuing this policy. Between 1907 and 1940, 18,500 mental patients were sterilized, half of them in the Golden State (Grob, 1994).

MENTAL HEALTH TREATMENTS DURING THE DEPRESSION AND WORLD WAR II

The period from 1929 to 1945 was tumultuous for mental health care in the United States. Resources available for institutional care were decimated by the Depression. But treatment innovations, primarily from Europe, again promised hope of cure. Some of the treatments would strike us as bizarre today. For example, an Austrian psychiatrist, Julius Wagner-Jauregg, observed that mental symptoms sometimes disappeared in patients who had typhoid fever. He drew blood from a soldier with malaria and injected it into several patients. The results were promising, and he received a Nobel Prize in 1927 for this work. Fever therapy, or malaria therapy, became popular in U.S. institutions and restored hope that mental illness could be cured. This optimism extended to other innovative approaches, such as insulin therapy, lobotomy, and use of electrical shock. Between 1935 and 1941 more than 75,000 patients received **shock therapy**. Surgery was less popular. About 18,608 patients underwent psychosurgery between 1936 and 1951 (Grob, 1994). Together, these therapies improved release rates for mental hospitals.

Events during World War II changed the mental health field. The war graphically demonstrated both the extent of mental illness among Americans and the influence of environmental stress. Over 1.75 million inductees were rejected by the military for psychiatric reasons (Grob, 1994). Despite this screening, many of the men sent into combat developed psychiatric symptoms. Military practitioners treated these men at the front, demonstrating that even extreme cases of what we might now call post-traumatic stress disorder (PTSD) could improve outside an institutional setting.

FEDERAL INVOLVEMENT IN MENTAL HEALTH

At the end of World War II the quality of care available through the nation's mental hospitals varied. In Kansas, the influence of the **Menninger Clinic** was felt soon after its founding in 1944. The Menninger brothers established an outstanding facility that continues to provide leadership in mental health care. They also advocated for improved care in the state's public institutions.

Residents in other states were less fortunate. An exposé of Oklahoma mental institutions by Mike Gorman, "Oklahoma Attacks Its Snakepits," was published in *Reader's Digest.* It became the basis for a famous 1946 novel called *The Snake Pit,* by Mary Jane Ward. This novel was adapted for a popular motion picture that starred Olivia de Havilland.

Together, these media events increased public concern regarding the quality of care in mental hospitals and triggered a call for increased federal involvement. The mental hygiene movement had already found a home in the federal government in 1930, when the U.S. Public Health Service created a Division of Mental Hygiene. Near the end of World War II, Robert H. Felix took over leadership of the division. He is widely recognized as the leading force in the 1946 passage of the National Mental Health Act.

The National Mental Health Act of 1946

The **National Mental Health Act** had three goals: to support research on psychiatric disorders, to train mental health personnel through fellowships and grants, and to provide grants to the states to establish clinics and demonstration programs. The act also required states to establish a single state agency for planning and administration of federal mental health funds. Under the act, the National Institute of Mental Health (NIMH) was established in 1949 as a branch of the Public Health Service. Robert Felix was its first director. One goal for NIMH leaders was to broaden the scope of mental health services beyond institutions. This community-based approach to treatment was more compatible with a public health approach to mental health. It served as the basis for the community mental health movement, which led to the discharge of thousands of mental patients from public facilities.

The 21st Century Cures Act

Promoted as a way of speeding up the development of effective medications, the 21st Century Cures Act has been hailed as landmark mental health legislation. The mental health components of the act were introduced in response to the 2013 Sandy Hook shooting, and the final version of the act was signed by President Obama in 2016. It emphasizes funding and promotion of evidence-based treatments, and mandates insurance parity for mental and physical health care. It also authorizes grants to increase the number of mental health professionals in the country, to fund assertive community treatment programs, and to expand drug and mental health courts. Finally, the act requires states to use at least 10 percent of their mental health block grants on early intervention for psychosis.

THE COMMUNITY MENTAL HEALTH MOVEMENT AND DEINSTITUTIONALIZATION

The idea of alternatives to traditional mental hospitals was not entirely new. In the mid-19th century, innovators such as John M. Gait had advocated community-based care for the chronically mentally ill. In Illinois a model facility, the Illinois Eastern Hospital for the Insane, later renamed the Kankakee State Hospital, was constructed in 1877 to house the chronically mentally ill. It featured a decentralized plan, with small outbuildings to house patients, and incurred about one-third the cost of larger centralized facilities. In 1885, Massachusetts developed a small board and care program for the "harmless insane," and by World War II, eight states had similar programs. They proved less costly than institutional care, and advocates such as social worker Edith Stern suggested that the quality of care was better in family-like settings.

During the 1950s, new treatment technologies raised enthusiasm for community-based care. These included psychotropic drugs that promised to control some of the most problematic symptoms of mental illness. One such drug was chlorpromazine, marketed as Thorazine, which helped control the symptoms of schizophrenia. It was followed by tranquilizers and antidepressants. The availability of these drugs and later psychotropic medications would enable the movement to deinstitutionalize mental patients.

Psychotherapies were also developed during this period. The effectiveness of psychotherapies in combat situations set the stage for their eventual acceptance by the mental health community. Despite initial skepticism, community-based approaches grew in popularity, along with the idea that treatment of mental illness could be effected outside institutions.

These changes set the stage for state legislation in support of community-based care. In New York, the Community Mental Health Services Act was passed in 1954 to provide state reimbursement of local mental health expenses. In 1957, California passed the Short-Doyle Act, designed to increase financial support for community services by providing a state-local match.

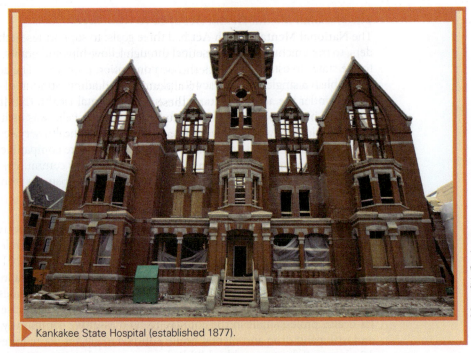

Kankakee State Hospital (established 1877).

© Boston Globe/Getty Images

The Kennedy administration advanced a federal plan for community mental health services. The first step in this plan was the 1961 release of the report of the Joint Commission on Mental Illness and Health. This report outlined the results of an extensive study of mental illness and its treatment. It offered the administration an Action for Mental Health Program that was both ambitious and expensive. The program would involve the federal government in diverse phases of mental health treatment, from prevention through aftercare.

Kennedy established a task force on mental health under NIMH leadership. This group advanced the concept of a comprehensive mental health center in each community that would provide a range of services and eliminate the need for mental institutions. The administration embraced this notion and held that the role of the federal government was not to operate the centers but to stimulate their establishment. Toward that end, the Mental Retardation and Community Mental Health Center Construction Act of 1963 provided a three-year authorization of $150 million for the construction of community mental health centers (CMHCs).

Americans were as enthusiastic about the construction of CMHCs as they had been about the establishment of mental hospitals. President Kennedy gave a special message to Congress describing this "bold new approach" to the treatment of mental health and mental retardation. There was evidence that self-help models such as those demonstrated by Fountain House in New York and Thresholds in Chicago (Beard, Propst, & Malamud, 1982) might help meet the needs of former mental patients. There was great hope that people with mental illness would be integrated into a welcoming community, with supportive services at hand. Two factors militated against the realization of this dream: the limited funding available for CMHCs and the very nature of serious mental illness.

During the 1960s and 1970s, the nation's fiscal resources were increasingly committed to the **Vietnam War** (Harrington, 1984). Only limited federal funding was available to construct CMHCs. Instead of the planned 2,000 centers, by 1980 only 754 were in place. Further, those CMHCs that were established did not effectively serve individuals with "severe and persistent mental illness" (SPMI). They were not residential facilities, but outpatient treatment centers based on the premise that patients would live independently in the community, perhaps with family members. But many patients with SPMI did not have families to receive them. Some family members were either unable or unwilling to cope with the challenges presented by severe mental illnesses.

Nonetheless, the number of people living in public mental hospitals began to drop. In part, this reduction occurred because the 1965 passage of **Medicaid** created a reimbursement mechanism for the elderly to live in nursing homes. Many elders were simply transferred from state mental hospitals into nursing homes (Morrissey & Goldman, 1986; Roberts & Kurtz, 1987). During the 1960s, the number of Americans living in nursing homes nearly doubled, from 470,000 to nearly 928,000.

The 1974 establishment of SSI as a federal entitlement provided further rationale for releasing mental patients into the community. It was believed that this federal safety net would provide the financial resources necessary for people with mental illness to live independently. But the 1980 disability amendments changed the definition of disability for SSI eligibility and called for a review of SSI recipients every three years. Those who were disabled by virtue of mental illness were especially hard hit. Although they represented 11 percent of SSI recipients, they constituted 30 percent of those deemed ineligible for the program after these reviews (Grob, 1994).

Later presidents would not share Kennedy's enthusiasm for expanding the federal government's role in promoting mental health. Johnson's Great Society emphasized fighting poverty and related ills. Nixon opposed the use of federal funds to establish CMHCs, and he unsuccessfully attempted to terminate the program. The Carter administration formulated the Mental Health Systems Act to create a framework for service delivery, but was unable to achieve full funding of mental health services. Reagan converted mental health and substance abuse programs into a block grant that was subsequently eliminated.

During the 1960s and 1970s, patients' rights advocates raised the argument that involuntary commitment to a mental facility was incarceration without due process. They successfully challenged involuntary commitment procedures in federal and state courts. These decades saw several landmark events restricting involuntary commitment. In 1969, California passed the Lanterman-Petris-Short Act to discourage commitment and lengthy confinement. The 1972 *Lessard* decision (*Lessard v. Schmidt*) in Wisconsin established the due process rights of patients faced with commitment. Similar to the rights of individuals faced with criminal incarceration, they included the right to timely notice of charges, notice of right to a jury trial, aid of counsel, protection against self-incrimination, and use of an evidentiary standard "beyond a reasonable doubt." One of the most well-known cases resulted in the *Wyatt v. Stickney* decision, which in 1972 established patients' right to be treated in the "least restrictive setting" (Roberts & Kurtz, 1987).

Several advocacy groups, such as the National Mental Health Association, the National Alliance of Mental Patients, the Network Against Psychiatric Assault, and the Coalition to Stop Institutional Violence, emerged to support the civil rights of mental patients. One of the most enduring, the National Alliance on Mental Illness, was established in 1979 to advocate for patients' rights and reduce the stigma associated with mental illness.

Pressures to reduce public funding of mental hospitals, optimism about community treatment, and public aversion to incarcerating mental patients against their will converged in a movement to "**deinstitutionalize**" mental patients. Deinstitutionalization involved moving severely mentally ill patients out of public mental hospitals and then closing all or part of the hospitals. It has been termed "one of the largest social experiments in American history" (Torrey, 1997, p. 8). In 1955, the peak year for hospitalization of people with mental illness, 558,239 patients lived in the nation's psychiatric hospitals. By 1994, there were only 71,619 patients in public mental hospitals.

While the nation was transferring patients out of public mental hospitals, private psychiatric facilities were flourishing, as were the psychiatric wards of general hospitals. As David Mechanic (1999) noted, "Between 1970 and 1992, the number of nonfederal general hospitals with separate psychiatric services increased from 797 to 1,616" (p. 130). By 1992, psychiatric facilities reported more than 1.7 million discharges after short stays (Graves, 1995). Private psychiatric facilities remain a growth industry, catering to patients with insurance coverage and organizing their services to optimize profits. The care they provide typically involves short stays, and their patients are more likely to have affective disorders such as depression. Public hospitals, by contrast, generally serve patients who need long-term care, including those with psychotic disorders, such as schizophrenia, and addiction disorders.

Clearly, deinstitutionalization did not represent a wholesale rejection of institutional treatment for mental illness. Low-income patients with intractable problems were released from hospitals, while those with private insurance and short-term difficulties had access to private institutional care. Indeed, some have argued that deinstitutionalization would be more accurately termed "transinstitutionalization," because it involved the transfer of people with chronic mental illness from public mental hospitals to nursing homes and criminal justice facilities (Torrey, 1997).

MENTALLY ILL OFFENDERS IN THE CRIMINAL JUSTICE SYSTEM

The U.S. criminal justice system is examined in depth in Chapter 9. Here, we will focus on a trend some refer to as the "**criminalization**" of mental illness, in which growing numbers of the mentally ill find themselves in U.S. jails and prisons. People with mental illness are overrepresented in prison populations, where the prevalence of mental illness is estimated to be four to five times that in the general population (Kim, Becker-Cohen & Serakos, 2015). The U.S. Department of Justice reported in 2006 that over half of prison and jail inmates suffered from a recent "mental health problem," with female inmates experiencing higher rates than males (Steadman et al., 2009; U.S. Department of Justice, 2006b). In 2007, Fisher and Drake pointed out "the startling reality that more individuals with mental illness are now committed to jails and prisons than are admitted to psychiatric facilities" (p. 545).

People with mental illness do poorly in prisons. Their behavior can disrupt already tense conditions, posing risks and demands that affect other prisoners as well as staff. Prison conditions are likely to exacerbate behavioral and affective symptoms of mental illness. Apart from that, they are often targeted for abuse by inmates and guards, and they have higher recidivism rates than other prisoners (AbuDagga et al., 2016).

From a pragmatic standpoint, it might seem reasonable to conclude that mentally ill offenders should be diverted out of the criminal justice system. As part of a trend known as "therapeutic jurisprudence" (Wexler & Winnick, 1996), diversion programs have been established to accomplish this goal. People with mental illness may be diverted at any point, from the prebooking stage (prior to formal charges), to postbooking interventions that attempt to prevent or reduce jail time. Most programs in the United States are post-booking diversions.

Diversion was the focus of 2000 legislation called America's Law Enforcement and Mental Health Project Act. This act provided statutory authority for the establishment of mental health courts (modeled on drug courts) to divert nonviolent offenders with mental illness out of the criminal justice system and into treatment. As of 2011, there were over 240 mental health courts operating in the United States (Kim et al., 2015 OK). Despite their popularity, there is still no clear evidence that diversion programs improve clinical outcomes or reduce recidivism among mentally ill offenders. There have been some promising outcomes, but these rely heavily on quasi-experimental designs so causality has not been established (Cowell, Broner, & Dupont, 2004; Kim et al., 2015 OK).

Other promising interventions include reentry programs that provide support and care to mentally ill offenders, and policies such as the Affordable Care Act that provide access to medical and mental health care (Kim et al., 2015 OK). These will be discussed in Chapter 9.

BOX 7.1   The Insanity Defense

In 1981, John W. Hinckley Jr. tried to assassinate U.S. President Ronald Reagan. Hinckley's attorneys entered a "not guilty by reason of insanity" plea and proceeded to successfully demonstrate that Hinckley had biological and behavioral symptoms of schizophrenia. Hinckley would spend his life in a psychiatric facility rather than face prison. The *Hinckley* decision set the stage for the 1984 Comprehensive Crime Control Act, which requires federal defendants to prove by "clear and convincing" evidence that they are unable to "appreciate the nature and quality or the wrongfulness of the act." This legislation included the Insanity Defense Reform Act, which set out sentencing provisions for federal offenders suffering from mental illness.

States vary in their approaches to determining whether someone with mental illness can be held liable for a criminal offense. Some use the M'Naghten Rule, under which the offender is presumed sane unless the defense can prove that the offender either did not know the nature of the act or was unaware at the time that it was wrong. Others rely on the Model Penal Code Rule, which does not hold mentally ill defendants responsible if they "lacked capacity either to appreciate the criminality of their conduct or to conform their conduct to the requirements of the law." Still other states rely on the Durham Rule, described as the most liberal approach, in which a person cannot be held responsible for an act that was caused by mental illness (Kim et al., 2015).

LO 7-4   Describe Factors That Influence Contemporary Approaches to Mental Illness

EP 3a
EP 4b

As we have seen, several threads run through the history of mental health interventions in the United States. The first is a perceived tension between the goals of the mental hygiene movement (prevention and health promotion) and the needs of people with serious mental illness. Many social workers are attracted to practices and activities that promote mental health. Specht and Courtney (1994) argue that this drains resources from programs that serve people with major psychiatric disorders. A second thread is the debate over the proper use of institutional or mandatory treatments for people with mental illness. Some argue that use of these approaches should be minimized because they infringe upon the civil rights of patients. Others note the vulnerability of (and sometimes the threat posed by) mental patients and suggest that the public need for safety has priority over individual freedom. Finally, a prevailing theme is the extent to which mental illness compounds the difficulties faced by vulnerable groups in the United States today.

PREVALENCE OF MENTAL ILLNESS

Three major national studies were conducted by NIMH to determine the prevalence of mental illness among Americans. The first was completed in the early 1980s. Called the Epidemiological Catchment Areas (ECA) study, it examined lifetime prevalence of major disorders in five communities: Los Angeles, California; New Haven, Connecticut; Baltimore, Maryland; St. Louis, Missouri; and Durham, North Carolina. While not strictly representative of the U.S. population, the sample numbered 20,000 and represented more than 1.6 million people living in these communities. The ECA study used a diagnostic interview schedule based on the *DSM-III* to examine a wide range of disorders (see Robins & Regier, 1991).

The second prevalence study, conducted by the NIMH from 1990 to 1992, was called the National Comorbidity Study (NCS). This study surveyed more than 8,000 people, aged 15 to 55, in a widely dispersed sample designed to be representative of the U.S. population. Interviewers used a revised version of the instrument developed for the ECA study (see Kessler et al., 1994).

The third study, named the National Comorbidity Survey Replication (NCSR), was conducted in 2005. It was based on a new nationally representative sample of over 9,000 people and used an instrument based on the *DSM-IV* as well as measures from the World Health Organization's World Mental Health Survey.

The NCSR indicated that the 12-month prevalence of any disorder was 26.2 percent. That is, in the year of the survey just over one in four respondents had symptoms that met *DSM* criteria for mental disorder, with the most common being anxiety disorders, followed by mood disorders, impulse-control disorders, and substance disorders. Fewer than half of these people received treatment. Of course, in some cases the problem was relatively minor. As David Mechanic explained, "…some psychiatric conditions are like the flu or a gastrointestinal disorder; they are relatively short-lived and do not greatly disrupt one's life" (1999, p. 39). This description applied to about 40 percent of those who reported a disorder with "mild" severity (Kessler, Chiu, Demler, & Walters, 2005).

On the other hand, NCSR findings suggested that 45 percent of those with one disorder met criteria for two or more disorders as well. These people would be described as having "comorbidity" and are considerably more likely to be seriously ill or disabled by their conditions (Kessler, Chiu, Demler, & Walters, 2005). Throughout the comorbidity studies the most common pattern involved a combination of addiction with one or more other disorders. Of course, treatment systems for substance abuse and mental illness are usually separate. These findings underscore the need for integrated services for those experiencing comorbid substance abuse and mental illness.

Results of the NCSR indicated that 41 percent of those with an identifiable mental illness sought some form of treatment. Among these, only a third received at least minimally adequate treatment. Those from underserved groups (the elderly, people of color, those with low incomes, those who lack insurance, and residents of rural areas) were most likely to have an unmet need for treatment (Wang et al., 2005).

NCSR results revealed a trend toward greater use of mental health services. In the 2005 NCSR 17.9 percent of the total sample reported accessing mental health services in the previous year. A decade earlier, the first NCS had reported service use by 13.3 percent, and the decade before that the figure was 12.3 percent. Of course, the adequacy and distribution of these services are still a concern (Wang et al., 2005).

Since 1971, the Substance Abuse and Mental Health Services Administration (SAMHSA) has conducted the annual National Survey on Drug Use and Health (NSDUH). It focuses on the use of illegal drugs, alcohol and tobacco, but now includes a few modules that consider mental illness in general (rather than specific conditions). The NSDUH surveys a nationally representative sample of about 70,000 adults and adolescents (aged 12 and older), but estimates related to mental illness are not provided for adolescents. In 2014, NSDUH estimates indicated that the 12-month prevalence of mental illness among Americans aged 18 or over was 18.1 percent. The estimated prevalence of serious mental illness was 4.2 percent (National Institute of Mental Health, n.d.). Taken together, the most recent prevalence estimates (those from the NSDUH and NCSR) suggest that roughly one in five Americans experiences mental illness of some kind in any given year. Their gender, age, and ethnic/racial distributions are presented in Figure 7.1.

FIGURE 7.1 Prevalence of Any Mental Illness Among U.S. Adults (2014)

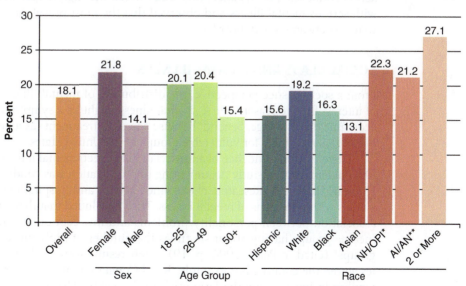

*NH/OPI = Native Hawaiian/Other Pacific Islander
**AI/AN = American Indian/Alaska Native

Source: National Institute of Mental Health (n.d.)
http://www.nimh.nih.gov/health/statistics/prevalence/any-mental-illness-ami-among-us-adults.shtml

BOX 7.2   Massacres and Mental Health

On December 14, 2012, 20-year-old Adam Lanza shot 20 young children and 6 adults at Sandy Hook Elementary School. At the time, this was the second deadliest shooting by a single person in U.S. history, the first being the 2007 shooting at Virginia Tech. Senior Seung-Hui Cho killed 32 people and wounded 17 others. Both Lanza and Cho may have suffered from mental disorders; some reported that Lanza had an autism spectrum disorder, and Cho had been diagnosed with severe anxiety disorder. Both of these massacres brought public scrutiny to America's mental health system.

Following the 2007 shootings the state of Virginia set out to transform its mental health system, an effort that took on new urgency when officials learned that in 2005, Cho had been subject to a temporary detention order based on a clinician's judgment that he presented a danger to himself or others. Following careful scrutiny of the mental health system, the emergency evaluation process was improved, criteria for involuntary commitment changed, mandatory outpatient treatment criteria tightened, and state funding for community mental health services increased (Bonnie, Reinhard, Hamilton, & McGarvey, 2013). Connecticut's Sandy Hook Advisory Commission held hearings on mental health issues related to the massacre. Meanwhile, the Senate gave lip service to improving the nation's mental health system.

Global prevalence data have been somewhat hard to come by. The instrument developed for the ECA study was adapted for use in other countries, and in 1998 WHO established a World Mental Health Survey Consortium to examine worldwide prevalence of serious mental illness. Their 2004 report, based on surveys of over 60,000 people in 15 countries at various levels of development, provided widely divergent estimates, ranging from 4.3 percent in the People's Republic of China to over 20 percent in the United States. But culture, language, and other differences make it difficult, if not impossible, to establish valid comparisons (WHO World Mental Health Survey Consortium, 2004). Of greater interest in this and other international studies are findings that prove consistent across countries. For instance, this study noted the high degree of disability associated with serious mental illness and observed that the most prevalent conditions worldwide were anxiety and mood disorders.

SOCIAL CLASS AND MENTAL ILLNESS

From a social justice perspective, the distribution of mental illness in the population is of interest for two reasons. First, mental illness might be a symptom or result of social or economic disadvantage. Second, because access to treatment (as a benefit of group membership) is a problem for vulnerable groups in the United States.

There is strong evidence of an association between mental illness and social class. The first epidemiological study documenting this association was conducted in 1934 at Johns Hopkins University. Researchers examined agency and hospital records to identify individuals with symptoms of mental illness. They concluded that there was an "unmistakable association between personality problems and low economic status, with the lowest income groups having about six times the number of problems as the highest income groups" (cited in Perry, 1996, p. 19). Their results were replicated in a series of studies across the country. For example, Rand Conger conducted a series of studies of farm families in Iowa during the farm crisis of the 1980s. His results demonstrated a strong association between economic distress and psychiatric illnesses (Conger et al., 1994).

More recent studies have also documented the association. These include the ECA study, the NCS, and the NCSR described above. Each of these national studies found that low socioeconomic status (SES) is associated with increased risk of mental illness in general and of depression, alcohol dependence, and schizophrenia in particular (Holzer et al., 1986; Kessler et al., 2005; Muntaner et al., 1998). Other studies have consistently reported higher rates of depression, schizophrenia, addiction, and other disorders among low-income populations (Dohrenwend, 1990; Eaton, 1985; Kessler et al., 1994; Robins et al., 1984).

Although the association between social and economic disadvantage and mental illness is well established, the underlying causal mechanism is under dispute. It is difficult to establish whether the stresses associated with low SES cause mental illness (the "social causation" argument) or the disabilities associated with mental illness cause a person to move down the SES ladder (the "natural selection" argument). Most likely, these two mechanisms work in tandem, with the extent of each effect determined by individual circumstances.

There is relatively little research documenting the natural selection argument, but many studies have reported the deleterious effects of economic, personal, and social stress on mental health. In 1973, Harvey Brenner published a famous study of the relationship between employment rates and mental hospitalization. He compared hospitalization rates for new cases of psychosis with employment rates in New York from 1910 to 1960 and found an inverse relationship. When the employment rate went down, admissions to treatment, especially among men, went up. When economic times improved, hospitalization rates declined. Of course it is not clear that the economic downturns actually caused mental illness. The economic stress may have simply exacerbated underlying conditions, overwhelming individuals' coping abilities. Nonetheless, the study did suggest an association between mental illness and economic conditions. Likewise, several studies have documented the adverse mental health consequences of unemployment (for example, Gray, 1985; Osipow & Fitzgerald, 1993).

So, while the mechanism is probably complex, it is clear that low-income Americans experience greater risk of mental illness. In the next two sections we will consider other risks commonly associated with mental illness: substance use, violence, and homelessness. These illustrate the way social problems intersect, while underscoring the potential ripple effects of effective interventions.

SUBSTANCE USE AND MENTAL ILLNESS

Mental illness and use of alcohol, tobacco, and illegal drugs frequently go together. Consider the high proportion of those diagnosed with schizophrenia who smoke cigarettes (estimated by the National Institute on Drug Abuse at roughly twice the rate of smoking among the general population) (NIDA, n.d.). Given how few people with mental illness receive effective treatment, it may not be surprising that many, like Tyler, whom we will meet in Chapter 9, resort to alcohol and illegal drugs to manage their symptoms. Of course, it is difficult to tell whether mental illness or substance abuse comes first. Perhaps drug abuse raises the risk of mental symptoms. Alternatively, genetic or biological factors may leave an individual vulnerable to both. Recognizing the close association, NIDA maintains that drug addiction should be considered a mental illness and the *DSM* includes a category of "substance use disorders" (NIDA, 2011).

The comorbidity of mental illness and substance use or abuse has significant implications for social work intervention, suggesting that mental health treatment ought generally to be prepared to address problems associated with alcohol and drug use, and vice versa. In the next section we will consider federal and state efforts to prevent mental illness and/or substance abuse.

PREVENTION OF SUBSTANCE ABUSE AND MENTAL ILLNESS

EP 4b

Prevention interventions reflect contrasting ideologies directed by different beliefs regarding the etiology and nature of mental illness and substance abuse. A universal or community-based approach involves the application of "primary" prevention to a wide swath of the population, in hopes of reducing the factors that contribute to mental illness and/or substance abuse. "Targeted" prevention strategies focus resources on groups regarded as "at risk" of developing these problems.

Twenty years ago, in a move reminiscent of the earlier Mental Hygiene Movement, the Institute of Medicine (IOM) released a seminal report arguing that adult mental illness is at least partly preventable and calling for expanded efforts in this regard (Munoz, Mrazek, & Haggerty, 1996). Most mental illness has its onset in childhood and adolescence, and research such as the **Adverse Childhood Experiences** (ACE) study has identified specific conditions and experiences associated with adult mental illness. In brief, the ACE studies suggest that depression, drug problems, alcohol use, and suicide attempts are all associated with child abuse and neglect and other forms of family dysfunction (Furber et al., 2015). To practicing social workers this might seem self-evident. The association does suggest that efforts to prevent mental illness and substance use might target families in the child welfare system, as well as children whose parents are mentally ill, in prison, or suffering from addiction. When resources are scarce, these targeted approaches may prove more cost-effective than universal or "primary prevention" interventions.

Prevention efforts funded by SAMHSA, the agency charged with mental illness and substance abuse prevention at the federal level, attempt to strike a balance between these universal and targeted approaches. SAMHSA administers the Community Mental Health Services Block Grant (MHBC), one of several funding mechanisms that support prevention. The grant requires states to set aside 5 percent of their allocation to fund early interventions for people with serious mental illness. SAMHSA funds a range of prevention programs, many of which are listed on a National Registry of Evidence-based Programs and Practices. Many of these programs take place in the schools. They range from broad-based efforts such as "Guiding Good Choices," a five-session curriculum for parents of children from 9 to 14 years old that teaches parenting skills related to preventing substance abuse, to "Students Taking a Right Stand," a more targeted approach that provides a range of interventions based on "an employee assistance model."

Some argue that mental illness and addiction fall within the ever-expanding realm of "personal responsibility." Interventions designed around this belief tend to take a "deterrent" approach to prevention. This is the approach that several states have taken in order to prevent pregnant women from abusing drugs. In an extension of the war on drugs (examined further in Chapter 9), these states have criminalized drug use by pregnant women. In their exhaustive study of this practice, Miranda, Dixon and Reyes (2015) report that the first known indictment of a pregnant woman for drug use occurred in California in 1977. An appeals court overturned the indictment. Since then, hundreds of pregnant women and new mothers have been prosecuted for drug use (Miranda et al., 2015). As of this writing, 18 states require health professionals to report suspected substance abuse during pregnancy as child abuse. Three states treat substance abuse during pregnancy as a crime under broad criminal statutes. Alabama and South Carolina prosecute under broad criminal statutes (i.e., manslaughter). Four states enforce mandatory drug testing of a pregnant woman if drug use is suspected (Iowa, North Dakota, Minnesota, and Kentucky) (Miranda et al., 2015). In 2014, Tennessee passed a "fetal-assault statute" that called for assault charges against pregnant women who used drugs. About 100 women were arrested under the law, and health professionals argued that many more were discouraged from seeking prenatal care. Fortunately, the statute included a sunset provision, and in 2016 the state legislature allowed it to expire (Jeltsen, 2016).

HOMELESSNESS AND MENTAL ILLNESS

The homeless mentally ill have become fixtures of America's urban landscape. They shuffle along city sidewalks, cutting a wide swath as they talk and gesture to companions who are invisible to others. Homeless Americans have higher rates of mental illness. This has been consistently documented since the early 1980s. In 2009, SAMSHA reported that 20 to 25 percent of homeless Americans suffered from severe mental illness, roughly four times the prevalence seen in the general U.S. population (National Coalition for the Homeless, 2009). When alcohol and drug addictions are included, the proportion undoubtedly rises. And, as we saw in Chapter 5, the Conference of Mayors reported that mental illness was the third largest cause of homelessness in 2008.

The United States is not alone in this regard. A 2008 systematic review looked at studies of homelessness and mental illness in Western Europe and North America and concluded that homeless people in the Western world have higher rates of alcohol and drug dependence as well as psychotic and personality disorders (Fazel, Khosla, Doll, & Geddes, 2008).

Homelessness, in itself, exposes people to an increased risk of victimization. The homeless who are mentally ill are especially vulnerable. Few studies have systematically documented the increased risk that mental illness brings to the homeless, yet common sense suggests that impaired thinking would undermine survival skills. Indeed, every major city in the United States has a horror story to offer (see Kates, 1985). Freezing to death in the winter is, as Torrey observed, "all too common" among homeless persons who are mentally ill (1997, p. 19). Torrey linked the increased incidence of homelessness among mentally ill persons directly to the deinstitutionalization movement, arguing that laws governing civil commitment have become irresponsibly restrictive.

In the past decade or so, housing policies under the McKinney-Vento Homeless Assistance Act of 1987 have increasingly focused on the chronically homeless, many of whom suffer from mental illness. "Housing First" initiatives offer permanent supported housing to this population (U.S. Department of Housing and Urban Development, 2007). Previous interventions emphasized control, calling on those suffering from addiction or mental illness to either remain stable or sober before permanent housing would be provided. But Housing First uses a "low demand" model that is based on the premise that housing is a fundamental right even while a person is actively abusing substances or experiencing the symptoms of mental illness. The success of this model in providing stable housing for the chronically homeless is fairly well established and should not be underestimated (for example, Tsemberis, Gulcur, & Nakae, 2004), but it remains to be seen whether Housing First contributes to a reduction in addiction and/or mental illness (Kertesz, Crouch, Milby, Cusimano, & Schumacher, 2009).

VIOLENCE AND MENTAL ILLNESS

Are people with mental illness more prone to committing violent acts than the general population? Perhaps the most definitive source of answers to this question is the ECA study mentioned above. The survey included questions about violent acts, such as hitting or throwing things at someone, causing bruises or injury, fighting, and using a weapon. Individuals with severe mental illness were compared with those who had no mental illness on these measures of violent behavior. Results suggested that people with a severe mental illness were

BOX 7.3   Preventing Home-Grown Terrorism

After Omar Mateen killed 49 people at the Pulse night-club in Orlando, many people wondered whether he was mentally ill. His wife speculated that he might be "bipolar," and a few psychiatrists suggested "anti-social" as a better descriptor (Hosseini, Girgis, & Khan-Pastula, 2016). We will probably never know about this case, but interest in preventing this particular brand of violence is growing, as is the development of community-based and deterrent approaches.

Sometimes called "lone wolves," young men who embrace violent extremism have been identified as a significant threat to American communities. In 2015, Attorney General Eric Holder commented that it was they who kept him up at night. Holder and Obama both argued that inclusive, tolerant communities are important tools in prevention of "homegrown terrorism" (Horsley, 2015). Holder's views are consistent with research by Sarah Lyons-Padilla and Michele Gelfand (2015), who described

those who expressed support for radical organizations as "culturally homeless." These authors argue for efforts to integrate bicultural individuals into the community and give them the opportunity for meaningful engagement.

Some European countries have taken a punitive or deterrent approach to citizens who travel to Syria to fight with the jihadists, denying them reentry or prosecuting them upon their return home. In contrast, Denmark is establishing community-based initiatives to prevent home-grown terrorism. The first program, known as "Women of Sahan," is run in the town of Odense. Women in Odense operate a hotline and community support program for mothers who are concerned that their children might be in the radicalization process (Temple-Raston, 2016). Another program, operated through the police department in the city of Aarhus, provides counseling, mentoring, and support to rehabilitate fighters who return home from Syria.

more likely than people with no mental disorder to commit all of the violent behaviors examined, a finding that has been repeatedly confirmed (Walkup & Rubin, 2013).

Media coverage of violent crimes committed by individuals suffering from severe psychiatric disorders supports the general perception that people with mental illness are dangerous. In some communities acts of violence by individuals suffering from mental illness have triggered calls to forbid anyone with a mental diagnosis from purchasing a gun. As advocates for people with mental illness have pointed out, such measures may unduly penalize Americans with mental illness. As in the general population, mentally ill persons who commit violent acts are a small minority.

Among people with mental illness, as in the general population, excessive use of drugs and alcohol substantially increases the risk of violence (Pickard & Fazel, 2013). Those who commit violent acts usually fail to comply with their medication regimens (Torrey, 2011). Indeed, the most common scenario found in media coverage involves an individual suffering from active psychotic symptoms who is not receiving treatment. Thus, as advocates sometimes struggle to point out, the violent act may be a result of limited treatment access rather than a consequence of mental illness per se.

LO 7-5   Describe the Structure and Financing of Mental Health Services in the United States

EP 5a
EP 8d

A variety of mental health services and treatments make up what some refer to as the "de facto mental health service system" (Regier et al., 1993; Surgeon General, 1999), that is, a system of services that has evolved without a central plan or policy to govern its development. The system has four components: the specialty mental health sector, the general medical/primary care sector, the human services sector, and the voluntary support network sector.

The specialty mental health sector is staffed by psychiatrists, psychologists, psychiatric social workers, and psychiatric nurses. The bulk of services are provided in outpatient settings, with inpatient care delivered in special psychiatric units in general hospitals. Private psychiatric hospitals and residential treatment centers also provide care for troubled children and adolescents. Public-sector facilities include state and county mental hospitals as well as CMHCs.

Although it is not primarily designed to meet mental health needs, the general medical/primary care sector is an important component of the service delivery system. The general medical sector often serves as an initial point of contact for adults with mental illness, and for some it is the only source of mental health services. Indeed, the 2005 NCSR suggested that general medical practitioners are by far the most common sources of treatment for Americans with mental illness. Among those who met *DSM* criteria, 23 percent reported receiving treatment from a general medical provider. Unfortunately, the survey also suggested that those who were treated in the general medical sector were considerably less likely than those in the specialty mental health sector to receive treatment that exceeded a minimal threshold of adequacy (Wang et al., 2005).

The human services sector consists of social services, rehabilitation facilities, school-based counseling, prison-based services, and religious counselors. This sector has been the primary source of mental health services for children, with adults less likely to use human services for mental health treatment (Wang et al., 2005).

The voluntary support network includes self-help groups and peer counselors. The 12-step program offered by **Alcoholics Anonymous** is an example of this type of service. In 1999 the surgeon general reported that this was a rapidly growing segment of the nation's mental health system. Nonetheless, it reaches only a small fraction of those afflicted with mental illness (Surgeon General, 1999). As we have seen, over half of those afflicted by mental illness do not receive treatment at all. Fragmented delivery systems and inequities in access leave many Americans without treatment.

FINANCING MENTAL HEALTH CARE

In 2009, the United States spent approximately $147 billion, over 1 percent of its GDP, for the treatment of mental illness and addiction. This represented a significant increase over the prior two decades, a change that was largely driven by increased spending on medications. Generally, about half of this spending has come from public sources, primarily state and local governments, with the remainder paid by private insurance firms and individuals. Passage of the Affordable Care Act was projected to increase overall spending, even as it slowed out-of-pocket spending (Mark et al., 2007; SAMHSA, 2014).

Like health costs, mental health expenditures have generally increased at a rate that exceeds inflation. In mental health, public financing has assumed a greater role while the share borne by private insurance has declined. Medicare and Medicaid, in particular, cover a growing proportion of U.S. mental health costs. The share contributed by Medicaid increased from 17 percent in 1986 to 28 percent in 2005 (Mark et al., 2011). Several initiatives expanded the federal role in financing mental health care. These include the Community Mental Health Block Grant, Community Support Programs, the PATH program for the homeless mentally ill, and the Comprehensive Community Mental Health Services for Children and Their Families program (U.S. GAO, 2000).

Medicaid has been described as "the single largest and most important medical program affecting persons with severe and persistent mental illness" (Mechanic, 1999, p. 194). The mental health services financed under Medicaid vary from state to state, with differences in both coverage and expenditures per Medicaid recipient. Historically, the use of Medicaid waivers and increased state-level control of the program have exacerbated regional disparities in service access. Under the Affordable Care Act, these disparities were heavily determined by state decisions about Medicaid expansion.

ACCESS TO TREATMENT

Access to mental health treatment is clearly a social justice issue. Apart from the uneven availability of services, both income and race determine access. Those who have insurance coverage for mental health care are more likely to receive treatment than those who do not. In light of this inequity, policy measures that expand access to coverage have significant implications for access.

As we saw in Chapter 6, the Affordable Care Act requires that all health plans include mental health and addiction parity, and these services are listed in the package of essential benefits delivered through the Health Insurance Exchanges. States that elected to participate in the Medicaid expansion also provided mental health coverage. Likewise, Medicare covers part of the cost of inpatient mental health care (Part A), as well as outpatient treatment (Part B) and medications (Part D). Medicare also provides for an annual depression screening from a participating provider at no cost to the patient (Centers for Medicare & Medicaid Services, n.d.b). Nonetheless, treatment access is still subject to persistent racial- and class-based disparities.

As indicated in Figure 7.1 earlier in this chapter, Americans of color report rates of mental illness that are generally comparable to or lower than those reported by whites.[3] Nonetheless, there is some evidence that people of color and those with low incomes experience more debilitating and more persistent mental illness. This may be attributed to their limited access to treatment. As McGuire and Miranda (2008) reported, "racial and ethnic minorities have less access to mental health services than do whites, are less likely to receive needed care and are more likely to receive poor quality care when treated." (p. 394).)

For years, this widely observed racial disparity in service access was explained by the argument that people of color experience much lower rates of mental illness. Yet, as shown in Figure 7.1, the results of the NSDUH refute this claim. Although people of diverse cultures may experience mental illness differently, the overall prevalence of mental illness is not markedly different, and individuals who identify with two different ethic/racial groups report considerably higher rates of mental illness. Underutilization may reflect the lack of people of color among mental health professionals, which results in language and cultural barriers to use. Of course it must also reflect economic disparities.[4]

Access to treatment can be a problem in other countries, as well. The 2004 report of the WHO mental health consortium noted that barely half of the serious cases identified in developed countries (35.5 percent to 50.3 percent) were in treatment, and in less-developed nations, the vast majority of cases (76.3 percent to 85.4 percent) received no treatment. Allocation problems were also noted. For instance, the consortium reported that although severity was associated with greater likelihood of treatment, "due to the high prevalence of mild and subthreshold cases, the number of those who received treatment far exceeds the number of untreated serious cases *in every country*" (p. 2581, emphasis added). Clearly, factors other than need for treatment—such as ability to pay—weigh heavily in the allocation of mental health care across the globe.

---

[3]There is some evidence that African-Americans have higher rates of schizophrenia than whites. Perhaps consequently, this group is overrepresented in state psychiatric hospitals (McGuire & Miranda, 2008).

[4]See the supplement to the 1999 surgeon general's report titled *Mental Health: Culture, Race, and Ethnicity* for a detailed look at access issues affecting people of color (http://www.surgeongeneral.gov/library/mentalhealth/cre/execsummary-1.html).

Contributed by Theresa L. Blakley, Union University, Jackson, Tennessee, and Emily Ann Hill, BSW, Union University Alumna

In 2006, when Tennessee cut 26,000 people with mental illness from its TennCare (Medicaid) program, Emily Hill and her fellow BSW students at Union University were outraged. As they investigated the situation their sense of injustice grew. Recipients who had both mental and physical illness were retained on the program but were limited to five prescription medications, forcing awful choices about whether to treat physical conditions such as diabetes or to purchase medication for the management of severe mental illness. Use of psychiatric emergency services spiked. Stories began to accumulate, like that of a man who was cut from TennCare and went into a manic episode. He drove a car into a building and died from severe head trauma. The police thought he must have been drunk, but instead he was suffering from the abrupt withdrawal of his psychotropic medications.

Vowing that they would "sleep when it's over," Emily and her classmates began an advocacy intervention with the support and direction of their social policy instructor,

Dr. Theresa Blakley. Since their efforts focused on educating legislators, one of the challenges they faced was, as Emily explained, "translating student outrage into language legislators could understand." Another challenge was mastering the legislative process and learning to read complex legislation. The BSW students joined forces with established stakeholders in Tennessee's advocacy community, such as AARP, NAMI, and business interests, and became part of an extensive lobbying campaign to reform the TennCare program.

Two important legislative changes resulted from their combined efforts. First, a joint resolution passed that called for a fiscal study of the program. Advocates were convinced that the study would reveal that TennCare cuts were ultimately more expensive than leaving the program's funding levels intact. The second result was passage of a bill promoted by AARP that softened the five-prescription limit. Another important result was the lessons learned. Emily and her classmates came to understand the power that social workers can exercise in influencing policy by establishing coalitions, lobbying with informed passion, and building respectful relationships with legislators.

MANAGED CARE AND MENTAL HEALTH SERVICES

As part of a trend toward privatization of public mental health services, managed care has become a vehicle for controlling the cost of public mental health services (Chalk, 1997). Medicaid recipients in most states are required to enroll with managed care providers, but states vary in their treatment of mental illness under managed care.

Two approaches to managed care have been applied to mental health services: *carve out* and *capitation*. Under a **carve-out** strategy, mental health services are treated from medical services. Either the managed care organization (MCO) or the state Medicaid authority contracts with local providers for mental health and substance abuse treatment in an approach known as managed behavioral health care (MBHC). State experiences with MBHC have varied, with some, such as Massachusetts, showing cost reductions, improved access, and treatment innovations, and others, such as Tennessee, experiencing major implementation problems (National Conference of State Legislatures, 2007).

Under **capitation**, the managed care provider receives a fixed amount per year for each Medicaid enrollee with diagnosed mental illness. Capitation of mental health services is complicated by the unpredictable trajectory and complex treatment requirements of mental illness. Several studies of the impact of capitation have demonstrated cost savings; however, the impact on client outcomes seems to be mixed (Cuffel et al., 2002). With privatization of mental health services there is some concern that the service delivery system may become more fragmented and that the corporate agendas of providers may interfere with their ability to concentrate fully on meeting the needs of clients (Carboni & Milward, 2012; Chalk, 1997).

LO 7-6   Become Familiar with the Role of Social Workers in the U.S. Mental Health System

EP 1a

Throughout the 20th century, social workers played an important role in the mental health system, and a growing proportion of social work professionals became mental health practitioners. Social work professionals were involved in most aspects of the service delivery system, from institutional treatment to community care. Indeed, in the 1990s, NIMH noted that social workers provided the lion's share of mental health care in the United States. This led to several initiatives that increased NIMH spending on social work infrastructure in mental health (National Advisory Mental Health Council, 1991). Two policies have had a direct impact on social workers in mental health practice: licensing and the duty to warn.

LICENSING

Licensing has had a significant impact on the availability of mental health treatment. Insurance reimbursement is typically available only for services provided by licensed professionals, and in most states a license is required for those using titles such as "counselor" or "social worker." Physicians have generally resisted expanding the licensed activities of other professionals in the mental health field. Similarly, psychologists, social workers, and nurses often compete for the legitimacy afforded through licensing.

Social work licensing procedures vary from state to state. Usually candidates for licensure must demonstrate that they have completed educational and practice requirements, and they must successfully complete an examination. With a license they may practice independently or in agencies that are reimbursed by federal or private insurers. Few states accept licenses issued in other states, and there is no national license for social workers. The National Association of Social Workers (NASW) offers a national credential for clinical social workers known as membership in the Academy of Certified Social Workers (ACSW), but this is not a professional license.

DUTY TO WARN

The **duty to warn**, with its attendant duty to protect, was established by the 1976 *Tarasoff v. Regents of the University of California* decision and subsequent rulings. Mental health practitioners whose patients present a significant threat of violence are required to take reasonable steps to protect the intended victims. Many see this requirement as a threat to confidentiality that can undermine patients' trust. Of course, in most settings practitioners must inform their patients of this duty. After an exhaustive review of research on the duty to protect, Appelbaum (1994) concluded that "[t]he duty to protect has complicated life for some clinicians, but it may have made life safer for some potential victims; and it has by no means been the disaster some authorities feared" (p. 99).

LO 7-7   Understand Emerging Policy Issues Related to Mental Health

EP 3a
EP 8d

Several policy issues have emerged in the field of mental health care. Three of these are discussed in this section: involuntary commitment of people with mental illness, outpatient commitment of people with mental illness, and insurance parity of mental health care.

INVOLUNTARY COMMITMENT

In the United States since the 19th century some people with mental illness have been confined against their will in institutions. As early as 1806, the state of Virginia passed a law to permit the **involuntary commitment** of mental patients. Justification for depriving these people of liberty stems from two sources: the police power of the state and the concept of *parens patriae* (state as parent). The policy motto "to serve and protect" captures the essence of the first justification. People with severe mental illness who pose a danger to others are committed to institutions for the safety of the public. Under **parens patriae**, the state is responsible for those who are unable to care for themselves. Here commitment is justified to preserve the safety of the person with mental illness.

Commitment cannot be undertaken lightly. U.S. law views the deprivation of liberty as one of the most serious applications of governmental power. A person who might be deprived of liberty has the right to due process, as outlined in the Fourteenth Amendment to the U.S. Constitution.

The due process rights of people with mental illness were not well established until 1975, when the Supreme Court ruling in *O'Connor v. Donaldson* clarified the conditions under which a state might commit someone for psychiatric care. The court found that "a State cannot constitutionally confine … a non-dangerous individual who is capable of surviving safely in freedom by himself or with the help of willing and responsible family members or friends" (Stavis, 1995). This decision has been widely taken to establish dangerousness (imminent danger to self or others) as a standard for involuntary commitment. This strict standard has come under scrutiny lately, as public concern for the untreated mentally ill persons has risen.

The National Alliance on Mental Illness (NAMI) and others have argued that this standard is too strict and that it interferes with the state's ability to protect people with mental illness (see Torrey, 1997). NAMI has suggested that civil commitment should be used in the case of people who are "gravely disabled," regardless of their dangerousness (Stavis, 1995).

MANDATORY OUTPATIENT TREATMENT

While civil commitment uses state coercion to compel those with mental illness to accept inpatient treatment, several measures have been established to compel or encourage people with mental illness to follow outpatient treatment regimens.

Involuntary outpatient commitment (IOC), or court-ordered treatment procedures, have been established in nearly all states, with North Carolina as the pioneer (Swartz & Swanson, 2004). Under IOC, a court orders a patient to comply with a specific outpatient treatment program. Thus, for example, a patient might be required to take medications and to participate in regular outpatient therapy. Proponents (including NAMI) argue that IOC improves the quality of life for mental patients, protects the community from patients who fail to comply with their medication regimen, and reduces the amount of time patients spend in mental hospitals. Opponents note that IOC deprives patients of the right to refuse treatment, requires excessive state intrusion, and is subject to abuse.

National surveys of IOC showed varied effectiveness. Perhaps the most significant barrier to successful implementation has been the reluctance of community mental health centers to assume responsibility for IOC patients, particularly those who are noncompliant (Torrey & Kaplan, 1995). Difficulties also stem from failure to specify what happens to patients who do not cooperate with their treatment plans, as well as concerns about liability and cost (Mechanic, 1999).

Conditional release and conservatorship/guardianship have also been used to encourage treatment compliance. Under conditional release programs, release from mental hospitals is based on compliance with an outpatient treatment regimen. Unlike IOC, conditional release is administered by the hospital superintendent rather than the court. Conservatorship and guardianship are widely used in California (Torrey & Kaplan, 1995). Under these procedures, a third party is appointed by the court. As conservator or guardian this person can then legally compel the patient to comply with a treatment program or involuntarily commit the patient for institutional care.

INSURANCE PARITY

The role of private insurance in financing mental health care has diminished slightly, which may have inspired legislative efforts to require mental health coverage (U.S. GAO, 2000). These initiatives, known as "parity" legislation, are discussed below.

Until the 1970s, most insurance companies covered mental illness on a par with physical illness (parity). Over time, companies found that their costs for mental health treatments were rising nearly twice as fast as their health-care expenses. Mental health treatment looked like a "bottomless pit," with unreliable diagnosis and potentially unlimited demand. Insurers began to reduce both the number of psychiatric visits covered and the amount paid for each visit and to establish "lifetime caps" on mental health care. By 1993, only 2 percent of private insurers offered parity for outpatient mental health treatment, and 20 percent offered parity for inpatient care (LaBruzza & Mendez-Villarrubia, 1994).

Private insurance coverage of mental health treatment is complicated by problems determining what constitutes "medical necessity." With respect to mental illness, medical necessity is hard to define. Is it medically necessary to provide psychotherapy to someone in the throes of divorce? What if the person suffers from schizophrenia? This is further complicated by the unpredictability of mental illness. Some patients may recover spontaneously without any treatment, while for others, lack of treatment may have tragic results.

Another complication in the parity debate is the **moral hazard** problem. The term "moral hazard" refers to a tendency for consumers to overutilize services if they are covered by insurance. This concept is relevant to physical illness, but it has been a more significant concern for mental disorders. The argument here is that psychotherapy can be personally fulfilling and may require years of treatment. Insurance companies use copayments and service limits to control overutilization.

As private insurers reduced mental health coverage, families and patients reported more difficulty securing care. NAMI has reported cases of individuals exhausting their lifetime mental health benefits in a single hospital stay. NAMI and others argue that differential coverage of mental health care is a form of discrimination against people with mental illness. So, with support from professional organizations such as the NASW, NAMI launched a campaign to advocate for insurance parity.

Insurance parity involves the use of government regulations to require insurers to offer the same benefits for mental disorders as they would for physical disorders. Parity applies to annual or lifetime limits, service or dollar maximums, copayments, and deductibles.

State legislatures took the lead in requiring mental health parity. As early as 1975, New Hampshire was one of the first states to mandate parity for certain diagnoses.

In 1996, the National Mental Health Parity Act was passed, requiring insurance plans that offered a mental health benefit to apply equal annual and lifetime limits to mental and physical illnesses. So, for example, private insurers could no longer set a $1 million lifetime limit for cancer patients and a $50,000 lifetime limit for mental illness. The law applied only to businesses with 51 or more employees, so it covered only a small fraction of the

U.S. labor force. It did not require health plans to cover or maintain coverage for mental illness. Substance abuse and drug addiction are excluded from the parity requirement. The law did not require parity with respect to visit limits or managed care provisions. It did not apply to insurance plans sold to individuals. Finally, if a company demonstrated that compliance resulted in an increased cost of at least 1 percent, their plan could be exempted from the parity requirement.

By 2008, nearly all states had passed some kind of mental health parity legislation. Though state laws varied in their definition of mental illness, coverage requirements, and exemptions, most provided more benefits than the federal statute required (NIMH, 2000). The Mental Health Parity and Addiction Equity Act of 2008 expanded parity requirements to include treatment limitations, copayments, and other financial requirements. The act did not require insurers to cover mental illness but did call for comparable treatment of mental and physical illness among plans that did provide mental health coverage. Small employers were exempt from the MHPAE's requirements. Consequently, about 20 percent of those with private insurance still had no coverage for mental health services and a third had no coverage for substance use disorders (U.S. Department of Health & Human Services, 2011).

The 2010 Affordable Care Act provided what some have described as "one of the largest expansions of mental health and substance use disorder coverage in a generation" (Beronio, Po, Skopec, & Glied, 2013). Mental health coverage is treated as an "essential health benefit." Insurance companies are required to provide coverage that is comparable to that for other health conditions. Mental health treatment is a mandatory service, and some psychotropic medications must be covered. Details regarding what diagnoses must be covered and what medications must be supplied were determined through the rule-making process.[5] By requiring parity and expanding access to health insurance, the ACA extended mental health coverage to an estimated 27 million Americans (Beronio et al., 2013). Of course, the threat of an ACA repeal could jeopardize these gains in years to come.

Closing Reflections

At the beginning of this chapter we looked at Rachel Sanders's experiences coping with serious mental illness. Several factors contributed to Rachel's success. Her family had the resources and commitment to sustain her. Although there were times when she lost all of her financial resources, Rachel was always able to rely on family support. Further, Rachel had insight into the nature of her illness and its treatment. Many people with serious mental illnesses are less fortunate. Lacking family, finances, and (at times) insight, they rely on what we have termed the de facto mental health system.

Mental health policies bring several tensions to the fore. The allocation of treatment is clearly a matter of distributive justice, and the proper role of government is a topic of debate. Mental health policy must distinguish between the seriously mentally ill (people with schizophrenia, manic-depressive illness, and other brain-related disorders) and the "worried well" (those who suffer from quality of life issues and emotional problems). The former would clearly fall under the rubric of "mental illness," and policies and services for them should be labeled accordingly. The latter are concerned primarily with "mental health." Torrey and others argue that mental health is a private, not a governmental concern, and scarce public resources should be reserved for mental illness.

---

[5]Please see the Bazelon Center's summary of health-care reform for details on the impact of PPACA on people with mental illness (http://www.bazelon.org/Where-We-Stand/Access-to-Services/Health-Care-Reform.aspx).

But need-based allocation rules can be problematic. Those who are most in need of care may lack insight into their illness. The tension between the liberty rights of people with mental illness and the public interest in their treatment is manifested in struggles over involuntary commitment. Mental health practitioners and policy makers struggle to sustain a just balance between these competing goals.

The history of mental health interventions in the United States has been marked by cycles of reform. The first came with the development of moral treatment and saw the expansion of the mental asylum. The second cycle, the mental hygiene movement, was marked by a focus on prevention. The third cycle, the community mental health movement, resulted in the deinstitutionalization of mental patients. As Morrissey and Goldman (1986) observe, "Each reform began with the promise that early treatment in the new setting would prevent the personal and societal problems associated with long-term mental disability" (p. 11). As each reform failed to fulfill its exaggerated promise, however, public disenchantment increased, and Americans became less willing to finance programs for people with mental illness. A new wave of reform was set off by the recognition that prisons have become *de facto* psychiatric institutions. Advocates and criminal justice officials recognize that jails and prisons are inappropriate settings for people with mental illness, and new diversion programs have been set up to address their concerns.

Reform cycles obscure a fundamental reality in the field of mental health: the fact that many people with severe mental illness cannot survive without care. Without expanded support and financing for mental health programs, they become flotsam drifting through the streets of U.S. cities. Perhaps with health-care reform, these cycles will translate into a more stable commitment to care for people with severe mental illness.

Think About It

1. What mental health services are available to your state's Medicaid recipients? What is the average expenditure per Medicaid recipient? Is mental health a "carved-out" service in your state?

2. What are the policy implications of the two proposed mechanisms used to explain the association between social class and mental illness in the United States? Assuming the "social causation" argument (that stress of living in poverty causes mental illness) what policy intervention would you expect to be most effective? On the other hand, what policies would be supported by the "natural selection" argument (mental illness causes poverty)? Do the nation's current policies reflect a preference for one of these points of view?

3. What steps could a private or public insurer take to reduce the "moral hazard" problem without denying needed treatment to people with mental illness?

4. Consider whether mental illness meets the criteria for collective action outlined by Abram de Swaan (see Part II introduction). Do you think improved public understanding of mental illness would change this situation? Why or why not?

Web-Based Exercises

For direct links to all the sites in these exercises, visit the *Foundations of Social Policy* Companion Site at www.cengagebrain.com and select the resources for Chapter 7.

1. Go to the website of the David L. Bazelon Center for Mental Health Law at http:// www. bazelon.org. What is the current agenda for this advocacy organization? What recent court cases are discussed? Select one of these to discuss with your class. Consider subscribing to the center's e-mail alert system, which provides alerts on policy issues in mental health.

2. Go to NAMI's website at http://www.nami.org and find their "Legislative Action Center." How do NAMI's concerns differ from those of the Bazelon Center? Do they overlap at all?

3. The World Health Organization has developed a "fact file" that provides snapshots of international mental health issues. Check it out at http://www.who.int/features/ factfiles/mental_health/en/index.html.

Competency Notes

As mentioned in the preface to this text, the Council on Social Work Education has designated nine core competencies and related practice behaviors that must be addressed by accredited social work programs. In these notes, I will specify the way chapter content addresses these competencies and behaviors. (This is designed to assist with the accreditation process.) Please refer to the "helping hands" icons for the locations of specific content in this chapter. Here you will find a brief explanation of how the accompanying content relates to the specified competency or practice behaviors.

The following list indicates where EPAS competencies and practice behaviors are addressed in this chapter.

EP 1a **Make ethical decisions by applying standards of the NASW Code of Ethics, relevant laws, models for ethical decision-making, ethical conduct of research, and additional codes of ethics as appropriate to context.** The role of social workers in the mental health system is described, licensing statutes are introduced, and ethical issues such as right to treatment and duty to warn are examined.

EP 3a **Apply their understanding of social, economic, and environmental justice to advocate for human rights at the individual and system levels.** The chapter introduces the idea that social construction of mental illness can serve oppressive ends, even as it disproportionately affects vulnerable groups (women and people of color). It also addresses the relationship between social class and mental health and human rights issues such as involuntary commitment.

EP 4b **Apply critical thinking to engage in critical analysis of quantitative and qualitative research methods and research findings.** Epidemiological research on the prevalence and risk of mental illness is described, and the ACE studies are introduced in some detail.

EP 5a **Identify social policy at the local, state, and federal level that impacts well-being, service delivery and access to social services.** The chapter introduces mental health policies, primarily at the federal level, that influence well-being as well as access to treatment.

EP 5c **Apply critical thinking to analyze, formulate, and advocate for policies that advance human rights and social, economic, and environmental justice.** Students are encouraged to consider the impacts of social trends and attitudes on mental health policies, with particular focus on the evolving role of social workers.

EP 8d   **Negotiate, mediate, and advocate with and on the behalf of diverse clients and constituencies.** The advocacy efforts of Dorothea Dix, as well as other specific examples of advocacy, are described here, and issues to which advocacy can be applied, including access to and the structure of mental health services are addressed.

Suggested Resources

Greenberg, G. (2013). *The Book of Woe: The DSM and the Unmaking of Psychiatry.* New York: Blue Rider Press.

Horwitz, A.V., Wakefield, J. & Spitzer, R.L. (2007) *The Loss of Sadness: How Psychiatry Transformed Normal Sorrow into Depressive Disorder.* New York: Oxford University Press.

Pickering, N. (2006). *The Metaphor of Mental Illness (International Perspectives in Philosophy and Psychiatry).* New York: Oxford University Press.

Torrey, E. F. (1997). *Out of the Shadows: Confronting America's Mental Illness Crisis.* New York: John Wiley & Sons.

www.bazelon.org. This site is maintained by the David L. Bazelon Center for Mental Health Law. It offers advocacy and reports in support of the civil rights of people with mental illness.

www.macarthur.Virginia.edu. Maintained by the MacArthur Research Network on Mental Health and the Law, this site is a good source of background information on developments in the area.

www.nami.org. This site is maintained by the National Alliance on Mental Illness (NAMI), the nation's foremost advocacy group for mentally ill persons and their families. It outlines NAMI positions on emerging issues in the field. The site is a great source for information on upcoming federal legislation.

http://www.samhsa.gov/about/cmhs.aspx. Maintained by the Center for Mental Health Services (CMHS) in the Substance Abuse and Mental Health Services Administration, this site provides access to government reports on a wide range of topics.

But the great Master said, "I see no best in kind, but in degree; I gave a various gift to each, to charm, to strengthen, and to teach."

—HENRY WADSWORTH LONGFELLOW, "THE SINGERS," 1849

Learning Objectives

This chapter will help prepare students to:

LO 8-1   Understand major approaches to defining disability and their policy implications

LO 8-2   Become familiar with the history of disability policies in the United States

LO 8-3   Become aware of trends in the prevalence of disabilities in the United States

LO 8-4   Understand how race/ethnicity and social class affect the experiences of people with disabilities

LO 8-5   Reflect on emerging issues in disability policy

EP 3a

It is a bit hard to know where disability policy fits within the organizational structure of this book. Disability is a risk we all share, yet people with disabilities are vulnerable to discrimination and disadvantage. In the introduction to Part II, I argued that the policy response to risks we all share is social insurance, while the policy remedies for vulnerable populations involve antidiscrimination policies and protective measures. Disability policies incorporate both approaches. Disability insurance provides all Americans with protection in the event we become disabled. On the other hand, the Americans with Disabilities Act focuses on eliminating discrimination. Paradox is one of the distinguishing features of this area of social policy. I think those of us who are *temporarily* able prefer to deny that we could become disabled in the blink of an eye or with the passage of decades. Hoping to shake that denial a bit, I have placed this chapter in Part II to emphasize our shared risk of disability.

LO 8-1   Understand Major Approaches to Defining Disability and Their Policy Implications

EP 5a

The human race is distinguished by variety in appearance, abilities, and desires. Some of us can do things others only dream of, while some cannot do what most people take for granted. Strictly speaking, "disability" refers to the absence of ability. Over time, the label "person with disability" has become an accepted way to describe a large and diverse group. As Longmore and Umansky (2001) put it, "Some are blind and some are deaf. Some walk with crutches and some are missing limbs. Some are paralyzed; a few have multiple disabilities" (pp. 3–4). Some were born with a disability, some trace their disability to an accident or illness, and for some the process of aging has meant loss of abilities. In all this diversity, people with disabilities share a collective identity and the common experiences of vulnerability, exclusion, and discrimination.

U.S. public policy reflects four (at times incompatible) approaches to defining disability:

- **Medical model.** Under this view, disability represents an impairment that results from loss or abnormality of physiological or anatomical structure or function due to an underlying medical condition. Intervention focuses on the treatment or management of the underlying condition. We will see this definition used in relation to children with disabilities in our discussion of the Individuals with Disabilities Education Act (IDEA).
- **Economic model.** From this perspective disability is about lost productivity. A person is disabled to the extent that he or she is unable to work, and the challenge for social policy is to provide income. Our nation's largest Disability Insurance (DI) program, operated under the Social Security Act, uses this approach to defining disability.
- **Functional model.** This model focuses on specific activities, such as walking or talking, and emphasizes physical rehabilitation or adaptation. The U.S. Census uses this approach when it generates estimates of the prevalence of disability among Americans, and the 1990 *Zebley* decision required the Social Security Administration to apply this model in identifying disability in children.
- **Ecological model.** Under this view, disability results from the interaction between individuals and their environments. This model calls for equal access to education, housing, services, and employment and for community integration of people with disabilities. The Americans with Disabilities Act (ADA) is informed by this perspective.

These definitions operate to varying degrees and, as we will see, they at times conflict in the public policies that determine the opportunities and resources available to people with disabilities. Of these supports, by far the most influential is Social Security Disability Insurance (DI), which was introduced in Chapter 4. For the purposes of DI:

> "Disability" means inability to engage in any substantial gainful activity by reason of any medically determinable physical or mental impairment which can be expected to result in death or which has lasted or can be expected to last for a continuous period of not less than 12 months. An individual shall be determined to be under a disability only if his physical or mental impairment or impairments are of such severity that he is not only unable to do his previous work but cannot, considering his age, education, and work experience, engage in any other kind of substantial gainful work (Social Security Administration, 1999).

Reflecting the conditions of 1956, when the program was established, this definition treats disability and work as mutually exclusive and thus places people at the onset of disability in a "Catch 22." It can take one to three years to establish eligibility for DI (which brings with it eligibility for Medicare), and during that time a claimant has a significant disincentive to seek rehabilitation or employment because either one of these could make them ineligible for DI benefits (Autor, 2011).

A HUMAN PERSPECTIVE   Alexis Mondragon

I met Alexis in the office of the Disabled Rights Action Committee, located at the back of a one-story strip mall. As I walked toward the building, I found my anxiety surfacing. I was afraid of Alexis—afraid of myself really, of doing or saying something that would hurt or offend her, of failing to connect. I'd heard that Alexis was a powerful woman with little patience for social workers. The voice that greeted me as I entered the building could come from no one else. She was giving orders in the tone of someone accustomed to authority.

Alexis is a strong woman. She radiates vitality from her motorized wheelchair. That day she wore a green sweatshirt that pictured a skeleton in a wheelchair and the words, "Not grateful and not dead yet." It set off her thick white hair beautifully. We shook hands and quickly found space for me to sit in the office foyer.

I was ready for a sad story, but Alexis gave me laughter. She was born in Pasadena 75 years ago and trained for a career in nursing. She joined the army as a nurse but caught polio in the early 1950s. The Salk vaccine was available. "It was there, but it wasn't there. Like the flu vaccine." She went to get the vaccine when she was pregnant, but the supply had run out. Later, she had her baby daughter vaccinated, but there wasn't enough for Alexis. So she made an appointment for the following week. In the interim she caught it. Laughing, Alexis said, "So you see! It was meant to be!" Since her husband was in the army, she spent nine months in the local army hospital, where she received good care. Though she was never in an iron lung, her husband told her that one was kept outside her room, just in case.

Alexis's mother-in-law cared for her baby during the following year while she was in rehab. She could have gone to Warm Springs, a hospital founded by President Franklin Roosevelt for polio patients, but elected to stay where she was. She didn't want to leave her husband. Her therapists had been trained at Warm Springs, and the care she received was outstanding. Alexis built up her upper body strength and found the water therapy especially helpful. After rehabilitation, she spent most of her time in a wheelchair.

Alexis returned to nursing, doing triage for two years for a private doctor. Laughing, she said of this period, "I talked to my sister who was alive at the time. She said, 'What do you do?' and I said, 'Oh, I tell people where to go and what to do.' And she said, 'Well, that sounds like something you could do.'"

Alexis's husband stayed in the army. They had two more children, and life went on. In 1961, when he was in his fifties, he was discharged from the army and moved into administrative jobs in the private sector. When his employer "went belly-up," he found it hard to get a new job. Alexis said, "He was over 50 and they would look at him and who cares what the law says."

Alexis went to work as an executive director for an advocacy group that focused on poverty issues. She explained that she was attracted to advocacy because she "always had a good sense of justice."

In 1990, Alexis developed post-polio syndrome, which has challenged her functioning. She explained that post-polio "takes you back to where you were." She has lost much of her upper body strength. The fibers that relay impulses to her muscles have deteriorated, and rehabilitation is no longer an option. Alexis says about 65 percent of polio patients develop post-polio syndrome. For her it has meant going from a manual wheelchair to a motorized chair—a difficult, but not overwhelming, transition. As she said, "I'm never down for very long." For Alexis the antidote to feeling down is doing what needs to be done. That, and "a husband who makes me laugh."

Advocacy on disability issues has been central to Alexis's life since the mid-1970s. She recalled one of her first actions. The goal was to change policies in the Department of Education. After extensive negotiations, an advisory committee was set up. Saying, "Be careful what you ask for," she explained that when representatives with disabilities serve on these committees "they are treated really nice." They get cookies and plaques and are asked their opinions. But since representatives with disabilities never get to vote and are unable to change policy, Alexis avoids serving on advisory committees, seeing them as a waste of time. If the advisory committee is not run by people with disabilities, it's "just a token thing.... All you can do is give advice."

Alexis works closely with American Disabled for Attendant Programs Today (ADAPT) (formerly American Disabled for Accessible Public Transit), a national advocacy group. ADAPT puts on a major action about twice a year, and Alexis has only missed four or five since

(continued)

1983 during a time when she was caring for her mother. ADAPT puts on demonstrations and, as Alexis describes it, "We tell them what we want.... Civil disobedience is where it's at." The actions are great fun—"like a family reunion." And Alexis can cite many examples of policy victories ADAPT has achieved through demonstrations.

Transit is a recurring theme in advocacy for people with disabilities. When President Carter was in office, he issued an executive order calling for wheelchair lifts on all public buses. The transportation authorities went to court and got an injunction prohibiting enforcement of the order. During the interim, the local busing authority had installed lifts on 23 new buses. When the court order came in, they bolted the lifts in place, making them useless. Responding to advocates' efforts, the busing authority did a test run in a very small community. Lifts were not used, so the authority claimed they were not needed. Tired of serving on committees and being ignored, advocates did a "crawl on." On Main Street they stopped buses, crawled up the steps, went to the next stop, and got off. They passed out leaflets. After two weeks with no results, people from neighboring states were invited to a conference, and at 5:00 p.m. advocates went out and stopped "every bus in the city." The media came, and Alexis had a much-publicized conversation with the transit director in which she said, "Everyone needs lifts on the buses. We don't want to be treated special." And so, she said, "We had the meeting, and the next thing we knew the lifts were ordered even before the ADA went into effect."

When I met with Alexis, ADAPT was focusing on the Medicaid Community Attendant Services and Support Act (MCASSA) and implementation of the *Olmstead* decision. As we will see in this chapter, these efforts are designed to enable people with disabilities to live in the community rather than in nursing homes.

Alexis remembers when Newt Gingrich agreed to sponsor the bill. He looked at the name and said, "Oh! My house! I understand that! Living in my house." (*Mi casa* means "my house" in Spanish.) MCASSA will allow the federal and state money used to keep a person in a nursing home to follow the person into the community, "with no worries about waivers." It would be available to the person for life. Earlier in the year, Alexis explained, "We finally got it heard by the Senate Finance Committee." ADAPT did a 144-mile march from Philadelphia to Washington, DC—the We Are People march. She described it as follows:

We charged 95 wheelchairs at night and marched all day long from 10 to 16 miles. It took us two weeks,

and we made a DVD of the march. We went and passed it out to everyone in Congress. When we went in we said we were just delivering the DVDs. We didn't say anything about taking over the finance committee. For six hours ADAPT chanted and sang. The room was packed and I couldn't get in. I was outside the room. But they chanted and sang and our demand was that they hear the bill. Grassley's folks came and tried to negotiate, and they refused to put it in writing. We'd been through this so many times, and they said, "You've got to trust us." They arrested us in the end. All they did was just cite us. Just downstairs in the cafeteria. Of course we knew we'd be out of there by 6:00 a.m. so they could serve breakfast. So they just gave us citations and released us. The fine was $50. I don't remember what the charge was—maybe failure to obey.

Alexis explained why people object to the term "handicapped." The origin of the term lies in the low status of people with disabilities in historic England. They spent their time begging, with "cap in hand." She also explained that in her state there is a hierarchy even within the disabilities movement, describing a "pecking order" in which people who walk with crutches enjoy high status in comparison with paraplegics and quadriplegics. People with cognitive impairment and developmental disabilities make up the lowest rung. She explained that people who bring their disability on themselves—for example, by having a car accident while driving under the influence—are sometimes treated as an "unworthy" class.

She objects to social workers, explaining that to this profession, people with disabilities are just "a service industry" of individuals who "need to be taken care of." This patronizing attitude is disempowering. Instead Alexis wishes social workers would "listen."

I was surprised, at the end of our interview, to hear Alexis and her colleagues speak disparagingly of Christopher Reeve. She explained to me that people in the movement had hoped that Reeve would be a strong advocate for people with disabilities, but he didn't fight on disability issues. Reeve fought "for a cure," and the improvements he made in his functional status were unrealistic for individuals without his wealth. Thus, Reeve failed to convey the idea that disability can be a natural part of life. Alexis compares "disability pride" to "gay pride," mentioning the rich culture of the disability community.

Alexis argued that the real disability is attitude. She compared "ableism" to racial prejudice, arguing that

(*continued*)

people who are able-bodied feel both afraid of and superior to people with disabilities. Reeve, she explained, "set us back by keeping the fear [of disability] alive."

A SOCIAL WORK PERSPECTIVE

Like Alexis, approximately 1.6 million Americans use wheelchairs for mobility. The vast majority use manual wheelchairs, and about 155,000 have motorized devices (Kaye, Kang, & LaPlante, 2002). Among people who use wheelchairs, polio is an uncommon condition. The most common are stroke (experienced by 11.1 percent of wheelchair users) and arthritis (10.4 percent) (Kaye, Kang, & LaPlante, 2002). In some ways, Alexis's experiences may not be typical. Health care has not been a problem for her because she and her husband are eligible for services provided by the Veterans Administration. As we will see, this is not the case for many people with disabilities.

Alexis is a powerful representative for people with disabilities. She likes advocacy because, as she explained, "It works." She is optimistic, seeing the Fair Housing Act and the Americans with Disabilities Act as essential tools for achieving equality for people with disabilities.

The connection between attitudes and policy became clear as I talked with Alexis, and my own attitudes toward people with disabilities moved from fear and pity to respect and acceptance. With attitudinal changes come policy changes that allow for equal access to public spaces, employment, and housing.

The expression "temporarily able-bodied" has special meaning in the context of population aging. As more Americans live to be very old, the number of people living with disabilities will inevitably grow. And, as Alexis's experiences illustrate, most of us are just one accident or major illness away from our disabled selves.

LO 8-2   Become Familiar with the History of Disability Policies in the United States

EP 5a
EP 5c

Long ago, people with severe disabilities simply did not survive. Babies born with serious impairments were subjected to infanticide, and others were abandoned when they threatened the survival of the group. Some people with mild disabilities were integrated into the community, performing what tasks they could. **Industrialization** brought a separation of home and workplace, and people with disabilities were not welcome in factories. They were either kept in isolation at home or sent out to fend for themselves on the streets.

Some saw the birth of children with disabilities as divine punishment for the parents' sins. Superstitions arose to explain this phenomenon, generally placing blame on the mother. So, for example, maternal drunkenness, masturbation, attempted abortion, and anxiety were believed to produce children with deformity or disability. Remnants of these beliefs can be seen today in the stigma and ostracism sometimes experienced by mothers of children born with disabilities (Green, 2003).

In 19th century America, people with developmental disabilities were labeled "idiots" or "lunatics." Their treatment paralleled that of the mentally ill, and they were seldom distinguished from people with mental illness. Institutions were established to house them, along with others seen as "dependent, defective, or delinquent." Some of these asylums offered education and rehabilitation, but many were strictly custodial.

Even now, the United States does not have a single coherent disability policy. Instead, laws and programs have developed piecemeal over the decades, responding to human needs and reflecting public opinions with various degrees of success. Here we will consider four types of policies: income supports for workers and veterans who become disabled, vocational training designed to enable people with disabilities to enter the workforce, education of children with disabilities, and laws to promote the rights of people with disabilities.

INCOME SUPPORTS FOR DISABLED VETERANS AND WORKERS

The first national disability program in the United States provided pensions to disabled veterans. As Scotch (2001) explains, these early pensions supported veterans of the Civil War who had fought for the North, along with their dependents. Veterans' pensions were justified not on the basis of need but on moral obligation. The nation owed support to young men who had sacrificed to defend it.

As industrialization progressed through the 19th century, factories became major employers, and job-related injuries increased. Workers who became disabled as the result of a job-related injury had to sue to receive compensation from their employers. However, the courts allowed employers a wide range of defenses, and the **burden of proof** rested on the employee. Injured employees had to prove that the injury was not the result of their own carelessness (contributory negligence), that a fellow worker did not cause the injury (fellow-servant rule), and that the injury was not caused by a risk that the worker should have been aware of, given the nature of the job (assumption of risk) (Berkowitz, 1987).

The hazards of industrialization increased, and courts became jammed with injury cases. Both employers and employees suffered from extensive delays and unpredictable results. The only ones who could count on being paid were the lawyers!

The **Progressive era** brought an attempt to reform this system through workers' compensation laws. To this day there is no national workers' compensation program in the United States. The first state program was established in Wisconsin in 1911, and by 1921, 45 states and territories had developed workers' compensation programs (Scotch, 2001). Workers' compensation was designed to introduce predictability and reduce the burden of litigation for both workers and employers. The basic structure remains unchanged. It is a system of compulsory insurance administered by local commissions, with awards predetermined by the nature and extent of the injury.

But disputes persisted then, as they do today. Some revolve around the extent of disability, as when a man with a back injury claims he is unable to work and the insurance company that denies his claim argues otherwise. Others question whether an injury was, in fact, job-related. One woman who slipped and fell 20 feet from her office was denied benefits on the grounds that her injury was not work-related (Berkowitz, 1987).

As we saw in Chapter 4, the 1935 **New Deal** offered insurance for some of the hazards faced by industrial workers, but disability coverage was not included due to objections from business and medical interests (Scotch, 2001). This coverage would be added in 1956 with the DI program. Although DI benefits were established as a federal entitlement, eligibility determination is managed by the states. Since its inception, the number of Americans served by the DI program has grown dramatically, as Figure 8.1 illustrates. This growth has led to pressures to limit coverage under DI and to encourage DI recipients to work.

BOX 8.1 Stopped in My Tracks

Like many able-bodied Americans, I walked past empty "handicapped" spaces with resentment that could be stifling when I was loaded with groceries or pressed for time. One such day I rushed past a new row of empty handicapped spaces into a restaurant to meet a colleague who used a wheelchair. I told her I wanted a special sticker of my own, and she said, "Okay, here's the deal. I'll trade you my handicapped sticker for your legs."

FIGURE 8.1   Social Security Disability Beneficiaries, 1960–2014

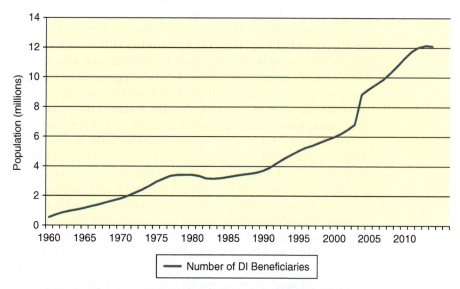

SOURCE: Social Security Administration (2015). *Annual Statistical Report on the Social Security Disability Insurance Program, 2011 – Disabled Beneficiaries and Nondisabled Dependents* (http://www.ssa.gov/policy/docs/statcomps/di_asr/).

ADDICTION AS DISABILITY

Prior to 1996, people who were disabled because of addiction had access to income support provided under DI and **Supplemental Security Income (SSI),** as well as food stamps and housing assistance. But increasingly punitive attitudes toward addiction, coupled with rising costs, led to erosion of these benefits.

First, the 1972 Social Security amendments that established SSI required that beneficiaries whose disability was caused by addiction receive payments through a representative payee and participate in treatment (Waid & Barber, 2001). Twenty-two years later, the Social Security Independence and Program Improvements Act of 1994 placed a three-year time limit on both SSI and DI benefits to people who were disabled because of addiction. The act also extended treatment requirements to DI recipients. It was a response to what many in Congress saw as "inappropriately diverting scarce federal resources from severely disabled individuals" and "providing a perverse incentive, contrary to the long-term interest of alcoholics and addicts, by providing them with cash payments so long as they do not work" (Lewin Group, 1998; Senate Committee on Finance, 1995). Finally, in 1996, Congress passed the Contract with America Advancement Act, which eliminated SSI eligibility for those who were disabled primarily as the result of alcoholism or addiction (Waid & Barber, 2001).

From 1974 to 1996, people who were addicted to drugs and/or alcohol could only receive SSI or DI benefits through a payee, and they were required to participate in treatment. Nonetheless, during the early 1990s, the number of SSI recipients whose disability stemmed from addiction increased substantially, from 24,000 in 1990 to 131,000 in 1995 and more than 200,000 in 1996 (Gresenz, Watkins, & Podus, 1998).

Some of this growth was due to "**cost shifting**" by states. In the early 1990s, several states encouraged people with addictions who were on state-financed general assistance (GA) programs to apply for SSI benefits. In Illinois, for example, the state paid for psychiatric evaluations for those who applied for SSI and financed a legal advocacy program designed to secure SSI benefits for this group (Katz, 1994). This strategy shifted the cost of their income maintenance from the state-funded GA programs to SSI, which is primarily funded by the federal government.

Growing numbers of beneficiaries brought concerns about possible misuse of both SSI and DI. An audit by the **General Accounting Office** suggested that, despite the treatment mandates, only a minority of people with addictions who received SSI were in treatment (U.S. General Accounting Office, 1994a). Representative payees were also scrutinized. These were the individuals charged with managing recipients' checks and ensuring that the recipients were in treatment. Audits revealed that many payees were not suited for these tasks, some were themselves addicts, and others were bartenders or liquor store owners (Cohen, 1994). This finding, along with the results of urinalysis of some cocaine addicts receiving SSI, strongly suggested that benefit checks were being used to purchase drugs and alcohol. Finally, rates of rehabilitation for substance abusers on both SSI and DI were extremely low (U.S. Department of Health and Human Services, 1994).

These findings supported the general notion that addicts were using public funds not to secure rehabilitation but instead to support their drug and alcohol habits. This belief, coupled with the popularity of a punitive stance regarding addiction, led to the 1996 passage of Public Law 104-121, which terminated SSI and DI benefits for those disabled by drug or alcohol addiction (see Sowers, 1998). Aid recipients with other disabling conditions were allowed to appeal the termination of their benefits.

Finally, all Social Security disability benefits to people with addictions were cut off. The Contract with America Advancement Act of 1996 eliminated eligibility for DI, SSI, Medicare, and Medicaid for those whose drug addiction or alcoholism was material to their disability. Later, passage of the 1997 welfare reform act would permanently deny welfare assistance and Food Stamps to people convicted of a drug felony.

In 1997, just over 209,000 individuals received termination notices, and 141,000 ultimately were cut off from SSI and DI (Gresenz, Watkins, & Podus, 1998). For these people, termination meant more than the loss of monthly income. They were no longer subject to the treatment mandate, no longer had contact with their representative payees, and no longer had medical coverage. This was the first time in the history of the Social Security program that the cause (rather than the extent or duration) of disability was used to deny eligibility. While some returned to their states' General Assistance (GA) rolls, others joined the ranks of the homeless and destitute.[1]

VOCATIONAL TRAINING

Apart from pensions and income supports, disability programs have historically offered training and rehabilitation to enable people with disabilities to reenter the workforce. Expanding on a post-World War I program for disabled veterans, the 1920 **Smith-Fess Act** established a vocational rehabilitation program for all Americans with disabilities. Through a federal-state partnership, the act authorized job placement, vocational training, and counseling services.

Clients were those aged 16 or over who had the potential for employment either in the labor force or in the home (Longmore & Umansky, 2001). As a result, the program engaged in creaming—screening out those whose disability, age, or other characteristics suggested little promise for employment. In addition, psychological tests were used to determine a person's potential for improvement. Congress and some program planners

---

[1]In a similar move, the Social Security Administration removed obesity from its "Listing of Impairments" in 1999. This rule change was designed to limit coverage to those whose obesity resulted in functional impairment, usually of the musculoskeletal system. Despite an initial decline, applications based on obesity impairment soon resumed their general increase (Stahl, Hyde, & Singh, 2016).

expected clients of vocational rehabilitation to be referred from workers' compensation programs, but this did not happen. As Berkowitz (1987) explains, "At the state level, workers' compensation programs remained close to the labor bureaucracy, and vocational rehabilitation became linked to the education bureaucracy" (p. 155). The cultures and procedures of the two programs were incompatible.

When DI was established in 1956, funds were made available to pay for vocational rehabilitation of program beneficiaries. But by the early 1960s, it became clear that few DI beneficiaries could be effectively served by vocational rehabilitation. Berkowitz (1987) reports, "In fiscal 1978, the state vocational rehabilitation agencies served 154,541 Social Security and federal welfare beneficiaries. They rehabilitated 12,268 people at an average cost of $7,976. As a result of rehabilitation, 6,346 people left the benefit rolls" (p. 162). Nonetheless, when SSI was established in 1974, funds from Social Security trust funds and general revenues were allocated to rehabilitate program beneficiaries—this despite the fact that eligibility for the program called for "permanent and total disability."

In part, continued funding was supported by the popularity of rehabilitation over income supports. Vocational rehabilitation was presented as the antithesis of welfare, taking people who would otherwise be dependent and returning them to productive employment. This argument was buttressed by a series of cost-benefit analyses arguing that money spent on vocational rehabilitation was returned in tax payments and welfare savings (Berkowitz, 1987).

Facing a fiscal crisis in Social Security and guided by a philosophy of fiscal conservatism, the Reagan administration practically eliminated the link between DI and vocational rehabilitation. The Omnibus Budget Reconciliation Act of 1981 established a new program that would cost an estimated 3 percent of the previous version. Under the new program, funding would be provided only after a participant had been employed for nine months. Decoupled from Social Security, vocational rehabilitation programs continued to receive federal funding amounting to over $1 billion per year (Berkowitz, 1987).

EDUCATION AND SUPPORT FOR CHILDREN WITH DISABILITIES

As we have seen, during the 19th century children who were born with developmental disabilities were either isolated in private homes or raised in asylums. No attempt was made to provide special educational programs for children with intellectual impairments.

As the concept of rehabilitation surfaced in the early 20th century, some children were enrolled in "hospital-schools"—living environments that combined physical treatment with a moral, vocational, and academic curriculum. The Widener Memorial School for Crippled Children, established in Philadelphia in 1910, was a model of this type of institution (Byrom, 2001). These asylums became important innovators in the use of adaptive

---

BOX 8.2   Baby Doe Protections for Infants with Disabilities

In 1982, a baby boy was born in Indiana with Down syndrome. His parents declined surgery to repair the esophageal problems, that led to his death. C. Everett Koop, then Surgeon General of the United States, held that the child was denied treatment because of his disability. As several similar incidents came to light, Dr. Koop was successful two years later in persuading Congress to redefine "medical child abuse" to include withholding care and treatment from infants born with disabilities. Under the "Baby Doe Amendment," parents' views and beliefs are irrelevant. Treatment is mandated unless the child is "permanently comatose" or treatment is "virtually futile." There is controversy about the extent to which the Baby Doe rules limit the ability of parents and physicians to consider the best interests of the child in making treatment decisions (see Moss, 1987; Kopelman, 2005).

equipment, and they attracted significant philanthropic funding. But they continued the widely accepted practice of segregating children with disabilities.

The 1954 Supreme Court decision in **Brown v. Board of Education of Topeka** alerted Americans to the problem of segregation on the basis of race, but it would be 20 years before this principle was applied to children with disabilities. As we will see in the next section, the civil rights movement of the 1970s brought a new activism to disability advocacy. Parents and organizations concerned with the rights of children with disabilities brought lawsuits arguing that, although the Constitution does not promise every child an education, the Fourteenth Amendment does establish the right to equal protection.

Two lawsuits were pivotal. The Pennsylvania Association for Retarded Children sued the state of Pennsylvania in 1971, successfully arguing that under the Fourteenth Amendment states were required to provide access to free public education to all children with mental retardation. This principle was extended in *Mills v. Board of Education of the District of Columbia*, when the court held that each child was entitled to free public education regardless of the nature or extent of disability (Fleischer & Zames, 2001).

In 1975, the **Education for All Handicapped Children Act** (renamed in 1990 the Individuals with Disabilities Education Act, or IDEA) required states to assess all children with disabilities and provide them with "appropriate elementary and secondary education." States were required to develop **individualized educational plans (IEPs)** for children with disabilities and to deliver education according to these IEPs. In addition to the principle of individualized education, IDEA called for integrating children with disabilities into the mainstream by requiring that education be provided in the "least restrictive environment."

Implementation of this landmark legislation has been difficult, to say the least. Chronically short of funds, schools have balked at providing the supports and modifications necessary to fulfill the goal of providing appropriate education for children with disabilities in the least restrictive environment. In this arena the very definition of disability for children comes into question. IDEA eligibility is based on 14 "categories of disability"[2] with the requirement that the disability "adversely affects educational performance." While a child need not be failing in school to be eligible for IDEA supports, the dual requirement of an identified condition that adversely affects educational performance can at times exclude children with disabilities from much-needed services. We see this in Amy's story (Box 8.3).

BOX 8.3   Amy's Story

Amy Rowley was an elementary school student who had very little hearing. An intelligent child, Amy was an A student in her mainstreamed classroom. The school provided a hearing aid, part-time interpreter, and tutors, which enabled her to succeed. But her parents felt Amy was not performing to her maximum potential and requested a full-time interpreter. In the 1982 case (*Hendrick Hudson Central School District v. Rowley*), the U.S. Supreme Court held against Amy's parents, interpreting the Individuals with Disabilities Education Act (IDEA) to mean not that each child receive an education tailored to achieve his or her maximum potential, but that the state was responsible for providing an "adequate" education. R. C. Smith, who wrote a book about the case, observes, "Amy was cursed in being deaf and bright, because she would always get by and always be told she was doing fine." (*Ragged Edge*, listed under Suggested Resources, published several articles about this case.)

---

[2]These include autism, deaf-blindness, developmental delay, emotional disturbance, hearing impairment, intellectual disability, multiple disabilities, orthopedic impairment, other health impairment, specific learning disability, speech or language impairment, traumatic brain injury, and visual impairment including blindness (http://nichcy.org/disability/categories).

Parents and associations have time and again resorted to litigation to force schools to comply with IDEA. Although these efforts have not always been successful, the tone of the debate is slowly changing from a focus on *needs* to an emphasis on *rights* of children with disabilities.

The 1990 Supreme Court decision in *Sullivan v. Zebley* was another landmark in the history of supports for children with disabilities. Prior to *Zebley* (as it is fondly known) a child could only be found disabled (and hence eligible for Supplemental Security Income) if he or she met medical criteria. That is, the child had to be diagnosed with a condition on the SSA's "Listing of Impairments." *Zebley* required that children with impairments that affected their ability to function in age-appropriate ways be deemed eligible for SSI, which dramatically expanded the pool of potential recipients. Initially, 452,000 children who had been denied SSI under the old eligibility process were notified of their potential eligibility. By 1996, child SSI participants had increased by nearly 1 million, effectively tripling enrollment (Garrett & Glied, 1997). Thus, by changing the definition of disability, the *Zebley* opinion increased the financial resources available to the families of hundreds of thousands of children.

In both *Zebley* and the IDEA litigation we see parents and advocates using arguments based on rights to secure resources for children. This approach represented an important development in the history of disability policy and, as we will see in the next section, it was part of a growing movement supporting equal rights for people with disabilities.

EP 8d

THE DISABILITY RIGHTS ERA

During the last three decades of the 20th century, civil rights became part of the national dialogue. Advocates for people with disabilities set out not to *secure help* but to *redefine disability* in American society. As a result, between 1970 and 1990, more than 50 pieces of disability legislation were passed (Longmore & Umansky, 2001), and a philosophy of independent living emerged to guide advocacy and facilitate service development (Hayashi, 2007).

This legislation largely resulted from the efforts of advocacy groups, such as the American Coalition of Citizens with Disabilities, the Association for Retarded Citizens (ARC), ADAPT, and Not Dead Yet. Some lobbied for equal access and filed suits in federal and state courts. Others, such as ADAPT, used tactics that had proven successful in the civil rights movement—blocking buses, picketing, and conducting sit-ins. The National Council on Independent Living, founded in Washington, DC, in 1982, now serves as a focal point for advocacy, and local independent living centers throughout the nation provide services and advocacy to promote independence.

BOX 8.4 Activism at Gallaudet

During the disability rights period, activism was not limited to national issues. In 1988, students at Gallaudet University, the premier institution of higher education for the deaf, protested the appointment of (yet another) hearing person as president of the university. As Longmore and Umansky (2001) reported, "They demanded a 'Deaf President Now!' and they won" (p. 11).

We have already discussed the major educational reform that marked this period, the Education for All Handicapped Children Act of 1975. Several other pieces of legislation were passed during the disability rights era:

- **The Architectural Barriers Act of 1968**. The ABA requires that buildings designed, built, leased, or renovated with federal funds after 1968 provide access for people with disabilities. Uniform Federal Accessibility Standards were established as guidelines under the act, calling for accessible walks, ramps, curb ramps, entrances, elevators, and restrooms.
- Section 504 of the **Rehabilitation Act of 1973**. Section 504 prohibits discrimination on the basis of disability by employers and organizations that receive federal funding. This applies to the delivery of benefits and services, as well as employment opportunities. Section 504 (as it is fondly known) was later expanded in the ADA.
- **Fair Housing Act of 1968 (as amended in 1988).** Title VIII of the Civil Rights Act, also known as the Fair Housing Act, prohibits discrimination on the basis of disability. The law applies to most housing, and among other things it requires that landlords allow tenants to modify housing (at the tenants' expense) to accommodate a disability. Buildings constructed after 1991 that include four or more units must meet special access requirements. This law is enforced by the Department of Housing and Urban Development (HUD).

AMERICANS WITH DISABILITIES ACT OF 1990

The Disability Rights Era culminated with passage of the Americans with Disabilities Act (ADA) in 1990. Under the Reagan administration, the National Council on Disability (NCD) held meetings with disability leaders in every state and issued recommendations that "Congress should act forthwith to include persons with disabilities in the Civil Rights Act of 1964 and other civil and voting rights legislation and regulations" (Fleischer & Zames, 2001, p. 89). Later, the NCD agreed that disability bias was a distinct type of prejudice that called for a separate law. An early version of the ADA was introduced in 1988. This version defined disability more broadly and had stricter antidiscrimination provisions than the bill that ultimately passed. For instance, it included a mandate that all buildings be accessible within two years.

As ultimately passed, the ADA bars discrimination by covered employers against qualified individuals and calls for "reasonable accommodation" in employment (Title I), public services and transportation (Title II), public accommodation (Title III), and the National Telephone Relay Service. Covered employers are companies that employ 15 or more workers. To be covered by ADA protections, an employee must be qualified, either with or without accommodation, to perform the essential functions of the job. Under the ADA, disability is defined as "a physical or mental impairment that substantially limits one or more ... major life activities." The term "impairment" refers to "any physiological disorder or condition, cosmetic disfigurement, or anatomical loss affecting one or more [body systems] or any mental or psychological disorder." The definition also applies to individuals who either have a record of impairment or are regarded as having an impairment, and it is compatible with the definition used in the Rehabilitation Act of 1973 (Faillace, 2004).

Implementation of the ADA rests with the U.S. Department of Justice Equal Employment Opportunity Commission (EEOC) and the courts. The Department of Justice reviews complaints and may pursue litigation on behalf of those whose ADA rights have been violated. Alternatively, individuals may pursue remedies through lawsuits. Procedures for filing an ADA complaint and a list of enforcement actions are available at www.ada.gov.

A growing body of case law has clarified—and at times confused—the definition of disability. The U.S. Supreme Court has heard several cases that involved interpretation of the ADA. Generally, these have focused on clarifying the definition of disability.

For example, in *Cleveland v. Policy Management Systems Corp.*, the court concluded that receiving DI benefits did not automatically make a person ineligible for ADA protections. Carolyn Cleveland argued that for DI purposes she was "totally disabled" but with reasonable accommodation could perform the "essential functions" of her job. The court supported her argument, stating that "despite the appearance of conflict that arises from the language of the two statutes, the two claims do not inherently conflict" (Fleischer & Zames, 2001, p. 103).

Another case clarified what is meant by a "major life activity." In 2002, the Supreme Court ruled on the case of *Toyota Motor Mfg., Ky. v. Williams*. Ella Williams was employed at a Toyota plant and requested accommodation for carpal tunnel syndrome. She later sued, claiming that she had been denied ADA accommodation. The Supreme Court found that, although her disability did limit her ability to perform some manual tasks, it did not limit her ability to perform major life activities such as household chores, bathing, and brushing her teeth, so she was not eligible for ADA protections.[3]

Two 1999 cases, *Sutton v. United Airlines* and *Murphy v. United Parcel Service,* introduced the notion of "corrective" or "mitigating" measures to narrow the definition of disability. In the *Sutton* case, two sisters who had applied for jobs as airline pilots were turned down because they did not meet the airline's uncorrected vision requirement. The court rejected their complaint, holding that with assistive devices (glasses) they could perform other jobs and so did not meet the ADA definition of disability. A similar finding in the *Murphy* case held that hypertension did not constitute a disability for ADA purposes because when corrected with medication it did not substantially limit important life activities.

The Olmstead Decision

One of the most significant ADA cases resulted in a ruling known as the *Olmstead* decision. In 1999, Lois Curtis and Elaine Wilson, patients in a state psychiatric hospital in Georgia, argued that they were inappropriately placed and could live in a community-based setting (Hayashi, 2004). They were not alone. At the time, nearly 2 million Americans with disabilities lived in institutional settings (Kaye, 2000). With adaptive equipment, a barrier-free environment, and some supports, many of these people could live in their communities. The Supreme Court ruled that medically unnecessary institutionalization of qualified people with disabilities amounted to discrimination under the ADA. In this case, qualified people were those who received public services.

Implementation of the *Olmstead* decision remains an important project for disability advocates and state policy makers. *Olmstead* called on the states to modify programs and services to eliminate inappropriate institutionalization of people with disabilities. States were required to make "reasonable modifications" but not "fundamental alterations" in programs, particularly Medicaid. The difference between the two has been disputed. The *Olmstead* opinion offers some direction, calling on states to develop an "effectively working plan" for placing people in less restrictive settings and "a waiting list that moved at a reasonable pace." Disputes over the definitions of "effectively" and "reasonable pace" have resulted in continued litigation, but most states have plans in place to facilitate the community integration of people with disabilities who rely on Medicaid (Rosenbaum & Teitelbaum, 2004).

---

[3]Supreme Court decisions in these and other cases are available through the Cornell University Law Schools Legal Information Institute. See http://www.law.cornell.edu/supct/cases/topic.htm. The Western New York Law Center has compiled a list of key decisions related to the ADA and Section 504. See http://www.wnylc .com/resources/courts/.

A HUMAN PERSPECTIVE   Advocacy: Thinking on Her Feet

Contributed by Jennifer Greenfield, Metropolitan Congregations United, St. Louis, Missouri, and Susan Tebb, Saint Louis University

Few MSW students have the chance to draft legislation, and when Jennifer Greenfield began her advocacy project she did not expect such an opportunity to come her way. In the spring of 2007, Jennifer was completing a practicum at Metropolitan Congregations United (MCU), an interfaith organization representing 62 religious congregations in metropolitan St. Louis. Her primary goal was to work on Medicaid reform during the 2007 state legislative session and to oppose a proposal known as the MO HealthNet that did not completely rescind the 2005 Medicaid cuts.

Under the slogan "MO HealthNet Is the Wrong Rx for Missouri," Jennifer's advocacy responsibilities included working with three disabled consumers who had been adversely affected by the 2005 cuts but who had never told their stories in public. She helped them prepare to give personal testimony at a rally. In addition, she wrote policy briefs and action alerts and testified before a House committee. At the rally and at church services throughout the city, participants signed prescription slips calling for comprehensive Medicaid reform, which were then placed in mock prescription bottles. During a lobby day the following week, she joined volunteers who delivered these mock prescriptions, along with the policy brief she had prepared, to all the Missouri legislators. She spoke directly with several legislators and helped a Medicaid consumer prepare testimony for a committee hearing.

The next week, the committee released a new draft of the MO HealthNet legislation that failed to address their primary concern: eligibility for 400,000 people who had lost Medicaid coverage or services in 2005. So Jennifer joined a Medicaid recipient to head back to the Capitol and deliver 10,000 petition signatures to the committee. Unexpectedly, the committee chair announced that testimony in support of full restoration of cuts would not be allowed that day. With just a few minutes to prepare, Jennifer identified a specific line item in the bill to target and proposed new language that reflected the MCU advocacy goals. She then presented the 10,000 signatures, in a stack of paper more than 1 foot tall, to the committee chair. Jennifer then went out to speak at a press conference. She was quoted in the *News Tribune* as saying, "We are concerned that despite weeks of hearings and debate, there is no discussion about restoring health care to the hundreds of thousands of people who are suffering because of cuts to Medicaid in 2005. Missourians want legislation that will ensure people with disabilities, children, seniors and the chronically ill have the care they need." The story of one woman with a disability who was affected by the cuts was also included. A few days later, Jennifer received a follow-up e-mail from the chair, noting that her proposed language had been included in the final committee version of the bill.

Jennifer's ability to think on her feet had direct results for people with disabilities who relied on Medicaid. The experience brought several important lessons. First, because the legislative schedule and process are highly fluid, it is not possible to plan advocacy strategies that will cover every contingency. Advocates must remain flexible and be skilled at making quick decisions if they want to be actively involved in developing legislation. In this case, the media served as a valuable ally, which suggests that cultivating relationships with reporters is an essential part of policy practice. Finally, by empowering and assisting those who are most vulnerable, social workers can have an important impact on policy decisions.

2010 Revisions to ADA

In 2010 the Department of Justice issued new regulations governing implementation of the ADA. Described by the Department as the "first major revision of its guidance on accessibility in 20 years," these regulations establish standards for accessibility in a wide range of settings, including recreational facilities, parks, and pools; they also expand nondiscrimination policies to address use of service animals and mobility devices, hotel room reservations, and provision of interpreter services through video conferencing (U.S. Department of Justice, 2011b).

One interesting case actually predated implementation of the new regulations. A civil action was brought by the Justice Department on behalf of Lee Anne Unchangco, who was denied the position of Children Social Services Worker III by the County of Ventura,

California, because she was deaf. In a consent decree, the county agreed to pay Ms. Unchangco $45,000; to provide staff training on the ADA, including the duty to make reasonable accommodation; and to go forth and discriminate no more (*United States vs. County of Ventura CA*, Consent Decree, http://www.ada.gov/ventura_ca.htm).

Interpretation of the ADA has generated a large body of case law, of which only a few cases are discussed here. Despite continuing litigation, the ADA's role as one of the nation's most important civil rights laws is undisputed. The act provides a legislative framework for integrating people with disabilities into all sectors of American society and a clear statement that discrimination on the basis of disability is not acceptable in the United States.

As was true of physical and mental illness, this chapter reveals the increased vulnerability of some segments of the U.S. population. In this case, older adults face a dramatically increased likelihood of disability, as do people of color and those with limited incomes. Before we consider the social justice implications of this distribution of risk, let's look at the prevalence of disabilities.

BOX 8.5   Mental Illness and Disability

Mental illness and mental impairment are important causes of disability around the world. In the United States, those with severe mental illness make up about a third of those who received benefits in 2008 through OASDI (Social Security Administration, 2009a). In 2005,

about 2.8 million people with severe mental impairments (including mental retardation) received SSI benefits (Sweeney & Fremstad, 2005). These benefits are often provided through "representative payees."

LO 8-3   Become Aware of Trends in the Prevalence of Disabilities in the United States

EP 5c

Overall disability rates have risen in the United States since 1970, in part due to population aging and in part to a rising incidence of disabling conditions among younger age groups (Kaye, 2000).[4] In 1996, Kaye and colleagues analyzed data from the National Health Interview Survey (NHIS) to report an upward trend in the proportion of Americans living with disabilities. In 1970, they reported 11.7 percent of the population experienced activity limitation, and by 1994, that figure had risen to 15.0 percent. The Centers for Disease Control and Prevention reported that in 2013, 53.3 million Americans (22.2 percent) reported a disability, with 12.0 percent reporting mobility impairment and 6.5 percent needing assistance with one or more activities of independent living (Centers for Disease Control and Prevention, 2015).

Those who wonder whether they are indeed "temporarily able-bodied" ought to consider the relationship between disability and age. As Figure 8.2 illustrates, less than 20 percent of Americans under age 15 had any disability in 2010. Less than 1 percent

---

[4]Disability prevalence estimates vary according to definitions and sampling procedures used, so census data can yield diverse prevalence figures. In 2008, questions about disability were added to the Current Population Survey conducted monthly for the Bureau of Labor Statistics. Those prevalence figures diverge from those revealed in the broader Survey of Income and Program Participation reported here.

FIGURE 8.2 Disability Rises with Age

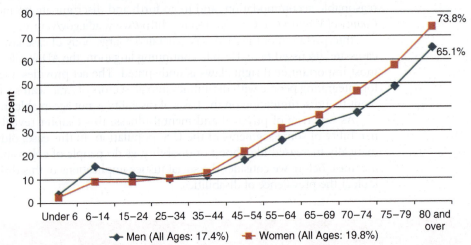

Source: U.S. Census Bureau. (2012). *Americans with Disabilities: 2010*. Table D-1: Prevalence of Disability by Sex and Age – All Races: 2010 (http://www.census.gov/people/disability/publications/sipp2010.html).

reported a disability severe enough to require assistance. That same year, however, the majority (70.5 percent) of people 80 years or older had a disability, and nearly a third (30.2 percent) needed assistance to cope with a severe disability. Gender differences are also pronounced in later years, with 73.8 percent of women 80 and over reporting a disability, compared with 65.1 percent of men.[5] Again, most women in this age group (59.9 percent) and nearly half of men (48.9 percent) reported a severe disability. As you can imagine, the high rate of disability among older adults has implications for a wide range of programs, from health-care services to housing developments.

LO 8-4 Understand How Race/Ethnicity and Social Class Affect the Experiences of People with Disabilities

EP 2a

The **prevalence** of disability depends on the definition that is used. The Behavioral Risk Factor Surveillance System (BRFSS) is an annual survey of more than 400,000 adults conducted by the CDC, who describe it as "the largest continuously conducted health survey system in the world." Since 2013 the BRFSS has included five questions related to disability. These give a rough idea of the prevalence of mobility, cognition, vision, independent living, and self-care disabilities among U.S. adults (Courtney-Long et al., 2015). The results are summarized in Table 8.1. In addition, we should note that in the BRFSS women reported higher rates of disability (24.4 percent) than men (19.8 percent) and, as we will see later those with high incomes report considerably lower rates of disability.

---

[5]Keep in mind that census data are based on self-report, so gender differences (and other observed differences) may reflect greater willingness to report having a disability and needing assistance.

TABLE 8.1 Overall Prevalence of Self-Reported Disability (BRFSS report)

Type of Disability	Question	Percent
Mobility	"Do you have serious difficulty walking or climbing stairs?"	13.0%
Cognition	"Because of a physical, mental, or emotional condition, do you have serious difficulty concentrating, remembering, or making decisions?"	10.6%
Independent Living	"Because of a physical, mental, or emotional condition, do you have difficulty doing errands alone such as visiting a doctor's office or shopping?"	6.5%
Vision	"Are you blind or do you have serious difficulty seeing, even when wearing glasses?"	4.6%
Self-Care	"Do you have difficulty dressing or bathing?"	3.6%

DISABILITY AND RACE/ETHNICITY

The most regularly updated data on race and ethnicity differences in disability rates comes from the **American Community Survey** (ACS), conducted by the Census Bureau. The questions have changed over the years, and since 2008 they are the same as those listed in Table 8.1, except that the ACS includes an additional question about hearing difficulty ("Are you deaf or do you have serious difficulty hearing?"). Those who identify with any one of the resulting six disability types are identified as having a disability.

African Americans and Native Americans reported the highest disability rates in the 2015 ACS. As Figure 8.3 illustrates, 16.8 percent of African Americans and 14 percent of Native Americans aged 5 and over were reported as having a disability, compared with 13 percent of those identified as White. Asian Americans and those who identified as Hispanic or Latino reported the lowest rates of disability: 6.9 percent and 8.7 percent, respectively.

There is evidence to suggest that in the U.S. labor market, people of color who have disabilities experience multiple disadvantages. In work based on national and state-wide samples, researchers from the University of San Francisco reported that disability status results in lower employment rates for people of color and that the difference in employment opportunities between those with and without disabilities is greater within minority populations (Trupin, Sebesta, & Yelin, 2000; Trupin & Yelin, 2005). Of course, it is difficult to distinguish race-based effects from the consequences of economic disadvantage.

Disproportionate racial representation in special education has been identified as a significant concern since the 1997 Reauthorization of the IDEA. One of the main goals of IDEA is to educate children in the "least restrictive environment" possible, and in most cases this would be the general classroom. Yet, African American children (and to some extent Hispanic students) are more likely than white students to be labeled "disabled," and among those who are identified as disabled they are more likely than whites to be removed from the general classroom for extended periods of "special education" (Turnbull, 2005).

Although the special education classroom may be appropriate for many children, there is concern that children of color are being mislabeled "learning disabled" when instead they may simply have different learning styles. Another concern is the possibility that children who pose problems of behavior management might be placed in special education to relieve pressures on the general classrooms. Of course, misidentification of children of

FIGURE 8.3 Disability and Race*

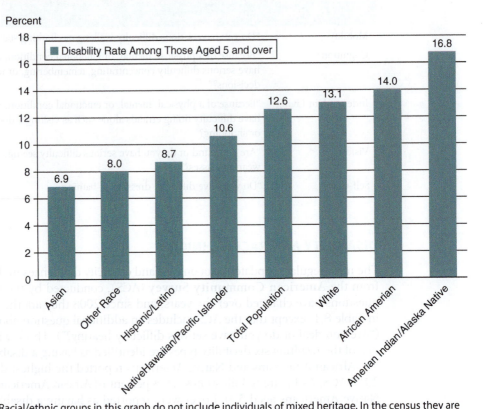

*Racial/ethnic groups in this graph do not include individuals of mixed heritage. In the census they are listed as "alone."
Source: U.S. Census Bureau. (2016). Americans with Disabilities: 2010. Table 2: Disability Rates by Gender, Race, and Hispanic Origin (http://www.census.gov/people/disability/publications/sipp2010.html, June 16, 2013).

color as learning disabled limits their educational and work opportunities and places them at risk for dropping out of school.

It may be difficult to establish the root causes of racial disproportionality in special education, but it is important to insure that a child's needs are kept at the forefront, rather than factors such as cultural insensitivity, under-resourced schools, inexperienced teachers, or racial bias. The 1997 and 2004 amendments to IDEA require states to monitor disproportionality, which has triggered vigorous dialogue about policy responses to this complex issue (Albrecht, Skiba, Losen, Chung, & Middelberg, 2012; National Education Association, 2007).

DISABILITY AND SOCIAL CLASS

The BRFSS results provide a vivid illustration of the long-standing tendency for disability rates to be higher among Americans with low incomes. As illustrated in Figure 8.4, this is the case across all five types of disabilities addressed in the survey.

Poverty is both a cause and a consequence of disability. In Chapter 5 we saw that poverty is associated with reduced access to health care. It may also be associated with increased exposure to environmental toxins and other threats that can result in disabling conditions.

FIGURE 8.4 Disability and Income

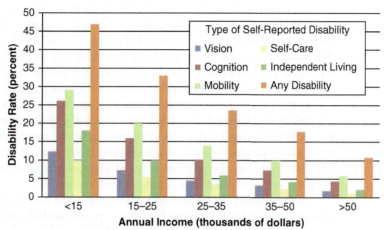

SOURCE: Data from Centers for Disease Control and Prevention (2015) *Prevalence of Disability and Disability Type Among Adults – United States, 2013* (https://www.cdc.gov/mmwr/preview/mmwrhtml/mm6429a2.htm).

On the other hand, people with disabilities are more likely to be unemployed and to have incomes below the poverty level. The U.S. Bureau of Labor Statistics reported that most Americans with disabilities (69.1 percent) were not in the labor force in 2013. Of those who were, 13.6 percent reported being unemployed, compared with a rate of 7 percent for people with no disability (U.S. Department of Labor, n.d.a).

The high rate of unemployment translates into poverty rates that are significantly higher than those of the general population. In 2011, 28.6 percent of Americans aged 15 to 64 who had a disability were in poverty, a rate that was double the poverty rate experienced by those with no disability (14.3 percent) (U.S. Census Bureau, 2012b).

As Margaret Nosek, a leading researcher on disabilities, noted, some people with disabilities must stay unemployed to retain their Medicaid eligibility. "We cannot work if we want health care," she explained (Brown, 2009). Those who do move from Social Security Disability or SSI to employment see their benefits reduced. Thus, the policies governing these programs reinforce the vicious spiral of poverty and disability in which each condition increases the likelihood of the other.

LO 8-5   Reflect on Emerging Issues in Disability Policy

EP 2b
EP 8d

Community integration has become a watchword for disability advocates throughout the developed world who seek to include people with disabilities in the lives of their communities. For instance, in the United Kingdom, an organization called the Promoting Social Inclusion Disability Working Group develops recommendations that support integration in employment, transportation, housing, citizenship, and education. In Australia, the Royal Rehabilitation Center operates a Community Integration Program designed to promote the inclusion of people with a wide range of disabilities. At the University of Pennsylvania, the Collaborative on Community Integration promotes the inclusion of people with psychiatric disabilities. These groups and other advocates argue that all people, regardless of ability, have the right to full community participation. For many, health care is a prerequisite to full participation.

Disability advocates have been united in support of the Medicaid Community Attendant Services and Supports Act (MCASSA—sometimes called the Community Choice Act). This legislation would expand residential options for people with disabilities, allowing them to choose community care with attendant services over nursing home care. As mentioned near the beginning of this chapter, MCASSA calls for the Medicaid money that would otherwise be spent on institutional care to follow the individual and pay for services in the community. The Act has been introduced in various forms (most recently as the Community Choice Act of 2009) but has not yet passed.

As the result of consistent advocacy on the part of ADAPT and other organizations, the Deficit Reduction Act of 2005 provided for establishment of the Money Follows the Person Rebalancing Demonstration Grant. In 2007, more than $1.4 billion was allocated to 31 states to move people out of institutional settings. Part of President Bush's New Freedom Initiative, the program allowed Medicaid beneficiaries in need of long-term care supports to receive them in a setting of their choice.

Of the Patient Protection and Affordable Care Act of 2010 (PPACA), one disability advocate said, "This is far more historic for people with disabilities than it is for the average American" (Diament, 2010). The health-care reform law did include several provisions that benefited people with disabilities. Expanded access to health insurance has proven to be a significant benefit. As we saw in Chapter 6, the law prevented denial of coverage for preexisting conditions. Further, by allowing adult children to remain on their parents' insurance plans until age 26, it improved coverage of young adults with disabilities. Health-care exchanges also provided a more affordable alternative to private coverage for people with disabilities. State Medicaid expansions are also important for people with disabilities. In addition to eligibility extensions, the act included a Community First Choice Option that offered states higher rates of federal matching funds if they eliminated caps on the number of people with disabilities who could be placed in the community (Smith, 2010).

As Figure 8.5 illustrates, since 1960 a growing (if still small) proportion of the U.S. labor force reports having a disability. This growth may reflect the aging of American workers (recall that disability rates increase with age). As the labor force absorbs a growing number of older and disabled workers, the demand for employers to accommodate their needs increases. Recall that the Americans with Disabilities Act requires covered employers to provide reasonable accommodations to employees with disabilities. The Department of Labor's Office of Disability Employment Policy provides access to a Job Accommodation Network (JAN) to provide guidance to employers seeking to meet ADA requirements, as well as applicants and employees with disabilities.

The DI program is also affected by changing perceptions of disability, as well as policy changes. In 1984, for instance, Congress directed the Social Security Administration to take a more liberal approach to determining the eligibility of applicants suffering from pain and mental illness. The resulting shifts are illustrated in Table 8.2, which presents the types of impairment associated with new disability awards in 1988, 2009, and 2011. Most noticeable in these figures is the rising proportion of awards made to people suffering from mental disorders and intellectual disabilities, as well as to those with musculoskeletal problems like arthritis. Keep in mind that there is no evidence of a comparable increase in the prevalence of these disorders, only in the program's response to them (Autor, 2011).

Regardless of the underlying causes, rising DI enrollment has led some to question the structure and operation of the program. The actuarial status of DI has emerged as a significant concern. As we saw in Chapter 4, the 2015 report of the Social Security Trustees called for immediate legislative action to avoid depletion of DI reserves and an automatic reduction in benefits. In response, the Bipartisan Budget Act of 2015 provided for the temporary diversion of a portion of the payroll tax that would otherwise have gone into

FIGURE 8.5 Workers with Disability as Percent of U.S. Labor Force

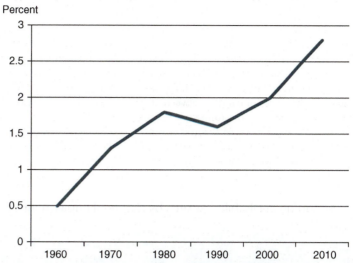

Source: Disabled Workers: Social Security Administration (2012). *Annual Statistical Report on the Social Security Disability Insurance Program, 2011 – Disabled Beneficiaries and Nondisabled Dependents* (http:// www.ssa.gov/policy/docs/statcomps/di_asr/). US Labor Force: Toosi, M. (2002), *A century of change: The US labor force, 1950–2050.* Bureau of Labor Statistics (http://www.bls.gov/opub/mlr/2002/05/art2full. pdf); and (for recent figures) Toosi, M. (2012). *Labor force projections to 2020: A more slowly growing workforce.* Bureau of Labor Statistics. (http://www.bls.gov/opub/mlr/2012/01/art3full.pdf).

BOX 8.6   Lessons from New Zealand

When New Zealanders are disabled by an accident, they are eligible for compensation and benefits provided by the country's Accident Compensation Corporation (ACC). Established in 1974 under the Accident Compensation Act, the ACC supplies a range of entitlements that cover medical care and rehabilitation and pay for some home modifications. It also provides an "independence allowance" or lump sum payment for those who suffer permanent impairment. ACC coverage is funded through taxes on wages (2 percent) and vehicles. Those covered under the scheme (virtually everyone in New Zealand, including visitors) do not have the right to file private suits for damages.

Establishment of the ACC had two interesting, if unintended consequences. First, auto insurance costs are quite low since there is no litigation in accident cases; and second, people who are disabled through accidents enjoy considerably more benefits than those who are disabled as a result of illness. A 1990 proposal to extend ACC coverage to those disabled by illness was not adopted.

---

the OASI reserves. From 2016 through 2018, the FICA tax directed toward the DI fund is scheduled to rise from 1.80 percent to 2.37 percent. This will postpone the depletion of the DI fund for an estimated 10 years, but the Trustees reported that "the DI Trust Fund [still] does not satisfy the test of short-range financial adequacy" as they renewed their call for legislative action to restore financial balance to the DI program. Of course, the trustees only identified two alternatives: an immediate increase of 2.58 percentage points in the payroll tax or an immediate and permanent reduction of 16 percent in benefits (Social Security Administration, 2016b).

BOX 8.7   Lesson from the Netherlands

During the 1990s over a third (34 percent) of 45- to 59-year-old Dutch men were receiving disability payments (Aarts, Burkhauser, & De Jong, 1996). The number of Dutch workers who claimed disability was so high that their claims came to be called "The Dutch Disease." The Dutch undertook a series of reforms between 2002 and 2006 designed to achieve the following results: transfer some of the costs of workers' sickness coverage to employers; reduce benefits substantially; and require a "Gatekeeper Protocol" in which the employer, worker,

and a physician develop a "return-to-work" plan within eight weeks of the disability claim. They also changed the financing mechanism for the program to "experience rating." As with unemployment insurance in the United States, Dutch employers who have large numbers of disability claims are charged higher rates for their disability insurance. Taken together, these policy changes set the stage for a significant drop in the number of Dutch workers applying for disability benefits (Autor, 2011).

TABLE 8.2 Proportion of Disability Awards by Nature of Impairment 1988, 2009, and 2011

Impairment Category	1988: Proportion of disability awards	2009: Proportion of disability awards	2011: Proportion of disability awards
Circulatory system (includes heart disease, hypertension, stroke)	17.6%	10.3%	8.5%
Mental disorders (includes mood disorders, schizophrenia, personality disorders, and intellectual disabilities)	20.9%	22.3%	32.3%
Musculoskeletal system and connective tissue (includes arthritis, amputation, back and bone disorders)	16.8%	31.2%	29.0%
Neoplastic (includes malignant growths)	13.2%	9.3%	n/a
Nervous system (includes epilepsy, Parkinson's, cerebral palsy, and multiple sclerosis)	8.4%	8.2%	9.4%
Respiratory system (includes asthma, tuberculosis, and cystic fibrosis)	5.6%	3.9%	2.9%
Injuries	5.1%	4.0%	n/a
Nutritional/metabolic (includes diabetes)	3.5%	3.5%	n/a
Infectious/parasitic (includes HIV from 1990)	0.7%	1.1%	n/a
Other	8.2%	6.2%	0.2%

Sources: 1988 and 2009 figures: *Social Security Disability Insurance Program Worker Experience, Actuarial Study No. 122. Entitlement to Disability Insurance Benefits*. Table 2: Disabled Worker Benefits Awarded: Percentage Distribution by Impairment Category (http://www.ssa.gov/OACT/NOTES/as122/as122_Body.html#48).
2011 figures: Social Security Administration (2012). *Annual Statistical Report on the Social Security Disability Insurance Program, 2011*. Table 21 Distribution by Diagnostic Group (http://www.ssa.gov/policy/docs/statcomps/di_asr/2011/sect01c.pdf).

On the other hand, some argue that the disincentive to work that is built into DI eligibility requirements denies beneficiaries the opportunity for rehabilitation and paid employment, thus contributing to program costs. Autor (2011) for example, argued that the notion that disability confers inability to work is archaic. Certainly, it is inconsistent with the basic objectives of the ADA: "The Nation's proper goals regarding individuals with disabilities are to assure equality of opportunity, full participation, independent living, and economic self-sufficiency."

Under this view, the DI program encourages dependency through powerful disincentives that discourage workers who become disabled from seeking rehabilitation, and at the same time DI offers no incentive to employers to provide accommodative supports. As we have seen, the Ticket to Work program initiated in 1999 was one effort to reduce the work disincentive with the promise of continued medical coverage during employment and restoration of benefits in the event of unemployment. But vanishingly few (0.01 percent) of those who enrolled in Ticket to Work were successfully integrated into the workforce, which suggests that DI recipients may indeed be unable to work.

This leaves policy makers few politically attractive alternatives. They might further tighten eligibility requirements (as when addicts were denied access). Or they could raise taxes and/or cut benefits (as the trustees recommend), or they might simply draw from the general fund to keep DI intact. More substantial changes could fundamentally restructure the program to emphasize early incentives and supports for rehabilitation and employment that target both workers and employers (Autor, 2011; Burkhauser & Daly, 2011). Alternatively, some have proposed replacing DI with a new social insurance program that would offer partial wage replacement for workers with disabilities who remain employed (MacDonald & O'Neil, 2006). The New Zealand and Dutch experiences may also be instructive in the next few years, when we may see some interesting developments in relation to disability insurance.

Closing Reflections

Some see a fundamental contradiction in disability policy (Berkowitz, 1987). Most of the public money in disabilities is spent to support people who are not working, leaving few resources allocated to training programs that would expand opportunities for people with disabilities to enter the labor force. Concern about "paying people not to work" is a recurring theme. Berkowitz offers a clear agenda for disability policy:

> If prejudices stand in the way of employment, then handicapped people must be protected by the vigorous enforcement of civil rights laws. If physical barriers prevent people from working or from taking part in other activities, then public policy must seek ways to remove the barriers. For those whose conditions make work impossible, public policy should promote independence and self-care. Being handicapped should not be equated with being helpless. We need to move disability policy beyond retirement and toward the participation of the handicapped in American life. (1987, p. 9)

But widespread prejudice against people with disabilities persists, and people with disabilities continue to battle unusually high rates of poverty, unemployment, and isolation. As Senator Edward Kennedy declared, "We must banish the patronizing mind-set that disabled people are unable. In fact, they have enormous talent, and America cannot afford to waste an ounce of it" (Fleischer & Zames, 2001, p. xvii).

Think About It

1. The 1996 decision to deny SSI and DI benefits to addicts reflects a belief that they should assume personal responsibility for their disability. Can you think of other situations for which the cause of a disability might be used to deny coverage (i.e., to enforce personal, as opposed to collective, responsibility)?

2. What has your state done to implement the *Olmstead* decision? Is there a plan in place to provide for community integration of people with disabilities?

3. Why do you think the language of the ADA extends protections to people who are "regarded" as having a disability? How would you determine whether someone who is regarded as having a disability merits ADA protections? Have any complaints on this basis been successful in the courts?

4. Retirement policies have important consequences for people who become disabled during their working lives. Disability is a cause of early retirement as well as unemployment in mid- to late life. Consider the relationship between disability and race. How do you think people of color are affected by increases in the age of eligibility for Social Security retirement benefits?

5. What do you see as the lessons from the New Zealand and Netherlands experiences with disability insurance? How might they transfer to the United States?

Web-Based Exercises

For direct links to all the sites in these exercises, visit the *Foundations of Social Policy* Companion Site at www.cengagebrain.com and select the resources for Chapter 8.

1. Go to the Ragged Edge website at http://www.ragged-edge-mag.com. Click on "advanced search." Under the second heading, "Search our libraries and archives," make sure "Ragged Edge Archives 2001–present" is selected, and enter "Amy Rowley." Read the material presented, and consider the question of educational equity for children with disabilities. Do you agree with the Supreme Court decision in this case? Why or why not?

2. Go to the Centers for Medicare & Medicaid Services (CMS) website at http://www .cms.gov. Open the page related to the Money Follows the Person Rebalancing Demonstration Grant (http://www.cms.gov/Regulations-and-Guidance/Legislation/Deficit ReductionAct/downloads/StateMFPGrantSummaries-All.pdf). Here you should find a downloadable copy of the summary of state MFP program applications. Open this document to find out what (if anything) your state has been doing as part of this initiative.

Competency Notes

As mentioned in the preface to this text, the Council on Social Work Education has designated nine core competencies and related practice behaviors that must be addressed by accredited social work programs. In these notes, I will specify the way chapter content addresses these competencies and behaviors. (This is designed to assist with the accreditation process.) Please refer to the "helping hands" icons for the locations of specific content in this chapter. Here you will find a brief explanation of how the accompanying content relates to the specified competency or practice behaviors.

The following list indicates where EPAS competencies and practice behaviors are addressed in this chapter.

EP 2a

Apply and communicate understanding of the importance of diversity and difference in shaping life experiences in practice at the micro, mezzo and macro levels. The chapter addresses racial and ethnic diversity, as well as social class and examines their relationship to the risk of disability.

EP 2b   **Present themselves as learners and engage client systems as experts of their own experiences.** The chapter describes disability movements that illustrate the expertise and power of people with disabilities.

EP 3a   **Apply and communicate understanding of the importance of diversity and difference in shaping life experiences in practice at the micro, mezzo and macro levels.** The chapter opens with a brief discussion of denial as a technique for distancing the "temporarily able" from people with disabilities.

EP 5a   **Identify social policy at the local, state, and federal level that impacts well-being, service delivery, and access to social services.** The chapter discusses a range of policies that have direct effects on this vulnerable population. The elimination of benefits for people with addiction is   discussed, along with other cost-cutting measures that disadvantage people with disabilities.

EP 5c   **Apply critical thinking to analyze, formulate, and advocate for policies that advance human rights and social, economic, and environmental justice.** Termination of benefits is presented as a mechanism of oppression, and the disproportionate disability risk experienced by people of color is discussed. The history of disability policy in the United States reveals the effects of changing trends and other developments .The chapter also touches on the reciprocal relationship between poverty and disability.

EP 8d   **Negotiate, mediate, and advocate with and on the behalf of diverse clients and constituencies.** The chapter addresses emerging issues that will call for social work advocacy. In addition, the disability rights movement is described to provide specific examples of advocacy efforts in this field.

Suggested Resources

Burkhauser, R. V., & Daly, M. (2011). *The Declining Work and Welfare of People with Disabilities: What Went Wrong and a Strategy for Change.* Washington, DC: AEI Press.

Fleischer, D. Z., & Zames, F. (2001). *The Disability Rights Movement: From Charity to Confrontation.* Philadelphia: Temple University Press.

Journal of Social Work in Disability and Rehabilitation. Distributed by Taylor & Francis, this journal offers a look at major issues affecting social work with and for people who have disabilities.

Nussbaum, S. (2013). *Good Kings Bad Kings* (A novel about disabled young people that won the PEN/ Bellwether Prize for Socially Engaged Fiction). New York: Algonquin Books.

Switzer, J. (2003). *Disabled Rights: American Disability Policy and the Fight for Equality.* Washington, DC: Georgetown University Press.

www.disabled-world.com. This site provides news and statistics for the worldwide disability community.

www.ncd.gov. Maintained by the National Council on Disability, the newsletter available here provides a glimpse into current policy developments.

www.ragged-edge-mag.com. *Ragged Edge* is an online magazine for the disability community, offering discussion of current issues and personal experiences. It's a lively and interesting read.

Crime and Criminal Justice

"Criminal justice" was a term she found more apt than it was meant to be.
—BARBARA NEELY

Learning Objectives

This chapter will help prepare students to:

LO 9-1   Understand the history of the U.S. criminal justice system

LO 9-2   Be familiar with the development of the U.S. juvenile justice system

LO 9-3   Be aware of contemporary trends in incarceration and their implications

LO 9-4   Be familiar with the basic structure and operation of the U.S. criminal justice system

LO 9-5   Become aware of the disproportionate representation of people of color throughout the U.S. criminal justice system

LO 9-6   Become aware of proposals to reform the U.S. criminal justice system

LO 9-7   Be familiar with the role social workers play in the U.S. criminal justice system

The mass incarceration of Americans is unprecedented. Our nation's incarceration rate is the highest in the world—and currently at the highest point in our own history with ripple effects on families and communities of the incarcerated, as well as our nation as a whole. As we examine the history of criminal justice we will trace the roots of this modern trend to the 1960s wars on crime and on drugs. We will examine the basic structure of the U.S. system to understand the roles of law enforcement, the courts, and correctional facilities and touch on recent developments related to each. Then we will go into some depth on the disproportionate representation of people of color, particularly African Americans, in the criminal justice system. We will turn to contemporary proposals to reform criminal justice in the United States and, finally, we'll consider the role of social workers, many of whom find employment in the burgeoning criminal justice system. But first, let's look Tyler Jennings, a self-described "convicted felon," and consider his experiences with the criminal justice system.

A HUMAN PERSPECTIVE   Tyler Jennings

A colleague introduced me to Tyler, a local criminal justice activist who describes himself as "a convicted felon." Tyler says that he has no regrets: "I do not regret my life at this point. I actually feel very privileged that I was given the opportunity … to learn about life on a whole other level … You couldn't pay to have my life. It's special. It's also crazy."

It all started in Denver, Colorado, where Tyler was born to loving parents from solid middle-class backgrounds. His childhood was happy. "I had no problems, you know … I didn't feel like I was a bad person." But when he was 10, Tyler's parents moved to another town, where his mom got a job as a high school principal. Then both parents joined an evangelical church. He explains, "That's pretty much where my life started to get all rocky." Tyler didn't fit in with the church group, and he resisted efforts to make him conform. "They were all gung-ho about the new religion, trying to be all on board with it … I didn't fit in and just started to get in trouble." Within a couple of years he was drinking alcohol, smoking pot, and experimenting with drugs.

Tyler links his experimentation to the DARE (Drug Abuse Resistance Education) Program at his school. "They started talking about doing psychedelic drugs and, like, being able to see purple elephants and things like that and little leprechauns. I was, like, 'Well, sign me up! I want to try that!" Within two years he was smoking pot regularly, sporting dreadlocks, and hanging out with skateboarders. He continued to earn good grades. Even when he was suspended from school, his mom made sure he kept up with his coursework. Nonetheless, Tyler spent more and more time in detention.

Then his parents found some pot in the house. As he explains, "My parents were like, 'You're just a silly stupid f****** drug addict. You're not going to amount to s***. You're going to go to prison or be dead.' So that's pretty much what I expected of myself." Tyler was 13 when his parents sent him to rehab. He hated it. The other kids were a lot older, and "They practiced a lot more abusive practices than I think they do now, like locking you in closets for like all day long with the lights off and, like, restraining you … I was, like, 'What kind of crazy dynamics is this shit?'" After a nasty incident involving his therapists left him with obvious bruises, Tyler's mother pulled him out of the program. "Because of that one incident, I was able to get my mom … And my mom was, like, 'Well, we aren't doing that anymore.' My parents decided to give me another try, but I was, like, … I didn't trust my parents anymore."

Tyler's parents made him go to church until he was "totally fed up with it all because I wasn't accepted by any one of them … They were very open to tell you that you weren't living like you should be…. You're going to go to hell." He continued to smoke pot, explaining that "It was not hard to find." He started his freshman year at the high school where his mother was principal, and he managed to get in trouble a lot. He sneaked alcohol into school and left the school building to smoke pot. "I really was a troublemaker," he said. During the second week of school he was suspended. At home, he took his parents' car and drove around at night. They didn't catch him because "They couldn't just stay awake all night, and I literally would stay awake all night and wait for them to fall asleep." He would drive off and smoke pot "just to get away … I literally felt like I was in prison."

Eventually, Tyler decided to run away from home. "I was going to be kicked out anyway, and you know where they were going to send me." His uncle and his father tracked him down. "They were looking for me—called the cops and everything. They found me … took me to the Boys Ranch," which differed from rehab in that "They used humiliation and different things." He spent a lot of time on the work crew, where "you just had to clean all day … they didn't even have enough stuff to clean, and they had this thing called the rock pile and you'd move the pile of rocks from one end of the field to the other and restack it. And … like, if they didn't feel like work crew was bad enough they'd take away your clothes and make you wear a blanket like a dress and tie a rope on you and walk you around like a dog." There was a school on site, and classes were held through the summer, so Tyler graduated from high school. "I was, like, a 16-year-old graduating from high school … did not have any skills." So he enrolled in the local community college, where he tasted freedom after "basically [being] incarcerated all my life, in my opinion." He got his own car and stopped going to class. When he failed all of his classes, his parents kicked him out of the house.

After that, Tyler was homeless for a month or so. He slept on friends' couches and did drugs "with the worst people you could possibly be with." He doesn't remember much about that time, only that his uncle found him and took him to lunch one day. The uncle let Tyler stay at his house on the condition that he join the Air Force. "I was, like, 'What the f*** do you mean?' 'Well, we think if you went into the military … they pay for you to go to college and you have a place to stay. You could travel the world.'

I was, like, 'F******-A yes! But I'm not going to be able to get in. I'm dirty for every drug there is.'"

Tyler did basic training in Texas. He had nearly made it through when he was "recycled" for insulting a girl at church. Recycling meant he was set back two weeks. But Tyler said it was the best thing that had happened for him because his Technical Instructor made him a Dorm Chief. "And that was when my time in the Air Force started getting good. I was seen as, like, a leader." He said, "This is when I really found out about how I was able to interact with people. I just develop trust and rapport. To get these other 50 people ... They would listen to me all the time." While he was in charge, his group was designated an "Honor Flight," which meant that they never failed an inspection and did excellent work on their written examinations. Tyler wore a ribbon at graduation to commemorate the Honor Flight, and his parents were there to watch him.

After graduation, Tyler went to Biloxi, Mississippi, for technical school. He trained for nearly a year before he "started hanging out with these crazy people from New Orleans." His friends were into cocaine. In retrospect, Tyler thinks that at 18 he was "just too young ... was just coming out of straight institutionalization." About this time, the Air Force decided to eliminate the position for which he was training, which gave him the option of taking an honorable discharge. He explained, "I didn't want to be in it ... I was, like, I want to smoke. I want to chill. I want to have a normal life. You know?" He had a girlfriend in New Orleans. He loved the South. But Tyler describes the decision as "the worst mistake of my life." Within 72 hours of being released from the military he was arrested on a beach for possession of cocaine. "That was really when all kinds of mess started for me which ended me up in prison."

Tyler got four years' probation and moved back to his parents' house. He returned to community college and on his "first spring break," got a DUI. "And I was still not 21 yet either." He spent a few days in jail, and Mississippi issued a probation violation, which required that he appear before a judge. Instead, he decided to run. He didn't get far before he was picked up and extradited "for the first time" to Mississippi. A security company called Wackenhut had the extradition contract. Tyler reports that, "It took, like, two and a half weeks to get to Mississippi in this little van, like, totally shackled ... The one lady that was driving was mad at us ... so she turned on static full blast and just turned it to the back so she didn't have to hear it. Full blast. Then wouldn't let us sleep, playing static at night. The van kept breaking down."

When he finally appeared before a judge, Tyler hadn't yet been charged and the judge said, "So you guys just f****** extradited him all the way down here?" Tyler says, "They had no choice other than to release me back on probation." Tyler's probation was extended and he was released to a halfway house in Alabama for three months until he could enter a residential treatment program for drug addiction. (By this time he was addicted to heroin.) He liked the halfway house because "They weren't restrictive. You could work all day long and come home. The only requirement was to go to one AA meeting. And the AA culture down there is actually really amazing ... I made a whole bunch of really good friends. Not bad at all."

But residential treatment didn't work well for him. He stayed seven months, "really trying to do good." The treatment center held "marathons" where "they locked everybody in the kitchen ... to sit there for days sometimes. Everybody goes around the room and cops to what they have done wrong. And I really wasn't doing anything wrong. I had seven years of prison over my head ..." By the third marathon, Tyler figured he was never going to make it through the program. He told a staff member he was going to leave, and the response was: "Well, that's your choice. See you later." So Tyler called some old friends and they picked him up at a gas station. He moved in with them and got a job doing construction work (for which he was paid under the table) and started saving for a trip to Mexico.

One of the friends was an addict, and after two months he and Tyler were smoking Mexican heroin every night. At about this time he had his first date with the woman who would become his wife. He found her amazing but kept in mind that he was going to Mexico. Then one day Tyler overdosed. He "sniffed a bunch of Xanax, so I was really out of it. Anyway, my friends just let me do three balloons of heroin." Someone called 911, the ambulance came, and Tyler was handcuffed to the hospital bed pending extradition to Mississippi.

"This time it was a huge bus ... This time they didn't let you go to the bathroom." There was a restroom in the bus for the drivers (four of them), but inmates weren't allowed to use it. Instead, they were permitted to relieve themselves when the bus stopped twice a day at fast food restaurants. But, Tyler said, "I was so terrified about going to prison it didn't matter that much." He spent the trip shackled to an OG (Original Gangster) Blood. "I had no idea who the guy was ... He just had a huge-ass scar over his face ... After day two, I was like finally going to ask a question, 'What happened to your face, Bro?' He's, like, 'Shut up, white boy, unless you want me to do it to you.'"

(continued)

Prison was not what Tyler expected. For one thing, he didn't have a cell. This prison was converted from an old army base, and instead of cells it was "open bay style." Two hundred and fifty people lived on a bay that had four rows of racks (beds). He explained, "With 250 people roaming around at night a lot can happen." There were no riots while he was there, and his relationship skills kept him reasonably safe. As a white person, he explained, "You are the minority, and they hate you." But "It wasn't bad for me … from day one in prison I was always being checked by the way up people in the organization: 'Is he an implant? Is he a cop? He doesn't have an accent. He can write. He doesn't hang out with other white people. He doesn't ever say anything racist …' You know, they were confused … The OG Blood [the guy he rode down with] was actually told by other organization members that he needed to figure out what the hell was going on with me … He was, like, 'That white boy is not a police officer.' He's, like, 'I rode down with him.' Whatever."

Gangs ran the place, with hierarchy and rules that reminded Tyler of the military: "chain of command and leadership and all that." Fighting was carefully controlled. "You'd have to go get clearance from one of these guys to go fight someone … because if you fought somebody unsanctioned, then the gangs would get involved because now you've brought heat on the zone." And there were rules for everything. "Even when you go to eat … it's not the prison guards you gotta worry about; it's the gangs … they don't want to have to stab you. They don't want to have to kill you. But they will definitely have to do that if you break security."

The gangs ran a tight ship. "Since it's open bays you would see if anything happened. It's got to be sanctioned … People get raped as punishment … and that's rare. They would more than likely just kill you." Tyler felt lucky there wasn't a riot during his time in prison, because that was when people get killed. He explained that stabbing, while fairly common, seldom proves fatal. On the other hand, he did see someone beaten to death. The simmering resentment between a black gang and the Aryan Brotherhood led to the death of one of the black Vice Lords. "Without even questioning, like, six of them go over and grab him and just beat him to death. One guy was like jumping on his leg until he broke his femur … I heard the whole thing going down, the bones and shit and I'm not even leaving my rack." No one intervened. The guards waited until it was over. The Crisis Response Teams were "never anywhere close …"

Tyler felt *really* lucky after Hurricane Katrina. The prison became overcrowded and he was released. "I was, like, "Give me the phone!" He dialed his mom, and "She started crying. Freaking out. Oh, she was terrified every day I was in there." He returned home and had to complete a year of Drug Court, which was "shit times, but not the worst … peeing in front of people." On Drug Court he couldn't even drink alcohol. He just worked construction and joined a sober riders' motorcycle club. And that, he said, "was great!"

He couldn't get a job or an apartment because of "Felonies and all that stuff … You could not even find an apartment in what is not the worst part of town … right across from the jail. You can find an apartment that's right there! Give you a nice view of where you're going back to!" His uncle gave him a job doing construction, and he returned to school to finish his associate's degree. Eventually, his Mississippi record was expunged at a cost of $10,000. "I was still a convicted felon for the first two years. And then it was just six months ago that I actually got my record expunged." Still, he couldn't vote or get a passport.

When he got out, Tyler married the woman he had met before going to prison. She was pregnant with their son Travis. Terrified at the prospect of becoming a parent, he started using heroin again. "I got myself physically dependent on it because I didn't know how to control the fear and anxiety." Eventually he got a job as a substance abuse counselor. "Everybody was just, like, 'You've been a drug addict; you would probably be a good counselor.'" Eventually he started "selling drugs to pay for drugs." As he explained, "I've also sort of got that criminal mentality. It's sort of hard to get rid of. The people I was messing with were very dangerous … being in prison sort of taught me how to manage that type of relationship." He and his wife fought about his drug use, and finally she cheated on him and he kicked her out.

Then, Tyler said, "I had to throw away every single thing I had been taught in my life about what happiness actually meant. Everything based off crazy religion and all these different things they had been pushing down my throat. Every therapist and every single person I ever talked to would try to sell me something. I finally threw everything out and was, like, 'What the hell is going to make me happy?'" It turned out that he had always wanted to blow glass. So he learned how, and he joined his town's art community.

Divorced now, with joint custody, Tyler is deeply committed to his son. "He's a good boy. He changed my life for sure … [I have] always been involved in my son's life. Never been a bad parent." Travis is 5 years old. The day before our interview, Tyler spent all day at birthday parties for Travis's two best friends. "The second party had a huge bounce house. I just got in and bounced. Good times! But those things are dangerous. They give you gnarly rug burns. I'm all torn up! Good times!" Tyler has Skype video chats with his son every night when they aren't together, "So I, like, get to see him and tell him goodnight, tell him I love him and talk about his day a little bit."

Between his son and his art, Tyler is in a good space. The future looks bright. He says, "I want to write some books … and then keep being a master glass blower, for sure, being involved in activism, trying to change the criminal justice system. We'll see. Like I said, we'll see how it plays out."

A SOCIAL WORK PERSPECTIVE

Tyler described himself as an "antisocial." His comments reflected a clear understanding of the way communities and families shape our behavior. He sees addiction as a way of coping with unmanageable emotions like anxiety, fear, or misery, and he advocates recovery rather than abstinence. At the same time, unlike most of the inmates in America, he grew up in a middle-class home. Even though his family sometimes gave up on him, they had the means to buffer his collision with the criminal justice system by vouching for him with police officials, assisting with his legal defense, providing funds to pay for his record to be expunged, and providing housing when he was released.

LO 9-1   Understand the History of the U.S. Criminal Justice System

America's criminal justice system (like its welfare system) initially mirrored that of England. In both cases, we see three key concepts intertwined: revenge, rehabilitation, and deterrence. Historian David Rothman traces the notion of revenge or punishment to the Calvinist doctrine of **original sin** (Rothman, 2002). By contrast, the intellectual origins of rehabilitation can be traced to the **enlightenment** notion of human perfectibility (Hirsch, 1992). Finally, the concept of **deterrence** goes back to an important Italian theorist named Cesare Beccaria, who offered the simple suggestion that if laws could be changed to deter crime, there would be no need for a punishment apparatus since they would inoculate the population from the desire to commit offenses. As we saw in Chapter 5, the welfare system exacts revenge through punitive treatment of its clients; it attempts rehabilitation through programs to improve their moral character or build up their **human capital**; and it enacts deterrence by pursuing the principle of "**less eligibility**." By contrast, the contemporary criminal justice system treats sentences, primarily as measures for exacting revenge, with a modest nod to rehabilitation in the form of drug treatment or prison education programs. Finally, the deterrence effect of punishments such as incarceration and the death penalty has received more lip service than empirical support. In the following sections we will observe the interplay of these three key concepts and the actions of several key individuals in the evolution of the U.S. criminal and juvenile justice systems.

COLONIAL JUSTICE

The first American settlers were not convicts, but Britain did transport thousands of convicts to the colonies between 1680 and the American Revolution. Many of these people were prisoners of war captured during the Scottish and Irish rebellions. Others had been charged with a variety of offenses, ranging from political crimes to vagrancy. These inmates arrived in prison ships, to the dismay of local citizens. Benjamin Franklin described convict transportation as "an insult and contempt, the cruelest, that ever one people offered to another," and suggested that Americans ship some of their rattlesnakes to England in exchange (Butler, 1896; Christianson, 1998, p. 50). Many of the transported convicts were sold as indentured servants, though history is rife with those who escaped to begin new lives in the Colonies.

One of the most intriguing was Miss Sarah Wilson, a maid who was condemned to die for stealing jewels from the royal apartments of the queen. She landed in Maryland in 1771 and was purchased by William Duval as a servant. But Sarah quickly escaped and traveled to South Carolina, where she presented herself as Princess Susanna Carolina Matilda, sister to the queen. In this guise, she "travelled from one gentleman's house to another … affecting the mode of royalty so inimitably that many had the honour to kiss her hand (Butler, 1896, p. 29). For several years she played the royal role, living extravagantly and defrauding the credulous of their funds. Duval captured Sarah once, but she escaped again in 1775 and eventually married a British Army officer. She was never convicted for her crimes and simply disappeared from the annals of history (Rolph, n.d.).

During this pre-revolutionary era, incarceration was not a primary form of punishment. As Adam Hirsch explained, "The wholesale incarceration of criminals is in truth a comparatively recent episode in the history of Anglo-American jurisprudence" (1992, p. xi). Although their charter called on the Massachusetts colonists to establish laws that were compatible with the laws of England, in practice Massachusetts and other colonies tended to develop their own approaches to the punishment of crime. Two such punishments were fines and public chastisement or "*admonition*." The colonies did inherit capital punishment from England's "**bloody code**," but they applied it sparingly and with a focus on moral crimes, as opposed to property offenses.

Fines were levied for a wide range of offenses, from doing needlework on the Sabbath to drunkenness to theft. Sometimes the fines were returned to the offender, subject to good behavior. Instead of a fine, some criminals were required to post a bond to insure good behavior, while others worked off their fines. Those who couldn't pay were required to engage in servitude, often for years, to work off their judgments. Some criminals were subject to lectures from the judge, known as **admonitions**. These might take place in public, and typically included a public confession and promise to reform (Hirsch, 1992). Others were subjected to public whippings, time in the stocks, branding (recall *The Scarlet Letter*), or banishment (also called "warning out").

The colonists did build jails, and by 1776 each of the 12 counties in the Massachusetts colony had its own. But these early jails served a wider range of purposes than they do today. For instance, prisoners of war were incarcerated in them, as well as political prisoners (such as those who remained loyal to the crown during the Revolutionary War). Jails were more likely to be filled with people awaiting trial or sentencing than by those serving time as punishment. The buildings themselves were poorly maintained and prisoners were frequently neglected or exploited, leading William Eden, who wrote *Principles of Penal Law* in 1771, to describe jailers as "a merciless race of men."

One such man, Zechariah Trescott, ran the notorious Suffolk County Jail in Boston until what might have been the nation's first prisoner revolt. Trescott had already been called before the legislature twice to answer complaints that he stole the food that family and friends brought for prisoners and that conditions in the jail were abysmal. Trescott "begged the legislature's forgiveness" and returned to his post, where he served for 10 years (Hirsch, 1992, p. 10). Finally the prisoners rebelled and took over the building. The militia was called upon to subdue the rebellion, and Trescott was at last discharged from his post.

BIRTH OF THE PENITENTIARY

Important demographic changes took place in post-revolutionary America. With reduced mortality and continued immigration, the population grew and became more transient. Slums and taverns on the outskirts of cities came to be seen as "sites of an alternative, interracial, lower-class culture … the very root of vice" (Meranze, 1996, p. 100). As populations moved from town to town and into the cities, community-based punishments such as admonishment or banishment became ineffective. Incarceration was introduced into state penal codes, initially as one of the several alternatives and later—along with fines and the death penalty—as the only sanctions available to judges. And so began the construction of state prisons and eventually penitentiaries.

By the 19th century, poorhouses and asylums for the insane were expanding, and two models of penitentiaries were in competition. The "Pennsylvania" model advocated solitary confinement to separate the inmates from their dysfunctional culture and help them to develop self-discipline. The "Auburn" model allowed inmates to work in congregate workshops during the day. Guards circled the workshops in hidden hallways wearing moccasins so the inmates would not know whether they were being watched (an idea that might have been borrowed from Jeremy Bentham's panopticon, described in Box 9.1). Dorothea Dix, whom we met in Chapter 7, favored the Pennsylvania system, but eventually the congregate Auburn model (named for a New York prison) prevailed.

Under the guise of moral reform, prisoners were subjected to tight discipline. They were not allowed to speak or interact in any way during the day, and violations brought on beatings. Prisoners were sorted by the severity of their crimes, and the most "hardened" were placed in solitary confinement. Riots were not uncommon in 19th century penitentiaries, and conditions were often criticized. From time to time the public was scandalized to learn about conditions in penitentiaries, but penal institutions continued to expand throughout the country.

Needless to say, conditions in 19th century penitentiaries were brutal by today's standards. Inmates were at risk of insanity, disabling injuries, or death. The punishments used to maintain order included bizarre practices such as "tying up," in which inmates were suspended by their wrists until they bled from the mouth, and the "water crib," in which inmates were placed face down in a coffin with their hands cuffed behind their backs while the coffin was slowly filled with water. The few female prisoners were not held in

BOX 9.1   Jeremy Bentham's Panopticon

As if anticipating the soon-to-come popularity of penitentiaries, English philosopher Jeremy Bentham conceived of an architectural design known as the "panopticon." Theoretically the design could apply to any type of institution where a few are responsible for minding many. Bentham described it as "a mill for grinding rogues honest and idle men industrious" (Bentham, 1843). The design did resemble a mill-wheel. It consisted of a circular building with a station in the middle from which prison guards could oversee the inmates arrayed in cells around the circumference. Central to the concept was the idea that the inmates could not see the guards, so they were never sure whether they were being observed. This architectural design was expected to be cheaper to operate than other prison structures since it required fewer staff and could generate income by requiring the inmates to perform menial labor. Despite Bentham's best efforts, however, the panopticon was never built in England. Actually, no true panopticon was ever constructed, although the *Presidio Modelo* in Cuba (build in the 1920s and now abandoned) bore a strong resemblance to Bentham's model, as did penitentiaries in France, the Netherlands, and Illinois. Some claim the panopticon influenced prison construction in other parts of the world as well.

separate facilities, so sexual abuse was common. Prisoners were often forced to work, a practice explicitly permitted by the Thirteenth Amendment (which abolished slavery in 1865, except as punishment for crime) (*Rothman, 2002*).

SOUTHERN JUSTICE

During the **antebellum era**, Southern states were slow to invest in penitentiaries and those that were constructed housed a disproportionate share of foreigners and slaves whose masters had sent them for correction. As Edward Ayers (1984) explained, after the Civil War the criminal justice system served as a vehicle by which states assumed control of newly freed African Americans. Towns that had not previously employed police forces hired returning Confederate veterans to take on the task of subduing this population. The broad mantle of "vagrancy" sufficed for many arrests, but new crimes were added, such as selling farm produce within the town limits or "using abusive language towards a white man" (Christianson, 1998, p. 171). After being thus swept off the streets, an African American man would soon find himself leased out as a laborer. Convict leasing was profitable for both the government and the employer, but the labor conditions were appalling and death rates, high.

Eventually most states eliminated convict leasing, often in response to public outcry. Such was the case in Florida. A young man named Martin Tabert had traveled from North

► The death of Martin Talbert brought an end to convict leasing in Florida.

Universal Images Group/Getty Images

Dakota to Tallahassee, where he was convicted for riding a train without a ticket. Tabert's family wired funds to cover his $25 fine ($338 in 2016 dollars). But the money was lost somehow, so he was sentenced to three months at hard labor at the Putnam Lumber Company. Cutting timber in the Florida swamps, he soon developed fevers, headaches, and oozing sores. One day he was so sick that he couldn't complete his assigned work, so the boss of the team, Walter Higginbotham, propped him up and whipped him with a leather strap. Tabert died the next day, and his parents raised an outcry. Higginbotham was tried for first-degree murder and then acquitted. The governor of Florida signed legislation to outlaw convict leasing in his state (Jones, n.d.).

Other Southern states moved from convict leasing to systems of chain gangs and state penal farms. In 1941, U.S. Attorney General Francis Biddle addressed convict leasing and similar practices when he issued the now-famous Circular No. 3591 directing U.S. attorneys in all jurisdictions to aggressively prosecute complaints of involuntary servitude (Price, n.d.).

FEDERAL JUSTICE

The Federal Bureau of Prisons was established in 1930, roughly 40 years after passage of the "Three Prisons Act" in 1891 had authorized the first federal prisons: Leavenworth (Kansas), Atlanta (Georgia), and McNeal Island (Washington). Today, federal prisons play a relatively minor role in the nation's incarceration boom. As we saw in Chapter 2, by 2016 they housed only 193,000 of the 2.3 million people incarcerated in the United States (Prison Policy Initiative, 2016). Federal policies, by contrast, have played an important role in promoting high rates of incarceration.

Following World War II the United States enjoyed an extended period of unprecedented economic growth. As we will see in Chapter 15, factory jobs expanded and Americans with only high school educations enjoyed a level of prosperity and security that has not been seen since. Some argue that this postwar affluence set the stage for the turbulence of the 1960s. Of course, this era also brought forth some of the nation's most progressive legislation: the Voting Rights Act of 1965, the Civil Rights Act of 1968, and the Great Society's War on Poverty.

The 1960s were also marked by civil unrest. In July 1964, a 15-year-old African American named James Powell was killed by a policeman in front of dozens of people. Two days later, an angry crowd marched on the Harlem police precinct, and six days of mayhem ensued (Flamm, 2016). A series riots ensued that summer in major cities throughout the East, and in 1965, the Watts neighborhood of Los Angeles was struck by five days of riots over an incident of police brutality (Horne, 1997). When Martin Luther King Jr. was murdered in 1968, the wave of riots that followed was given a name: the "Holy

---

BOX 9.2   Michel Foucault's *Discipline and Punish*

French philosopher Michel Foucault published *Discipline and Punish: The Birth of the Prison*, in 1975. In it, he traces the roots of prison systems to changes in technology and power that shaped Western cultures. He sees the prison system as part of a "continuing trajectory of subjection." He begins his argument by characterizing torture as theater or ceremony and crime as an attack on the sovereign state. Punishment, in this view, is an expression of the omnipotence of the sovereign. Chain gangs, while gentler than public torture, still provided a physical display of the state's control over the convict's body. Foucault examines the prison environment, which is characterized by constant observation and measures designed to tame the individual and create "docile bodies." Finally, Foucault argues that the carceral system (with its prison technology) is part of a surveillance network that includes schools, hospitals, factories, churches, and military institutions; all designed to shape individuals to meet the needs of the social machine.

BOX 9.3   The Harlem Renaissance

As African Americans moved north to fill positions in the factories gearing up for World War II, the 1920s and '30s brought an explosion of creativity known as the Harlem Renaissance. Writers like Langston Hughes, Rudolf Fisher, Nella Larsen, and Arna Bontemps wrote about the lives of African Americans in a manner that Hughes described as the "expression of our individual dark-skinned selves." Painters like Aaron Douglas, Lois Mailou Jones, and Jacob Lawrence sought new forms to represent, as Aaron Douglas said, "the very depths of the souls of our people." Musicians like Duke Ellington, Bessie Smith, and Cab Calloway promoted new forms of jazz that appealed to African Americans and white Americans alike. Together, this artistic burst led Alain Lock to declare in 1926 that "Negro life is seizing its first chances for group expression and self-determination." The Harlem Renaissance faded with the Great Depression but left a lasting mark on American culture.

Week Uprising." It was also described as the "greatest wave of social unrest since the Civil War" (Levy, 2011, p. 6). These race-related protests were accompanied by college students demonstrating over the escalation of the Vietnam war.

These events were nationally televised, and middle-class Americans in "the heartland" were subjected to nightly broadcasts with images of looting, shooting, and fires in cities far away. A Harris poll conducted in 1968 reported that 81 percent of voters felt that "law and order have broken down." Interestingly, respondents attributed the breakdown to "organized crime" (61 percent); "negroes who start riots" (59 percent); "communists" (51 percent), "anti-Vietnam demonstrators" (38 percent); "national leadership" (37 percent); "hippies and student protestors" (29 percent), "right-wing demagogues" (20 percent), and "police brutality" (13 percent). Sociologists Dennis Loo and Ruth-Ellen Grimes (2004) argue that public opinion was manipulated by the media and other elites and that Goldwater and other politicians of the era cloaked their race-based agenda beneath an anti-crime platform that was seen as more palatable than one based on opposition to civil rights.

Scholars differ on the underlying rationale for the rising focus on law and order. Some trace it to the demographic and social shifts associated with the Great Migration. Between 1910 and 1970, six million African Americans moved from Southern states to urban centers in the Northeast, Midwest, and later in the West. This historic population shift responded to "push" factors (economic downturns, Black Codes, and Jim Crow laws in the South) as well as "pull" factors (employment opportunities associated with WWI and WWII). It transformed the racial mix of Northern urban centers. African American enclaves developed and became centers of black culture and black resistance (Alexander, 2012; Hinton, 2016; Muller, 2012). Some, like Loo and Grimes (2004) point to a moral panic engineered by the press and politicians. Hinton argues that Republicans turned to "the racially coded politics of crime control to appeal to disenchanted white voters" (Hinton, p. 7). Perhaps the civil rights movement and its progressive legislation triggered a backlash similar to that observed in the 2016 presidential election.

EP 4b

There is also reason to believe crime rates were rising in the United States. As Figure 9.1 illustrates, the FBI **Uniform Crime Reports** for the 1960s do indicate higher rates of violent crime. But, as Elizabeth Hinton (2016) points out, these are based on *arrests* and could be attributed to increased surveillance, police presence, and reporting. Perhaps this is what led Egil Krogh (Nixon's crime guy) to comment that "the crime problem is more apparent than real" (Hinton, 2016, p. 25).

FIGURE 9.1 Violent Crime* in the United States, 1960–2015

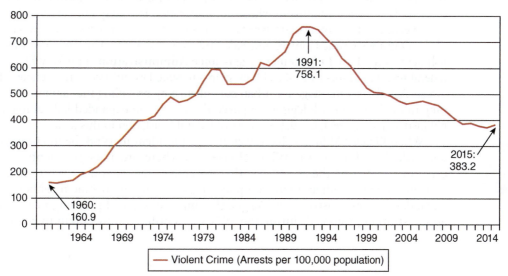

*Includes Murder, Rape, Robbery, and Aggravated Assault.
SOURCE: *United States Crime Rates 1960–2015*. Data compiled by DisasterCenter.com. From FBI UCS Annual Crime Reports
(http://www.disastercenter.com/crime/uscrime.htm).

In 1973, the Bureau of Justice Statistics initiated the **National Crime Survey** (NCS), which has been conducted annually ever since. The survey is based on a nationally representative sample of 90,000 households (about 160,000 people). Staff interview people about the number and nature of "victimizations" they have experienced during the prior six months. Although the survey is not a perfect measure (since people may choose not to report victimization to the interviewer), it provides a more nuanced view of violent crime than the Uniform Crime Reports. According to the NCS, the rate of violent crime gradually increased by 8 percent from 1973 to 1981 (from 36 to 39 victimizations per 1,000 people aged 12 to 39). During the same period, the UCR reports depicted an increase of 42 percent (from 417.4 per 100,000 to 594.3). Most of this increase was reported by African American victims and leaders in the African American community who typically supported the law and order initiatives (Bureau of Justice Statistics, 1987; Hinton, Kohler-Hausmann, & Weaver, 2016).

BOX 9.4   Edgar Hoover's COINTELPRO

As McCarthy's anti-communist campaign was winding down, the Federal Bureau of Investigation launched its COunter INTELligence PROgram, a well-known instance of government surveillance. Under Director J. Edgar Hoover, agents set out to interfere with individuals and organizations that were considered "subversive," using covert and, at times, illegal tactics. Targets included Rev. Martin Luther King, Jr., as well as anti-Vietnam War organizations, feminist groups, those involved in the civil rights movement, and others. Wiretaps were used, as well as bugs to collect "information" that the FBI could then use in a campaign of rumor, innuendo, and sabotage. In one infamous example documented by King biographer Taylor Branch, the FBI reportedly sent a package of audio recordings and a letter encouraging Dr. King to commit suicide.

During the 1964 presidential campaign Goldwater introduced a "law and order" rhetoric that would influence presidential politics for decades (Hinton, 2016). He lost to incumbent Lyndon Johnson, whose administration is widely remembered for the War on Poverty. But Johnson also declared a "war on crime" in 1965 and oversaw saw passage of the Omnibus Crime Control and Safe Streets Act of 1968. This law authorized establishment of the **Law Enforcement Assistance Administration** (LEAA), which managed federal research grants as well as block grants to state law enforcement agencies. The Safe Streets Act also set the stage for urban surveillance by providing the nation's first wiretapping rules. This hallmark legislation paved the way for an expanded federal role in criminal justice. Please see Table 9.1 for a list of federal legislation in this area.

EP 5a

When Richard Milhous Nixon was elected president in 1968, he too brought a "law and order" platform to the White House. But where previous presidents were interested in eliminating the conditions that fostered crime, Nixon set out to manage and contain crime through an increased police presence in low-income neighborhoods and expanded prison construction. We see the impulse of racial profiling in a strategy his administration promoted during the 1970s. Scientific findings (akin to contemporary

TABLE 9.1 Federal Crime Legislation

Year of Passage	Title
2006	Adam Walsh Child Protection and Safety Act
1970	Comprehensive Drug Abuse Prevention and Control Act
1970	Controlled Substances Act
2004	Crime Victims' Rights Act
2010	Elder Justice Act
1994	Jacob Wetterling Crimes Against Children and Sexually Violent Offender Registration Act
1974	Juvenile Justice and Delinquency Prevention Act
2004	Law Enforcement Officers Safety Act
2004	Mentally Ill Offender Treatment and Crime Reduction Act
1968	Omnibus Crime Control and Safe Streets Act
1996	Prison Litigation Reform Act
2003	Prison Rape Reduction Act
2003	Prosecutorial Remedies and Other Tools to End the Exploitation of Children Today Act (PROTECT)
1984	Sentencing Reform Act
2006	Sex Offender Registration and Notification Act (SORNA)
2006	Sober Truth on Preventing (STOP) Underage Drinking Act
2000	The Victims of Trafficking and Violence Prevention Act
1891	Three Prisons Act
2010	Tribal Law and Order Act
1984	Victims of Crime Act (VOCA)
1994	Violence Against Women Act
1994	Violent Crime Control and Law Enforcement Act

"risk factors") were used by law enforcement to profile youth who were likely to commit crimes. Elizabeth Hinton (2016) quotes one LEAA administrator of the era: "It is expected that the predictive techniques will enable the police to better anticipate criminal activity and act to prevent it" (p. 23). The St. Louis Program was one of several initiatives that targeted youth on the basis of their race, class, and age. Those who insisted on spending time with "groups of questionable purpose" were arrested for loitering and detained (Hinton, 2016, p. 23).

Hinton (2016) argues that riots and direct action by organizations like the Black Panthers, the Revolutionary Action Movement, and the Young Lords alienated white liberals and shifted their focus from poverty to crime. Indeed, some have argued that antipoverty measures were simply a means of suppressing urban unrest (Piven & Cloward, 1971). Meanwhile, block grants funded through the Safe Streets Act provided the resources for greater surveillance (both electronic and undercover), an increased police presence, expanded sting operations, and a militarized response to riots.

A NEW WAR

Faced with reports of growing heroin addiction among U.S. servicemen in Vietnam, and a mandate to "get tough" on crime, Nixon declared "war on drugs" in 1971.[1] He promised to dramatically escalate intervention in illegal trafficking of marijuana and narcotics.

The use and distribution of marijuana and certain narcotics was initially subject to tax: narcotics via the 1914 **Harrison Narcotics Tax Act** and marijuana via the **Marihuana**

BOX 9.5 Registering Sex Offenders: Public Safety or Public Shaming?

Horrendous crimes often trigger moral panic that leads policy-makers to conclude that something (anything?) must be done. In 1994, the abduction of 11-year-old Jacob Wetterling led to passage of an act named after him that requires states to maintain registries of sex offenders for a minimum of 10 years following conviction and for life in "particularly serious offenses. Two years later, another abduction, this time of a 22-year-old, resulted in **Megan's Law,** which requires that those registries be available to the public. Supporters argue that these laws keep the public safe. In some states, they are not allowed to be within close vicinity of schools, day care centers, libraries, places of worship, or other public facilities.

So men, like my neighbor, who was convicted of fondling his step-daughter, are required to register their addresses, often with photos and general descriptions of their offenses on a public data base. They are labeled risks to public safety, often for the rest of their lives.

The consequences can range from unpleasant to dire. In a 2005 survey of registered offenders, significant percentages reported they had lost a job (42 percent), lost or been denied a place to live (38 percent), been treated rudely in a public place (32 percent), lost a friend (56 percent), or receive harassing or threatening mail (22 percent) or phone calls (17 percent) (Tewksbury, 2005).

As criminologists are well aware, the vast majority of sex offenses are committed by perpetrators who are known and often related to their victims. The crimes that grab the headlines and the victims for whom legislation of this kind is named are rare exceptions. Indeed, most studies have concluded that these laws have no significant effect on public safety (Harris, Lobanov-Rostovsky, & Levenson, 2016). Organizations seeking to eliminate registration include Women Against Registry, Human Rights Watch, Reform Sex Offender Laws, and the ACLU.

---

[1]Given the partisan divides of recent years, it is worth noting that Nixon worked with a Democratic Congress through both of his terms in office. So both wars (on crime and drugs) had bipartisan support.

Tax Act of 1937. Over the years a total of 200 laws were passed to regulate the use of illegal drugs. Nixon consolidated these, promoting passage of the **Comprehensive Drug Abuse Prevention and Control Act of 1970**. Title II of this law (also known as the Controlled Substances Act) has been the keystone of the war on drugs. It categorized controlled substances into five "schedules" based on their risk of abuse, their medical use, and their safety. Schedule I drugs—those assumed to have the highest risk of addiction and no accepted medical use—currently include heroin, LSD, marijuana, mescaline, ecstasy, psilocybin, and GHB. States were required to pass laws that were compatible with the CSA, and possession and distribution of Schedule I drugs became subject to both state and federal prosecution. Nixon also appointed the nation's first "Drug Czar" and established the **Drug Enforcement Agency (DEA)** under the Department of Justice in 1973 to enforce the CSA.

The war on drugs escalated during the 1980s. Ronald Reagan took office in 1981 and America's "number one problem" (drug abuse) was tackled through a zero tolerance policy, mandatory sentencing for drug offenses, and rising enforcement efforts (Congressional Research Service, 2014). Meanwhile, Nancy Reagan promoted an antidrug campaign best remembered for its slogan, "Just Say No." The DARE (Drug Abuse Resistance Education) Program was adopted in schools throughout the country despite a lack of evidence in support of its efficacy.

Later in this chapter we will return to the history of the war on drugs and consider its impact on incarceration trends. To complete our history of the criminal justice system, we will now turn to the development of the juvenile justice system in the United States.

LO 9-2   Be Familiar with the Development of the U.S. Juvenile Justice System

JUSTICE FOR THE DANGEROUS CLASSES

Early American courts did not differentiate between juvenile and adult offenders. The juvenile court movement of the 19th century (which coincided with emerging awareness of children as victims of abuse) led to the creation of separate courts and institutions for children that emphasized education and rehabilitation. Of course, given the widespread belief that the blame for delinquency lay with the individual child, these institutions often meted out severe punishment and extremely difficult living conditions.

Eventually the limitations of punishment as a deterrent became clear, and these institutions began to emphasize rehabilitation through the use of indeterminate sentences, probation and parole, and training and counseling. When offenders were released, they usually went straight into employment that had been arranged for them and remained on parole so that their reentrance into the community would be carefully controlled. This system was applied in the New York State Reformatory at Elmira in the 1870s. Studies found that four out of five of the reformatory's "graduates" did not return to a penal institution. Soon other states established similar juvenile facilities.

The world's first full-fledged juvenile court was created in Cook County (Chicago) in 1899. (Denver, Colorado, established its juvenile court a year later.) The aim was to reduce the stigma of juvenile crime and create new mechanisms for dealing with offenders. Hearings were informal, with no lawyers, oaths, or robes. The judge was placed in the role of a "parental guide," as defined by statute: "The care, custody, and discipline of the children brought before the court shall approximate as nearly as possible that which they should receive from their parents, and ... as far as practicable they shall be treated not as criminals but as children in need of aid, encouragement and guidance" (Trattner, 1989, p. 118). Clearly, this system depended heavily on the benevolence of juvenile court judges. Their authority greatly exceeded that of judges in adult court. Later this approach was criticized as stripping children of their constitutional rights and placing them at the mercy of not-so-benevolent judges.

The *Gault* case, decided by the U.S. Supreme Court in May 1967, dramatically changed the operation of juvenile courts. On January 8 at about 10 a.m., 15-year-old Gerald Gault and a friend were taken into custody by the sheriff of Gila County, Arizona. They were accused by a neighbor of making phone calls "of the irritatingly, offensive, adolescent, sex variety" [*In re Gault,* 387 U.S. 1; 18 L. Ed. 2d 527; 87 S. Ct. 1428 (1967)]. At the time, Gerald was on probation as a result of having been with another boy who had stolen a wallet. Gerald's parents, who were both at work at the time of the incident, were not notified that their son had been arrested. Gerald was taken to a detention facility. When the parents came home, they sent his older brother to look for Gerald and learned that he was in custody. The parents went to the detention facility and were told that a hearing would be held the following day. There was no record of the hearing, and three to four days later Gerald was released, with no explanation. A note from the arresting officer indicated that the judge had set a date a week later for "further hearings on Gerald's delinquency." Gerald's mother requested that the woman who complained about her son be present at the hearing, but she was told that the complainant's presence was not necessary. At the end of the hearing, the judge committed Gerald as a delinquent to the State Industrial School "for the period of his minority [that is, until age 21]." The child was to be confined for years for making lewd phone calls, an offense that for an adult would result in a fine of $5 to $50 or not more than two months' imprisonment.

Concluding that "unbridled discretion, however benevolently motivated, is frequently a poor substitute for principle and procedure," the Supreme Court held that "neither the Fourteenth Amendment nor the Bill of Rights is for adults alone" and set forth procedural requirements for juvenile cases. These included timely notice of charges, the right of the child to legal counsel, the right to confront and cross-examine complainants, and protection against self-incrimination. At the same time that it imposed these due process requirements on juvenile courts, the Supreme Court upheld the constitutionality and desirability of other measures: the separation of juveniles from adult offenders, the practice of "sealing" juvenile records so they will not affect adult eligibility for civil service and other privileges, and the informality of juvenile court proceedings. These procedures remain in place today.

THE JUVENILE JUSTICE AND DELINQUENCY PREVENTION ACT OF 1974

The **Juvenile Justice and Delinquency Prevention Act** of 1974 (JJDP) (PL 93-415) has become the vehicle for reforming the juvenile courts. First, the act changed the courts' treatment of youth convicted of less serious offenses called "**status offenses.**" Status offenses are behaviors that can be regulated because of a youth's "status" as a minor. They vary from state to state but typically include curfew violations, truancy, and failure to respond to parental authority. Until 1974, children who committed status offenses were incarcerated in detention facilities with those guilty of more serious crimes. The JJDP Act required states to separate status offenders from those guilty of criminal acts. As a result, as many as 40 percent of youths who were status offenders were diverted from detention facilities (Clement, 1997).

In 1988, the JJDP was amended to address the disproportionate representation of minority youth in the juvenile justice system. Unlike the diversion of status offenders, this initiative has been relatively unsuccessful. The Office of Juvenile Justice and Delinquency

Prevention (OJJDP) summarized research on the topic, noting that "[i]n every state studied, minority males had a higher probability rate of incarceration before age 18 than their white peers" (Roscoe & Morton, 1994, p. 1).

Both African American and Hispanic youth are still disproportionately represented in the nation's detention centers. In 2003, African Americans had the highest youth incarceration rate. That year, 754 African American youth out of every 100,000 were detained. This compares to rates of 496 for Native American youth, 348 for Hispanic youth, 190 for Caucasian youth, and 113 for Asian youth (U.S. Department of Justice, 2007c). In 2006, African American youth accounted for 16 percent of youth in the United States, but they were 28 percent of juveniles arrested, 30 percent of those brought to trial, and 37 percent of youth placed in secure detention in the United States (Chapin Hall Center for Children, 2009).

As several studies have demonstrated, the overrepresentation of minority youth reflects the way they are "processed" in the juvenile justice system. Youth of color are more likely to be arrested, more likely to be charged, and more likely to be detained. Jeffrey Butts of the Urban Institute explains, "At each stage of the process, there's a slight empirical bias. And the problem is that the slight empirical bias at every stage of the decision-making accumulates…. [B]y the time you reach the end you have all minorities in the deep end of the system" (Center on Juvenile and Criminal Justice, 2007). These remarks echoed several previous studies of the treatment of minority youth (see, for example, Leonard, Pope, & Feyerherm, 1995).

OTHER FORMS OF CHILD VILLAINY

American children are still the "dangerous classes" when they engage in behavior that is threatening to the broader society, often through membership in youth gangs. When children become extremely threatening, the response of the nation's juvenile justice system is to "certify" them as adults so they can be tried and punished accordingly.

Youth Gangs

Once confined to the urban core of a few major cities, youth gangs have been reported in every state in the nation. The OJJDP has conducted Youth Gang Surveys of police and sheriff's departments across the nation to monitor the prevalence of gangs. The 1990s saw a steady decline in the number of gangs reported that extended to 2002. From 2002 to 2007 the number of gangs increased to the point where it exceeded 27,000. Youth gangs tend to be concentrated in larger cities and surrounding suburbs, although gang problems have been reported in smaller cities and rural counties as well (National Youth Gang Center, 2009).

Experts suggest that youths join gangs for several different reasons. Observing that most of the nation's gangs originated in inner cities, some experts emphasize poverty and hopelessness, suggesting that gang membership offers a chance for economic advancement. The recent expansion of gangs in affluent suburbs has led some observers (for example, Monti, 1994) to emphasize the role of family dysfunction in gang involvement, noting that gang members often come from families affected by divorce, substance abuse, and abuse or neglect of children. The gang, they suggest, becomes a surrogate family—one with clear roles, loyalties, and responsibilities.

Regardless of the reasons for joining, once children are part of a gang, they are widely feared. There is a rational basis for that fear. As the OJJDP reported, "Gang members account for a disproportionate share of delinquent acts, particularly the most serious offenses" (Thornberry & Burch, 1997, p. 1). This observation stems from the Rochester Youth Development Study. Researchers followed a sample of 1,000 seventh- and eighth-grade boys and girls, primarily from high-crime areas. Interviewing children over

EP 4b

a four-year period, they found that about 30 percent reported being a member of a street gang at some point prior to finishing high school. The same 30 percent committed 65 percent of the delinquent acts carried out by the entire group, including 70 percent of drug sales and 69 percent of violent crimes (Thornberry & Burch, 1997).

Often gang members commit delinquent acts while engaging in income-producing activities known as "gang enterprise." A review of gang structure and activities prepared by Urban Dynamics (1999) indicated that the availability of cocaine and the ease with which it can be converted to "crack" created a lucrative business for gang members. Traditional gang enterprises, such as extortion, robbery, and burglary, were then replaced by drug sales. The net effect for a hard-core gang member without a high school diploma can be a high tax-free income that makes the minimum-wage job he or she might be able to perform in the legal economy seem laughable. As Barry Feld (1999) explains, "For many urban black youths, employment in the illegal economy provides an alternative to joblessness and poverty" (p. 197).

The nation's gang prevention efforts, largely orchestrated through law-enforcement authorities, have included the expansion of Community Oriented Policing Services (COPS). Often police focus on "hot spots" such as public housing units, assigning extra patrol officers there. Other programs have mobilized community organizations to strengthen efforts to keep children in school. Still other communities have established physical blockades to prevent traffic from moving through areas with a high incidence of drive-by shootings. At the same time, youth convicted of serious gang-related offenses face punitive treatment in the justice system.

Certification of Serious Youth Offenders as Adults

The violent crimes committed by hard-core gang members have fueled public fear of serious youth offenders and given momentum to a movement to "get tough with these kids." One policy response has been the "waiver of juvenile court jurisdiction," or the "certification" of some youth offenders as adults. These processes remove the offender from the juvenile court system and place the youth under the jurisdiction of adult correctional authorities. Prosecution of youths as adults is based partly on a belief that these youthful offenders are not amenable to rehabilitation through the juvenile justice system and partly (in conjunction with the growing emphasis on "victims' rights") on an emphasis on retribution that has gained popularity. The net result is a series of policy decisions, beginning in the late 1980s, designed to move serious young offenders out of the juvenile justice system and into the criminal courts.

Typically, a prosecutor will ask the juvenile court judge to "waive jurisdiction" in the case of a serious young offender who (1) is not amenable to rehabilitation and (2) represents a threat to public safety. States vary in the amount of discretion granted to the judge. In some cases, the age and seriousness of the offense might require that juvenile court jurisdiction be waived. For example, if a 15- or 16-year-old were to commit a murder, the case would automatically be referred to the criminal (adult) court. Other states provide for "prosecutorial discretion," in which the prosecutor, not the judge, may decide whether to try the case in juvenile or adult court. An emerging focus in these procedures has emphasized not the age of the offender but the nature of the offense. As a result, children charged with heinous crimes have been tried in adult courts and sentenced to adult prison and to death.

International observers were appalled by the willingness of U.S. courts to impose the death penalty on children. The practice went against provisions of the United Nations Convention on the Rights of the Child and several other international treaties. Nonetheless, prior to a 2005 Supreme Court ruling, the laws of 38 states and the federal government authorized the death penalty for murders committed by individuals between the ages of 16 and 18. Between 1973, when a Supreme Court ruling revived the death penalty, and 1999, 180 juvenile death sentences were imposed. Thirteen people were executed

---

BOX 9.6 John Lee Malvo

John Lee Malvo was arrested on October 24, 2002, in connection with a series of sniper attacks on the Washington, DC, beltway that killed 10 people. He was 17 years old at the time. His first trial was held in Virginia, one of the seven states that executed juvenile offenders. Malvo's lawyers used a plea of "not guilty by reason of insanity" to introduce evidence suggesting that Malvo had been brainwashed by John Allen Mohammad, the other perpetrator in the attacks. A jury convicted Malvo of capital murder and recommended life imprisonment without parole.

John Lee Malvo's childhood has been described as "miserable, impoverished, and lonely." His case raises the question of childhood culpability and underscores the dilemma faced when children commit atrocious acts. Does a horrible childhood justify murder? Are children subject to the same moral expectations as adults?

EP 2a

during this period for crimes they committed between the ages of 16 and 18, with the states of Texas and Florida reporting the most executions.

Racial disparities in the criminal justice system were reflected in death sentences given for juvenile crimes. Young people of color were disproportionately represented among those receiving the death sentence. Among 71 people on death row in 2004 for juvenile crimes, nearly two-thirds were people of color. The victims of their crimes were typically white adults (Death Penalty Information Center, 2004).

Citing "evolving standards of decency," the Supreme Court held in the 2005 case of *Roper v. Simmons* that the Constitution bars capital punishment for crimes committed before the age of 18. An opinion drafted by Justice Anthony M. Kennedy described the rationale for the 5-to-4 ruling. The opinion noted that "it is fair to say that the United States now stands alone in a world that has turned its face against the juvenile death penalty." In his scathing dissent, Justice Antonin Scalia wrote, "I do not believe that the meaning of our Eighth Amendment, any more than the meaning of other provisions of our Constitution, should be determined by the subjective views of five members of this court and like-minded foreigners."

From a social justice perspective, abusive parents and youthful criminals can be seen not as victims or villains but as flip sides of the same coin: the inevitable result of systemic failures that can be addressed through social policy.

LO 9-3   Be Aware of Contemporary Trends in Incarceration and Their Implications

Here, we will consider two trends that have and will continue to influence U.S. criminal justice policy. First, the dramatic rise in the U.S. incarceration rate, and second, developments in the waning war on drugs.

INCARCERATION NATION

In 2015, the United States had 5 percent of the world's population and over 20 percent of the world's inmates (ACLU, n.d.). Stated otherwise, the number of Americans who are in jails and prisons at any given time is disproportionately high by global standards. As Table 9.2 illustrates, roughly 716 out of every 100,000 Americans were incarcerated in state and federal prisons and jails in 2016. The United Kingdom is a distant second, incarcerating 147 per 100,000. Among the 2.3 million Americans incarcerated in 2016, most (1.4 million)

TABLE 9.2 Incarceration Rates Among Founding NATO Members

Nation	Incarcerations per 100,000 Population
United States	716
United Kingdom	147
Portugal	136
Luxembourg	122
Canada	118
Belgium	108
Italy	106
France	98
Netherlands	82
Denmark	73
Norway	72

Source: Prison Policy Project, States of Incarceration: The Global Context (http://www.prisonpolicy.org/global/).

were in state prisons. Another 650,000 were in local jails (mostly awaiting trial), and only about 211,000 were in federal prison (Prison Policy Initiative, 2016). Figure 9.2 illustrates the trend toward rising U.S. incarceration that began in the 1980s and extended to the mid-2010s. By comparing this graph to Figure 9.1, you can see that, as Travis, Western, and Redburn (2014) explain, "Incarceration trends do not simply track trends in crime." (p. 44). Instead, rising incarceration is generally attributed to two developments: the war on drugs and changes in criminal justice policy (Travis, Western, & Redburn, 2014).

WAR ON DRUGS REVISITED

The war on drugs certainly contributed to rising incarceration rates during the last two decades of the 20th century. Arrests for drug-related crimes increased dramatically during the 1980s, and by 2009 the UCR reported 1.3 million arrests for use and possession, and another 310,000 for manufacture and sale (Snyder, 2011). As a result, by 2016 nearly half a million people were in prisons and jails for drug offenses. They account for nearly half of the inmates in federal prisons, but a smaller fraction (about 15 percent) of state prisoners have drug offenses as their most serious charges.

As we saw in Chapter 5, drug offenders have been singled out for special punishment. Under the PRWORA, those convicted of felony drug offenses are banned for life from receiving TANF and SNAP benefits or living in public housing. Notably, this lifetime ban was passed by a unanimous voice vote in response to an amendment offered by Senator Phil Gramm (R-TX). States were allowed to opt out of the ban, and eight chose to do so. Others have modified the ban to permit those with felony drug convictions to receive benefits under certain conditions. By 2015 only three states (Arizona, Michigan, and Virginia) still imposed a full ban on drug offenders. Nonetheless, the Sentencing Project (2015) estimated that between its enactment and 2011 the ban affected over 180,000 Americans, with a disproportionate impact on women and people of color.

The destructive impacts of the war on drugs led a group of 22 world leaders and intellectuals to release a detailed report concluding that "The global war on drugs has failed, with devastating consequences for individuals and societies around the world" (Global

FIGURE 9.2 Americans in State and Federal Prisons, 1960–2015

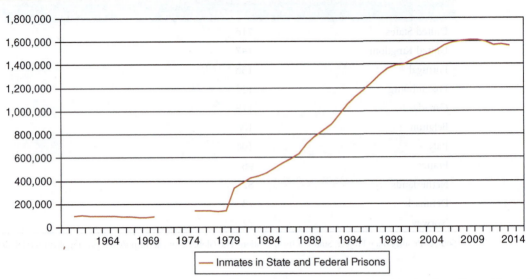

SOURCE: Bureau of Justice Statistics, Key Statistics, Correctional population counts by status 1980–2014 (http://www.bjs.gov/index .cfm?ty=kfdetail&iid=488); Bureau of Justice Statistics, Historical Corrections Statistics in the United States, 1850–1984 (https: //www.bjs.gov/content/pub/pdf/hcsus5084.pdf).

EP 4b

Commission on Drug Policy, 2011). They recommended replacing "the global drug prohibition regime" to policies and strategies that were more fiscally responsible, such as harm reduction, drug abuse prevention, and rehabilitation programs.

In this context, proposals to decriminalize use and distribution of marijuana have been quite successful. In 1996, following passage of Proposition 215, the California legislature passed the Compassionate Use Act, which allowed those with chronic illness to use cannabis if it was prescribed by their physicians. The federal government prevailed in its suit charging an Oakland cannabis cooperative with violations of federal law (*United States v. Oakland Cannabis Buyers' Cooperative*, 2001). The Supreme Court ruled in a second case (*Gonzales v. Raich*, 2005) that cannabis providers were in violation of federal law. And so began another brief skirmish in the war on drugs as DEA agents targeted medical cannabis dispensaries. The Obama administration brought a shift in priorities by declaring, "Put simply, an enforcement-centric 'war on drugs' approach to drug policy is counterproductive, inefficient, and costly." While the administration did not support decriminalization of drugs, it did favor an increased focus on prevention and treatment of addition (White House, n.d.b).

As of this writing, 28 states and the District of Columbia have eliminated penalties for the medical use of marijuana; eight states and the District have legalized recreational use (Wallace, 2016). The impacts of legalization remain unclear. RAND researchers did predict a sharp decline in the cost of marijuana but expressed uncertainty regarding the potential impact on government revenues and the demand for treatment (Kilmer et al., 2010). One uncertainty stems from the conflict between federal and state drug laws. The Trump administration has not yet signaled whether it intends to aggressively enforce the federal laws.

The potential impact of legalization can be gauged by looking at the precedent set by the Dutch. In the Netherlands, marijuana use is not only legal but widely available through "coffee shops." MacCoun and Reuter (2001) concluded that legalization per se did not increase cannabis use. Indeed, it separated sales of legal cannabis from those of illegal "hard" drugs, which curtailed the already weak association between cannabis and other drugs. That is, by making marijuana legal, the Dutch eliminated its already minor role as a "gateway" to more addictive drugs.

A broader precedent has been set by several Latin American countries. Personal use of drugs, or possession of small amounts without an intent to distribute, are decriminalized in Argentina, Mexico, Brazil, and Uruguay. In 2009, Ecuador's new constitution declared drug addiction to be a public health problem and mandated an approach based on prevention and treatment (Youngers & Walsh, 2009). Argentinian leaders, in particular, recognized that those imprisoned in their country for drug offenses tended to be (a) minor players in the drug industry and (b) disproportionately female. So, without abandoning efforts to interfere with drug trafficking, Argentina is taking a public health approach to drug abuse (Transnational Institute, n.d.). This balance between interdiction and public health efforts is also consistent with the April 2016 Resolution of the UN General Assembly titled "Our joint commitment to effectively addressing and countering the world drug problem" (United Nations General Assembly, 2016).

CHANGES IN CRIMINAL JUSTICE POLICY

The crime rate determines who might be at risk of incarceration, but criminal justice policy determines how that risk will play out. Heightened surveillance and police presence in urban neighborhoods may increase the probability of arrest, and sentencing guidelines establish the consequences.

During the period of rising incarceration, arrest rates for all offenses except drug crimes held steady or declined. Burglary was steady at 14 per 100 offenses. Arrests for rape declined from about 44 per 100 offenses in 1984 to 24 per 100 in 2010. Robbery held steady at 26 to 31 arrests per 100 offenses; and aggravated assault at about 52 per 100. Arrest rates for murder declined from 100 to 80 per 100 offenses (Travis, Western, & Redburn, 2014).

Sentencing guidelines have long been identified as an important cause of rising incarceration rates. Generally speaking, the probability of an arrest resulting in a prison sentence rose steadily from 1980 to 2010, particularly for drug and violent crimes. This reflected the expansion of **determinate sentencing** that took place from the mid-1970s to the mid-1980s, and the imposition of harsher sentences for drug and violent crimes that were put in place from the mid-1980s to the mid-1990s (Travis, Western, & Redburn, 2014).

Three-strikes laws, also known as **habitual offender** laws, were popular during the 1990s as they promised to take "bad guys" off the streets. These statutes require that judges take into account prior offenses in sentencing. Typically, these statutes mandate **sentencing enhancements** such as "20 years to life" for a third felony conviction. Washington was the first state to enact a three-strikes law, passing a public initiative (Initiative 593) in 1993. California followed suit the next year[2] with Proposition 184. Another 22 states passed similar statutes by 2004, some of them calling for life sentences without possibility of parole on the third offense. But none was as sweeping as the California law, in which a "strike" did not necessarily have to be a violent felony.

---

[2]The overwhelming support for Proposition 184 has been attributed to a terrible crime committed in California the previous year. A convicted felon named Richard Allen Davis kidnapped and murdered a young girl. This instance supports the argument that tough crime laws are a response to moral panic (Taibbi, 2013).

BOX 9.7   Three Strikes, You're Out!

In 1994, California voters overwhelmingly supported a Three Strikes law that required a life sentence for anyone who was convicted of a third felony. Shane Taylor got his first strike when he was 18. He was arrested twice; first, for attempted burglary of an empty residence, and then for burglary of an empty residence. He said both crimes were related to his drug use. After he was released Shane got married, found a job as a cook, and had a child. But in 1998 he was convicted for possession of $10 worth

of meth. Shane's daughter, Alisha, was 4 years old. Shane served over 15 years of the sentence before California voters approved another proposition designed to allow for release of prisoners like him. In a *New York Times* documentary called "Three Strikes of Injustice," Shane said he was "over the moon" to be able to return to his family. The judge who sentenced him said he was "really sorry." Stanford's Three Strikes Project reports that recidivism among released three-strikers hovers around 2 percent.

The result was a drastic increase in the state's prison population. One study by the Stanford Law School indicated that over 4,000 inmates were serving life sentences for nonviolent offenses. The California statute faced a challenge that it violated the constitutional prohibition on cruel and unusual punishment, but it was upheld by the Supreme Court (*Lockyer v. Andrade, 2003*). In 2012, the state's voters moderated their three-strikes law via Proposition 36, which allowed for the release of over 1,000 nonviolent offenders (Justice Advocacy Project, n.d.).

In 1994 Congress passed and President Clinton signed into law the **Violent Crime Control and Law Enforcement Act**, which calls for mandatory life imprisonment for anyone who is convicted of a "serious violent felony" (murder, manslaughter, sex offense, kidnapping, robbery, or an offense that includes the use or significant risk of force) in federal court and who has two or more convictions in federal or state courts of which at least one is also a "serious violent felony." In 1995, Tommy Lee Farmer became the first person convicted under the law. A convicted murderer released on parole, he was sentenced to life in prison without the possibility of parole for trying to rob a convenience store. President Clinton interrupted his vacation to announce the sentence to the press. Two decades later in July 2015 Clinton said he regretted signing the bill (BBC News, 2015). We will revisit the question of sentencing reform following a brief review of the structure and processes that characterize the criminal justice system in the United States.

LO 9-4   Be Familiar with the Basic Structure and Operation of the U.S. Criminal Justice System

THE CARCERAL STATE

This section examines the current structure and operation of America's "**carceral state**." The term refers to the criminal justice apparatus of the country, which consists of three key components: law enforcement (police); the courts (lawyers and judges); and corrections (jails, prisons, parole, and probation). As with many government functions (see Chapter 2), the carceral state operates at federal, state, and sometimes local levels.

Law Enforcement

Federal police powers are limited by the Constitution to those involving foreign affairs and interstate commerce.[3] The Department of Justice (DOJ) is the umbrella agency charged with federal law enforcement. Most of its policing activities are done through subsidiaries: the Federal Bureau of Investigation (FBI), Drug Enforcement Administration (DEA), Bureau of Alcohol, Tobacco, Firearms and Explosives (ATF), and the United States Marshals Service. At the state level, law enforcement activities are carried out by state police or highway patrols, often within a Department of Public Safety. County or municipal police and sheriffs' offices may also be involved in local enforcement. Two trends have marked 21st-century law enforcement: the militarization of police and the rise of community policing.

As weapons have become more widely available, both criminals and police have resorted to ever-more-sophisticated guns and body armor. The DEA, in particular, is highly militarized, with a history of conducting operations overseas, often in tandem with the Department of Defense (Drug Enforcement Administration, n.d.). The militarization of police was accelerated by the expansion of the "1033 program" under the National Defense Authorization Act of 1997. The act allowed the military to transfer its excess equipment to civilian law enforcement agencies. Over 8,000 agencies participate in the program, which has transferred over $5 billion worth of gear (including assault rifles, grenade launchers, bayonets, night-vision equipment, bomb detonator robots, helicopters, airplanes, camouflage gear, and armored vehicles) to local law enforcement agencies (Defense Logistics Agency, n.d.; Musgrave, Meagher, & Dance, 2014). The use of unmanned aerial vehicles (drones) for domestic police work is not common in the United States, but several police forces have applied to the FAA for permits, raising concerns about invasion of privacy that have led several states to pass laws specifically mandating warrants for drone surveillance (McNeal, 2014).

Community Policing

In the wake of Ferguson and other instances of police brutality, community policing has come to the fore. This decades-old approach seeks to establish a collaborative relationship between community residents and police around a range of issues, including those (like abandoned cars and neglected properties) that relate more to preserving order than to crime. One key goal is to reduce fear of crime through a highly visible police presence that is tailored to the characteristics and needs of the community. Community policing is also designed to reduce hostility toward police in high-crime neighborhoods. Finally, there is an expectation that residents will assist the police in identifying and apprehending crime suspects (Bureau of Justice Assistance, 1994).

While community policing has not had a significant impact on crime itself, it does seem to enhance residents' satisfaction and trust in the police (Gill et al., 2014). This approach has been institutionalized through the establishment of the Office of Community Oriented Policing Services within the Department of Justice. But some argue that community policing is actually order-maintenance policing—that it engages police more intensely in the maintenance of social order, increasing arrest rates for "social control" crimes like graffiti, curfew, and loitering violations in high-crime (aka low-income) neighborhoods (Hinton, 2016; Sharpe, 2013).

---

[3]As soon as a suspect crosses state lines he or she becomes subject to federal jurisdiction and, as we saw in the case of marijuana, interstate commerce can be quite broadly defined to include a range of activities related to illegal drugs.

BOX 9.8   The "Stop Snitching" Movement

Law enforcement officials describe the "stop snitching" movement as an effort by drug dealers to silence informants. Rap star Cameron Giles sees it as a way to promote his music. The slogan has appeared on T-shirts, sometimes worn by defendants in court. But community activists have a different point of view. David M. Kennedy, director of the Center for Crime Prevention and Control argues that the "no snitch" ethic reflects distrust of law enforcement in residents of low-income communities and a desire to take back control of their neighborhoods. As he explained to NPR, "It has become mainstream thought in many minority, especially African-American communities, that law enforcement is the enemy, and good people do not treat with the enemy" (National Public Radio, 2008).

THE COURTS

As with law enforcement, criminal courts in the United States operate at both federal and state levels. Federal courts have jurisdiction over cases in which the United States is a party, those involving violations of the Constitution or federal laws, those between residents of different states in which at least $75,000 is involved, and bankruptcy, copyright, patent, and maritime cases. Most judges in federal courts are appointed for life by the president. The U.S. attorney general's office is responsible for prosecuting federal crimes in cases that are heard by the federal judiciary. The U.S. attorney general is appointed by the president for a four-year term and maintains offices in each of 94 federal districts. The vast majority of federal defendants do not go to trial. Instead, over 90 percent of offenders plead guilty in exchange for a more lenient sentence. Those who do go to trial may appeal to the U.S. Supreme Court, though very few such appeals are actually heard.

Most criminal trials take place in state courts before judges who may be either elected or appointed, depending on the state's procedures. State attorney generals' offices prosecute criminal cases, and public defenders are available to those who cannot afford to pay for representation. State cases may be appealed up to the state supreme court, which is the final authority on state law.

Victims' Rights

Even as he was aggressively pursuing the war on drugs, Ronald Reagan set up the Task Force on Victims of Crime to formalize process that provide support for crime victims. The **Victims of Crime Act** of 1984 (VOCA) established a process for funding victim services through fines paid by federal criminal offenders, and codified victims' rights. In 2004, George W. Bush signed a **Crime Victims' Rights Act** (CVRA), which established victims' rights in relation to court and parole proceedings. Under CVRA, victims are notified and, within reason, allowed to participate in criminal proceedings. The Act also provided for restitution and a range of services, including emergency assistance, counseling and social service referrals. It also secured (Offices of the United States Attorneys, 2016).

While proponents argue in favor of preventing additional harm to victims, critics of this "victim-inclusion" approach express concern that the involvement of victims may introduce excessive emotionality into court proceedings and interfere with the rights of defendants by giving preference to the victims' desires for either vengeance or forgiveness. Legal scholar Vik Kanwar (2001/2002) examined the expressive function of the criminal justice system and concluded that victim-centered approaches shift the debate about capital punishment increasingly toward a focus on the victim's desire for "closure."

CORRECTIONS

America's correctional system is a behemoth with the following components:

- 102 federal prisons
- 2,259 juvenile correctional facilities
- 3,283 local jails
- 1,719 state prisons
- 79 Indian country jails
- Uncounted territorial prisons, military detention facilities, and immigrant detention centers
- 52 parole boards
- 87,950 probation officers
- Thousands of forensic social workers

(Bureau of Labor Statistics, 2015c; National Association of Social Workers, 2010; Prison Policy Initiative, 2016)

The 2.4 million Americans living in jails and prisons are only the tip of the iceberg. At any given time, nearly 7 million people are under the jurisdiction of the correctional system (either incarcerated or on probation or parole). Of course, the number of lives touched by corrections is even greater. For instance, over half of incarcerated men and two-thirds of incarcerated women have left behind minor children (Petersilia, 2000).

In Chapter 2 we examined the privatization of U.S. prisons, noting that it is a multi-billion-dollar industry. Here, we will simply note that the average cost of a year's detention in a federal prison was $30,620 in 2014 (Bureau of Prisons, 2015) and the 2017 budget request for the U.S. Bureau of Prisons was $7.3 billion (Congressional Research Service, 2016).

EP 3a

"Civil Death"

In ancient Greece and Rome, ostracism or "civil death" was the penalty for serious crimes. In addition to **disenfranchisement**, the criminal might also lose all claims to property. In medieval jurisdictions punishment often included banishment, or exclusion from community activities.

In modern America, many people like Tyler experience a kind of civil death. Despite the national commitment to universal suffrage, convicted felons in 12 states permanently lose the right to vote. Indeed, only Maine and Vermont do not restrict the voting rights of people who are convicted of a felony (including those in prison). As a result of this **felony disenfranchisement**, an estimated 5.85 million Americans, including a disproportionate number of African Americans, are prohibited from voting (Sentencing Project, 2016). By international standards, this represents a violation of human rights. In 2005, the European Court of Human Rights decided that a ban on voting in prison violates the right to free and fair elections. Further, courts in Canada, Israel, and South Africa have ruled that restriction (let alone denial) of voting rights is unconstitutional (Sentencing Project, 2016).

Reentry and Recidivism

Apart from losing the right to vote, those with felony convictions often struggle to reenter the community "outside." No doubt this contributes to the risk of reoffending: about two-thirds of all parolees are rearrested within three years, and most rearrests happen within the first six months (Petersilia, 2000; Urban Institute, 2005). As Tyler explained, finding housing after being released from prison can be difficult. Most property management groups will not rent to anyone whose conviction is less than 10 years old, and the same applies to small landlords who run background checks. Offenders who committed drug crimes are barred from public housing. As a result, many parolees (an estimated 10 percent in California) are homeless.

Further, those who have been incarcerated are subject to high rates of unemployment. One five-city survey found 65 percent of employers would not knowingly employ someone with *any* type of prior conviction. In California parolees are barred from law, real estate, medicine, nursing, physical therapy, and education. In Colorado they need not apply for positions as dentists, engineers, nurses, pharmacists, physicians, or real estate agents (Holzer, 1996).

Ripple Effects

EP 2a

The ripple effects of the incarceration behemoth can extend in unexpected directions. Reentry and recidivism contribute to social disorganization in disadvantaged neighborhoods. Gang conflicts in prison are often released with the prisoner and explode in the community (Petrosilia, 2000). Elijah Anderson argued that the large numbers of former prisoners in low-income communities results in moral authority being vested in young men with "street smarts" rather than parents or community leaders. Further, epidemics of drug-resistant tuberculosis, HIV, and even meningitis in disadvantaged neighborhoods have been traced to crowded prisons (Petersilia, 2000). Finally, mass incarceration removes millions of low and unskilled workers from the economy, lowering the U.S. unemployment rate a notch or two. As we will see in the next section, these ripple effects are greatest for individuals, families, and communities of color, particularly African Americans.

LO 9-5   Become Aware of the Disproportionate Representation of People of Color Throughout the U.S. Criminal Justice System

DISPROPORTIONATE REPRESENTATION

African Americans, Hispanics, and Native Americans are overrepresented in the U.S. criminal justice system. This intractable phenomenon, known in forensic circles as **disproportionate minority contact** or DMC, has generated the abiding mistrust Barbara Neely expressed in the epigraph to this chapter.

The juvenile justice figures are stark: in 2010, African Americans made up 17 percent of the U.S. juvenile population but accounted for 31 percent of all arrests. Although youth arrests have dropped since 1996, this disparity has remained steady: African American youth remain twice as likely to be arrested as white youth. Property offenses like burglary, car theft, and arson are the most common charges against youth, and in 2011 African American youth were 2.5 times as likely as white youth to be arrested for a property offense. When it came to status offenses, African American youth were 269 percent more likely than whites to be arrested for curfew violations. Then, in sentencing, they were 4.7 times more likely to be confined in residential facilities. Disparities for Hispanic and Native American youth are comparable. States are required, under the 1988 amendments to the Juvenile Justice and Delinquency Prevention Act, to monitor racial disparities and to address them when they reach a specified level. Yet the disparities persist (Office of Juvenile Justice and Delinquency Prevention, 2014; Sentencing Project, 2014).

Similar conditions prevail in the adult corrections system. In 2009, African Americans were 2.5 times more likely than whites to be arrested. African Americans represented 13 percent of the population yet made up 28 percent of arrests, 40 percent of individuals confined in jails and prisons, and 42 percent of the people on death row. African

Joshua Lott/Getty Images

African Americans like Michael Brown are 13 percent of the population and 24 percent of those fatally shot by police.

Americans are given harsher penalties than whites for a range of crimes, and the race-based disparities accumulate as they move through the criminal justice system to the point that African Americans were six times as likely, Native Americans four times as likely, and Hispanics twice as likely as whites to be confined to prisons (National Council on Crime and Delinquency, 2009).

Two broad theoretical approaches attempt to explain race-based disparities in criminal justice: the **differential offending framework** and the **differential treatment framework**. The differential offending framework focuses on the offenders themselves, suggesting that people of color are (due to individual and contextual risk factors) more likely to commit crimes. Research in this area has identified unstable and disadvantaged communities, poor schools, delinquent peers, single parents, and greater exposure to violence as risk factors that disproportionately affect people of color. The differential treatment framework focuses on decisions made by law enforcement and judges that result in higher arrest rates and harsher sentences for people of color. This approach emphasizes the role of implicit biases and explicit behaviors (such as racial profiling) in determining criminal justice events that can range from labeling African American youth "likely criminals" to targeting African American neighborhoods for surveillance and arresting men on charges of loitering (Office of Juvenile Justice and Delinquency Prevention, 2014).

Racial disparities within the criminal justice system are both pervasive and persistent. This leads some, like Angela Davis and others in the prison abolition movement, to advocate the elimination of what they call the "prison-industrial complex." Organizations like Critical Resistance seek to "challenge the belief that caging and controlling people makes us safe." (See Davis and Rodriguez, 2000.) Meanwhile, others seek to address this and related problems through criminal justice reform.

LO 9-6

EP 3a
EP 5c

Become Aware of Proposals to Reform the U.S. Criminal Justice System

CRIMINAL JUSTICE REFORM

Criminal justice reform is one of few issues that secured bipartisan support during the Obama administration. Widespread concern about the cost of mass incarceration (estimated at $60 billion per year) as well as the injustices associated with mandatory sentencing has generated an unusual consensus in favor of change. In 2015, a coalition of ordinarily competing interests (the ACLU, the Center for American Progress, the Koch family, and the MacArthur Foundation) developed a resolution for criminal justice reform that focused on rehabilitation and employment opportunities for former inmates. In the 2016 presidential campaign, Hillary Clinton declared her support for reform, observing, "Families are being torn apart by excessive incarceration. Young people are being threatened and humiliated by racial profiling. Children are growing up in homes shattered by prison and poverty… We need to listen" (Hillary Clinton Campaign, n.d.). President Trump did not weigh in on the issue.

The high degree of interest in criminal justice reform is evident in the number of related bills that were introduced in the 114th Congress, including the following:

- The Sentencing Reform and Corrections Act (S 2123), which was designed to reduce federal mandatory minimum drug and gun sentences
- The Solitary Confinement Study and Reform Act (HR 2299, 2330), which established a commission to study the impact of solitary confinement and recommend national standards
- The National Criminal Justice Commission Act (HR 2330), which would establish a commission to review "all areas of the criminal justice system" and recommend changes to "prevent, deter, and reduce crime and violence, reduce recidivism, improve cost-effectiveness, and ensure the interests of justice"
- The Safe Justice Reinvestment Act (HR 2944), for which a summary is not provided
- The Justice Is Not for Sale Act (S 2054; HR 3543), which caps prison phone call rates and connection charges and amends the conditions of parole
- The Criminal Consequences of Early Release Act (S2514), which requires the department to report on recidivism among federal prisoners who are released early
- The Youth Justice Act (HR 2728), which calls on the Office of Juvenile Justice and Delinquency Prevention to develop an evidence-based plan to improve the juvenile justice system

This array illustrates an incremental approach to criminal justice reform that is currently in favor. Among the many proposals brought forward, the Sentencing Reform and Corrections Act (S 2123) has gained the most traction, including extensive bipartisan negotiations that may continue during the Trump administration. While the final version remains in doubt, any measure that reduces mandatory minimum sentences and addresses reentry problems is likely to have some impact on incarceration rates in the United States.

BOX 9.9 Operation Peacemaker

In 2007, Richmond, California was a war zone with over 40 homicides a year; eight times the national average. The city considered bringing in the National Guard to help get the violence under control. That was before Operation Peacemaker began offering $1,000 monthly fellowships to young criminals to prevent gun violence. "Neighborhood change agents," all of whom have been incarcerated for drug offenses, are charged with keeping the peace. They mentor the "fellows," teens who are suspected of violent crimes but have not yet been prosecuted. DeVone Boggan, founder of the program, describes the teens as "babies growing up in a war zone." Some call the program "cash for criminals," but Boggan points to his results. By 2014, gun violence in Richmond had fallen and 94 percent of the fellows were still alive. Nearly 80 percent had not even been suspected of a new gun crime.

Restorative Justice: An Alternative Approach

The restorative justice movement seeks to promote rehabilitation through a "reconsideration of the relationships between citizens, the state, and the community" (Karp & Frank, 2016, p. 51). The goal of restorative justice is to repair the harm done by a crime and repair the relationships between offender, victim, and community. Proponents of this approach argue for dialogues that promote the reintegration of criminals into their communities through practices such as victim–offender mediation programs and diversion efforts. Thirty-seven states have passed statutes that establish restorative interventions in various contexts, often in connection with juvenile justice programs. At the federal level the Youth PROMISE Act, with bipartisan support, proposes to fund a series of restorative justice programs designed to break the school-to-prison pipeline. And there is growing evidence that restorative justice techniques can enhance victim satisfaction and reduce recidivism (Pavelka & Leach, 2014).

LO 9-7   Be Familiar with the Role Social Workers Play in the U.S. Criminal Justice System

FORENSIC SOCIAL WORK

Thousands of social workers hold administrative and direct service roles in criminal justice. Social workers advise the courts on disposition of juvenile cases and sentencing of adults, serve as probation and parole officers, operate diversion programs for mentally ill offenders, staff drug courts, provide counseling to crime victims and rehabilitation services to drug offenders, oversee reentry programs, and work with communities to address the root causes of crime. Yet, as a recent report by NASW argues, "The profession has had limited impact on shaping criminal justice policies and assuming leadership roles" (NASW, 2010, p. 2). To some extent, this reflects our aversion to the "get tough" policies of recent decades. In this context, as Roberts and Springer argued, social workers in criminal justice faced a key ethical challenge as they "weigh[ed] the needs of the justice system against those of the offender" (2007, p. 46). But these policies have been widely discredited, and U.S. policy makers are searching for new approaches to achieving criminal justice—approaches that are based on evidence rather than ideology. This poses a unique opportunity for social workers to weigh in on behalf of disadvantaged individuals and communities.

Closing Reflections

The mass incarceration of Americans could be seen as an unintended consequence of the wars on crime and drugs. Certainly, it was not an explicit goal of either of these initiatives. Faced with rising crime rates and a moral panic, U.S. politicians set out to ensure that the "bad guys" were locked up. If they are in prison—the argument went—they are not out committing crimes. Some even suggested that incarceration served a deterrent function, discouraging potential criminals in the community. But the financial and social costs of mass incarceration have proven too high.

Of the three key criminal justice concepts introduced at the opening of this chapter (revenge, rehabilitation, and deterrence), rehabilitation has received the least attention in the U.S. criminal justice system. Our nation tolerates vast expenditures for incarceration while investing only minimally in treatment. As a result, U.S. prisons have become "colleges of crime" rather than venues for reform. Yet, as social workers know very well, investing in rehabilitation generates a surer return than either revenge or deterrence. At this juncture, several promising approaches have been proposed, from a rollback of mandatory minimum sentences to the expansion of restorative justice programs. Social workers are well positioned to contribute to the national debate about what form criminal justice should take in the remaining decades of the 21st century.

Think About It

1. What is your state's policy on the voting rights of people with felony convictions? Has it changed lately? Should it?

2. Has "moral panic" over a horrendous crime struck your state? Was there a policy response? What have been the long-term consequences?

3. Does your state regulate police use of drones? How?

Web-Based Exercises

For direct links to all the sites in these exercises, visit the *Foundations of Social Policy* Companion Site at www.cengagebrain.com and select the resources for Chapter 9.

1. The National Sex Offender Public Website. Named for Dru Sjodin, a college student who was raped and murdered by a registered sex offender, enables the user to search either by name or within a 1 to 3 mile radius of an address. Go to: https://www.nsopw.gov/en/Search and enter your home address and indicate a radius of three miles. Note the number of offenders identified. Now choose one offender (by clicking on a house) and see what you can learn about him. Is it enough to determine whether he is a risk to you? Compare your results with those of your classmates.

Competency Notes

As mentioned in the preface to this text, the Council on Social Work Education has designated nine core competencies and related practice behaviors that must be addressed by accredited social work programs. In these notes, I will specify the way chapter content addresses these competencies and behaviors. (This is designed to assist with the accreditation process.) Please refer to the "helping hands" icons for the locations of specific content in this chapter. Here you will find a brief explanation of how the accompanying content relates to the specified competency or practice behaviors.

The following list indicates where EPAS competencies and practice behaviors are addressed in this chapter.

EP 2a   **Apply and communicate understanding of the importance of diversity and difference in shaping life experiences in practice at the micro, mezzo and macro levels.** This chapter provides extensive treatment of race-based disparities in the criminal justice system, as well as the implications of mass incarceration for disadvantaged communities.

EP 3a   **Apply their understanding of social, economic, and environmental justice to advocate for human rights at the individual and system levels.** The chapter introduces several approaches to criminal justice reform to inform social work advocacy efforts. It also explores specific injustices associated with the current system.

EP 4b   **Apply critical thinking to engage in critical analysis of quantitative and qualitative research methods and research findings.** The chapter introduces two approaches to crime measurement and summarizes several studies related to gang membership and the impacts of legalization of marijuana.

EP 5a   **Identify social policy at the local, state, and federal level that impacts well-being, service delivery, and access to social services.** The chapter discusses the widespread community impacts of federal laws related to the war on crime and the war on drugs.

EP 5c   **Apply critical thinking to analyze, formulate, and advocate for policies that advance human rights and social, economic, and environmental justice.** The discussion of criminal justice reform invites students to engage in consideration of possible improvements to the contemporary system.

Suggested Resources

Bernstein, N. (2013). *Burning Down the House: The End of Juvenile Prison*. New York: The New Press.

Critical Resistance (criticalresistance.org) "seeks to build an international movement to end the prison industrial complex by challenging the belief that caging and controlling people makes us safe."

Gilmore, K. (n.d.). *Slavery and Prison – Understanding the Connections*. History Is a Weapon. http://www.historyisaweapon.com/defcon1/gilmoreprisonslavery.html.

Hinton, E. (2016). *From the War on Poverty to the War on Crime: The Making of Mass Incarceration in America*. Cambridge, MA: Harvard University Press.

Patterson, G. T. (2012). *Social Work Practice in the Criminal Justice System*. Philadelphia: Routledge.

Prison Culture (www.usprisonculture.com/blog/. This blog aims to document "how the current prison industrial complex operates and to underscore the ways that it structures American society."

Stevenson, B. (2014). *Just Mercy: A Story of Justice and Redemption*. New York: Spiegel & Grau.

Wilson, J. Q., & Petersilia, J. (2011). *Crime and Public Policy*. New York: Oxford University Press.

Zeher, H., & Toews, B. (Eds.). (2004). *Critical Issues in Restorative Justice*. Monsey, NY: Criminal Justice Press.

Vulnerable Populations: Discrimination and Oppression

▶ Occupy Wall Street activists mark two-year anniversary of movement.

Spencer Platt/Staff/Getty Images News/ Getty Images

In the mosaic of American life, each one of us is in some sense a minority. But some groups have been singled out for discrimination and oppression that members of more privileged groups have been spared. The words *discrimination* and *oppression* are sometimes used in vague, emotionally charged ways that can obscure their meaning. So let's begin with definitions.

In a broad sense, **discrimination** means "the quality or power of finely distinguishing," but defined more narrowly, it means "making a difference in treatment or favor on a basis other than individual merit." It can reflect our **implicit bias**: an attitude we may be unaware of that nonetheless influences our reactions to people in other groups. During the 2016 presidential campaign, Hillary Clinton argued that "Implicit bias is a problem for everyone. Not just the police." This triggered a firestorm of controversy as Americans struggled (as many social work students do) to grasp the possibility that one could hold prejudicial attitudes without even knowing it. A growing body of evidence suggests that Clinton was right. In 1998, a computerized **Implicit Association Test** was released, and studies using this measure have linked implicit bias to explicit prejudice as well as discriminatory behavior (Egloff & Schmukle, 2002; Green et al., 2007; Greenwald, Poehlman, Uhlmann, & Banaji, 2009).

Discrimination assumes policy relevance when it is based on *categorical* rather than *individual* characteristics and when the difference in treatment occurs within a limited range of activities specified by law. Under U.S. law, several categories of persons are *protected,* and discrimination directed toward individuals *because* of their inclusion in these categories is prohibited. In addition to race and national origin, **protected categories** include gender, religion, age, and disability. At present, sexual orientation and gender identity are not protected categories under federal law.

As the chapters in Part III reveal, U.S. social policy has at times served as a tool *for* discrimination and oppression. Only in recent history have we expected government not only to refrain from discrimination but also to take steps to eliminate it. These changes have at times triggered a backlash marked by claims of **reverse discrimination**.

Oppression constrains a person's opportunities and restricts development and self-determination. As Adams, Bell, and Griffin (1997) pointed out, "Oppression fuses institutional and systemic discrimination, personal bias, bigotry, and social prejudice in a complex web of relationships and structures that saturate most aspects of life in our society" (p. 4). It contributes to a hierarchical society in which the privileged benefit from the subordination of other groups. Oppression robs society of the talent and energies of thousands of people, even as it restricts individual opportunities for sustenance and fulfillment.

Oppression can be subtle, as when a high school counselor discourages an African American student from enrolling in a college preparatory class or when a Latina cannot imagine herself as president of the United States. Oppression can also take more obvious forms, as when the U.S. Congress, through the Defense of Marriage Act, denied gay and lesbian couples the right to marry, or when a corporation routinely promotes white employees over people of color.

In its most insidious form, oppression invades the hearts and minds of vulnerable individuals, causing them to limit their expectations and moderate their demands. When this **internalized oppression** is operating, we see members of oppressed groups perpetuating stereotypes and punishing or ignoring those who question the status quo. We see poor people blaming themselves for their situations, Native Americans dismissing other Native Americans as lazy alcoholics, or gays rejecting other gays for behavior that marks them as "too queer."

Sometimes oppression in the United States has led to traumatizing events, such as the genocide of Native Americans, the internment of the Japanese during World War II, and the enslavement of African Americans. Several authors have suggested that these "cultural" or "collective" traumas leave lasting marks, shaping expectations and worldviews for generations (Alexander et al., 2004; Erikson, 1976; Weaver & Brave Heart, 1999).[1]

Oppression leaves vulnerable people with limited access to the benefits of group membership and greater risk for poverty, disease, disability, and death. This is the case, for example, when people of color are denied employment opportunities, when the basic needs of children are neglected, when women are paid less than men for the same work, when the vulnerabilities of older adults are ignored, when those who identify as GLBTQ are subjected to violence and intimidation, and when working people are deprived of the fruits of their labor.

While it is in some ways easiest to discuss vulnerable populations on the basis of single characteristics such as gender or sexual orientation, it is important to acknowledge that each one of us embodies multiple, intersecting identities. An "intersectional perspective" challenges us to take this complexity into account in our understanding of social justice. As Denis (2008) explained, "Intersectional analysis involves the concurrent analyses

---

[1] I am indebted to Rita Takahashi for background on cultural trauma.

of multiple, intersecting sources of subordination/oppression, and is based on the premise that the impact of a particular form of subordination may vary, depending on its combination with other potential sources of subordination (or privilege)" (p. 677). Sometimes the impact of multiple identities may be additive, as when an African American woman's risk of poverty is compounded by age and gender. And sometimes the available remedies for discrimination are inadequate to deal with oppression based on multiple identities such as gender, race, and sexual orientation. High socioeconomic status may buffer people of color from some effects of pervasive racism, but not all, as we saw in 2009 when Harvard professor Henry Louis Gates was arrested while struggling to release a jammed front door at his own home.

We will touch on issues of intersectionality in Part III as we consider identities associated with vulnerability in the United States. We will consider people of color (Chapter 10), those who identify as LBGTQ (Chapter 11), children (Chapter 12), women (Chapter 13), and elderly people (Chapter 14). Part III will conclude with a focus on working Americans (Chapter 15). Not everyone who works for a living experiences systematic discrimination, but the workplace can be exploitive, and events such as the Great Recession have brought the vulnerabilities of working Americans into sharp relief.

E PLURIBUS UNUM

Learning Objectives

This chapter will help prepare students to:

LO 10-1 Understand the social construction of race and theories of racism

LO 10-2 Become aware of the changing racial profile of the United States and the shifting role of government vis à vis race and ethnicity

LO 10-3 Reflect on the role of history in shaping the current experiences of African Americans

LO 10-4 Reflect on the role of history in shaping the current experiences of Hispanic or Latino Americans

LO 10-5 Reflect on the role of history in shaping the current experiences of Asian Americans

LO 10-6 Reflect on the role of history in shaping the current experiences of Native Americans

LO 10-7 Understand the role immigration plays in shaping and reflecting race relations in the United States

LO 10-8 Analyze and critique hate crime legislation

LO 10-9 Understand the background and impacts of English-only laws

LO 10-10 Describe the differential impact of standardized testing on people of color

LO 10-11 Become aware of factors that can interfere with the voting rights of Americans of color

E pluribus unum—"of many, one"—historically referred to the union of the states. But it applies equally well to the unity within diversity that has come to characterize this country. The United States is the most ethnically diverse country in the world—soon to be a nation with no clear racial majority. This diversity is a source of strength, vitality, and creativity. But intolerance mars the nation's fabric. Racial prejudice and hatred are a national plague, with periodic outbreaks and remissions. Thousands of Americans are victims of hate crime each year. But more insidious and pervasive than hate crimes is institutionalized racism, a subtle form of discrimination that denies people access to basic necessities such as education, housing, and employment. This type of discrimination lies at the root of the higher risk of poverty, illness, and premature death experienced by many people of color.[1]

LO 10-1   Understand the Social Construction of Race and Theories of Racism

EP 2a
EP 5c

Most scientists agree that race is a **social construct** with little basis in human genetics or biology (Cox, 1970; Fields, 1982; Wilson, 1996). The notion that there were "types" of humans, and the use of the word "race" to refer to those types, have been described as European inventions. Wilson (1996) notes that "the word 'race'—meaning different human species—appeared in the English language at precisely the time when Britain began to colonize other lands" (p. 48).[2] Perhaps treating people who looked different as other races made it easier to justify exploiting them.

To say that race is a social construct is not to underestimate its impact. Race has profound meanings in the United States, even if they are primarily economic, historical, and political (see Goldberg, 1993; Gossett, 1965; Omi & Winaut, 1994). During the early part of the 19th century, Alexis de Tocqueville (1835) observed the persistence of racial prejudice and division in the United States and predicted race war in the nation's future. At times we have come close to fulfilling his prediction.

Ethnicity has been used in several contexts to single out groups that may not be racially distinct but are characterized by shared culture, common history, values, attitudes, and behaviors. Thus, for example, ethnicity was used to marginalize certain groups of European immigrants, such as Italians and Irish, who were sometimes referred to as "ethnics." It was used by Nazis in their persecution of Jews. Today the term *ethnicity* has lost much of its pejorative flavor and is simply used to describe groups with distinctive cultural and historical traditions.

Of course, the United States is not the only nation in which the construct of race serves as a tool for social stratification. Throughout the Americas, social and economic opportunities are concentrated among those of European descent, leaving indigenous, immigrant, and mixed-racial groups at a disadvantage. This is the case in Brazil, for example, where people of mixed and African descent have shorter life expectancies, lower educational attainment, and diminished occupational opportunities (Fernandes, 2004; Reichmann, 1999). Similar patterns have been observed in other Latin American nations (Appelbaum, Macpherson, & Rosemblatt, 2003; Wade, 1997). Some view this inequality as the enduring legacy of colonialism (see, for example, Avalos, Affigne, & Travis, 1997; Wilson, 1996).

Changes in the U.S. census illustrate our evolving understanding of racial identity. Responding to the census, Americans select a race category that we feel best describes us. Over the years, the census has offered at least 26 different categories. The first official

---

[1]A note regarding the politics of language: Many labels are offensive because (in my opinion) the very process of labeling is inherently offensive. None of us chooses to be described first on the basis of our racial ancestry. We prefer to be known as individuals, not as categories. Yet categories are relevant to social policy. Resources are allocated using race-based categories. The language used in this book is designed to emphasize the value of diversity and support the goal of a racially just United States.

[2]The beginnings of Britain's colonization of other lands can be traced to the late 1500s.

When I called the Calvary Baptist Church to schedule an appointment with Reverend Davis, his booming voice greeted me from the answering machine: "It's a great day at Calvary Baptist. We have services every Sunday at 11:00, and we would love to see you there." With that welcome, I went on to request an hour of his time for an interview that would go into a book on social policy. I knew he was a busy man and I couldn't expect a leisurely discussion. This would have to be a highly focused interview.

I met Reverend Davis at his church office, which was crowded with memorabilia from the Reverend's career. On the walls were elegant drawings of African Americans, a birthday card made by one of his children, a few inspiring quotes, and a picture of Reverend Davis from 1974 when he became pastor of the church. Piles of books were stacked on the floor. The furniture was worn, but the computer was state-of-the-art. As I arrived, his secretary was leaving, so Reverend Davis warned me he would have to answer the phone himself. During our hour together Reverend Davis received a dozen phone calls, all of them important, all brief and to the point. Sometimes he would answer with "Grand Central Station ...," which aptly described his office—Command Central for his urgent calling.

France Davis was born in 1946 in Georgia, the eighth of nine children. He grew up on a cotton and corn farm and attended African American schools. His parents were adamant that their children receive more education than they had received. Mr. Davis had completed third grade, and Mrs. Davis, eighth grade. Both insisted that their children at least consider going to college.

Of his parents Reverend Davis said, "Other people use celebrities as role models. I use my parents.... They modeled participation and involvement in the community and society in which I grew up." Although they were unable to register to vote during his early years, France's parents were always active in the affairs of their community, and when they were able to register, they participated in the electoral process. They set the stage for their son's success through their teaching and guidance. Reverend Davis recalled, "They taught us early to strive for balanced living; to get oneself academically prepared, but also spiritually prepared and then economically, socially, and politically aware. The goal was always to be best, and as African Americans we were taught that to be the best you had to be twice as good as anybody else."

After finishing high school in 1964, he went to Tuskegee University in Alabama, the school founded in 1881 by Booker T. Washington. He became involved in the civil rights movement, participating in Martin Luther King's Selma to Montgomery March and student activities on campus. He also wrote for the student newspaper, which gave him "a platform from which to talk about some of the issues."

Reverend Davis remembers his involvement in the civil rights movement as a great adventure. He had no support from his family; in fact, Reverend Davis believed that if his mother had known what he was doing, she "would probably have disowned me ... [at least] she would have tried to get me to quit." There was some danger involved. "There was the Klan, and even the Alabama National Guard with their Confederate flag." But, as Reverend Davis put it, "I didn't have anything to lose. I didn't own anything, so no one could take anything away from me. I didn't have a job, so no one could fire me." Besides that, Reverend Davis was accustomed to the threat posed by hate groups, having grown up, as he put it, "in Klan country."

The greatest success Reverend Davis remembers from those days came in the march from Selma to Montgomery. The march "was a major achievement and undertaking in a place where the governor of the state had argued that admission to the white school would come over his dead body. So there was a sense of 'here we are, in his face' ... we were right out in front of the capitol building. He was probably standing at a window looking at us. We were in his face and there was a real sense of accomplishment."

Other efforts were not always successful. One time Reverend Davis and some of his fellow students went into Mississippi to register voters. They were turned back at the airport in Mississippi, as outside agitators. "We were turned away because we were outsiders.... Someone had told them we were coming, so they were there and they just put us on a plane back out.... We were always considered outsiders.... One of the common strategies of the other side was to define certain people as outsiders and then to make them of no effect."

Overall, though, the civil rights movement was a deeply satisfying experience for Reverend Davis. "We had a great time at it, and got a lot done.... There was a sense of being part of that which was causing change of a major structural part of our society. What we were changing was the ways laws were interpreted from 1896 with the *Plessy v. Ferguson* Supreme Court decision. We were pulling down strongholds that were related to that [decision] so it was a sense of accomplishment, but also a sense of adventure."

(continued)

A HUMAN PERSPECTIVE   The Reverend France Davis (*Continued*)

Forced to withdraw from college due to lack of funds, Reverend Davis joined the U.S. Air Force and served for four years during the Vietnam conflict. Of this experience, he said, "Life in the service was exciting, and the travel in particular was educational. I probably learned more in four years of military travel and experience than I did in the previous years of college and high school. I saw the world in many ways and traveled to different countries. I saw the way people lived. So it was an opportunity to see people living all across the country and different places I never thought I'd be … to see how life was different, and as a result of that I concluded that there was no such thing as 'normal'; everything is relative…. What's normal for me is just that—therefore no one is inferior or superior." Reverend Davis learned to speak Thai, and he made friends in every community in which he lived.

After leaving the service, Reverend Davis entered several colleges in California. He says he "took school seriously, and enrolled in four colleges full-time." Somehow, Reverend Davis found time for involvement in the student movements at U.C. Berkeley. He also met his future wife during this period.

Then, in 1972, he was recruited by the University of Utah to serve as a teaching fellow. He describes his entry into the state as "difficult," reporting that he was "turned down for a place to stay … due to my skin color and cultural differences." His response reflected his personal commitment to social action. "As had been my custom before, I just decided to do something about it. I knew it wasn't right, and so I set about to take whatever action was necessary to get the person's attention." With the assistance of a university administrator, Reverend Davis "reminded [the landlords] that they were contractors with the university. Second, we reminded them that it was illegal to discriminate against a person because they were of a particular skin color or culture." Reverend Davis's efforts were successful, and he was offered housing. He took some pleasure in turning down that offer. "The forces of the university were behind what I was talking about, and so with that understanding, they backed off…. They offered me, as a result of our pressure, any place that they had before it was done, but I, of course, refused." Reverend Davis accepted housing in the university's International House and enjoyed a congenial year there before he was married.

In 1974, the Reverend Davis was asked to "fill in" at Calvary Baptist when their pastor resigned and they were looking for his replacement. Reverend Davis said, "Since they haven't found anybody, I'm still filling in…. That's the way it is." His "filling in" has been marked by

accomplishments. The congregation has outgrown its current building, and construction of a new one is set to begin "any day." The church sponsors several important community-service projects, including a 30-unit housing project for the elderly and a preschool reading program. His own volunteer activities have included organizing to establish a Martin Luther King holiday in the state and a Martin Luther King Boulevard in its capital city, as well as serving on numerous boards and commissions.

As a member of the Board of Corrections, Reverend Davis has worked to reduce **racial profiling** by police departments. He is stopped by an officer once a month or more, usually in the daytime and sometimes at night. When the officers find out that the black man they just pulled over is a Baptist minister, they apologize. "They apologize when they find out that I have a name, credentials. But the unfortunate thing about that is that it suggests that people who don't have the credentials get a different kind of treatment. That's why I'm concerned about it." He says, "One of the problems with it [profiling] is getting anybody to admit that they're doing it…. There aren't any hard facts being collected." Reverend Davis hopes for passage of a bill that will require police to collect data on the racial backgrounds of people they pull over and cite for traffic violations.

When I asked Reverend Davis about the role of the church in social change, he offered the following perspective:

I think first and foremost the role of the church is a spiritual role. It's designed to help people be all they can be from the inside out—to help them to come to grips with who they are themselves, to understand their own heritage and their own being. That's first and foremost the role of the church in any community. But in addition to that, whatever it is that causes people to hurt is where the church ought to be. So if people are hurting spiritually, if they hurt physically, or with regard to housing or economically or socially or politically…. Fairness and justice issues are at the top of the table, and it is the role of the church to be the voice for the voiceless—to represent the lost, the least, and the last. Those three groups tend to have not much voice in the community, so it is the role of the church to help them be represented and to give them voice.

Reverend Davis feels that education is the best tool for combating racial prejudice: "I think much of what people do in terms of racial hatred and the problems of discrimination is based in ignorance." In his role as church leader and advocate for the African American community, Reverend Davis has been the target of racial hatred. He has a folder with vile hate mail that has come to the church, and the church building has been defiled with racist graffiti. These actions have led him to conclude that "some folk are just filled with meanness and hatred, and we have to find another way to deal with those. I don't know what that is."

Coping with racial hatred requires learning not to take it in and let it devour you. I asked Reverend Davis whether the hate mail enraged him. He replied, "I'm accustomed to it, so it doesn't enrage me. I expect this horror—it's life as I've learned it…. It's upsetting, though. As long as they leave it here at my office [it's not as threatening], but every now and then somebody finds out where I live and they take it to the house, leave it at the door … but I've lived with this since I was born. I was born in Klan territory."

His experiences with racial hatred do not influence the way Reverend Davis feels about people. "I've learned to just consider the source of events, and I rationalize that the person that does that sort of thing is just probably angry and frightened, so what they direct toward me is what they feel toward themselves. They just hate themselves, so they need the hate of somebody else. I refuse to participate in their games." Indeed, Reverend Davis believes that this is an important skill for African American children to learn. In the church preschool program children are taught "not to take things personally, to rise above them."

Reverend Davis takes a long-term view of race relations in the United States. When I asked what it would take to heal race relations, he replied, "I think it's going to take a few generations passing off the scene, first of all. I think people of my generation and older are not likely to change much. So we're going to have to, as did the children of Israel in the Bible, die before we get to the Promised Land." He does not expect race issues to be resolved during his lifetime but hopes "we can get more young people understanding that difference does not mean 'less than'; it's just difference. 'Variety,' as my Daddy would put it, 'is the spice of life.'"

Reverend Davis sees education as a top issue for the African American community. His advice for advocates interested in race issues is to "help to ensure that everyone learns to read and write—that they have a fair chance to get a good education." He is concerned about discrimination in education and employment, noting that policies must "ensure that people who have been discriminated against, who have been left out, are no longer." He argues that "some creative mind has got to come up with something that does not create as much backlash as affirmative action." Another critical issue for the African American community, in his opinion, is securing adequate, affordable housing.

By the end of our hour together, I knew Reverend Davis needed to move on to his next commitment. It was time for me to get out of the way so he could get back to the important work at hand. It is the work of a lifetime preparing for a time when racial hatred, discrimination, and bigotry are historical anomalies rather than daily experiences.

A SOCIAL WORK PERSPECTIVE

The Reverend France Davis is a role model and community leader. His parents raised him and his siblings in a loving, stable environment with high expectations and clear commitments. Like many parents who come from disadvantaged backgrounds, they told their children, "You have to be much better than the others for your abilities to be recognized." They also taught their son to understand racial hatred in ways that were constructive rather than self-defeating. They prepared him not only to survive in a racist world but also to strive for a better world. The result is a committed activist who has become indispensable to his congregation and his community.

Social policies have had a profound impact on Reverend Davis's life, even as he has influenced them. As he noted, his parents were unable to vote when he was small, and he attended segregated schools. The civil rights movement, of which he was a part, not only established African American electoral rights but tore down the "separate but equal" farce that resulted from the *Plessy v. Ferguson* decision. Housing policies also affected Reverend Davis. In retrospect, he felt that he would have been unable to secure housing as a young African American man in a predominantly white town without the assistance and support of a university vice president.

Racial profiling has touched Reverend Davis's life as it has touched the lives of many people of color. Eliminating racial profiling may not seem as noble a cause as eliminating barriers to voter registration, but we vote only once a year. In some communities, people of color going about their business may be stopped by police several times a day. Each time, they risk being cited or even arrested for something they didn't do.

Reverend Davis devotes his professional career to spiritual leadership and his civic volunteer career to social justice. Equal access to education and employment ranks high on his list of priority issues, as does housing access. But equally important, if less tangible, is his desire to work toward a society in which "difference is just that: difference."

census, conducted in 1790, had three racial categories: "free white," "free other," and "slaves." The 1820 census added the term "colored," as well as questions about nativity, with a new category for "foreigners not naturalized." By 1850, the color question distinguished between slaves who were "black" and those who were "mulatto." Categories for Chinese and American Indians were added in 1879, and by 1890 the race question included a range of options: White, Black, Mulatto, Quadroon, Octoroon, Chinese, Japanese, and Indian. In 1900, a question was added to indicate the "fraction of a person's lineage that is white." Through the 20th century, categories were added and race and ethnicity were split to permit separate identification of race and Hispanic origin. In 1930, for the first and only time, "Mexican" was treated as a separate category. Census designers struggled to enumerate people of mixed racial origins until the 2000 census when, for the first time, Americans were allowed to select more than one racial category (U.S. Census Bureau, n.d.b).

RACISM

Overt racism is based on the belief that some racial groups are inferior to others. As a lens through which some view the world, it is often used to justify racial oppression. Social scientists have long speculated on its origins. Some, like Reverend Davis, attribute racism to lack of familiarity or ignorance. On the other hand, critical theorists focus on economic institutions. As we will see, these perspectives offer divergent views on the origins and future of racism, with some arguing that it will naturally disappear and others emphasizing the need for intervention.

Those who use ignorance to explain racism argue that it is simply an early stage in the historical process of cultural assimilation—the inevitable result of early contact between disparate groups. For example, Park (1974) argues that racial conflict surfaces in the early stages of cultural contact and recedes with the process of assimilation. He identifies four stages in the assimilation process: initial contact between racial and ethnic groups, competition between these groups, accommodation, and assimilation. The first two stages are marked by conflict and racism, which fades away in the later stages. Gordon (1964) elaborates on the later stages, arguing that assimilation proceeds in three stages: cultural assimilation (the minority culture is accepted or tolerated by the majority culture), marital assimilation (interracial marriages occur in large numbers), and prejudice-free assimilation (the final stage, when notions of racial superiority disappear).

Market theorists, who analyze the impact of competitive forces on discriminatory practices, share the view that racism will simply disappear. For example, Sowell (1981) argues that in a free market, firms that discriminate against talented minorities pay a higher price for a less productive labor force. In a competitive market, this inefficiency should ultimately either eliminate these firms or force them to change their discriminatory practices. Of course, Sowell assumes a perfectly competitive market in which those of all races enjoy equal access to training and educational opportunities.

Noting a significant decline in racism during World War II, Willhelm (1970) argued that when the demand for labor increases, racism diminishes, and when jobs are scarce it increases. This argument does not explain the intense racism that marked the antebellum South, when slave labor was in high demand, nor does this labor-based approach explain this nation's efforts to exterminate Native Americans.

In a contrasting view, other critical theorists attribute racism to economic exploitation, arguing, as Wilson (1996) did, that [racism] is a modern historical phenomenon, grounded in alienating, exploitative, and oppressive economic arrangements. It arose in a particular stage in history, after the dissolution of feudalism, after the Protestant Reformation, and with the rise of a new economic order undergirded by the intense drive to accumulate wealth.... It [this drive] fueled the genocide against Native Americans and propelled the Atlantic slave trade. Modern racism emerged out of slavery and colonialism. These economic institutions created clear demarcation lines between the oppressed and the oppressor, which overlapped with color lines. The oppressed were not only separated from the oppressors, the oppressed were primarily people of color. The notion that people of color were of a different species and were inferior to their oppressors served to legitimize the oppressive arrangement and to desensitize the dominant group to the plight of the oppressed (p. 37).

Wilson argued that racism is the result of oppressive economic arrangements. It provides justification for the suppression of one group for the benefit of another. Support for this argument is found in the history of both African slaves and European immigrant groups in the United States. Most of us understand that the notion of Africans as subhuman served to justify the brutal exploitation of slavery. But it is easy to forget that when Irish and European Jews immigrated to the United States they were characterized as inferior.

Class conflict theorists also attribute racism to economic conditions, but instead of focusing on oppressive economic relationships they focus on competition between classes. This might take place between company owners and working classes or between managers and laborers, with the privileged classes promoting racism to maintain and justify their advantaged positions. Under this view, racism will persist as long as inequality and the accumulation of wealth and privilege are tolerated.

LO 10-2   Become Aware of the Changing Racial Profile of the United States and the Shifting Role of Government Vis à Vis Race and Ethnicity

EP 2a

The United States has been populated by immigrants in a series of waves that began with the arrival of the first Native Americans in the Pleistocene era and continued through successive arrivals from Western Europe, Africa, South and Central America, Asia, and other points across the globe. We will consider immigration through a lens of race/ethnicity in this chapter and examine its implications for labor in Chapter 14. But first, let's examine how history has shaped contemporary American race relations.

Already the world's most racially and ethnically diverse nation, the United States is projected to become even more diverse in coming decades. The Census Bureau projects that by 2042 people of color will make up over half of the U.S. population, with the most dramatic growth among those who identify as Hispanic or Latino. This group is expected to nearly triple in size and to increase from 15 percent in 2008 to nearly a third (30 percent) of the population by 2050. Similarly, the number of Americans who identify as multiracial is expected to triple. Modest growth is projected for Asian Americans, African Americans, and Native Americans as well (U.S. Census Bureau, 2008). These trends are illustrated in Figure 10.1.

For much of its history the U.S. government was an agent of **racial oppression**. Even leaders who professed belief in equality and liberty supported racist institutions. For instance, Stephen A. Douglas, a Democratic senator in 1858, stated the prevailing view of

FIGURE 10.1 Changing Racial Composition of the U.S. Population, 2010–2050

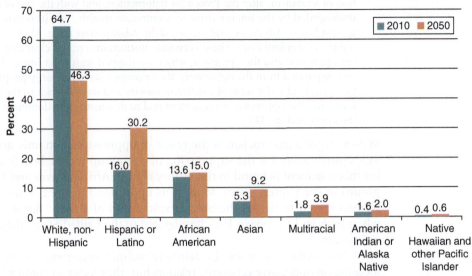

SOURCE OF DATA: U.S. Census Bureau, 2008 National Population Projections: Summary Tables—Table 4: Projections of the Population by Sex, Race, and Hispanic Origin for the United States: 2010 to 2050 (http://www.census.gov/population/projections/data/national/2008/summarytables.html).

his time clearly when he said, "[T]his government of ours is founded on the white basis. It was made by the white man, for the benefit of the white man, to be administered by white men" (Loewen, 1995, p. 154). Even a cursory review of U.S. history reveals centuries of government support for racial oppression, from legislation that perpetuated slavery and segregation to race-based immigration policies.

Today some look to government to heal racial divisions, reduce discrimination, and ensure equal opportunities for people of color. Policies in this tradition include the Freedmen's Bureau Bill of 1865; **affirmative action**, established by John F. Kennedy's executive order in 1961; the **Civil Rights Act of 1964**; and the **Voting Rights Act of 1965**. We will discuss these initiatives and related policies in the following sections.

Despite these efforts, the transition to racial equality is far from complete. Even as the United States becomes a "majority-minority" nation, people of color are disproportionately represented among those living in poverty, among clients of child welfare services, and among detainees of juvenile and criminal justice facilities; we see racial disparities in employment and health-care access; and many of our schools and neighborhoods are still segregated by race.

LO 10-3   Reflect on the Role of History in Shaping the Current Experiences of African Americans

EP 2a
EP 5c

The history of most African Americans is distinct from that of other people of color (including Native Americans) in that many of their ancestors were transported to America against their will. As we will see in this section, slavery was followed by other forms of government-sanctioned oppression. The civil rights movement led most Americans to recognize the injustice of these practices.

BOX 10.1   Thaddeus Stevens (1792–1868)

Thaddeus Stevens, a white Republican senator from Pennsylvania, worked for racial equality throughout his career. At his request, he was buried in a cemetery that served both whites and African Americans. His tombstone was a final chance to make his case. It says, "[F]inding other cemeteries limited as to race by charter rules, I have chosen this that I might illustrate in my death the principles which I advocated through a long life."

SLAVERY AND ITS AFTERMATH

During most of the 17th century, laborers on plantations in colonial America were indentured servants from Europe. In time, the supply of indentured servants diminished, and the slave trade accelerated to the point where the population of African slaves exceeded the European population in southern colonies. Public policies of the late 17th century began to distinguish European servants from African slaves, meting out differential punishment for offenses (Stampp, 1956). For example, in 1705 a Virginia law required dismemberment of "troublesome" slaves while at the same time prohibiting masters from whipping European servants, naked, without a court order (Morgan, 1975). In one of the most brutal public policies recorded in the United States, several colonies enacted legislation mandating castration of slaves who made repeated attempts to escape.

The American Revolution brought a new understanding of freedom and equality. While some were able to restrict their notions of freedom to white men, other revolutionary leaders found this more difficult. In his first draft of the Declaration of Independence, Thomas Jefferson included a clause that was critical of the slave trade, in his complaints against King Edward: "he has waged cruel war against human nature itself, violating its most sacred rights of life and liberty in the persons of a distant people who never offended him, captivating and carrying them into slavery in another hemisphere, or to incur miserable death in their transportation thither" (National Humanities Center Resource Toolbox, n.d.). Of course, his southern compatriots insisted on the deletion of this clause.[3]

In states with the least economic investment in slavery, an abolitionist movement flourished and legislatures enacted laws to restrict or abolish slavery. These laws were enacted in New York, Massachusetts, New Jersey, Pennsylvania, Connecticut, and Rhode Island. Meanwhile, southern leaders seized on the notion of property rights to argue that the government had no right to deprive them of their slaves (because they were property). In the South, black slavery was seen as a prerequisite to white freedom.

After the Revolution, the new Constitutional government was designed by men of property. Enumerating the wealth of the members of the Constitutional Convention, Dye and Ziegler (1996) estimate that nearly a third were plantation owners and slaveholders. In deference to their economic interests, the Constitution did not prohibit or restrict slavery. In fact, it reinforced the institution. For example, in population counts to determine congressional representation, each slave was to be counted as three-fifths of a person. This increased the political clout of property holders who held the franchise in slave states.

---

[3]Jefferson went on to author legislation in Virginia that allowed for the gradual emancipation of slaves. Yet, among his slaves, the only ones he freed were his children—and he did that on his deathbed. He left their mother, Sally Hemings, enslaved for the rest of her life.

The Constitution also required that runaway slaves who made it to free states be returned to their owners upon demand. Article IV, Section Two, stated that "No Person held to service or Labor in one State, under the Laws thereof, escaping into another, shall, in consequence of any Law or Regulation therein, be discharged from such Service or Labor, but shall be delivered up on Claim of the Party to whom such Service or Labor may be due." Since slaves were recognized as property, the Fifth Amendment, which protected property from arbitrary governmental seizure, helped to sustain the institution. Finally, under the Naturalization Act of 1790, U.S. citizenship was defined in terms compatible with the European worldview. The act required applicants for citizenship to be of good character and *white*.

The first federal involvement in abolitionist efforts came in 1808, when the international slave trade was banned. Even then, Congress did not alter the terms of domestic slavery. The **Fugitive Slave Act of 1850** and the **Dred Scott decision of 1857** established an obligation to return escaped slaves and denied equal citizenship to African Americans.

State laws in the South not only treated slaves as property; they also restricted the activities of white residents to sustain the institution of slavery. Thus, for example, state laws prohibited whites—even slave owners—from teaching slaves to read or write. Owners were also prohibited from freeing their slaves unless the slaves left the state. Finally, interracial marriage, even between free adult blacks and whites, was strictly prohibited.

Although the Civil War (1861–1865) did bring an end to slavery, it was not fought for that purpose. It was a war of independence for the South and a struggle to maintain the Union for the North. President Lincoln explained his priorities in a letter to the editor of the *New York Tribune*:

> I would save the Union. I would save it the shortest way under the Constitution. The sooner the national authority can be restored; the nearer the Union will be "the Union as it was." If there be those who would not save the Union, unless they could at the same time save slavery, I do not agree with them. If there be those who would not save the Union unless they could at the same time destroy slavery, I do not agree with them. My paramount object in this struggle is to save the Union, and is not either to save or to destroy slavery. If I could save the Union without freeing any slave I would do it, and if I could save it by freeing all the slaves I would do it; and if I could save it by freeing some and leaving others alone I would also do that. What I do about slavery, and the colored race, I do because I believe it helps to save the Union; and what I forbear, I forbear because I do not believe it would help to save the Union. I shall do less whenever I shall believe what I am doing hurts the cause, and I shall do more whenever I shall believe doing more will help the cause. I shall try to correct errors when shown to be errors; and I shall adopt new views so fast as they shall appear to be true views. I have here stated my purpose according to my view of official duty; and I intend no modification of my oft-expressed personal wish that all men everywhere could be free (Abraham Lincoln Online, n.d.).

One month later, Lincoln used his war powers to issue the Emancipation Proclamation which freed slaves in southern states. Hundreds of thousands of African Americans contributed to the northern war effort, which saved the Union and put an end to slavery.

The postwar period was certainly not marked by racial equality. Southern landholders maintained control over county and state governments, and with the end of federal reconstruction, they passed **Jim Crow**[4] laws designed to "keep Negroes in their place." The first

---

[4]Jim Crow was not a real person. The term is a pejorative way of characterizing African Americans that was coined by a white minstrel named Daddy Rice. He would blacken his face and dress in rags, then dance and sing while purporting to imitate African Americans. His most popular song, "Jump Jim Crow," was an insulting parody of African American culture.

Jim Crow law, passed in 1888 in Louisiana, declared that African Americans could not be seated with whites on railway cars. In addition to laws like this that sharply enforced racial segregation in public facilities, state and county laws established other oppressive practices, including the credit system used in sharecropping, debt peonage, convict leasing, segregated schools, and voting restrictions.

Credit and Sharecropping

Under **sharecropping**, those who worked the land owned very little, not even their tools. They paid a percentage of their crops as rent and borrowed tools and animals from the landowner. The credit system used in sharecropping was particularly onerous. Croppers received advances for their seed, supplies, and household goods. The interest rates charged on these advances were outrageous, ranging from about 53 to 71 percent (Mandel, 1992). In addition to interest, landowners charged inflated prices for goods they sold to the croppers, who often had no alternative to the planter-owned stores.

Debt Peonage

Under sharecropping and related practices, a landowner could virtually ensure a lifetime of debt for his tenants. Early in the 20th century, nearly every southern state had a system of **debt peonage**. Under state laws, leaving the land without paying debts was defined as labor fraud and was punishable by imprisonment. This legislation provided landowners with a pool of forced labor—tenants who could not leave the land because of their debts. The extent of debt peonage has been disputed. Some argue that the practice was rare and had died out by the Depression. But Daniel (1972) cites cases as recent as the 1960s.

Convict Leasing

The practice of **convict leasing** has been described as "comparable to the worst horrors of slavery" (Wilson, 1996, p. 88). Under this system, landowners and other employers would bid on contracts to use convicts on chain gangs for their labor. The convicts, the vast majority of whom were African Americans, had virtually no protection from abuse and lived in appalling conditions (Lichtenstein, 1996). They labored under the supervision of armed guards. Convict laborers had extremely high mortality rates. Camejo (1976) reported that as many as one in four laborers died each year in Arkansas during the 1880s. The practice was phased out by the 1950s, but chain gangs were revived for a brief period in the 1990s when several states decided to "get tough on crime." In Alabama a threatened lawsuit by the Southern Poverty Law Center brought an end to the practice.

Segregated Schools

Education is widely seen as a tool for empowerment, and race-based oppression has historically focused on denying education to people of color. Prior to the Civil War, southern states enforced laws that prohibited teaching an African American to read or write. During Reconstruction, federal efforts did not address equal access to education, and the Supreme Court contributed to unequal access through its ***Plessy v. Ferguson*** decision.

Homer Plessy was a light-skinned African American who bought a first-class ticket on the East Louisiana Railway. When he tried to take his seat, he was ordered to go to the "colored" section. He refused and was jailed. When the case was reviewed by the Supreme Court in 1896, the Court held that "if Plessy be a colored man and be so assigned, he has been deprived of no property, since he is not lawfully entitled to the reputation of being a white man" (quoted in George, 2000, p. 7). The Court introduced the idea that "separate but equal" facilities were lawful, a principle that would have an enduring impact on the educational opportunities of African American children.[5]

Until the middle of the 20th century, the nation's segregated educational system relegated African American children to ill-equipped classrooms with outdated textbooks. Transportation and meal services available to white children were not provided in the "colored" schools. Access to higher education and professional training was severely limited. It was in this seriously underfunded system that Reverend Davis's parents were educated.

In 1954, the Supreme Court finally rejected the principle of separate but equal in its ***Brown v. Board of Education*** decision. On behalf of the National Association for the Advancement of Colored People (NAACP), Thurgood Marshall (later a Supreme Court justice himself) argued that segregation produced enduring damage in African American children, scarring them for life with a sense of inferiority (an example of the *internalized oppression* discussed in the introduction to Part III). Chief Justice Earl Warren delivered the Court's unanimous decision to order desegregation of the nation's schools.

But desegregation was not a simple matter. Three years would pass before the school board in Little Rock, Arkansas, reluctantly concluded that they would have to desegregate their Central High School. Nine African American children were handpicked to attend the all-white school. On Wednesday, September 4, 1957, the school was surrounded by members of the National Guard and an angry mob. Eight of the children entered as a group under police protection. The ninth child, Elizabeth Eckford, did not have a phone and was not informed of the group's plans. She approached the school alone. Eckford described the experience in her book *Growing Up Southern* (Mayfield, 1981).

Voting Restrictions

In the southern states, voting restrictions disenfranchised large blocs of African American voters. These barriers included poll taxes that had to be paid annually. A voter could be required to pay poll taxes for previous years as well as the current year before being allowed to register. Some jurisdictions required property ownership for voter registration, while others established complex literacy requirements. Some areas established poll taxes that applied only to African Americans. African Americans who did show up to vote were subjected to harassment, intimidation, and even violence. These measures kept millions of African Americans, like Reverend Davis's parents, out of the voting booth until the civil rights movement of the 1960s.

BOX 10.2   Dr. Charles Richard Drew (1904–1950)

Dr. Charles Richard Drew became world-renowned for perfecting the technique for separating blood plasma from whole blood so it could be used more readily. Countless lives were saved. At the age of 45, Dr. Drew was critically injured in an auto accident in North Carolina.

A persistent urban legend holds that when he was taken to a hospital he was denied treatment because he was African American. This rumor was used in a *M*A*S*H* episode, but it is unsubstantiated. Dr. Drew was treated but died from his injuries.

---

[5]The *Plessy v. Ferguson* decision was not unanimous. Justice John Marshall Harlan wrote an eloquent dissent, stating that "the arbitrary separation of citizens, on the basis of race, while they are on a public highway, is a badge of servitude wholly inconsistent with the civil freedom and equality before the law established by the Constitution. It cannot be justified upon any legal grounds" (quoted in George, 2000, p. 8).

Elizabeth Eckford's first day of school, 1957, Little Rock, Arkansas.

Bettmann/Corbis

THE NEW DEAL

Seen by many as a progressive movement toward equality, the New Deal included several provisions explicitly designed to maintain racial privilege. President Franklin Roosevelt faced a solid bloc of white southern congressmen who refused to support any Social Security legislation that included African Americans (Duster, 1996). As a result, the Social Security Act of 1935 excluded domestic servants and agricultural workers—jobs predominantly filled by African Americans. The Wagner Act of 1935, which established the right of unions to collective bargaining, was revised to permit racial exclusion. Similarly, the 1934 National Housing Act exacerbated racial segregation in housing by permitting the use of race as a criterion for granting loans.

THE CIVIL RIGHTS MOVEMENT

Most people locate the peak of the civil rights movement in the summer of 1964, but its origins lie deep in U.S. history. Several events set the stage for that summer, including the Montgomery bus boycott of 1955–1957 and the activities of the freedom riders of 1961. In 1962, President Kennedy sent federal troops to enable James Meredith to enroll at the University of Mississippi, and in 1963 Reverend Martin Luther King, Jr., wrote his seminal argument for nonviolent resistance, "Letter from Birmingham Jail." But it was in July of 1964 that the Civil Rights Act passed (despite a Senate filibuster), outlawing race-based discrimination in public accommodations, employment, voting, and schools. This legislation set the stage for progress toward racial equality in the United States.

CURRENT REALITIES

Noting increases in the proportion of African Americans who complete college, become homeowners, and are employed in executive or managerial positions, commentators speak of the rise of the African American middle class (for example, Pattillo-McCoy, 1999). Indeed, there has been progress at the upper end of the income distribution. In 1970, only 10 percent of all households and 4 percent of African American households enjoyed annual incomes of $100,000 or more (in 2014 dollars). By 2014, 25 percent of all households and 13 percent of African American households had achieved this level of affluence. Whereas the general population saw a 150 percent increase in its likelihood of being affluent, African American households saw a 225 percent rise. This is illustrated in Figure 10.2. Of course, progress has been tenuous and slow. Racial inequality persists, and affluent households are hardly typical.

Median income is the most commonly used measure of the financial situation of typical households, and African American households have a lower median income than the general population. As Figure 10.3 indicates, the median 2014 income for African American households was the nation's lowest at $35,653, compared with $53,657 for all households. African American households also have a higher risk of poverty. The 2014 income distribution for African American households indicated that one in five (20.1 percent) had incomes under $15,000 (see Figure 10.4), compared with 12.6 percent of all households.

Household income of African Americans is influenced by household composition and the gender gap in wages. African Americans have more female-headed households than other groups in the United States. Nearly half (43 percent) of African American families were headed by a woman in 2014, compared with one in five (19 percent) for the general population (U.S. Census Bureau, 2015c). And, of course, households headed by women are

FIGURE 10.2 Rising Affluence by Race, 1970–2014 (Households with Annual Incomes of $100,000 or More in Constant 2014 Dollars)

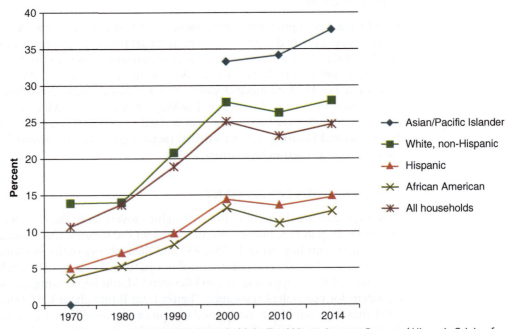

SOURCE OF DATA: U.S. Census Bureau (2015). Households by Total Money Income, Race, and Hispanic Origin of Householder: 1967 to 2014 (http://www2.census.gov/programs-surveys/demo/tables/p60/252/table3.pdf).

FIGURE 10.3 Median Annual Household Income by Race, 2014

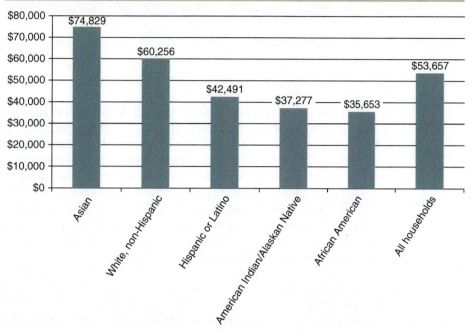

Source of Data: U.S. Census Bureau (2015). Households by Total Money Income, Race, and Hispanic Origin of Householder: 1967–2014 (http://www2.census.gov/programs-surveys/demo/tables /p60/252/table3.pdf); American Indian/Alaskan Native data from U.S. Census (2015). FFF: American Indian and Alaska Native Heritage Month: November, 2015 (http://www.census.gov/newsroom /facts-for-features/2015/cb15-ff22.html).

FIGURE 10.4 Income Distribution by Race, 2014

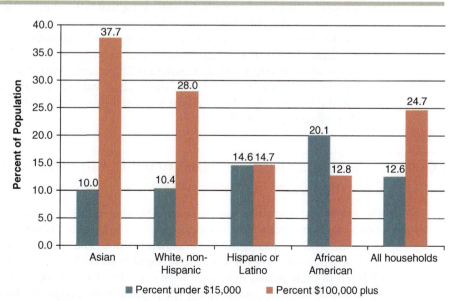

Source of Data: U.S. Census Bureau, Household Income, Table 696: Money Income of Families— Percent distribution by income level in constant (2009) dollars: 1980 to 2014 (http://www.census .gov/compendia/statab/2012/tables/12s0695.pdf).

BOX 10.3   Ralph Bunche (1904–1971)

Ralph Bunche, African American, negotiated the first cease-fire in the Middle East, for which he received the 1950 Nobel Peace Prize.

at greater risk for poverty. For example, in 2015, households headed by a single female had a 28.2 percent risk of poverty, compared with rates of 5.4 percent for married couples and 14.9 percent for households headed by a single male (U.S. Census Bureau, 2016). Further, as we will see in Chapter 15, African American women earn lower incomes even at comparable levels of educational attainment, and they are underrepresented in highly paid occupations.

Chapter 6 addressed the African American experience with health disparities, higher infant mortality rates, greater cancer morbidity and mortality, and lower life expectancies. Apart from its obvious disadvantages, reduced life expectancy translates into lower Social Security benefits over a lifetime. So, one effect of these health disparities for African Americans is diminished return on their payroll taxes.

Reverend Davis's experiences only hint at the dire consequences of implicit bias. On August 4, 2014, Darren Wilson, a 28-year-old white police officer in Ferguson, Missouri, shot and killed Michael Brown, an 18-year-old African American who had stolen some cigarillos from a convenience store. Michael Brown was unarmed. His death sparked peaceful protests that were fanned by tensions between the majority African American town and the majority white police. Within days the protests turned unruly. Businesses were looted and vehicles vandalized. Later, in November, a grand jury refused to indict Wilson, and Ferguson once again erupted in protests that echoed throughout the country. The expression, "Hands up! Don't shoot!" repeated by protesters reflected the widespread belief that Brown was attempting to surrender when he was shot.

After Ferguson, the "Black Lives Matter" movement worked to raised awareness of African American men's risk of being shot by police. At the same time, some commentators pointed to "the Ferguson effect," suggesting that police became less "proactive," leaving citizens at greater risk (MacDonald, 2016).

The *Washington Post* reviewed news reports, public records, and Internet databases and concluded that 991 Americans were killed by police in 2015. Among them, African Americans were overrepresented, making up 26 percent (258). Ninety-six percent of the victims were men (Washington Post, 2016). That year, 42 police officers were shot and killed in the line of duty (Officer Down Memorial Page, 2015). The racial composition of the fallen officers is not available.

LO 10-4   Reflect on the Role of History in Shaping the Current Experiences of Hispanic or Latino Americans

EP 2a
EP 5c

The term "Hispanic or Latino" refers to a person's ethnic and cultural origins. Hispanic Americans come from Spanish-speaking countries. Their history and culture reflect the global influence of Spain during its imperialist period. The Spanish (like other colonial powers) married members of the indigenous populations of their country's colonies. In Mexico, children of these mixed marriages were considered **mestizos**, with features of both the Spanish and the indigenous peoples. The population of indigenous Tamo-Arawak in Puerto Rico was quickly decimated by war and disease, which led the Spanish to bring in slaves from Africa. Subsequent interracial marriages led some Puerto Ricans to identify themselves as black. Thus, "Hispanic Americans" may have different racial identities and different experiences of U.S. racism. Puerto Ricans immigrating to New York may find themselves identified as black, whether or not they self-identify in this way. Their access to housing and jobs may more closely resemble that of African Americans than of other Hispanic groups.

The nation's Hispanic population has diverse origins and backgrounds. Some lived in the Southwest before it was part of the United States. Others emigrated from Spanish-speaking areas—initially Mexico, and more recently Latin America, Puerto Rico, and Cuba. In the 2010 census over half (63 percent) of Hispanic Americans reported that their origins were in Mexico. Just under a tenth (9 percent) traced their origins to Puerto Rico. Others reported origins in Central America (7.9 percent), South America (5.5 percent), and Cuba (3.5 percent) (U.S. Census Bureau, 2011a).

This diversity complicates our understanding of Hispanic claims on U.S. social policy. Should they be considered an indigenous group that has experienced disadvantage and oppression (and is therefore entitled to affirmative efforts to remedy past injustices)? Or should they be viewed as a group that, like other immigrants, can be expected to achieve economic and social parity in the process of assimilation? Is policy needed to improve the status of Hispanic Americans in the United States? Or will the process of assimilation mitigate the need for public intervention? In the following sections we will consider the diverse histories of Hispanic Americans, including immigrants from Mexico, Puerto Rico, Cuba, and Latin America.

MEXICAN AMERICANS

While other European nations were colonizing the northeastern region of what is now the United States, the Spanish government established its colonial presence in the southwestern region and in Mexico. The Spanish encouraged the settlement of California, recruiting settlers from Mexico who were willing to move north, so by the late 18th century the Mexican presence in California and the Southwest was well established.

Like Britain, Spain lost its American colonies, and the Mexican Revolution brought that nation's independence in 1821. At that time the land area of Mexico was about twice what it is today, encompassing the current states of California, New Mexico, Arizona, Texas, Colorado, and Utah. Mexican society was rigidly hierarchical, with those who possessed Spanish land grants, the "dons," enjoying a pastoral and aristocratic lifestyle for which those at the bottom, the indigenous peoples, supplied labor.

American visitors, and even settlers, were initially welcomed. As their numbers grew and their intent to claim territory became clear, Mexico outlawed American immigration. Nonetheless, Americans continued to arrive in violation of Mexican law, leading one commissioner in Texas to complain, "The incoming stream of settlers is unceasing" (Takaki, 1993, p. 173).

This influx lasted until the Mexican–American War was declared in 1836. Conflict first broke out in Texas, where the Mexican government had outlawed slavery. This enraged slaveholding Texans who, under the leadership of Sam Houston, forced the Mexican government to cede the state. The "Lone Star Republic" was established as an independent nation, with Houston as its leader.

The Texas victory was widely interpreted as an advance for the Anglo-Saxon race. Stephen Austin had declared war with Mexico inevitable, viewing it as a conflict between a "mongrel Spanish-Indian and negro race" and "civilization and the Anglo-American race." Likewise, Sam Houston declared that the Lone Star Republic would reflect "glory on the Anglo-Saxon race" (Takaki, 1993, p. 174).

For Mexico, the war was devastating. The United States annexed Texas in 1845 and extended U.S. borders to the Pacific. In the 1848 Treaty of Guadalupe Hidalgo, Mexico ceded Texas and the Southwest Territories.

U.S. control of the area led to several measures designed to make life difficult for people of Spanish or Mexican descent. California passed a series of "Greaser Acts," declaring that those Spanish and Indian people who were not "peaceful and quiet" were vagrants subject to imprisonment. The acts also imposed a "Mexican Miners Tax" that exacted fees from all Spanish-speaking miners. Although the treaty's provisions afforded Mexicans the vote, barriers that included poll taxes, language restrictions, and intimidation were used to reduce their political participation. Even the dons were subject to oppression. Landholdings that derived from Spanish land grants were challenged by American squatters. The U.S. court review was lengthy and expensive, and even if their title was declared legitimate, owners frequently had to sell their land to pay legal expenses.

As a result of these and similar policies, Mexicans in California and the Southwest lost their property and their social standing, and those who stayed were often reduced to the status of menial laborers. Even in these jobs, they encountered discrimination. Mexican workers in most industries (such as mining and railroads) were systematically paid less than "Americans" (whites) in the same jobs. A system of debt peonage was instituted, similar to that used to tie African Americans to southern farms. Living in company towns, many were forced to buy clothing, food, and other supplies from company-owned stores. The high price of these goods left workers so deeply in debt that they essentially became slaves to the company. In Chapter 15 we will examine the history of Chicano laborers in the United States.

There was also tension around the education of Chicano children. Employers wanted to restrict access to education to ensure a continuous supply of cheap labor. Parents longed for their children to become educated so they would enjoy a better standard of living. Most school districts restricted educational opportunities of Chicano children, channeling them into technical and domestic classes. Some of the larger districts established separate schools for Chicanos similar to those to which African Americans in the South were relegated. Meanwhile, the nature of Hispanic immigration into the United States began to change as residents of Puerto Rico, Cuba, and Latin America relocated to the United States.

IMMIGRANTS FROM PUERTO RICO, LATIN AMERICAN COUNTRIES, AND CUBA

The second-largest group of Hispanic Americans has origins in Puerto Rico. Their island was ceded to the U.S. by Spain in 1898, and since 1917 those born in Puerto Rico have been, citizens of the United States. While they do hold a presidential primary, residents of Puerto Rico are not represented in the Electoral College so they cannot vote for president. Those who establish residency in a state can vote for president there. Migration from Puerto Rico swelled during the 1940s and 1950s as young men left to serve in World War II and became aware of economic opportunities on the U.S. mainland. Today, nearly two-thirds of Puerto Ricans live on the U.S. mainland, primarily in the Northeast (Chavez, 1991; U.S. Census Bureau, 2011a).

Latin American immigrants, primarily from the Dominican Republic, El Salvador, and Nicaragua, have increased the diversity of the U.S. Hispanic population. Many have fled political instability caused by the collapse of regimes (such as that in El Salvador) that were supported by the United States. Others fled after U.S.-supported regimes were installed (as in Nicaragua). Many immigrants in this situation struggle to secure refugee status because recognition of their oppression might imply indictment of the U.S.-supported regime.

Generally regarded as "elite" Hispanic immigrants, the ranks of Cuban Americans have included many landowners, professionals, and businesspeople. Since the 1960s, Cubans have immigrated in waves and remain concentrated in Florida. Unlike Mexican immigrants who seek economic improvement, Cubans tend to be "political" refugees looking for a different political system. Among older Cubans, many anticipated returning to Cuba with the end of the Castro regime (Perez, 2013). Their hopes of return have been complicated by the embargo imposed by the United States when Fidel Castro overthrew the **Batista regime** in 1958. The embargo placed severe restrictions on travel and commercial dealings with Cuba. In 2009, the Obama administration eased the travel ban to enable Cuban Americans to travel freely to Cuba, and in 2011 rules were amended to permit all Americans to visit Cuba as part of organized tours. As of this writing the financial embargo remains in place. When U.S. goods are exported to Cuba, payment is required in cash because credit is prohibited. Despite the embargo, and despite objections from the Castro regime, the United States maintains a Cuban landholding at Guantanamo Bay on property leased to it under the 1903 Cuban–American treaty.

CURRENT REALITIES

The nation's Hispanic population has changed. Today it is more heavily composed of immigrants. Chavez (1991) reported that in 1970 barely one in five Hispanic Americans was foreign-born. By 2014 that figure had risen to 35 percent (U.S. Census Bureau, 2014). Whereas early Hispanic immigrants came almost exclusively from Mexico, more recent waves have brought migrants from Cuba, Puerto Rico, and Latin America (primarily El Salvador and Nicaragua). Where Mexican immigrants are primarily economic refugees, seeking to escape poverty, those from Cuba and Latin America are primarily political refugees. They tend to include more professionals and members of landed classes. Nonetheless, foreign-born immigrants typically experience greater economic deprivation than native-born Americans of Hispanic descent (Bean & Tienda, 1987; Chavez, 1991).

Although the Hispanic American population in the United States has grown increasingly diverse, broad economic and health indicators suggest the group as a whole continues to experience disadvantages. For example, as Figure 10.3 indicates, the median income for Hispanic households was $42,491 in 2014, compared with a median of $53,657 for the general population. Likewise, the income distribution presented in Figure 10.4 indicates that Hispanic households were more likely to have incomes below $15,000 and less likely to have incomes above $100,000 than the general population.

As we saw in Chapter 6, life expectancy for Hispanic Americans as a whole is generally comparable to or better than that of the white population. The same is generally true of infant mortality, although this indicator does illustrate the diversity of the Hispanic American population. For instance, in 2013 nearly six (5.96) out of every 1,000 infants born in the United States died before their first birthday. Among Puerto Ricans, infant mortality was slightly lower, at 5.93 per 1,000. Rates for other Hispanic groups were considerably lower. Mexican American mothers lost 4.9 infants per 1,000, while those from Central and South America lost 4.3. Those from Cuba had the lowest infant mortality rate: 3.02 per 1,000 (National Vital Statistics System, 2015).

LO 10-5   Reflect on the Role of History in Shaping the Current Experiences of Asian Americans

EP 2a
EP 5c

Asian immigrants traveled across the Pacific in response to the demand for labor in the rapidly expanding economy of the western United States. The Chinese came first, entering California just before the Gold Rush of 1849. They were followed by large numbers of Japanese people, whose emigration was carefully managed by their government. Immigrants from Korea, the Philippines, and other Asian and Pacific Island locations came in smaller numbers. In the following sections we will consider the experiences of Chinese and Japanese immigrants to the United States.

CHINESE IMMIGRANTS

Chinese immigrants came to this country in search of the "Gold Mountain," a land of beauty and wealth. Their native land was suffering from poverty and chaos caused by the opium wars with the British. To finance these wars, and to pay the large indemnities charged by Western imperialist powers, the Chinese (Qing) government imposed high taxes. Many farmers lost their land, and food shortages led to widespread famine.

During the latter half of the 19th century, hundreds of thousands of young Chinese men—primarily illiterate laborers—came to the United States. They were attracted by stories of countrymen who had spent a few years working in the United States and returned with fabulous wealth. These and related stories were propagated by labor brokers—entrepreneurs hired by American firms to recruit Chinese laborers. Contrary to myth, there is no evidence that Chinese men were kidnapped and brought to America as "coolies" (Takaki, 1993). Most stayed in California, but some made their way to southern states where they served as an alternative to African American labor.

Initially the Chinese were welcomed and their contributions appreciated. They did not represent a political threat, since the Naturalization Act of 1790 reserved citizenship for whites, and the Chinese immigrants did jobs that no white person wanted to perform. Chinese laborers worked in the mines under cramped and dangerous conditions. When mining became less profitable, they were hired by the railroads. As Chinn and colleagues (1969) explain, the Central Pacific Railroad line was a Chinese achievement. Again, Chinese workers labored under extremely difficult conditions, laying track through Donner Summit during the winter of 1866.

Thousands of Chinese (nearly one-fourth of California's Chinese population in 1869) settled in San Francisco, where they established a thriving community known as Chinatown and helped the city to become a leader in manufacturing. Chinese were also successful as agricultural laborers in California's Central Valley.

Their conspicuous effectiveness and relative success led to resentment on the part of white labor organizations, which lobbied for passage of the Chinese Exclusion Act in 1882.[6] The act prohibited immigration by Chinese laborers. It was the first piece of immigration legislation that expressly forbade immigration from a specific nation.

Chinese continued to be targets of resentment and eventually moved into self-employment, opening small businesses such as restaurants, grocery stores, and laundries. Chinese laundries represented an especially good niche for former laborers. Few white men saw this occupation as an economic threat because it was incompatible with their view of the male role. Yet laundry required only a minimal investment and did not demand high levels of skill or literacy—an excellent alternative to facing the racial tensions of the labor market.

Racial tension persisted in other venues, however, and Chinese were seen as potential threats to the "purity" of the white race. In 1880, California passed a law prohibiting

---

BOX 10.4   Gen Yeo Wong (1910-2016)

Gen Yeo Wong came to the U.S. when he was 10, as a "paper son." A modernist painter, Wong's work is on display at the Art Institute of Chicago. But he is best known as the creator of the landscapes used in Disney's Bambi movie.

---

[6]The Chinese Exclusion Act was renewed in 1892 and extended indefinitely in 1902. It went out of effect with the passage of the Immigration and Naturalization Act of 1924.

marriage between a white person and a "negro, mulatto, or Mongolian" (Osumi, 1982). These "**anti-miscegenation**" laws remained on the books in some states as late as 1999.[7]

For economic and cultural reasons, women did not emigrate from China. They had no value in the labor market and were accustomed to living within the narrow confines of their homes. Well-born Chinese women were nearly unable to walk due to the practice of binding their feet into "rosebuds." A few Chinese men were able to bring their wives to the United States, and thousands of Chinese women were sold into prostitution. Nonetheless, the population of Chinese immigrants was predominantly male.

JAPANESE IMMIGRANTS

The Japanese immigration experience differed from that of the Chinese in several respects. First, it began later. The initial wave of Japanese immigrants came to the United States in 1885, roughly 40 years after the beginning of Chinese immigration. Second, their country of origin was not a relatively undeveloped region but an emerging world power. Japan had defeated the Russians in 1905 and commanded a measure of respect for its military and economic potential. Third, while the Chinese government was not involved in emigration, Japanese emigration was carefully orchestrated and monitored by the Japanese government, which was ready to intercede diplomatically if its citizens were abused (Daniels & Kitano, 1970). These differences led to a less difficult immigration experience for the Japanese, particularly as it was affected by federal policies.

These advantages did nothing, of course, to reduce the impact of American racism or mitigate the demands of the American economy on Japanese immigrants. Like the Chinese, the Japanese fled economic deprivation and sought a better standard of living. Another similarity was the widespread belief, if not expectation, that Japanese emigrants were only temporarily residing in the United States.

Like the Chinese, the Japanese came to the United States as laborers. Thousands worked in the sugar cane fields of Hawaii, and others became agricultural laborers in California. The agricultural skills of the Japanese were considerable, and they introduced new techniques and crops to the states' fast-growing agricultural economies.

Unlike the Chinese, Japanese women came to the United States to work alongside their husbands. In Japan they had already become accepted members of the industrial labor force, and a wife was an asset in the immigration process. As a result, the first generation of Japanese immigrants (the *Issei*) settled and raised a second generation of U.S.-born Japanese Americans (the *Nisei*).

Like the Chicanos, Japanese immigrants saw education as the key to their children's advancement. Also like the Chicanos, the Issei encountered resistance in their attempts to secure a public education for their children. In San Francisco the resistance was especially strident. In 1906, in the middle of an anti-Japanese campaign by the *San Francisco Chronicle,* the board of education ordered all Japanese students (both native- and foreign-born) to attend the segregated "Oriental School" that had been established in Chinatown. Daniels and Kitano (1970) note that the furor was disproportionate to the number of Japanese children in San Francisco schools: "Only a very few students were involved—at the time of the order there was a grand total of ninety-three Japanese students distributed among twenty-three different public schools, and twenty-five of them were native-born citizens" (p. 48).

---

[7]South Carolina and Alabama were the last states to eliminate statutes prohibiting interracial marriage. South Carolina did so in 1998 and Alabama in 1999. These laws were declared unconstitutional by the U.S. Supreme Court in 1967.

The school board's order created an international uproar. The U.S. ambassador to Japan received official protests from the Japanese government, which maintained that the action violated treaties protecting the rights of Japanese citizens in the United States. President Theodore Roosevelt summoned the San Francisco school board to Washington and "with a combination of threats, pleas, cajolings, and promises, succeeded in having the school board rescind the offending order" (Daniels & Kitano, 1970, p. 48). Roosevelt also succeeded in persuading the California legislature to refrain from passing anti-Japanese legislation.

In return for protecting the rights of Japanese citizens, Roosevelt exchanged a series of notes with the Japanese government that have come to be known as the Gentlemen's Agreement. The Japanese agreed to limit emigration of laborers and farmers to the United States. This concession quieted calls for national legislation to restrict Japanese immigration on the model of the Chinese Exclusion Act. The Gentlemen's Agreement did allow for wives to join their husbands in the United States, and as a result, thousands of "picture brides" made up the last of the Japanese immigrants. These women had long-distance arranged marriages to men with whom they had exchanged only photographs prior to meeting as husband and wife in the United States.

Of course, the Japanese government's protection of its citizens in the United States did not pave the way to U.S. citizenship. In a telling example of judicial racism, the U.S. Supreme Court denied the citizenship petition of Takao Ozawa. In 1922, Ozawa (a graduate of the University of California and a young man of good character and light complexion) petitioned for citizenship. Under the Naturalization Act of 1795, naturalization was limited to "free, White persons." This race-based criterion was extended in 1870 to permit naturalization of "aliens of African nativity and to persons of African descent." The Court ruled that Ozawa's complexion, however light, did not qualify as "white," and he was not of African descent. Thus, Ozawa was ruled ineligible for naturalized citizenship.

The Court ruled, in *Ozawa v. United States,* that "white" meant "Caucasian." As Daniels and Kitano (1970) report, however, the same Court ruled "shortly thereafter, that an applicant from India, who was ethnographically a Caucasian although his complexion was of a mahogany hue" was not entitled to citizenship because "White did not mean Caucasian at all, but meant, rather, 'white' as commonly understood" (p. 54). This court served as what Daniels and Kitano called "the last bulwark of racism" until its membership changed in the 1930s and 1940s through appointments by President Franklin Roosevelt.

CURRENT REALITIES

Asians and Pacific Islanders are typically grouped together by the census, despite their heterogeneity. Economic indicators provide some support for the popular view of Asian Americans as a "model minority." For example, as indicated in Figure 10.3, the median household income of Asian households in 2014 was the nation's highest, $74,829. Likewise, as Figure 10.4 indicates, in 2014 Asian households were more likely than others to have incomes above $100,000 and slightly less likely to report incomes below $15,000 per year.

Several factors contribute to the higher median household income among America's Asian population. First, this group is more likely to have more than two workers within a household. Second, as we will see in Chapter 15, workers of Asian descent tend to be overrepresented in the ranks of managerial and professional workers. Finally, Asian Americans have historically had a relatively high rate of business ownership (Population Reference Bureau, 1999).

As we saw in Chapter 6, life expectancy and infant mortality among Americans of Asian and Pacific Island descent are generally favorable in comparison with the general population and with non-Hispanic white Americans.

LO 10-6   Reflect on the Role of History in Shaping the Current Experiences of Native Americans

EP 2a
EP 5c

The history of U.S. policy in relation to indigenous peoples can be divided into five stages: initial contact and treaty making (1532–1828), removal and relocation (1828–1887), forced assimilation (1887–1945), termination (1945–1961), and self-determination (1961 to present) (Deloria & Lytle, 1983). Each stage has been marked by a powerful desire on the part of some European immigrants to appropriate communal lands and natural resources for personal economic gain.

INITIAL CONTACT AND TREATY MAKING

When Columbus encountered Native Americans,[8] he is quoted as having remarked:

> They [Native Americans] are the best people in the world and above all the gentlest—without knowledge of what is evil—nor do they murder or steal. They are very simple and honest … none

BOX 10.5   The Great Law of Peace

Contrary to popular views of Native Americans as savages, some of the English colonists recognized that they had developed effective methods for governance. Indeed, historians agree that the U.S. Constitution drew as much from the Native Americans as it did from the Europeans (Schaaf, 1990). Their argument is compelling in part because neither Britain nor other major originating nations had faced the challenge of uniting disparate political entities. In creating their new nation, the colonists faced just that challenge. Each colony had a distinctive history and culture, yet they all needed to work together if the nation was to succeed. This challenge had been effectively addressed by tribal confederacies on the eastern seaboard of North America.

The Great Law of Peace governed a confederation of Iroquois tribes (also called the Haudenasaunee Six Nations). For centuries, these tribes strove for balance of power and supported the idea of the inherent rights of people, including freedom of speech and religion. Their council-based system of governance was of great interest to colonial leaders, including George Washington and Benjamin Franklin.

While serving as Indian Commissioner for Lancaster, Pennsylvania, during the mid-1700s, Benjamin Franklin studied the Iroquois system of governance. In 1744, minutes of the Lancaster, Pennsylvania, Provincial Council

reported that Onondaga leader Canasatego advised the council to form a league similar to the Iroquois confederacy, saying, "[O]ur Wise forefathers established Union and Amity between the Five Nations. This has made us formidable; this has given us great Weight and Authority with our neighboring Nations. We are a powerful Confederacy; and by your observing the same methods our Wise Forefathers have taken, you will acquire such Strength and power. Therefore whatever befalls you, never fall out with one another" (Friends Committee on National Legislation, 1987). Further, Schaaf (1990) notes that the "Albany Plan of Union" proposed by Benjamin Franklin in 1754 reflects the structures of the Iroquois confederacy's Grand Council. (Dr. Paul Wallace, an ethnohistorian, wrote extensively about the governance structures of the Iroquois and Algonquian peoples. See also Parker, 1916 and Weatherford, 1988.)

On the 200th anniversary of the signing of the U.S. Constitution (September 1987), a concurrent resolution to the 100th Congress set out to "acknowledge the contribution of the Iroquois Confederacy of Nations to the Development of the United States Constitution and to reaffirm the continuing government-to-government relationship between Indian Tribes and the United States established in the Constitution." Senator Daniel Inouye and colleagues introduced the resolution.

---

[8]Some tribes object to the term "Native American," feeling that it is too broad and includes Native Hawaiians and other indigenous people in land now occupied by the United States. Today, many prefer to use "Native American" when referring to indigenous tribes of the continental United States and "Alaska Native" to describe native peoples of Alaska. Michael Yellow Bird argues that the terms "Indian," "American Indian," and "Native American" are "counterfeit identities." He advocates the use of "First Nation" and "Indigenous Peoples" (Yellow Bird, 2001); however, these terms have not been widely accepted.

of them refusing anything he may possess when he is asked for it. They exhibit great love toward all others in preference to themselves. They would make fine servants. With 50 men we could subjugate them all and make them do whatever we want. (Phillips & Phillips, 1992, p. 166)

When Europeans established their first colony in Virginia, the area was inhabited by an estimated 14,000 members of the Powhatan tribe (Takaki, 1993). For these agricultural people, corn was a dietary staple, as it was for many of the tribes encountered by the European immigrants. During what John Smith later called "the starving time" (winter of 1607), the Powhatans shared their food with the immigrants and taught them principles of survival. Later, the Iroquois Federation would teach the colonists important principles of governance by sharing "the Great Law of Peace" (see Box 10.4).

In return, the Europeans declared Native Americans "heathens" and promoted their view of the race as "backward" and "savage." This view helped to justify atrocities committed by the Europeans, who were eager to steal the land under cultivation by Native Americans.

European interest in Native American lands initially stemmed from the popularity of tobacco in England. In 1613, the colony in Virginia sent its first shipment of tobacco to London. Within seven years, annual tobacco exports had increased to 60,000 pounds (Takaki, 1993). The Native Americans' already-cleared fields would, when converted to tobacco, produce riches for the immigrants. Europeans' lust for land and their capacity for declaring other races "inhuman" set the stage for well-documented brutalities.

With the passage of the **Naturalization Act of 1790**, Native Americans were classified as "domestic foreigners" and denied citizenship. The task of working with these internal nations was assigned to Congress through the Constitution and affirmed later in the 1802 Indian Trade and Intercourse Act, which provided that no Native American land would be ceded to the United States except through treaties with Congress.

REMOVAL AND RELOCATION

Cotton grows well in the southeastern United States. European demand for the fiber was high in the 19th century, so European immigrants eagerly claimed territory in that part of the country. The states of Alabama, Mississippi, and Louisiana were carved out of Native American territory for cultivation of cotton. Between 1814 and 1824, 11 "treaties of cessation" were negotiated, forcing tribes in this area to relocate west of the Mississippi. A popular justification for appropriating Native American lands was the argument that the Native Americans did not fully "use" the land.

Faced with the threat of extermination, Native American nations fought back. The Indian Wars progressed, and violence by Native Americans was seen both as evidence of their "savagery" and as justification for their annihilation. President Andrew Jackson (a veteran of the Indian Wars) encouraged this view, allowing states to appropriate Native American lands for distribution to white settlers in contradiction to the Indian Trade and Intercourse Act as well as an 1832 Supreme Court ruling.[9] One example of Jackson's practice of ignoring federal law came when the state of Mississippi abolished the sovereignty of the Choctaw nation. The federal government then collaborated in the state's effort to deprive Choctaw of their land through the Treaty of Dancing Rabbit Creek in 1830. Tribal leaders, threatened with extermination, had no choice but to approve the treaty, which required the Choctaw to cede their land (10,423,130 acres) to the federal government and move west of the Mississippi.

---

[9]Jackson is quoted as having responded to objections that he was acting in opposition to the Supreme Court by saying, "Let the Supreme Court enforce its ruling."

Alexis de Tocqueville described the exodus of the Choctaw from Mississippi:

> It was then the middle of winter and the cold was unusually severe; the snow had frozen hard upon the ground, and the river was drifting huge masses of ice. The Indians had their families with them, and they brought in their train the wounded and the sick, with children newly born and old men upon the verge of death. Three or four thousand soldiers drive before them the wandering races of the aborigines; these are followed by the pioneers, who pierce the woods, scare off the beasts of prey, explore the courses of the inland streams, and make ready the triumphal march of civilization across the desert (de Tocqueville, 1835, pp. 352–364).

The federal government made a profit from the sale of the Choctaw lands. Since this sale was in violation of the treaty, the Choctaw sued in federal court. In 1890, they were awarded a settlement of nearly $3 million, most of which went to pay their lawyers (Wright, 1928).

In one of many similar incidents, one-fourth of the Cherokee Nation died on the Trail of Tears as a direct result of betrayal and manipulation sanctioned by the president and Congress. Cherokee lands covered what is now called Georgia. In 1829, the Georgia state government passed a law extending their authority to Cherokee lands. Aware that this action was a violation of federal law, Chief Ross of the Cherokee Nation wrote to President Jackson pleading for his protection. Jackson instructed his Indian commissioner, J. F. Schermerhorn, to negotiate a treaty to move the Cherokee. Schermerhorn presented the treaty to a Cherokee council that was carefully crafted to include only those Cherokee who were inclined to approve it. (Chief Ross was jailed for the occasion.) A tiny fraction of the Nation attended the Council. None of the tribal leaders were present. The treaty was ratified. Even some federal officials acknowledged it as a fraud. Nonetheless, Congress ratified the treaty, and the president approved it. And, as a result, most of the Cherokee Nation set out, in the middle of one of the worst winters on record, to resettle west of the Mississippi on land they had never seen.

As the Western expansion progressed and railroads were built, the lands west of the Mississippi captured the imagination of the U.S. government and its citizens. The railroads made extensive use of public policy to advance their interests, securing the rights to millions of acres of land that lay adjacent to their tracks and fostering passage of the 1871 Indian Appropriation Act. This act declared that "hereafter no Indian nation or tribe within the territory of the United States shall be acknowledged or recognized as an independent nation, tribe, or power, with whom the United States may contract by treaty" (Walker, 1874, p. 5). The act denied the very existence of tribes as legitimate political units, eliminating the need to negotiate treaties and paving the way for the railroads' expansion. This act was accompanied by federal policy that forcibly placed Indians on reservations, where they could be trained as agricultural workers and assimilated into the broader society.

FORCED ASSIMILATION

Under the reservation system, land was assigned to the tribes with the assurance that they would not be subject to attack by U.S. military forces as long as they were within reservation boundaries. Of course, the problem with the system was whites' insatiable appetite for Native lands. Thus, in 1887, the **Dawes Act**, also known as the Indian Emancipation Act, was passed to eliminate the reservation system. White "reformers" argued that true assimilation would come only with private, not tribal, ownership of land. Under this act, each head of household who was at least one-half Native American would be given a 160-acre parcel. If a reservation had more parcels than households, the "surplus" parcels would be sold to white settlers. The net effect of the act was removal of thousands of acres from

Native American pupils of Carlisle Indian Industrial School, circa 1900 (central Pennsylvania).

the reservation system. Not only were "surplus" parcels sold, but settlers purchased or stole property from individual tribal landowners. Tribal leaders recognized the threat the Dawes Act posed to tribal survival, and some, like Chief Lone Wolf of the Kiowas, went to court to argue that the parceling out of land was in violation of previous treaties. In 1903, the Supreme Court declared that the federal government could abrogate treaty provisions. This allotment procedure reduced Native lands from 138 million to 48 million acres (Limerick, 1987).

In 1924, U.S. citizenship was conferred on all tribal members. Later, as part of Franklin Roosevelt's New Deal, Native Americans were offered an opportunity to regain tribal control of what remained of their reservation land through the 1934 Indian Reorganization Act (also known as the Howard-Wheeler Act). This law restored the political legitimacy of tribes (in the eyes of the U.S. government) and encouraged the maintenance of Native American culture on reservation lands. Reorganization meant that tribes would enjoy self-government on their lands and that some funds would be allocated for purchase of additional tribal lands. The law included a provision that required ratification by a majority of tribal members. Most tribes did approve reorganization, but some (most notably the Navajo, Crow, and Seneca) chose to remain outside the system.

General Richard Pratt's motto, "Kill the Indian, Save the Man," was the watchword of a movement to assimilate Native Americans by removing children from their homes and placing them in boarding schools run either by the government or by messianic Christian denominations. Pratt founded the first Native American boarding school in 1879, the Carlisle Indian School, in Pennsylvania. Three years later, U.S. Indian Commissioner Thomas Morgan supported the effort, commenting that it was "cheaper to educate Indians than to kill them" (Kelley, 1999).

Tens of thousands of Native American children were placed in these schools. The children were subjected to a harsh daily schedule, with only limited time devoted to education and the remainder to hard labor. They were strictly punished for revealing any evidence of their culture, such as carrying a medicine bundle or speaking a native language. The children were trained to be domestic servants and agricultural laborers.

BOX 10.6   Wilma Mankiller (1945–2010)

Wilma Mankiller organized the residents of the impoverished and demoralized 300-family town of Bell, Oklahoma, to develop a clean water supply that was connected to every house. She went on to be elected chief of the Cherokee Nation.

This assimilation program peaked in the United States in 1931, when nearly one-third of Native American children were in boarding schools. It continues today in boarding schools operated by the government. Most of these are located on the Navajo reservation. The schools are now managed primarily by Native Americans, many of whom are alumni. As a result, students can expect a less punitive, more culturally congruent experience (Limerick, 1987).

TERMINATION

The brutalities of removal, the reservation system, and the boarding schools are well documented, as is the duplicity with which U.S. officials treated Native American tribes. Between 1778 and 1871, some 370 Native American treaties were ratified by the U.S. Senate.[10] Many were abrogated or ignored. The legacy of this duplicity still colors relations between Native Americans and the U.S. government.

Federal recognition is critical for tribes seeking to establish services and provide benefits to their people. There are 562 federally recognized tribes in the United States and about 148 groups seeking federal recognition. The process of attaining federal recognition is difficult and arbitrary. During the 1950s and 1960s, the federal government pursued a policy of "termination," discontinuing recognition of several tribes (Churchill, 1998; Yellow Bird, 2001). At the same time, a program of relocation dispatched Native American people from reservations to cities with the goal of forcing them to assimilate into mainstream society.

A direct result of this policy is seen today in the numbers of Native American people living off reservations. In 1900, over 99 percent of federally recognized Native Americans lived on reservations. By 1970, nearly half (44.5 percent) lived off reservations. Recent estimates suggest that over half of Native Americans—from 55 to 70 percent—live off the reservation (Churchill, 1998; Walters, 1999).

The betrayals committed by government representatives were not condemned by most white U.S. citizens at the time. Intelligent, well-meaning people were persuaded that Native Americans were less human than whites—that they were "savage." The whites' insatiable greed for Native land stemmed from an economic system that allowed for the accumulation of private wealth at the expense of communal and environmental values. It was reinforced by religious values that emphasized the superiority of Christianity. Finally, it was fostered by a failure to see, as Reverend Davis said, that "difference is just that: difference. Not better or worse, just different."

---

[10]These treaties are compiled in a volume entitled *Indian Treaties, 1778–1811,* available through the Diplomatic Branch of the National Archives and Records Services, Washington, DC.

CURRENT REALITIES: SELF-DETERMINATION

Today, policies affecting Native Americans in the United States are administered by the Bureau of Indian Affairs (BIA). Figures from the 2000 census estimate a Native American population of 2.4 million (U.S. Census Bureau, 2001). For census purposes, a Native American is someone who reports that he or she is a Native American. The BIA recognizes 562 tribes, including hundreds of village groups in Alaska. The process of tribal recognition is lengthy and often contentious.[11]

Tribes that are officially recognized by the federal government are considered **internal, dependent nations**. As a result, most transactions on reservations are not subject to state income tax or sales taxes. Residents of reservations do not pay local property taxes. Native Americans living on a reservation do have the right to vote in state and local elections, though several western states (including Arizona and Utah) have attempted (so far unsuccessfully) to disenfranchise reservation residents within their jurisdictions. Under federal law, tribal lands are held in trust by the Secretary of the Interior. Revenue from grazing and mineral leasing is returned to the tribes as "trust income."

Tribes are understandably sensitive about efforts to undermine their sovereignty. This influenced the Sioux tribe's successful (as of this writing) protest against the Dakota Access pipeline. State efforts to regulate gaming on reservations also raise sovereignty issues. So Native American advocates were alarmed by passage of the 1988 Indian Gaming Regulatory Act by Congress, which allowed for state regulation of gaming on reservations.

Sovereignty issues also come up in relation to child protective services. The 1978 **Indian Child Welfare Act (ICWA)** was designed to prevent removal of Native American children from their tribes and families. Under the ICWA, tribes have primary jurisdiction over Native American children who enter the child welfare system, and state authorities are required to give preference to kin and tribes in finding homes for those who are removed due to abuse or neglect. Advocates complain that states are reluctant to designate children as Indian, claiming that even enrolled children living off-reservation are "not Indian enough" to be subject to ICWA provisions. Further, the Multiethnic Placement Act (passed in 1994) is seen as weakening the federal mandate to seek Native American homes for Native American children. (This topic is discussed further in Chapter 12.)

Prior to the 2000 census, the last careful count of the nation's Native American population had been mandated by the Dawes Act in 1887. Census counts during the interim undercounted the Native American population, and as a result much was written about the so-called "vanishing race" (Churchill, 1998; Johansen, 2002; Thornton, 1987, 1996). Using a strategy familiar to social workers since the Settlement House days, the U.S. Census Bureau hired Native American people to collect data for the 2000 census, and Native Americans were encouraged to participate in the census at powwows and other cultural events, urban Native American centers and clinics, schools and universities, and other settings.

As a result of these efforts, more than 4.1 million people told the 2000 census takers that they were at least part Native American, which is double the 2 million who reported Native ancestry in the 1990 census and 14 times the official figure of about 300,000 a century ago. Most of this growth was due to a change in census procedures. Census 2000 was the first in which respondents were allowed to choose more than one race. A total of 1.6 million Americans identified themselves as part American Indian/Alaska Native, which accounted for most of the increase. But even when those identifying as part American Indian/Alaska Native are not included, census 2000 documented a 25 percent increase in the number of Americans identified as Native American people since the 1990 census (Johansen, 2002; Thornton, 1987, 1996; U.S. Census Bureau, 2002a).

---

[11]The BIA bases recognition decisions on a group's continued cultural existence. But some tribes do an end run around the BIA, seeking recognition through a direct act of Congress. Given the high value of gambling for tribes, recognition decisions have significant commercial implications.

Available data offer a stark portrayal of the economic status of the first Americans. In 2014, Native Americans had the highest poverty rate of any race or ethnicity in the United States (28.3 percent), and the median household income for households headed by Native Americans and Alaska Natives was the nation's second lowest, at $37,227.

Native Americans live in diverse settings—in hogans in the deserts of Arizona, Utah, and Nevada; in concrete block houses on reservations; in urban apartments; and in suburban homes. Current estimates suggest that over half of Native Americans—between 55 and 70 percent—live off the reservation, many in urban centers such as New York and Los Angeles (Churchill, 1998; Ogunwole, 2002; Walters, 1999). Urban Native Americans generally enjoy higher incomes and better health than those living on reservations.

Reservations offer better access to tribal community and the Indian Health Service (IHS), but living conditions can be difficult. Many homes have no electricity, refrigeration, or indoor toilets. Transportation can also be problematic, and many rely on poorly maintained dirt roads that become impassable in rain or snow. Finally, communication can be a challenge, broadband, traditional wireline phone service, cell phone coverage, radio, and TV broadcast services are limited on Tribal lands (Federal Communications Commission, 2013).

Under the Indian Self-Determination and Educational Assistance Act of 1975, tribes are permitted to manage health programs that were formerly under the purview of the IHS. Many have taken advantage of this opportunity, and as Roubideaux (2002) reports, "approximately half of the IHS budget is now managed by tribes" (p. 1402). But access to health care is problematic, even on reservations. As the National Indian Health Board (2004) notes, IHS funding has lagged behind need and even basic fairness. Indeed, the federal government spends nearly twice as much on each federal prisoner's health care as it does on a per capita basis for Native Americans and Alaska Natives. Further, per-person IHS expenditures between 2000 and 2013 were approximately $2,849, while the comparable figure for the general U.S. population was $7,713 (Indian Health Service, 2014). Limited access to health care, coupled with poverty and harsh living conditions, have contributed to higher than average rates of morbidity and mortality and reduced life expectancy for indigenous peoples (Centers for Disease Control and Prevention, 2007a).

EMERGING POLICIES

The history of people of color in the United States is rife with examples of prejudice and government-sponsored oppression. With the exception of Asian Americans, people of color are overrepresented in the nation's criminal justice and child welfare systems and underrepresented in educational settings. Has the nation moved forward in recent decades? Is racism a thing of the past? In the remainder of this chapter we will examine some emerging policy developments that may help address these questions. Let's start with a look at U.S. immigration policy from the perspective of race and ethnicity.

LO 10-7   Understand the Role Immigration Plays in Shaping and Reflecting Race Relations in the United States

EP 3a
EP 8d

In June of 2013 the U.S. Senate passed the **Border Security, Economic Opportunity, and Immigration Modernization Act** of 2013. The controversial bill offered a path to citizenship for undocumented immigrants and thus represented a significant departure from earlier policies that focused on deportation. The Congressional Budget Office estimated that enacting the bill would provide net savings of !135 billion by 2023. (CBO, 2013).

TABLE 10.1 Milestones in Race-Based Immigration Policies

Naturalization Acts of 1790, 1795, and 1798
- Restricted citizenship and voting rights to free whites

Chinese Exclusion Act (1882)
- Suspended Chinese immigration
- Barred Chinese from naturalization
- Provided for deportation of Chinese who immigrated illegally

Immigration and Naturalization Act of 1924
- Imposed permanent numeric limit on immigration
- Established a quota system based on national origins

Immigration and Naturalization Act of 1952
- Continued national origins quotas

Immigration and Naturalization Act Amendments of 1965
- Repealed national origins quotas
- Set per-country limits and overall ceiling on number of immigrants from the Eastern Hemisphere
- Imposed ceiling on immigration from Western Hemisphere (for the first time)

Immigration and Naturalization Act Amendments of 1976
- Extended per-country limits to nations in Western Hemisphere

1996 Immigration Acts
- Increased patrols and barriers along U.S.–Mexico border
- Denied SSI and Food Stamps to documented immigrants
- Denied most public services to undocumented immigrants

Border Security, Economic Opportunity, and Immigration Modernization Act of 2013 (proposed)
- Provided a path to citizenship for undocumented immigrants
- Increased patrols and enforcement along U.S.–Mexico border

Prior to 1882, the United States had an open immigration policy. Anyone could relocate to this developing nation.[12] For over a century the nation has refined its immigration policy in pursuit of three stated goals: exclusion (excluding groups considered undesirable by the majority), economic advancement (promoting domestic economic interests), and humanitarian relief (providing a haven for the oppressed and permitting families to remain together). We will focus on economic advancement in Chapter 15. Here, let's consider policies that specifically target minority racial or ethnic groups. These are summarized in Table 10.1 and, as we will see, most (but not all) have served the goal of exclusion.

While provisions to exclude communists and homosexuals would come later, the nation's first immigration restrictions targeted the Chinese. As we have seen, the Chinese Exclusion Act of 1882 suspended immigration from that nation when Chinese laborers began to be widely perceived as a threat by American workers.

Later, the **Naturalization Act** of 1924 established a quota that favored immigrants from western and northern European nations. Based on the argument that immigrants from these nations were more readily assimilated, this act was actually designed to reduce immigration from southern and eastern Europe. But the quota system remained in effect until the 1970s and it served to restrict immigration by people of color throughout that period. Since then, the face of U.S. immigration has changed considerably, as we can see in Figure 10.5. During this half-century, the foreign-born population of the United States has shifted from a primarily European group to one largely composed of immigrants from Latin America and Asia. This is a direct result of the elimination of the national origins quota system (U.S. Census Bureau, 2012d).

---

[12]Of course, citizenship and voting rights were restricted. Under the Naturalization Acts of the late 1700s, only free whites could be citizens and only free white males could vote (Davis & Cloud-Two Dogs, 2004).

FIGURE 10.5 Origins of Foreign-Born Population, 1960 to 2007 (Percent Distribution by Region of Birth)

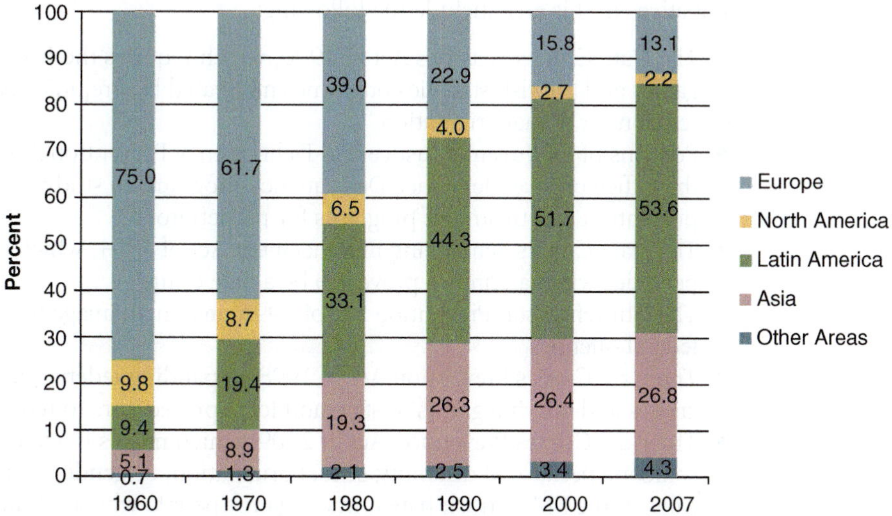

Source of Data: U.S. Census Bureau (2010). Race and Hispanic Origin of the Foreign-Born Population in the United States: 2007 (http://www.census.gov/prod/2010pubs/acs-11.pdf).

During the last 50 years the foreign-born population of the United States has increased, both in size and as a percentage of the total. In 1960, about one in 20 U.S. residents (a total of 9.6 million) was born in a different country; today, the 40 million foreign-born Americans make up about one in eight, or 13 percent of the total (U.S. Census Bureau, 2012c).

Immigrants from Mexico make up the largest share of foreign-born Americans, about 29 percent in 2010. During the late 20th and early 21st centuries, the largest group of immigrants came from Mexico. But since the Great Recession, annual arrivals of Asian immigrants have come to exceed those from Latin America and Mexico. This may reflect limited economic opportunities as well as hostility toward Hispanic immigrants that manifested in repeated attempts to restrict the flow of undocumented immigrants over the U.S.–Mexico border. Other signs of hostility include the English-only initiatives discussed later in this chapter and, of course, the success of Donald Trump's vitriolic Presidential campaign, which was marked by a promise to "build a wall" between Mexico and the United States.

LO 10-8   Analyze and Critique Hate Crime Legislation

EP 5c
EP 8d

In July 2013, jurors in a Florida court found George Zimmerman not guilty in the shooting death of 17-year-old Trayvon Martin, an unarmed African American. Relying on the 2009 expansion of federal jurisdiction over hate crimes described below, the U.S. Justice Department considered a second prosecution under federal hate crime statutes.

Under current federal law, crimes committed because of a person's membership in a protected group (based on race, ethnicity, religion, or national origin) can result in more severe penalties. These hate crimes are seen as more grievous than others because in addition to harming their immediate victims they instill fear in people with similar characteristics. Although a 1969 statute offered federal prosecution of crimes against racial, ethnic, or religious minorities engaged in federally protected activities (such as voting or attending public school), most federal legislation in this area dates to the 1990s. Federal initiatives in this area include the following:

- The Hate Crimes Statistics Act of 1990, which requires the Justice Department to gather and publish statistics on crimes motivated by prejudice based on race, ethnicity, religion, or sexual orientation
- Portions of the Juvenile Justice and Delinquency Prevention Act of 1992 directing the Office of Juvenile Justice Delinquency Programs to study hate crimes and develop prevention and treatment programs for perpetrators
- The Hate Crimes Sentencing Enhancement Act of 1994, which calls for increased penalties when a crime is proven to be a hate crime
- The Church Arson Prevention Act of 1996, making damage to religious property a federal offense
- The Hate Crimes Prevention Act of 1998, expanding federal jurisdiction to violent hate crimes and offering grants to state and local prosecutors to reduce hate crimes
- The Hate Crimes Prevention Act of 2009, which makes it a federal crime to attack someone because of disability, sexual orientation, or gender identity. The act also calls on the FBI to track hate crimes against people who are transgendered. It extends federal jurisdiction over hate crimes by dropping the requirement that the crime be committed while the victim is engaged in a federally protected activity. The constitutionality of this act has been challenged (for instance, in the case of *Glenn v. Holder*), but as of this writing it has not undergone review by the Supreme Court.

Nearly all states have passed hate crime statutes that mirror federal law, allowing harsher penalties for crimes targeting people based on their race, ethnicity, religion, or national origin. About half of the hate crime statutes at the state level include sexual orientation (see www.adl.org for a map of state hate crime provisions).

Hate crime legislation is controversial. Proponents argue that harsher sentences for hate crimes are fair because these crimes are more damaging than similar offenses not motivated by hate. They suggest that stiffer penalties may deter perpetrators. Opponents compare hate crimes to "thought" crimes, arguing that it is impossible to demonstrate reliably that a crime was motivated by hatred and that efforts to do so infringe on the right to freedom of speech (see Troy, 1998).

In the wake of the attacks of September 11, 2001, hate crimes against Americans who are (or are perceived to be) Islamic increased dramatically. The FBI reported that anti-Muslim hate crimes increased from 28 in 2000 to 481 in 2001 (Federal Bureau of Investigation, 2000, 2001). Human rights organizations documented thousands of incidents, ranging from murder to airport harassment and destruction of property. In a 2004 report, the Council on American-Islamic Relations (CAIR) reported increased harassment of people perceived to be Muslim, with a growing number of incidents involving government officials acting under the purview of the USA PATRIOT Act (CAIR, 2004).

The FBI issues a report each year called Hate Crime Statistics. The 2008 version revealed that most hate crimes reported that year were motivated by racial bias (51 percent); nearly one in five (19.5 percent) reflected a religious bias; 17 percent reflected sexual orientation bias; and 11.5 percent reflected a bias related to ethnicity or national origin. Roughly 1 percent involved bias against disability (Federal Bureau of Investigation, 2009). In 2013, the Department of Justice reported that hate crimes motivated by religious bias had increased considerably (Langton, Planty, & Sandholtz, 2013).

LO 10-9   Understand the Background and Impacts of English-Only Laws

EP 5c
EP 8d

English-only proposals surfaced as early as 1780, when John Adams proposed that the Continental Congress establish an official academy to "purify, develop, and dictate usage of English" (ACLU, 1996). His proposal was rejected as undemocratic. With the 1803 purchase of the Louisiana Territory, President Jefferson tried to impose an English-only policy on French speakers in that territory. The uproar from the territory led to a quick retreat, and Louisiana entered the Union in 1812 as the only state with a non-English-speaking majority (Kloss, 1998). The Californios (Spanish speakers who resided in California when it was conquered) were less successful. Although the state's constitution recognized Spanish language rights and guaranteed bilingual publication of state laws, the following year saw the Gold Rush. Spanish speakers became a minority, and "greaser laws" were passed to harass them (Leibowitz, 1969). "English only" became the law of the land in the new state of California. Finally, the forced assimilation of Native Americans into the English-only world involved taking Native American children to boarding schools far from home, where they were punished for speaking their own language.[13]

The English-only movement resurfaced in the 1980s, with proponents arguing that the English language needed legislative protection from the encroachment of other tongues and that "creeping bilingualism" threatened the very foundations of American culture. Legislation was advanced at the federal and state levels to restrict the use of other languages for government business.

Proponents of official English are generally political conservatives—the same people who favor immigration restrictions and would deny services to legal immigrants. In the early 1980s, a constitutional amendment was proposed that would have banned the use of languages other than English by federal, state, and local governments. It never reached a vote. Later, in 1994, Republican leadership in the House of Representatives passed a measure that prohibited the use of languages other than English by the federal government. Threatened with a presidential veto, the measure died without Senate action (Crawford, 1992). Since then there have been several unsuccessful attempts to pass federal English-only statutes. English-only proponents have been more successful at passing state legislation, and as of this writing, official English requirements have been established in most states.

Proponents of English-only legislation offer several arguments. First, they suggest that bilingual education delays or prevents acquisition of English by immigrants. They assert that immigrants today, unlike those of the past, refuse to learn English and insist on government-sponsored bilingual programs. Second, they argue that the United States is at risk of becoming balkanized (divided into smaller, often hostile units) like Quebec or India. Idaho Senator Steve Symms introduced an English-only amendment to the U.S. Constitution, arguing that "countless hundreds of thousands have lost their lives in the language riots of India. Real potential exists for a similar situation in the United States" (Crawford, 1992, p. 395). Finally, proponents suggest that English is a "common bond" holding Americans of diverse backgrounds together.

None of these arguments is based on evidence, and most are designed to appeal to anti-immigrant and racist feelings. Educational studies consistently demonstrate that non-English-speaking students do better in school and learn English more quickly in bilingual or structured English immersion classrooms (Ramirez, Yuen, & Ramey, 1991).

---

[13]English-only efforts were also initiated in the U.S. territories of Puerto Rico and Guam. Less successful in Puerto Rico, these policies nearly eradicated the indigenous language of Guam.

BOX 10.7   Navajo Code Talkers, World War II

In a vivid illustration of the benefits of language diversity, Navajo Marines during World War II used their language for top-secret communications. It was the only code the enemy was unable to break. The Navajo Code Talkers took part in every assault by the U.S. Marines between 1942 and 1945. They are recognized in a permanent exhibit on the Pentagon Concourse. The 1990 Native American Languages Act (PL 101-477) recognized the right of indigenous peoples to use their native languages as mediums of commerce and instruction. Native Americans speak 250 different tribal languages and for many, English is a second language.

There is no evidence of language-based political organization (aside from the English-only movement) in the United States. Finally, national pride in the United States tends to be more strongly associated with ideals such as individual freedom and achievement than with the English language. As James Crawford, who has studied the English-only movement for a decade, notes, "English-only arguments are so value-laden in their distaste for diversity, so crude in their analogies with other nations, so credulous about the power of social engineering, and so bereft of factual evidence that they are difficult to take seriously" (Crawford, 1996, p. 4).

Millions of Americans do take these arguments seriously, however. Scholars differ on the reasons for this phenomenon. Some argue that the movement attracts people with racial prejudices and anxieties about cultural change (see Schmid, 1992). Others suggest that support for English-only legislation reflects an upsurge in national pride (see Citrin et al., 1990).

The effects of English-only legislation vary, depending on whether the laws simply declare English the official language or bar the use of other languages. The official declaration of the prominence of English has had little practical effect, but some legislation passed by the states has banned bilingual ballots and bilingual instruction in public schools, some cities have passed ordinances prohibiting the use of other languages in private signs, and some have eliminated the use of courtroom translation. All of these practices have made life more difficult for Americans for whom English is a second language (ACLU, 1996).

LO 10-10 Describe the Differential Impact of Standardized Testing on People of Color

EP 3a
EP 8d

On the surface, standardized tests appear race-neutral. Designed to measure general aptitude, most are not used to promote discrimination. But the consequences of standardized testing consistently operate against people of color.

The intelligence tests used today are based on the Stanford-Binet test, which emerged during the heyday of the "eugenics movement." This movement advanced the view that high intelligence, like other desirable traits, was genetically based and less present in "inferior" races. The creator of the Stanford-Binet test, Lewis Terman, used it to support the notion that northern Europeans were superior to other races. He argued that high scores were correlated with moral behavior and that higher IQs explained the economic dominance of northern Europeans.

Employment testing was used during the 1960s in hiring and promotion decisions. In addition to measuring proficiency in specific skills, these tests often purported to measure general aptitude or intelligence. Because of limited educational opportunities, people of color did poorly on the tests. When the "intent" of the testing process was examined, the process appeared race-neutral; however, the "consequences" of the testing were disadvantageous to racial minorities. In 1966, the Equal Employment Opportunity Commission (EEOC) issued guidelines stipulating that tests with these consequences were in violation of Title VII of the 1964 Civil Rights Act unless the employer could demonstrate that they accurately predicted job performance.

LO 10-11   Become Aware of Factors That Can Interfere with the Voting Rights of Americans of Color

EP 3a
EP 8d

Although few would directly question an American's right to vote, recent decades have seen the passage of restrictions that effectively disenfranchise people of color. The 2013 Supreme Court decision in **Shelby County v. Holder** brought the issue of voting rights to the fore. In it, a 5-4 majority overturned a key section of the 1965 Voting Rights Act.

Recall that long after the Civil War southern states used a range of tactics to keep African Americans from voting. These ranged from poll taxes and literacy tests to physical threats and intimidation. In response, the Voting Rights Act required that jurisdictions with a history of racial discrimination (as determined by a formula that assessed the use of literacy tests and records of low voter registration and turnout by minorities) submit any proposed changes in voting laws to the Justice Department for preclearance. Nine states (most in the South) and parts of seven more states were subject to preclearance. In this process the onus was on the states to demonstrate that the changes would not interfere with the rights of minority voters.

Although the Court's majority did not overturn the process of preclearance itself, it ruled that the formula approved by Congress in 2009 was out of date. Thus, congressional action to revise the formula would be required before preclearance could once again take effect.

In her dissenting opinion, Justice Ginsberg acknowledged that "first-generation barriers to minority voting rights" such as poll taxes and literacy tests had been eliminated, but she warned against "second-generation barriers." Ginsberg cited numerous examples of discriminatory practices that were corrected or prohibited through the preclearance process. One occurred in Kilmichael, Mississippi, where the mayor and all-white city council decided to cancel the 2001 local elections after a large number of African Americans declared their candidacy for office. The Justice Department intervened, and the town elected its first African American mayor (Supreme Court, 2013c).

Other "second-generation" practices include redistricting that eliminates voting districts with a majority of African American or Latino voters, moving polling places out of minority neighborhoods, eliminating the option of early voting, and establishing complex or duplicative registration requirements. There is evidence that laws requiring voters to produce identification at the polling place may reduce turnout among people of color (de Alth, 2011). Nonetheless, these voter ID laws are generally popular with the voting public and have been passed in several states.

In a practice known as "felony disenfranchisement," nearly 6 million Americans have lost their right to vote due to felony convictions (Sentencing Project, 2012). Indeed, several states *permanently* deny the right to vote to anyone convicted of a felony, although some have devised complex procedures through which the right can be restored. Given racial disparities in rates of arrest, conviction, and sentencing, people of color are disproportionately represented among the disenfranchised. In Florida, for instance, the Sentencing Project reported that nearly a quarter (23 percent) of African Americans of voting age cannot legally vote. The practice of felony disenfranchisement was held constitutional by the Supreme Court in the 1974 case of *Richardson v. Ramirez* (Brennan Center, n.d.).

Closing Reflections

Race and ethnicity have long been fault lines in American society and, as we have seen, racial discrimination leaves many people of color at a disadvantage. Yet over the past few decades, and particularly during the economic boom of the 1990s, many people of color moved into the middle class. This was a significant accomplishment, both for the United States as a whole and for the individuals involved.

But economic advancement divides ethnic communities along class lines, fueling arguments that people of color who are not economically successful are personally flawed. Some people of color, frequently second- and third-generation members of successful families, have become vocal opponents of public income supports and affirmative action (see, for example, Linda Chavez's 1991 work, *Out of the Barrio,* or comments by Justice Clarence Thomas). They argue, in essence, "If I could make it, so can you." This raises concern that the coming years may see less cohesiveness within racial and ethnic communities as they fracture along class lines.

America is on the verge of being a "minority majority" nation. Apart from the semantic challenge of retraining ourselves not to refer to people of color as "minorities," this demographic change is reshaping the political dynamics of the nation. The reelection of President Obama in 2012 was widely attributed to his success in attracting Latino voters, and pressure to establish a pathway to citizenship for undocumented immigrants stems in part from this new reality. Some will no doubt find the politics of a minority-majority America disconcerting (to say the least). Let us hope that social workers will enter this new arena well prepared to advance the interests of our clients and our profession.

Think About It

1. Use the history of racial oppression in the United States to evaluate the major theories of racism discussed in this chapter. Does history support the idea that racism is the result of ignorance or of market competition? What do you see as the roots of racism? Do you think racism will be eliminated in your lifetime?

2. Do you think past injustices (such as the internment of the Japanese during World War II) entitle people to some kind of remedy? Is an apology in order? Economic reparation? To whom is it due? Should descendants of former slaves receive some kind of reparation? Why or why not?

3. Do you think a class-based society is more or less fair than one in which race is the basis of social allocations?

Web-Based Exercises

For direct links to all the sites in these exercises, visit the *Foundations of Social Policy* Companion Site at www.cengagebrain.com and select the resources for Chapter 10.

1. Go to the website of the Southern Poverty Law Center (www.splcenter.org). Click on the "What We Do" tab to read about the center's activities. Consider recent developments in the SPL's battle against hate groups, and the center's work on behalf of immigrants.

2. Go to the website of the U.S. Census Bureau (www.census.gov). Click on "Poverty" (under "People and Households," which is located at the bottom of the page); then

click on the "Data" tab near the top of the page. Under "Current Population Survey, Annual Social and Economic Supplement (CPS ASEC)" you will find "Historical Tables." On the "Historical Poverty Tables" page you will find a wealth of information. Click on "People" for Table 2: "Poverty Status, by Family Relationship, Race, and Hispanic Origin," which presents trends in poverty rates by race from 1959 to the most recent year available. With this table, you can compare the most recent racial differences in poverty with past disparities. Have conditions improved or deteriorated?

3. Go to the Advancement Project's voter protection map (http://www.advancement-project.org/map) and check on voter ID requirements in your state. Do you think these requirements affected the results of any recent elections?

4. Go to the Sentencing Project website (www.sentencingproject.org) and check on felony disenfranchisement in your state. Do any residents permanently lose the right to vote based on felony offenses? How would a person in this situation go about restoring this right?

Competency Notes

As mentioned in the preface to this text, the Council on Social Work Education has designated nine core competencies and related practice behaviors that must be addressed by accredited social work programs. In these notes, I will specify the way chapter content addresses these competencies and behaviors. (This is designed to assist with the accreditation process.) Please refer to the "helping hands" icons for the locations of specific content in this chapter. Here you will find a brief explanation of how the accompanying content relates to the specified competency or practice behaviors. The following list indicates where EPAS competencies and practice behaviors are addressed in this chapter.

EP 2a   **Apply and communicate understanding of the importance of diversity and difference in shaping life experiences in practice at the micro, mezzo, and macro levels.** The chapter treats race as a social construct and examines the role of race in shaping opportunities and experiences at micro, mezzo, and macro levels. It also emphasizes the increasing diversity of the U.S. population.

EP 3a   **Apply their understanding of social, economic, and environmental justice to advocate for human rights at the individual and system levels.** Knowledge of the range of contemporary issues that affect can inform students' human rights advocacy at both individual and system levels. In addition, this chapter reveals the role of social values and structures (particularly government) in maintaining privilege.

EP 5c   **Apply critical thinking to analyze, formulate, and advocate for policies that advance human rights and social, economic, and environmental justice.** The chapter addresses the construction of racism, as well as its implications. This, in addition to an understanding of the history of policies affecting people of color in the United States will inform students' analysis of contemporary policies.

EP 8d   **Negotiate, mediate, and advocate with and on the behalf of diverse clients and constituencies.** Issues that call for effective advocacy are described, including immigration, the English-only movement, hate crime legislation, and use of standardized testing.

Suggested Resources

Davis, K. E., & Bent-Goodley, T. B. (2004). *The Color of Social Policy*. Alexandria, VA: Council on Social Work Education.

Jones, J. (2013). *A Dreadful Deceit: The Myth of Race from the Colonial Era to Obama's America*. New York: Basic Books.

Kaplan, H. R. (2011). *The Myth of Post-Racial America: Searching for Equality in the Age of Materialism*. New York: Rowman & Littlefield.

Kotkin, J. (2010). *The Next Hundred Million: America in 2050*. New York: Penguin Press.

Resendez, A. (2016). *The Other Slavery: The uncovered story of Indian enslavement in America*. Boston: Houghton Mifflin Harcourt.

Takaki, R. (2008). *A Different Mirror: A History of Multicultural America*. Boston: Back Bay Books.

Wilson, C. A. (1996). *Racism: From Slavery to Advanced Capitalism*. Thousand Oaks, CA: Sage.

www.airpi.org. The American Indian Policy Center is a nonprofit organization that was founded in 1992 for the purposes of research, policy development, and education on Native American issues. The site offers some outstanding policy papers written from a Native American perspective.

www.bia.gov. This is the official website of the Bureau of Indian Affairs, which is part of the Department of the Interior. It offers some useful background information, written from what some might consider a defensive posture.

www.Kirwaninstitute.osu.edu. Sponsored by Ohio State University, this site includes state-of-the-art information on implicit bias.

www.naacp.org. The National Association for the Advancement of Colored People describes itself as the nation's "largest and strongest civil rights organization." The NAACP's site offers information about the organization, as well as news briefs and access to their magazine, *Crisis*.

www.splcenter.org. The Southern Poverty Law Center is a nonprofit organization whose mission is to "combat hate, intolerance and discrimination through education and litigation." At the site, you will find information on current events and projects, "intelligence reports" on hate groups in the United States, and educational material for teaching tolerance.

11

Gay, Lesbian, Bisexual, and Trans Individuals

I will scatter myself among men and women as I go.
I will toss a new gladness and roughness among them,
Whoever denies me, it shall not trouble me,
Whoever accepts me, he or she shall be blessed, and shall bless me.
WALT WHITMAN, "SONG OF THE OPEN ROAD"

Learning Objectives

This chapter will help prepare students to:

LO 11-1 Know how our understandings of sexual orientation and gender have evolved

LO 11-2 Become familiar with the history of policies that affect families of GLBT individuals

LO 11-3 Become aware of the history and current status of legislation governing discrimination against GLBT individuals

LO 11-4 Know the history of anti-GLBT violence and hate crime legislation in the United States

LO 11-5 Understand the impact of HIV/AIDS on the GLBT community and social policy measures to address the epidemic

LO 11-6 Become aware of recent developments in policy related to GLBT individuals

LO 11-7 Understand the issues affecting GLBT individuals from a social justice perspective that recognizes the role and responsibilities of social workers

The struggle for equal rights for GLBT (gay, lesbian, bisexual, or trans) Americans came to public awareness in 1969, when New York City police raided a gay bar (Stonewall Inn) in Greenwich Village. The ensuing rebellion marked the beginning of the gay rights movement. Since that time, most Americans have seen television coverage of annual gay pride parades held in major cities throughout the country. These parades support a view of GLBT Americans as colorful figures in the national landscape. Such images can obscure the realities experienced by Americans who are GLBT, which can include violence, employment discrimination, lack of health benefits, and legal barriers to family formation.

A HUMAN PERSPECTIVE   Mike Dixon

Born during the early 1950s in northern California, Mike has known he was gay since the age of 8 or 9. He said, "I always felt 'different' from other kids, but I didn't really have a word for it. I did know that I shouldn't talk about it with anyone, and so I just kept whatever it was to myself." He has a vivid memory of the moment he realized he was gay. "I looked down and saw this older kid. He was swimming and only had shorts on. I got this overwhelming urge to grab him around the middle and hug him…. From that point on, I realized that I wasn't like the other boys I knew, but I didn't dare say why— even to myself."

Life in elementary school was rugged. Mike hated team sports, gym, and recess. Recess was especially awful "because that is when I would routinely get beat up by the bullies in school." But he loved working with his father and uncle in their heating business. "I used to go to work with them when I was a kid. I really loved doing this, and especially loved getting to 'do something' like rolling out pipe, soldering, digging holes for water pipes."

Mike said "things were a little better" when he got to high school. "The teachers were more intelligent, and I didn't feel like I was going to be picked on all the time … there were other kids like me—sort of brainy and withdrawn —and we hung out together." Still, he "got into drugs" in high school and nearly flunked out. Teachers identified him as an "underachiever," and eventually he graduated with a low C average. His sexual identity was not an important issue during high school. "I never had sex with anyone while I was in high school. I never even really thought about it. It never dawned on me that I could actually act on my desires—it was a hetero world, but even that was something that was taken for granted, and I didn't question why it was so." In retrospect, Mike said, "I have to say that I thought high school was a waste. I hated that place, and the conformist attitudes they tried to shove down my throat."

Mike graduated in 1968. After leaving home to attend college, he came out "to myself and a few other people I knew. I never came out formally to my parents." He felt that his mother "got it" without being told, but she never said anything. He said, "My father was kind of oblivious, and it turned out that he was completely cool about it when I came out to him around 1979, after my mother died." Mike's father liked all of his boyfriends and took care to include them in invitations and celebrations. Of his only sibling Mike said, "I came out to my sister around this time, and she didn't give a shit." Later his sister told him she resented his lifestyle, "like being queer

was about partying, spending money, and having a good time."

During college, Mike "met this guy in a class" and they moved in together. They didn't really consider themselves a "couple" because they were so different. "He was a real political hippie and I was a sort of brain-nerd-sass-ass-intellectual." Still, he had "a pretty good life for an 18-year-old," and they found jobs in a printing plant. Mike worked there for almost nine years, putting himself through college.

Mike enjoyed college. "I really liked the atmosphere of college and was far more interested in what was going on in class and in talking to the people I met there." But the prospect of being drafted and sent to Vietnam threw a shadow over this period of his life. When his deferment was changed and Mike received a new draft card, he had a horrible fight with his parents. He told them he planned to go to Canada if he was called to Vietnam, and "[t]hey did not understand that I didn't think it was my 'duty' to go off and get killed in Johnson's war. That was a confusing, almost psychotic time in my life. I went to work four nights per week, studied like mad so I wouldn't get kicked out of school, and just prayed that the draft board didn't call me."

Time passed, and the draft was replaced by the lottery. Mike's number was 332. "That did it," he said, "I was free!" He graduated the next year and moved to Holland with a friend he had met in school. The year in Holland was great. "We lived in Delft, I learned Dutch, and just spent all day hanging out and drawing pictures of old buildings. I lived on my 'retirement' check—some paltry union pension rebate—that they gave me when I quit the printing company." Then Mike got a call that his mother was dying. He flew back, and "she was dead within a week."

Mike stayed in the United States and enrolled to do graduate work in art. Here he met his first serious boyfriend. It was "… this kid in one of my drawing classes … we had a torrid affair that lasted about nine months … then he left me for a younger guy…. I was devastated. I spent the next year in an alcoholic isolation that only snapped when I got arrested for drunk driving … that sort of shocked me out of my swoon, but I never forgot that kid for ten years." Mike got into therapy, an experience that changed his life and his outlook on himself.

Nonetheless, he said, "I think I was still in love with him [first boyfriend] when I moved in with my 'second' boyfriend, after I moved to San Francisco in 1980." He met "Bob" through a mutual friend, and they hit it off right away. "He had this idea that we should start a catering company—I was a good cook, and he had worked in hotels and knew the business, somewhat. We borrowed $5,000 from a friend, bought a used van and a couple of cases of cocktail glasses, had some cards printed at my old printing company, and we were in business.... We moved in together in 1981 and worked like dogs until he died in 1990."

The business was successful. "We had the reputation of being one of the top five caterers in San Francisco, and we did it at the right time (the '80s) when people were spending money like it was water. We bought a huge house in the East Bay, with a pool. We went to Europe twice, went on long trips to New England and the South, went to Hawaii every winter for three weeks, and generally lived as if there were no tomorrow."

But Mike's partner had AIDS. "When I think back on it, he must have had AIDS when we met. Then, in about 1985, he started to get opportunistic infections. He got weaker and weaker, until finally he could not get out of bed without help. I kept the business together through his illness, and when I got a call during some job that he was not expected to make it through the night, I went and sat with him until he died. I went to Hawaii with his ashes … then I came back home. I put the house up for sale, sold the catering business, and just withdrew again."

Mike described the impact of AIDS on the San Francisco gay community: "During this time about every male I knew died. I went to eight or ten 'memorials' (funerals were considered un-PC) during that year-and-a-half period. It was one a month for a while. I kept thinking, 'I'm next,' but kept testing negative. One after another, everyone I knew died of AIDS. That period in San Francisco gay history is famous now—people started calling it the Plague, but that seemed too lighthearted, somehow. It was just awful. Everyone anyone knew was dying these hideous deaths. The gay community was trying to mobilize, but there was not a lot of organization. We were all grieving—no one's story was any more heart-breaking than anyone else's. We were all wrecks. Most people I knew got through a few deaths, and then they died themselves. Mayor Feinstein came and spoke at Bob's funeral. They were business friends, and she couldn't believe that 'even Bob' would die. Straights just didn't get it. They seemed to just be unable to conceive of how huge it was, and of what it felt like to have your whole world die grisly deaths with only medical help and no social support other than that which we gave to one another. When we catered cocktail parties and dinners, I would overhear well-heeled straights saying things like, 'We have to do something about this! Pretty soon we are all going to get it if we aren't careful.' Little did they know—if some of those ladies knew what we knew about their husbands and sons, they would have been a little more respectful, I think."

After three years of "onslaught," Mike decided to move to the South with a friend, Tom. They bought a Civil-War-era house in Tarboro, North Carolina, where, as Mike said, "We experienced no discrimination … in fact, it was the opposite. We got along with everyone, and even did some cooking—I wouldn't call it catering—around town. We knew everyone, and our house was a sort of central meeting place because it was right in the middle of town." Then, in 1995, Tom got really sick. "He knew what it was all about, and having seen dozens of his friends get sick too, he decided to forgo treatment and just let things 'take their course.' He was dead in two months, of acute sepsis and an encephalitic HIV infection. In other words, he went crazy, and then died of blood poisoning."

When Mike met his current partner through mutual friends in 1996, it was "love at first sight … we had everything in common except our age—he is ten years younger than me. He and I felt like we had found the people we had been looking for all along. We still feel this way and never get tired of each other's company. We are in love with each other, and that has a way of making the past make sense. I certainly don't regret a second of my past, and if our relationship now is the result of all that living I did, then it was well worth the wait. I cannot imagine being so lucky as to be living with someone so wonderful in such a mutually complementary way. Believe it or not, we have never had a major fight, nor have we ever even had a negatively charged emotional exchange."

Rather than oppressed or victimized, Mike feels that gay men are lucky and enjoy tremendous freedom. "I think society expects little of us, as a group. We don't have that onus of having to have kids if we don't want it, and we aren't expected to join that work-and-spend cycle that most heterosexual families are in. There is little outside pressure on our family—of the two of us and two dogs. We live our lives, pay our taxes, and take care of the yard. The cars are in good repair, and once in a while we go on vacation to some nice place. We cook our own food, clean our own house, and maintain pretty good relationships with our neighbors."

He can cite very few experiences of discrimination. Once, after they knew Bob had AIDS, he and Bob applied for health insurance. "We knew he had AIDS, but the world hadn't caught up with the idea that it was truly a fatal disease. We applied for a small business policy, and they came over and interviewed us. The agent got it right away that we were a 'couple,' and they turned down the application with no explanation. I called and asked them

(continued)

A HUMAN PERSPECTIVE   Mike Dixon (*Continued*)

why, and they gave me some gobbledygook about being too small a business. I called the state office of consumer affairs, described the situation, and asked for their advice. They said that we were definitely discriminated against—in the city of San Francisco, insurance companies were not allowed to discriminate on the basis of sexual orientation, even then—but they said that we would have an almost impossible time proving it. They knew that insurance companies were trying to weasel out of policies they had already written to gay businesses because of the fear of AIDS claims, and there wasn't anything they were willing to do about it."

Discrimination has not been an important influence in Mike's life. "I have bought and sold houses, lived in a small southern town, lived in a conservative suburb in the East Bay, traveled all over the place with other men—in short, done everything everyone else does, and I have never felt discriminated against personally."

In his late forties, Mike decided to pursue a career in social work because, as he puts it, "It is one of the very few things we can do for each other that truly makes a difference in our lives—both the social worker's and the client's." In the MSW program he had what he describes as his first real experiences of feeling discriminated against. He said that "judgmental marginalization would be a better way to put it." In one class, a fellow MSW student announced that he would have trouble working with gay men "because that would be like asking me to work with child molesters or rapists." Mike said he couldn't believe his ears. When the school administration did not respond appropriately, Mike took matters in his own hands. "I confronted the student later, and we had a meeting of the minds. In short, I told him that if he and his buddies made it uncomfortable for me in class, I was going to get an attorney and make it very uncomfortable for them and the school … that ended it."

His advice to a GLBTQ person dealing with discrimination is simple: "Get a lawyer. Even though we don't have the law on our side, the public humiliation of having everyone know that you bash fags is probably enough of a deterrent in this day and age. … I would tell them not to bother with the 'let's get together and talk about this' routine. Bigotry is bigotry and ought to be dealt with accordingly. You can be friends after you have a level playing field. For homosexuals the field is never level. We are a particularly hated minority, and it is an uphill battle … better to get the big guns right away and save yourself the trouble of mediation in a world that does not really count you as a whole person anyway."

Possibly as an aftereffect of the trauma of the AIDS epidemic, Mike feels that the "mainstream" gay community is attempting to "normalize" their experience. "It is as if they are saying, 'We're just like you, but with this one tiny difference'. Neither Peter nor I believe that. We believe that we are not like the rest of the American culture—we are very different from it."

He believes homophobia is inevitable, and he attributes it in part to individuals' lack of clarity about their own sexuality and groups' need to define themselves as "right" by defining others as "wrong." His critique of social work education is biting: "Day after day, we tackle heterosexual family problems, heterosexual child problems, and heterosexual individual problems. All the intervention models seem to be constructed around heterosexual ideals and thinking. The sexual orientation angle has just been completely ignored. It is conservatively estimated that 8 to 10 percent of the population is lesbian, gay, or mostly homosexually oriented bisexual … this is a huge minority. The 'out' representatives are perhaps less than a quarter of that—maybe 2 to 3 percent at most. This minority crosses all ethnic, cultural, and racial lines—it is a minority of everyone. Certain occupations and avocations have a larger-than-average representation of homosexuals. I think social work is one of them." Mike says he "cannot envision a day when I, and those who come after me, will feel the real freedom of not being hated by someone—not for anything I have done or said, but simply because of who I am."

For a long time, Mike and his partner felt that the absence of marriage equality was not a significant issue. As Mike explained, "Who would want any authority regulating their material life, let alone their emotional life? We are together because we love each other, not because a state or a church has sanctioned our commitment. We are two men who choose to unite, and we are not trying to 'be like' the straight world because we are not straight." But when I ran into them at a marriage equality celebration in June 2013, Mike told me they had just married and were utterly thrilled—not to emulate the straight world—but to celebrate their own unique commitment.

A SOCIAL WORK PERSPECTIVE

Mike's life underscores the uniqueness of human experience and the difficulty of making broad generalizations about the homosexual population. As a member of the gay community of San Francisco, Mike experienced the overwhelming grief of the HIV/AIDS epidemic. He drew strength and creativity from that experience, even as it brought repeated personal losses. Mike's experiences with the AIDS pandemic were shared by many GLBT Americans of his generation.

A self-professed libertarian, Mike asks only that public policy not intrude on his personal life. For him, experiences of discrimination and laws that declare his lifestyle unacceptable have little relevance. Yet, as Mike readily acknowledges, these laws have a much different impact on members of the gay and lesbian communities who are attempting to raise children. Mike sees hatred of homosexuality as inevitable and expects little from public policies that strive to eliminate it.

But in some ways Mike's experiences are unique to his race and gender. As a white male, he has had access to privileges and resources unavailable to women and people of color. For many—particularly women of color who identify as lesbian or trans—experiences of discrimination are intensified by multiple jeopardies.

LO 11-1   Know How Our Understandings of Sexual Orientation and Gender Have Evolved

EP 5c

Western notions of sexual orientation and gender have changed considerably. As we will see, **same-sex attraction** has long been part of human experience, but it has only been a defining aspect of identity since the 19th century. On the other hand, our understanding of gender—long seen as a stable binary and widely considered central to identity—has shifted in recent decades.

SEXUAL ORIENTATION

Attraction between members of the same gender has probably always been part of human sexuality. Homosexual activity, particularly among men in ancient times, is well documented, and cultures have had a wide range of responses to same-sex attraction.

Homosexuality has been variously defined as "sin," "psychopathology," "preference," and "orientation." The term was first applied in the mid-19th century by Viennese author Karoly Maria Benkert to refer to the "Uranians" described by Karl Heinrich Ulrichs, a biologist in Hanover, Germany. Fascinated by findings of androgyny in early stages of human embryonic development, he concluded that homosexual attraction had congenital roots and identified what he called a "third sex" consisting of people who experienced same-sex attraction. In 1864, Ulrichs issued a pamphlet (using a pen name) that called for **legalization** of same-sex marriage (Greenberg, 1988).

Understanding the causes of same-sex attraction has considerable influence on public attitudes and social policy. Ulrichs's tolerant views stemmed from his belief that homosexuality was an inborn trait and that people who couldn't help being attracted to same-sex partners should not be punished. Under this view, children (and other innocents) cannot be "converted" to homosexuality. The fear that children will be corrupted by exposure to homosexuals is frequently used in persecution campaigns. Advocates of more tolerant public policies generally adhere to the notion that homosexuality is an inborn trait rather than an acquired characteristic.

Freud explained same-sex attraction in psychological rather than biological terms, locating its origins in early childhood experiences (Osborne, 1993). By attributing same-sex attraction to parenting, Freud helped expand the stigma associated with homosexuality in Victorian times to include parents and families. Further developments in psychiatric theory would result in homosexuality being treated as a psychopathology. This view was

Despite widespread public opposition to same-sex relationships, in 1996 South Africa became the first nation to
prohibit discrimination on the basis of sexual orientation
in its constitution. As a result, the nation now permits
same-sex marriage and protects gay and lesbian citizens from discrimination in employment. South African
Bishop and Nobel Laureate Desmond Tutu has spoken
ardently in support of equal rights for homosexuals.

pivotal in the persecution of homosexuals, particularly by the U.S. Immigration and Naturalization Service. It persisted for decades, waning only with the 1973 decision by the
American Psychiatric Association to remove homosexuality from its *Diagnostic and Statistical Manual*.

Contemporary theories of same-sex attraction incorporate aspects of **biological determinism**, childhood experiences, and culture. Recent biological studies have
identified possible genetic precursors (see Murphy, 2005) and described embryonic
developments associated with trans identity (see Qazy, 2006). Psychological theorists
have focused on childhood experiences and young-adult socialization (see Friedman
& Downey, 2002). Others have pursued an integrative approach, arguing for the
interaction of biology, culture, and individual development (see Frank, 2007). Meanwhile, advocates of both gay rights and gay persecution continue to base at least part
of their rhetoric on categorical (frequently inaccurate) statements about the causes of
homosexuality.

Ultimately, the causes of same-sex attraction and trans identity are irrelevant to the
case for equal rights. Persecution of individuals on the basis of any aspect of personal
identity (gender identity, race, religion, or sexual orientation) is antithetical to democratic
values, to the guarantees of the U.S. Constitution, and to the international understanding
of human rights.

GENDER

Americans' views on **sexual orientation** have changed dramatically during the past 50
years. So, too, have our notions of gender and gender identity. Broadly speaking, we can
identify three ways to understand gender: gender essentialism, sexual identity theories,
and postmodern theories of gender.

An essentialist view treats gender as a binary concept (male versus female) that is
dictated by nature. Under this view, male and female gender roles and gender expressions
stem directly from this simple biological reality. Deviation from traditional gender expression is seen as abnormal or unnatural.

When sexual identity is placed at the forefront, people are seen as having a stable
identity based on three components: sex, gender, and sexual orientation. Here, "sex" refers
to physiology, the biological manifestation of a person's genetic and hormonal arrangement. "Gender" refers to feelings and behaviors. These include "gender identity" (the
internal sense of who we are), "**gender expression**" (the way we communicate gender
identity, such as through clothing, hair styles, or mannerisms), and "**gender role**" (cultural

expectations of how we interact with others). Finally, "sexual orientation" refers to the interaction between our gender identity and the people we find attractive (homosexual, heterosexual, asexual, pansexual, and so on).

Postmodern theories of gender, espoused in particular by Judith Butler, reject both the **binary** treatment of gender and the notion of a stable identity. Under this view, categorizing bodies as male or female supports an archaic social construct. Likewise, gender and sexual identities are seen as fluid over the course of a lifetime. Rejection of the gender binary opens up the possibility of interacting with people as unique individuals, even as it frees everyone to express themselves as they choose (Butler, 2004).

Of course, most U.S. policies are based on the binary view of gender (male versus female), although recognition of a variety of possible identities is seen in some antidiscrimination statutes. Postmodern theories may be reflected in the policies of the future as they call on society and social policy to "get beyond" gender.

A SEXUAL MINORITY

GLBT individuals are clearly a minority in the United States. Mike mentioned a widely used estimate that gay and lesbian men and women constitute 8 to 10 percent of the U.S. population. This figure probably comes from two Kinsey reports, *Sexual Behavior in the Human Male* (Kinsey, Pomeroy, & Martin, 1948) and *Sexual Behavior in the Human Female* (Kinsey et al., 1953). Based on his studies, Alfred C. Kinsey estimated that 13 percent of men and 7 percent of women engaged in sex primarily with same-gender partners for part of their lives. He went on to estimate that about 4 percent of men were exclusively homosexual throughout their lives. Although Kinsey's methods have been questioned (his study surveyed only volunteers and did not have a random sample), his figures were later duplicated in other studies (see Barnett, 1973; Michael et al., 1994).

Nonetheless, it is difficult to estimate the number of people who identify as **gay**, **lesbian**, **bisexual**, **trans**, or **queer**. In 1992, Michael and colleagues surveyed a random sample of Americans about their sexual behavior. With a response rate above 80 percent, this is probably (as they claim) the most recent definitive study of the topic. Their results varied, depending on whether attraction, behavior, or identity was considered. About 6 percent of men in this study said they were attracted to other men; about 5 percent said they had had sex with another man since turning 18; and about 3 percent of men said they considered themselves homosexual or bisexual. Similarly, about 10 percent of women said they were attracted to other women; about 4 percent said they had had sex with another woman after age 18; and about 1.4 percent of women said they thought of themselves as homosexual or bisexual (Michael et al., 1994).

Census data do provide some indication of the number of people who live in same-sex couple households. In 1990, the response "unmarried partner" was added to the relationship item in recognition of the growing number of couples who live together without getting married. From 2005 on, the American Community Survey enumerated same-sex households in the United States. Estimates based on 2014 data indicated 783,100 same-sex couple households in the United States, among whom 43 percent were married and a slight majority (52 percent) were households of women (U.S. Census Bureau, 2015c). Further details are presented in Figure 11.1 (U.S. Census Bureau, n.d.a).

FIGURE 11.1 Same-Sex Couple Households in the United States, 2014

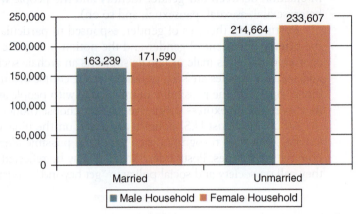

Source: U.S. Census Bureau (n.d.). *American Community Survey Data on Same Sex Couples* (http://www.census.gov/hhes/samesex/data/acs.html, accessed October 20, 2016).

LO 11-2   Become Familiar with the History of Policies That Affect Families of GLBT Individuals

EP 3a
EP 5c

In some ways the history of policies affecting GLBT Americans parallels the civil rights movement. In both cases government authorities have at times served as agents of oppression; in both cases, the rights of a minority have weighed against the opinions of the majority; and in both cases the courts have played an important and controversial role. Here we will consider policies related to sodomy, marriage, and family formation.

Perhaps due to our Puritan heritage, sexual practices and diverse approaches to family formation have been divisive in the United States. This is certainly true of policies that affect the GLBT population.

SODOMY

Sodomy laws specifically forbade some physical expressions of affection between people of the same sex, even in the privacy of their own homes. The nation's first sodomy law was enacted in Virginia in 1610 and carried the death penalty (Galas, 1996). Only 50 years ago, every state in the Union had sodomy laws on its books. Some states still have such laws, even though they were declared unconstitutional by the Supreme Court.

In 1986, sodomy laws were challenged in the *Bowers v. Hardwick* case. Michael Hardwick was arrested on sodomy charges after police entered his house to serve a warrant for not paying a fine for drinking in public. Another tenant let the police in, and they found him in bed with another man. Hardwick was convicted of sodomy and jailed. His lawyers appealed to the Eleventh Circuit Court of Appeals, arguing that the conviction violated Hardwick's right to privacy. Citing the importance of privacy in previous cases such as *Roe v. Wade*, they succeeded in overturning the verdict in the Eleventh Circuit. The State of Georgia appealed to the U.S. Supreme Court, which ruled against Hardwick. In a closely divided opinion (5-4), the Court held that the right of privacy did not apply to homosexual conduct.

BOX 11.2   U.N. Human Rights Commission Rules on Sodomy Laws

In 1994, nine years before the U.S. Supreme Court overturned the nation's sodomy laws, the United Nations Human Rights Commission ruled that such laws were in violation of the International Covenant on Civil and Political Rights (ICCPR). The Commission held that the term "sex" in Articles 2(1), 17, and 26 of the ICCPR must be interpreted to include sexual orientation and, therefore, laws that criminalized same-sex contacts between consenting adults are in violation of the covenant (see *Toonen v. Australia,* Communication No. 488/1992, U.N. Doc. CCPR/C/50/D/488/1992-1994).

In the 2003 case of *Lawrence v. Texas,* the Supreme Court overruled a Texas sodomy law in broad terms and in effect apologized for the 1986 decision. The vote was 6 to 3. Justice Anthony M. Kennedy said that gays are "entitled to respect for their private lives. The state cannot demean their existence or control their destiny by making their private sexual conduct a crime." In a sweeping victory for the rights of Americans who experience same-sex attraction, the decision clearly established that state sodomy laws were unconstitutional.

MARRIAGE EQUALITY

Mike and his partner were not alone in feeling that the lack of a legal sanction for their relationship was not a significant disadvantage. Rimmerman (2000) noted that "same-sex marriage is not a crucial issue for many [gay] movement members" and suggested that those for whom it is central represented the more conservative elements of the movement (p. 51).

But for many GLBT Americans, the absence of legal recognition for a relationship had direct and sometimes devastating consequences. This was the case, for example, when a gay man died without leaving a will and his partner of 30 years was disinherited. It occurred when a lesbian mother died and her partner lost custody of the child they were raising together. It deprived thousands of people from receiving health insurance coverage through their partner's employer. So perhaps it is not surprising that between 2013 and 2014 the number of same-sex couples who reported they were married increased by over 83,000 (U.S. Census Bureau, n.d.a).

Marriage confers access to a wide range of rights and benefits. Recognizing its importance, Chief Justice Earl Warren wrote a landmark opinion for the Supreme Court in 1967 that said, "The freedom to marry has long been recognized as one of the vital personal rights essential to the orderly pursuit of happiness by free men. Marriage is one of the 'basic civil rights of man,' fundamental to our very existence and survival" (*Loving v. Virginia,* Supreme Court of the United States, 1967). With this opinion, the Supreme Court struck down laws in 16 states that prohibited interracial marriage and confirmed a fundamental right to marry.

Twenty-four years later, three same-sex couples in Hawaii appeared in the local Department of Health to apply for marriage licenses. When a health official denied their requests, they filed suit. The case, known as *Baehr v. Lewin,* made its way to the Hawaii Supreme Court in 1993, which sent it back to the lower court after ruling that under Hawaii's Equal Rights Amendment a standard of "strict scrutiny" must be applied to any measure depriving people of basic civil rights. The court found that the outcome in *Baehr v. Lewin* could not stand this level of scrutiny. The favorable decision did not establish a

▶ Marriage equality is now the law of the land.

fundamental right to same-sex marriage, and it was invalidated in 1998 when Hawaiian voters supported a constitutional amendment to ban same-sex marriages.

Under the **full faith and credit clause** of the U.S. Constitution, states must recognize and enforce (give "full faith and credit" to) contracts from other states. Antigay activists were concerned that civil unions might be "exported" throughout the United States. A federal law known as the **Defense of Marriage Act** of 1996 was drafted to address this concern.

The Defense of Marriage Act (DOMA) was introduced during an election year (1996) by Representatives Steve Largent (R-OK) and Bob Barr (R-GA) in the House and Senator Don Nickles (R-OK) in the Senate. The bill passed both houses by overwhelming majorities and was signed into law (in the middle of the night) by President Bill Clinton. DOMA did two things. First, it defined marriage for purposes of federal law as "a legal union between one man and one woman as husband and wife" and "spouse" as a "member of the opposite sex who is husband or wife." The law denied federal benefits, such as Social Security, to partners in same-sex marriages. It did not interfere with state policies about same-sex marriage, but did indicate that no state would be required to recognize a same-sex marriage from another state.

Advocates questioned the constitutionality of DOMA, arguing that the constitution's full faith and credit clause could not be superseded by legislation. Others held that DOMA was incompatible with the Supreme Court ruling in *Romer v. Evans*.

Meanwhile, developments in the states took the same-sex marriage debate in another direction. During the 12 years from 1997 to 2009, marriage or civil unions for same-sex couples were legally established in Massachusetts, Vermont, Connecticut, New Jersey, New Hampshire, and Iowa. In most of these states, legislation was prompted by judicial rulings concluding that denying same-sex couples the right to marry was not permitted under the

BOX 11.3   Same-Sex Marriage: An International Perspective

In 1989, Denmark became the first nation to offer legal recognition to same-sex unions. Other Nordic countries followed suit, and in 2001 the Netherlands became the first nation to legalize same-sex marriages. Since then Belgium, France, Germany, Canada, Luxembourg, the United Kingdom, South Africa, and Slovenia have recognized same-sex commitment, either through civil unions or through marriage. On the other hand, some countries, such as Australia, Uganda, and Latvia, have officially banned same-sex marriage. (See www.ilga-europe.org for information on the status of same-sex unions in European nations.)

state constitutions. A look at developments in Vermont and Massachusetts will illustrate the processes involved.

In 1997, several gay and lesbian couples in Vermont filed a lawsuit after they were denied licenses to marry (*Baker v. State of Vermont*). Two years later, in 1999, the state Supreme Court decided that state law discriminated against homosexual couples and ordered the legislature to correct the problem either by allowing same-sex couples to marry or by establishing a parallel **domestic partnership** status in which couples could register their relationship and enjoy the same rights as heterosexual couples. The state legislature drafted a bill to establish **civil unions** for same-sex couples. After extensive debate, the bill was signed into law by Governor Howard Dean in April 2000.[1]

The policy climate in Massachusetts was also favorable for same-sex marriage. In the 2003 case of *Goodridge v. Department of Public Health*, the state Supreme Court ruled that there was no constitutional basis to deny gay and lesbian couples the right to marry. The court gave the legislature six months to rewrite the state's marriage laws so they would be consistent with the Massachusetts constitution. The legislature voted to ban same-sex marriages but allow civil unions, making theirs the second state in the Union to offer this alternative. But the court rejected this approach, holding that civil unions did not satisfy the requirements of the state constitution. In a contentious session, the state legislature approved a constitutional amendment that would prohibit marriage by same-sex couples but would allow for civil unions. Massachusetts law required that the amendment be approved by two subsequent legislative sessions before it could be presented to the public for a vote (Liptak, 2004). In 2006, the amendment was defeated. Thus, under the *Goodridge v. Department of Public Health* ruling, same-sex marriage would remain legal in the state of Massachusetts at least until 2012 (Philips, 2007).

In 2009, the state mounted a DOMA challenge in the case of *Massachusetts v. United States Department of Health and Human Services*. A year later, U.S. District Court judge Joseph Tauro ruled that DOMA violated the Tenth[2] Amendment to the Constitution and fell outside of congressional authority. In deciding a companion case (*Gill et al. v. Office of Personnel Management*) Tauro further declared that "[a]s irrational prejudice plainly never constitutes a legitimate government interest, this court must hold that Section 3 of DOMA

---

[1]Signing the bill took a measure of courage on Governor Dean's part, since he was up for reelection that year. Dean won reelection in November after a contentious campaign.

[2]"The powers not delegated to the United States by the Constitution, nor prohibited by it to the States, are reserved to the States respectively, or to the people."

as applied to Plaintiffs violates the equal protection principles embodied in the Fifth Amendment to the United States Constitution." The decision was automatically stayed pending appeal by the federal government.[3]

In the 2004 election, President Bush called for an amendment to the U.S. constitution that would prohibit same-sex marriage. This proposal never gained traction at the federal level but was highly successful among the states. Prior to 2004, constitutions in five states (Alaska, Louisiana, Missouri, Nebraska, and Nevada) had been amended to ban same-sex marriage. In 2004, voters in eleven more states (Arkansas, Georgia, Kentucky, Michigan, Mississippi, Montana, North Dakota, Ohio, Oklahoma, Oregon, and Utah) approved constitutional amendments. Eventually, 41 states passed laws and/ or constitutional amendments banning same-sex marriages. Of course, this did not mean that the issue was settled in these states. The California experience is illustrative.

California Proposition 22 was named "the Knight Initiative," after state senator Pete Knight, one of its ardent proponents. The initiative said, "Only marriage between a man and a woman is valid or recognized in California." This deceptively simple phrase sounds almost like a statement of fact. Its proponents argued that Prop. 22 was not "antigay" but "pro-family," suggesting that it was possible to support gay rights generally and vote for this marriage initiative.

Their efforts were effective. The Knight Initiative passed in 2000 by a wide margin (61 to 39 percent). Later in 2004, city officials in San Francisco openly challenged the law, performing hundreds of marriages before opponents won a court injunction forcing them to stop and nullify the marriages. In March 2005, Judge Richard Kramer of the Superior Court of California reversed this ruling, a decision that was upheld by the Supreme Court of California in June 2008. This decision legalized same-sex marriage in the state and sent more than four thousand couples to the altar.

Two weeks prior to the Supreme Court ruling, a ballot initiative known as Proposition 8 was approved for the November ballot. Prop. 8, titled "Eliminates Right of Same-Sex Couples to Marry Act," would amend the state constitution. It passed by a slim majority (52 percent).[4] In subsequent legal challenges, the state Supreme Court upheld the proposition but affirmed the legality of marriages performed before it passed. The next year, 2009, the California legislature passed (and Governor Schwarzenegger signed) SB 54, the "Marriage Recognition and Family Protection Act." In addition to affirming the legality of marriages performed before Prop. 8, the law called for recognition of marriages performed outside of California after Prop. 8. Couples in these unions are entitled to all the rights, benefits, and obligations of marriage, except for use of the term "marriage." In August 2010, U.S. District Judge Vaughn Walker ruled in a San Francisco court that Prop. 8 was in violation of the U.S. Constitution.

On June 26, 2013, the Supreme Court allowed Walker's decision to stand, invalidating the referendum in the case of the *Hollingsworth v. Perry* (Supreme Court of the United States, 2013a). This was a watershed day for marriage equality as the court also ruled in *United States v. Windsor* that DOMA violated the Fifth Amendment guarantee of equal

---

[3]Tauro's decision in this case makes for interesting reading. It is available at http://metroweekly.com/poliglot/2010/07/08/2010-07-08-gill-district-court-decision.pdf.

[4]Some have argued that the historic turnout of African American voters who supported Barack Obama may have been responsible for passage of Proposition 8 (see Grad, 2008). A report by Equality California found a majority of African American (and Latino) voters backed the proposal, as did an even larger majority of Republicans and religious voters. Called *California's Proposition 8: What Happened, and What Does the Future Hold?*, the report is available through the National Gay and Lesbian Task Force at www.thetaskforce.org.

▶ While a slim majority of Americans now favor marriage equality, there has been some backlash against it.

protection. On behalf of the 5-4 majority, Justice Anthony Kennedy wrote, "By seeking to displace this protection and treating these persons as living in marriages less respected than others, the federal statute is in violation of the Fifth Amendment" (Supreme Court of the United States, 2013b, p. 26). Thus, same-sex couples who are legally married under state law cannot be denied federal benefits such as Social Security, family leave, immigration, and tax exemptions. Of course, the court did not invalidate laws in the majority of the states that did not recognize same-sex marriage.

For that, Americans waited another year. In June 2015, the Supreme Court invalidated all state bans on same-sex marriage and required all states to recognize marriages performed in other states. In *Obergefell v. Hodges*, a 5-4 majority held that denying the right to marry to same-sex couples violated the due process and equal protection clauses of the Fourteenth Amendment. Under this decision, all states were required to issue marriage licenses to same-sex couples.

Backlash: Preserving Religious Liberty

Shortly after the *Obergefell v. Hodges* ruling, a county clerk in Kentucky named Kim Davis made headlines by refusing to issue marriage licenses to same-sex couples. Davis was jailed briefly. She appealed her conviction, but after a year asked the court to dismiss her appeal. Kentucky passed a law removing clerks' names from marriage licenses which, according to Davis, eliminated her religious objections (Siemaszko, 2016). Nonetheless, even a year after the court's ruling, several counties in Alabama and Texas still refused to issue marriage licenses to same-sex couples.

Religious objections were also raised by the owners of an Oregon bakery called "Sweet Cakes by Melissa," when they refused to prepare a wedding cake for a lesbian couple. The owners of Sweet Cakes argued that they were not discriminating against the couple, but simply following their religious convictions. The state of Oregon saw things differently. In 2007, the state had passed the Oregon Equality Act, which prohibited discrimination on the basis of sexual orientation and gender identity in employment, housing, and public accommodations. The Oregon Bureau of Labor and Industries ruled that Sweet Cakes could not deny the couple service, "just as they cannot legally deny service based on race, sex, age, disability or religion." (Wong, 2015). A hefty fine was levied and paid through a highly successful fundraising effort. In itself, this case is not unique; several businesses have refused to serve same-sex couples, and opposition to GLBT rights is often justified on the basis of religion. The Sweet Cakes case illustrates some of the issues at stake when deeply held religious convictions clash with the civil rights of those who identify as gay, lesbian, bisexual, or trans.

Indeed, after the legalization of same-sex marriage, **"Religious Freedom and Restoration Acts" (RFRAs)** were introduced in 16 states. Designed to protect organizations, businesses, and in some cases individuals with deeply held religious convictions from charges of discrimination, the bills passed in Indiana and Arkansas. RFRAs are modeled on federal legislation that passed unanimously in 1993. The federal RFRA requires that government have a "compelling interest" before it infringes on religious freedom, and that it apply the "least restrictive" means of doing so. Prior to 2015, similar statutes were on the books in 19 states. As we will see in Chapter 13 (Women), the Supreme Court referenced RFRA in its *Burwell v. Hobby Lobby Stores* decision that enabled private businesses to decline to provide the contraceptive care required by the Affordable Care Act.

Many Americans oppose same-sex marriage, just as many opposed interracial marriage in 1967 when the Supreme Court struck down laws against it (Richards, 1999). Like marriage, rights that affect family formation for GLBT Americans have also been contentious in the United States.

PARENTING

The advent of marriage equality has gone a long way towards smoothing the pathway to parenting for gay and lesbian couples who, unlike Mike and his partner, would like to become parents. Results from the 2014 American Community Survey indicate that about 16 percent of same-sex couples have children living with them (22 percent of lesbian and 10 percent of gay households) (U.S. Census Bureau, n.d.a).

Like marriage, parenting is widely considered a "fundamental right." The right to raise one's children has been affirmed in several Supreme Court cases (see *Meyer v. Nebraska,* 1923; *Pierce v. Society of Sisters,* 1925; *Lassiter v. Dept. of Social Services,* 1981). Yet discrimination against gay and lesbian parents was once common in child custody and visitation decisions following divorce proceedings, and in some states same-sex couples were denied access to adoption prior to 2016.

Sodomy laws were once used as justification for denying parenting rights of homosexuals, with the illegality of a couple's presumed sexual conduct used as evidence of moral failure. As we have seen, the Supreme Court declared these laws unconstitutional in *Lawrence v. Texas.* Later arguments were based on the widely held belief that gays and lesbians are inadequate parents.

This belief lacks empirical support. It would be impossible to conduct a perfectly controlled and representative study comparing the parenting effectiveness of same-sex marriages and heterosexual marriages, and the sampling procedures of most studies in this field have been quite limited (Regnerus, 2012). Furthermore, there is no compelling evidence that children raised with same-sex parents experience significant developmental deficits (Biblarz & Stacey, 2010; Gartrell & Bos, 2010; Tasker, 2010). In light of this, courts in numerous cases have found that opponents of same-sex marriages fail to establish that same-sex parenting has adverse effects on children (Joslin, 2011).

ADOPTION

Same-sex couples can become involved in two types of adoption proceedings: "stranger adoption" and "second-parent" adoption. Stranger adoption occurs when a same-sex couple or GLBT individual offers to provide a permanent home to a child whose biological parents are unable or unwilling to do so. Such adoptions typically involve children in state custody. Second-parent adoptions arise when the partner of a child's biological parent seeks legal recognition of his or her relationship with the child.

After the 2015 Supreme Court decision legalized same-sex marriage, a few states (including Alabama, Florida, Mississippi, Michigan, and Nebraska) continued to ban adoption by gay or lesbian couples until March 2016, when a federal judge ruled that Mississippi's ban was unconstitutional.

DIVORCE

One remaining area of potential uncertainty for same-sex couples and their children arises when marriages dissolve. The question of what constitutes a "parent" comes up in disputes over custody, visitation, and child support. Non-biological or **"second parents,"** who have not married their partners or adopted their children may be especially vulnerable in these situations. Historically, some courts have denied custody and visitation to former partners of biological parents, regardless of their involvement in raising the children, and some argue that same-sex divorce continues to privilege biological parents (Goldberg, Moyer, Black, & Henry, 2015; Holtzman, 2013).

LO 11-3   Become Aware of the History and Current Status of Legislation Governing Discrimination Against GLBT Individuals

EP 3a
EP 5c
EP 8d

Until 1975 gay men and lesbians could not work for the federal government, period. Disclosure meant immediate dismissal, so those who did have federal jobs were forced to conceal their sexual orientation. Frank Kameny was the first federal employee to challenge this policy (Galas, 1996).

In 1957, Mr. Kameny worked as an astronomer with the U.S. Army map service. He had a Ph.D. from Harvard and was well qualified for the position. But within a year after starting his job, Kameny was fired because his supervisor suspected that he was gay. As Kameny told it,

> I was called in by some two-bit Civil Service Commission investigator and told, "We have information that leads us to believe that you are a homosexual. Do you have any comment?" I said, "What's the information?" They said, "We can't tell you." I said, "Well, then I can't give you an answer. You don't deserve an answer. And in any case, this is none of your business." I was not open about being gay at the time … but I was certainly leading a social life. I went to gay bars…. They issued a letter: They said they were dismissing me for homosexuality. I was in shock. (Galas, 1996, p. 62)

Kameny waged a three-year battle to get his job back. His appeals to the Civil Service Commission, U.S. District Court, and U.S. Court of Appeals were all denied, and the U.S. Supreme Court refused to hear his case. These defeats inspired a lifetime of activism. In the early 1960s, he began organizing gays in Washington, DC, to battle employment discrimination. Finally, in 1975, the U.S. Civil Service Commission reversed its discriminatory policy.

In 1982, Wisconsin became the first state to pass legislation banning employment discrimination based on sexual orientation. Then in 1993, Minnesota included both sexual orientation and gender identity in its Human Rights Act. In time, 21 states would pass laws prohibiting employment discrimination on the basis of sexual orientation. Meanwhile, antigay activists began organizing countermeasures.

During the early 1990s, referendums seeking to limit the rights of gays and lesbians were introduced in several states, including Arizona, Maine, Michigan, Missouri, Nevada, and Washington, where supporters were unable to secure enough signatures to get them on the ballot. Antigay organizers were more successful in Colorado and Oregon.

COLORADO AMENDMENT TWO

In 1992, a right-wing organization called Colorado for Family Values—an offshoot of the Traditional Values Coalition of Anaheim, California, and the Eagle Forum—spearheaded a campaign to pass the Colorado initiative known as Amendment Two (O'Rourke & Dellinger, 1997). Amendment Two was designed to repeal existing state and local laws that protected GLBT individuals from discrimination and to ban any future protective statutes. Activists on both sides agreed that passage of Amendment Two would have historic impacts on the rights of GLBT Americans. Proponents argued against granting "special rights" to homosexuals. Opponents of the initiative argued that the issue was not about special treatment, but protection of basic civil rights.

The initiative passed by a margin of 53 to 47 percent in November 1992. Some observers felt the public was ill informed about the amendment. They suggested its passage reflected voters' opposition to "special rights," not their desire to deny GLBT citizens basic civil rights.

The amendment never went into effect. Nine days after it was passed, gay rights activists sued for an injunction against its enforcement. The injunction was granted in January 1993. Amendment Two was declared unconstitutional by the U.S. Supreme Court in 1994, in a 6-to-1 decision. In *Romer v. Evans,* the Court ruled that Amendment Two violated the equal protection clause of the Fourteenth Amendment to the Constitution. Justice Kennedy wrote the opinion (echoing the dissent in *Plessy v. Ferguson*) that the Constitution "neither knows nor tolerates classes among citizens." The opinion found the argument that Amendment Two simply denied homosexuals special rights "implausible," saying:

> The amendment imposes a special disability on those persons alone. Homosexuals are forbidden the safeguards that others enjoy and may seek without constraint. They can obtain specific protection against discrimination only by enlisting the citizenry of Colorado to amend the state constitution…. We find nothing special in the protections Amendment Two withholds. These are protections taken for granted by most people either because they already have them or do not need them; these are protections against exclusion from an almost limitless number of transactions and endeavors that constitute ordinary civic life in a free society. (*Romer v. Evans,* p. 1627, cited by O'Rourke & Dellinger, 1997, p. 137)

The Court found that Amendment Two inflicted "immediate, continuing, and real injuries that outrun and belie any legitimate justifications that might be claimed for it." Further, justices inferred that "the disadvantage imposed is born of animosity toward the class of persons affected" (O'Rourke & Dellinger, 1997, p. 138).

OREGON INITIATIVES

While the Supreme Court considered Amendment Two, another antigay rights initiative was underway in Oregon. It was not the first of its type. As Douglass (1997) noted, "During a three-year period from 1991 to 1994, Oregon voters considered state and local ballot measures dealing with homosexuality on thirty separate occasions" (p. 17). The antigay measures introduced in Oregon were promoted by an organization called the Oregon Citizens Alliance (OCA).

The Alliance had considerable success passing local initiatives before they decided to introduce two statewide initiatives. In 1991, Ballot Measure 9 proposed to amend the Oregon constitution to define homosexuality as "abnormal, wrong, unnatural, and perverse." The measure would have prohibited local and state governments from encouraging homosexual behavior and, like Colorado Amendment Two, would have prohibited state and local governments from extending civil rights protections to GLBT Americans. OCA's campaign suggested that homosexuality posed a threat to the state's children and argued that gays and lesbians should have "no special rights." In this progressive state, opponents to the measure were many, and they were organized. Measure 9 was defeated by a 57 percent majority (Galas, 1996). Three years later, in 1994, OCA put Ballot Measure 13 before the Oregon voters. A toned-down version of the earlier initiative, this measure was defeated by a 51 percent majority (Galas, 1996). The Oregon defeats coincided with voters in Idaho rejecting a similar measure, entitled variously "Stop Special Rights" and "Proposition One" (Levine, 1997).

ANTI-DISCRIMINATION STATUTES

Protections from discrimination are piecemeal in the United States. As of this writing, 20 states and Washington DC have laws that prohibit discrimination in housing or employment and 19 prohibit discrimination in public accommodation[5] on the basis of sexual orientation or gender identity. Thirteen states provide similar protection from credit

---

BOX 11.4   Local Governments and Businesses Take the Lead

The term "domestic partnership" describes a committed relationship that is not characterized by either marriage or a civil union. It may be applied to either same-sex or heterosexual relationships and, depending on the context, can provide access to benefits. Hundreds of U.S. businesses provide employee benefits to domestic partners, as do some local jurisdictions. San Francisco became the first U.S. city to recognize domestic partnerships after the murder of Harvey Milk in 1979. Other cities, including West Hollywood and Berkeley, followed suit. Today several states, including California, Oregon, Nevada, Washington, Hawaii, Maine, and Wisconsin, also recognize domestic partnerships. Of course, under DOMA, federal benefits such as Social Security could not be extended to domestic partnerships.

Some local governments and businesses went further by passing their own antidiscrimination policies. In Salt Lake City, for instance, an ordinance passed in 2009 prohibits discrimination in housing and employment based on sexual orientation or gender identity.

---

[5]Oregon's antidiscrimination statute does include public accommodation, and it was on that basis that the Sweet Cakes ruling was made.

discrimination. A few states have anti discrimination statutes that address only sexual orientation. Absent statutes, some cities have nondiscrimination ordinances or executive orders (Movement Advancement Project, n.d.).

In states without a statute, discrimination against GLBT individuals in employment, housing, and public accommodation is perfectly legal. Any GLBT resident can be denied a job, and apartment, or a wedding cake for identifying as gay, lesbian, bisexual, or trans.

It is hard to document the rate of employment discrimination affecting GLBT individuals. Self-report studies suggest that between 15 and 43 percent of gay and lesbian workers have experienced some form of employment discrimination. Studies of trans people report similar or higher levels (Badgett et al., 2007). Researchers who have looked at complaints in states that prohibit sexual orientation discrimination report the rate is comparable to the rate of complaints of race- or sex-based discrimination (Rubenstein, 2002). Other researchers have sent out fictitious résumés for job seekers. In one large-scale study, résumés indicating experience with GLBT organizations were significantly less likely to receive a positive response than comparable résumés without the GLBT markers. This study reported regional and state differences indicating less discrimination in western and northeastern states; but perhaps most interesting was the significant difference between states with antidiscrimination statutes and those without. While discrimination was observed in both cases, it was less likely in states where these legal protections were in place (Tilcsik, 2011).

Under the Obama administration, the Equal Employment Opportunity Commission interpreted Title VII of the Civil Rights Act, which prohibits employment discrimination on the basis of sex, as barring discrimination based on gender identity or sexual orientation. This interpretation was an executive decision, and was not subjected to Supreme Court review; but between 2012 and 2016 it was used to address complaints of employment discrimination and harassment against GLBT individuals.

Seeking a more permanent solution, gay rights activists have advocated for federal protection through the **Employment Non-Discrimination Act** (ENDA). This bill would prohibit employment discrimination on the basis of sexual orientation. ENDA was first introduced in 1994 by Senator Edward Kennedy with about 30 cosponsors in the Senate. It has had the support of the nation's largest labor union, the AFL-CIO, as well as numerous business interests (Sweeney, 1999). Hearings have documented the pernicious effects of employment discrimination against gays and lesbians, and the bill has been reintroduced almost every year since.

By the time you read this, ENDA may be the law of the land. If so, it will prohibit discrimination in hiring, firing, promotion, compensation, and other employment decisions on the basis of sexual orientation or gender identity. It will not apply to the military, religious organizations, or businesses employing fewer than 15 people, nor will it establish affirmative action for sexual minorities.

Unlike the controversy surrounding same-sex marriage and parenting, most Americans oppose employment discrimination on the basis of sexual orientation. Support for antidiscrimination measures has grown steadily in recent decades. In 2013, Republican pollster Alex Lundry surveyed over 2,000 registered voters from all 50 states and reported that a majority in all states supported protections for gays and lesbians in the workplace (Haberman, 2013). And in the last decade the list of corporations, cities, and towns that have passed their own antidiscrimination policies has continued to grow.

THE BOY SCOUTS OF AMERICA

The Boy Scouts' decades-long effort to exclude gay men and boys from the ranks of its volunteers culminated with the 1990 expulsion of James Dale by a New Jersey branch.[6] Dale had been a Boy Scout since he was 8 years old. As a high school senior, he had attained the rank of Eagle Scout. Before leaving for college he applied for an adult membership. As a college student he was openly gay and became involved in gay rights activism. In his sophomore year his membership was revoked because the Boy Scouts "specifically forbid membership to homosexuals."

The Boy Scouts had a longstanding tradition of excluding gay men and lesbians, but New Jersey law prohibited discrimination on the basis of sexual orientation by public agencies and businesses. Arguing that they were a private organization, the Boy Scouts took the case all the way to the Supreme Court, which ruled in their favor in 2000 (*Boy Scouts of America v. Dale*).

Although the Supreme Court's decision was widely held as a defeat for gay rights, communities throughout the nation expressed their outrage by withholding support from the Boy Scouts. Several towns held that, since the Boy Scouts were a private organization, they could not make use of public resources, such as educational and recreational facilities. Further, United Way chapters in some communities either reduced or eliminated their support for the Boy Scouts.

Perhaps as a result, in 2013 the 1,400 members of the Boy Scouts of America's National Council approved a resolution removing the membership restriction on youth who identify as gay. In a press statement, BSA explained the decision, "The Boy Scouts of America will not sacrifice its mission, or the youth served by the movement, by allowing the organization to be consumed by a single, divisive, and unresolved societal issue." (Boy Scouts of America, 2013). In February 2014, 17-year-old Pascal Tessier of Maryland became the first openly gay Eagle Scout. The ban on gay scout leaders was lifted in 2015.

LO 11-4   Know the History of Anti-GLBT Violence and Hate Crime Legislation in the United States

EP 5c
EP 8d

In 1978, Harvey Milk, San Francisco's first gay city supervisor, was murdered by Dan White. White also killed Mayor George Moscone, presumably for his support of gay rights. White had campaigned on an antigay platform for his position on the board of supervisors and had been the only member of the board to vote against the city's antidiscrimination ordinance.

Milk was one of the nation's early victims of antigay hate crimes. The FBI reports that violence against gays has escalated in recent decades. Only a few of these crimes come to public attention; one example was the 1998 murder of Matthew Shepard in Wyoming. Nevertheless, more than a thousand "bias-motivated incidents" against gays and lesbians are documented each year.

Not all of these incidents represent severe violence, but the Southern Poverty Law Center (SPLC) noted an increase in murders of homosexuals at the end of the 1990s. The

---

[6]Mr. Dale's was one of several cases that resulted from the Boy Scouts' practice of denying membership to homosexuals.

SPLC reported that figures from the National Coalition of Anti-Violence Programs documented 14 antigay murders in 1996 and 33 in 1998. These statistics led the SPLC to conclude that "gay men and lesbians suffer from extraordinarily high levels of violence based on their sexual orientation" (SPLC, 1999).

The upsurge in violence against gay men and lesbians triggered an effort to include sexual orientation in federal hate crime legislation. In 1999, Senator Edward Kennedy, along with 39 Democrats and 5 Republicans, sponsored legislation that would have added gender, disability, and sexual orientation to federally protected categories. Known as either the Matthew Shepard Act or the Local Law Enforcement Hate Crimes Prevention Act, a version of the bill was reintroduced in each successive Congress. In 2007, the bill passed both the House and the Senate but was vetoed by President Bush. It finally passed and was signed in 2009 by President Obama. The Hate Crimes Prevention Act of 2009 expands federal hate crime coverage to include crimes motivated by a person's actual or perceived sexual orientation or gender identity.

Under the Act, the FBI is required to issue annual reports on hate crimes in the United States. In 2014, the report indicated that, among 5,479 reported hate crime incidents, 18.6 percent related to sexual orientation bias and another 1.8 percent to gender identity. Taken together, incidents related to sexual orientation and gender identity are second only to racial bias as a source of hate crime incidents reported in the United States (Federal Bureau of Investigation, 2016).

Opponents of hate crime legislation cite concerns about freedom of speech, arguing that hate crimes are "thought" crimes—invasive and hard to prove. This argument has been central to the objections of conservative religious organizations and the American Civil Liberties Union (ACLU). Supporters argue that stricter hate crime legislation will reduce violence and harassment, if not hate itself.

LO 11-5   Understand the Impact of HIV/AIDS on the GLBT Community and Social Policy Measures to Address the Epidemic

EP 8d

As Mike's story illustrates, the HIV/AIDS epidemic was devastating for the gay community. In addition to multiple losses, it spawned a wave of antigay sentiment.

Fear of contracting AIDS intensified discrimination against gay men. Many who worked in food services and other fields that involved contact with other people were summarily fired. Others were denied housing or health care. Indeed, as we saw in Chapter 6, the discrimination spawned by AIDS extended beyond gay men to include anyone affected by the disease. Because of this, the Americans with Disabilities Act of 1990 (ADA) provides specific protections for people with HIV/AIDS. The ADA prohibits discrimination in housing, health care, and employment, and it requires workplace accommodation for those who are ill.

Since the first cases were reported in 1981, an estimated 1.9 million Americans have been infected with HIV and over 698,000 have died (Kaiser Family Foundation, 2016). Most of those infected and killed are gay and bisexual men. For the past decade, the rate of new infections in the United State has held steady at about 50,000, and an estimated 1.2 million Americans were living with the disease in 2016 (Kaiser Family Foundation, 2016). As we saw in Chapter 6, ADA protections are important as these survivors navigate the health-care system.

LO 11-6   Become Aware of Recent Developments in Policy Related to GLBT Individuals

EP 3a
EP 5c
EP 8d

Recent decades have seen a good deal of progress toward equal treatment of GLBT individuals. We have already touched on the movement toward marriage equality and efforts to end employment discrimination. Here we consider advances and lingering issues affecting people in the military and those who identify as trans.

GLBT INDIVIDUALS IN THE MILITARY

In 1778, Lt. Gothold Frederick Enslin became the first man to be dishonorably discharged from the military for homosexuality. As testament to his shame, his sword was broken in half over his head. He marched out of Washington's camp at Valley Forge to a slow drumbeat (Galas, 1996).

The U.S. military had a clear policy calling for the dishonorable discharge of homosexuals until the early months of the Bill Clinton administration. That policy was based on the view that homosexuality was a mental illness and that homosexuals were therefore "unsuitable for military service" (Shilts, 1993). In addition, the presence of homosexuals was believed to be detrimental to troop morale. These beliefs conflicted with a 639-page report prepared for the Navy in 1957. Known as the Crittenden Report, this document concluded that homosexuality did not interfere with effective military service. The report was not widely publicized until it resurfaced in 1976 (Shilts, 1993).

Prior to the Bill Clinton administration, thousands of people were forced out of the military because they were gay (Shilts, 1993). Until the 1970s, these discharges were private affairs. Then, in 1975, Sergeant Leonard Matlovich decided to mount a challenge. A decorated Vietnam veteran, Matlovich was serving as a race relations instructor for the Air Force. He noted similarities between previous discrimination against blacks and current discrimination against homosexuals. In both cases, military authorities argued that the minority soldiers would prove untrustworthy and would threaten morale. Matlovich felt his outstanding service record was proof against this assertion. The Air Force disagreed, and when Matlovich informed them of his sexual orientation, discharge proceedings began. Matlovich challenged the discharge in federal court but was unsuccessful. He appealed the adverse ruling to the U.S. Court of Appeals, which ruled in his favor and called for the Air Force to reinstate him. The Air Force was reluctant to do so, offering him a $160,000 cash settlement instead. Matlovich accepted the settlement, feeling that his case would not fare well in the Supreme Court. He died of AIDS in 1988. Matlovich's tombstone bears this inscription: "A Gay Vietnam Veteran—When I was in the military they gave me a medal for killing two men, and a discharge for loving one" (Galas, 1996).

Following Matlovich's lead, growing numbers of young gay men and lesbians fought their military discharges. When Bill Clinton campaigned for president, he promised to issue an executive order rescinding the ban on homosexuals in the military. After the 1992 election, the religious right began organizing, with strong support in the Senate Armed Services Committee, veterans' groups, and the Pentagon. The political costs of overturning the ban looked overwhelming to the new president. The resulting compromise established "**Don't ask, don't tell, don't pursue**" as the military's policy on homosexuality (Rimmerman, 2000).

A HUMAN PERSPECTIVE   Advocacy: Victory in Washington State After 29 Years of Effort

Contributed by Janice Laasko, University of Washington, Tacoma, and Forrest Robert Stepnowski, BASW, Bachelor's of Arts in Social Welfare University of Washington, Tacoma

Many Americans are not aware that, in the absence of state legislation to the contrary, it is perfectly legal to discriminate on the basis of sexual orientation in employment, housing, public accommodations, and other arenas. Gay and lesbian Americans have been terminated from employment, evicted from housing, denied access to health care and financial credit, and refused access to public areas because of their sexual identity. Twenty-nine years ago the GLBT community in the state of Washington began advocating for the addition of sexual orientation to the state's nondiscrimination statute. Undergraduate social work student Forrest Robert Stepnowski and his colleagues took up the effort in 2005, lobbying for passage of House Bill 2661, which would add the words "sexual orientation" to the state's antidiscrimination law. They felt their efforts were consistent with the NASW Code of Ethics and supportive of their personal values. A significant part of the campaign was educational. The students

developed fact sheets on HB2661 and distributed them widely. Each student resolved to contact at least 12 people, asking for their support. They set up a table on campus for three days to distribute the fact sheets and seek support. A phone chain that was developed in the early stages of the lobbying effort proved vital when one legislator announced that she was reconsidering her previous support for the bill. The phone tree was mobilized and her office received nearly 100 calls urging her to stand firm in her support. The students participated in a lobby day at the capitol and attended committee hearings.

On January 27, 2006, while the students were in their social policy class, word came that the bill had passed. Their group's only GLBT member burst into tears, reflecting on the wide impact of their actions.

The students reported that the experience taught them about the legislative process and how best to utilize their personal strengths to influence legislators. Most importantly, they learned that they could make a real difference on behalf of disenfranchised and vulnerable populations. (Forrest was a 2006 winner in the Influencing State Policy contest.)

The compromise allowed gays and lesbians to serve in the military but placed restrictions on their behavior. They could not tell anyone they were homosexual or engage in hugging, kissing, or dancing with someone of the same sex, even when off duty. In 1994, the policy was challenged by six military personnel who were discharged. They argued that the policy violated their rights of free speech and equal protection. A U.S. District Court judge agreed and ordered the military to reinstate them (Galas, 1996).

The armed forces are among the nation's largest employers. Thousands of gays and lesbians are members of the military, devoting years and risking their lives to protect this nation. The "Don't Ask, Don't Tell" policy confined them to a tightly closeted existence. President Obama pledged to do away with the ban, and in October 2010 U.S. District Judge Virginia Phillips ruled "Don't Ask, Don't Tell" unconstitutional. Finally in December 2010, Congress repealed "Don't Ask, Don't Tell"; however, as the case of Chelsea Manning (formerly Bradley Manning) illustrates, members of the military who identify as trans still have few protections.

TRANS RIGHTS

The term *trans* is not a medical or psychiatric diagnosis.[7] Rather, it is an umbrella term that refers to people whose gender identity or expression differs from conventional expectations of masculinity and femininity. The appearance, behavior, and characteristics of trans individuals often do not match traditional expectations. Usually, trans individuals

---

[7]The DSM does not treat transgender feelings as a mental disorder unless they cause "distress or disability." In such a case, the diagnosis Gender Identity Disorder may be applied.

find that their personal gender identity is not compatible with their physical gender. Many (but not all) seek medical treatment that includes the use of surgery and/or hormones to bring their bodies into alignment with their identities. Others engage in cross-dressing and other nontraditional means of expression. The terms **gender variant** and **gender nonconforming** are sometimes used to describe this population. These terms do not describe a person's sexual orientation, which may be homosexual, heterosexual, bisexual, or asexual.

Because they more visibly threaten traditional norms, trans Americans are especially vulnerable to discrimination and even violence. The National Coalition of Anti-Violence Programs reported that hate crimes against trans people tend to be especially brutal (Church & Minter, 2000). This underscores the importance of legal protections, yet the inclusion of gender identity in antidiscrimination bills has at times fractured the advocacy community. Some argued protections specific to trans were unnecessary, while others have suggested that they were not feasible. But the phrase "gender identity or expression" is now included in most state antidiscrimination statutes as well as the federal hate crime law, and it has been part of ENDA for several iterations.

Protection of trans rights can be challenging, even with a supportive administration. The recent application of Title IX to a trans issue is instructive. Where Title VII of the Civil Rights Act prohibits discrimination in employment, Title IX addresses discrimination in education. It has been used to strengthen efforts to prosecute sexual assault cases on college campuses, and in May 2016 served as the basis of the controversial "Dear Colleague" letter from the U.S. Department of Education that required public schools to allow trans students to make use of the bathroom that corresponded to their gender identity. Two school districts and 13 states immediately filed suit, and within three months, a federal judge in Texas issued a preliminary injunction barring the administration from enforcing the "guidance." The judge ruled that the administration had engaged in rulemaking without going through the regulatory process called for by the Administrative Procedure Act (see Chapter 2 for details on rulemaking). As of this writing, it is unclear whether the administration will appeal the injunction. This development underscores the importance of nondiscrimination legislation that includes protections for gender identity.

Apart from discrimination, many trans individuals struggle to secure appropriate medical care. The Human Rights Campaign has documented cases in which people have been denied health insurance coverage based on their trans status. A majority of commercial health insurance plans have "transgender exclusions" that deny coverage for medical care necessary to accomplish gender transition (Human Rights Campaign, n.d.). In 2008 the American Medical Association addressed these issues in its policies, saying, "Our American Medical Association supports public and private health insurance coverage for treatment of gender identity disorder as recommended by a physician (Res. 122; A-08)" (American Medical Association, n.d.).

LO 11-7   Understand the Issues Affecting GLBT Individuals from a Social Justice Perspective That Recognizes the Role and Responsibilities of Social Workers

EP 5c

The NASW Code of Ethics is clear on the profession's attitude toward discrimination on the basis of sexual orientation, stating that "Social Workers should not practice, condone, facilitate or collaborate with any form of discrimination on the basis of ... sexual orientation."

Mike's experiences during his social work training were, sadly, not unusual. For some social workers the possibility of serving GLBT clients poses a dilemma. Their personal or religious beliefs conflict with their professional obligations. The Social Work Code of Ethics prohibits active involvement in discriminatory conduct. It also discourages us from condoning discrimination on the basis of sexual orientation. The challenge for social workers who find this problematic is to ensure that their personal biases do not intrude into their professional activities.

TABLE 11.1 Prominent Gays, Lesbians, and Bisexuals

Leonardo da Vinci (1452–1519) A gifted artist, da Vinci is acclaimed for the beauty of his paintings and the novelty of his inventions. Little is known of his private life except that he was devoted to beautiful young men.

Mutsuo Takahashi (1937–) Internationally renowned poet and playwright Takahashi has won numerous awards for his poetry, much of which celebrates the dignity of homoeroticism.

Walt Whitman (1819–1892) Whitman's poetry is widely interpreted as homoerotic, though he was silent on the topic of his own sexuality.

Peter Ilyich Tchaikovsky (1840–1893) Tchaikovsky's lasting compositions include *Swan Lake, The Nutcracker,* and *The Sleeping Beauty.* He was reportedly tormented by his homosexuality, but in his will Tchaikovsky named his companion, Bob, as his sole heir.

Oscar Wilde (1854–1900) Wilde's literary legacy includes *The Picture of Dorian Gray* and *The Importance of Being Earnest.* Wilde was prosecuted for sodomy and died in exile.

Jane Addams (1860–1935) A pioneer in the field of social work, Addams founded Hull House in Chicago. Her most intimate relationship was with Mary Rozet Smith, her companion for 40 years. The two traveled and lived together. Addams won the Nobel Peace Prize in 1931 for her leadership in the international women's peace movement.

Gertrude Stein (1874–1946) Stein's lifetime intimacy with Alice B. Toklas led her to personify lesbian identity for many during the early 20th century and beyond. An author and critic, Stein enjoyed considerable influence in the artistic community.

Virginia Woolf (1882–1941) The author of literary criticism, novels, and plays, Woolf is probably best known for her collection of essays, *A Room of One's Own.* After suffering several nervous breakdowns, Woolf committed suicide by drowning herself.

Ruth Benedict (1887–1948) Benedict was a cultural anthropologist. Her partner and collaborator, Margaret Mead, may be a more familiar figure. Mead and Benedict worked closely together, and Benedict left a lasting mark on her field.

Barbara Jordan (1936–1996) Lawyer, politician, and congresswoman, Jordan was awarded the Presidential Medal of Freedom in 1994.

Alan Turing (1912–1954) Turing was a mathematician whose research and theoretical formulations set the stage for the development of the digital computer. Turing died of cyanide poisoning in a possible suicide.

James Baldwin (1924–1987) Author of *Notes of a Native Son, Nobody Knows My Name,* and *The Fire Next Time,* Baldwin benefited from the support of his lover, Lucien Happersberger.

Andy Warhol (1928–1987) Best known for his painting of a Campbell's soup can, Warhol left a lasting mark on American contemporary art. Warhol was open about his sexuality, if reclusive in general.

Rev. Peter Gomes (1942–) Current Harvard University chaplain who came out as a gay man in 1991. He is a nationally known lecturer and advocate for gay rights

Harvey Milk (1930–1978) Known as the first openly gay official elected in the United States, Milk was a strong advocate for small business and minorities during his tenure as a San Francisco supervisor. Milk was murdered by Dan White, an antigay activist.

Barney Frank (1940–) In 1987, Frank was serving his fourth term in the U.S. House of Representatives when a reporter asked him whether he was gay. Frank answered in the affirmative and braced himself for the end of his political career. Instead, he was reelected in 1988 by a strong majority.

Elton John (1947–) Elton John identified as bisexual until the late 1980s, when he came out as gay. His first marriage to another man ended in divorce, and he subsequently married his long-time partner, filmmaker David Furnish, in a 2005 ceremony in the United Kingdom.

Sources: Russell (1996); BBC (2005); Rogers (2000); GLBTQ.com (n.d.).

Closing Reflections

Some have argued that GLBT individuals need not suffer from discrimination because their status is "invisible." If they did not disclose that they were GLBT, they would not be subject to oppression or persecution. If they would just go back into the closet, all would be well. But life in the closet is stifling, lonely, and scary. Eskridge (1999) has aptly referred to "the apartheid of the closet."

In this chapter we have documented the progress of federal and state policies that affect people who are gay, lesbian, bisexual, or trans—people have made outstanding contributions to our nation's culture and our daily lives (see Table 11.1). And public opinion is shifting. Growing numbers of Americans object to discrimination in employment. People with HIV/AIDS are no longer denied care on the grounds that, as Senator Jesse Helms said in his 1995 fight to reduce federal funding for HIV/AIDS, their "deliberate, disgusting, revolting conduct" was to blame for their illness (Galas, 1996, p. 84). Finally, despite some backlash, marriage equality is the law of the land. These are signs of progress, and the social work profession is beginning to take its place at the forefront of the struggle to secure equal rights for GLBT Americans.

Think About It

1. In 2012, the Michigan House of Representatives passed HB 5040, the "Julea Ward Freedom of Conscience Act." The Act arose when a counseling student at Eastern Michigan University was discharged from the graduate program in counseling when she refused to provide gay-affirmative treatment to a client because it was against her religious beliefs. Under HB 5040, public institutions of higher education would have been prohibited from disciplining students who refuse to counsel clients around "goals, outcomes, or behaviors that conflict with a sincerely held religious belief." Would you support or oppose a measure like this in your state? Why?

2. If you were advocating for GLBT rights, what would be your top-priority issue? Why?

3. Does your university include sexual orientation and gender identity/expression in its nondiscrimination policy? Does your city? Your state?

4. Do the health insurance plans available through your state's insurance exchange provide coverage for medical treatment of gender identity disorders?

Web-Based Exercises

For direct links to all the sites in these exercises, visit the *Foundations of Social Policy* Companion Site at www.cengagebrain.com and select the resources for Chapter 11.

1. Does the United Nations recognize a fundamental right to marry a member of one's own sex? Go to http://www.un.org/Overview/rights.html or Google "Universal Declaration of Human Rights," and read Article 16 carefully. What do you think? Now review Article 2. Does this change your mind? What about material presented in Box 11.2?

2. Visit the website for the Transgender Law and Policy Institute (www.transgenderlaw.org), and choose the "Litigation: Case Law" page. From the page menu, choose an area of litigation and review the cases listed. Do you think case law in this area is moving toward or away from supporting the civil rights of transgendered individuals? Why?

3. Go to the website of the National Gay and Lesbian Task Force (www.ngltf.org) and check the press releases under the PRESS tab to see what current issues the organization is working on.

4. Go to the website for Lambda Legal (lambdalegal.org). Scroll down and click on the U.S. map under "In Your State." Now select your state in the map and read about the current status of relationship recognition, employment protections, and parenting laws that affect GLBT residents. Are there any pending cases that might change these policies?

Competency Notes

As mentioned in the preface to this text, the Council on Social Work Education has designated nine core competencies and related practice behaviors that must be addressed by accredited social work programs. In these notes, I will specify the way chapter content addresses these competencies and behaviors. (This is designed to assist with the accreditation process.) Please refer to the "helping hands" icons for the locations of specific content in this chapter. Here you will find a brief explanation of how the accompanying content relates to the specified competency or practice behaviors.

The following list indicates where competencies and practice behaviors are addressed in this chapter.

EP 3a   **Apply their understanding of social, economic, and environmental justice to advocate for human rights at the individual and system levels.** The chapter describes violations of human rights, and the roles of exclusion, stereotyping, discrimination, and violence in the oppression of those who identify as GLBT. It also describes the development of policies to advance the human rights of this population.

EP 5c   **Apply critical thinking to analyze, formulate, and advocate for policies that advance human rights and social, economic, and environmental justice.** This history of policy development in this area illustrates how shifting values have influenced heteronormative privilege. Students' analytic skills will be supported by the chapter's exploration of changing views of homosexuality and the impact that shifting understandings of its origins have had on policy.

EP 8d   **Negotiate, mediate, and advocate with and on the behalf of diverse clients and constituencies.** The history of advocacy in this area should both inform and motivate students' advocacy efforts.

Suggested Resources

D'Emilio, J., Turner, W. B., & Vaid, U. (2000). *Creating Change: Sexuality, Public Policy, and Civil Rights.* New York: St Martin's Press.

Kosciw, J. G., Greytak, E. A., Bartkiewicz, M. J., Boesen, J. J., & Palmer, N. A. (2012). *The 2011 National School Climate Survey: The Experiences of Lesbian, Gay, Bisexual and Transgender Youth in Our Nation's Schools.* New York: Gay, Lesbian & Straight Education Network (GLSEN).

Stockton, K. B. (2009). *The Queer Child, or Growing Sideways in the Twentieth Century (Series Q).* Durham, NC: Duke University Press.

www.hrc.org. The Human Rights Campaign is dedicated to promoting gay and lesbian rights. Their website offers action alerts and a searchable index of HRC publications.

www.ngltf.org. The National Gay and Lesbian Task Force is a leader in the struggle for gay rights. Their site provides news and issue alerts, as well as publications with useful background material on target issues.

www.path.org. The World Professional Association for Transgender Health (WPATH) offers material on research and advocacy related to transgender and transsexual health issues.

www.transgenderlaw.org. The Transgender Law and Policy Institute engages in advocacy and policy analysis on behalf of transgendered Americans. Their site provides an introduction to policy and legal issues and an update on current initiatives.

When the voices of children are heard on the green
And laughing is heard on the hill,
My heart is at rest within my breast
And everything else is still.
WILLIAM BLAKE, "NURSE'S SONG"

Learning Objectives

This chapter will help prepare students to:

LO 12-1 Become aware of how history, culture, and economics have influenced Western conceptions of childhood

LO 12-2 Understand contemporary issues that influence adoption in the United States

LO 12-3 Become aware of the background and contemporary issues affecting the education of children in the United States

LO 12-4 Understand how children in the United States have been victimized through poverty and violence

LO 12-5 Become aware that children of color are disproportionately represented in the U.S. child welfare system

LO 12-6 Know the role social workers play in policy practice related to children

Children have played diverse roles in American society, from menial laborers to conscientious students, from dangerous villains to innocent victims. Once considered the private responsibility of their parents, children's welfare is now widely recognized as a matter of public interest. The well-established principle of *parens patriae* (state as parent) reflects government's compelling interest in the welfare of children. Indeed, many believe "it takes a village" to raise a child and parents should not be expected to shoulder the responsibility alone.

A HUMAN PERSPECTIVE   Lorenzo Martinez

Lorenzo is a vivid child, with jet-black hair and sparkling dark eyes. He has seen more of life than most 15-year-olds and often has trouble understanding or interpreting his experiences. Lorenzo lives with his paternal grandfather and grandmother (whom he affectionately calls "Nini"), his 14-year-old sister, and her 4-month-old baby.

Lorenzo's family is of Mexican descent, and his grandparents speak both Spanish and English. They celebrate traditional Mexican holidays and watch Spanish stations on television. Lorenzo considers himself Mexican but does not believe he has ever faced discrimination because of his heritage.

Lorenzo is the oldest of six children born to Margaret and Garcia Martinez. His mother was 14 years old when he was born, and his father was 16. Both parents have been convicted on drug charges, and over the course of several years all six of their children have been removed from their home. Lorenzo blames his mother for his parents' drug problems, saying that his father tried to quit from time to time, but his mother was deeply embedded in a drug culture and made her living by selling drugs. He remembers his parents' home as "always filled with drugs." He said he used to eat the seeds as his parents sat at the kitchen table sorting and bagging marijuana for sale. He remembers an uncle making him "take a hit" off a joint when he was 4 but says he didn't begin smoking regularly until he was in the sixth grade.

Lorenzo has not lived with his parents since he was in the third grade, when he moved in with his paternal grandparents. He says he doesn't know why he was moved. "It's just always been that way." A few years after he moved in with them, his grandparents became his legal guardians. Lorenzo thinks this was required by his school. Like all of his siblings, Lorenzo is supposed to visit his mother only under supervision. He says he feels "pretty close" to his mom, however, and he goes to see her whenever he wants, with or without supervision. But she still has problems. A few months ago she had a baby with another man. The baby was born with drugs in his system and was removed from her custody.

Lorenzo is outgoing and enjoys being with his friends. He moved frequently during elementary school but always had friends to hang out with. Since his father had been involved in a gang, he "courted"

(jumped) Lorenzo into the same gang. Lorenzo was courted when he was 13 but has known this gang since early childhood. His girlfriend is the sister of one of his homeboys, and Lorenzo sees the gang as a way of life. He says all of his cousins, nephews, and acquaintances are involved in the gang and that his favorite things to do are "hanging out with my homeboys" and smoking marijuana.

A few years before this interview, Lorenzo's father was murdered. Lorenzo is not sure why, but he believes it was not gang-related. His father was involved in the gang, but a policeman told Lorenzo the murder was drug-related. This distinction seems important to Lorenzo, who is still a gang member but is not involved in selling drugs. Lorenzo was close to his dad and misses him. He remembers that his dad sometimes worked odd jobs in construction and attended technical school for a while. His mom used to work at fast-food restaurants sporadically.

In sixth grade, Lorenzo came to the attention of the local law enforcement authorities. He says he used to "get blazed" daily with his friends and began to commit crimes. He has been convicted for shoplifting, carrying a weapon in school (brass knuckles), possession of a stolen vehicle, and probation violations (dirty urinalysis, breaking curfew, running away). He has been in a youth detention center on three separate occasions for one week each time, has spent five days doing community service (shoveling snow from sidewalks), and narrowly escaped a youth work camp when his uncle pled in front of the judge to have him sent instead to an inpatient psychiatric facility. He spent three weeks there in the winter prior to our interview, followed by a week in an outpatient program.

Although Lorenzo feels that he has been treated reasonably by the juvenile justice system, his grandmother disagrees. She said, "The system is a joke.... These kids that have just minor offenses are treated worse than animals." Upon reflection, Lorenzo decided that the police don't give gang kids a second chance. "Once the police connect you with a gang you are automatically guilty of a crime. They seem to think that kids can never change."

Lorenzo strongly believes that kids could be kept out of the juvenile justice system if they knew more about "how awful it is." He thinks elementary school children should be taken on field trips to youth detention facilities and that guest speakers should show slides of children there. He feels pictures or videos of "the bad stuff" will work: "Get the kids at their sad times, when they're crying…. When you're in that cell, that's when it really hits you."

At the time of our interview, Lorenzo was on probation. He felt responsible for his behavior, saying, "Everything I did I chose…. I had a good home, good teachers at school … the only problems I had were ones I created." He also resolved to "stay clean" and leave the gang. Of course, Lorenzo knew that leaving the gang would be difficult. He expected to be given a hard time and to eventually get "jumped out." He was enrolled in an alternative high school and planned to finish school there, where he hoped it would be easier for him to stay away from gang activities and drugs. He planned to stay with his girlfriend and had just begun a job in the fast-food business. Lorenzo's long-term goal was to be a therapist: "Once I saw that cool office I decided I wanted to kick back and eat M&M's all day!" He thought he might be able to get a football scholarship and attend college.

A SOCIAL WORK PERSPECTIVE

Lorenzo's extended family is clearly a strong resource in his life. His placement with grandparents is an example of "kinship care," an established practice in the child welfare system. Whenever possible, children who enter state custody are placed with members of their extended family. Lorenzo's grandparents had the resources and were willing to take him in, and his uncle argued on his behalf in juvenile court. He describes his grandparents' place as "a good home," and his grandmother appears deeply concerned about his experiences with the juvenile justice system.

On the deficit side of his equation are Lorenzo's parents. Clearly a troubled couple, they combined teenage parenthood, a gang lifestyle, and serious drug abuse in one dysfunctional package. One can only speculate about Lorenzo's experiences during the eight years when he was in his parents' care. But it is striking to note that his experience with counseling seems to have led Lorenzo not to attribute his situation to childhood trauma but to assume personal responsibility for following in his parents'

footsteps. This perspective may reflect the attitudes he has encountered in a juvenile justice system that is increasingly inclined to blame (and punish) children for their misbehavior.

Lorenzo's life has been touched by two major components of the nation's child welfare system. First, child protective services intervened on behalf of Lorenzo and his siblings to remove them from their parents' home. In Lorenzo's case, the preference for kinship care brought him to a stable, supportive environment, his grandparents' home. Lorenzo's situation illustrates a potential advantage of kinship care. It afforded him access to the support of other members of his extended family, such as the uncle who intervened on his behalf in court.

The second child welfare component Lorenzo encountered was the juvenile justice system. Children of color, like Lorenzo, are disproportionately represented in all phases of the juvenile justice system, but particularly in detention facilities. Both Lorenzo and his grandmother felt that the system treated children—particularly those in gangs—like criminals and that the police did not believe in a child's capacity to change. This treatment may reflect a growing tendency on the part of the justice system to emphasize punishment over rehabilitation when dealing with serious youth offenders. It may also reflect increased fear on the part of the public and the police that criminal acts by youth gangs are spiraling out of control.

Why did Lorenzo join the gang? Was it for a sense of belonging? For structure and a role? For economic advancement? For access to drugs? Because of his father's involvement? Specialists in gang behavior have identified each of these factors as potential reasons for youth involvement in gangs. Children in gangs commit roughly twice as many crimes (especially violent crimes) as similarly "at-risk" children who do not belong to gangs. They are, therefore, more likely than others to be labeled "villains" and to be subjected to the worst punishment the system has to offer.

In Lorenzo we see multiple problems: substance abuse, child abuse or neglect, gang involvement, and criminal behavior. His future, like that of other children in similar situations, will depend on the capacity and willingness of his family and community to invest resources in him, as well as on his own resilience.

LO 12-1   Become Aware of How History, Culture, and Economics Have Influenced Western Conceptions of Childhood

EP 5a

Throughout most of human history there was no place for childhood as we know it. The art of ancient and medieval times suggests that most children were seen as small-scale adults. With the exception of Greek art, this perspective was evident throughout the ancient world. As Philippe Aries explained in his classic work, *Centuries of Childhood*, "The realistic representation of children or the idealization of childhood, in grace and rounded charms, was confined to Greek art." Aries observed that later medieval artists portrayed children as little adults, and suggested that this lack of distinctive representation indicates that "childhood was a period of transition which passed quickly and which was just as quickly forgotten" (Aries, 1962, p. 34).[1]

From the 12th through the 14th centuries, artists began to portray children, first in religious art and later in secular art. They were shown mingling with adults in a variety of settings depicting work, play, and relaxation. According to Aries, this mingling indicated that the world of children was not separated from that of adults.

But children were not treasured as individuals. Observing that portraits of children were rare, Aries noted that "childhood was simply an unimportant phase of which there was no need to keep any record." High mortality rates discouraged strong attachments to young children. "The general feeling was, and for a long time remained, that one had several children in order to keep just a few" (p. 38). The death of a child was considered a "necessary wastage," and it was not until the 18th century that this idea faded from Western thought.

Aries dates the transformation in attitudes toward childhood to the 17th century, when children began to appear in paintings, and groupings in family portraits placed them in the center. Children's clothing also changed, from small imitations of adult dress to a distinctive, childlike style. This change was particularly evident for boys, as Aries noted: "The idea of childhood profited the boys first of all, while the girls persisted much longer in the traditional way of life which confused them with the adults" (p. 61). With this transformation came two distinct approaches to children. The first, practiced within the home by children's caregivers, involved "coddling" and "playing" with children—enjoying their antics and giving them pleasure. The second, encouraged by public authorities and moralists, focused on discipline and direction. Thus, children were treated not only as sources of amusement[2] but as future citizens who required direction and education. The family became a vehicle not only for the transmission of names and estates but also for the education of children. The concern of public and religious authorities of this era recognized the government's stake in children's upbringing in an early manifestation of the principle of *parens patriae,* or state as parent.

In time, children were removed from adult society to spend their time at home or school. This created childhood as we know it—a sort of hiatus, a time of preparation and (for some) a time of fun. It also transformed the family, raising its emotional, moral, and intellectual importance, and sharpened the distinction between private and public spheres.

---

[1]Discussion in this section draws heavily from Aries's comparative study of modern and medieval families.

[2]As sources of amusement, prepubescent children were often caressed and teased about their sexual organs in a manner that would be unacceptable today. An example comes from the diary of a 16th-century physician who wrote of Louis XII's childhood. When the child was one year old, the physician reported that "[h]e laughed uproariously when his nanny waggled his cock with her fingers." Later the child copied the trick. He called a page and "shouted, 'Hey, there' and pulled up his robe, showing him his cock" (Aries, 1962, p. 100).

CHILDREN AS ASSETS AND THE DANGEROUS CLASSES

Throughout U.S. history, children have often been viewed as assets. The idea of children as economic assets prevailed during colonial and postcolonial times, when they performed labor for their families and employers. As we will see in Chapter 15, this role has diminished in the United States through legislation that regulates child labor. But children are still assets, most notably as the linchpins of family formation.

The Europeans who settled in North America during the 17th century brought with them European views of children as little adults. Indeed, childhood in colonial America brought few special protections from family or government. Because of the contrast between the attitudes we now hold and those that prevailed in colonial America, many people have the impression that children were treated as property during that era. It would be more accurate, however, to say that they were seen as economic assets.[3] Children's labor contributed to family well-being, and their fathers or masters (in the case of indentured servants and apprentices) had the legal right to their custody and control. Fathers and masters were also legally responsible for the education and moral upbringing of children in their custody. Mothers had no legal rights to their children if the father was alive, and only limited rights after his death.

The rights afforded to children themselves were limited as well. Misbehavior was severely punished. Some children found their way into poorhouses, and others were sold as indentured servants (Mason, 1994). State involvement in the lives of children was limited but not unheard of. Criminal charges brought against adults for child abuse were recorded as early as 1655 (Watkins, 1990). That year, a master in Massachusetts was found guilty of maltreatment that resulted in the death of his 12-year-old apprentice. He was punished severely. Bremner (1970) reports on other cases in which children were removed from homes that had been deemed unsuitable. It was more common to bring criminal charges against masters to whom children were apprenticed than against parents. Parents were charged only in cases of grievous abuse, described by Thomas as "punishment that was grossly unreasonable in relation to the offense, when the parents inflicted cruel and merciless punishment, or when the punishment permanently injured the child" (Thomas, 1972, p. 304).

Colonial America had no established authority charged with protecting children. Instead, those responsible for enforcing criminal laws responded to crimes against children. Similarly, there was no systematic procedure for identifying children who were abused or neglected. No laws required reporting of child maltreatment. Cases came to the attention of the authorities through accidents of fortune: a visit from an especially public-spirited neighbor, the arrival of a census taker, or a complaint from a teacher. This lack of a structure or a system of child protection persisted until the establishment of the New York Society for the Prevention of Cruelty to Children during the 19th century (this topic will be discussed later in this chapter).

The Industrial Revolution brought overcrowding to U.S. cities, which were notorious for producing the "**dangerous classes**," a term Charles Loring Brace used to describe the children of urban slums. In 1853, Brace founded the Children's Aid Society and developed the practice of **placing out** poor urban children.[4] Thousands of these children (most of whom were Roman Catholic) were sent to live on farms and work for families

---

[3]The exception to this statement is children born into slavery, who were treated as property to an extent not permitted with biological children and indentured servants.

[4]There are some striking parallels between the Children's Aid Society's "placing out," the practice of international adoption, and the forced enrollment of Native American children in boarding schools. In each case, disenfranchised children were/are removed from their homes by powerful people "for their own good."

BOX 12.1 | Nebraska's Abandoned Children

It started out as a perfectly reasonable proposal. In 2008, Nebraska legislators passed a safe-haven law to allow parents to abandon their children at a safe place such as a hospital, without fear of prosecution. Similar laws had already been passed in other states, but in Nebraska legislators neglected to define the word "child." By the time they scrambled to narrow the definition to new-borns, at least 34 children, many of them teenagers and some from other states, had been abandoned by their parents. Many of the abandoned children had a history of mental illness. Notably, Omaha is the home of Boys Town, the country's original safe haven.

with "strong Christian (i.e., Protestant) values." This practice was harshly criticized. Brace attributed the criticism to "ignorant Roman Catholics" who spread rumors that the children were sold as slaves, given new names, and converted to Protestantism (Brace, 1872, p. 234). As a result, said Brace, the poor themselves opposed the practice. In his 1872 treatise on his work, Brace said, "Most distressing of all was, when a drunken mother or father followed a half-starved boy, already scarred and sore with their brutality, and snatched him from one of our parties of little emigrants, all joyful with their new prospects, only to beat him and leave him on the streets" (p. 235).

Opponents noted that the Children's Aid Society did not carefully investigate the foster homes, that the foster families sometimes mistreated the children, and that many of the children were never heard from again.

Over the course of 25 years, the society removed 50,000 children from the streets of New York. Poor families protested the practice. The Roman Catholic Church charged the agency with using this practice to convert Catholic children to Protestantism. Later, many of the receiving states objected to having indigent youth dropped within their borders. Eventually, placing out was abandoned in favor of asylums.

CHILDHOOD IN MODERN AMERICA

In the modern United States, few see children as economic assets, but they are nonetheless sought after. Many adults derive satisfaction from being a parent, and some use adoption to add children to their families.

LO 12-2 Understand Contemporary Issues That Influence Adoption in the United States

EP 2a
EP 5a
EP 5c

Adoption has become widely accepted, both as a method for providing loving homes to needy children and as an approach to creating or expanding families. But national policy controversies have erupted around transracial or transcultural adoption and adoption by GLBT parents.

TRANSRACIAL OR TRANSCULTURAL ADOPTION

Most transracial or transcultural adoptions in the United States have involved white parents adopting children of color. The vast majority of these are international adoptions, but in a significant proportion, Native American and African American children have been adopted by white parents.

International Adoption

International adoptions peaked in 2004, when the State Department issued over 22,000 visas for **orphan immigrants**, most of them from mainland China (31 percent) and Russia (23 percent). At that time, international adoptions were fairly routine and predictable. But as corrupt practices came to light and international tensions increased, countries like Russia, China, South Korea, Romania, Vietnam, and Guatemala curtailed or reduced U.S. adoptions. As a result, the number of international adoptions in the United States has fallen precipitously. By 2014, the number of orphan visas had dropped to 6,408. The single largest source of orphans was still mainland China (32 percent), followed by Ethiopia (11 percent) and Ukraine (8 percent) (U.S. Department of State, 2015).

Faced with concerns about corrupt adoption practices (particularly children who were not orphaned being kidnapped and sold for adoption), an international protocol known as the **Hague Adoption Convention** was adopted. The convention went into effect in the United States in 2008. Among other things, it established a system for accrediting adoption agencies and called for protections to ensure that consent to adoptions is given freely and in writing, with consideration for the child's wishes and, where feasible, written consent from the child, as well as determination that prospective adoptive parents are eligible and suitable to adopt. (The full text of the convention is available at www.hcch.net.)

Domestic Transracial Adoption

Transracial adoption was rare prior to the 1964 Civil Rights Act. One exception was the **Indian Adoption Project**. Operating between 1958 and 1967, it was a joint effort between the Bureau of Indian Affairs and the Child Welfare League of America (CWLA). Federal funds were used to place Native American children who were living on reservations in mainstream homes. One of numerous efforts to place Native American children in foster or adoptive homes off the reservation, the Indian Adoption Project placed 395 children in white adoptive homes before it was shut down (Fanshel, 1972). In 2001, the CWLA Board of Directors passed a resolution expressing "deep regret for its participation in any activities that were intended to break up Indian families, promote assimilation, and/or disregard Indian tribal governments" (Kreisher, 2002a).

While transracial Native American adoptions were on the decline, the adoption of African American children reached a peak. In 1971, 2,574 African American children were adopted by white parents (Cox, 1994). The following year, the National Association of Black Social Workers (NABSW) expressed vehement opposition to the practice. They saw it as "an insidious scheme for depriving the black community of its most valuable resources: its children" (Day, 1979). There was also concern that white parents might be unable to prepare African American children to cope with prejudice and discrimination. Committed to meeting the needs of the black community, the NABSW argued that adoption agencies applied white middle-class norms when they evaluated prospective adoptive parents, and as a result, African American families were denied the opportunity to adopt so African American children were unnecessarily placed in white homes.

Although African American families adopted at a rate 4.5 times greater than white families, the number of African American children available for adoption continued to exceed the number of African American families available as potential adoptive placements. Most of these children had been removed from their biological families by the public child welfare system. At the same time, several studies demonstrated that African American children raised by white parents developed healthy racial identities and most did not experience adjustment problems (Simon, 1994). As a result, during the 1990s, a consensus formed among child welfare professionals that agency policies and preferences against transracial adoption were denying African American children permanent homes.

In 1994, President Clinton signed the **Multi-Ethnic Placement Act** (MEPA) (PL 103-382). The law is designed to "prevent discrimination in the placement of children in **foster care** and adoption on the basis of race, color, or national origin; to decrease the time children wait to be adopted; and to ensure agency recruitment of a pool of foster and adoptive parents who reflect the racial and ethnic diversity of the children available for adoption" (Pecora et al., 2000, p. 41).

Unfortunately, federal funds were not provided to assist in recruiting minority families, either as foster or adoptive parents. Significant barriers remained, including the lack of minority professionals in the child welfare system; the high proportion of single-parent, low-income families within the African American community; rigid requirements and fees; and pervasive institutional racism (Crumbley, 1999).

In 1994 (the year that MEPA passed), the NABSW revised its position on transracial adoption:

> We believe that too many children are placed in foster care unnecessarily and that often they remain in foster care too long…. When all reasonable efforts have been made to keep the child and family together, and when family preservation, family reunification, and relative placement have failed, then, and only then, should we seek adoption. Adoption should be within the same race. Transracial adoption should only occur after clearly documented evidence of unsuccessful same-race adoption. (Crumbley, 1999, p. 96)

While acknowledging the benefits of adoption over foster care, the NABSW did not accept the argument that suitable adoptive families were not available in the African American community. They argued that when an agency makes special efforts to recruit African American families, same-race placement of African American children could be as high as 94 percent (NABSW, 1994).

In 1998, most (52 percent) of the foster children in the United States were African American (Administration for Children and Families, 2006). Recent years have seen some progress in the placement of foster children, in general, and African American children in particular. Since 2005, the number of children in foster care has gone down by about 100,000 and by 2014, African American children were about 24 percent of the population in care (Children's Bureau, 2015). Of course, African American children are still overrepresented in foster care.

Adoption by Gays and Lesbians

Historically, child welfare authorities in the United States confronted thorny issues as they considered gays and lesbians as prospective adoptive parents. Until the 1950s and 1960s, only married Caucasians between 21 and 35 years of age who had no biological offspring were considered suitable adoptive parents (Kreisher, 2002b). But the opportunity to adopt children was gradually extended to include unmarried women and men, people of color, people with disabilities, older individuals, and families with children. Reflecting growing awareness of the numbers of children in foster care who await adoption, the tagline for a 2002 ad campaign developed for HHS captures the agency's more open approach: "You don't have to be perfect to be a perfect parent."

Adoption by gay and lesbian persons runs counter to several myths: the idea that homosexual parents are likely to molest children sexually, that children adopted by homosexuals will be pressured to become homosexual, and that the children will be living in "immoral" environments. There is no empirical literature to support these claims. **Perpetrators** of child sexual abuse are predominantly heterosexual, and there is no evidence that the sexual orientation of a child is determined by that of his or her parents. Other opponents of gay/lesbian adoptions argued that children would be teased by their peers from more traditional families. Proponents of this argument usually found anecdotal evidence to support this claim, but there is no established research pointing to negative developmental effects. Indeed, the intolerance reflected in harassment and bullying of children in nontraditional homes may reflect dysfunction in the homes of the bullies, rather than in the homes of their victims.

With the advent of **marriage equality**, policies that prohibit adoption by gay and lesbian individuals and couples are going by the wayside, yet the historic controversies over transracial and gay/lesbian adoption illustrate the powerful role that ideology and values play in social policy debates. Both supporters and opponents can cite cases in support of their positions. Of course no one would suggest that we randomly assign children to adoptive homes, which means that social scientists cannot provide a definitive answer regarding the effects of transracial and gay/lesbian adoptions. Perhaps we can influence dialogue by shifting the lens to a more macro perspective that considers what constitutes a good society—whether "the problem" may be lodged not in these new family forms but in the intolerance and prejudice they encounter in the broader society. As we will see, prejudices like these often play out in the educational system.

LO 12-3   Become Aware of the Background and Contemporary Issues Affecting the Education of Children in the United States

EP 5a
EP 5c

Philippe Aries (1962) discussed the establishment of schools as a force that defined and extended childhood for western Europeans during the 12th through 17th centuries.[5] Girls were excluded from schools, but boys of various ages and classes were allowed to participate. Less formal and structured than modern schools, these institutions provided basic literacy skills and a smattering of Latin over periods that might extend as long as four or five years. The most well established were religious schools designed to prepare young boys for careers in the clergy. Another significant educational institution, dating back to the medieval period, was apprenticeship. Many boys learned crafts through lengthy periods of apprenticeship under masters. Indeed, in 1562 England passed the Statute of Artificers, designed to force poor children into apprenticeships. An early poverty prevention policy, this law was designed to reduce the need for public assistance.

European immigrants brought the practice of **apprenticeship** to colonial America as a means of replenishing the skilled labor force. The first compulsory education law in colonial America involved apprenticeship. It was passed in 1642 by the Massachusetts Bay Colony. The act required that the selectmen of each town attend to the "calling and employment of children" and "especially of their ability to read and understand the principles of religion and the capital laws of the country" (Good, 1962, p. 28). This education was to take place not in schools, but primarily in homes and shops.[6] Schools were established in a haphazard fashion that reflected the many competing demands on communities. They operated irregularly, with terms seldom lasting more than three months, and curricula were organized around whatever reading and writing materials were at hand.

The **Massachusetts Bay Colony** passed an act in 1647 to establish educational consistency throughout the colony. The act required that towns with at least 50 families maintain an elementary school (then called a "dame" school because it was operated by a woman, often a widow). Towns numbering at least 100 families were required to provide a secondary school. Towns that failed to comply with the act were fined. Evidently, some

---

[5]Most of the material in this section is drawn from H. G. Good's seminal work, *A History of American Education* (1962).

[6]Good argues that this law represented the beginnings of public involvement in children's upbringing in the New World.

towns found it easier to pay the fine than to establish a school (Good, 1962). Similar laws eventually spread throughout the colonies. As towns grew, they were divided into school districts, each with its own governing board and elementary school. The practice of establishing local school districts continues to this day.

Several great thinkers in revolutionary America (Thomas Jefferson, Benjamin Rush, Samuel Knox, and Noah Webster) saw education as fundamental to nation-building. Education could secure liberty and democracy and set the stage for the nation's economic expansion. As Thomas Jefferson said of education's role,

> The object is to bring into action that mass of talents which lies buried in poverty in every country for want of means of development, and thus give activity to a mass of mind, which in proportion to our population, shall be the double or treble of what it is in most countries. (U.S. Commission on Civil Rights, 1967, pp. 94–95)

Education would help unite the states into a nation, but there was much debate over the form it should take. Should it be centralized at the federal level or treated as a local endeavor?

The Tenth Amendment to the Constitution left education to the states and discouraged federal interference.[7] As a result, the nation's earliest statutes involving education are found in state constitutions. When the Constitution was ratified, six of the new states included educational provisions in their constitutions. The most detailed was in Section 44 of the Pennsylvania constitution:

> A school or schools shall be established in every county by the legislature, for the convenient instruction of youth with such salaries to the masters, paid by the public, as may enable them to instruct youth at low prices; and all useful learning shall be duly encouraged and promoted in one or more Universities. (Good, 1962, p. 88)

In this early stage of the nation's history, state efforts could supplement private schools, and some states provided free education for the poor. But the notion of universal, free public education had not yet caught hold.

Free and universal public education was a uniquely American invention. It was more compatible with the nation's democratic ideals than the class-based systems in England and Europe. Because there was no model to follow, the establishment of the American school system was neither quick nor smooth. Indeed, during the nation's first few decades, no organized constituency supported the concept.

The **unionization** of factory workers created the nation's first organized force for free public education. In 1828 (following the depression of 1819), the **Workingmen's Party** was organized in New York and Philadelphia. In Philadelphia the party's initial advocacy efforts focused on establishing independent newspapers, libraries, public lectures, and debates. In 1829, the organization issued a report that addressed public education. It rejected the idea of providing free instruction only to the poor and argued for free and universal elementary schools "in which teaching was not to be restricted to 'words and figures' but would also attempt to form rational self-governing character" (Good, 1962, p. 120). The report proposed establishment of local school boards that were elected by and answerable to the people they served. The Workingmen's Party in New York had a socialist wing, and in 1825, party members proposed the establishment of free public boarding schools for all children as a vehicle for eliminating class differences in the new republic. Ultimately, the movement for public education expanded beyond the laboring classes to include advocates from diverse walks of life.

Opposition to public education came primarily from the privileged classes. Some argued that apprenticeship made universal education both impossible and unnecessary.

---

[7]This does not prevent Congress from authorizing funds for educational endeavors.

Others suggested that the laboring classes should work so that the rich could cultivate their minds. Many objected to the use of taxes to finance schools, seeing it as "an arbitrary division of the property of the rich with the poor" (Good, 1962, p. 122). Public schools, it was argued, would be corrupt and inefficient.

Despite opposition, the public education movement grew, and after 1830, several states had expanded public education and retreated from their funding of private schools. Several cities (Philadelphia, Baltimore, and Cincinnati, for example) established public schools through special legislation passed prior to state action. Eventually, however, state constitutions were amended (or established in newer states) to direct legislatures, as Illinois does, "to provide for a thorough and efficient system of free schools whereby all the children of this State may receive a good common school education" (Good, 1962, p. 143).

States' public educational systems developed individually, in piecemeal fashion. As a result there was considerable variation. The most striking variation involved the segregation of African American children and Caucasian children in southern educational systems (to be discussed later in this chapter). Over time, these regional differences have blurred, and a national pattern of public education has emerged (Good, 1962). One aspect of the national pattern that we now take for granted is compulsory attendance.

COMPULSORY ATTENDANCE LAWS

Massachusetts passed the first **compulsory attendance** law in 1852, requiring that children between the ages of 8 and 14 attend school for 12 weeks each year. The law permitted exceptions for children of poor families, those who were ill, and those who were being "otherwise educated." Children were also excused from the 12-week requirement if local schools were not open that long. The law called for fines if parents did not comply, but punitive action was rare. It was not until 1900 that compulsory attendance laws were enacted in a majority (32) of the states, and it would be another 18 years before the movement for compulsory schooling would reach all 48 contiguous states.

Compulsory education was controversial for two reasons. First, many objected to government interference with parental authority. Second, these laws prevented children from working in industrial and farm settings at a time when many parents relied on their children's labor for income. Several attendance laws were subjected to constitutional challenges. They were upheld, with opinions reflecting the view that the state had a compelling interest in the education of children.

By 1918, all states had passed statutes requiring school attendance. Over the years, these laws have expanded the duration of required schooling and become more similar. Today most states require about nine months of regular attendance annually for children from age 5 or 6 to 16 years.

AN EXPANDED FEDERAL PRESENCE

During the 20th century, the federal government began to exert more influence over public education. Federal involvement included the forced desegregation of schools in the South, subsidized higher education for veterans, financial supports such as the National School Lunch Program, and mandates imposed by **No Child Left Behind**.

Federal education programs are typically administered or supervised by the Department of Education, established by Congress in 1867 to provide educational information to state and local education authorities. Congress later reduced annual appropriations for the department and downgraded it to an Office of Education, later a Bureau of Education within the Department of the Interior. There it remained until 1929, when Herbert

Hoover's National Advisory Committee on Education recommended the establishment of a cabinet-level Department of Education.

DESEGREGATION

Late in the 19th century, after **Reconstruction**, 17 southern states required that black and white children attend separate schools. Four other states permitted districts to engage in segregation. The U.S. Supreme Court supported the practice in an 1896 case. The case, known as *Plessy v. Ferguson,* did not directly involve school segregation, referring instead to a Louisiana law that required separate railroad cars for African Americans. The Court's opinion brought in the schools, however, stating that "separate and equal" facilities did "not necessarily imply the inferiority of either race," and cited "separate schools for white and colored children" as an illustration of the principle (Good, 1962, p. 577). With this judicial blessing, districts in the South and the North developed racially segregated schools.

▶ Linda Brown (of *Brown v. Board of Education*) in a segregated classroom, Monroe Elementary School.

Carl Iwasaki//Time & Life Pictures/Getty Images

In time it became abundantly clear that the separate schools for African American and white children were hardly equal. African American teachers were poorly paid, facilities were inadequate, and children's educational attainment suffered accordingly. On May 17, 1954, in its decision on *Brown v. Board of Education,* the Supreme Court reversed its earlier position, declaring that **racial segregation** in public education was unconstitutional. The Court said, "We conclude that in the field of education the doctrine of 'separate but equal' has no place.

Separate educational facilities are inherently unequal," and concluded that segregation violated the equal protection guarantees provided by the Fourteenth Amendment.

Citizens' (sometimes violent) opposition to the Court's decision has been well documented (see Bouma & Hoffman, 1968; Crain, 1968; Damerell, 1968; Rubin, 1972). Opponents of desegregation argue that (1) it does not significantly improve academic achievement of minority children, (2) it effectively denies children access to neighborhood schools, and (3) schools play an insignificant role in the reduction of racial inequality (Scott, 2003).

The nation's progress toward school desegregation has been halting and remains incomplete. Twelve years after the *Brown v. Board of Education* decision, the U.S. Office of Education concluded that "the great majority of American children attend schools that are largely segregated—that is, almost all of their fellow students are of the same racial background as they are" (U.S. Commission on Civil Rights, 1967, p. 2). Decades later, Jonathan Kozol (1991) documented abysmal conditions in the inner-city schools that served children of color. A continuing challenge for U.S. educators has been the effort to ensure equal access to education for children of all races. Head Start is an early-intervention approach designed to reduce inequality in American education.

HEAD START

One of the most significant federal investments in education, Head Start was established as part of the 1965 **War on Poverty** programs. It is managed by the Administration on Children and Families within the **U.S. Department of Health and Human Services**. Head Start offers comprehensive child development services to preschool children from low-income families. The program operates by extending grants to nonprofit and community organizations that administer individual programs. Eligibility requirements vary, but most spaces are reserved for children who come from families with incomes below the federal poverty limit. Programs also vary in the types of services they offer. Head Start programs have some required components, including educational and social services for families. Most establish links with social service providers serving low-income families in their communities. Parental involvement is another hallmark of Head Start programs.

Head Start is extremely popular, and this is reflected in federal appropriations for the program. Annual allocations grew from $96.4 million in 1966 to over $8.2 billion in 2015, when the program served just under a million children between the ages of 3 and 5—a modest increase over the 733,000 served in 1966 and a decline in the proportion of the eligible population served (See Figure 12.1). Indeed, the 2009 **American Recovery and Reinvestment Act** included an additional $2.1 billion appropriation for Head Start. But Head Start has never reached all eligible children, and in 2014–2015 reached only 41 percent (National Head Start Association, 2016).

Evaluation of the program has traditionally focused on the cognitive and academic achievements of the children involved. In 2000, the **Rand Corporation** reported on long-term effects of Head Start participation using national data from the Panel Study of Income Dynamics. Their analysis indicated that for whites, Head Start participation was associated with greater likelihood of completing high school and attending college, while African American participants were less likely to have been charged with, or convicted of, a crime (Garces, Thomas, & Currie, 2000). A congressionally mandated Head Start Impact Study demonstrated significant gains for children in the program across a range of areas, including prereading skills, social-emotional development, and physical health (Administration for Children and Families, 2005).

Head Start does have its critics. Based on the rising cost per child (over $8,000 in 2015), a comparative study by staff of the American Enterprise Institute noted that Head Start is more expensive than other pre-kindergarten programs (Besharov, Myers, & Morrow, 2007). Another

FIGURE 12.1 Head Start Enrollment and Appropriations, 1966–2015

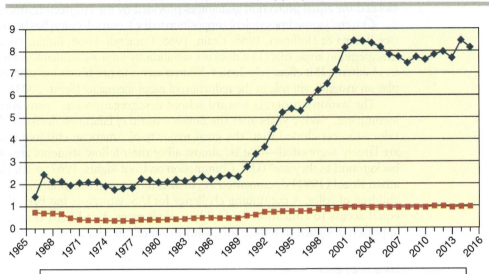

—◆— Federal Appropriations (in billions of constant 2016 dollars) —■— Enrollment (in millions)

Sources: Administration for Children and Youth, DHHS, Head Start Enrollment History Figures (https://eclkc. ohs.acf.hhs.gov/hslc/data/factsheets/2015-hs-program-factsheet.html, accessed October 20, 2016). Inflation adjustment computed using Bureau of Labor Statistics CPI inflation calculator (http://data.bls.gov/ cgi-bin/cpicalc.pl, accessed October 20, 2016).

conservative think tank, the Heritage Foundation, trumpeted results of an HHS impact study indicating "few sustained benefits" from participation (The Heritage Foundation, 2010).[8]

Nonetheless, President Obama consistently favored expansion of early childhood education programs like Head Start; and over the past few years, more states have been funding public preschool initiatives. By 2015, only five states (Idaho, Montana, New Hampshire, South Dakota, and Wyoming) did not use some state funding for prekindergarten programs (Education Commission of the States, 2016).

EDUCATING CHILDREN WITH DISABILITIES

Most of us are aware that the 1954 Supreme Court decision in *Brown v. The Board of Education of Topeka* addressed school segregation.[9] But the case also had implications for the education of children with disabilities because it established the principle of equal access to educational opportunity (Yell, Rogers, & Lodge Rodgers, 1998). Nonetheless, 20 years would pass before these implications were addressed. In 1975, Gerald Ford signed the Education for All Handicapped Children Act requiring states that received federal funds to provide "free and appropriate public education" to children with disabilities. Later, in 1990, this act was incorporated in the Individuals with Disabilities Education Act (IDEA). Under current law, states must provide:

- Free and appropriate public education for all children with disabilities, regardless of the severity of the disability

---

[8]For copies of the report itself see HHS's 2010 report, *Head Start Impact Study: Final Report* (http://www.acf.hhs. gov/programs/opre/hs/impact_study/reports/impact_study/executive_summary_finl.pdf).

[9]I am indebted to Elizabeth LaMont, doctoral candidate at the University of Utah, for providing background information for this section.

- An **individualized education program (IEP)** for every eligible child
- Access to education in a regular classroom if possible
- Related services necessary to support the child in an educational environment (such as counseling, therapy, health services, and rehabilitation)
- Parental rights to participate in planning and consent to any change in educational programming
- **Due process** procedures to allow parents to appeal placement and other decisions
- Confidentiality of records

Nonetheless, state and federal resources for education are limited and, as we saw in Chapter 8, parents of children with disabilities must exercise vigilance (and sometimes engage in litigation) to secure the "free and appropriate public education" to which their children are entitled.

MODERN EDUCATIONAL REFORMS

Recent educational reforms have addressed two aspects of public education in the United States: school financing and school choice.

School Financing

Throughout their history, American public elementary and secondary schools have been financed through local and state **appropriations**. Federal contributions typically represent only a small fraction of education budgets. State money comes from either general tax revenues or property taxes. The U.S. Department of Education reported that total funding for K-12 public education in the United States in 2008–2009 was $661 billion, about 4.6 percent of the gross national product (National Center for Education Statistics, 2009). Most of that comes from a combination of state funds (about 45 percent) and local taxes (another 45 percent). About 7 percent comes from federal sources and 2 percent from private sources (National Center for Education Statistics, 2004).

Inequality has been a hallmark of school financing in the United States. In his landmark book, *Savage Inequalities,* Jonathan Kozol (1991) noted "a certain grim aesthetic in the almost perfect upward scaling of expenditures from poorest of the poor to richest of the rich within the New York City area: $5,590 for the children of the Bronx and Harlem, $6,340 for the nonwhite kids of Roosevelt, $6,400 for the black kids of Mount Vernon, $7,400 for the slightly better-off community of Yonkers, over $11,000 for the very lucky children of Manhasset, Jericho and Great Neck" (pp. 122–123).

State funding models for education do little to address these inequalities. The "foundation program" was introduced in the early 1920s to balance local control with state support for education. Under this approach, the initial funds required to operate public schools are drawn from a local tax based on the value of homes and businesses within the district. In affluent districts this amount is sufficient to meet the schools' needs. In less affluent districts, where the tax rate is the same, lower property values result in less revenue. State funds are then allocated to bring financial resources of the poorer districts up to the "foundation" level—a level that, in theory, is roughly equal to the amount used in the wealthy districts. Of course, the needs of poorer districts are often greater because children experience higher rates of family dysfunction and community stress. Needs aside, poorer districts receive less funding because states set the "foundation level" to provide a bare minimum, not to establish an adequate educational foundation.

Kozol (1991) vividly documented the educational minimum provided for children in poor districts:

> Christopher approaches me at the end of class. The room is too hot. His skin looks warm and his black hair is damp. "Write this down. You asked a question about Martin Luther King. I'm going to say something. All that stuff about the dream means nothing to the kids I know in East St. Louis. So far as they're concerned, he died in vain. He was famous and he lived and gave his speeches and he died and now he's gone … don't tell students in this school about the dream. Go and look into a toilet here if you would like to know what life is like for students in this city." I do as Christopher asked…. Four of the six toilets do not work. The toilet stalls, which are eaten away by red and brown corrosion, have no doors. The toilets have no seats. One has a rotted wooden stump. There are no paper towels and no soap. Near the door there is a loop of wire with an empty toilet-paper roll. (p. 36)

Disparities in school finances have resulted in lawsuits against most states. One of the earliest was filed in Texas in 1968. In a **class action suit** *(Rodriguez v. San Antonio Independent School District),* plaintiffs charged that the unequal financing of education violated the equal protection clause of the U.S. Constitution. After years of litigation, the state was forced to change its method of school financing. Similar outcomes have been observed throughout the nation. During the last four decades of the 20th century, more than 40 school finance cases were heard in state supreme courts (Center for Education Reform, 1999).

At the federal level, Title I of the Elementary and Secondary Education Act of 1965 (EASE) was designed to address the difficulties experienced by schools in low-income neighborhoods. Title I is the largest single source of federal funding for K-12 education, representing 21 percent of the 2015 budget request for the Department of Education (U.S. Department of Education, n.d.a). Funds are used to provide teachers, tutoring, labs, parent involvement activities, prekindergarten programs, and other resources for schools in which at least 40 percent of students qualify for free or reduced-price lunch programs. These are aptly termed "Title I schools."

No Child Left Behind

The **No Child Left Behind Act** of 2001 (NCLB) revised the ESEA to hold public schools accountable for their students' mastery of core subjects, particularly reading and mathematics. Although its testing requirements applied to all public schools, NCLB imposed special requirements on Title I schools. Under the act, each state was required to test student progress in reading and math annually in grades 3 through 8, and at least once during grades 10 through 12. Title I schools were required to demonstrate "adequate yearly progress" across several student groups. Schools failing to make progress were placed on the dreaded "Schools in Need of Improvement" list, and those on the list for two years or more faced sanctions. Appropriations under the act amounted to a significant increase in federal funding for education. The act also included requirements for teacher qualifications and protections for school prayer.

The reauthorization of the No Child Left Behind Act in 2007 triggered intense debate. The law had done little to ease educational disparities. Its testing and penalties were controversial, and implementation challenged many school districts. Teachers objected that the act was forcing them to "teach to the test" (National Education Association, n.d.). In 2004, the General Accounting Office had reported that districts were sometimes unable to provide viable alternative schools to students from Title I schools that had been sanctioned with school choice (U.S. General Accounting Office, 2004). Some districts learned to "game the system" through manipulation of testing procedures.

Sonda Dawes/The Image Works

▶ Promotional materials for No Child Left Behind in front of the U.S. Department of Education

Recognizing widespread dissatisfaction with NCLB, in 2011 the Obama administration announced modifications to the implementation of the statute. A waiver system was established to provide some flexibility to states that were unable to reach NCLB benchmarks, and 43 states and the District of Columbia received waivers (U.S. Department of Education, n.d.b). In addition, with $4 billion from the American Recovery and Reinvestment Act of 2009, a four-year competitive grant program known as "Race to the Top" was established to encourage school reform. Eleven states and the District of Columbia secured **Race to the Top** grants, which were used to spearhead an intense process of system reform. While there is some evidence of increased high school completion rates in these states, the grants' impacts on student achievement have not been rigorously evaluated (U.S. Department of Education, 2015).

Hoping to build agreement for national curriculum standards at the state level, the National Governors Association began work on a "Common Core" of educational standards in math and literacy. The NGA released the standards in 2009. As of this writing, 42 states had signed on (Common Core State Standards Initiative, n.d.).

Lotteries

No doubt 19th-century educational reformers would have been astonished by the concept of using gambling revenues to finance the public schools. In 1964, New Hampshire became the first state to establish a **lottery**. Since then, 36 more states and the District of Columbia have set up lotteries (North American Association of State and Provincial Lotteries, 1999). Most devote part of their proceeds to education. In Georgia lotteries support college funds called "Hope" scholarships. The practice of allocating some proceeds to education has increased public support for the lottery.

In no case does lottery funding provide a substantial portion of the educational budget. In California, less than 2 percent of the 2006–2007 budget for public schools was drawn from the lottery (Education Data Partnership, 2007). Further, most states with lotteries have used the funds not to *increase* but to *replace* state dollars that had been going to education, resulting in little to no net growth in school funding (Strauss, 2012).

As the government has moved into the gaming business, social workers and other helping professionals have become aware of gambling's toll. Compulsive gamblers have been compared to alcoholics in their capacity to ignore the costs of their problem behavior. Apart from the growing problem of compulsive gambling, professionals are concerned that those who participate in the lottery (the vast majority of whom lose money) come primarily from poor and working-class backgrounds. Thus, the lottery is a regressive way to finance public education.

School Choice: Tuition Vouchers and Charter Schools

Traditionally, children in the United States have been assigned to the school serving their neighborhood. School choice reforms give parents the opportunity to select the school that their children will attend. At its most basic level, school choice enables parents to send their children to any public school within the state. More complex and controversial school choice reforms include **tuition vouchers** and **charter schools**.

Under existing tuition voucher programs, the state or local school district provides parents with a portion of the educational funding allotted to their children and allows them to use these funds to enroll their children in the school of their choice. In some states tuition vouchers can be used only for secular schools, while in other jurisdictions parents may use the vouchers to send their children to religious schools.[10] Tuition voucher programs have been vigorously opposed by teachers' unions at local and federal levels. Opponents of the programs argue that they damage public schools by diverting needed funds and by draining away the most academically motivated students. As a result, they argue, schools in poorer districts will deteriorate even further.

Proponents argue that giving parents in low-income areas the opportunity to send their children to schools outside their neighborhoods equalizes educational opportunities and gives neighborhood schools the motivation to improve. School choice is the educational reform of preference for libertarians, most notably Milton Friedman (Friedman, 1955). According to Friedman, "a society that takes freedom of the individual, or more realistically the family, as its ultimate objective, seeks to further this objective by relying primarily on voluntary exchange among individuals for the organization of economic activity" (p. 1). Libertarians argue that parents should be given vouchers and the opportunity to purchase education in any licensed school, public or private.

Whereas tuition vouchers address the "demand" side of the education equation by enabling parents to shop for schools, charter schools address the "supply" side. Enthusiastically endorsed by Bill Clinton in 2000, the charter school movement has now become fairly entrenched, although it remains controversial.

---

[10]The use of public funds to send children to religious schools has been subjected to several court challenges. In a 1998 case, the Wisconsin Supreme Court ruled in favor of the practice.

Thirty-nine states have passed laws that allow for the establishment of charter schools through a charter or contract that sets specific academic goals that must be met. Each school receives an allotment from the school district for students who choose to attend. Charter schools are, therefore, public schools, although some see them as an effort to "privatize" public education.

Exempt from district curriculum requirements and governance, charter schools are managed by a charter board. Of course, the per-pupil allotment for charter schools is either the same as in established public schools or a lesser amount, and charter schools often face high start-up expenses to acquire buildings and purchase equipment. Therefore, their financial situation may be unstable. Opponents of charter schools argue that they are not feasible alternatives for low-income families and that they siphon affluent and academically motivated students away from the traditional public schools.

The impact of charter schools on public education has not been determined. A 2004 report released by the American Federation of Teachers argued that student achievement in charter schools lagged behind that in traditional public schools (Nelson, Rosenberg, & Van Meter, 2004). On the other hand, a 2011 meta-analysis conducted by the National Charter School Research Project at the University of Washington suggested that in some areas charter schools were outperforming traditional public schools (Betts & Tang, 2011). Even today, rigorous research on the impacts of charter schools is quite limited (Center for Public Education, n.d.). Without it, the debate tends to revolve around political and ideological arguments on the nature and value of public education. Meanwhile, charter schools continue to play a significant role in U.S. educational reforms.

LO 12-4   Understand How Children in the United States Have Been Victimized Through Poverty and Violence

EP 2a
EP 5c

Public response to child victimization in the United States has been marked by episodes of high interest, followed by extended periods of indifference or inattention. American children have been victims of both poverty and violence.

POVERTY AND CHILDREN, PAST AND PRESENT

In colonial times, children who were impoverished through parental death or other circumstances often were sold as indentured servants. In theory, this practice was designed to teach children a trade or skill, but more often indentured servants were assigned menial tasks and functioned virtually as slaves until they reached the age of release (21 or 24 for boys; 18 for girls). During indenture, parents lost their custody rights, so children were sold only under dire circumstances. During the 19th century, institutional alternatives were established in major cities. Instead of being indentured, impoverished children were sent to orphanages, almshouses, or poorhouses.

A harbinger of change came in 1909, when James E. West, a friend of President Theodore Roosevelt who had been raised in an orphanage, persuaded the president to convene a Conference on the Care of Dependent Children. The conference brought the needs of these children to national attention, setting the stage for the development of a public child welfare system (Trattner, 1989). Its keynote statement proclaimed, "Home life is the highest and finest product of civilization…. [C]hildren should not be deprived of it except for urgent and compelling reasons" (Trattner, 1989, p. 194). The conference led to a reduced emphasis on institutionalization and an increased use of adoption and foster homes for children in need. It also was the first in a series of conferences of its kind, held every 10 years until 1981, when it was canceled by the Reagan administration. Despite support from advocates such as the Child Welfare League of America, there has not been a White House conference on children since 1971.

The U.S. Children's Bureau was established in 1912, three years after the first White House Conference on Children, despite fierce opposition from business interests who feared it would signal the end of child labor. They were prescient.

Julia Lathrop, a former Hull House resident and member of the Illinois State Board of Charities, took over as director of the agency. She chose infant mortality as the agency's initial focus. It seemed to be a relatively noncontroversial issue. After all, if the federal government spent $1.25 million a year for the Bureau of Animal Husbandry, shouldn't it devote some of its resources to care for the nation's children?

The matter quickly became controversial, however. In 1918, based on research by the Children's Bureau, Jeanette Rankin (the first woman to serve in Congress) introduced the Sheppard-Towner Bill. The bill called for the federal government to offer grants-in-aid to states that would provide health care and education to disadvantaged mothers. Opponents accused Lathrop of being part of the recent Bolshevik revolution and charged that the state was taking over the upbringing and medical care of children. Medical societies attacked the bill, its sponsor, and the staff of the Children's Bureau. In one of the debate's more vitriolic statements, Senator Thomas Reed of Missouri argued that if the bill passed, "female celibates would instruct mothers on how to bring up their babies" (Trattner, 1989, p. 199). Despite these views, after three years of debate and the ratification of the Nineteenth Amendment granting women the right to vote, the bill passed in 1921 and was signed by President Warren G. Harding.

Under the bill's mandate, between 1921 and 1929 nearly 3,000 maternal and child health centers were established in 45 states (Trattner, 1989, p. 199). State health departments were strengthened, and infant and maternal mortality rates dropped significantly. Despite the act's effectiveness, Congress refused to renew funding in 1929, bowing to the opposition of both medical professionals and the new president, Herbert Hoover. Later, Title V of the 1939 Social Security Act would again establish federal grants-in-aid that enabled the Children's Bureau to resume its work in maternal and child health. This program operates today under the auspices of the Department of Health and Human Services.

As we saw in Chapter 5, children in the United States face a higher risk of poverty than any other age group. On an international level, the United States has a higher rate of child poverty than any other nation in the Organisation for Economic Co-operation and Development (OECD) (see Table 12.1). Modern policies regarding child poverty in the United States reveal deep ambivalence. On the one hand, the notion of children suffering is unacceptable. Thus, development of educational programs, health care, and even social services for children in poverty seldom encounters serious opposition. On the other hand, the nation has long been inclined to blame adults for their indigence. Most children in poverty are intimately linked to an adult in poverty. Therein lies the ambivalence. If what it takes to move a child out of poverty is financial assistance to a member of the undeserving poor, the nation balks.

This ambivalence is evident in the history of income maintenance programs funded under the Social Security Act. Initially, Title IV of the act established a federal-state grant-in-aid program called Aid to Dependent Children (ADC). In 1962, the name of the program was changed to Aid to Families with Dependent Children (AFDC). This change reflected growing awareness of the role of the family in children's lives, and it also underscored the reality that aid was provided to families, not directly to children themselves. In 1996, the federal entitlement provided under AFDC was converted to a block

TABLE 12.1 Poverty Rates in Households with Children: 2013*

OECD Average: 13.3			
Nation	**Percent in Poverty**	**Nation**	**Percent in Poverty**
Australia	13.0	Japan	16.3
Austria	10.2	Luxembourg	12.4
Canada	16.5	Mexico	19.7
Czech Republic	10.3	Netherlands	10.5
Denmark	2.7	New Zealand	12.8
Finland	4.6	Norway	6.8
France	11.3	Portugal	18.2
Germany	9.8	Sweden	8.5
Greece	18.7	United Kingdom	9.9
Italy	17.7	**United States**	**20.5**

*Poverty thresholds set at 50 percent of median income for the population.
Source: OECD (2013) OECD Family Database, OECD, Paris - Child Outcomes (CO2.2A Child Income Poverty Rates, 2013 or nearest available year). (http://www.oecd.org/social/family/database.htm, October 21, 2016).

grant called Temporary Assistance to Needy Families (TANF). As discussed in Chapter 5, the name change is the tip of the iceberg of the changes initiated by the TANF program. Nonetheless, it is important to note that the word "children" has, for the first time since 1935, been eliminated from the name of the program that provides income security for needy families.

The consequences of child poverty are far-reaching. Children in low-income families face higher health risks, in part due to substandard housing and limited access to health care. Their educational opportunities are severely truncated. Finally, children in households with poverty-level incomes experience significantly higher rates of neglect and violence than those living in more affluent settings.

VIOLENCE AGAINST CHILDREN, PAST AND PRESENT

The latter part of the 19th century was a time of outcry for public intervention to address child abuse and neglect. In 1875, the case of "Mary Ellen" brought child abuse to public attention and led to the creation of the New York Society for the Prevention of Cruelty to Children (NYSPCC). The case has become the stuff of myth, based on the mistaken belief that in the absence of laws to protect children, those designed to protect animals were applied to protect a child. This myth has been repeated in several social work texts (for example, DiNitto, 1995; Kadushin, 1974). Yet, as Watkins (1990) demonstrated, laws to protect children were on the books as early as the 17th century. What was lacking was an entity to assume responsibility for their enforcement. The NYSPCC became that entity, and during the first 20 years of its existence, it intervened in more than 230,000 cases, with enough impact to provoke criticism of its aggressive efforts to protect abused and neglected children.

Sallie Watkins (1990) presented the facts in the Mary Ellen case. In 1864, the infant was left with the Department of Charities by a woman who claimed to have no knowledge of how to reach her parents. Mary Ellen was indentured to a family at the age of 18 months. Mary Connolly was her mistress and her abuser. Nine years later, Mrs. Etta Wheeler was visiting in poor neighborhoods when she heard complaints about a child being horribly abused. She posed as a census taker and investigated the situation in December 1873. Appalled by the child's condition, Mrs. Wheeler sought help from the police and several charitable organizations before finding an ally in Mr. Henry Bergh, president of the **New York Society for the Prevention of Cruelty to Animals** (NYSPCA). Mr. Bergh intervened in the case as a private citizen, not as a representative of the NYSPCA. The laws he invoked to remove Mary Ellen were those designed to protect people in custody. A judge issued a special warrant that led to Mary Ellen's removal from the home and the subsequent trial of her guardian, Mrs. Connolly. When searches for her parents proved unsuccessful, Mary Ellen was placed in the care of Mrs. Wheeler. She married at the age of 24, had two children, and lived into her eighties. Her abuser, Mrs. Connolly, was sent to a penitentiary for one year.

Mary Ellen's experiences were important, not because they changed the laws regarding abuse of children, but because they raised public awareness of the problem and led to the establishment of the NYSPCC.

The NYSPCC was the first organization of its kind in the world and the beginning of an "anticruelty" movement that spread throughout the United States and Europe. By 1910, more than 200 such societies had been established (Costin, 1992). The movement soon encountered a tension that to this day pervades the field of child welfare: the conflict between family privacy and child protection. The NYSPCC operated by aggressively removing children from homes and placing them in institutions. Institutionalization of children placed the organization in direct conflict with the deep-seated American preference for parental authority and family life. (As mentioned earlier, this value was articulated in the famous resolution on home life from the 1909 Conference on the Care of Dependent Children.) This conflict, coupled with social and economic conditions in the post–World War I period, drew attention away from the problem of child abuse. The ensuing period of indifference to the issue would last for several decades.

In the 1960s, child abuse was "discovered" once again. A pediatric radiologist named John Caffey reported a new "syndrome" in infants that included subdural hematomas along with atypical fractures of limbs and ribs (Caffey, 1946). In 1962, C. Henry Kempe gave this condition a name: "battered child syndrome." With this label, child abuse resurfaced as a public concern (Kempe et al., 1962).

In its rediscovered form, child abuse was considered more a medical than a social problem. Responding to the advocacy of medical professionals, states quickly passed legislation dictating a public response. Legislation was also enacted at the federal level. The Child Abuse Prevention and Treatment Act of 1974 (CAPTA) established mandatory reporting procedures under which health and human service professionals were required to notify state authorities of suspected or known cases of child abuse or neglect. The act also established the **National Center for Child Abuse and Neglect**, and it provided funding to serve troubled families.

As a direct result of federal and state legislation, more cases of abuse and neglect came to the attention of authorities, and greater numbers of children were removed from their homes. In the case of Native American children, the situation became especially egregious. In a practice that was reminiscent of the Indian boarding schools discussed in Chapter 10, Native American children removed from their homes were often placed with Caucasian foster families. Critics saw foster placement as another attempt to eradicate Native American culture, harming the very children the system was supposed to protect.

In response to these concerns, the Indian Child Welfare Act of 1978 (PL 95-608) established tribal jurisdiction over Native American children who enter the child welfare system. Tribes exercise their jurisdiction in diverse ways, but at a minimum the act calls for the placement of Native American children in foster and adoptive homes that reflect the Native American culture and for the provision of assistance (financial and educational) to enable the tribes to administer their own child welfare and family support services.

As the child welfare system matured, the practice of removing children from abusive and neglectful homes brought more children into foster care. Policy makers became concerned about this increase, noting that decades of research had illuminated flaws in the nation's foster care system. In the late 1950s, Henry Maas and Richard Engler (1959) had suggested that extended stays in foster care could produce behavior problems. Support for their view was offered at a 1963 conference sponsored by the Child Welfare League of America and the National Association of Social Workers. At this "Institute on Child Welfare Research," social scientists suggested that separating children from their parents and placing them in foster care was not always in the best interest of the child (Fanshel & Shinn, 1978). They documented an alarming phenomenon called "foster care drift," observing that children often languished for years in foster care, with little stability or planning for their future.

To address this problem, the 1980 Adoption Assistance and Child Welfare Act (PL 96-272) established clear procedures and timelines for the management of children who enter into state custody. Within 18 months of the child's placement, a dispositional hearing would be held to place the child in the least restrictive, most family-like setting that was available and appropriate. States were required to make "reasonable efforts" to reunify families. Funds were provided for reunification services, which included a wide range of supportive activities, from parenting education and stress management to budgeting and case management. If progress toward reunification was not made, the law required states to begin "permanency planning" on behalf of the child. That is, the state agency was required to develop a plan for the permanent placement of the child in long-term foster care, guardianship, or (if parental rights were terminated) adoption. The law was codified as Titles IV-B and IV-E of the Social Security Act and is still in force.

The 1980 law forced child welfare workers to make painful decisions. No longer could they wait and hope that abusive parents would change. Instead, for a limited time, workers became active partners with biological parents in an effort to preserve the family

---

BOX 12.2   The End of Childhood

For some people, turning 18 brings new privileges like the right to vote, join the military, or buy a gun; for many the responsibilities of adulthood are postponed well into their twenties. But for the nation's most vulnerable children the age of majority brings an abrupt withdrawal of supports they have relied on for a long time, in some cases as long as they can remember. These include youth who are involved with the juvenile justice system, those with physical disabilities or mental illness, and children in foster care (Osgood, Foster, & Courtney, 2010).

Since 1999, the number of children who "age out" of foster care each year has been steadily increasing, and by 2011 it was well over 20,000. Despite the availability of state and federal programs to help prepare them for the transition out of foster care (for example, Title IV-E Independent Living funds, Chafee Foster Care Independence Program, state reentry programs) these "veterans" of the system are prone to negative outcomes, including pregnancy, incarceration, poverty, and homelessness (Dworsky et al., 2012).

unit. Researchers and program administrators began to develop services and methods that would accomplish reunification. The Homebuilders program in the state of Washington was one model effort to support "family preservation"—that is, the reunification of children with their biological parents. This program developed a model of intensive services to families to prevent foster placement. Initial research on family preservation efforts was promising. Families were reunified and parenting improved (Pecora et al., 1995).

Growing enthusiasm for **family preservation** led to the 1993 passage of the **Family Preservation and Support Services Act** (PL 103-66), which provided increased funding for reunification services. Each state received an amount of money based on the number of children receiving food stamps. Unfortunately, the Homebuilders model has been hard to duplicate in other settings (Littell, 1995). Perhaps as a result, the nation's enthusiasm for family preservation seems to have reverted to an inclination toward child removal.

The **Adoption and Safe Families Act** of 1997 (PL 105-89) emphasized that the first priority in making decisions involving child welfare is the safety of children. While authorizing limited funding ($305 million in 2001) for family preservation, the law contained several provisions designed to encourage adoption, including incentive payments for states that exceed their average number of adoptions; expanded health coverage for adopted children with special needs; new, shorter, 12-month timelines for permanency hearings and filing for termination of parental rights; and modifications in provisions requiring reasonable efforts to preserve and reunify families. Under these modifications, states need not make such efforts in cases that involve "aggravated circumstances" (including but not limited to abandonment, torture, chronic abuse, and sexual abuse); cases in which parents committed (or aided, abetted, or attempted to commit) either murder or manslaughter of a child; cases involving felony assault that resulted in serious bodily injury to a child; and cases in which parental rights to the child's sibling have been involuntarily terminated. In essence, this law established several categories of "undeserving" parents and excused states from the responsibility of trying to preserve their families. In these cases, states must hold permanency hearings within 30 days (not 12 months) of a child's removal.

Reauthorization of the **Child Abuse Prevention and Treatment Act** (CAPTA) in 2010 included significant modifications. First, it expanded the requirement that health care providers refer newborns affected by prenatal drug exposure make "appropriate referrals" to child protective services to include referral of newborns diagnosed with fetal alcohol spectrum disorder. Second, the CAPTA reauthorization established that no plan for reunification is required when a parent has committed sexual abuse or is a registered sex offender. Thus, it is likely that agencies will proceed to alternative permanency planning in cases of sexual abuse. Third, CAPTA calls for criminal background checks of all other adults living in the household of prospective foster care or adoptive parents. Fourth, the act requires states to report on their efforts to encourage family involvement in CPS decisions (already mandated through family group conferencing in some states) and to promote collaboration between CPS and domestic violence and substance abuse programs.

Children of color, especially African American children, are overrepresented in the public child welfare system (Chipungu & Bent-Goodley, 2004). This is only one result of the institutional racism that pervades both American society and the child welfare system itself. As we saw in Chapter 5, African American, Hispanic, and Native American children are more likely to live in poverty. African American and Hispanic children are also more likely to have a parent who is incarcerated (see Chapter 9). In the child welfare system, cases involving African American children are more likely to be reported, investigated, and substantiated. African American children are more likely than white children under similar circumstances to be removed from their homes and remain in care and less likely to be reunified with their families (Chapin Hall Center for Children, 2009). Due to these accumulated factors, children of color, who make up one-third of the general population of children in the United States, represent over half of children in foster care (Administration for Children & Families, 2015).

The history of the U.S. child welfare system also reveals ambivalence toward the parents involved—a tendency to see them as either victims or villains. The nation puts no restrictions on procreation.[11] Americans must complete more training to become drivers than to become parents. This would suggest a "right" to raise children—one that many would intuitively endorse. Some, due to mental illness, substance abuse, or poverty, are unable to fulfill their parental obligations. Motivated by enthusiasm for biological parenting, child welfare agencies have undertaken what in some cases has amounted to heroic measures to achieve "family preservation." On the other hand, some view abusive or neglectful parents as villains, not victims. This view supports prompt removal of children from abusive homes, as well as punishment of the perpetrators. In some ways, it represents a return to the nation's 19th-century approach exemplified in the case of little Mary Ellen.

Although rates of violence have been declining worldwide, American children are more likely to be victims than children in other industrialized countries. Many take their own lives, while others are the victims of homicide, often at the hands of those charged with their care.

Among developed nations, the United States has a relatively high rate of child mortality. In 2009, the OECD reported a death rate for U.S. teens (aged 15 to 19) of 132 per 100,000, which was the third highest rate among the 26 member countries. For younger children, aged 1 to 4 years, the U.S. rate (61 per 100,000) is fifth highest. Child death rates for OECD nations are presented in Table 12.2.

Among American children under 5 the risk of being killed is highest for the youngest children, with parents being the most likely perpetrators. In 1996, homicides of children aged 5 and under reached a 40-year high. Although the rates have declined since then, a racial disparity persists, with African American children more than twice as likely to be murdered as those of other races (U.S. Department of Justice, 2011a).

Rates of death due to both homicide and suicide increase with age up to 24 years. In 2014, suicide was the second leading cause of death among Americans aged 10 to 24. Although suicide rates among girls have risen, boys remain at greatest risk (Centers for Disease Control and Prevention, 2015b). This is the case in other countries as well (McLoughlin, Gould, & Malone, 2015).

Attempts to explain youth suicide and homicide tend to focus on individual pathology. Studies have identified risk factors such as substance abuse and mental illness (Cash & Bridge, 2009; Davidson & Linnoila, 2013). Although these have clear implications for social work practice, they say little about the potential role of public policies in addressing these parallel trends. Yet research on the contribution of economic factors suggests an important role for social policy. As Holinger and others (1994) have noted, "Poverty appears to be the most consistent underlying risk factor in communities with high homicide rates" (p. 150). Economic factors such as unemployment are among the most important in determining both youth suicide and youth homicide rates. Clearly, efforts to reduce poverty and economic vulnerability will have the secondary benefit of reducing the violence experienced by America's children. In addition, improved psychiatric treatment and reduced access to guns have been cited as social changes that might reduce the likelihood of suicide (World Health Organization, 2002).

---

[11]China is probably the only nation in the world in which most people must seek government approval before becoming biological parents. Even in China, this policy is unpopular.

TABLE 12.2 Child Death Rates in OECD Nations (Deaths per 100,000 Population)

Nation	1–4 years	5–9 years	10–14 years	15–19 years
OECD Average	55	29	33	94
Australia	51	23	25	90
Austria	39	24	24	104
Belgium	87	45	55	160
Canada	44	21	28	91
Czech Republic	43	17	32	87
Denmark	44	26	33	87
Finland	41	29	26	90
France	43	20	25	78
Germany	44	21	23	78
Greece	59	44	43	128
Hungary	61	33	32	79
Iceland	24	18	26	66
Ireland	65	35	40	115
Italy	57	33	39	108
Japan	50	21	20	56
Korea	59	35	29	62
Luxembourg	21	16	14	69
Mexico	145	57	69	140
Netherlands	50	24	28	65
New Zealand	60	27	36	133
Norway	44	22	27	83
Poland	53	32	36	92
Portugal	82	49	56	125
Slovak Republic	85	38	34	86
Spain	48	24	30	81
Sweden	39	21	26	69
Switzerland	57	29	36	108
United Kingdom	47	21	27	75
United States	61	29	37	132

Source: OECD (2009). Comparative Child Well-Being Across the OECD. (http://www.oecd.org/els/family/ 43570328.pdf, accessed September 8, 2013).

BULLYING

In 2013, about one in five (21.5 percent) of students aged 12 to 18 reported that they had been bullied at school—generally through ridicule, name-calling, or insults (National Center for Education Statistics, 2016). Those who identify or are perceived as gay, lesbian, or trans are especially vulnerable to bullying, leading Katherine Van Wormer and Robin McKinney to describe the United States as "a toxic environment for gender nonconforming girls and boys" (2003; p. 410). Many face parental rejection and peer bullying, a combination that can lead to distress, homelessness, and—in the worst case—suicide. Several highly publicized cases of bullying and suicide have focused attention on the nation's schools, leading the U.S. Secretary of Education to issue several guidance letters to remind school administrators of their responsibility to address bullying and harassment as matters of civil rights (U.S. Department of Education, 2010, 2014).

EP 2a
EP 4b
EP 5c

Teen Pregnancy

Teen pregnancy creates two high-risk children: a child-mother and an infant. The mother is less likely than older mothers to receive adequate prenatal care. She is also less likely to finish high school and more likely to depend on public assistance (National Campaign to Prevent Teen Pregnancy, 2006). Children born to teenage mothers have lower birth weights, are more likely to perform poorly in school, and experience higher rates of abuse and neglect (George & Lee, 1997; Maynard, 1996; Wolfe & Perozek, 1997). Sons of teen mothers are more likely to spend time in prison, while daughters of teens are more likely (like Lorenzo's sister) to become teen mothers themselves (Maynard, 1996).

Now at historic lows, the teen pregnancy rate in the United States peaked in 1991, at 116.5 pregnancies per 1,000 teens aged 15 to 19. It declined to a record low of 52.4 pregnancies per 1,000 teens in 2011. Seeking to understand this decline, the Guttmacher Institute researchers examined data and surveys regarding teen sexual behavior and concluded that it was primarily due to increased use of contraception, although greater abstinence was a contributing factor. Teen pregnancy rates among Hispanic Americans and African Americans remain considerably higher than those among Asian and Caucasian Americans (Sedgh et al., 2015).

Teen birth rates have dropped along with pregnancy rates. Births to American females aged 15 to 19 peaked in 1957 at 96 births per 1,000 females (Guttmacher Institute, 2002). In 2011, the National Center for Health Statistics reported a rate of 31 births per 1,000 teens (NCHS, 2012). Trends in teen birth rates are illustrated in Figure 12.2.

FIGURE 12.2 Teen Birth Rates in the United States: 1991, 2000, 2006, 2015

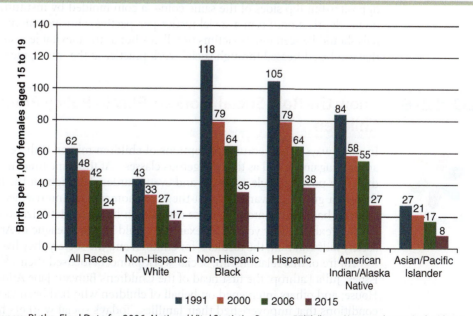

SOURCES: Births: Final Data for 2006, *National Vital Statistics Reports, 57*(7) (http://www.cdc.gov/nchs/data/nvsr/nvsr57/nvsr57_07.pdf); Births: Final Data for 2011, *National Vital Statistics Reports, 62*(11) (http://www.cdc.gov/nchs/data/nvsr/nvsr62/nvsr62_01.pdf).

Like other issues in child welfare, the problem of teen pregnancy challenges the division between private familial matters and the public interest. Most Americans believe teenagers should abstain from sex, but they also feel that sexually active teens should have access to contraception (Princeton Survey Research Associates, 1997). Most also believe that teens should seek information about sex and reproduction from their parents, but sometimes this does not happen. Teen pregnancy has consequences, not only for the family involved but for the broader community. Recognizing the public interest in preventing teen pregnancies, U.S. schools typically offer rudimentary education on sex and reproduction. These educational efforts generate controversy, particularly when coupled with proposals to educate teens about contraception or to provide contraceptive devices. Abortion is even more controversial. Although abortion is legal in the United States, most states require that teenagers seeking abortions have parental approval (Guttmacher Institute, 2013a, 2013b).

The United States reports the highest rates of teen pregnancy and teen births in the developed world outside the former Soviet bloc. (Sedgh et al., 2015). This observation has been consistent for decades despite declining rates of teen pregnancy and birth in the United States, and it is generally attributed to lower contraceptive use in America (Guttmacher Institute, 2002; Sedgh et al., 2015). There is some evidence that lower rates of teen pregnancy and birth in Europe are associated with the availability of free contraception (Part et al., 2013).

LO 12-5   Become Aware That Children of Color Are Disproportionately Represented in the U.S. Child Welfare System

In Chapter 9 we learned that children of color are overrepresented in the juvenile justice system. This chapter echoes that theme, as we see that African American and Hispanic children are more likely to experience teen pregnancy, even as they are disproportionately involved in the child welfare system. This suggests that victim and villain are not polar opposites but flip sides of the same coin—a coin molded by institutional racism and economic deprivation. From a social justice perspective, abusive parents and youthful criminals should be seen not as victims or villains but as the inevitable result of systemic failures that can be addressed through social work practice at the micro, mezzo, and macro levels.

LO 12-6   Know the Role Social Workers Play in Policy Practice Related to Children

EP 3a

In some ways, 21st-century perceptions of children mirror 19th-century views. Children are once again viewed as the "dangerous classes." At the same time, many of America's children face poverty, neglect, abuse, and even murder. Throughout the field of child welfare, there is a growing awareness that these phenomena are intertwined. A growing body of research has documented the close association between victimization of children and the violence exhibited by youth (for example, Child Welfare League of America, 1997). When society fails children, the results—for children and the society they live in—are devastating.

Aware of this relationship, social work pioneers focused their efforts on child welfare issues. Julia Lathrop, the first head of the Children's Bureau; Jane Addams, founder of Hull House; and others intervened on behalf of children who had been victimized by the social conditions that impoverished their families. Today's social workers have the opportunity to continue the profession's long tradition of progressive advocacy on behalf of children. In the areas of child protective services, education, and juvenile delinquency, reasoned advocacy is needed as much today as it was in the 19th century.[12] In some ways, the tools for this advocacy effort remain the same: state-of-the-art research that documents conditions and evaluates programs and passionate advocates who can communicate the implications of that research to policy makers and the public.

Advocates have also discovered the power of litigation for improving the policies and programs that affect the nation's children. The use of the courts for social advocacy was alluded to in the discussion of school finance, which described how inequalities have been challenged by a series of class action lawsuits. These suits have also been used to improve services for abused and neglected children. Several state child welfare agencies have been targets of class action suits, and a few have come under judicial supervision. This direct oversight of executive functions places the judiciary in a new role. It also frequently has the effect of increasing the financial resources available for child welfare services.

Closing Reflections

The United States is a dangerous place for children, and American children face greater risks than their age peers in other industrialized nations. Approximately one in five American children live in families with poverty-level incomes—the highest child poverty rate in the developed world. The nation's infant mortality rate is also higher here than in other developed nations. Finally, American children face an unparalleled risk of neglect, abuse, suicide, and murder—all of this in the most affluent nation on earth.

The well-being of the nation's children depends less on resources than on political will. George Henry Payne observed that "the general history of the child … moves as from one mountain peak to another with a long valley of gloom in between" (Costin, 1992, p. 194). This certainly applies to policies affecting America's children. Social workers have long attempted to harness the energy and commitment of the peak times to sustain the nation's children through extended periods of indifference.

Today, social workers in child welfare confront Herculean tasks. Aware of broad social trends that might preclude effective parenting, they help troubled people learn to raise their children. In a system that seems increasingly punitive toward low-income parents, they help judges, administrators, and policy makers understand that the interests of a child overlap the rights of the parents. Aware of the educational failures that lead poor children to drop out of school and the economic transformations that have left them without viable employment options, they strive to keep disadvantaged youngsters out of gangs. Facing public skepticism about the effectiveness of "throwing money at education," they sustain local, state, and federal support for Head Start.

In child welfare, social workers embody the principle of *parens patriae*. They serve as the arms of the state, reaching out to remove children from dangerous settings. The broader challenge now is to convert those settings into communities and homes capable of nurturing human beings—to transition from removing children from impoverished and neglectful settings to building healthy, sustainable communities for children and their families.

---

[12]There is a tendency to pit children's needs against those of the elderly. The nation has roughly twice as many citizens under the age of 18 as it does over the age of 65 (Pecora et al., 2000). Yet our financial commitment to the elderly (through Medicare, Social Security, and related programs) dwarfs our investment in children's education and care. See Chapter 14 for a discussion of the politics of intergenerational equity in the United States.

Think About It

1. What does your state constitution say about education? Has the state fulfilled its commitment in this area?

2. Do you think public child welfare agencies should allow gay and lesbian adoptions? If so, how should the agency manage public debate around the issue? Should it quietly allow a few qualified gay and lesbian couples to adopt? Would it be better to hold public forums on the topic? If agency policies prevent adoption by gay and lesbian couples, is the agency vulnerable to lawsuits?

3. Do you think school choice programs undermine public education? Who uses these programs? Are they serving low-income families? Why do you think the teachers' unions oppose vouchers?

4. What macroeconomic and social trends do you think contribute to youth violence in the United States? Have social policies contributed?

5. How have issues of diversity influenced child welfare policy in the United States?

6. Is there an established "right to parenthood" in the United States? Should everyone have the right to bear and raise their biological children?

Web-Based Exercises

For direct links to all the sites in these exercises, visit the *Foundations of Social Policy* Companion Site at www.cengagebrain.com and select the resources for Chapter 12.

1. Go to the website of the Child Welfare League of America (www.cwla.org) and do a search for material on "international adoptions." What are the trends in international adoption? From the CWLA's perspective, what are the domestic and international policy issues affecting this type of adoption? Now do a Google search on "policy issues in international adoption." What organizations are posting material on this topic? How do their perspectives differ from that of the CWLA?

2. Visit the website of the Children's Defense Fund (www.childrensdefense.org) and list the policy concerns mentioned on the home page. This will give you an idea of the fund's advocacy priorities. Do they match your view of the most pressing problems affecting the nation's children? Why or why not? What sort of advocacy steps does the fund want you to take? Do you think these will be effective? Why or why not?

3. Go to the OECD website (www.oecd.org) and search for "comparative child well-being." You should find a report that offers a country-comparison of a range of well-being measures across 30 OECD countries. Download the pdf file and skim the report. Select a measure of interest to you and see how the United States compares with other similar nations.

Competency Notes

As mentioned in the preface to this text, the Council on Social Work Education has designated nine core competencies and related practice behaviors that must be addressed by accredited social work programs. In these notes, I will specify the way chapter content addresses these competencies and behaviors. (This is designed to assist with the accreditation process.) Please refer to the "helping hands" icons for the locations of specific content in this chapter. Here you will find a brief explanation of how the accompanying content relates to the specified competency or practice behaviors.

The following list indicates where EPAS competencies and practice behaviors are addressed in this chapter.

EP 2a   **Apply and communicate understanding of the importance of diversity and difference in shaping life experiences in practice at the micro, mezzo, and macro levels.** The chapter addresses racial disproportion in the child welfare system, as well as the vulnerability of children of color in relation to several social indices.

EP 3a   **Apply their understanding of social, economic, and environmental justice to advocate for human rights at the individual and system levels.** The chapter discusses emerging notions of the proper role of government versus family in child welfare. Content on disparities (and bullying) in the education system and the challenges associated with educating children with disabilities prepares students to advocate for human rights in these areas.

EP 4b   **Apply critical thinking to engage in critical analysis of quantitative and qualitative research methods and research findings.** Research findings are referenced and research methods are critiqued in several sections, including those on charter schools and teen pregnancy.

EP 5a   **Identify social policy at the local, state, and federal level that impacts well-being, service delivery, and access to social services.** Policies discussed in this chapter (particularly adoption and education policies) are designed to advance the well-being of children and their families.

EP 5c   **Apply critical thinking to analyze, formulate, and advocate for policies that advance human rights and social, economic, and environmental justice.** The history of policies that affect children has been influenced by changing conceptions of children and shifting attitudes toward their behavior. The chapter also discusses emerging notions of the proper role of government versus family in child welfare.

Suggested Resources

Davidson, L., & Linnoila, M. (Eds.). (2013). *Risk Factors for Youth Suicide.* New York: Routledge.

McAuley, C., Pecora, P. J., & Rose, W. (Eds.). (2006). *Enhancing the Well-being of Children and Families Through Effective Interventions: International Evidence for Practice.* London & Philadelphia: Jessica Kingsley Publishers.

O'Connor, S. (2001). *Orphan Trains: The Story of Charles Loring Brace and the Children He Saved and Failed.* New York: Houghton Mifflin.

Public Broadcasting System. (2005). *Aging Out: A Documentary.* (http://www.pbs.org/wnet/agingout/index-hi.html)

www.adoptioninstitute.org. The Evan B. Donaldson Adoption Institute is a nonprofit organization committed to improving adoption policy and practice. The policy page offers issue papers on a range of current policies related to adoption.

www.childrensdefense.org. The Children's Defense Fund considers itself "America's strongest voice for children." This website offers CDF reports and summaries on topics ranging from child care to gun control.

www.cwla.org. The Child Welfare League of America is the nation's oldest and largest nonprofit organization, committed to "developing and promoting policies and programs to protect America's children and strengthen America's families." Their website offers a list of publications that can be browsed by subject, as well as current news on a wide range of issues related to child welfare.

www.ed.gov. The home page of the U.S. Department of Education offers a tremendous array of publications with an excellent search engine. It is a good source of general information and a good way to become familiar with the current administration's position on issues affecting education.

www.teenpregnancy.org. This site is maintained by the National Campaign to Prevent Teen and Unplanned Pregnancy. It offers current reports on topics related to teen pregnancy in the United States, as well as links to related sites.

CHAPTER

13

Women

If I were asked…to what the singular prosperity and growing strength of that people [Americans] ought mainly to be attributed, I should reply: To the superiority of their women.

ALEXIS DE TOCQUEVILLE, *DEMOCRACY IN AMERICA*

Learning Objectives

This chapter will help prepare students to:

LO 13-1 Know about past and present social policies affecting women's roles as wives and mothers

LO 13-2 Know about past and present social policies concerning women's reproductive rights

LO 13-3 Know about past and present policies regarding violence against women

LO 13-4 Become aware of policy issues affecting women in the workplace

LO 13-5 Become aware of policy issues affecting women in the military

LO 13-6 Reflect on women's struggle for political equality

LO 13-7 Understand some of the challenges women face in the social work profession

The status of women in the United States is neither singular nor static. A woman's situation is determined by factors apart from gender, such as culture, class, and sexual orientation. Therefore, it is probably more appropriate to speak of the "statuses" of American women. These statuses evolve and change in response to social movements and economic trends. Despite this diversity and flux, gender is pivotal in the allocation of resources, rights, and responsibilities in the United States and abroad. Thus, it is an important consideration in the pursuit of social justice.

LO 13-1   Know About Past and Present Social Policies Affecting Women's Roles as Wives and Mothers

EP 1b
EP 5c

A recurring theme in policies that affect women as wives and mothers is the fear that government intrusion will violate the sanctity of the home. Americans have always distrusted government intervention, and the notion that "a man's home is his castle" has run counter to public policy efforts on behalf of women. To a great extent, early American public policy treated wives and mothers as the wards of their husbands. In this section, we will examine the impact of this perspective in relation to property rights and credit, divorce, reproductive rights, domestic violence, and rape.

PROPERTY RIGHTS AND CREDIT

From the 17th through the early 19th century, married women were subject to a common-law doctrine called "**coverture**." This principle was based on biblical notions of the unity of spouses and simply held that a man and his wife were "one person in the law" (Rhode, 1989, p. 10). The "one," of course, was the husband. Wives could not hold, acquire, control, bequeath, or convey property; enter into contracts; or initiate legal actions. Indeed, they could not legally withhold their wages from their husbands. The gender-based division of activity that was enforced by coverture had as its rationale a set of norms that have been described by historians as the "doctrine of separate spheres." According to this view, women were best suited to private roles within the home, while men's character traits prepared them for public roles. Accordingly, women were legally barred from higher education, most professions, and public office. There were individual exceptions to these rules, such as women who ran taverns or were active in business. Often these women operated as "agents" for their husbands.

As it turned out, strict restrictions on married women's property rights impeded commerce in the emerging nation. This was the case, for example, when a deserted wife could not sell her property or enter into contracts. Thus, beginning in 1839, state legislatures began to remove the most blatant restrictions on women's legal capacity. Several jurisdictions enacted married women's property acts, which granted wives certain powers. Nonetheless, even as late as 1970, men continued to be given preference over women in the selection of guardians, trustees, and executors of estates (*Reed v. Reed*, 404 U.S. 71 [1971]).

Limitations on women's property rights contributed to restrictions on their ability to borrow money. As long as married women could not enter into contracts, they could not take out loans. Just over 45 years ago, many divorced women lacked credit records and thus were unable to borrow money. The Equal Credit Opportunity Act of 1974 prohibited discrimination in lending on the basis of sex. The Federal Trade Commission issued "Regulation B," which spells out the procedures for implementing the act's provisions. Among these is the requirement that credit records for husbands and wives be maintained separately, each reflecting the experiences of the couple. Further, organizations must disclose the reasons whenever credit is denied.

DIVORCE

Historically, the federal government has not been a major force in developing family law in the United States. As a result, divorce statutes vary from state to state. Further, many of the hard decisions in a divorce are made by individual judges using state law as a reference point. In this section, we will consider three aspects of divorce: the grounds under which it is granted, the division of marital resources, and child custody. Divorce laws have undergone substantial changes in each of these areas.

Annie Boone works for a grassroots organization called Justice, Economic Dignity, and Independence for Women (JEDI Women) (the same organization that helped Melissa in Chapter 1). Walking into its storefront offices, the visitor enters a beehive of activity. Men and women bustle through the main hall from office to office, displaying a sense of purpose and commitment. Annie serves as JEDI Women's lead organizer, a full-time position that carries health benefits but no pension coverage. Her office is in the middle of all the activity, and she found it challenging to carve out time for our interview.

Annie is energetic and capable, with a rapid-fire manner of speaking. Her face framed by bouncy brown curls, Annie dresses in jeans and looks much younger than her age (late thirties). She has testified before the state legislature and the U.S. Congress and spoken to audiences numbering in the hundreds. She is frustrated by the insensitivity of lawmakers and shows contempt for women who don't understand life outside of their "Cinderella stories."

Hers is not a Cinderella story. Annie experienced abuse at the hands of her father, her husband, and her sons. She raised four children on public assistance and wrote an article about her experiences called "A Wedding Band Is a Never-Ending Circle, and So Is Abuse" for the *Georgetown Journal on Fighting Poverty*. In it she relates,

> I grew up thinking my only role in life was to become Betty Crocker—a good wife and a caring mother for my children. This message was inbred in me from the day I was born. A wife and a mother were all I ever wanted to be. I was never informed that … I should get as much schooling as I possibly could so that if something happened between my husband and myself, I could always take care of myself. The husband was the breadwinner of the family, and what he said went, whether you liked it or not. Women were to stay home, take care of their children, cook, and stay pregnant. (p. 13)

Annie's father was illiterate. Although he never abused his wife physically, he was very abusive with the children. His desire to control Annie was so powerful that he nailed her bedroom window shut and installed a lock on the outside of her bedroom door. As Annie said, "If he really wanted me in my bedroom, I was in my bedroom." She described one incident:

> You know, he loved me to death, but his violence was, like, out of control. I can remember when

I came home late one time from school and … he was upset because I didn't clean my room … When I came in the door he started yelling at me, so I went up to my room and I slammed my bedroom door. He came in there and he was just irate, and he started pulling all my clothes out of the drawers and … kicking me in the back, you know, with his steel-toed boots.… Abuse was pretty much the norm, you know.

Annie met her future husband, Jim, when she was 14. He wasn't violent before they married. "He was a sweetheart, you know, a charmer." The tension between Annie and her father escalated until "just about a half a year before I turned 16, I came home and all my stuff was on the front porch, and my dad said, 'I have just had enough. I don't want you around our house until you learn to abide by my rules.'" Annie decided to move in with her boyfriend. When her father threatened to file statutory rape charges against Jim and tell the police that his daughter had run away, Annie decided to get married. Annie said she "fit into being a wife rather easily." Jim wanted to have 12 kids. Annie worked, but Jim was unable to hold a steady job. He didn't enjoy work. He was "into drugs and alcohol too. So that kind of takes away your motivation to want to do things."

The first hint of trouble in the marriage was Jim's desire to control Annie's contacts with her friends. His eventual physical abuse was no secret to Annie's parents. As she relates, "I was pregnant with my oldest, and my ex-husband had beaten me up pretty bad, and I called home and I said, 'I need to come. I just need to come home.'… I didn't know at the time I was pregnant.… I knew I was feeling really sick. I'm sure it was just morning sickness, but on top of him assaulting me and being in a strange environment… they sent me a plane ticket.… When I came back here, I had so much makeup on to cover up all the bruises, you know. I was just totally embarrassed by that and, um, I walked in the door and my mom said, 'You know, it'd be a really good idea if you'd go wash off that… makeup so we can see how bad you've been assaulted this time.'"

Annie's parents did not encourage her to leave Jim. She explains, "They [imposed] a lot of their religious beliefs on me.… Women's roles in life were to stay married and have kids." In her article, Annie describes the pivotal incident that led to her divorce: "One message my parents taught me well was that marriage is a commitment for life to be faithful. I was faithful, but was always accused of cheating with other men. I found out that my

(continued)

husband had gotten my roommate pregnant and that they were having an affair in my own home. After I confronted my husband about this and he admitted to having an affair with her, I was determined to leave. The violence was out of control.... [T]he next morning my family had five trucks out to my home and I was out of his life in less than one hour." Annie lived with her parents, briefly, and she came to regret bringing them into the "war zone." Jim stalked the house, picking fights with family and friends. Finally, Annie applied for public assistance to secure a home for herself and her children. She did not tell the caseworker that she was a victim of domestic violence, and the caseworker did not ask.

Of course, Jim was not (and still is not) completely out of Annie's life. Over the years he has told the children that if it weren't for their mother, they could live as a family. This has been especially hard on the boys, generating resentment that translated into destructive behavior. Annie's second son, Jacob, has an attention deficit disorder and hyperactivity, as well as a conduct disorder. Annie feels some personal responsibility: "Watching my children and the pain they've gone through and kind of feeling like I inflicted some of that, you know. I made some bad choices about, you know, my life and having kids so young.... I was never taught any of that."

Once she did leave her husband, Annie found another source of stress in the caseworkers who entered her life.

Caseworkers, even though they want to sometimes help, they're not so helpful, you know, and I got so tired of all the caseworkers that wanted to make my life better, and really what they were doing was creating more hassles for me, you know.... I asked the courts for help because my son was just out of control. Cops were at my house all the time. I felt like I was losing my sanity. I felt like I had to be around him 24/7, you know. And I was really striving for a better life.... I'd get a job and I'd get laid off because, you know, he kept gettin' in trouble at school and I'd have to go and take care of his problems, you know ... so I always kind of felt like we were a family at war, and it was something that always bothered me because I spent so much energy trying to diffuse all that anger, you know, and I felt like it was created by all the anger they'd seen at such a young age. And it just escalated as they got older.... I mean, my sons had abused me quite a few times.... I did everything in the community that I could ... because this was just becoming too overwhelming.

Well, finally they appointed me this caseworker and she came out to my home....So on her first appointment with me she comes to my house, and you know, I've cleaned everything from top to bottom because I'm afraid ... you know, the system here is ... to cause more havoc.... When you walked in my house you smelled Pine-Sol and bleach.... And my girlfriend was sitting on the couch and this caseworker from hell walks in the door and says, "I want you [to the girlfriend] to leave. This is a private meeting between me and Annie. And I really, Annie, want you to put that incense out, it's making my sinuses just go crazy." And I thought, "Oh God!" you know. "I'm asking for help, not more destruction." So, anyway, she sets up this plan for me and Jacob to abide by.

The plan required that Annie spend all her time with her children, with no opportunity to find respite or continue her education. Annie finally convinced the caseworker that she needed to go to school.

Annie worked to become self-sufficient. "Even back when I left my husband, there were certain things that I'd do to try and become self-sufficient. Like, I didn't have a car at the time.... The day care was ten blocks from me. That's a lot to walk with a 4-year-old and little kids. So I had to take a bus that went from my house to downtown and then came back, for 10 blocks. It took me two hours to get to school and two hours to get back every night." Ultimately, Annie received her GED and completed a clerk-typist program with straight B's. "That's not bad with four kids, you know."

On public assistance Annie received $563 per month to support her family of five. Among the continuing challenges she faced was difficulty laundering clothes. Usually she washed them in the bathtub and hung them "all over the house" to dry. On the few occasions that she could afford to use a laundromat, she walked, pushing a borrowed shopping cart full of her family's clothes. "That was so humiliating, you know?"

While on assistance, Annie had two destructive relationships. The first was with a man who bought her a car. He claimed that a case of malaria from his tour of duty in Vietnam had left him sterile. When Annie became pregnant, he insisted the child was not his. He was violent with Annie and one day took her car out and torched its interior. He finally moved out, and when Annie moved, she lost touch with him. The second relationship lasted eight years. Bob was physically abusive, but as Annie explained, her self-esteem was so low that she thought she "deserved" the abuse. It was not until her work with JEDI Women had convinced her of her own worth that Annie was able to agree that Bob should leave.

Why didn't she just leave him? Annie believes that as long as benefits are inadequate, public assistance will leave women vulnerable to predatory men. A man who can contribute transportation, food, and even a little cash to the household may enable a woman who would otherwise become homeless to pay the rent or give her children a few "extras" like new clothes or a day at the movies. As a result, women on welfare tolerate abuse that others might find unacceptable.

One day I heard about JEDI and I called Deeda and I talked to her…. I said, "You know, there's gotta be something wrong with this whole scenario." She affirmed that I'm not the only woman out there that's going [through these difficulties]…. See, I'd tell myself that for years, is that I really felt like I was just born from hell or something because my whole life had been hell, you know … and Deeda's like, "Uh-huh.… There's a lot of injustice that happens to women, you know."… My first thing I ever did with JEDI was a protest…. I was just told that they were doing a news conference at the Capitol and that I should come…. I went to the Capitol and I was standing in the group and they were doing like a skit. And it all related to my life, and it was like, "Whoa! This group's awesome. This is what I need!" … and at the same time I kept thinking, "God, I hope I don't get arrested out here being in this" but the more involved I got, the more issues that I found that weren't just me, and that's when I decided that women really needed to be more vocal about what's going on with their lives.

Annie told her children about her plans to speak out about the domestic violence she had experienced. At first her boys were angry, but the girls participated in JEDI Women events and were pictured in a newspaper article about their mother's activism.

Annie is optimistic about her family's future. Her oldest son is showing signs of new maturity. Now in his senior year of high school, he has been attending school more regularly, and Annie hopes he will graduate. Jacob is in a juvenile facility, "locked up for things that are really not his fault." But he has announced to members of his gang and opposing gangs that he isn't going to be involved in gangs anymore. Her oldest daughter called her father, "and she said, 'I'd never marry a man like you. I want somebody that's gonna be responsible and pay their child support if we ever got a divorce…. I just don't think there's a man qualified to meet my expectations, so I don't think I'll ever get married. I'll just go to

school.'" Annie's youngest daughter is "hanging around girls that are sexually active," but Annie plans to enroll her in a program this summer that educates teenagers about the harsh realities of single parenting. Annie hopes none of her children experience violence. "I just have a lot of expectations for my children, and I hope that being with me has taught them something. If nothing else, to be vocal about what's going on."

For herself, Annie dreams of going to law school and working with victims of domestic violence. She has some money for college coming from her two years as a VISTA volunteer, and she anticipates that when her youngest child turns 18 she will be free to pursue this dream. Annie is enjoying a measure of financial security and independence for the first time in her life. She is dating a very nice man who doesn't drink, shows no signs of violence, and pays child support for his three children. Although she would certainly not rush into it, marriage is a possibility. But, as she points out, the relationship would have to be strong to endure the schooling she envisions completing.

A SOCIAL WORK PERSPECTIVE

Like Annie, most women on public assistance have been victims of domestic violence. Estimates of the proportion of mothers receiving public assistance who have experienced domestic violence range from roughly half (Curcio, 1996) to more than two-thirds (Allard et al., 1997; Raphael, 1996). Violence forces many women and children to leave their homes and places them at the mercy of public and private service agencies. Further, as Annie suggested, women experiencing abuse are at greatest risk of injury and death after they have left home (Fleury et al., 1998; Owens, 1999).

Annie's experience with public assistance would not be possible today. She was on Aid to Families with Dependent Children (AFDC) for 11 years. With current work requirements and lifetime assistance limits, women now must secure employment as quickly as possible (see Chapter 5). Further, all states stipulate that mothers who are seeking public assistance must identify their children's father(s). This requirement enables the state to collect child support on the children's behalf. Sometimes mothers are allowed to keep a portion of the payments, and the rest is used to offset the cost of the family's welfare benefits (Garfinkel, 1992). Although "good cause" exemptions to this requirement may be granted, they are rare (Pearson & Griswold, 1997). Thus, the state's interest in collecting child support from noncustodial fathers may further endanger women leaving abusive relationships.

(continued)

A HUMAN PERSPECTIVE   Annie Boone (*continued*)

Annie's training in clerical services prepared her to join the majority of employed women. Continued occupational segregation leaves most female workers in the service sector, often in jobs without benefits or pension coverage. Unlike millions of Americans, Annie has health insurance through her employer. Like approximately two-thirds of working women, however, she does not have pension coverage. At the moment, Annie is enjoying the support and relative security of employment in a nonprofit advocacy organization. She also has a long-term plan for financial security. Despite fears that going back to school may cost her the first healthy relationship she has ever had with a man, Annie is determined to earn the credentials necessary to secure her long-term financial well-being.

The grounds under which divorce is granted have come full circle. Under Roman and early Anglo-American doctrine, consensual divorce (now known as "no-fault" divorce) was granted. Later, as divorce came to be seen as an ecclesiastical matter, the grounds were restricted. Early 19th-century American courts identified bigamy, impotence, and adultery as grounds for divorce. By mid-century, desertion and cruelty were added, although most courts did not identify "domestic chastisement" (wife beating) as cruelty. Grounds for divorce were liberalized in the 20th century with the establishment of no-fault divorce.

Class often determined a couple's access to divorce. In New York, for example, where adultery was the only legal grounds for divorce until 1966, wealthy couples either established residence in other states (like Nevada) that offered more liberal grounds or conducted elaborate courtroom charades to meet New York requirements. Less affluent couples were left with separation as the "poor man's divorce."

Procedures for dividing marital assets, assigning alimony, and awarding child custody have reflected the social norms governing gender relations both within and outside of marriage. Most states are "**common-law**" property jurisdictions, in which spouses' earnings during marriage are treated as separate property rather than joint assets. This practice stands in contrast with "**community property**" jurisdictions, which hold that all property acquired during the marriage is jointly owned by both spouses.[1] Until 1970, divorce in "common-law" jurisdictions significantly disadvantaged wives who did not work.

In 1970, the Uniform Marriage and Divorce Act was developed by the National Conference of Commissioners on Uniform State Laws (NCCUSL), a deliberative body that develops and disseminates model legislation for consideration by state legislatures. Although the legislation has seldom been adopted in its entirety (Schneider, 1991), many provisions of the act were incorporated by state legislatures. These included provisions requiring "equitable division" of marital resources. In many cases, this equitable division reflects the "one-third rule," in which wives are entitled to one-third of the property accumulated during the marriage. The husbands' greater share reflected their larger monetary contribution to the marital assets and ignored the wives' work during their "second shift."

In theory, a divorcing woman (or man) who did not receive substantial property might be entitled to lifetime alimony. In practice, however, as DiFonzo (1997) noted, "the most striking aspect of alimony was its scarcity" (p. 62). Data accumulated by the U.S. Census Bureau suggest that around the turn of the century (1897–1906) alimony was requested in 13.4 percent of cases and awarded in only 9.3 percent. Nationwide data from the turn of

---

[1] Community property laws view marriage as a joint enterprise, with husband and wife equal partners, regardless of employment status. Most community property states are in the West, and most were once part of Mexico. Jennifer Stuntz (2005) traced the origins of these laws to Spain.

the century to 1922 suggest that the proportion of divorcing wives receiving alimony was consistently below 15 percent (Jacobson, 1959).

The divorce rate in the United States doubled during the 1960s and 1970s, and courts increasingly used female participation in the labor force to deny alimony. Indeed, a stated goal of the Uniform Marriage and Divorce Act was to "minimize alimony as well as acrimony." As a result, permanent alimony is becoming a thing of the past. Several states have passed laws that allow for modification of alimony awards if the recipient is cohabiting with someone, and others place time limits on alimony (American Academy of Matrimonial Lawyers, 2007).

Children and Divorce

The principles by which courts award **custody** of children reflect the changing roles of fathers and mothers. Early Anglo-American doctrine gave custody to the father, who essentially had a property right in the child. During the Industrial Revolution, the monetary value of a child's labor diminished, and American doctrine gradually evolved from "**paternal preference**" to "**maternal presumption**." Courts became unwilling to remove children "of tender years" from their mothers. For older children, the tendency was to focus on parental fitness. By the 1980s, two-thirds of states had officially abolished maternal preferences in favor of a "Best Interest Standard." Most had established some form of joint-custody legislation, and in contested cases, men were winning custody one-third to one-half of the time (Weitzman & Maclean, 1992).[2]

Over time, then, custody provisions have gone from viewing children as the property of the father to viewing them as the charges of the mother. Thus, for nearly 40 years most states have applied the Best Interest Standard, in which the judge determines which arrangement best meets the child's needs (Scott & Emery, 2013). For the past decade, the American Law Institute has promoted a gender-neutral "approximation standard" that emphasizes the caregiving role. Under this standard, the court seeks to allocate custodial time so that it matches the proportion of time each parent spent caring for the child prior to the separation (Sanders, 2010).

Reforms that have made divorce law more gender neutral may have also reduced women's bargaining power (Laufer-Ukeles, 2008). Today, wives can no longer threaten to contest the grounds of the divorce or reveal proof of the husband's infidelity to get a better settlement. Similarly, the elimination of the presumption in favor of maternal custody may lead women to give up their property claims to avoid a protracted child custody battle (Weitzman & Maclean, 1992). The loss of maternal preference has left women vulnerable when they do not conform to traditional stereotypes of the "good mother." Women who have had extramarital relationships or who are lesbian risk losing their children. Further, some courts have been hostile to "overly ambitious" women whose careers absorb much of their energy and time, while others have refused custody to women without work interests on the grounds that they lack financial means. Nonetheless, in the vast majority of divorces custody is awarded to the mother; hence the popular maxim: "In a divorce, men become single and women become single parents." But, as Phyllis Chesler pointed out, "this doesn't mean that mothers have won their children in a battle. Rather, mothers often retain custody when fathers choose not to fight for it" (2011, p. xi).

As single parents, very few divorced women can rely on their children's fathers for support. Even when support is awarded, many divorced men fail to meet their obligations. A study of 2002 census data reported that only 38 percent of custodial parents received any child support, and two-fifths of these reported that they did not receive all that was

---

[2]As Deborah Rhode (1989) noted, some fathers who are denied legal custody of their children obtain de facto custody by abducting them.

due. Annual child support ranged from $2,100 for those who received partial payments to $5,800 for parents who received all they were owed (Pirog & Ziol-Guest, 2006).

In recognition of this long-standing trend, the Office of Child Support Enforcement was established in 1975 (under Title IV-D of the Social Security Act) to address the problem. At the same time federal funding was provided to states to establish offices to enforce payment of child support. Later, the 1984 Child Support Amendments and Family Support Act of 1988 required states to implement child support guidelines and automatic withholding of wages. Finally, sections of the 1996 PRWORA legislation were designed to facilitate interstate collaboration in enforcement of child support orders for TANF participants.

Serving over 17 million children in 2004, the Child Support Enforcement Program is generally seen as a tool for improving child well-being. While the program does lift some children out of poverty, its redistributive aspects are seldom considered. Child support enforcement does not take into account the resources and obligations of the noncustodial parent, and in some cases it is simply a transfer of funds from low-income noncustodial fathers to state governments or from second families of noncustodial parents to first families. (See Chapter 5 for a discussion of child support collection and welfare benefits.)

Collaborative or mediated divorces have emerged as a popular alternative to adversarial proceedings. Couples who use this approach work with a neutral party—usually a divorce mediator—to negotiate the details of their separation, including distribution of property, child custody arrangements, and child support. Critics of **divorce mediation** have suggested that women fare poorly because they have less bargaining power than men, although there does not seem to be empirical evidence to support this assertion (Bryan, 1994; Shaw, 2010).

An International Perspective on Marriage and Divorce

We frequently hear that the United States has the highest divorce rate in the world and that half of all marriages in the United States end in divorce. While the United States may have the world's highest divorce rate, we also have the highest marriage rate. On the other hand, available statistics do *not* indicate that half of all marriages end in divorce. Some may be tempted to compare the nation's 2011 divorce rate (3.6 per 1,000 population aged 15 to 64) with the marriage rate (6.8) and conclude that "half of marriages end in divorce." But this is an inappropriate comparison since the divorce rate reflects *all* prior marriages, not just those made in 2011. It is more accurate to say "that twice as many people were married as were divorced that year." Trends in marriage and divorce rates for the United States and other developed nations are presented in Figure 13.1.

LO 13-2   Know About Past and Present Social Policies Concerning Women's Reproductive Rights

EP 3a
EP 5a
EP 5c

Humans have used measures to control fertility for several millennia, and only in modern times have birth control and abortion become emotionally charged political and moral issues. In the United States, increased use of abortion and contraception coincided with the shift from a rural to an industrial economy. With this shift, children were seen less as economic assets than as potential financial burdens to their parents.

ABORTION AND BIRTH CONTROL

According to Deborah Rhode (1989), early opposition to abortion and contraception stemmed from two concerns: first, the fear that when sex was separated from procreation

FIGURE 13.1 Marriage and Divorce Rates in Developed Nations

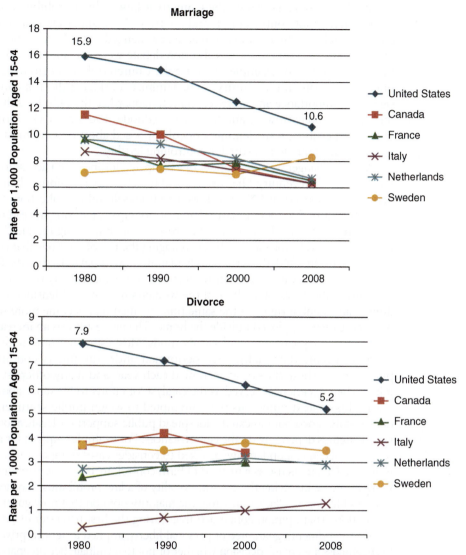

SOURCE: U.S. Census Bureau, 2012 Statistical Abstract, Table 1336: Marriage and Divorce Rates by Country: 1980 to 2008 (http://www.census.gov/compendia/statab/2012/tables/12s1336.pdf).

the result would be widespread promiscuity, venereal disease, and social instability; and second, the belief that if the "better" classes were able to control their fecundity while immigrants and working classes were not, the result would be an "inferior" race. Spearheading the opposition to abortion were physicians, who secured the high moral ground by arguing that abortion was unsafe for mothers, despite the fact that during the late 19th century (as today) abortion was considerably safer than childbirth. Physicians' opposition to abortion may have had an economic incentive. At the time, they faced significant competition from midwives in both reproductive health and obstetrics. Physicians' campaign against abortion exploited the myth that these "nefarious acts" were most often committed by midwives. Thus, physicians' opposition may have been part of a larger effort to discredit lay health providers (Reegan, 1997).

In 1873, Congress passed the **Comstock Law**, which prohibited the distribution of information about contraception and abortion. Most states also passed statutes making abortion a felony. These statutes remained unchanged until the late 1960s. It is interesting to note that key actors in today's abortion debate were considerably less involved during the 19th century. For example, the Catholic Church did not begin to actively oppose the practice until late in the century. Some feminists of the era did not consider the issue of significant importance and were reluctant to jeopardize the fight for suffrage over an issue they saw as "too narrow … and too sordid" (Rhode, 1989, p. 204). During the early years of the 20th century, some feminists openly opposed abortion, and most considered abstinence the appropriate measure for controlling fertility.

Margaret Sanger was the founder of a campaign for increased access to birth control during the early 20th century. She was inspired to her advocacy efforts when she witnessed the death of an impoverished New York woman from self-induced abortion. Sanger's arguments for birth control did not emphasize feminist principles, focusing instead on the health benefits for mothers and children and the prospect for "improving the race." She enlisted support from medical professionals by encouraging the use of methods that could be controlled by physicians. In 1940, the term "family planning" was coined to shift the focus of the debate on contraception away from women's anatomy and sexual activity (Rhode, 1989, p. 205).

During the 1960s, members of the women's movement identified **reproductive freedom** as an essential right. At the same time, women had become more sexually active and were more often employed outside the home. The net result was an increase in the numbers of unwanted pregnancies and illegal abortions. Most estimates indicate that about 1 million abortions occurred annually, often performed under unsanitary conditions by unskilled practitioners. Thousands of women died each year, and many others suffered permanent injury. Their experiences served as the catalyst for efforts to liberalize abortion statutes.

In this context numerous polls attempted to weigh public sentiment regarding abortion. Results varied but indicated widespread public support for legalization of abortion, with varying figures depending on the circumstances. For example, support for abortion tended to be greater when respondents were asked to consider cases of rape or incest than when they were asked about its use as a method of birth control. In 1973, the Supreme Court heard *Roe v. Wade*, a case involving the constitutionality of a law prohibiting abortion except to save a mother's life. Justice Blackmun wrote the majority opinion that now governs women's access to abortion. That opinion concluded that during the first trimester of pregnancy, the Fourteenth Amendment's guarantee of personal liberty implied a right to privacy "broad enough to encompass a woman's decision whether or not to terminate her pregnancy." Restrictions on that right required a compelling state interest in protecting either maternal or fetal life. At the time, the risk of abortion exceeded the risk of childbirth during the second and third trimesters, and fetal viability occurred during the third trimester. Thus, the Court permitted regulation of late-term abortion based on the state's interest in protecting the life of the mother.

The decision, which satisfied neither feminists nor fundamentalists at the time, serves as the foundation for existing law governing women's access to abortion. It also set the stage for ongoing debate. The backlash against *Roe v. Wade* led to passage of the Hyde Amendment in 1977. Henry Hyde (R-Illinois) introduced the amendment to a federal appropriation act to prohibit use of appropriated funds for abortion unless the mother's life was endangered by the pregnancy. Since then the amendment has been attached to each year's federal spending bill, with exceptions for rape, incest, and severe health damage added or removed as Congress saw fit.

The 1980 election of Ronald Reagan further eroded women's access to abortion. During his tenure, President Reagan appointed half the members of the federal bench and

BOX 13.1 Women's Health

Reproductive issues and organs tend to dominate the study of women's health while other, equally vital issues have been neglected (see Inhorn, 2006). Two policy issues merit consideration: the exclusion of women from health research, and the disparate treatment of women by health insurance companies. Prior to the 1990 establishment of the NIH Office of Research on Women's Health, women were simply left out of biomedical studies and clinical trials funded by the federal government. Consequently, treatment regimes were (and to some extent still are) based on male physiques and experiences (Munch, 2006). Prior to passage of the Affordable Care Act, women also faced disparities in the individual health insurance market, where companies used "gender rating" to charge them higher premiums. Companies argued that this practice was economically rational, since women generally use health care more than men did.

made three appointments to the Supreme Court, in each case trying to select people who did not support *Roe v. Wade* (Melich, 1998).[3]

These appointments set the stage for two major Supreme Court decisions on the issue. In 1989, the Supreme Court upheld a restrictive abortion statute enacted in Missouri *(Webster v. Reproductive Health Services)*. Then in 1992, the Court ruled that the usual standard applied to protection of constitutional rights ("strict scrutiny") did not apply to women's right to abortion. Instead, the court ruled that states could restrict access to abortion as long as the restrictions did not "unduly burden" the woman *(Planned Parenthood of Southeastern Pennsylvania v. Casey)*.

A spate of restrictions have since been approved by state legislatures, including mandatory waiting periods, parental notice and consent requirements, counseling requirements, and bans on **partial birth abortions**. In 1997, for example, 33 states enacted restrictions on abortion. In a few cases, these states also expanded funding for programs that provide access to contraception, a measure seen by some as a practical approach to reducing the need for abortion. But public funding for contraception is itself controversial. Particularly controversial has been funding of programs that provide birth control education and contraceptive devices to teenagers.

Access to abortion has been further restricted by Congress. These restrictions usually involve the use of federal funding for abortions, and they are generally waived if the procedure is necessary to save a woman's life or if the pregnancy is the result of incest or rape. As of this writing, restrictions have been applied to federal employees (whose insurance plans may not cover abortion); servicewomen stationed overseas (who may not obtain an abortion in a military medical facility); women in federal prisons (who may not use prison funds for abortion); women residing in the District of Columbia (who cannot use federal or local funds for abortion); and Medicaid recipients (who, under the Hyde Amendment, may not use their health coverage for abortion). In each instance, the prohibition does not apply if the pregnancy is the result of rape or if the woman's life is endangered. Efforts to apply criminal sanctions to physicians who perform "partial birth" abortions were passed repeatedly in Congress and vetoed by President Clinton between 1996 and 2000. In 2003, Congress passed the Partial Birth Abortion Ban, and it was signed into law by President Bush. The bill did not include an exception for cases in which the mother faced a medical emergency, so it was subjected to a Supreme Court challenge in the 2006 case of *Gonzales v. Carhart*. The 5-to-4 ruling upholding the ban has been attributed to the replacement of Sandra Day O'Connor with Justice Samuel Alito.

---

[3]Two of Reagan's appointees (Kennedy and O'Connor) did not prove to be as strongly opposed to *Roe v. Wade* as had been anticipated.

A Human Perspective   Advocacy: Defeating the "Meth Moms" Bill

Contributed by J. R. Seaman, Lewis-Clark State College, Coeur d'Alene, Idaho, and Sarah Knott, Walsh and Associates, Coeur d'Alene, Idaho.

In 2006, the Idaho legislature was debating a bill that euphemistically came to be called the "Meth Moms Bill," written to make drug use by pregnant women a felony. Stating that "it is a permissible inference that a pregnant female has consumed a controlled substance if during the pregnancy the female tests positive for the presence of a controlled substance or if the female or her newborn child tests positive for the presence of a controlled substance upon the birth of the newborn child," the bill explicitly allowed for incarceration but offered no guarantee of treatment. Indeed, punishment rather than rehabilitation was the sponsor's goal. Across the state, coalitions formed to oppose the legislation. Despite intense lobbying by the human services community in opposition to the bill, it passed the senate. The only hope for defeating the bill was to convince members of the house to vote against it.

BSW student Sarah Knott set out to do just that. First, she completed a research project on the etiology of female substance abuse, the effects of incarceration on substance-abusing pregnant women, and whether pregnant women would forgo prenatal care to avoid the threat of imprisonment. With these facts in hand, Sarah educated other students and encouraged them to speak with any legislators they could buttonhole at the Capitol. "Talking points" were developed, and students were encouraged to get key points across within two minutes of initiating a conversation. Some legislators were so impressed with the facts that Sarah and her colleagues had diligently researched that they wrote back to the students. One student, for example, received a note from State Senator Phil Hart: "As of yesterday, we held SB 1337 in our Judiciary Committee of the House.... In plain language, that means we killed the bill for the year." He went on to thank her for informing him of the issues and noted that "we just don't have the time or staff to handle too many issues at once." The effort was a small victory for women that was won by committed students, human services advocates in Idaho, and informed legislators.

Sarah and her fellow students learned that legislation often addresses derivative problems rather than their root causes. In this case attention was directed to punishing mothers addicted to methamphetamines rather than to alleviating the problems that led to their addiction. The success of their efforts persuaded students that an informed advocate who can intelligently address decision makers can make a difference. Research was vital to this process, and the students' ability to marshal facts and communicate them effectively contributed to a successful advocacy intervention.

Abortion also featured in the 2010 health-care reform debates. Anti-abortion advocates among congressional Democrats stalled the Affordable Care Act (ACA), insisting that it would allow for use of federal funds for abortions. In a carefully orchestrated compromise, they were persuaded to support the ACA when the White House issued an executive order affirming the Hyde Amendment. Under the act, no health-care plan is required to cover abortion, and states may deny coverage of abortion through the insurance exchanges.

Debates over **reproductive rights** are emotionally charged, and compromises are rare. Opponents of legal abortion argue that a fetus of any age should be seen as an innocent human being. They view abortion as murder, and a few go so far as to advocate violence against clinics and physicians. The notion of fetal rights leads not only to the view that abortion is murder but also to the argument that maternal behavior that is damaging to the fetus should be prosecuted. So, some suggest, maternal drug use during pregnancy should be treated not only as a crime in its own right, but as an assault on a human being.

AN INTERNATIONAL PERSPECTIVE ON ABORTION

The World Health Organization (WHO) reported a worldwide decline in the rate of induced abortions from 40 per 1,000 women aged 15 to 44 in 1990–1994 to 35 per 1,000 women aged 15 to 44 in 2010-2014 (see Figure 13.2). Most of that decline occurred

FIGURE 13.2   Induced Abortion Rates Worldwide

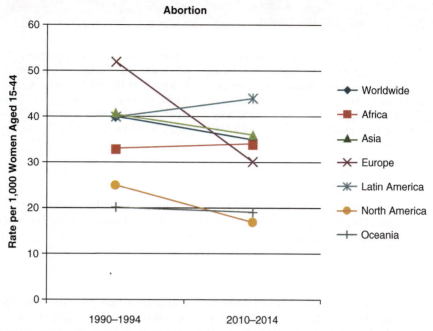

Source: Guttmacher Institute (n.d.), *Induced Abortion Worldwide* (https://www.guttmacher.org/fact-sheet/induced-abortion-worldwide).

between 1995 and 2003, with many nations showing no significant decline in the early years of the 21st century. At about the same time, the U.S. abortion rate declined from 25.0 in 1993 to 13.2 in 2012 (Guttmacher Institute, 2013a). In 2008, the Eastern Europe sub-region reported the highest abortion rate, at 43 per 1,000 women of childbearing age. The world's lowest rates were observed in North America, Australia/New Zealand, Eastern Asia, Northern Europe, and Western Europe. Observing that abortions take place throughout the world "regardless of the status of abortion laws," the WHO notes that "morbidity and mortality resulting from abortion tend to be high in countries and regions characterized by restrictive abortion laws" (WHO, n.d.b, p. 4).

INVOLUNTARY STERILIZATION

The success of the family planning movement fueled a campaign for involuntary sterilization of thousands of poor and developmentally disabled women. With the development of relatively safe surgical sterilization techniques, states passed a wave of compulsory sterilization laws. These laws were reviewed and sustained in a 1927 decision by the Supreme Court (*Buck v. Belt*). The case involved the sterilization of Carrie Buck, the supposedly "feeble-minded" daughter of a "feeble-minded" mother. Buck had just given birth in an institution to a feeble-minded child. Concluding that "three generations of imbeciles are enough" (Rhode, 1989, p. 205), Justice Holmes wrote the majority opinion supporting sterilization. As it turned out, evidence that Buck was "feeble-minded" was equivocal because the girl had been institutionalized to conceal her pregnancy, which was the result of a rape. Although the Supreme Court later cast doubt on the legality of the practice, it was used extensively by welfare officials who

BOX 13.2   Women in Leadership: Sima Samar, Minister of Women's Affairs, Afghanistan

Sima Samar served as Minister of Women's Affairs for the interim administration in Afghanistan. Trained as a physician, she has turned to politics to advance the interests of women in her country. Samar describes this as her primary mission. Since 1989, she has defied authorities by operating schools and health clinics for women. In 2001, Samar received the John Humphrey Freedom Award for her work. She was appointed head of the Afghanistan Independent Human Rights Commission by Mr. Hamid Karzai, who was then Chair of the interim Afghan government. Samar has been mentioned as a potential recipient of the Nobel Peace Prize.

required "voluntary consent" to sterilization as a condition of receiving aid. Sterilization, particularly of poor minority women, continued until the 1980s, when it was curtailed by federal regulation.

PRESCRIPTION EQUITY

For years, private health insurance companies that provide coverage for prescription medications have denied coverage for contraceptives. With the advent of an **erectile dysfunction** drug called Viagra, the issue really came to the fore. Women's organizations, advocates, and several members of Congress argued that companies that provide prescription coverage should not be allowed to exclude contraceptives.

In 1998, Congress extended contraceptive coverage to federal employees enrolled in the Federal Employees' Health Benefits Program. The following year, Senator Barbara Boxer and her colleagues introduced the Equity in Prescription Insurance and Contraceptive Coverage Act. The text of the bill noted that "private insurance provides extremely limited coverage of contraceptives: half of traditional indemnity plans and preferred provider organizations, 20 percent of point-of-service networks, and 7 percent of health maintenance organizations cover no contraceptive methods other than sterilization" (sec. 112, Findings (9)). The act did not reach the floor for a vote that year,

The debate over contraceptive coverage reached a flash point following passage of the Affordable Care Act, which required most employer health plans to cover contraceptive care with no copayment required. Several religious leaders objected to this provision, arguing that it required them to fund practices they found morally reprehensible. Following their protests, in July 2013 the Obama administration issued rules exempting religious employers from the requirement.

The rules exempted nonprofit religious organizations from the contraceptive mandate but required their insurance companies to offer contraceptive coverage separately (U.S. Department of Health and Human Services, 2013). This sleight of hand was not acceptable to a group of for-profit companies not afforded the accommodation, most prominently the owners of a craft supply chain called "Hobby Lobby" who filed suit against the administration. Hobby Lobby's lawyers relied on the **Religious Freedom Restoration Act** to argue that the contraceptive mandate violated the First Amendment right to free exercise of religion. In a tightly worded opinion, the Supreme Court ruled in *Burwell v. Hobby Lobby Stores, Inc.* that "closely held" corporations were exempt from the contraceptive mandate.

LO 13-3 Know About Past and Present Policies Regarding Violence Against Women

EP 1b
EP 3a
EP 5a
EP 5c

Murder and assault of women have long been recognized as unacceptable, but only during recent decades have wife abuse and acquaintance rape been viewed as acts of violence. In this section we will look at domestic violence and rape as issues that continue to affect American women.

DOMESTIC VIOLENCE

Today wife beating is condemned as domestic violence, but it was referred to as "**domestic chastisement**" in 19th-century America. Wife beating was explicitly sanctioned by some early Christian ecclesiastics, who noted that "[i]t was preferable for husbands to punish the [wife's] body and correct the soul than to damage the soul and spare the body" (Rhode, 1989, p. 238). Since husbands were legally responsible for their wives' behavior, common law recognized a husband's right to discipline his spouse, provided that he "neither kill nor maim her." A few American courts defined the boundaries of that right: a husband was permitted to whip his wife as long as he used a switch no thicker than his thumb. (The phrase "rule of thumb" comes from this stipulation.)

Divorce was an option only if the abuse was extreme and unprovoked. It was not available to women who continued to live with an abusive husband or who were judged to have "provoked" the abuse either through "passionate language" or refusal to have sexual relations. Because women had few legal avenues for dealing with spousal violence, their best recourse was community disapproval. When the severity of the beatings exceeded locally acceptable standards, a wife might seek assistance from family members or community leaders. This situation continued fundamentally unchanged until the late 20th century.

The battered-women's movement of the early 1970s focused on providing refuge for victims and raising public awareness of the problem. For years, organizations like the Salvation Army had provided shelter to battered women, but their primary focus was on addressing the problems caused by alcoholism rather than domestic abuse. In 1973, women's advocates succeeded in opening the first shelters specifically designed for battered women: Transition House in Boston and Rainbow Retreat in Phoenix (Dobash & Dobash, 1992).

With these beginnings, a social movement to address domestic violence was born. Emerson and Russell Dobash (1992) have identified three general goals of the movement: "assisting victims, challenging male violence, and changing women's position in society" (p. 29). The number of organizations working to assist battered women grew exponentially. In 1977, there were 163 groups operating 130 shelters, and by 1989, the number of programs had reached 1,200, with shelters housing 300,000 women and children per year (Dobash & Dobash, 1992).

BOX 13.3 Women in Leadership: Nabeela Al-Mulla, First Arab-Muslim Woman Representing Any Country as an Ambassador to the United Nations

Nabeela Al-Mulla, Kuwait's ambassador to the United Nations, presented a required report in January 2004 to the Committee on the Elimination of Discrimination Against Women. Ironically, the report indicated that Kuwaiti women lack the right to vote or run for office, yet it was presented by the first Arab-Muslim woman representing any country before the United Nations.

BOX 13.4   Francine Hughes

On March 9, 1977, Francine Hughes was arrested for setting fire to her house while her ex-husband was sleeping. He died in the blaze, and she was charged with murder. During her trial she recounted her 12-year experience with an abusive husband, and the jury found Hughes not guilty by reason of temporary insanity. Her case, resulting in both a book (*The Burning Bed* by Faith McNulty) and an NBC-TV movie, contributed to growing recognition of domestic violence as an issue of national concern.

The battered-women's movement grew from local and regional efforts to national initiatives in 1977 when a White House meeting was held to bring together activists and federal representatives. Within six months, the Commission on Civil Rights held hearings to consider whether battered women received equal protection under the law. Activists argued that because the legal system and police did not protect women, they were deprived of their liberty and property when forced to flee from abusive homes. More than 600 people attended the hearings, listening to presentations from 30 speakers. Among the issues discussed were law enforcement's response to domestic violence cases, oppression of women as a root cause of the violence, the potential for treating battering men, the incidence of husband abuse, and federal funding for shelters.

The National Coalition Against Domestic Violence (NCADV) focused on attempting to secure federal funding for shelters. They encountered opposition in Congress from representatives who argued that the government had "no business intruding into family disputes" (Rhode, 1989, p. 243). Over these objections, Representative Barbara Mikulski introduced the Family Violence Prevention and Treatment Act in 1978. Despite support from the Carter administration, the bill failed, and after the 1980 election of Ronald Reagan its chances for passage diminished. Finally, during the 1983–1984 congressional session, Mikulski condensed the bill and introduced it as an amendment to the Child Abuse Prevention and Treatment Act. It passed, providing states with $65 million over three years for abuse prevention and victim services, as well as $2 million each year for police training.

The 1990s saw a dramatically increased federal response. The 1994 Violence Against Women Act expanded the funding available for training law enforcement officials, established interstate domestic violence as a federal crime, and confirmed that sex-based violence violates a woman's civil rights.[4] In 1996, President Bill Clinton established the National Domestic Violence Hotline (1-800-799-SAFE) through an executive order. In the first year and a half of its operation, the hotline received more than 120,000 calls. The Centers for Disease Control and Prevention (CDC) estimates that 1.3 million women are physically assaulted by an intimate partner each year, and the FBI reports that a third of homicides against women are committed by their partners (CDC, 2003; FBI, 2008).

Protective Orders

In all 50 states, women who experience domestic abuse may seek a restraining order or **protective order** from the court. While procedures vary from state to state, these orders

---

[4]The Violence Against Women Act was declared unconstitutional by U.S. District Judge Jackson Kiser in Virginia, leading the National Organization for Women to argue that the judge's ruling is further evidence of the need for an Equal Rights Amendment.

typically do not require definitive proof of abuse. Often a victim's statement, backed up with police reports, photographs of injuries, or medical reports, will suffice for the court to order the perpetrator to stay away. (The order might also prohibit contact and may even call for restitution.) Once the order has been served, the perpetrator can be arrested for any violation.

The effectiveness of protective orders may depend on the willingness of police to enforce them. Like too many other women, Jessica Gonzales found the police in her home town (Castle Rock, Colorado) less than helpful in this regard. In 1999 she was involved in a nasty divorce, and the court issued a restraining order that required her husband to stay at least 100 yards away from her and her daughters except during specified visitations. One day, her husband kidnapped the children in violation of the order. Gonzalez notified police (she called them several times) but they did not take action. The husband later killed the daughters and engaged in a fatal shoot-out with police. In 2005 the U.S. Supreme Court heard Gonzalez's lawsuit against Castle Rock and ruled that Gonzalez did not have a constitutional right to police protection and supported the police departments' discretion with respect to restraining orders.

Several states have established criminal sanctions for violation of protective orders, and some specifically require police to make arrests. In Montana, for instance, the state Supreme Court held that police officers can be found liable if a victim of domestic violence is harmed because they failed to enforce a protective order. The same holds in Tennessee.

SEXUAL VIOLENCE

Unlike domestic violence, rape has long been recognized as a legal offense. However, it was primarily seen, not as an offense against a woman, but as an affront to the men in her life—her father or husband. Based on a view of rape as a threat to the patrilineal system of inheritance, U.S. rape law "builds on a history of class, race, and gender biases" (Rhode, 1989, p. 245). The social status of both victims and assailants has historically been influential in determining the legal consequences of the crime. Thus, in the United States, the rape of black women by white men was scarcely treated as a crime, while hundreds of black men were lynched when they were accused of raping white women (NAACP, 1969). Between 1945 and 1965, a death sentence was 18 times more likely for convicted black rapists with white victims than for any other combination (Rhode, 1989).

Women who charge strangers with rape have traditionally been subjected to a high level of scrutiny and a requirement that they demonstrate their resistance. Until the passage of "rape shield" laws in the late 1970s, a woman's sex life was considered permissible evidence in court. Defendants used accounts of past behavior to establish that a woman was "unchaste" and probably had incited the rape through her behavior or dress. Failure to energetically resist a rapist was interpreted by some courts as an indication of consent. Thus, women were victimized twice: once by a rapist and once by a legal system that insisted on putting rape victims on trial. Today **rape shield laws** help prevent material regarding a woman's sexual history from being introduced by the defense during a rape trial.

For years, spousal rape simply was not a crime. Under the principle of coverture, man and wife were one—and how could a man rape himself? Later arguments held that, by getting married, women consented to intercourse upon demand and thus could not charge their husbands with rape. Opponents of prosecution of spousal rape continued to argue that the event itself was exceedingly rare and prosecution would involve the state meddling in "normal sexual relations" or voyeurs "behind the bedroom door" (Rhode, 1989, p. 250).

Spousal rape and **acquaintance rape** depart from our common understanding of the crime. Yet in the vast majority of reported sexual assaults the offender is known to the victim (U.S. Department of Justice, 2014). Many women do not view forced sexual intercourse with a husband or date as a crime, so spousal and acquaintance rape often go unreported. But these acts are crimes in all 50 states. In California, for instance, any sexual intercourse that is "accomplished forcibly, or by the threat of force without consent" (California penal code) is considered rape. But the application and interpretation of this law often depends on the nature of a woman's relationship with the offender as well as her sexual history. Rape shield laws may not apply if a woman has had previous sexual relations with the offender (Anderson, 2004).

During the past 45 years, the nation's laws have become less tolerant of violence against women. The rape shield laws mentioned above were passed by state legislatures in the 1970s. These, along with the 1994 **Violence Against Women Act**, were important milestones.

In a more recent trend, several states (most notably California) have passed affirmative consent laws to more clearly define sexual assault. Under Title IX of the Civil Rights Act, universities have a special obligation to prevent sexual harassment and sexual assaults. This underscores the need to clarify what is meant by sexual consent. Campus assaults that involve the use of "date-rape drugs" have challenged the once-popular "no means no" prevention approach, as an unconscious victim can hardly say "No." This approach has now been replaced by "yes means yes" based on the argument that silence cannot be construed as consent (as the defense claimed in the 2016 case of Stanford student Brock Turner, convicted for sexually assaulting an unconscious woman). Further changes to University responses to sexual assault might follow passage of the bipartisan Campus Accountability and Safety Act which, as of this writing, was pending before the Senate.

Of course, these laws serve women who have already been victimized. Rape and the threat of violence hurt not only the women who are direct victims but also women who constrain their movements and activities to avoid becoming victims.

American social policy has clearly influenced the costs and rewards incurred by women in their roles as students, wives, and mothers. These laws reflect and influence broad changes in the social consensus about what constitutes justice in intimate relationships. Today, women can enjoy property rights and secure credit independently, regardless of their marital status. Divorce is available to more women than ever before. Public policy and public opinion reject the notion that a married woman should submit to "domestic chastisement" or rape, and that sexual assault is a natural part of college life. Women enjoy a measure of control over their reproductive futures, and public policy has taken initial strides toward reducing the tensions experienced by mothers in the workplace.

LO 13-4   Become Aware of Policy Issues Affecting Women in the Workplace

EP 3a
EP 5c

Today, most American women combine marriage, motherhood, and work. As a result, many policies and practices that affect women at work influence their other roles, just as resources to support their other roles affect women's ability to succeed in the labor market. Of course, a growing number of women do not marry and do not have children. A recurring challenge for U.S. public policy has been not only to enable the majority to combine family and work roles but to do so without disadvantaging the minority who are pursuing a different life path.

Progress toward equal employment rights in the United States has been uneven at best. Attempts to expand government regulation of private employers confront deeply ingrained American beliefs about the fairness of the free market and the integrity of the entrepreneur. Public policy in this arena is often marked by ambivalence, reluctance, and denial. Nonetheless, our conceptions about what constitutes justice in the workplace have changed considerably. While pay equity may remain a distant goal, working women are no longer paid less simply because of their gender. Steps are being taken to reduce the career sacrifices that working women undergo when they become mothers. During retirement, many women enjoy the benefits ensured by pension reforms. Finally, the costs of labor force participation need no longer include the risk of being subjected to sexual harassment. These and other issues affecting women in the labor force are discussed further in Chapter 15.

LO 13-5   Become Aware of Policy Issues Affecting Women in the Military

EP 3a

The wars in Iraq and Afghanistan brought many debates, including those about the role of women in the U.S. military. Throughout the nation's history, women have served in the military, sometimes by pretending to be men. Today, more women are serving in the armed forces than ever before. The Pew Research Center reports that from 1973 to 2010 the number of women in active duty increased from about 42,000 to 167,000, with their proportion of the active duty personnel rising from 2 percent to 14 percent (Patten & Parker, 2011).

Involving women in combat is controversial in the United States. Opponents argue that women are unable to manage the physical demands of combat and that their presence will undermine cohesion of the forces. Few mention aloud the underlying belief that combat service is inconsistent with culturally accepted gender roles. Supporters note that, according to most studies, women who are properly trained and conditioned are able to meet the physical demands, and they suggest that excluding women from combat roles is a form of discrimination.

U.S. military policy has moved toward permitting women to serve in combat roles. In 1992, the Defense Authorization Act repealed the long-standing combat exclusion applied to women pilots in the navy and air force. In 1993, the combat exclusion for women on combat ships was ended. Finally, in 1994, Defense Secretary Aspin approved a general policy that would allow army women to serve with ground combat units during fighting. This has led to increased combat exposure for women, from 7 percent among veterans of the pre-1990 era to 24 percent of post-1990 women veterans (Patten & Parker, 2011).

Drafting women is also controversial. In 1980, President Carter reinstated the draft registration process, recommending that Congress amend the Military Selective Service Act to permit registration and conscription of women. Congress declined to amend the act and allocated funding for registration of men only. Several men sued, challenging the constitutionality of the act, and their case went all the way to the Supreme Court. In June 1981, the Court held in *Rostker v. Goldberg* that Congress had acted within its constitutional authority in allowing for registration of men and not women. Congress may have the opportunity to reconsider its position. The Universal National Service Act was introduced several times, most recently in 2013. It calls for all young people, including women, to perform a period of military service or a "period of civilian service in furtherance of the national defense and homeland security."

Women's increased presence in the military has brought rising concern over sexual harassment and sexual assault. In 1991, this issue came to media attention with the Tailhook scandal. This related to a series of incidents that took place during a conference of the Tailhook Association, held in Las Vegas, Nevada. The subsequent outcry and investigations never entirely settled the issue, but the scandal did end the careers of several senior military officials and aviators (Zimmerman, 1995).

Since Tailhook, there have been several major scandals at military academies, including 1996 events at the Aberdeen Proving Ground in Maryland that resulted in rape convictions against three officers (Clines, 1997) and 2003 allegations of sexual assault at the Air Force Academy (Schemo, 2003). In response to these problems the 2004 National Defense Authorization Act called for establishment of a task force to investigate and generate recommendations. The Task Force report was released in 2005. In addition to calling for culture changes in the military, it recommended measures to support victims' rights, hold offenders accountable, and train all military personnel about sexual harassment (Defense Task Force on Sexual Harassment and Violence at the Military Service Academies, 2005).

More recently, in 2013, the Pentagon released a study based on a survey of active-duty service members. Results indicated that as many as 26,000 were sexually assaulted in 2013. Only a small fraction of the incidents were reported and even fewer resulted in prosecution (Steinhauer, 2013). The same year, the Military Justice Improvement Act was introduced in the House and Senate to require changes in the way military courts process rape cases.

LO 13-6   Reflect on Women's Struggle for Political Equality

EP 3a
EP 5c

Initially, women were not considered "citizens" or even "persons" under the Constitution of the United States. As Rhode (1989) notes, "When the framers of America's founding documents spoke of men—of 'men … created equal' and 'endowed … with certain unalienable rights'—they were not using the term generically" (pp. 19–20). Women were not alone in this regard, sharing their exclusion with Native Americans and slaves. Women's progress toward full citizenship in the United States has seen two major reform efforts. One was successful and the other was not. The first was the campaign for women's right to vote, and the second was the campaign for passage of the Equal Rights Amendment (ERA).

SUFFRAGE

The right to vote, or **suffrage,** the defining characteristic of full citizenship, was denied American women until 1920. It was a long time coming. Signs of discontent surfaced as early as 1848, when the first convention to discuss women's rights convened in Seneca Falls, New York. Two years later, the National Women's Rights Convention, planned by Lucy Stone, Lucretia Mott, and Abby Kelley, drew a thousand people. Sixteen years later, suffragists presented petitions bearing 10,000 signatures to Congress, asking for an amendment prohibiting disenfranchisement on the basis of sex. During the same year, 1866, the American Equal Rights Association was formed to pursue voting rights

BOX 13.6   Women in Leadership: Massoumeh Ebtekar, Vice President of Iran, 1997–2005

Massoumeh Ebtekar holds a Ph.D. in immunology. Born in 1960, she is married with two children. Ebtekar was among the students who occupied the U.S. embassy in Tehran during the Carter administration. In 1981 she was appointed editor-in-chief of the English newspaper *Kayhan International.* She served as vice head of the National Committee of the Fourth World Conference on Women in 1995, headed the communication network of women's nongovernmental organizations in Iran, and was Iran's first female vice president.

for women and African Americans. In 1868, when the Fourteenth Amendment was ratified, the word "male" was used for the first time to define a citizen for the purposes of voting. That same year, the first federal women's suffrage amendment was introduced in Congress.

During the years between introduction and passage of the Nineteenth Amendment, suffragists mounted a campaign that included marches and picketing, hunger strikes, fiery protests, and parades. At one especially clever protest in 1919, the National Woman's Party established a "watchfire for freedom" in which they burned every speech President Wilson had given about democracy. Suffragists were arrested by police, attacked by mobs, and reviled from many pulpits. Anti-suffragist organizations were formed to prevent women from securing the right to vote.

Opponents of suffrage (many of whom were women of means) argued that it would jeopardize traditional values—that allowing women to vote would run "counter to the dictates of biology, the experience of evolution and the will of the Creator" (Rhode, 1989, p. 14). They thought domestic disaster would ensue. In a version of the "slippery slope" argument, anti-suffragists suggested that once women had the vote, they would want to enter the workplace, where mingling of the sexes would result in promiscuity. Thus, women's suffrage would pave the way to anarchy and free love. Others suggested that involvement in the public sphere would be hard to reconcile with the demands of the private sphere. Finally, some argued opposing points: either wives would vote the same way their husbands did, in which case their votes would make no difference, or wives would vote differently from their husbands, which would lead to domestic strife.

The suffrage movement found fertile ground during the settlement of the West. Wyoming granted women voting rights in 1869, while it was still a territory. Colorado followed, adopting women's suffrage in 1893. Colorado was followed in quick succession by the states of Utah (1896), Idaho (1896), Washington (1896), and California (1911). By the end of 1914, women had voting rights in nine western states and Kansas. Six years later, the Nineteenth Amendment was ratified by 36 states and signed into law.

BOX 13.7   Nineteenth Amendment to the Constitution

"The right of citizens of the United States to vote shall not be denied or abridged by the United States or by any state on account of sex."

Suffragettes marching for the vote in New York.

Bain Collection/Library of Congress Prints and Photographs Division Washington, D.C. [LC-USZ62-53202]

THE EQUAL RIGHTS AMENDMENT

Three years after the right to vote had been secured, the National Woman's Party (NWP) began working to establish a constitutional amendment protecting the civil rights of women. **The Equal Rights Amendment (ERA)** was authored by Alice Paul, head of the NWP. The original text of the amendment stated, "Men and women shall have equal rights throughout the United States and every place subject to its jurisdiction. Congress shall have power to enforce this article by appropriate legislation." In 1923, the ERA was introduced in Congress by Senator Charles Curtis and Representative Daniel Read Anthony, Jr., both Republicans from Kansas;[5] Anthony was the nephew of suffragist Susan B. Anthony. In response to dogged lobbying by the NWP, the ERA was introduced in each subsequent session of Congress.

Most moderate women's organizations, including the **League of Women Voters**, the Women's Trade Union League, the National Consumers League, and the newly created Women's Bureau within the Department of Labor, opposed the ERA. They worried that its passage would void protective legislation that restricted the number of hours women could be required to work and established minimum pay requirements for women.

---

[5]Members of the Republican Party supported the ERA well into the 1970s. The amendment was endorsed by the party in its 1940 platform. Indeed, Republican support for women's concerns historically exceeded that of the Democratic Party. The reversal on the part of Republicans dates to the Reagan era, when systematic efforts by conservative Republicans effectively silenced the party's progressive element. The transformation of the party's positions vis-à-vis women was well documented in Tanya Melich's 1998 book, *The Republican War Against Women*.

BOX 13.8 Equal Rights Amendment

The text of the Equal Rights Amendment, as revised by Alice Paul in 1943 and passed by Congress in 1972, reads as follows: "Equality of rights under the law shall not be denied or abridged by the United States or by any state on account of sex."

The amendment was revived in 1967 with the establishment of the **National Organization for Women (NOW),** which pledged to battle for passage. Four years later, the ERA was approved without amendment by the House of Representatives. It had the endorsements of the National Education Association and the United Auto Workers. In 1972, the amendment passed the Senate. Although it passed both houses with substantial margins, two senators (Sam Ervin and Emmanuel Celler) were successful in setting a time limit of seven years for ratification.

With the clock ticking, NOW's campaign began. In light of Congress's overwhelming endorsement, the amendment seemed headed for early state ratification. Within months, 20 state legislatures had ratified it, often with minimal debate. It received a boost in 1973 with the endorsement of the AFL-CIO. During the late 1970s, however, the ERA lost its momentum. Anti-ERA groups began to surface, such as Phyllis Schlafly's National Committee to Stop ERA.

Schlafly, herself a lawyer, worked for a right-wing organization and devoted her considerable energies to defeating the amendment. Flying throughout the nation, she became the spokesperson for traditional values. Arguments against the ERA held that women would lose their preferential treatment with respect to family and military obligations. Wives would be legally required to work; divorcing women would lose presumptions in favor of awarding them custody of small children; and women would be subject to the draft and forced into combat. The ERA, it was argued, would permit homosexual marriage and require unisex public bathrooms. Finally, the states' rights argument was raised by some who believed the amendment represented unwarranted intrusion of the federal government into a policy area best left to state governments.

In response, NOW organized a convention boycott, supported by more than 450 pro-ERA organizations. Participating organizations refused to schedule meetings or conventions in states that had not ratified the ERA. It was at this point in the struggle, on July 9, 1977, that Alice Paul, author of the ERA, died at the age of 92. In 1978, with intense lobbying by women's organizations, the House of Representatives approved an extension of the ERA deadline to June 30, 1982.

The ERA battle extended (as many do) from legislatures to the courts, when in 1978, the attorney general of Missouri filed an antitrust suit against NOW's boycott. A year later a federal judge ruled that NOW's activities were protected by the First Amendment and did not violate antitrust laws. This decision was upheld by the U.S. Court of Appeals, and the Supreme Court declined to hear Missouri's appeal. In the late 1980s the legality of NOW's boycott was established. In other court action, legislators from Idaho, Arizona, and Washington filed suit challenging the legality of the ERA extension and seeking to validate states' right to rescind their earlier approval of the amendment. The case was assigned to Judge Marion Callister, who held a high office in the Church of Jesus Christ of Latter-Day Saints (the Mormons). The church actively opposed the ERA, and Judge Callister ruled the ERA extension illegal and rescission legal. Seventeen days later, the Supreme Court granted a unanimous stay, prohibiting enforcement of the Callister decision.

BOX 13.9   Women Heads of State (as of November 2016)

* Indicates the country's first female head of state.

Country	Head of State
Austria	Co-Acting President Doris Bures
Argentina	President Cristina Fernandez de Kirchner
Bangladesh	Prime Minister Sheikh Hasina
Chile*	President Michelle Bachelet
Croatia	President Kolinda Grabar-Kitarovic
Estonia	President Kersti Kaljulaid
Germany*	Chancellor Angela Merkel
Jamaica*	Prime Minister Portia Simpson-Miller
Latvia	Prime Minister Laimdota Straujuma
Liberia*	President Ellen Johnson Sirleaf
Lithuania*	President Dalia Grybauskaite
Malta	President Marie-Louise Coleiro Preca
Marshall Islands	President Hilda Heine
Mauritius*	President Ameenah Gurib
Nepal	President Bidhya Devi Bhandari
Norway	Prime Minister Ema Solberg
Poland	Prime Minister Ewa Kopacz
South Korea	President Park Geun-hye
Switzerland	President Eveline Widmer-Schlumpf
Taiwan	President Tsai Ing-wen
Trinidad and Tobago*	Prime Minister Kamla Persad-Bissessar

SOURCE: Roberto Ortiz de Zarate, Women Prime Ministers. Terra.es archive (http://archive.is/R64Ci, accessed September 29, 2013).

On June 30, 1982, the ERA was stopped three states short of ratification. Since then the amendment has been reintroduced time and again. Debate over the amendment continues, with opponents emphasizing that legislation of the past three decades has made the ERA unnecessary. Under this view, statutes such as Title VII of the Equal Rights Act of 1964, the 1963 Equal Pay Act, and the Equal Credit Opportunity Act of 1974 have provided remedies for the most glaring acts of discrimination against women. ERA supporters, including NOW, argue that the amendment is needed, if only for symbolic purposes, to enshrine women's rights in the Constitution.

LO 13-7   Understand Some of the Challenges Women Face in the Social Work Profession

EP 5c

Like Deeda Seed, founder of JEDI Women in this chapter's case study, many social workers devote themselves to the advancement of women. Within the profession itself, however, women experience the very discrimination that advocates struggle to eliminate. Most social workers are women, but they are consistently paid less than men. In 2011, the NASW report titled *Social Work Salaries by Gender* concluded that the gender gap in salaries remains a problem for the profession (NASW, 2011). Using data gathered from over 22,000 social workers, the report documents gender disparities across all practice settings and at all income levels. Earlier studies have placed the gender gap among licensed social workers at approximately 14 percent (Whitaker, Weismiller, & Clark, 2006). Clearly, as Gibelman and Schervish (1995) and others noted years ago, it is time for the profession to "get its own house in order" (p. 628).

Closing Reflections

Advertisements for Virginia Slims cigarettes used to annoy many people by declaring, "You've come a long way, baby." Apart from the patronizing "baby," the slogan has a ring of truth. Women in the United States have come a long way in a protracted struggle that has taken its toll. Progress has been achieved largely through the efforts of thousands of women and men who participated in one of the great social movements of our time, the "women's movement." This chapter began by recounting the experiences of Annie Boone, who survived abuse to raise her children and build her own economic security. We chronicled the historical developments related to women's roles as wives and mothers, as workers and citizens. We outlined the contemporary issues that face American women and ended the chapter with a brief look at the position of women in the social work profession.

American women have achieved tremendous progress as wives and mothers, as workers, and as citizens. Today we can scarcely imagine being unable to vote, and the notion of coverture is inconceivable. And with the democrat's nomination of Hillary Clinton, we came close to having our first woman president. Further, as we will see in Chapter 15, the past half-century has seen progress in the rights of working women. Like women in many other industrialized nations, American women have come a long way, but we are overrepresented among the nation's disadvantaged and victimized. Clearly, we still have a long way to go.

Think About It

1. To what extent do you think genetic or physical differences between men and women contribute to their different roles and rewards in the U.S. workplace?

2. Is the notion of equal pay for comparable work compatible with your view of social justice?

3. Are low-income mothers among the "deserving poor"? Why or why not? Consider the U.S. welfare system—under what circumstances would low-income mothers be considered deserving in this context?

4. Why do you think women in the military would be interested in serving in combat roles?

Web-Based Exercises

For direct links to all the sites in these exercises, visit the *Foundations of Social Policy* Companion Site at www.cengagebrain.com and select the resources for Chapter 13.

1. Women in combat: Go to www.americanrevolution.org (a Revolutionary War site maintained by the History Channel). In their "Scholar's Showcase" you'll find an essay by Tina Ann Nguyen on the role of women in that war. It's titled "American Athenas: Women in the Revolution" and offers some interesting and seldom-told stories about women's roles in the revolution. They weren't just wringing their hands and keeping house!

2. Women in leadership: Use Google to learn more about one of the women listed in the "Women in Leadership" boxes in this chapter. Begin your search by entering her name and country of origin.

Competency Notes

As mentioned in the preface to this text, the Council on Social Work Education has designated nine core competencies and related practice behaviors that must be addressed by accredited social work programs. In these notes, I will specify the way chapter content addresses these competencies and behaviors. (This is designed to assist with the accreditation process.) Please refer to the "helping hands" icons for the locations of specific content in this chapter. Here you will find a brief explanation of how the accompanying content relates to the specified competency or practice behaviors.

The following list indicates where EPAS competencies and practice behaviors are addressed in this chapter.

EP 1b **Use reflection and self-regulation to manage personal values and maintain professionalism in practice situations.** Values and beliefs regarding the proper role of women have at times interfered with progress toward equal rights and have influenced policies on a wide range of topics from women's suffrage to domestic violence. This topic sensitizes students to the oppressive impacts of outmoded beliefs.

EP 3a **Apply their understanding of social, economic, and environmental justice to advocate for human rights at the individual and system levels.** The chapter describes policies that govern credit, divorce, and reproductive rights, all of which illustrate justice-related principles that can inform advocacy. It helps students identify oppression of women in a variety of forms, from "protective legislation" to the struggle for equal rights. It also presents examples of historic and contemporary advocacy efforts on behalf of women's rights, ranging from the suffrage movement to a BSW student's struggle to prevent criminalization of meth-addicted mothers.

EP 5a **Identify social policy at the local, state, and federal level that impacts well-being, service delivery, and access to social services.** Policies discussed in this chapter have direct bearing on the well-being of women and their families.

EP 5c **Apply critical thinking to analyze, formulate, and advocate for policies that advance human rights and social, economic, and environmental justice.** This chapter helps students analyze the impacts of social and demographic trends and political developments that have influenced policy issues.

Suggested Resources

Chesler, P. (2011). *Mothers on Trial: The Battle for Children and Custody.* Chicago: Lawrence Hill Books.

Kristof, D.F. & WuDunn, S. (2020). *Half the Sky: Turning oppression into opportunity for women worldwide.* Vintage: Reprint edition.

www.dol.gov/wb/. Maintained by the Women's Bureau in the U.S. Department of Labor, this site offers information of interest to "working" women, not only in the United States but around the world.

www.now.org. The National Organization for Women provides an astonishing array of information through its website. Visitors to the site can sign up to receive NOW action alerts.

www.owl-national.org. This site is home to the national office of the Older Women's League. It is an outstanding source of information on policy issues of importance not just to older women but to women of all ages.

www.pay-equity.org. This site is maintained by the National Committee on Pay Equity (NCPE), which acts as a clearinghouse for pay equity news and information. The site offers NCPE publications and updates on data and activities having to do with fair wages.

14 Older Adults

Our society must make it right and possible for old people not to fear the young or be deserted by them, for the test of a civilization is the way that it cares for its helpless members.
—PEARL S. BUCK

Learning Objectives

This chapter will help prepare students to:

LO 14-1 Understand how old age has been defined

LO 14-2 Consider how social and economic factors influenced the status of older adults in colonial America

LO 14-3 Appreciate historic shifts in Americans' attitudes toward older adults

LO 14-4 Reflect on the origins of contemporary programs and policies that affect older adults

LO 14-5 Examine contemporary attitudes toward aging and older adults

LO 14-6 Become familiar with the demographic and economic realities that shape aging today

LO 14-7 Become familiar with contemporary programs and policies that affect older adults in the United States

LO 14-8 Reflect on specialized issues affecting health care for older adults

LO 14-9 Become aware of the unmet need for social work professionals to serve older adults

The aging of the world's human population is unprecedented. Never before have so many people lived to be so old. Of course, old age itself was not unheard of. A few noteworthy individuals have always survived to advanced age, but mass aging is a new phenomenon. For this reason, older adults and their families have been described as "modern pioneers" (Shanas, 1980). Nations throughout the world are seeking the best ways to provide for the needs of older citizens and tap into their expertise. At the same time, we face an alarming tendency to blame older adults for social and economic problems and to view their presence among us as a threat. Robert Butler coined the term "ageism" to describe negative stereotypes and attitudes toward older adults and the process of aging. Ageism is widespread, even among elders. Stereotyping and denigrating advanced age is a relatively new form of oppression—a departure from more traditional appreciation of old age.[1]

As more people survive into old age, the population of older adults is becoming more heterogeneous. The health status of older adults reveals great variety. Many suffer from debilitating chronic conditions, but others compete in the Senior Olympics. The same is true of economic well-being. Some older adults (predominantly women, the very old, and people of color) live in abject poverty, but others (like Warren Buffett) number among the world's most affluent and powerful. This diversity complicates the task of program and policy development, bringing into question the continued use of age as the basis of eligibility for public programs.

LO 14-1   Understand How Old Age Has Been Defined

EP 2a
EP 5c

Demographic and social changes have had a tremendous impact on the role and status of older adults in the United States, changing even what we *mean* when we refer to "the aged." Like so many human categories, old age is socially constructed. Prehistoric people who survived past their reproductive prime may have been considered "old." During the colonial era, Americans had short life expectancies, so the few who survived beyond 40 years were seen as aged. At the beginning of the 20th century, U.S. life expectancy at birth had increased to 48 years, pushing up the definition of old age (Brody, 1971). By the dawn of this century, the nation's definition of "old age" had been extended by several decades.

Today's definition places the onset of old age somewhere between the ages of 50 and 80. Eligibility for membership in AARP begins at 50. At 62 Americans are eligible to begin collecting Social Security benefits. Eligibility for programs funded under the Older Americans Act begins at age 60. Medicare eligibility begins at age 65. Observing the growing proportion of Americans who were reaching the age of 65, Bernice Neugarten (then in her sixties) coined the term "young old" to describe those from 65 to 75 years of age and "old old" to refer to those over 75. More recently, the term "oldest old" has been used to describe people over the age of 80. Perhaps someday centenarians (one of the fastest-growing age groups) will be termed the "incredibly old."

Have you heard that "today's 60 is yesterday's 40"? How about "You're only as old as you feel"? These popular maxims reflect the improvements in health and functional status enjoyed by many older adults. Although, as we will see, physical vulnerability remains a hallmark of later life, growing numbers of people in their sixties, seventies, and eighties enjoy vigorous health. This new reality influences our definition of old age as well, and many consider themselves "old" only when they begin to experience mental and physical declines, coupled with functional, social, or economic dependence. This poses a challenge to public policy, which seeks measurable and "objective" criteria for allocating resources and services.

---

[1]A note on language is in order. Some object to the use of the words "aged" and "old" to refer to "people of advanced age." Yet these terms are widely used in policy discourse and in the lexicon of daily life. I cling to the hope they will one day have the honorable connotations they deserve.

Mrs. Sylvia Johnson, an 80-year-old African American woman, lived 12 blocks from the White House in a DC public housing unit. I met her through a volunteer organization serving the aged in her neighborhood. Wilma, the outreach worker, took me for an initial visit two days before my scheduled interview. At that time, Mrs. Johnson's one-room apartment was crowded with her homemaker Wilma, Amy (a volunteer with a housing advocacy group), and me.

On the day of the interview, Wilma gave me detailed directions, including where to cross the street, and instructed me to "call in" as soon as I arrived so she wouldn't worry. I was one of few white people in the area. Homeless young men shuffled by, deciding not to bother asking me for money. Young men in cars zoomed down the street, making as much noise as possible. A few old people passed, walking as quickly as they could. Apartment units in the area were surrounded by wire fences, with bars on the windows at street level.

Entering the building, I was scrutinized by three men who had been in the foyer during my first visit. The security guard remembered me. Still, he studied my ID and told me to write my name, agency, destination, and arrival time on his sign-in sheet. After signing in, I took the elevator to the fourth floor, where the hall was deserted. Mrs. Johnson's apartment, like most in the building, bore evidence of years of neglect. There were holes in the walls where plaster had come off. Water ran continuously from the kitchen and bathroom faucets. Closet doors had come off their hinges and were propped against the wall. Walls carried several layers of grime, and cockroaches had the run of the place. The heating system worked, though, and the apartment was warm enough to keep a visitor in a light sweat.

Mrs. Johnson was heavy and had lost both legs and much of her eyesight to diabetes. She spent her time in a hospital bed, with blinds drawn. I entered the darkened room to find her lying in bed, the stumps of her legs against the foot of the bed, her head cocked to the side of her pillow, her eyes staring at the wall. She nodded slowly when I asked if she was okay.

Mrs. Johnson asked for some water. When I found a chipped mug and brought her water, she said it was too cold. I offered some ginger ale I'd seen on the counter. She drank five cups and then said she was hungry. After inspecting the refrigerator, I offered a bologna sandwich with mayonnaise. The bologna was open and dry in the refrigerator, not sealed in plastic. I found a plate and fixed the sandwich, while a half dozen cockroaches explored the counter. She ate eagerly, consuming all but the last corner of crust.

Mrs. Johnson did not have the strength to lift herself out of bed. The mattress was covered with plastic, and she lay on a disposable absorbent towel called a "chuck" that is used in hospitals. Under her bed two of these had been discarded, along with a crumpled hospital gown.

Mrs. Johnson had a homemaker who came four hours a day from Monday through Friday. Funding for this service came from Medicaid and the Older Americans Act. On weekends her son Louis gave what care he could. Louis drank too much, and some said he used crack. A few days before the interview he had been barred from the building for a year because he had assaulted a resident. Louis had no place else to sleep and had clearly spent the preceding night on Mrs. Johnson's sofa. The morning before I came he left, locking his mother in. When I called in, Wilma warned me not to stay too long because there would be trouble if Louis showed up. With Wilma's advice in mind, I put my tape recorder at the foot of the bed and began to talk with Mrs. Johnson about her life.

Sylvia Johnson was born in 1913 in Camden, South Carolina. She told me that she was the fourth of 12 children, all of whom were "mean." No one in town picked on them because they were all so mean. Her daddy was big—over 200 pounds. He worked in the construction trade. Her mother was pretty nice, but if you misbehaved she would "get Daddy on you." What Daddy would do was never clear because Sylvia never dared find out.

Sylvia went to school and finished the eighth grade. While she was visiting her sister-in-law in DC, she met her future husband, a much older man. She decided to quit school and marry him. People teased her about marrying someone old enough to be her grandfather, but Mrs. Johnson thought he was a good man to marry. He gave her money, and she'd never had money before. She was happy with her choice. "I had a good husband.... Well, like he know better than to try to beat me, you know."

Mrs. Johnson had four sons. Her children knew better than to make her mad because she was "mean as a dog." People didn't bother her much because she was so mean. "Mean as a dog" is a phrase she used often to describe herself. Her sons grew up mean, and they protected their mama. She never worked. But her husband had jobs and "things like that." They lived in a house on

(continued)

A HUMAN PERSPECTIVE   Sylvia Johnson (*Continued*)

the edge of town. Then he died of "asthma, something like that." It made Mrs. Johnson cry to see him in such pain. Two of her sons died too.

Midway through the interview I was startled by a loud knock on the door. Two police officers wanted to look in the closet for Louis's coat. I didn't think to ask for a search warrant. They found the coat, examined it, and left. The closet was jammed full of men's clothes, with no women's clothes in sight.

Several people wanted Mrs. Johnson moved to a nursing home. I asked her whether she would like to go someplace where people could take care of her and bring her food. She said, "No." As we talked she often mentioned that people didn't "bother" her. I asked whether they had bothered her in the hospital. "Oh, no. They were nice." One woman brought her food, and when Mrs. Johnson didn't like it, she brought in some country food. Would Mrs. Johnson like to go someplace like a hospital? "No, because this is more like a home." Not that it was a home, just more like one. Mrs. Johnson clearly preferred the apartment over a nursing home.

Because Louis had been violent, several people had accused him of abusing his mother. This she denied. No one had ever hurt her, because she was so mean and her sons were so mean. "Louis? He wouldn't hurt his mama. He's a good boy."

Mrs. Johnson used to watch TV for the stories, but as her eyesight deteriorated she found it harder to follow the plots and just watched the pictures—despite their being out of focus.

What did Mrs. Johnson like best about herself? "I'm alive." Many people she had known were dead, but she wasn't, and she felt there must be a reason for that. Maybe because she helped people when she could. "Maybe there's … one star got in my hat…. I was always … you know, nice to people. I used to take children, take care of 'em."

Mrs. Johnson considered herself neither unfortunate nor poor. "You know, I'm the richest somebody in the world…. I thank God for bein' here, you know. I'm proud … a lot of folks … they're dead and gone." Reflecting on her life, she said, "It's all right, you know, like I've gotten married and everything and had a good life…. I'm knowin' folks, you know, they're getting married and they're just messed over and they get on welfare; but I did not go for none of that."

Did she think about death? "Hush your mouth." Did she worry about it? "No." Mrs. Johnson didn't worry about anything. Nor did she need anything. If she had more money, she'd probably buy something but she wasn't sure what, because she hadn't bought anything in a long time. Mrs. Johnson didn't long for anything. But she would love to go back to the country with its cool, clean air.

A SOCIAL WORK PERSPECTIVE

At the time of our interview, Mrs. Johnson seemed to be in dire straits. With severe functional limitations, an extremely low income, and limited family support, she depended on public services to meet her most basic needs. Most people who knew her—neighbors, the building security guard, and her outreach worker—would have felt more comfortable if Mrs. Johnson would have agreed to move to a nursing home where she could receive 24-hour care. Medicaid would cover the costs of institutional care. But Mrs. Johnson did not want to go into a nursing home. She wanted to stay in the apartment.

Five months after our interview, Mrs. Johnson was still in the apartment. No steps had been taken to admit her to a nursing home. Her outreach worker doubted that this was even an option, given limitations on Medicaid beds in the area. Repairs to her apartment had not been made because funding for public housing in the district was limited. As her building manager explained, residents could enter all the repair requests they liked, but when there was no drywall, no plumbing supplies, "no nothing" in the warehouse, repair personnel could not do much.

Mrs. Johnson's situation combined lifelong poverty, family dysfunction, and severe health problems. But integral to her self-esteem was the fact that she had never been on "welfare." Her living circumstances made others uncomfortable. She lived in public housing in an impoverished neighborhood. We became aware of her situation because her neighborhood was served by an active home-visiting agency. Surely other elders, equally dependent and equally neglected, were invisible because there was no outreach worker to knock on their doors twice a week.

LO 14-2   Consider How Social and Economic Factors Influenced the Status of Older Adults in Colonial America

EP 5c

Public policy reflects popular beliefs and attitudes toward older adults. Before tracing the development of contemporary programs and policies we will briefly consider the status of older adults in early America, focusing on three groups: Native American elders, African American elders, and European American elders.

America's **colonial era** extended from the arrival of the Mayflower on November 11, 1620, well into the next century. Short life expectancies defined the experiences of the three main subgroups, all of whom faced hostile environments. For Native Americans the arrival of European immigrants radically decreased life expectancy by exposing them to diseases and war. African Americans under slavery had extremely short life expectancies. The usual life span of a slave during this period has been estimated at 28 to 32 years (Mintz & Kellogg, 1988). Short life expectancies also marked the lives of early European immigrants, particularly in the South.

As a result of these circumstances, there were few old people in colonial America. Benjamin Franklin lived well into his eighties, but when he died in 1790 he had few age peers. Even as late as 1830, those over age 60 made up only 4 percent of America's population (Haber, 1983). Shorter **life expectancy** did not mean that *no one* reached extreme old age, however. Indeed, there are recorded cases among Native American tribes of individuals who reached 95 to 103 years (Simmons, 1945), but they were the exceptions, not the rule. As we will see, culture was (and continues to be) a strong determinant of values related to age.

NATIVE AMERICANS

Respect for advanced age was an integral part of many Native American cultures. Legends illustrate the powers enjoyed by Native American elders, who were central figures in many stories of creation. Among the Hopi, two aged goddesses were believed to have created all living things, and an old Spider Woman is said to have invented arts and crafts (Simmons, 1945). The Menomini, Creek, and Omaha all have held that old men were the first recipients of magical powers and healing arts.

Tribal food taboos often served the interests of older adults, reflecting their influence on this important aspect of the culture. The most choice, nutritious tidbits were withheld from the young. Elders often enforced and, some claim, manipulated these taboos. Among the Omaha, for example, the tender part of buffalo intestine was considered harmful to youths, and young people were warned against eating bone marrow. Old men warned that it would cause sprained ankles in the young and could be eaten only by those past their prime (Simmons, 1945, p. 27).

Native American groups varied in their responses to those of advanced age. The Omaha Indians retained their elders in leadership positions long after they began to fail physically. For them, knowledge and experience were pivotal in determining an elder's status (Simmons, 1945).

Nevertheless, honor for the aged did not preclude abandoning those who became helpless. In times of need, some tribes were forced to euthanize or abandon their elders. As Simmons (1945) observed, "Among all people a point is reached in aging at which any further usefulness appears to be over and the incumbent regarded as a living liability. 'Senility' may be a suitable label for this.... All societies differentiate between old age and this final pathetic plight. Some do something positive about it. Others wait for nature to do it or perhaps assist nature in doing it" (p. 87). Native Americans, particularly nomadic tribes, were forced to abandon those who reached the "helpless stage" of life. Typically, an elder would be left with a cache of supplies and fuel. The Omaha, for example, did not abandon their aged on the open prairie but left them at a campsite with the promise of return. Less common than abandonment was euthanasia. Sometimes the Hopi, who placed a high premium on their elders, would "help them to die" in an honorable, if violent, act of mercy.

Personal wealth often determined the quality of old age. Among the Navajo some elders accumulated wealth in the form of both tangible goods (horses, sheep, cattle, and goats) and intangible resources like knowledge of medicinal herbs, healing ceremonies, and magic. Knowledge and healing powers could be exchanged for gifts or fees.

In most Native American tribes, the aged poor were cared for. Among the Crow, for example, Edward S. Curtis reports that "[s]ometimes one man killed as many as 15 buffalo in a run. He would then cry, 'I do not take the arrows back, nor the skin'; it was then known that all but a few, which he kept for himself, were for the use of the poor old people who had come hurrying out from the camp when the butchering began.... After a hunt, a broad, level stretch of land was dotted with dead buffalo, men butchering, old men hurrying to and fro receiving a piece of meat from this one and that" (Simmons, 1945, pp. 21–22).

The willingness of a tribe or clan to support dependent elders often depended on the availability of food. As Simmons notes, "[A]mong the Hopi no aged person needed to fear starvation *as long as his many relatives had food to spare* and he was able to go to their houses to eat" (italics added, p. 23). It seems that a tribe's care of needy elders depended at least in part on the resources available.

Gender also influenced the status of older adults. Across tribes, gender differences in prestige tended to mirror those observed in relation to wealth. Where women had access to wealth, they enjoyed high status. It was more typical, though, for men to control wealth and have higher status than women. As Simmons notes, "[P]roperty rights of aged women show greater variations and seem to be more strongly influenced by the prevailing type of social organization" (p. 49). Women accumulated more property in groups characterized by matrilineal patterns of inheritance and descent. Women also fared better among groups that relied on collection, hunting, and fishing than among farmers and herders. Based on these observations, Simmons concludes, "In the simpler beginnings aged women seem to have had a more nearly equal chance to acquire property, but with the development of society their mates and brothers have found it possible to get and to control more property" (p. 49).

Despite a general cultural disposition toward honoring age, the status of individual elders in Native American tribes was determined by knowledge and skill, wealth, and gender. Further, the treatment of needy elders was influenced, at least to some extent, by tribal resources.

AFRICAN AMERICANS

The brutalities of slavery dictated short life expectancies for African Americans who were kidnapped as young adults. Although those born in the colonies lived longer, slaves who survived to advanced age had no assurance of comfortable retirement. As Andrew Achenbaum (1986) reports, "If the law did not forbid it, some slave owners 'emancipated' superannuated blacks, thereby 'freeing' *themselves* of caring for aging slaves. Others heartlessly banished their worn-out slaves like old horses to eke out an existence on their own" (p. 29, italics added).

Young African Americans generally treated their "aunts" and "uncles" with deference and support. As Frederick Douglass recounted,

> "Uncle" Toby was the blacksmith, "Uncle" Harry the cartwright, and "Uncle" Abel the shoemaker … these mechanics were called "Uncles" by all the younger slaves, not because they really sustained any relationship to any, but according to plantation etiquette as a mark of respect, due from the younger to the older slaves. Strange and even ridiculous as it may seem, among a people so uncultivated and with so many stern trials to look in the face, there is not to be found among any people a more rigid enforcement of the law of respect to elders than is maintained among them. (Gutman, 1976, p. 218)

Older slaves often exercised near-absolute authority over the younger members of their communities. Herbert Gutman tells of an incident that illustrates this authority: "A white met an aged man on a Mississippi plantation and learned from his *owner* that Uncle Jacob was a regulator on the plantation; … a *word* or a *look* from him, addressed to younger slaves, had more efficiency than a *blow* from the overseer" (p. 219). Older women were often appointed to care for children, teaching them prayers, hymns, and lessons along the way. As Leslie Owens explains, "A beginning lesson was to respect slave elders, particularly the aged" (1976, p. 204).

The respect accorded to aging members of slave communities may be traced in part to West African traditions, in which elders were repositories for information about family and community history, folklore, and ritual traditions (Gutman, 1976). The practice of referring to unrelated elders using familial terms was also adaptive. It helped create a "fictive" kin system among slaves that could help them to endure separation from blood relatives (Owens, 1976).

It is unclear what status differentials were observed among aged African Americans. Possibly because of severe external oppression, there is no evidence of greater status being awarded on the basis of either possessions or gender.

EUROPEAN IMMIGRANTS

One persistent myth holds that European immigrants who reached advanced age in early America enjoyed high social status and strong family ties. Instead, as Carol Haber (1983) pointed out, "In early America … the relationship between age and honor was neither direct nor simple. For some, great age contributed to their high status; for others it led only to ridicule and neglect" (p. 9). Lacking programs and policies to define them as "old," 19th-century elders were judged by their individual attributes. Among Europeans, property, gender, and occupation were critical in defining a person's social status.

Older people with rich estates enjoyed commensurate prestige. Historians have studied seating in early American town halls as a measure of social status. The best seats, those closest to the front, typically went to senior landholders. In an agricultural economy, where the primary means of securing a living was through land, control of property implied social stature as well as authority over family members. Thus, for example, an aged father might determine the timing of his son's or daughter's marriage. He might even select his child's spouse. But authority did not necessarily translate into affection. As Fischer (1977) noted, veneration "is a cold emotion." Younger generations may have respected the old, but they maintained an emotional distance.

A mother's authority and power derived almost exclusively from her spouse, and aged widows found themselves at the mercy of their children. To reduce mothers' vulnerability, some jurisdictions passed laws giving widows one-third of their husband's estates. Some husbands went to great lengths to specify precisely what property was to be included in their wives' shares. For example, when Adam Deemus of Allegheny County, Pennsylvania, made a will in 1789, he left his wife "the privilege to live in the house we now live in until another one is built and a room prepared for herself if she chuses [sic], the bed and beding [sic] she now lays on, saddel [sic] bridle with the horse called Tom: likewise ten milch [sic] cows, three sheep...." (Haber, 1983, p. 20). Some went further, stipulating that children would receive their inheritance only after providing acceptable support and care to their mothers. Such was the case in Timothy Richardson's 1715 inheritance. He did not receive his father's estate in Woodburn, Massachusetts, until he agreed to "give, sign, and pass unto his mother, the widow of the diceased [sic], good and sufficient security" (Haber, 1983, p. 20).

Many aged Americans did not own large estates. In the absence of pensions or mandatory retirement laws, workers were expected to labor as long as they could. The loss of occupation meant not only the loss of a livelihood but also a decline in prestige as the retired worker gave up a principal means of social integration. Far from being an opportunity for leisure, retirement was the sign of impending poverty and death.

Status differentials among European American elders are fairly well documented and seem to have been determined by gender, wealth, and occupation. Nonetheless, like Native Americans and African Americans, European immigrants had a general norm that supported respect for the aged. This norm would erode in subsequent years as attitudes toward aging shifted.

LO 14-3 Appreciate Historic Shifts in Americans' Attitudes Toward Older Adults

EP 5c

Attitudes toward aged *individuals* varied in colonial America as they do today. Nonetheless, most historians and social critics agree that values and attitudes were generally more positive toward the aged as *a group* during the nation's formative years than they are today, suggesting a transformation in cultural values related to age. Some trace diminished respect for older adults to the American Revolution (Fischer, 1977), while others date it within the last half of the 19th century (Achenbaum, 1978; Haber, 1983).

Signs of the transformation were apparent in several developments during the late 18th century (Fischer, 1977). First, seating in town meetinghouses was revised. Age was no longer taken into account. Instead, desirable seats were assigned solely on the basis of wealth. Second, the nation's first **compulsory retirement law** was passed in New York in 1777. Third, census takers observed a shift in what is referred to as "**age heaping**." This process results in higher-than-expected population counts in certain age groups and is the cumulative result of individuals lying to census takers about their age. In early America people tended to report being older than they were, but after the revolutionary period census data revealed a bias toward reporting younger ages. Finally, some argued that the fashion in clothing during this era came to favor youth (Fischer, 1977).

Other signs date the transformation to the late 19th century, when popular and scientific writing came to describe the aged as ugly and disease ridden, rather than as stately and healthy. Paradoxically, the medical advances that contributed to longevity also focused attention on age-related disease and decline. As a result, instead of exalting their moral and practical wisdom, commentators began to equate age with illness and conclude that older people had nothing to contribute to society (Achenbaum, 1986).

What caused this transformation in attitudes? Many have concluded that industrialization lowered the status of elders in today's society (Achenbaum, 1986; Shanas, 1968). New practices in business and manufacturing technology stressed speed and efficiency, traits incompatible with the aging process. The industrial workforce had few jobs that could accommodate older adults, and thus between 1851 and 1861 the old experienced the greatest decline in both economic and occupational rank of any age group (Haber, 1983). Further, rapidly changing technology made the knowledge and skills of aged workers obsolete. Younger workers no longer looked to their elders for training and advice.

But industrialization alone could not account for the reduced status of the older adults. As Fischer (1977) points out, in Japan—a nation that underwent rapid industrialization—the status of the aged has remained quite high. Further, signs of diminished respect for elders appeared in the United States before the industrial revolution.

Several other factors may have contributed. The War of Independence set the stage for revolutionary ideas. Change became not only possible, but valued. So rejection of the old political order entailed rejection of traditional ideas that held age as the basis of prestige (Fischer, 1977). As some Americans began to accumulate fortunes, wealth may have replaced age as a way of discriminating among people. And, as we have seen, advancing medical knowledge may also have contributed. As diseases and physical losses associated with age were documented, older people came to be seen as incapacitated and worthless (Achenbaum, 1986).

Finally, the diminished status of older adults may have been caused by changed relationships with their children (Haber, 1983). Parents in colonial times were seldom without children. The birth of the first grandchild followed closely or even preceded that of a couple's last child. As women limited their family sizes and planned the timing of childbirth, the line dividing generations grew more distinct and the "empty nest" became more common. With no children to raise, the older generation no longer had a central function. Urbanization tended to limit family size and diminish parental authority. In a city an older son who resisted his father's authority could simply leave home and find a job—an option that had not been available when the sole source of income was the family farm.

In sum, age alone did not determine the status or well-being of adults in early America. All three of the cultural groups considered here showed evidence of a general norm of respect for the aged. Native Americans typically expressed their veneration through myths and food taboos, providing care for needy elders as resources permitted. Elders served as fictive kin in slave communities, assisting in the education and direction of younger slaves. Among European immigrants, the status of the aged was closely tied to their control of property, and landed elders wielded authority over their offspring. The status of European American elders showed signs of decline as early as the latter part of the 18th century. Historians hold different opinions regarding the causes of that decline, attributing it to revolutionary ideas, accumulated wealth, industrialization, urbanization, and changing family roles.

LO 14-4   Reflect on the Origins of Contemporary Programs and Policies That Affect Older Adults

EP 5a

The programs and policies developed for indigent elders in the new nation reflected both American attitudes toward age and the nation's beliefs about poverty. Public relief focused on the European elders who, when they became indigent, were treated as poor, not old.

PUBLIC RELIEF FOR NEEDY ELDERS

Being old and poor has always put Americans in a precarious situation. The township records of early colonies illustrate the status of indigent elders. In these documents, the wealthy are listed by both first and last names, and the poor are called by their last name with the prefix "old." Thus, while "Thomas Moore" might be a man of means, his poor cousin would be referred to as "Old Moore."

Public relief for indigent elders in the United States was initially modeled on England's Elizabethan Poor Laws. These laws did not allow for differentiation on the basis of age. Elders were treated the same as any other group of poor people. Their sustenance was the responsibility of the parish or local community, which provided either "outdoor relief" (money to pay rent or buy goods) or "indoor relief" (lodging in a poorhouse).

With urbanization, the population of cities increased, as did the number of indigents within a city's borders. Philadelphia, for example, saw dramatic growth in its poorhouse population. Prior to 1750, fewer than 50 paupers per year were admitted, but by 1815 this number had risen to 2,250. Roughly a third of these were destitute because of old age (Haber, 1983), but age was not yet used to distinguish among the poor. Older adults were lodged in the almshouse or poorhouse among other worthy poor—people who were disadvantaged through no fault of their own.

Beginning in the 1830s, the notion of a homogeneous class of indigents was challenged. Reformers who served the urban poor became interested in more efficient use of resources and decided to focus their efforts on those most capable of reform, the "redeemable poor." The aged were not included in this category. In 1855, for example, the New York Association for Improving the Condition of the Poor (NYAICP) declared that it would assist only five groups: industrious laborers, indigent widows and deserted wives with children, educated single females, the sick and the bereaved who would improve, and mechanics who suffered temporary loss of employment (NYAICP annual report, 1855, p. 37, cited by Haber, 1983). The association resolved "to give no aid to persons who, from infirmity, imbecility, *old age,* or any other cause are likely to continue unable to earn their own support and consequently to be permanently dependent" (italics added, p. 38). Urban charity organization societies (COS) took the same position. In 1892, Amos Warner expounded on the hopelessness of work with the aged: "In work with the aged one is conscious that for the individuals dealt with there is no possibility of success" (Haber, 1983, p. 40).

Thus, while COS and other philanthropies were sending young laborers back to rural areas and attempting to retrain or rehabilitate others, the aged were confined to public almshouses. In time they made up a growing proportion of the almshouse population. By 1904, over half of the residents in almshouses throughout the nation were over 60 years old (Haber & Gratton, 1994).

Over time, age came to be associated with destitution (particularly by charity professionals).[2] In 1902, Homer Folks, New York City's commissioner of charities, announced a new name for the city almshouse: the Home for the Aged and Infirm. He intended to send the message that the residents of this facility were not the lazy able-bodied, but those who were simply too old or sick to earn a living. **Institutional care** was less expensive than **outdoor relief** for the aged, and so the almshouses came to be seen as the most appropriate setting for needy elders.

As "homes" or "asylums" were populated by the aged and infirm, they took on a more medical focus. The line between hospital and almshouse blurred, and "old-age homes" began to offer medical care in addition to room and board, setting the stage for development of the facilities we now call nursing homes.

---

[2]Three classic books illustrate this tendency to associate age with poverty: *Pauperism and the Endowment of Old Age* and *The Aged Poor in England and Wales,* both published in the 1890s and written by Charles Booth, and *Old Age Dependency in the United States,* written during the same era by Lee Welling Squier.

INFORMAL ASSISTANCE AMONG AFRICAN AMERICANS

During the **antebellum era** many African American elders lived in abject poverty. Unable to access the relief provided to European American elders, African Americans relied on informal community supports. Organizations known as benevolent societies were developed in collaboration with homes for the aged. These mutual-aid societies worked to keep African Americans off public relief and to provide for a decent burial. Society members paid annual dues and in return were given sickness and death benefits, which could then be turned over to a home for the aged. For example, in 1864 Quakers and African Americans founded the Home for Aged and Infirm Colored Persons in Philadelphia to provide care for "worthy" and "exemplary" African Americans "who in their old age from sickness or infirmity have become more or less dependent upon the charities of the benevolent" (Pollard, 1980, p. 231). For at least 27 years, the home provided lodging and care to members of Philadelphia benevolent societies, and in return, the societies turned members' benefits over to the Home. The number of these societies mushroomed. Philadelphia alone had more than 100 societies serving more than 7,000 members (Pollard, 1980). During the latter part of the 19th century, the resources of benevolent societies were strained by the longevity of their members. Ultimately, these societies were replaced by insurance firms with greater financial reserves. Nonetheless, benevolent societies represented a significant resource for older African Americans, serving as a hallmark of the community's response to need.

PUBLIC PENSIONS FOR VETERANS

The 19th century set the stage for many of our current approaches to the care of needy aged. Agencies that focused on the redeemable poor gave up on elders, reserving their energy and resources for young people with some hope of employment. Poor elders increasingly found themselves "warehoused" in institutional settings—precursors of today's nursing homes. One class of elders was favored by public policy initiatives, however: military veterans.

Public pensions for veterans were the nation's first federal retirement programs. In 1829 (more than a century before the passage of the Social Security Act), federal legislation awarded pensions to veterans of the Revolutionary War. Notably, this act was passed 46 years after the end of the war, ensuring that few would collect the pensions and that those who did would be very old. Later, provisions were made for survivors of the War of 1812, the Indian conflicts, and the Mexican War to receive federal pensions. These pensions were funded through general tax revenues and did not represent a significant drain on the public purse.

This changed when Civil War veterans were added to the federal pension program. Their addition (only 25 years after Appomattox), meant thousands of potential recipients might receive pensions, placing a huge drain on public revenues. Faced with this potential drain, the U.S. Pension Bureau stressed that the money was only for those in dire need, establishing severe restrictions on eligibility. Applicants had to prove they were "suffering from a mental or physical disability of permanent character, not the result of their own vicious habits, which incapacitates them from the performance of manual labor in such a degree as to render them unable to earn support" (Haber, 1983, pp. 110–111).

Administration of these restrictions was complex. Physicians disagreed about the character and cause of disabilities, and many decisions were appealed and reversed. In 1904, **Theodore Roosevelt** officially included every aged veteran in the pension program and declared that those who reached the age of 62 would be considered half disabled; at age 65 they would be considered two-thirds incapacitated, and those over 70 would be considered totally disabled. Thus, chronological age replaced functional ability in determining who would receive a pension. This dramatically eased the administration of the program, replacing physician examination with a simple review of birth records (Haber & Gratton, 1994). By establishing the ability of the federal government to operate a pension program, federal pensions for veterans set the stage for Social Security.

Contemporary policies affecting older adults reflect several of the themes introduced in this brief history. Among them are a tendency for publicly funded services to focus on the majority population, a willingness to make special provisions to meet the needs of veterans, the administrative complexity of using functional status as a measure of need, an inclination to apply institutional solutions to economic and social problems, and the impact of economic resources on community willingness to support indigent elders.

LO 14-5   Examine Contemporary Attitudes Toward Aging and Older Adults

EP 3a
EP 5a
EP 5c

International visitors to the United States often hold the stereotype that Americans do not value or care for the aged—that we put them in "warehouses." But American attitudes toward older adults are complex, rooted in cultural norms that dictate respect for the aged but also distracted by contemporary pressures. In this section we will consider two divergent views of the nation's aged: "intergenerational equity" rhetoric that paints older Americans in negative terms and a "productive aging" discourse that offers a more favorable view.

INTERGENERATIONAL EQUITY

The last few decades of the 20th century saw strident debate over "**intergenerational equity**," which has become a catchword for political commentators predicting an "age war" or a "**generational conflict**" over the allocation of scarce resources. According to this view, "greedy geezers" have taken up more than their share of public funds, and America's youth have been deprived as a result. This argument was largely confined to the United States and was not seriously advanced in any other nation (Kingson & Quadagno, 1997). It surfaced in a context of relative economic scarcity as U.S. economic growth slowed considerably during the 1970s, with limited increases in productivity and rising inflation.

Notably, the intergenerational equity argument was advanced, not by advocates for children, but by an elite group of political and business leaders. In 1984, Senator Dave Durenberger (R-MN) founded an organization called Americans for Generational Equity (AGE) with a stated goal: "to promote the concept of generational equity among America's political, intellectual and financial leaders" (Quadagno, 1989). Financial support for AGE came primarily from "banks, insurance companies, defense contractors, and healthcare corporations" (Quadagno, 1989, p. 360), and with that support the organization mounted an effective campaign of inflammatory propaganda that included articles with titles such as "Older Voters Drive Budget," "U.S. Coddles Elderly but Ignores Plight of Children," and "The Tyranny of America's Old" (Cook, 1996). AGE staff members also wrote books, such as *Born to Pay* by Phillip Longman (1987). Although AGE no longer exists, it did influence the debate about public support for programs that serve older adults (Quadagno, 1989). Similar work is carried out by the Concord Coalition, founded by Pete Peterson (former chair of President Clinton's Tax and Entitlement Reform Commission).

Robert Binstock offered an explanation for the popularity of the intergenerational equity argument. He observed a broad shift in the portrayal of the aged around 1978, and suggests that initially older adults were described using a "**compassionate stereotype**" that presented them as poor, frail, and needy. They appeared as vaguely pathetic figures, clearly in need of assistance. During the 1980s, however, the media, public commentators, and scholars began describing elders as rich, healthy, and politically powerful. Their need for public resources became open to dispute. This shift served as the foundation for an emerging stereotype that Binstock (1983) called the "aged as scapegoat," in which a wide range of political, social, and economic problems are blamed on senior citizens.

We see an echo of the intergenerational equity argument when pundits and policy makers point to the "**aging tsunami**" that threatens to engulf the nation. Calling for **entitlement reform**, they argue that the resources devoted to older Americans—Social Security benefits and Medicare in particular—are unsustainable drains on the federal budget.

PRODUCTIVE AGING: AN ATTITUDE SHIFT

During the 1990s, a growing number of professionals and academics in the field of aging began to advance the concept of **productive aging**. Their efforts, in part designed to counter the effects of the "**greedy geezer**" rhetoric, underscore the potential and the actual contributions of older adults. According to this view, the "**new aged**" are healthier and more financially secure than any previous generation, and as a result, they are in a better position to contribute to the well-being of their families, their communities, and their society. Within this tradition, older adults are portrayed as vital individuals who are eager for meaningful involvement (Perlmutter, 1990; Rowe & Kahn, 1998).

Central to this viewpoint is the notion that societal barriers, such as age discrimination in employment or inaccessible public buildings, make it difficult for elders to provide meaningful contributions. Thus, advocacy in the field of productive aging would focus on removing those barriers and increasing opportunities for engagement. This more positive view of age stands in sharp contrast to the critical view presented in the intergenerational equity rhetoric (Bass, Caro, & Chen, 1993; Butler, Oberlink, & Schechter, 1990; Morrow-Howell, Hinterlong, & Sherraden, 2001). Nonetheless, the impact of this perspective on support for public programming has not been assessed.

LO 14-6 Become Familiar with the Demographic and Economic Realities That Shape Aging Today

EP 3a
EP 5a
EP 5c

In addition to reflecting attitudes, modern public policies are influenced by demographic and economic realities. In this section we will examine how these factors have shaped policies and programs for older Americans.

THE GRAYING OF AMERICA

The 20th century saw unprecedented growth in the number and proportion of older adults. When the century opened, those aged 65 or older numbered 3 million—roughly 4 percent of the U.S. population. By 2000, the population 65 or older numbered 35 million, or 12.4 percent (U.S. Census Bureau, 2002b). The United States is not alone in the graying of its population. Nations throughout the world are seeing similar changes, and in many, like the United States, the situation is exacerbated by unusually high post–World War II birth rates.[3] The American **baby boom** cohort consists of individuals born between 1945

---

[3]As the austerity of the Great Depression and the war years was replaced by economic security and in some cases affluence, many industrialized nations had baby booms. The dates vary, but each nation saw dramatically increased birth rates.

and 1964. This group has moved through the system of age-based public services "like a pig in a python," and during the first half of the 21st century baby boomers are expected to accentuate the underlying growth in America's senior population, such that by 2030 nearly one in five Americans is projected to be 65 or older (U.S. Census Bureau, 2010a).

The baby boom was a temporary aberration in the long-term trend of declining fertility. It was followed in the 1970s by a new and more enduring demographic reality: the "**baby bust**." Fertility rates in the United States appear to have stabilized at levels well below those seen previously. Despite fertility declines, the U.S. population continues to grow through immigration and improved life expectancy.[4]

More Americans are surviving childhood, and greater numbers are living to advanced ages. These two trends have dramatically increased life expectancies. In colonial America, life expectancy for the population as a whole was less than 40 years. As we saw in Chapter 6, life expectancy in the United States rose to 78 years by 2008, and it stands at 78.8 years today. This is largely the result of public health measures that have reduced infant mortality. Taken together, declining fertility and increased longevity have caused unprecedented growth in the nation's older population.

EP 2a

The aging population has increased not only in numbers but also in diversity. Today's older adults are proportionately older, more female, and more ethnically diverse than ever before. Between 1930 and 2000, the fastest-growing subgroup within the aged population was those 75 and older; however, from 2000 to 2010 older adults of color increased from 11 percent to 14 percent of the aging population and the proportion over age 75 declined slightly (from 48 percent to 46 percent). These trends are illustrated in Figure 14.1.

FIGURE 14.1   Rising Diversity Among Older Adults

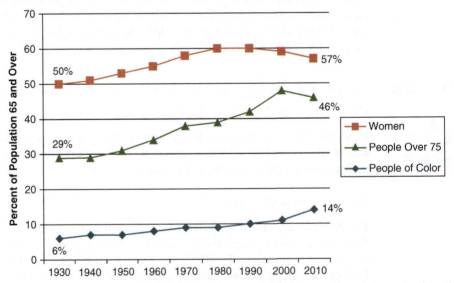

Source: U.S. Bureau of the Census (1998). Statistical Abstract of the United States and Census Briefs on the Older Population (for 2000 and 2010) (http://www.census.gov/prod/cen2010/briefs/c2010br-09.pdf).

[4]Population dynamics in the United States stand in sharp contrast to a number of nations that are facing serious population declines. These include Russia and several former Soviet states, as well as Japan, Italy, and some African nations.

INCOME AND AGE

Older adults in the United States today face a lower risk of poverty than their parents did. In 1959, more than one in three (35 percent of) Americans aged 65 or over had incomes below the federal poverty threshold. By 2015 that figure had dropped to 8.8 percent. This decline is illustrated in Figure 14.2. As we will see, the dramatic decline in poverty among American elders is largely attributable to the Social Security Act. Yet some Americans continue to experience financial vulnerability in their later years, and the very subgroups that have experienced the fastest growth (the very old, people of color, and women) have the highest rates of poverty.

Poverty in Late Life

With respect to elders living in poverty, this country fares poorly in international comparisons. In 2007, international researchers studied the economic status of older adults in seven industrialized nations.[5] They used 50 percent of median income as a poverty measure and concluded that the United States had the highest rate of poverty (Sierminska, Brandolini, & Smeeding, 2007). Their findings are summarized in Table 14.1.

In the United States the very old have lower incomes, primarily because at older ages we see a disproportionately high number of single women. The relationship between age, marital status, and income is illustrated in Figure 14.3. The very old are also more likely to live on incomes below poverty. Americans 80 years or older had a poverty rate of 12 percent in 2013, and 45 percent lived on incomes that were less than twice the poverty rate. Among the very old, women have a higher risk of poverty than men. In 2013 the poverty rate for women over 80 was 23 percent, and for men it was 14 percent (Cubanski, Casillas, & Damico, 2015).

FIGURE 14.2   Poverty Among Americans 65 and Older, 1959–2015

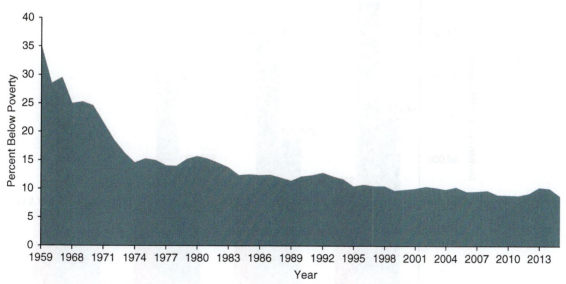

SOURCE: U.S. Census Bureau (2016). Historical Poverty Tables – People: Table 3. Poverty status by age, race, and Hispanic origin (http://www.census.gov/hhes/www/poverty/data/historical/people.html).

---

[5]Nations studied included Canada, Sweden, France, Italy, Germany, the United States, and the United Kingdom.

TABLE 14.1 Poverty Among Older Adults: International Comparisons

Nation	Percentage That Are "Income Poor"
United States	23.2%
United Kingdom	14.9%
Italy	11.7%
Germany	10.8%
Sweden	7.3%
Finland	6.1%
Canada	5.2%

Source: Sierminska, Brandolini, & Smeeding (2007).

At the intersection of age, gender, and race, older women of color experience high rates of poverty in the United States. This is illustrated in Figure 14.4. As the figure indicates, people of color experience higher rates of poverty in their later years. African American and Hispanic elders have the highest rates of poverty. In 2010, the poverty rate for African American women was 20.5 percent, while the rate for Hispanic women was 20.9 percent.

FIGURE 14.3   Age, Marital Status, and Income of Older Adults, 2014

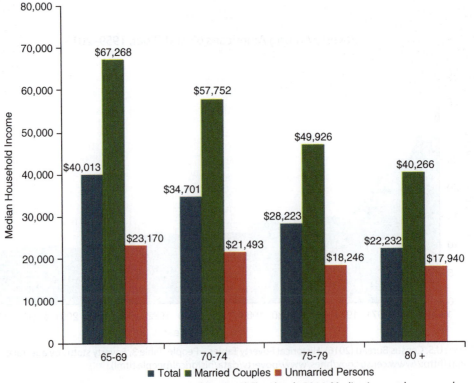

Source: Social Security Administration (n.d.). Income of the Aged Chartbook: 2014, Median income by age and marital status, 2015 (http://www.ssa.gov/policy/docs/chartbooks/income_aged/2014/iac14/ html#table20).

FIGURE 14.4   Poverty Among Older Adults by Gender and Race

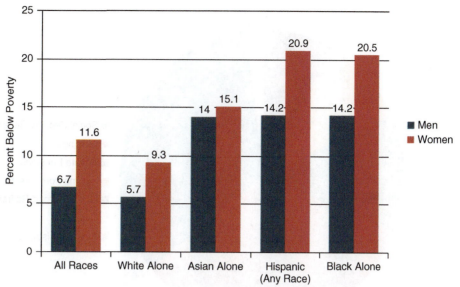

Source: U.S. Census Bureau, Current Population Survey, Annual Social & Economic Supplement. POV01: Age and Sex of All People, Family Members and Unrelated Individuals Iterated by Income-to-Poverty Ratio and Race: 2009 (http://www.census.gov/hhes/www/cpstables/032010/pov/new01_000.htm).

By 2013, the overall rate for African Americans was 17.6 percent; for Hispanics, 19.8 percent; and for older whites, 7.4 percent (Administration on Aging, 2014).

Likewise, older women living alone in the United States are consistently among the poorest of the aged, faring worse than older couples. The highest risk of poverty among the aged was experienced by Hispanic women who lived alone, among whom nearly half (40.8 percent) had incomes below the poverty threshold (Administration on Aging, 2011; Kaiser Family Foundation, 2015b). African American women who lived alone also experienced an elevated risk of poverty, with an overall poverty rate of 30.7 percent. Clearly, those with the highest risk of poverty are most likely to benefit from antipoverty programs.

Social Security has been termed the nation's most effective antipoverty program. Its impact was demonstrated in a seminal study by the Center on Budget and Policy Priorities (Porter, Latin, & Primus, 1999). Researchers analyzed five years of census data (1993–1997) to determine the number of elders in each state who would have been poor if they had not had Social Security benefits. Results indicated that Social Security lowered the number of elders in poverty from 15.3 million to 3.8 million in 1997. Without Social Security, nearly half (47.6 percent) of the U.S. older population would have been poor. The study also revealed that 60 percent of those lifted from poverty by Social Security were women. Because women live longer than men, the fact that Social Security benefits are indexed to inflation is especially important to them.

Retirement Income
The importance of Social Security to the nation's elders becomes even more clear when we consider the sources of income for this age group. Sources of "aggregate" income (for all seniors) are presented in Figure 14.5. As we can see, Social Security was the largest single source of retirement income, providing 34 percent of the income received in 2010.

FIGURE 14.5   Sources of Aggregate Income of Older Americans

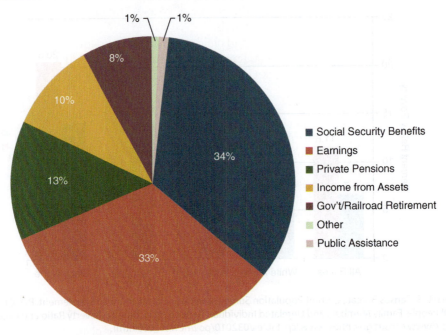

SOURCE: Social Security Administration (n.d.). Income of the Population 55 or Older, 2014 (http://www.ssa .gov/policy/docs/statcomps/income_pop55/2010/sect10.pdf).

The importance of this program cannot be overstated. In 2014, 85 percent of couples and 84 percent of single adults aged 65 and older in the United States received Social Security benefits. Most older adults in America (64 percent in 2014) received more than half of their income from Social Security. Social Security benefits made up *90 percent or more* of the income received by about one in five older couples (21 percent) and nearly half (43 percent) of single adults 65 and over. (Social Security Administration, 2016c).

Earnings are a significant (and growing) source of income for older Americans, representing nearly a third (32 percent) of aggregate income. We will expand on this topic in Chapter 15. Private pensions represented only 13 percent of income for adults aged 55 and over in 2014; income from assets, about 10 percent; government and railroad retirement benefits, 8 percent; and public assistance, less than 1 percent (Social Security Administration, 2016c).

In this section, we have considered the complex array of attitudes and conditions that shape policies that affect older adults in the United States. American attitudes toward older adults reflect traditional values and contemporary tensions. The result can be paradoxical, alternating between resentment (of greedy geezers) and hope (for productive aging). At the same time, we face challenging material conditions: unprecedented growth in an older population that is becoming increasingly diverse, and economic conditions in which some enjoy affluent retirement lifestyles while others live in abject poverty and most depend heavily on Social Security. In the following section we will consider programs and policies for older adults in the United States.

LO 14-7   Become Familiar with Contemporary Programs and Policies That Affect Older Adults in the United States

EP 5a
EP 5b

Programs for older adults that are authorized under the Social Security Act were introduced in Chapter 4. These include OASDI, Medicare, Medicaid, and Supplemental Security Income—integral parts of the nation's safety net. In the following sections we will consider the Older Americans Act and public policies governing private pensions. We will also look at health policy issues focused on older adults: long-term care, rationing of care by age, end-of-life care, and assisted suicide.

THE OLDER AMERICANS ACT AND AGE-BASED SERVICES

The **Older Americans Act (OAA)** was passed just prior to the escalation of the Vietnam War and the economic downturns of the 1970s. It represented a national commitment to meeting the needs of the aged. Although its goals were exalted, OAA funding was limited. Nonetheless, the act established a national network of providers and governmental authorities charged with the care of the aged. The history and structure of this network and some tensions inherent to OAA programs are discussed here.

Prior to the 1965 passage of the OAA, the aged received limited social services through programs that had not been specifically designed for them. As early as 1950, President Truman initiated the first National Conference on Aging. Participants called for greater government involvement in meeting the needs of the aged. Continuing interest led President Eisenhower to create the Federal Council on Aging in 1956 to coordinate federal activities related to aging. Successful passage of the OAA has been attributed to the 1961 White House Conference on Aging. The conference brought experts on aging and advocates for older adults to Washington, DC, from across the nation, raising awareness of issues affecting the aged. In 1962, Representative John Fogarty of Rhode Island and Senator Pat McNamara of Michigan introduced legislation to establish an independent U.S. Commission on Aging. The Kennedy administration objected to creation of an independent agency. In 1963, the act was reintroduced, this time proposing an Administration on Aging (AOA) under the Department of Health, Education and Welfare. Again, the proposal was defeated.

The 1965 proposal reflected the 1963 version, but this time the bill received bipartisan support and the OAA was signed into law by President Johnson on July 14, 1965. In his remarks upon signing the bill, the president suggested the legislation would provide "a coordinated program of services and opportunities for our older citizens" (U.S. House of Representatives, 1988, p. 2). Of course, the goals of the OAA were considerably loftier. They are presented in Box 14.1.

OAA programs were placed under the jurisdiction of the **Administration on Aging**, a federal agency within the Department of Health, Education and Welfare (HEW) (now Health and Human Services). Originally, the head of the AOA was a commissioner on aging who reported to the Secretary of the HEW, but in 1993 Fernando Torres-Gil received presidential appointment as the first assistant secretary for aging. This appointment established the AOA as a more autonomous federal agency. In 2012, the AOA was merged with the Office on Disability and the Administration on Developmental Disabilities to form the new **Administration for Community Living**.

Initial funding was modest. In 1966, total appropriations under the OAA amounted to $6.5 million. By 2016, however, the AOA appropriation exceeded $1.9 billion. A comparison of the 1966 and 2016 appropriations reveals the growing complexity of programs operating under the OAA. The 1966 appropriations funded two categories: Title II, Grants

BOX 14.1   Older Americans Act of 1965: Declaration of Objectives

"[I]n keeping with the traditional American concept of the inherent dignity of the individual ... the older people of our Nation are entitled to, and it is the joint and several duty and responsibility of the governments of the United States, the several states and their political subdivisions, and of Indian tribes to assist our older people to secure equal opportunity to the full and free enjoyment of the following objectives:

1. An adequate income in retirement in accordance with the American standard of living.
2. The best possible physical and mental health which science can make available and without regard to economic status.
3. Obtaining and maintaining suitable housing, independently selected, designed and located with reference to special needs and available at costs which older citizens can afford.
4. Full restorative services for those who require institutional care, and a comprehensive array of community-based, long-term care services adequate to appropriately sustain older people in their communities and in their homes, including support to family members and other persons providing voluntary care to older individuals needing long-term care services.

5. Opportunity for employment with no discriminatory personnel practices because of age.
6. Retirement in health, honor, dignity—after years of contribution to the economy.
7. Participating in and contributing to meaningful activity within the widest range of civic, cultural, educational and training, and recreational opportunities.
8. Efficient community services, including access to low-cost transportation, which provide a choice in supported living arrangements and social assistance in a coordinated manner and which are readily available when needed, with emphasis on maintaining a continuum of care for vulnerable older individuals.
9. Immediate benefit from proven research knowledge which can sustain and improve health and happiness.
10. Freedom, independence, and the free exercise of individual initiative in planning and managing their own lives, full participation in the planning and operation of community-based services and programs provided for their benefit, and protection against abuse, neglect and exploitation."

for State and Community Programs on Aging ($5 million), and Title IV, Training, Research and Discretionary Projects and Programs ($1.5 million). The 2016 appropriations are detailed in Table 14.2.

OAA Programs Today

The OAA established the administrative structure for the delivery of social services to the aged. Under the authority of the AOA, each state or territory operates its own state office on aging. The network is further divided into area agencies. Thus, every jurisdiction in the United States has a designated authority responsible for programming for the aged. This tremendous accomplishment can be attributed to (and is dependent on) a partnership of federal, state, and local governments. Eligibility for services funded under the OAA is based solely on age. Anyone aged 60 or over may participate, regardless of income or assets.

The funding formula for OAA programs is based on the proportion of the nation's aged who reside in each state. As a consequence, states with large senior populations, such as Florida and California, enjoy higher OAA appropriations than states with relatively young populations, such as Alaska and Utah. Under the act, Area Agencies on Aging must avoid providing services themselves. Whenever possible, they must contract with private and public entities.

Funded by their appropriations, states sustain a network of OAA services, including those described in Title III of the act:

TABLE 14.2   2016 Appropriations Under Title III of the Older Americans Act

Program	2016 Funding (in Thousands of Dollars)	Percent of Total
Health and Independence for older adults	1,256,444	86
Nutrition Services	834,753	57
Home and Community-Based Supportive Services	347,724	24
Preventive Health Services	19,848	1.4
Chronic Disease Self-Management Education	8,000	0.5
Elder Falls Prevention	5,000	0.3
Native American Nutrition and Supportive Services	31,158	2.1
Aging Network Support Activities	9,961	0.7
Holocaust Survivor Assistance	2,500	0.2
Caregiver and Family Support Services	176,777	12
Family Caregiver Support Services	150,586	10
Native American Caregiver Support Services	7,531	0.5
Alzheimer's Disease Supportive Services Program	4,800	0.3
Alzheimer's Disease Initiative	10,500	0.7
Lifespan Respite Care	3,360	0.2
Protection of Vulnerable Adults	32,532	2.2
Long-Term Care Ombudsman Program	15,885	0.1
Prevention of Elder Abuse and Neglect	4,773	0.3
Elder Rights Support Activities	11,874	0.8

Source: Administration for Community Living (2016). *FY 2016 ACL Budget Table*. (Enacted). (http://www.acl.gov/About_ACL/Budget/ACL-FY2016-budget-table.aspx).

1. *Access services.* Transportation, outreach, information, and referral.
2. *Supportive services.* Health (including mental health), transportation, housing repair, community-based services to prevent institutionalization, legal assistance, exercise programs, health screening, preretirement counseling, and "any other necessary services for the general welfare of the older people."
3. *Nutrition services.* Congregate meals in senior centers and home-delivered Meals on Wheels.

In addition, a National Caregiver Initiative, passed in 2000, authorizes services to family members caring for frail elders.

Tensions Surrounding OAA Programs

Targeting of OAA services has been a source of tension. As indicated earlier, the act requires that services be made available to all Americans aged 60 or over, regardless of their income or assets. Yet funding for these services amounts to less than $50 for each potential recipient (Americans aged 60 or over). Clearly, OAA services cannot meet the needs of *every* older American, so allocation of scarce resources is an ongoing challenge. A careful look at 2016 appropriations gives insights into AOA priorities.

Congregate meals delivered in senior centers illustrate this tension. Consistently the single largest item in the AOA appropriation, these meals provide important socialization opportunities as well as a nutritional supplement. Yet congregate meals have been criticized as failing to serve cultural minorities and frail elders. The social climate in most senior centers reflects the majority culture in the area.[6] Although not overtly hostile, the activities, food, and atmosphere may not be familiar or welcoming to people from minority cultures. Similarly, frail elders—those who are most in need of assistance to maintain their independence—may be physically unable to participate in congregate meals or senior center programs.

In response to this tension, the 1987 amendments to the OAA added Section 305 of Title III to require that states "(E) Provide assurances that preference will be given to providing services to older individuals with the *greatest economic or social need, with particular attention to low-income minority individuals*" (italics added). Subsequent appropriations revealed an increased emphasis on cultural minorities and vulnerable individuals. Between 1986 and 2001, grants to Indian tribes more than doubled, going from $8.3 million to $23.5 million (Administration on Aging, 2001; U.S. House of Representatives, 1988). Programs serving frail and vulnerable elders were also initiated, including in-home services for the frail, elder abuse prevention, and long-term care ombudsman services. Later, the National Caregiver Support Program was added to OAA programs. With funding in excess of $160 million, this program delivers assistance, training, and respite to family members caring for the frail.

The 1987 requirement that OAA services focus on those with the greatest need created a new tension. Seniors in greatest need are the least likely to provide the political support needed to increase program budgets. The popularity of OAA services has been linked in part to their ability to serve mainstream, middle-class seniors. An ongoing challenge for OAA programs is sustaining political support while nonetheless targeting those who are most in need.

OAA programs are also directly affected by changing perceptions of the nation's aged. When seniors are perceived as "greedy geezers," Americans become more critical of programs that use age-based eligibility criteria, particularly if these programs fail to meet the needs of the most vulnerable elders. The challenge for the OAA network will be to respond credibly to this criticism while maintaining the integrity and political viability of programs funded under the act.

PUBLIC POLICIES AND PRIVATE PENSIONS

Many Americans are familiar with public programs such as those operated under the OAA, but they may be unaware of the laws governing the establishment and operation of private pensions. Yet, these policies affect the financial security of millions of older adults. The term "private" is a misnomer when applied to pensions. Few personal assets are as profoundly affected by public policy as pensions.[7] Although the first company pension plan was established in 1875 (by the American Express Company), most were developed after passage of the Revenue Act of 1921. This law encouraged the development of private pensions by exempting both employer contributions and pension fund income from federal income taxes.

---

[6] In some places an entire catchment area might serve predominantly minority residents. This is the case, for example, when a city's African American neighborhood has its own senior center. These centers tend to serve an African American clientele, and congregate meals reflect the predominant culture in the surrounding neighborhood.

[7] See Schulz (1995) for a detailed discussion of private pensions.

During the 1940s and 1950s private pensions mushroomed. The number of workers covered rose from about 4 million in the late 1930s to 10 million in 1950. This expansion was the result of wage and price controls imposed to limit inflation during World War II. With wages capped, one of the few ways companies could attract qualified workers (themselves in limited supply) was to offer generous fringe benefits such as pensions and health insurance. Thus, two public policy initiatives—wage controls and tax deductions—set the stage for the expansion of private pensions.

There were several problems with the early pensions: (1) they tended to treat top executives more favorably than regular employees; (2) workers often lost their benefits as a result of mergers, closures, and bankruptcies; (3) in some spectacular scandals, pension reserves were mismanaged and lost; (4) some workers were fired just months before they became eligible for a pension; and (5) workers' survivors (most of them widows) received no income from pensions upon the death of the worker.

In 1974, Congress addressed these problems by passing comprehensive legislation to regulate pensions. The **Employee Retirement Income Security Act (ERISA)** limited the number of years of employment an employer could require before a worker had the legal right to receive pension benefits—before the worker became "vested." It strengthened standards governing the management of pension funds. It restricted the extent to which employers could use pensions only to reward "key employees"—that is, highly paid executives. As we will see in Chapter 15, ERISA was amended in 1984 by the Retirement Equity Act to require that plans provide the option of a Joint and Survivor Annuity. This stipulation provides a modicum of income security to survivors.[8]

Another major public policy affecting pensions was the 1974 establishment of the **Pension Benefit Guaranty Corporation (PBGC)**. Created through Title IV of ERISA, the PBGC manages a mandatory insurance program for pension benefits so that in the event of bankruptcy, workers do not lose all of their pension rights. Prior to the establishment of the PBGC, workers lost their pension if their employer went out of business. For example, when Studebaker terminated its pension plan in 1963, more than 4,000 auto workers lost part or all of their pensions (PBGC, 2001). When Braniff Airlines went out of business in 1982, however, the PBGC insured vested employees and provided benefits up to a maximum of about $1,500 per month (Schulz, 1995).

Although business representatives opposed each of these regulatory reforms, the laws did not slow the growth of pensions. Twenty million workers were covered in 1960 and 35 million in 1979. By 1995, an estimated 42 million workers, roughly half of the labor force, were covered by pension plans (Schulz, 1995). The growth in pension coverage slowed during the 21st century, in part reflecting the decline of unions. In 2013, only 13 percent of non-union workers in the private sector were covered by pension plans, compared with 67 percent of unionized workers. Of course, pension coverage is higher in the public sector, reaching 78 percent of the 2013 workforce (Morrissey, 2013).

Of course, many workers are still not covered. Most of them are employed in trade and service industries. Key factors determining whether workers will be covered are their union status and the number of people employed by the company. Workers without pensions are usually not union members and work for firms with relatively few employees. Women and minorities are overrepresented among workers who do not enjoy pension coverage. In this chapter's Human Perspective box, it is clear that Mrs. Johnson and her husband did not have pension coverage. (Women's experiences with pensions are discussed further in Chapter 15.)

---

[8]ERISA also enabled some employees to establish Individual Retirement Accounts.

The nature of pensions has changed since the 1980s. Most of those set up prior to 1960 were "**defined benefit**" programs. That is, they promised monthly benefits based on earnings and years of service. These plans offered workers a measure of security. They were insured by the PBGC, and most workers knew how much retirement income they could anticipate. But they imposed financial demands on employers, who are legally obligated to deliver pension benefits. During the 1980s, many employers began to offer "**defined contribution**" pension programs, under which a specified amount is deposited into a tax-sheltered retirement account for the worker. The 401(k) account is an example of a defined contribution plan. Such plans are not insured by the PBGC, and the retirement income they will generate is influenced by fluctuations in financial markets.

In 1980, defined benefit plans covered the vast majority (80 percent) of workers who had pension coverage. But their numbers have declined markedly. According to the Teacher Insurance and Annuity Association, the proportion of private-sector employers who offered a defined benefit plan declined from 50 percent in 1998 to 5 percent in 2015, a trend that accelerated as many plans were terminated during the Great Recession (Sullivan, 2016). This change has reduced retirement security for those workers fortunate enough to have a pension.

The spectacular failure of the Enron Corporation in 2002 illustrated the risks of defined contribution plans. Like many companies, Enron offered employees a 401(k) plan that was heavily invested in company stock. When the stock plummeted in value, employees lost their retirement savings. The resulting litigation and controversy led to passage of the Pension Protection Act of 2006.

Described as a "sweeping reform" of the nation's pension laws, the act regulates, to some extent, employers (such as Enron) who offer company stock as an investment in defined contribution plans. Through its financial provisions, the act reduces the extent to which companies can underfund their defined benefit pensions. The act also makes it easier for companies to automatically enroll employees in defined contribution plans, requires greater disclosure about the performance of retirement accounts, and regulates the extent to which employers can advise employees about investment of their pension contributions. Finally, the act permanently increased contribution limits for IRAs and 401(k)s. While the act contains a number of helpful technical improvements, it does little to extend coverage to low-income workers who most need to save for retirement.

BOX 14.2   New Pension Insecurities?

In July 2004, United Airlines announced that it was halting all payments into its defined benefit pension plans, subject to bankruptcy and reorganization. United proposed to jettison its pension obligations by transferring pensions to the Pension Benefit Guaranty Corporation (PBGC). On behalf of the union that represented United ground workers, Robert Roach Jr. suggested that "instead of terminating pensions, maybe we should explore terminating the employment of United's top management, who have mired the company in bankruptcy for more than two years" (*Washington Post*, March 12, 2005). United's action set the stage for similar moves by established airlines coping with increased competition from new airlines (without significant pension obligations), reduced demand since 9/11, and rising fuel costs. U.S. Airways shifted its pension plan to the PBGC in 2003, as did several failed steel companies. The solvency of the PBGC has come into question and with it the security of pension income for thousands of American workers. The pensions of public employees are also vulnerable, as we saw in the 2013 bankruptcy of Detroit.

ADULT PROTECTIVE SERVICES

In 2010, a nationally representative sample of 5,777 older adults was surveyed by telephone regarding their experiences of abuse and neglect. The authors of this National Elder Mistreatment Study summarized their results by saying that "slightly more than 1 in 10 of our community-residing, cognitively intact elderly persons reported experiencing some type of abuse or potential neglect" (Acierno et al., 2010, p. 294). Specific results indicated that 5.2 percent of older adults experienced financial abuse by a family member during the year of the study; 5.1 had experienced potential neglect; 4.6 percent, emotional abuse; 1.6 percent, physical abuse; 0.6 percent, sexual abuse (Acierno et al., 2010).

Public intervention in cases of elder abuse and neglect dates to the 1961 White House Conference on Aging, which recommended the study of "ways to facilitate the provision of protective services to older people" (Senate Committee on Aging, 1961, p. 59). In the decade that followed, the Administration on Aging funded several demonstration projects to test models for delivering these services, but the real impetus for states to establish APS services was the 1974 passage of Title XX of the Social Security Act, which provided funding for social services if states met five goals, which included "preventing or remedying neglect, abuse, or exploitation of children and adults unable to protect their own interests" (Mixson, 2010). By 1985 nearly all states had a designated office charged with providing protective services to older adults; however, the 1987 conversion of Title XX into the Social Services Block Grant (SSBG) reduced funding even as it increased state discretion in allocating federal funds. Competing demands (such as child protection services) limited the resources available to address cases of elder abuse.

This history is reflected in the network of state APS programs. Resources are chronically limited, and states vary in their definitions, their eligibility requirements, and their interventions. The federal role in this area is limited. Under the Elder Justice Act of 2009 (part of the Affordable Care Act) an elder abuse coordinating council is established and federal detection and prevention efforts are assigned to the Secretary of Health and Human Services. While the law authorizes funding for research, programs, and training, its funding is quite limited. The Older Americans Act includes definitions of elder abuse and authorizes funding for the National Center on Elder Abuse, which disseminates information and awards grants under the Administration on Aging. APS services in the United States face challenges in the management of self-neglect cases, as well as concerns regarding the effectiveness of mandatory reporting.

Self-Neglect

Most APS cases involve self-neglect (Ernst & Smith, 2011)—that is, older adults who fail to secure "goods and services necessary to maintain physical health, mental health, emotional well-being and general safety" (Wiehe, 1998, p. 135) often due to untreated mental illness or limited financial resources. Paula Mixson reframed these as instances of "societal neglect" (2010, p. 29), arguing that they cannot be effectively addressed without reforms to the nation's social service and financial infrastructures. John Regan's 1985 observation remains apt today: "The creation of an Adult Protective Services program does not establish for these victims a promised land flowing with benevolence and abundant services" (p. 3).

Even as they underscore the failings of the U.S. safety net, self-neglect cases reveal a tension between the values of safety and freedom that is pervasive throughout APS services. Too often, it seems that securing an older adult's safety involves compromising his or her freedom. Despite a stated preference for maintaining clients in the "least restrictive environment," older adults who become APS cases may face heightened risk of institutional placement. These considerations may lead some older adults to endure neglect (and even abuse) rather than seek APS services.

Consider the findings of a seminal evaluation of protective services conducted by the Benjamin Rose Institute (Blenkner, Bloom, & Nielson, 1971). This experimental study compared clients in an APS program with those receiving routine services available in the community. Results indicated that although APS services did not prevent deterioration or improve mental or physical competence, they did increase the likelihood of institutionalization (Blenkner et al., 1971). Likewise, a study of APS case outcomes found that cases were most frequently resolved through the hospitalization, nursing home placement, or relocation of the victim (Wolf & Pillemer, 1989).

Mandatory Reporting

In most states social workers and other professionals who work with older adults are required to report cases of suspected elder abuse or neglect to the appropriate governmental authority. Mandatory reporting was designed to improve case detection, and the number of reported cases did increase following passage of mandatory reporting legislation. Unfortunately, funding for APS services typically did not (Daly, Jogerst, Brinig, & Dawson, 2003). High rates of re-referral suggested that APS staff were unable to follow up on reports, leading several observers to note the futility of reporting in the absence of effective intervention services and supports (Mixson, 2010).

This tension led Paula Mixson (2010) to suggest that the benefits of mandatory reporting result not from the mandate, but from public education and awareness regarding elder abuse and neglect. She suggests eliminating the mandate while retaining provisions that prohibit false reports and provide liability protection for those who report in good faith. Despite skepticism from Mixson and others, this requirement enjoys widespread public approval (Dakin & Pearlmutter, 2009) which might stem from a belief that government must "do something."

Nonetheless, many argue that APS services in the United States struggle with a lack of coherence (Mixson, 2010). Self-neglect clients who comprise most of the caseload present practical complexities and ethical dilemmas. On the other hand, elder abuse that involves assault, battery, theft, or fraud may be a matter for criminal authorities. APS workers find themselves operating in the margins, assessing complex and ambiguous situations and striving to improve the living conditions of vulnerable adults as they reconcile competing interests and coordinate the services of a wide range of health, mental health, and law enforcement providers.

LO 14-8   Reflect on Specialized Issues Affecting Health Care for Older Adults

EP 3a
EP 5b

In Chapter 6 we examined the serious fiscal pressures confronting the Medicare program. In the following sections we will touch on some specialized issues related to health care for the aged, including long-term care, rationing health care by age, end-of-life care, and assisted suicide.

LONG-TERM CARE

As Joshua Weiner noted, "One of the great successes of the twentieth century has been the prevention and treatment of acute illnesses" (1996, p. 51). Unfortunately, this cannot be said of the chronic illnesses that affect millions of aged Americans. Our health-care system has struggled to meet the care needs of those who face lingering illness and disability. Most older adults manage chronic illness by relying on family caregivers who provide care at considerable personal and financial cost. As we have seen, the Older Americans Act provides some resources to assist in **community-based care**. In addition, most states use funding available through Medicaid Home and Community-Based Care Waivers to offer limited coverage for in-home services and alternatives to nursing homes, such as assisted living facilities that provide care for elders who need some help to live independently (National Association of State Units on Aging, 2005). In part as a result of these initiatives, the number of older adults living in nursing homes for 90 days or longer declined from 1.21 million in 1999 to 1.06 million in 2004 (Kasper & O'Malley, 2007).

But for those who require it, nursing home care is expensive. Private rooms averaged $77,745 per year in 2007 (MetLife, 2007). While a few can pay for nursing homes on their own, either with personal resources or by using long-term care insurance, most nursing home care is paid for by Medicaid.[9] The Kaiser Commission reported that 68 percent of 2004 nursing home costs were paid by Medicaid. Of course, Medicaid has income and asset limits, so patients who need coverage must "spend down." In other words, they must deplete their assets and income until they meet Medicaid's eligibility limits.

Prior to passage of the Medicare Catastrophic Coverage Act of 1988 (MCCA), those who needed Medicaid coverage for long-term care faced a risk known as "spousal impoverishment." In the process of spending down to become eligible themselves, they left the community-dwelling spouse in poverty as well. Under the MCCA and other federal statutes, state Medicaid programs are now required to allow spouses to retain income up to a certain level—usually 150 percent of the federal poverty threshold. The spouse is also allowed to keep some of the couple's assets. Although most MCCA provisions were repealed, these spousal impoverishment measures remain in effect.

Older adults wishing to preserve assets for their heirs sometimes transfer those assets prior to entering a nursing home. As a result, state and federal funds intended to provide medical care of the poor have been spent to cover the care of Americans who are better off financially. State and federal policies discourage this type of transfer, which has become an accepted part of estate planning in legal circles. The MCCA and subsequent federal statutes have stringent provisions governing the transfer of assets. Medicaid eligibility will be delayed if, during the "look-back period" of five years prior to applying for coverage, applicants disposed of assets for less than fair market value. This provision does not ordinarily apply to a house transferred to a spouse or other relatives.[10] Generally, policy in this area has been designed to encourage those who can afford it to purchase long-term care insurance instead of relying on Medicaid.

Private insurance companies have offered long-term care policies since 1982. Though less popular than health insurance, this type of coverage has been growing both in availability and popularity. Government policy has contributed to that growth as the federal government and several states offer tax reductions and other incentives to encourage the purchase of long-term care insurance.

---

[9]Most states require Medicaid applicants who apply for nursing home admission to be screened to ensure that the placement is appropriate. Individuals who request placement for primarily social reasons (such as the lack of a committed caregiver) or mental health reasons (such as depression) are denied admission.

[10]Medicaid eligibility is not affected by the transfer of a house to the following relatives: a spouse, a child under 21 years of age, a disabled or blind adult child, an adult child who lived in the house and cared for the patient for at least two years before the patient was institutionalized, or a sibling who has equity in the house and has lived in it for at least one year before nursing home placement of the homeowner.

BOX 14.3   The Eden Alternative

The Eden Alternative is a new approach to long-term care designed to humanize nursing homes. The movement started in 1991 when Dr. William Thomas founded the first "Edenized" nursing home in New York. Dr. Thomas identified three "plagues" of old age: loneliness, helplessness, and boredom. Edenized nursing homes are designed to eliminate all three. They look more like homes than medical facilities and include children and pets in their programming. Thomas aggressively promotes his Eden Alternative, which some say is just part of a general trend to humanize care in nursing homes. Although this approach is widely seen as promising, initial research studies provide only limited evidence of improvement on standardized outcome measures (Bergman-Evans, 2004; Coleman et al., 2002). For more information, see Thomas (1996).

In their early days, long-term care policies were problematic. Companies used deceptive sales tactics, and policies had small print that exempted major conditions such as Alzheimer's from coverage (National Policy and Resource Center on Women and Aging, 1996). Partly as a result of government intervention and partly due to consumer education, these practices have improved. Still, few older adults have long-term care coverage, and private insurance pays for the care of only a small fraction of long-term nursing home residents—less than 3 percent in 2004 (Kasper & O'Malley, 2007). This situation may change in the future. As we saw in Chapter 6, the Affordable Care Act included a long-term care insurance program known as the CLASS Act; however, this measure was repealed.

RATIONING HEALTH CARE BY AGE

Some people advocate withholding medical care from older adults on the grounds that their care is expensive and their social contributions are limited. According to this view, late life medical care involves lavish expenditures for individuals who have little to contribute to society—a situation that is particularly galling in view of the unmet health needs of infants and children. Former governor Richard Lamm of Colorado and others have suggested that medical treatment be withheld after a certain age (see Callahan, 1987, 1990). Through acceptance of a "**natural life course**," we might allocate scarce resources more effectively (Daniels, 1988). In a less diplomatic statement of the same view, Lamm has been widely quoted as arguing that old people "have a duty to die and get out of the way" (Slater, 1984, p. 1). By doing so, they would presumably free up money to provide medical care for the young.

In opposition to age rationing of health care, Jahnigen and Binstock (1991) argued that it would be wrong to deny lifesaving care to a class of people defined only by their age. According to this view, clinical decisions about care should be based on individual considerations. As C. Everett Koop suggests, "Age is far too loose a criterion. Look at me. One of the main reasons I was rebuffed during my nomination to the office of surgeon general was because I was 'too old.' I was just a youngster of sixty-five.... Of course, this did not sit very well with the man who nominated me. President Reagan had just passed his seventieth birthday" (Binstock & Post, 1991, p. ix). Opponents of age-based rationing suggest that denying health care on the basis of age would deny some people life or functioning for significant periods, at a cost not only to the elders themselves but to their family members and friends. They further suggest that the fiscal crisis in health care is not entirely due to the graying of America, but also to systemic factors such as inflation in medical costs and expenditures for technological developments.

END-OF-LIFE CARE

Although most Americans prefer to die at home, the majority still die in hospitals. The number of deaths in hospitals has declined since the 1980s. Public policy decisions were instrumental in this shift, which some attribute to Medicare's prospective payment system and the use of **diagnosis-related groups** or DRGs (Sager et al., 1989). Under this view, the pressure to discharge patients has moved dying people out of hospitals.

Yet others acknowledge that without community-based supports such as those provided under hospice programs, fewer people would be dying at home (Tolle et al., 1999). **Hospice care** got a significant boost with the 1982 passage of the Tax Equity and Fiscal Responsibility Act, or TEFRA. This legislation added hospice care to the benefits covered by Medicare, making hospice available to everyone who has a life expectancy of six months or less under Medicare Part A.

Public policy has also established the framework for patients to provide advance directives regarding their end-of-life care. The two approaches most often used are a living will and a durable power of attorney. A living will is designed to outline specific requests about medical procedures that a person may or may not want in the case of incapacity. A durable power of attorney is used to designate a representative for the purpose of directing medical care if a person is unable to express his or her own wishes. Unlike a "simple" power of attorney, the durable power of attorney remains in effect if its executor becomes incompetent or disabled.

All states now recognize the living will as legally enforceable. Indeed, the Patient Self-Determination Act of 1990 requires health-care institutions participating in Medicare and Medicaid to provide patients with written information regarding living wills. These institutions must ask whether patients have an advance medical directive and document the reply in their medical records.

ASSISTED SUICIDE

Dr. Jack Kevorkian, a retired pathologist in Michigan, probably did more than anyone else to bring the topic of **assisted suicide** to public attention. Dr. Kevorkian acknowledged assisting in the suicides of at least 92 people—most of them women—ranging in age from 26 to 89 (Euthanasia Research and Guidance Organization, 1998). In 1999, he was convicted of second-degree homicide for his involvement in the death of 52-year-old Thomas Youk.

Several organizations are working hard to secure legal protection for physicians who help patients commit suicide.[11] These advocates make several arguments in support of their cause. First, they suggest that the suffering associated with some terminal diseases is unbearable and cannot be relieved, stripping such patients of dignity and depriving their life of meaning. Second, advocates argue that physicians (like Dr. Kevorkian) are already helping patients commit suicide and that "decriminalizing" their actions would open them to public scrutiny and ensure that decisions are made in a balanced way that protects the interests of terminally ill patients. Finally, they note that a nation such as the United States, which places a high value on individual dignity, should not deprive terminally ill persons of assistance in ending their lives. (See Orentlicher, 1996, for a detailed review of legal aspects of these arguments.)

---

[11]Groups that support assisted suicide include Americans for Death with Dignity; Choice in Dying; Death with Dignity, National Center; and Euthanasia Research and Guidance Organization.

Opponents[12] of assisted suicide offer several arguments. First, they argue that it is the duty of medical practitioners to relieve terminally ill patients of the suffering attendant to their diseases. If physicians have an easy out in the form of assisted suicide, they will not make the heroic efforts necessary to relieve pain. Second, they suggest that assisted suicide is one step down a slippery slope that could lead to euthanasia of undesirable or disabled elders. Finally, they suggest that terminally ill patients who are in unremitting pain are not competent to make an informed decision regarding the value or meaning of their life.

Oregon was the first state to legalize physician-assisted suicide. In November 1994, Oregon voters made theirs the first state in the nation to legalize physician-assisted suicide, passing Measure 16 by a slim margin (51 percent in favor and 49 percent opposed). The new law was immediately challenged by a group of patients who declared that it violated their constitutional rights. Federal District Court Judge Hogan ruled in their favor, issuing a permanent injunction against the law. In February 1997, the Federal Ninth Circuit Court reversed Hogan's ruling. The court did not rule on the constitutionality of the statute but decided the patients did not have "standing" to bring the case. In October 1997, the Supreme Court refused to hear the case.

Two cases decided by U.S. courts of appeals offered contradictory opinions. In the first, *Quill v. Vacco*, three New York physicians and their patients challenged the constitutionality of that state's laws prohibiting physicians from providing drugs to hasten death. In April 1996, the U.S. Court of Appeals for the Second Circuit held that "physicians who are willing to do so may prescribe drugs to be self-administered by mentally competent patients who seek to end their lives during the final stages of a terminal illness" (*Quill v. Vacco*, 1995, pp. 2–3). In contrast, the constitutionality of the State of Washington's law against physician-assisted suicide was upheld in a 1995 ruling by the U.S. Court of Appeals for the Ninth Circuit. The opinion states that the court found "no basis for concluding that the statute violates the constitution" (*Compassion in Dying v. State of Washington*, 1995, p. 4).

In 2001, the Bush administration weighed in when Attorney General John Ashcroft issued a new interpretation of the Controlled Substances Act. Ashcroft held that the act granted him authority to prohibit prescriptions for drugs administered under Oregon's Death with Dignity Act. A lawsuit was filed in Oregon, and a U.S. district court judge ruled against Ashcroft in 2002. The case meandered up to the U.S. Supreme Court, which heard arguments and, on January 17, 2006, affirmed the lower court's decision upholding the Death with Dignity Act.[13]

Since then, physician-assisted suicide has been legalized in five additional states via three distinct approaches: voter referendum, court decision, and state statute. In Washington, the Death with Dignity Act was approved by voters in 2008. Colorado voters approved Proposition 106 in 2016. In Montana, the Supreme Court held that existing state law allowed for physician-assisted suicide. Then legislatures in two more states passed statutes: Vermont in 2013 and California in 2015. Other states have instituted or are considering statutes to legalize the practice, and by the time you read this the number of states that permit physician-assisted suicide may have grown.

---

[12]Opponents of assisted suicide include the Roman Catholic Church; Not Dead Yet; the International Anti-Euthanasia Task Force; and Americans Disabled for Attendant Programs Today.

[13]The interested reader will find a summary of laws around the world governing assisted suicide at http:// www. assistedsuicide.org/suicide_laws.html.

LO 14-9   Become Aware of the Unmet Need for Social Work Professionals to Serve Older Adults

EP 3a
EP 8d

The United States does not have enough qualified social workers to serve its aging population, a problem that is expected to worsen in the near future. The Department of Health and Human Services has estimated that between 60,000 and 70,000 professionally trained social workers will be needed to serve older people and their families in 2020 (National Institute on Aging, 1987). Historically, the number of social workers providing services to the nation's aged has been less than half that number (Greene, 1989; Petersen, 1988). This suggests the need for a significant increase in the number of social workers trained to work with older people.

Few schools of social work offer specialized training in aging, however, and those that do offer such programs find that student interest is low (Lubben, Damron-Rodriguez, & Beck, 1992; McCaslin, 1987). Unless there is an increase in the production of professional-level social workers who are prepared to serve the aged, people from other fields such as nursing and gerontology will fill roles ordinarily reserved for social workers, such as case manager, counselor, discharge planner, and program administrator. Most social workers in aging find that the rewards of working with the nation's elders are greater than they anticipated.

Closing Reflections

EP 2a

Public policies and programs for older adults reflect public attitudes. When **compassionate stereotypes** prevail, aging programs tend to expand. In the context of "greedy geezer" rhetoric, they often contract. Apart from attitudes, the material realities of age drive policies and programs.

Twenty-first-century realities for this age group are complex. Foremost is its tremendous growth. The aging of baby boomers is beginning to place unprecedented demands on public programs for the aged. Many in this cohort are economically well-off, enjoying the accumulated benefits of an advantaged life, a phenomenon known as **"cumulative advantage"** (Crystal & Shea, 1990). These advantages render suspect the use of age-based eligibility requirements for publicly funded benefits. As a result, programs ranging from Social Security and Medicare to services provided under the OAA are subjects of intense public scrutiny.

At the same time, the effects of lifelong oppression, termed "cumulative disadvantage," restrict the opportunities and resources available to vulnerable subgroups of the aging population (Crystal & Shea, 1990). Older women of color, like Mrs. Johnson, have extremely high rates of poverty. Age itself brings disadvantages. Even normal physical aging processes can leave a person dependent on health care to manage pain and disability. In the decades to come, a growing proportion of the senior population will consist of the very old, women, and minorities—the groups most vulnerable to these disadvantages and those most likely to depend on public programs and services. It is important that social workers continue to serve as advocates for these disenfranchised and vulnerable elders.

Think About It

1. Consider Mrs. Johnson's experiences with public policies and programs. In what ways do they reflect the themes discussed in the historical sections of this chapter? What modern policies and programs have influenced her living conditions? In what ways do gender and race determine the resources available to Mrs. Johnson?

2. Federal, state, and local governments devote considerable resources to measures that assist older people. These range from health services to the popular Meals on Wheels programs. At the same time, many observers feel the nation has neglected the needs of vulnerable children. How would you justify spending public resources on programs for the aged?

3. A central tension in OAA programs is the need to use scarce funds to serve those in greatest need, while the political viability of these programs stems from their middle-class constituency. If you were the director of a state office on aging, how would you respond to the mandate to serve those in greatest social and economic need?

4. Consider three aged people, all of whom have incomes below the federal poverty threshold. Helen is a widowed homemaker who raised four children. Her children are all doing well, but her husband's terminal illness in the early 1980s has left her impoverished. Sandra worked all her life in a nonunion factory. She has no pension and now is too disabled to work. Betty is a lifelong alcoholic. Married three times, never for more than three years, she has moved from place to place, working at low-paying jobs. She has two children but doesn't know where they are. Describe the public income supports on which these individuals might draw. Now list these three individuals in order of priority—who has the greatest claim on public resources?

5. Medicare currently offers health coverage to elders of all income levels, and this coverage is better than most policies that low- and many middle-income workers could afford to purchase on their own. Yet funding for Medicare comes from a tax on wages. Do you think this is fair? Why or why not? Would you propose to finance health care this way? Or would you recommend a different approach?

6. Do you think age should continue to be used (instead of frailty or vulnerability) as the basis of eligibility for Older Americans Act programs? What about Adult Protective Services? Why or why not?

Web-Based Exercises

For direct links to all the sites in these exercises, visit the *Foundations of Social Policy* Companion Site at www.cengagebrain.com and select the resources for Chapter 14.

1. Go to the Social Security Administration's Income of the Aged Chartbook: 2014 located at http://www.socialsecurity.gov/policy/docs/chartbooks/income_aged/. Based on the information provided, answer the following questions.
   1. In what ways do aged households with asset income differ from those without?
   2. How do members of various racial and ethnic groups differ in source and amount of retirement income?
   3. Does marital status affect retirement income? If so, how?
   4. How would you describe the distribution of income in retirement? What are the most common income levels?

II. Estimate your longevity on the Living to 100 Life Expectancy Calculator (www.livingto100.com) and see what advice this site has to offer about lifestyle and other considerations. The results might surprise you. If you want to know more, choose "about" on the upper menu and learn about the fascinating results coming from the New England Centenarian Study at Boston University.

Competency Notes

As mentioned in the preface to this text, the Council on Social Work Education has designated nine core competencies and related practice behaviors that must be addressed by accredited social work programs. In these notes, I will specify the way chapter content addresses these competencies and behaviors. (This is designed to assist with the accreditation process.) Please refer to the "helping hands" icons for the locations of specific content in this chapter. Here you will find a brief explanation of how the accompanying content relates to the specified competency or practice behaviors.

The following list indicates where EPAS competencies and practice behaviors are addressed in this chapter.

EP 2a **Apply and communicate understanding of the importance of diversity and difference in shaping life experiences in practice at the micro, mezzo, and macro levels.** The chapter discusses the rising diversity of the population of older adults, as well as role of Social Security in reducing poverty and ends with a call for social work advocacy on behalf of vulnerable elders.

EP 3a **Apply their understanding of social, economic, and environmental justice to advocate for human rights at the individual and system levels.** The chapter introduces ageism as a mechanism for oppression of older adults and discusses the concept of cumulative disadvantage to explain the vulnerabilities that result from a lifetime of oppression.

EP 5a **Identify social policy at the local, state, and federal level that impacts well-being, service delivery, and access to social services.** The chapter describes the services established under the Older Americans Act, as well as policies that authorize funding and regulate long-term care and hospice care. It also examines pension policies and their implications.

EP 5b **Assess how social welfare and economic policies impact the delivery of and access to social services.** The chapter addresses the underlying social and economic realities that set the stage for the policies that fund social services to older adults.

EP 5c **Apply critical thinking to analyze, formulate and advocate for policies that advance human rights and social, economic, and environmental justice.** Central to this chapter is the relationship between public attitudes toward older adults and the development of policies and programs to serve them. The chapter also discusses trends that influence the demand for services to the aged.

EP 8d **Negotiate, mediate, and advocate with and on the behalf of diverse clients and constituencies.** This chapter discusses the growing need for social workers providing services to the nation's older people and their families.

Suggested Resources

Achenbaum, W. A. (1986). *Social Security Visions and Revisions*. Cambridge: Cambridge University Press.

Binstock, R. H., & Post, S. G. (Eds.). (1991). *Too Old for Health Care: Controversies in Medicine, Law, Economics, and Ethics*. Baltimore: Johns Hopkins University Press.

Hudson, R. B. (Ed.). (1997). *The Future of Age-Based Public Policy*. Baltimore: Johns Hopkins University Press.

Kingson, E. R., & Berkowitz, E. D. (1993). *Social Security and Medicare: A Policy Primer*. Westport, CT: Greenwood Publishing Group.

Richardson, V. E., & Barusch, A. S. (2006). *Gerontological Practice for the Twenty-First Century: A Social Work Perspective*. New York: Columbia University Press.

Schulz, J. H. (1995). *The Economics of Aging* (6th ed.). Westport, CT: Auburn House.

www.aarp.org. The official site of AARP, this is a gold mine of information about aging. AARP's legislative issues link provides up-to-date information about issues that affect the aged.

www.agingsociety.org. This is the site of the National Academy on an Aging Society, a policy institute operated by the Gerontological Society of America (www.geron.org). The academy's mission is to promote "education, research, and public understanding" on issues that affect the aged. Its publications are well balanced and carefully researched.

www.aoa.gov. Maintained by the U.S. Administration on Aging, this site is an excellent source of information on programs funded under the Older Americans Act.

CHAPTER

15

Working Americans

I can look at history and say that we are evolving into a more just world. I know that it doesn't look so good today, but over a hundred years it does change tremendously. But it changes because millions of people make a decision to make a difference, to think differently, to demand justice, to demand justice for other people, to not look the other way, and I just need to be a part of that.

LAS VEGAS COCKTAIL WAITRESS AND UNION ORGANIZER (CHANDLER & JONES, 2003)

Learning Objectives

This chapter will help prepare students to:

LO 15-1 Become familiar with the history of labor in the United States and abroad

LO 15-2 Understand how historic developments like the Cold War and the Civil Rights Movement influenced the Labor Movement

LO 15-3 Appreciate the influence of affirmative action on American workers

LO 15-4 Become familiar with immigration policies and their influence on American workers

LO 15-5 Become familiar with the history of U.S. policies protecting women and children in the workplace

LO 15-6 Become aware of the historic role of social workers in the labor movement

LO 15-7 Reflect on contemporary realities that shape the experiences of U.S. workers

LO 15-8 Become familiar with U.S. policies that affect vulnerable groups in the workplace

LO 15-9 Understand key provisions of U.S. labor policies

LO 15-10 Understand the impact of globalization on workers in the United States and elsewhere

Most Americans work for a living, bartering our time and energy in a market that tends to favor employers. The "organization man" was once a figure of disdain, representing the sacrifice of individualism to the demands of the workplace; now we look back at him with nostalgia. He evokes memories of a time when workers—particularly white-collar workers—could expect to remain with the same employer for their entire career. Few contemporary workers enjoy this degree of employment stability, and all too often the interests of employee and employer are diametrically opposed.

EP 3a

LO 15-1   Become Familiar with the History of Labor in the United States and Abroad

The history of labor is the history of our nation, ranging from the forced labor of slaves to the technical performance of aerospace engineers. In this section, we will briefly focus on key developments in the U.S. labor movement, as well as legislation and court decisions that had pivotal impacts on work experiences. We will then examine in more detail the history of affirmative action, immigration, and policies protecting women and children. This section closes with a look at the historic alliance between the social work profession and the labor movement.

EP 2a
EP 3a
EP 5c

LO 15-2   Understand How Historic Developments Like the Cold War and the Civil Rights Movement Influenced the Labor Movement

Many aspects of employment are determined not by laws but by contracts or agreements between employers and employees. Advocates of free enterprise argue that it is inappropriate, even *unconstitutional*, for the government to intervene in these private contracts.[1] But the power differential between employee and employer is usually so great that the contract is less a matter of mutual agreement than of employer fiat. Unions shore up the power of employees, enabling them to bring greater clout to the bargaining table. Union actions have improved conditions for workers in a wide range of industries.

In many ways, the history of the U.S. labor movement is international. As Frank (2004) explains, "[U]nions, the basic institutional unit of U.S. labor history, were transnational from day one" (p. 99). Labor unions crossed borders, in part because leaders were concerned that overseas workers who were not unionized might undercut domestic workers, and also because they recognized that the mutual interests of workers transcended nationality. Some established international "secretariats" that exchanged information with overseas workers, solicited financial help during strikes and discouraged foreign workers from becoming scabs. Apart from these practical considerations, some unions shared a vision of working-class solidarity. Recall Karl Marx's famous call, "Proletarians of all countries, unite!" As this quote suggests, in its early years the U.S. labor movement drew inspiration from communist philosophy and leadership from the socialist movement.

In the 1860s, American unions participated in the **International Workingmen's Association (IWA)**, known as the "First International," sending a delegate from the iron molders' union to the IWA's first congress in Geneva in 1866. Their concerns were both pragmatic and idealistic, combining worries about foreign strikebreakers with a push toward solidarity. The organizational framework would not survive beyond the 1870s, but historians credit the First International with providing a forum for labor leaders to make contact and develop a common agenda for change. The call for international labor legislation surfaced in the First International and would reappear in subsequent organizations as well (Lorwin, 1929).

---

[1]These arguments generally invoke the contract clause (Article 1, section 10, clause 1) of the Constitution, which prohibits states from passing laws that retroactively impair contract rights.

A HUMAN PERSPECTIVE   Sam Tobin

Sam's hefty frame towers over me as I greet him on the tiny front porch of his new townhouse on the outskirts of Omaha. Dressed casually in an old T-shirt and paint-speckled jeans, he warns that I will need to speak loudly. The rock and roll days of his youth left him with a hearing impairment. Besides that, he has lost all of his hair, so looks a bit older than his 33 years. I increase the volume to compliment him on the little red geraniums planted along the foundation. In a sweet, hopeful gesture, someone—his wife Hannah, as it turns out—has put a lot of effort into those seedlings.

Sam's mother raised him alone, relying mostly on public assistance. His dad worked construction jobs. Sam hated school, finding English and math particularly loathsome. At 14 he started playing drums with a friend after school. His high school music teacher thought he had talent and bought him a set of drums, fueling a dream of rock and roll stardom. After graduation he got a day job as a groundskeeper at a local school, playing drums at night for local bands. Sam earned some good reviews and lots of applause. That's how he met Hannah. She was singing with a band, and they decided to become a team. Attraction flared, and they were married within a month.

Along with two other music lovers, Sam and Hannah cobbled together a band and set out in a trailer to tour the country. "I was dreaming I was going to be a musician and I left and said, 'I'm never coming back. I'm going on tour. I'm gonna be a rock star. Bye bye!'" Sam recalls. They played at night clubs and colleges and made a demo CD. Sam said it was a fun time, but "it sure didn't pay us much!" In the highly competitive music market they had a hard time getting gigs. Their debts grew, and they never did seem to break even, let alone get ahead. "We hardly made $150 a week," Sam explains. "We had a couple of bad tours and realized that music could not fill our stomachs. The band members started getting frustrated and the band disintegrated." He figures, "The system doesn't support artists. The music industry is not favorable to new artists. It's all about number crunching from foreign companies. That's all they see. So I burned out on music. It was fun as a hobby, but it's another thing when it's your job. It loses its sweetness. I'm not as passionate about it as I used to be. Maybe when I get older...."

Sam and Hannah moved to California and found "real" jobs. She worked in a chocolate factory, and he worked in a UPS store. Even without the dream of stardom, life was pleasant, and they enjoyed the gentle climate. Then Hannah got pregnant with their daughter, Cecelia. Sam was delighted but soon realized that even on two incomes they could not afford child care. Hannah asked her employer for shift work, but instead she was laid off. Her employer offered no explanation, just "Sorry, we can't do that for you. We're gonna have to let you go." Now there was no way the couple could afford rent and the new baby. Sam had to sell his drum set to pay the rent. So they decided to return to Nebraska where the cost of housing was much lower and Hannah's family could help out in a pinch.

But the return home had its bittersweet moments. The only job Sam could find was his old job—as groundskeeper at the school. So he ate a little crow and is now able to chuckle at the irony. Hannah found a job as a custodian. Sam says, "We did not want to claim bankruptcy, so we planned how much both of us would need to earn to pay off all our debts." Sam worked for a while without a contract. During this time he broke his ankle at home. He couldn't work, so he had to take leave without pay. He also was hit by the medical bills, since health insurance had not yet been arranged. The family's temporarily reduced income coupled with medical expenses set them back financially. Luckily, they received a good income tax refund that covered their expenses for a while.

"We are not in a position to save any money right now and live from paycheck to paycheck," Sam says, explaining that his job doesn't pay much. But it is full-time and he gets health benefits and has flexible hours. "I get designated breaks and stuff like that. I'm not fired as easily because it's a government job. Not like in a private job, like if a boss doesn't like you he can fire you or lay you off. That happened to me a couple of times. I get all holidays." Sam is determined to keep the job, and hopes that Hannah will be able to go to college and study nursing. Eventually, he would like to go to college too. Sam thinks the American job market favors college-educated people.

School may have to be postponed, since the couple just had another baby, a son named Joshua. Sam plans to tell his son, "Your dad had to cut lawns for ten years because he did not attend school." He says he will caution both children to stay in school and to "create a strong household with a work ethic. Living on minimum wage is not fun. I had no one behind me to support me. There were counselors in school, but they did not give me any direction. Now I will be a counselor for my kids."

Sam is optimistic about the future, saying, "I have a lot of faith in my wife, in myself." Still, he acknowledges the growing economic inequality in the United States: "What I see is separation of the classes like back in the old days

(continued)

when there used to be serfs and royalty. It's getting to be more like that, the haves and the have-nots. It's a hard hurdle to get over. Education is the only hope you have. Unless you have a lot of capital or business savvy, you're just going to be clawing at the wall. It's all about education."

Sam is glad he did follow his music dream, and hopes to return to it "if I can afford to retire at 50 or 55." His advice for policy makers is "The main thing is benefits. It's all about benefits. Make sure employees have benefits. … America's health system is out of control because of skyrocketing costs of health insurance…. Y'know, it costs more, and it's just so easy for the small business owner to lose their money that they just … I don't know. … It's about insurance. Because like at our work there are 'hourlies' without insurance, like when I was on hourly … you've got people working full-time with no benefits."

A SOCIAL WORK PERSPECTIVE

Sam hit the nail on the head when he said, "It's all about benefits." As we will see, union leaders and policy makers agree with him that the rising cost of health care is still one of the most important issues affecting working people in America.

Sam is also correct in his assessment that education could make an important difference in the financial security of his family. Of course, in today's labor market professional status does not guarantee financial stability. But in recent decades education has been the one thing standing between workers and income declines. During the 1980s, for example, the only men who saw real wage increases were those with at least six years of college, and those without any post-secondary education experienced significant wage declines (Bluestone, 1994). Still, the odds may be against Sam completing college. Between 2007 and 2011, only 28 percent of the U.S. population over age 25 held college degrees (U.S. Census Bureau, n.d.c). And one study reported that only 6 percent of college students from low-income families completed four-year degrees (Zweig, 2000).

Sam has spent some time in the "secondary labor market" of temporary and part-time jobs. These account for about a third of all jobs in the United States (Reisch & Gorin, 2001). Like Sam, most people in the secondary labor market do not belong to unions, and many enjoy neither job security nor pension and health care benefits.

The First International was followed by the "Black International," formally known as the International Working People's Association. For a few years in the 1880s, this anarchist group advocated for international worker solidarity. It was followed in 1889 by the "Second International," which began with a congress of socialist labor leaders, primarily from Germany and France. Americans participated in these meetings, but the advent of World War I shattered the organization. As Frank puts it, "Nationalism trumped working-class internationalism abruptly and brutally" (2004, p. 102). Worker organizations that did not support the war effort paid the price in government suppression and public hostility.

Nonetheless, a "Third International" was founded in the 1920s to unite socialist and labor leaders. Americans participated in this Soviet-based organization, and during this era many left-thinking intellectuals (like Bertha Reynolds) visited Russia.

Perhaps the most international of U.S. unions was the Industrial Workers of the World, known as IWW, or the "Wobblies." They organized factory workers rather than craftsmen and had locals in South Africa, Australia, Chile, Canada, Mexico, and the United States. Similarly, the Knights of Labor founded several Canadian locals in the 1880s. In contrast, the American Federation of Labor, which has been the dominant union in the United States since the early 20th century, is primarily a national enterprise.

The years during and immediately following the **Great Depression** have been described as a "working-class interlude in American labor history" (Greenstone, 1969, p. 71). The 1935 Wagner Act—described by some as the most important labor law in American history—established workers' rights to organize unions and negotiate with management (Farhang & Katznelson, 2005). Also known as the **National Labor Relations Act (NLRA),** this law acknowledged workers' rights to organize and join labor unions, to collectively bargain, and to strike. It set up the **National Labor Relations Board**, an independent federal agency, to administer the act and to certify unions. The act forbade employers from interfering with employees exercising their right to organize and engage in **collective bargaining**, from attempting to dominate a labor union, from refusing to bargain "in good faith," and from discriminating against union members in hiring. In 1937, the Supreme Court upheld the NLRA (*NLRB v. Jones & Laughlin Steel Corp.*), setting the stage for a period of growth in union membership.

Critics complained that the NLRA did not restrict union tactics, particularly the use of "**sit-down strikes**," in which workers occupy factories and halt production. The effectiveness of this approach is self-evident, but it was declared unconstitutional by the Supreme Court in 1939 (*NLRB v. Fansteel Metallurgical Corporation*). In the elections of 1946, the Republican Party won majorities in both houses of Congress. Traditionally pro-business, the Republicans set out to dismantle NLRA protections by passing the **Taft-Hartley Act**, also known as the Labor-Management Relations Act of 1947.

Taft-Hartley allowed the president to seek a court injunction to block or prevent strikes that he felt would endanger national health or safety.[2] It also created an 80-day "cooling-off" period, during which strikes that might create a "national emergency" could be prohibited. The act also prohibited secondary boycotts, sympathy strikes or boycotts, and "closed shops" (which hired only union members). The law permitted "union shops," in which employees are required to join a union, as long as union shops were not prohibited under state law. This clause set the stage for passage of "right-to-work" laws at the state level that prohibited union shops. Reflecting the times, Taft-Hartley also required union officers to take an oath that they were not communists.

THE COLD WAR

In 1946, more than a third (35 percent) of non-farm workers in the United States belonged to unions (Cherny, Issel, & Taylor, 2004). By 2015, only 11.1 percent of wage and salaried workers were union members (Bureau of Labor Statistics, 2016a). While Taft-Hartley contributed to the decline of unions in the United States, beliefs and attitudes with their roots in the **Cold War** period played a role as well.

The term "McCarthyism" has been used to describe the anticommunist crusade that held Americans in its thrall during the late 1940s and 1950s. Communists, particularly those with ties to the Soviet Union, were portrayed as traitors, and public furor reached fever pitch in 1956 when Nikita Khrushchev addressed Western ambassadors at a Moscow reception and mouthed his infamous phrase, "We will bury you." McCarthy himself was a senator from Wisconsin who spearheaded the anticommunist witch hunts that targeted unions affiliated with the Communist Party. But McCarthy was not alone. The "war on communism" had several fronts, marshalling the efforts of churches, right-wing journalists, employers, and federal officials (Schrecker, 2004). Thousands of workers lost their jobs, and some were blacklisted and lost their careers.

McCarthyism deprived labor of some of its most talented leaders, and, perhaps more damaging, the pervasive anticommunist rhetoric pulled the ideological rug out from under

---

[2]Presidents have invoked Taft-Hartley in attempts to stop strikes 35 times, and they were successful on all but two of these occasions. Most recently, President Bush invoked Taft-Hartley when negotiations between port operators and the International Longshore and Warehouse Union broke down (Wagner, 2002).

the movement. Those seeking broad social reform could no longer rally around the banner of worker solidarity. But other issues and other banners would fill the void.

THE CIVIL RIGHTS MOVEMENT

Two broad social and economic changes set the stage for the civil rights movement of the 1960s: the migration of Southern agricultural workers to Northern cities and the organizing experiences of African American union members. Cotton prices dropped sharply during the first half of the 20th century, and methods for harvesting and processing the fiber became mechanized. As a result, hundreds of thousands of agricultural workers, many of them African Americans, left the rural areas of the South and moved to urban areas in the North. They sought employment in industrial settings, often in union jobs.

This movement to urban settings provided opportunities for socialization and organization. African American workers were no longer dependent on planters for employment and goods. This influx of new members also led some of the nation's unions to embrace interracial solidarity.

The role of unions in the struggle for racial equality has been debated. Citing examples of racially exclusive unions such as the **American Federation of Labor (AFL)** and the railroad unions, some argue that the racism of white members made unions hostile to African American workers. Others suggest that racially exclusive unions were the result of pressure from local communities and factory owners. Community hostility to racial integration was expressed in antiunion violence. Several leaders of integrated unions, both African American and white, were lynched or otherwise murdered with the cooperation of local law enforcement officials. Racism in unions was also fostered when factory owners brought in African American workers as strikebreakers.

Chicago 2005: Members of the United Steelworkers and American Postal Workers Unions join hands at an AFL-CIO solidarity rally.

© Karin Hildebrand Lau/Shutterstock.com

Nonetheless, the history of the union movement does provide examples of solidarity between white and African American union members. The **United Mine Workers of America (UMW)** enrolled white and African American members who worked side by side in the coal mines of Appalachia. As Foner (1981) notes, African Americans served in leadership roles at both local and national levels of the UMW. The Noble Knights of Labor, a federation of unions, was also deeply committed to racial solidarity, as was the Industrial Workers of the World (IWW). These unions held integrated meetings, even in the South where local statutes prohibited such activities.

Thus, while some leaders and participants in the civil rights movement came from churches and schools, others came from unions. They brought with them the lessons learned from union organizing as well as considerable financial support. The **United Auto Workers**, for example, contributed about $160,000 to the Southern Christian Leadership Conference to help cover bail expenses from the Birmingham demonstrations of 1963 (Wilson, 1996).

The civil rights movement brought the federal government into the realm of race relations with the passage of vitally important legislation. In Chapter 10 we noted the effects of the Civil Rights Act of 1960 and the Voting Rights Act of 1965 on the voting rights of African Americans and other people of color. Here we will observe that the **Civil Rights Act of 1964** prohibited discrimination in employment based on race, color, religion, sex, and national origin. These statutes negated state and local laws that enforced segregation and set the stage for historic confrontations between federal and state officials. But, as we will see, the federal government had already weighed in on employment discrimination through the executive order that established affirmative action.

LO 15-3 Appreciate the Influence of Affirmative Action on American Workers

EP 3a
EP 5a

Cedric Herring (1997) offers a succinct definition of **affirmative action**: "Affirmative Action consists of activities specifically to identify, recruit, promote and/or retain qualified women and members of disadvantaged minority groups in order to overcome the results of past discrimination and to deter employers from engaging in discriminatory practices" (p. 6).

This broad definition was made specific by two major policy initiatives. The first consisted of executive orders issued under the Kennedy, Johnson, and Nixon administrations requiring that firms doing business with the federal government engage in affirmative action. The second was Title VII of the 1964 Civil Rights Act, which prohibited discrimination by private employers and unions (Pedriana, 1999).

On March 6, 1961, President Kennedy signed Executive Order 10925, which prohibited government contractors from practicing racial discrimination and required that they take "affirmative action" to ensure that there was no discrimination. The order established the President's Committee on Equal Employment Opportunity (PCEEO) to enforce the law. Although other presidents had issued nondiscrimination orders in the past, none had included the clause requiring affirmative action. While establishing an obligation for employers to take action, the order did not specify what this might entail. In essence, it required that federal contractors "do something" without specifying exactly what "something" was. Only one specific action was required: employers had to document the racial composition of their workforce.

Lockheed Corporation was the subject of the first complaint filed under Order 10925. The NAACP complained that the company practiced blatant and pervasive racial discrimination. In response, the firm developed an aggressive "Plan for Progress" that included recruiting and training people of color, reviewing promotion procedures, and establishing vocational programs in local schools.

"Plans for Progress" became a watchword for the PCEEO, and companies that voluntarily developed these plans were guaranteed that they would not be subjects of investigation. Many did so, but the results were disappointing. The Southern Regional Council conducted an evaluation and concluded that the plans were ineffective. Indeed, there was some evidence that firms completing the plans had worse records on equal employment than those that did not (Pedriana, 1999). Ultimately, the most influential feature of Order 10925 was its record-keeping requirement, which resulted in a "unique national profile of the employment distribution of race" (Graham, 1990, p. 60).

With support from the Kennedy administration, Congress passed Title VII of the Civil Rights Act of 1964, which prohibited employment discrimination on the basis of gender or race and established the **Equal Employment Opportunity Commission (EEOC)** to enforce the law (Box 15.1). Affirmative action was called for in cases of intentional violation. As Pedriana (1999) notes, Title VII included the following language:

> If the court finds that the respondent has intentionally engaged in or is intentionally engaging in an unlawful employment practice … the court may enjoin the respondent from engaging in such unlawful employment practice, and order such affirmative action as may be appropriate. (p. 11)

Even this language was fairly broad, and it was left to the courts and the EEOC to interpret and implement the title. Central to their interpretations was defining "discrimination." The law prohibited, but did not define, the practice. Early interpretations focused on discriminatory intent. Firms that intentionally and obviously discriminated on the basis of race were concentrated in the South, where separate locker rooms, cafeterias, and washroom facilities were the norm and where African Americans were concentrated in low-paid jobs. The approach based on intent was effective at eliminating these more obvious instances of discrimination.

Over time, a focus on institutional discrimination led to redefinition of the term to focus less on intent and more on the consequences of discrimination. Attention shifted to broader employment practices, such as seniority systems and employment testing, that led to racial inequality in the workplace. Indeed, under this view, employment discrimination was part of a broader pattern of oppression that included inferior educational opportunities, exclusion from informal job networks, and limited access to apprenticeship and mentoring opportunities.

Two federal court rulings supported a focus on consequences rather than intent. In *Quarks v. Philip Morris,* the district court ruled against the company's argument that "the present consequences of past discrimination" were not covered by the Civil Rights Act, saying, "Congress did not intend to freeze an entire generation of Negro employees into discriminatory patterns that existed before the act" (Pedriana, 1999, p. 16).

BOX 15.1   Title VII of the Civil Rights Act of 1964

"It shall be an unlawful employment practice for an employer to fail or refuse to hire or to discharge any individual or otherwise to discriminate against any individual with respect to his compensation, terms, conditions, or privileges of employment, because of such individual's race, color, religion, sex, or national origin; or … to limit, segregate, or classify his employees or applicants for employment in any way which would deprive or tend to deprive any individual employee of employment opportunities or otherwise adversely affect his status as an employee, because of such individual's race, color, religion, sex, or national origin."

Then, in *Griggs v. Duke Power Company*, the Supreme Court unanimously ruled against the company's promotion requirement of a high school diploma and its use of employment testing. Establishing what is now known as "the doctrine of disparate impact," the Court ruled that

> [t]he objective of Title VII is plain from the language of the statute. It was to achieve equality of employment opportunities and remove barriers that have operated in the past to favor an identifiable group of White employees over other employees. Under the act, practices, procedures or tests neutral on their face and even neutral in terms of intent cannot be maintained if they operate to "freeze" the status quo of prior discriminatory employment practices. ... Congress directed the thrust of the Act to the consequences of employment practices, not simply the motivation. (Pedriana, 1999, p. 17)

Under the doctrine of disparate impact, businesses that had racial and gender disparities in the workplace could be subject to costly and time-consuming litigation. To avoid litigation, many firms followed the EEOC's guidelines and developed voluntary affirmative action plans. These plans frequently included race-based hiring and promotion goals, now known as "quotas." Few firms were subject to court-ordered affirmative action, and those that were the subject of court mandates had fairly egregious discriminatory practices (Pedriana, 1999).

Quotas were used more often in the enforcement of presidential orders regarding government contractors. In 1965, President Johnson issued Executive Order 11246 to replace Kennedy's Order 10925. This order created the Office of Federal Contract Compliance (OFCC) to enforce nondiscrimination in government contracting. Under the order, firms could be required to set and meet hiring quotas. These requirements were especially controversial for construction firms, which traditionally segregated their trades along racial lines. These firms were required to set hiring goals in each of the trades, with the result being the maligned practice of "hiring by the numbers."

President Nixon's contributions to affirmative action were substantial. Indeed, as Troy Duster (1996) points out,

> Nixon did more than any other president to promote and institutionalize affirmative action. While John Kennedy issued the initially limited executive orders in 1963, and while Lyndon Johnson had maneuvered through Congress the 1964 civil rights legislation that mandated selected forms in the workplace, it was Nixon who demanded and required that corporate America institute programs of affirmative action. (p. 41)

Insiders' accounts of the Nixon administration have argued that the president's motive was political: to drive a wedge in the traditional Democratic alliance of labor and African Americans (see Ehrlichman, 1982; Haldeman, 1994).

In sum, both Title VII and the presidential orders governing federal contracting increased employment opportunities for people of color. Probably the greatest impact of Title VII came with the courts' establishment of the doctrine of disparate impact. Under this doctrine, even race-neutral practices that resulted in racial disparities were potential subjects of litigation. This led many firms to voluntarily adopt and implement affirmative action plans. The use of hiring quotas was most often a response to federal contracting requirements established under presidential orders.

The expansion of affirmative action occurred in an economic climate of expanded opportunity and, as Duster (1996) and others (Ezorsky, 1991; Northrup, 1970; Quadagno, 1994) have argued, it worked. Affirmative action expanded minorities' access to employment, particularly in public-sector jobs and the building trades. Duster (1996) argued, "It is empirically demonstrable that affirmative action provided a way out of poverty for hundreds of thousands, even millions, of poor blacks" (p. 56).

But by the late 1970s, unemployment rates had risen, real wages were declining, and conditions were ripe for a backlash. This backlash was spearheaded by leaders in California (Nixon's home state), who argued that affirmative action was unfair.

At a time when jobs were disappearing and admission to California's public universities was increasingly competitive, these arguments were persuasive. Affirmative action received a serious challenge in the 1978 case of *Regents of the University of California v. Bakke.* In this case, a 37-year-old white engineer (Allan Bakke) had been twice denied admission to the university's medical school. The school reserved 16 of its 100 entering positions for minorities, and some of the 16 admitted when Bakke was denied had lower admissions test scores than he had. The case was decided by the U.S. Supreme Court in a split decision that represented a carefully crafted compromise.[3] The justices held that the California admissions policy was unconstitutional because it used a quota system based on race. The Court left open the question of whether a race-sensitive admissions policy could be crafted that would not be held unconstitutional (Ball, 2000).

The year 1991 saw a major shift in the composition of the Supreme Court. That year, Thurgood Marshall—the first African American justice on the Court—retired at the age of 82. Marshall was known as a liberal justice and a staunch supporter of civil rights. As a lawyer, he had successfully argued the case of *Brown v. Board of Education* before the Supreme Court. George Bush nominated Clarence Thomas to replace Marshall on the bench. Thomas had earned his conservative credentials while serving as chairman of the EEOC during the Reagan administration. In that role he halted the use of class action discrimination suits. Thomas opposed all race-based legislation and expressed his opposition to affirmative action during his confirmation hearings. He was confirmed by a four-vote margin in the Senate, the closest in 20th century history, and now sits as a reliable vote against affirmative action.

Meanwhile, other attacks on affirmative action involved political processes. In 1995, the regents of the University of California, under the leadership of Republican Governor Pete Wilson, voted to abolish affirmative action in college admissions. A year later, voters in California passed Proposition 209 by a narrow margin. This measure outlawed the use of race, sex, ethnicity, or national origin as a reason for discriminating against or granting preferential treatment to any person or group. Later, similar initiatives passed in Washington State (Initiative 200) and Florida (the One Florida Initiative).

In June 2003, the Supreme Court upheld the constitutionality of affirmative action in university admissions by a one-vote margin in the case of *Grutter v. Bollinger.* Arguing that "universities occupy a special niche," the Court opinion endorsed racial diversity on campuses and found a compelling state interest in maintaining that diversity: "In order to cultivate a set of leaders with legitimacy in the eyes of the citizenry, it is necessary that the path to leadership be visibly open to talented and qualified individuals of every race and ethnicity." At the same time, in the 2003 case of *Gratz v. Bollinger,* the Court, by a three-vote margin, rejected the use of a point system based on race, finding it was too close to a quota system. The difference between these cases lay in the way affirmative action was implemented. In the first case the University of Michigan law school treated race as a factor in an individualized, holistic review of each file. In the second, the University of Michigan undergraduate admissions offices automatically assigned points to applications from people of color.

---

[3]The Supreme Court refused to order the university to admit Bakke, but he did obtain such an order through a California court. Bakke was admitted to the UC Davis Medical School and graduated in 1992.

Today the pendulum has swung away from affirmative action. As we will see later in this chapter, people of color are still disproportionately concentrated in low-wage jobs. Yet, there is widespread opposition to the use of racial quotas in hiring. Opponents have successfully argued that affirmative action:

- Stigmatizes women and minorities whose colleagues perceive them as having been hired not for their qualifications but to satisfy affirmative action quotas.
- Is no longer necessary, as discrimination in employment no longer exists.
- Results in "reverse discrimination" against men and whites.
- Does not help the truly disadvantaged.

As Reverend Davis explained in Chapter 10, in today's political environment it will take creativity to devise a new approach to equal opportunity in employment that is both effective and politically feasible.

LO 15-4 Become Familiar with Immigration Policies and Their Influence on American Workers

EP 2a
EP 3a
EP 5c

U.S. immigration policy serves several broad policy goals. In Chapter 10 we considered immigration in the context of race relations. Here, we will focus on immigration policy designed to manage the supply of labor.[4]

Immigration policies explicitly designed to promote domestic economic goals surfaced in the Immigration and Naturalization Act of 1952, which established quotas for workers with needed skills. This practice is now a well-established part of U.S. immigration policy. Indeed, Microsoft's Bill Gates has argued against further restrictions on immigration, suggesting they would "prevent companies like ours from doing business in the United States" (Close Up Foundation, 1998). Major milestones in U.S. immigration policy related to employment are summarized in Table 15.1.

Of course, there is some overlap between race-based and employment-based immigration policies. As we saw in Chapter 10, exclusion was used in response to competition from Chinese laborers.[5] The experiences of Mexican immigrants illustrate the use of immigration to meet U.S. demands for labor.

As early as the 19th century, Mexican laborers in the United States began to organize unions and declare strikes to improve working conditions. The strikes were supported by *mutualistas,* labor organizations that helped members pay for hospitalization and funeral expenses, provided low-interest loans, and offered support in times of need. For example, when 3,500 miners (most of them Mexican) went on strike against the Clifton-Morneci mines, mutualistas gave food, clothing, and other supports to strikers. In this case, despite use of the National Guard to break the strike, workers were successful at extracting a wage increase.

During the early 20th century, while laborers in the United States were struggling for wage parity, Mexico was wracked by civil war. The Diaz government was overthrown in

---

[4]Ideology and sexual orientation have also been grounds for prohibiting immigration. Fear of communism led to the 1952 passage of the McCarran-Walter Act, which prohibited immigration by people who subscribed to this ideology. McCarran-Walter was overturned in 1990. Until 1990, U.S. immigration policy also allowed for the exclusion of homosexuals.

[5]The Chinese Exclusion Act was renewed in 1892 and extended indefinitely in 1902. Its effect ended with the passage of the Immigration and Naturalization Act of 1924.

TABLE 15.1   Milestones in U.S. Immigration Policy Related to Employment

Immigration Act of 1891
- Provided for national control of immigration
- Established Bureau of Immigration under the Treasury Department
- Provided for deportation of undocumented immigrants

Immigration and Naturalization Act Amendments of 1952
- Established quota for workers with needed skills

Immigration and Naturalization Act Amendments of 1965
- Established seven-category reference system based on family unification and skills

Immigration Reform and Control Act of 1986
- Instituted employer sanctions for knowingly hiring undocumented workers
- Tripled employment-based immigration
- Provided legal status to about 3 million undocumented immigrants who arrived before 1982

1996 Immigration Acts
- Denied SSI and food stamps to legal immigrants
- Denied most public services to undocumented immigrants

Enhanced Border Security and Visa Entry Reform Act of 2001
- Increased background checks required for visas
- Increased budget and personnel for border security

Sources: Close Up Foundation (1998); Congressional Research Service (2002); Fox & Passel (1994).

1911 by Madeira, who was soon overthrown by General Victoriano Huerta. Huerta was forced into exile as two other generals battled revolutionaries Pancho Villa and Emiliano Zapata. The war was especially hard on civilians, and thousands fled to the north to avoid starvation, torture, or murder.

The northward migration continued. Mexican laborers were well received, particularly in southern California and Texas, where they soon made up most of the construction and agricultural labor force. Differential pay scales persisted, and Anglo workers were typically paid more for the same work than Mexican immigrants, referred to as **Chicanos**. Chicanos were generally restricted to unskilled jobs and found it virtually impossible to move into managerial positions.

The Depression ended U.S. demands for Mexican labor, and a policy of **repatriation** ensued. Chicanos who applied for welfare were given aid only upon agreeing to return to Mexico. Buses and boxcars were used to transport entire families—including children born in the United States—to Mexico. An estimated 400,000 Chicanos were repatriated during the Depression (Moquin, 1972).

World War II brought exploding demand for labor, and in 1942, the **Bracero Program** was introduced to encourage Mexican men to come north and work as contract agricultural laborers. Under an executive agreement between the United States and Mexico, approximately 350,000 men entered the United States to do agricultural work (Chavez, 1991). The program ended in 1960. Under the North American Free Trade Agreement (NAFTA) signed in 1993, citizens of Canada and Mexico who are offered professional jobs in the United States are eligible for special work visas if their professions are on the NAFTA list.

National debate about undocumented immigration has ebbed and flowed, with some observing the huge economic contribution of undocumented workers and others seeking to exclude them as lawbreakers. Some efforts have targeted employers. For instance, the

BOX 15.2   Cesar Chavez (1927–1993)

Cesar Chavez organized the United Farm Workers (UFW) in 1966 to advocate on behalf of migrant workers. An AFL-CIO affiliate, UFW has been responsible for improved living conditions and benefits for migrant workers throughout the country.

1986 Immigration Control and Reform Act (IRCA) established sanctions for the "knowing" hiring of undocumented immigrants. At the same time, the IRCA provided a pathway to legal status (sometimes called "amnesty") for about 3 million undocumented immigrants.

An important part of the immigration debate concerns eligibility for public service, a significant concern for low-wage workers and their families. Concern over the cost of services provided to immigrants, particularly undocumented immigrants, has led to eligibility restrictions affecting both groups.

In the 1982 decision in *Plyler v. Doe,* the Supreme Court invalidated a Texas law that allowed school districts to charge tuition to undocumented immigrants whose children attended public schools. In its ruling (drafted by Thurgood Marshall), the Court held that depriving these children of education would ultimately prove costly to the government, as uneducated children would likely rely on welfare in adulthood.

Political pressure to restrict public services to immigrants culminated in 1996 welfare reform legislation (discussed in Chapter 5) that would have denied Supplemental Security Income (SSI) and food stamps to legal immigrants and excluded undocumented immigrants from most public services. Amid the ensuing uproar, some of the law's more draconian measures were repealed. The Balanced Budget Act of 1997 restored SSI eligibility to most legal immigrants who had lost it under the 1996 law. In 1998, PL 105-185 restored food stamp eligibility to some legal immigrants.[6] Nonetheless, the rights of immigrants, both documented and undocumented, to receive public services that citizens take for granted are now open to dispute.

Immigrants do jobs that many Americans cannot or will not perform, while providing a buffer against the population erosion that would otherwise result from declining fertility. As Marcelo Suarez-Orozco noted, as the baby boomers retire, "It is most likely that immigrant workers will once again be summoned, this time to take care of retired citizens, to pay into the Social Security system, and to help the country maintain its economic vitality" (Suarez-Orozco, 2006, in *Moving Forward)*. At the same time that U.S. policy has often reflected the prejudices of the times, immigration continues to enrich our nation's cultural heritage.

"Immigration reform" means different things to different people. To some, it means pathways to citizenship for people who lack documentation. To others, it means the construction of walls at U.S. borders. Some advocate permitting temporary guest workers to enter the country, through efforts like the Bracero programs of the 1940s and 1950s. Some promote legislation like the **DREAM Act**, which would provide a "conditional path to citizenship" for young adults. Meanwhile, others support statutes that call on local police to identify people who are in the country without documentation so they can be subjected to an "expedited removal" process. Politicians on both sides of the fence generally conclude they have a lot to lose by tackling immigration reform (see Suarez-Orozco, 2006; Waldinger, 2006).

---

[6]The Balanced Budget Act was mentioned in Chapter 5.

In 2012, Congress again failed to pass the DREAM Act. So, in what the *New York Times* called "a sweeping exercise of executive authority," President Obama signed an **executive order** that established a program called "**Deferred Action for Childhood Arrivals**" (DACA) that removed the threat of deportation and provided work permits for young people (between the ages of 16 and 31) without documentation who were brought to the United States as children (Preston, 2012). A 2013 report by the Brookings Institute reported that over half (59 percent) of those eligible (estimated at nearly 1 million) submitted applications within the first year of the program. A strong majority (72 percent) had been approved within the year, and only 1 percent were denied (Singer & Svajlenka, 2013). Apart from a sense of fairness, the fundamental rationale for this immigration program was that these young adults would take the opportunity to pursue their careers and contribute to the U.S. economy.

Of course, with the 2016 election of Donald Trump the future of DACA is uncertain. While the elimination of programs authorized by statute requires congressional action, executive orders can be removed with one stroke of the presidential pen. By the time you read this, DACA may no longer be in effect.

LO 15-5   Become Familiar with the History of U.S. Policies Protecting Women and Children in the Workplace

EP 2a
EP 3a
EP 5c

A central focus of public debate and public policy during the late 19th and early 20th centuries was protecting women and children in paid employment.[7] Women have always worked, but under what historians call the "doctrine of separate spheres," middle-class women and girls of the 19th century were largely restricted to domestic activities (Lasch, 1979). Children of tender years usually were kept at home, but economic necessity forced some to enter the workforce. In this section we will consider the history of policies that developed in the United States to protect women and children in the workforce.

WOMEN IN THE U.S. LABOR FORCE

One recurring challenge to public policies supportive of women has been Americans' belief (or hope) that if the free market were unburdened by government regulation, it would ultimately provide fair conditions for all. In the workplace, American public policy has evolved from restricting women's job activities through **protective legislation** to prohibiting discrimination on the basis of gender through Title VII.

When women began entering paid employment in large numbers, they were routinely paid less than men who held the same jobs. For example, when the federal government bought its first typewriters in 1867, it established a classification for clerk typists. Within this classification, women received $600 per year and men $1,200 per year (Simpson, 1985).

Working women were excluded from most trade unions, so they established their own organizations. Unions in traditionally female occupations (laundresses, cap makers, and shoe workers) multiplied, and during the early 1900s, the Women's Trade Union League was established to promote the establishment of women's unions. Women also formed "protective leagues" to enhance working conditions and "abolish the sweatshop." Their successes set the stage for protective legislation.

---

[7]A detailed history of women in the U.S. labor force is beyond the scope of this chapter. The interested reader will find material in Kessler-Harris (1990), Wandersee (1981), Ware (1981), and Weiner (1985). All of these sources were consulted extensively during the preparation of this section.

Protective Legislation for "Working Girls"

The turn of the century has been characterized as the era of the "working girl." In 1890, roughly one in five women, most of them young and single, were employed outside the home, usually in domestic service. Critics of female employment argued that these women were rendering themselves either unfit or unable (if not unwilling) to assume their natural roles as wives and mothers (Weiner, 1985). In 1910, the U.S. Senate's study of employed women and children asked, "Is the trend of modern industry dangerous to the character of women?" (Kessler-Harris, 1990).

Protective labor laws were passed in the United States, Europe, and Australia during the post-World War I era amid rising concern that women were displacing men in manufacturing jobs and popular arguments that work diminished women's reproductive capacity. These laws restricted the number of hours women could work and regulated their wages. Though widely seen as an advance for working women, they had a paternalistic feel, implying that women might be safer if they remained outside the workforce (see Wikander, Kessler-Harris, & Lewis, 1995).

The impact of the laws was debated. Some argued that wage requirements kept women out of middle- and upper-level positions. There were reports of women being fired as soon as they completed apprenticeships and became eligible for higher wages. Women complained that restrictions in the hours they could work limited their ability to compete effectively for jobs (Weiner, 1985).

Ultimately, the wage restrictions were overturned by the courts. In 1923, the Supreme Court overturned wage regulations in the District of Columbia, invoking the freedom-of-contract argument (*Adkins v. Children's Hospital;* Weiner, 1985). Consequently, protective laws gradually were either overturned or disregarded.

Working Mothers and the New Deal

The widespread movement of married women into the labor force emerged as a significant trend in the United States during the 1920s. Prior to this period, even in families with very low incomes, fewer than one in four married women worked outside the home. African American women were the conspicuous exception to this rule. At all economic levels, a much higher proportion of African American wives and mothers worked.

Why did wives go to work? Wandersee (1981) argues that the increased employment of married women can be traced to an emerging ethic of consumption. With the development of mass marketing, the concept of an "American standard of living" became, as Wandersee puts it, "[something] all could aspire to, many would attain, and some would never know" (p. 21). The changing character of home life also contributed. As the home was transformed from a unit of production to a unit of consumption, women who needed productive roles sought them outside the home.

During the Great Depression, the federal government restricted employment of married women in the civil service through Section 213 of the Federal Economy Act. In the interest of "spreading the wealth," this legislation prohibited more than one member of the same family from working in the civil service. Within a year, more than 1,600 workers, three-fourths of them women, lost their government jobs. Nearly every state introduced bills to prevent employment of married women. As a 1936 Gallup poll indicated, most Americans supported these practices (Abramowitz, 1996).

Despite their presence in the labor force, women were excluded from most New Deal legislation on behalf of workers. For example, the Fair Labor Standards Act (FLSA), which regulated working hours, set a minimum wage, and prohibited child labor, specifically exempted domestic service from its provisions. The National Industrial Recovery Act (NIRA), designed to "get industrial production moving again," covered only about half of employed women. Indeed, Wandersee noted that women who were most in need of protection—domestic laborers, laundresses not employed in laundries, and dressmakers not employed in factories—were among those excluded from the NIRA's labor protections. Later, the Social Security Act of 1935 excluded domestic workers, failing to provide coverage for approximately 30 percent of working women, many of them women of color (Wandersee, 1981).

Failure of the New Deal legislation to address women's needs reflected strong disapproval of working women, particularly those who were married. This attitude was articulated by leaders of the unions that supported the Roosevelt administration. Central to their arguments were two concerns: (1) that working women would displace working men and (2) that by working, women jeopardized the natural order of civilization.

Samuel Gompers, head of the American Federation of Labor during this era, focused on the first concern when he said, "In industries where the wives and children toil, the man is often idle because he has been supplanted" (Kessler-Harris, 1990, p. 19). The second concern was expressed by a contributor to a labor journal called the *American Federationist*: "Woman's greatest security is to be found in the home, and where rests the security of women rests the security of life, the security of civilization" (Wandersee, 1981, pp. 69–70). Another labor paper argued that "sisters and daughters" should not leave home, even for congenial workshops and factories, and vowed to check this "most unnatural invasion of our firesides" (Abramowitz, 1996, p. 189).

Both concerns were expressed in a 1937 petition by the legislature of North Dakota. In it, legislators asked that the Department of Labor study the growing problem of "homekeeping" women entering paid employment:

> Whereas the employment of women in paid work outside the home has increased materially in recent years; and
>
> Whereas the home-keeping women going into commercial and industrial work was mentioned by the report of the Biggers Committee on National Unemployment as one of the causes of the unemployment problem; and …
>
> Whereas we all recognize the services rendered by the women of our homes in the building of character:
>
> Therefore be it Resolved, that the House of Representatives of the State of North Dakota, the Senate Concurring, hereby petition the … Department of Labor … to use its influence toward the securing of data on women employed outside the home … and thereupon to make a survey and a study of the problems of the home-keeping women, to find the reason for the tendency to leave home for commercial and industrial work and to make recommendations to reduce and, so far as possible, eliminate this tendency in modern living. (*Congressional Record*, Vol. 84, p. 1271)

Of course, policies and attitudes toward working women shifted when World War II brought exploding demand for labor. "Rosie the Riveter" was emblematic of a broad-based campaign to encourage women to abandon their vaunted domesticity and contribute to the war effort. And women responded. About 6 million of them entered the workforce for the first time.

The presence of female workers changed U.S. workplaces. For the first time, makers of steel-toed shoes had to produce them in women's sizes. The women themselves were changed as well. In oral histories from the period, many reported that they discovered new capabilities and overcame fears as the result of their work experiences (Harvey, n.d.). Though many left the workplace when the war ended, public attitudes toward working women would never be the same (see the Regional Oral History Office of Bancroft Library for oral histories of women of this era at http://bancroft.berkeley.edu/ROHO/ projects/ rosie/).

Palmer, Alfred T./Library of Congress Prints and Photographs Division Washington, D.C. 20540 USA [LC-DIG-ppmsca-12895]

▶ WWII women at work poster. Alfred Palmer, photographer, 1943.

Working Women and the Great Society

Decades later, public policy reflected the shift in attitudes and beliefs about working women. In 1964, President Johnson signed the first piece of congressional legislation that acknowledged gender discrimination as a significant social problem: Title VII of the Civil Rights Act. Popular myth holds that Title VII was introduced by an opponent of civil rights as a joke, or with the intention of scuttling the act completely. Indeed, the "sex amendment" (as it was known) was introduced by a southern Democrat, Representative Howard W. Smith of Virginia. While the Civil Rights Act was being debated on the House floor, Representative Smith rose and offered a one-word amendment to Title VII, which prohibited discrimination in employment. The word was "sex," and it added women to the categories of individuals protected under the act. Evidently the amendment triggered several hours of "humorous debate," which Jo Freeman (1991) reports was later described as "Ladies' Day in the House." The amendment passed by a vote of 168 to 133.

Freeman and other historians agree that Smith's motivation in introducing the amendment was not humor. Instead, she argues, he was responding to tenacious lobbying by the National Women's Party (NWP). Composed of an elite group of highly educated and well-off women, the NWP was a consistent presence in the Capitol halls. They argued that sex discrimination was pervasive in the U.S. labor market, and if they did not succeed in persuading legislators to adopt their views, they undoubtedly persuaded Congress that the NWP would not go away empty-handed. Thus, when Representative Smith introduced the sex amendment, he was bowing to pressure. As we saw in Chapter 13, the NWP also lobbied unsuccessfully for passage of the Equal Rights Amendment (ERA).

As soon as the sex amendment passed the House, women's organizations throughout the nation organized to support it. Unlike the ERA, this provision received the endorsement of the Women's Bureau and the League of Women Voters. It passed the Senate and was signed into law, to the utter indifference of the Equal Employment Opportunity Commission (EEOC). The EEOC considered the inclusion of sex "a fluke" that was "conceived out of wedlock." As Freeman notes, EEOC staff "tried to ignore its existence" despite the fact that one-third of the employment complaints filed during the commission's first year of existence (1965) charged discrimination on the basis of sex (1991, p. 164).

The EEOC's indifference set the stage for the founding of the National Organization for Women (NOW). As Rhode (1989) tells it, NOW was founded during the 1966 Conference of Commissions on the Status of Women. Frustrated by the EEOC's tolerance of help-wanted advertisements that discriminated on the basis of sex, "twenty-eight disaffected conference participants each paid five dollars to join a group that Betty Friedan spontaneously christened NOW. Its purpose, as recorded on the first accessible napkin, was 'to bring women into full participation in the mainstream of American society now'" (Rhode, 1989, p. 58). NOW began by fighting sex-classified help-wanted advertisements. Bowing to NOW's efforts, the EEOC eventually declared that the practice violated Title VII, a view that was upheld by the Supreme Court in 1973.

It is an understatement to say that public attitudes and policies toward working women have changed. Despite these changes, as we will see in later sections of this chapter, working women in the United States have achieved neither wage parity with men nor proportionate representation across occupations. Before we explore this topic more thoroughly, let us briefly consider the development of child labor policies in the United States.

CHILD LABOR: A TARGET OF REFORM

During the late 19th and early 20th centuries, reformers began to focus on child labor. Their concern reflected changes both in social expectations of childhood and in the conditions under which children were laboring.

The 1900 census revealed about 2 million children working in factories, mines, and other settings in the United States (U.S. National Archives & Records Administration, 2007). This finding triggered a national movement to end child labor. The National Child Labor Committee was founded in 1904 to prevent exploitation of children in the labor market. Their efforts were pivotal in focusing public attention on the issue. Ultimately, labor unions, the Consumers Union, and eventually even industrial management went on record opposing the practice. Some laws were passed by the states, but there was growing demand for federal legislation.

In 1872, the **Prohibition Party** had included a plank in its platform opposing child labor. Later, Republicans, Democrats, and Progressives all went on record calling for a federal law prohibiting the employment of children. Child labor was an early focus of the Children's Bureau, which documented conditions in factories where children worked. In 1906, Senator Beveridge, a Republican from Indiana, proposed to use the federal government's authority to regulate interstate commerce to ban the interstate sale of products made with child labor. The nation's first child labor bill, known as the **Keating-Owen Child Labor Act** of 1916, was based on this proposal.

The bill was approved by Congress and signed by President Woodrow Wilson. But it proved controversial and was subjected to a Supreme Court challenge in the case of *Hammer v. Dagenhart*. The same Supreme Court justices who established the principle of **"separate but equal"** in *Plessy v. Ferguson* declared Keating-Owen unconstitutional.

BOX 15.3   Child Labor Continues in the United States

After the 1930s, child labor was eliminated from U.S. factories. But millions of children have continued to work illegally (Levine, 2003), and Human Rights Watch (2000) reports that hundreds of thousands of children are legally employed as agricultural workers. The minimum age for a child to work on a farm is 12 years, although younger children can work with parental consent. Agricultural work is the nation's second most hazardous occupation (after mining, from which children are prohibited).

They also invalidated the second child labor law passed as part of the Revenue Act of 1919, which attempted to use the taxing authority of Congress to regulate child labor.

These Supreme Court rulings derailed federal attempts to reform child labor practices for nearly two decades. An attempt to ratify a Child Labor Amendment to the constitution was stalled in the 1920s, and the federal effort to restrict the use of child labor was not resuscitated until the 1938 passage of the **Fair Labor Standards Act**. This act, too, was the subject of a Supreme Court challenge, and in 1941 the Court upheld the law, reversing its earlier position (see *U.S. v. Darby*). As we will see near the end of this chapter, child labor today is regulated by policies at both the federal and the state levels.

LO 15-6   Become Aware of the Historic Role of Social Workers in the Labor Movement

EP 3a

Social work has a long history of concern for labor issues. As part of the Progressive movement, social work leaders such as Florence Kelley, Lillian Wald, Mary van Kleeck, and Helen Hall supported workers' causes through their writings and advocacy, and social workers were active in movements to support labor (Karger, 1988). Under Jane Addams's leadership, the work of Hull House took into account the needs and problems faced by working Americans. As we saw in Chapter 4, Frances Perkins's role in the Roosevelt administration was pivotal, ensuring that New Deal programs responded to the needs of workers. This tradition of knowledge and understanding of work's impact on individuals and communities helps distinguish social work from other mental health professions (Reisch, 1987).

It is probably fair to say that since World War II the labor movement has not been a central focus of social work practice and advocacy. The profession's attention to workplace issues has shifted to **employee assistance programs (EAPs),** where social workers primarily serve the interests of management. In EAPs, the focus is on personal difficulties, such as substance abuse, that interfere with job performance rather than on workplace problems such as low wages or discrimination (Chandler & Jones, 2003).

Recent decades have seen a decline in the power of unions throughout the country. As many as 22 states are "**right to work**" states (sometimes called "right to fire" states). In these jurisdictions, employees may not be required to join a union. Even if a majority votes in favor of union representation, individual employees may elect not to join. This limits the resources available to unions, which must nonetheless represent all employees in contract negotiations. Further, most states are "employment at will" states, in which employers can hire and fire at will and are not required to provide justification.

Nonetheless, the right to organize and to bargain collectively remains a well-established doctrine in U.S. labor policy. The process of organizing and bargaining can be highly contested (Cutcher-Gershenfeld et al., 2007). It begins with a petition, or "cards," signed

BOX 15.4   Mary van Kleeck

Considered a "communist sympathizer," Mary van Kleeck was pivotal in the left-wing "rank-and-file" movement in social work during the 1930s, arguing that the New Deal reforms did not go far enough in empowering and protecting workers. She resigned shortly after her appointment to the Advisory Council for Roosevelt's National Recovery Administration (NRA) to protest the president's decision to eliminate a clause in the legislation that protected labor's right to strike in industries covered by NRA codes (Selmi & Hunter, 2001). Many of her insights have relevance today. For instance, in her well-known 1934 paper, *Our Illusions Regarding Government,* van Kleeck held that in a capitalist system "government is essentially dominated by the strongest economic power and becomes the instrument to serve the purposes of the groups possessing that power."

by a substantial proportion of employees (at least 30 percent). Once these signatures are collected, the union submits a petition to the National Labor Relations Board, requesting that a secret election be held to permit employees to vote on whether to certify the union as their bargaining agent. Following a successful election, the union has one year to negotiate a collective bargaining agreement. Unions claim that these lengthy procedures allow employers to undermine organizing efforts through unfair labor practices such as firing employees who support unions and refusing to bargain in good faith. A recent study indicated that even when a substantial number of employees request union representation, most organizing efforts are not successful. John-Paul Ferguson reviewed the trajectories of over 22,000 organizing drives that filed election petitions from 1999 to 2005 and found that only one in five resulted in a contract between the business and the union (Ferguson, 2008). Since 2007. the **Employee Free Choice Act** has been introduced to ease the road from petition to contract. An original sponsor of the act, President Obama expressed continuing support for its provisions, but it is unclear how this measure will fare under the Trump administration.

The right to **collective bargaining** came under attack in the wake of the Great Recession. As private-sector jobs disappeared, the relative security enjoyed by public-sector employees was a likely target for envy; and, faced with declining budgets, state officials chafed at union contracts that locked in benefits and wage increases. Here, we will focus on developments in Wisconsin, bearing in mind that other states, including Ohio, Idaho, Iowa, Michigan, Indiana, New Hampshire, Kansas, and Tennessee, have seen similar efforts to reduce the power of public employee unions (Reuters, 2011). Reflecting the times, these measures do have a partisan aspect. Public employee unions have long been sources of support for Democratic candidates; consequently, any measure that reduces their political strength tends to advantage Republicans.

In 2010 the Wisconsin legislature passed Act 10, a controversial measure championed by Republican Governor Scott Walker that curtailed collective bargaining rights of public employee unions (except for police and firefighters), prohibited payment of dues through payroll deductions, and required annual recertification of unions. In response, union members turned to public protests and more than 100,000 occupied the state capitol—an action that prefigured Occupy Wall Street later that year and was termed "the Madison uprising" by one author (Aronowitz, 2012, p. 1). In June 2012, a union-backed effort to recall Governor Walker failed when his democratic challenger, Mayor Tom Barrett of Milwaukee, received only 46 percent of the vote (Davey & Zeleny, 2012). Meanwhile, with their membership dropping, the unions filed several lawsuits, but in 2014 the State Supreme Court upheld Act 10 (Stein, 2014).

In 2006, the largest drug-testing site in North America was shut down by fire and health authorities in Florida. Evidently, a company known as SFBC International was using a former Holiday Inn to house undocumented immigrants who were paid to participate in drug trials. This was not the first time treatment of "volunteers" in drug trials had come to the attention of authorities. In 1996, the *Wall Street Journal* reported that the Eli Lilly Company was hiring people from a local homeless shelter to test experimental drugs. With growing pressure to bring drugs to market quickly, drug trials are increasingly being carried out by private companies under contract to pharmaceutical companies. These testing firms hire vulnerable workers willing to submit to a range of tests as part of human trials for new drugs. Known as "guinea-pigging," the work is hazardous and largely unregulated. Since 2002, Bob Helms has been involved in "guinea pig activism." A former union organizer, Helms has established a "jobzine" that provides information and support to these workers. *Guinea Pig Zero* offers interesting reading at www.guineapigzero.com (Elliott, 2008).

Of course, many employees are not represented by unions, some are not fluent in English, and some do not understand their rights. These workers are the natural focus of social work intervention. By providing worker education, we can empower these workers and their families and reduce the dissolution, violence, and suffering that result from job stress and disruption. Through partnerships with unions we can help organize for better working conditions and enable workers to secure the rights to which they are entitled. Through our advocacy efforts we can expand (or at least preserve) legal protections for people who work for a living. There is much rewarding work to be done in this field, with great potential for advancing the cause of social justice.

Since the 1970s, a growing number of social work practitioners and scholars have turned their attention to the labor movement, recognizing that social work and organized labor share common goals and methods (Molloy & Burmeister, 1990; Selmi & Hunter, 2001). The 1996 welfare reform legislation offered further impetus to the alliance between social work and labor by thrusting clients of social workers into paid employment (Chandler & Jones, 2003).

At times it has been unclear what professional roles might be available for social workers in the labor movement. It is all very well to engage in advocacy, but without paid roles for practitioners it is unlikely that labor will become a professional priority (Selmi & Hunter, 2001). Unions have typically not delivered social services and thus have not been in a position to employ social workers.

There are a few examples of successful alliances between social work professionals and organized unions. During World War II, Bertha Reynolds organized a service program for the National Maritime Union that employed social workers on its staff (Reynolds, 1975). In the early 1990s, the Hunter College School of Social Work initiated an action research project in collaboration with Local 1199 of the Hospital and Health Care Employment Union. Researchers documented the needs of home care workers, and results were used in collective bargaining to secure much-needed benefits. The union then funded a service program to meet ongoing needs of its members (Donovan, Kurzman, & Rotman, 1993). After 9/11, Americans cut down on travel and Las Vegas was hit hard. Fifteen thousand members of the Culinary Union were laid off. The union responded by setting up a "Helping Hand Center" housed in a huge tent in their parking lot. Unemployment services set up an office there, as did the power company and United Way. In this way, union members who had been laid off could have a variety of needs met in one site (Chandler & Jones, 2003).

From a broad perspective, social work is part of the social protection afforded to Americans, mitigating the effects of the labor market on workers and their families. Our profession also has a strong history of alliances with the labor movement. Given the growing vulnerability of workers in today's economy, it is vitally important that these efforts continue.

LO 15-7   Reflect on Contemporary Realities That Shape the Experiences of U.S. Workers

EP 3a
EP 5a

Having completed our brief survey of the history of U.S. labor, we now turn to some contemporary realities that affect workers. These were brought to the fore by the **Great Recession** of 2007–2010 and its aftermath, in which the United States lost over 8 million jobs (Bureau of Labor Statistics, 2010). Indeed, few Americans were untouched by the recession. In March 2010, the Pew Economic Policy Group reported on a survey of a random sample of one thousand Americans. Results suggested that 46 percent had either lost their jobs or had a family or close friend who had lost a job due to the financial downturn. Over half (53 percent) had lost some, most, or all of their savings (PEW Economic Policy Group, 2010).

In the following sections we turn first to factors of general relevance, including the role of work in preventing poverty, the effects of inequality on U.S. workers, unemployment trends, the implications of rising productivity, and the rising cost of employee benefits. Then we will look at conditions specifically affecting women and people of color in the workforce.

WORK AS AN ANTIPOVERTY STRATEGY

The status of American workers is inextricably linked to the fate of the nation's poor. As we saw most recently in the Great Recession, rising unemployment pushes more Americans into poverty. But for millions of Americans, work does not provide an exit from poverty. Roughly one-fourth of full-time workers do not earn enough to raise a family of four above the poverty threshold (Mishel, Bernstein, & Boushey, 2004), and the majority of households with incomes below the poverty threshold include at least one worker (U.S. Census Bureau, 2003a). Of course, women and people of color are more likely to earn poverty-level wages than white men.

In 2015, 870,000 American workers earned the federal minimum wage of $7.25 per hour, and another 1.7 million had wages *below* the federal minimum. Together, these workers made up 3.3 percent of hourly employees in the United States (Bureau of Labor Statistics, 2016b). Figure 15.1 illustrates the historic relationship between minimum wage levels and the proportion of Americans living in poverty. As this figure indicates, the real value of the minimum wage has steadily declined since the late 1970s, even as the proportion of Americans living in poverty has increased.

INEQUALITY AND U.S. WORKERS

Since the 2008 government bailouts, most Americans have been sensitized to the differential between the average worker's pay and the compensation awarded to chief executive officers (CEOs); however, some are not aware that this reflects a long-term trend. Inequality among nations and between Americans increased during the second half of the 20th century, and at the beginning of the 21st century inequality was greater than it had been since the government began monitoring the income gap in 1947 (Blumberg,

FIGURE 15.1 Trends in Value of Minimum Wage and U.S. Poverty Rate

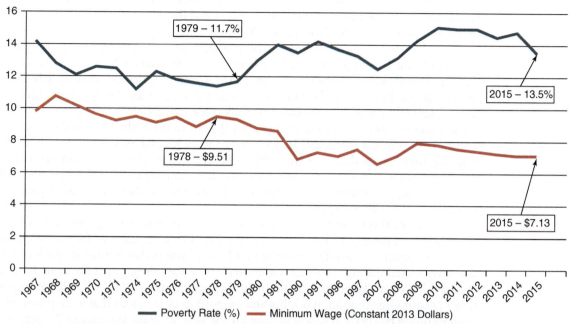

SOURCE: Minimum wage levels: U.S. Department of Labor, Wage & Hour Division, History of Federal Minimum Wage Rates under the Fair Labor Standards Act, 1938–2015 (http://www.dol.gov/whd/minwage/chart.htm) adjusted using CPI Inflation Calculator from Bureau of Labor Statistics.. Poverty statistics from Figure 5.2.

1980). As we saw in Chapter 5, this trend accelerated through the 1980s and persisted (but slowed) during the economic growth of the 1990s. The Center on Budget and Policy Priorities (CBPP) reported, "Nationwide, from the late 1970s to the late 1990s, the average income of the lowest-income families fell by over 6 percent after adjustment for inflation, and the average real income of the middle fifth of families grew by about 5 percent. By contrast, the average real income of the highest-income fifth of families increased by over 30 percent" (Bernstein et al., 2000, p. vii).

The causes of rising inequality are complex, involving broad economic and social trends as well as policy decisions that disadvantage low-income Americans. Economic trends that increase investment income and profits clearly benefit the affluent. At the same time, when policy makers unravel the safety net, fail to raise the minimum wage, or diminish labor protections, they further disadvantage low-income Americans. Regressive tax structures at the local, state, and federal levels also accelerate the trend toward greater inequality.

EP 4b

As a result, the United States today is a nation of extremes. In 2015, over 43 million Americans lived on incomes below the poverty threshold (see Figure 15.1). The same year, the IRS received over 410,000 tax returns reporting income over $1 million, and 16,000 reporting incomes in excess of $10 million (Internal Revenue Service, n.d.a). In 2014, the average compensation package for CEOs of S&P 500 companies increased by over 30 percent to an average of $22.6 million, 373 times the pay received by typical American workers (Mullaney, 2015). Stated differently, it would take the average worker 373 years to earn what the typical CEO brings home in a year. (Please see Anderson et al., 2008, for a discussion of public policies that support excessive CEO compensation.)

THE DECLINE OF U.S. MANUFACTURING

Rising inequality diminishes the cohesiveness of American society, as the wealthy become unable to fathom the plight of low-wage workers and the poor become less able to believe in the American dream that hard work will bring them prosperity.

The election of Donald Trump has been widely attributed to this sense of hopelessness and to the frustration among "working class" Americans, which traces back to the decline of manufacturing jobs (i.e., Cohn, 2016). During the decades immediately following World War II, American manufacturing was a dominant force in the world economy. Indeed, half of the world's manufacturing took place in the United States, in part because the factories of other major industrial nations (Japan, German, the U.K., and Russia) were decimated by the war (Smil, 2013). So, during the 1950s and '60s, many Americans who had only high school diplomas were able to secure well-paid union jobs in manufacturing. Thirty years later, these opportunities were less available to their children, and today manufacturing jobs seldom provide the security and income those living in major industrial cities have come to expect.

Some trace this trend to the "exporting" of U.S. manufacturing jobs to developing countries, most notably China, Mexico, and other "low wage nations" (Scott, 2015). The Trump campaign successfully persuaded millions of voters that it was the result of trade deals negotiated during the Obama administration. Certainly, our trade deals have not included important labor (and environmental) protections (see AFL-CIO, 2015; International Labour Organization, n.d.). But the proportion of U.S. jobs that were provided by manufacturing has been in steady decline for the past 50 years; from about 25 percent in 1966 to 9 percent in 2014 (Baily & Bosworth, 2014; Scott, 2015). At the same time, the manufacturing share of the U.S. GDP has remained constant. That is, U.S. manufacturers have been producing the same amount of "goods and value" relative to the nation's economy with fewer workers. Automation and technological advances have resulted in rising productivity.

RISING PRODUCTIVITY

Rising productivity is a long-term trend in the United States. From an economic perspective, productivity is measured as output per hour worked or output per worker. The U.S. economy has become more productive on both measures. More efficient or "lean" production and technological developments have made it possible to produce both goods and services with less human labor (Head, 1996).

The implications of rising productivity for workers are mixed. One might expect to see wages rise when an hour of work results in greater output. But this has not been the case. With the possible exception of the 1995–2000 economic boom, real wages in the United States have been stagnant (or declining, in the case of low-wage workers) since 1979. Most recently, as Lawrence Mishel and Heidi Shierholz explained, "During the Great Recession and its aftermath (i.e., between 2007 and 2012), wages fell for the entire bottom 70 percent of the wage distribution, despite productivity growth of 7.7 percent" (Mishel & Shierholz, 2013, not paginated).

One might also expect the time spent working to decrease in light of increased productivity. Historically, technological advances have led to shorter work weeks. The hours worked each week dropped from 80 to 60 during the 19th century, and from 60 to 40 during the 20th century. Faced with rising unemployment, the European Commission favored shortening the work week (Commission of the European Communities, 1982). The idea is catching hold in France and other nations, where a four-day work week has been proposed.

BOX 15.6   Take Back Your Time Day

In 1926, Henry Ford revolutionized labor practices by introducing the five-day work week. Ford argued that workers needed leisure time if they were to consume the goods his factories produced. Today the United States is no longer a leader in reducing the work week. Each year the average worker in this country puts in about nine weeks more on the job than European workers do. Several organizations urge Americans to protest by taking the day off around October 24, nine weeks prior to the end of the year. The results, they argue, would be more jobs, along with environmental gains that would come from lower consumption. For more information on the movement to reduce the American work week, visit www.shorterworkweek.com or the Shorter Work Time Action Page (www.swt.org).

Proposals for a shorter work week have not been well received in the United States, however, and American workers have responded to stagnant wages by working longer hours, increasing their average annual work time by 181 hours (the equivalent of 4.5 weeks) between 1979 and 2007 to a total of 1,868 (Mishel, 2013).

Originally designed to allow for rare extensions of the work week in cases of emergency, overtime is now used to expand the ordinary work week. This practice reflects the high cost of employee benefits. It is less expensive, even with overtime, to have one worker put in extra hours than to hire an additional worker.

"IT'S ALL ABOUT BENEFITS"

In 2007, the Heritage Foundation proclaimed that "compensation is keeping pace with rising productivity" (Sherk, 2007). How can this be true, given the stagnation in wages? The key term here is "compensation." Although wages have not increased with rising productivity, the cost of employee benefits has. Indeed, the rising cost of employee benefits more than absorbs the gains from rising productivity. As Sam said, "It's all about benefits."

Mostly, it's about health benefits. The Kaiser Family Foundation reported that premiums for employer-sponsored health insurance have been increasing four times faster, on average, than worker earnings since 2000 (Kaiser Family Foundation, 2006). About half of American workers in private industry had employer-sponsored health insurance in 2009 (Bureau of Labor Statistics, 2009a), and health insurance premiums are one of the fastest-growing costs faced by U.S. companies, absorbing a growing share of the total compensation package for workers. In 2016, health insurance benefits cost 7.6 percent of total compensation compared with 1999, when they averaged 5.4 percent (Bureau of Labor Statistics, 2016c). Typically, these costs are passed on to employees, who experience lower wages and/or are required to pay higher shares of their premiums.

Health insurance premiums are frequently on the agenda when union officials and company management sit down in collective bargaining situations. Arguing that they are not in the health insurance business, employers ask workers to pay an ever-increasing share of ever-increasing premiums. Unions explore the possibility of providing health insurance themselves. Managers bemoan the rising cost of health care. Some contracts include clauses that release companies from responsibility for health insurance premiums in the event that government-sponsored care becomes available. Negotiators for the steelworkers echo Sam's remark, "It's all about benefits" (Holland, 2007).

FIGURE 15.2 Unemployment Trends in the United States, 1923–2015

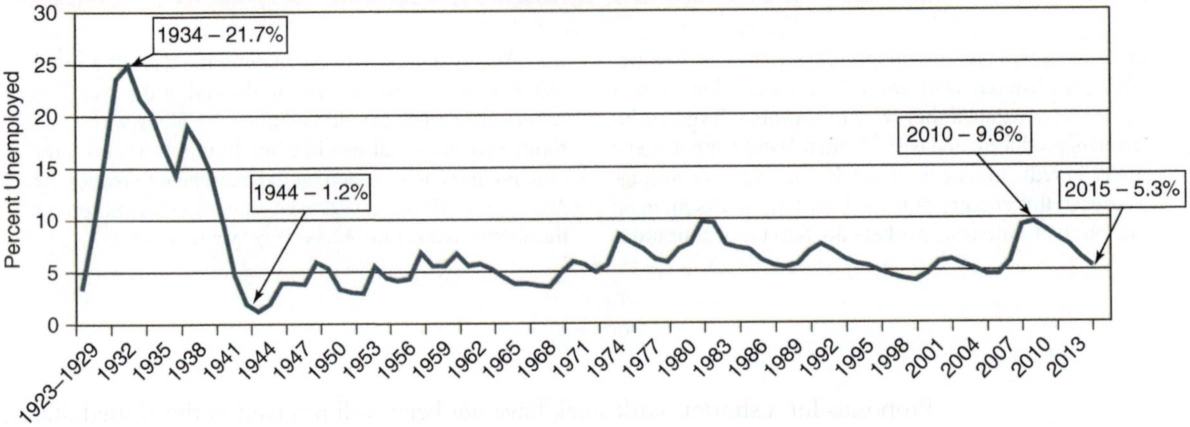

SOURCES: 1923–1942: BLS, Compensation from before World War I through the Great Depression (http://www.bls.gov/opub/cwc/cm20030124ar03p1.htm); 1942–2015: Bureau of Labor Statistics, Labor Force Statistics from the Current Population Survey, Employment status of the civilian noninstitutional population, 1945 to date (http://www.bls.gov/cps/cpsaat01.htm, accessed Nov. 18, 2016).

UNEMPLOYMENT IN THE UNITED STATES

The most recent (2007–2010) recession, variously attributed to excessive lending, deregulation of financial markets, rising oil prices, and speculation, brought the vulnerability of workers into harsh relief. The International Labour Organization (ILO) estimated that at least 20 million jobs were lost globally by the end of 2009 (ILO, 2009). The United States alone saw the loss of approximately 8.4 million jobs. The U.S. unemployment rate, which had been fairly steady at 5 percent for years, surpassed 10 percent in October 2009 for the first time since 1983 (Bureau of Labor Statistics, 2010).

As we will see later in this chapter, many workers are not covered by unemployment insurance, and those who are covered find the benefits limited. Thus, millions of families lost their homes to foreclosure. And, of course, in the United States unemployment can mean loss of health insurance and increased risk of suicide (i.e., Kposowa, 2001).

In 1932, during the height of the Great Depression, one in four U.S. workers was unemployed. Next to that figure, even the post-recession rate of 10 percent appears small. Trends in U.S. unemployment rates are illustrated in Figure 15.2.[8]

By international comparison, unemployment in the United States was slightly below average for OECD nations in late 2016. Whereas the United States reported a rate of 4.9 percent, the mean for the 28 nations that made up the European Union was 6.3, with the lowest rate (2.9 percent) reported in Iceland and the highest (19.3) in Spain (OECD, n.d.b).

It is important to keep in mind that U.S. unemployment figures are based on a very specific definition and do not include workers who are underemployed or those who are no longer seeking work ("**discouraged" workers**).[9] U.S. unemployment figures are based on a monthly survey known as the Current Population Survey, in which a representative sample of about 60,000 U.S. households are interviewed. A person is considered unemployed if

---

[8]The European Union uses a similar definition of unemployment (Eurostat, 2007), and when Japan's definition is adjusted to conform to the U.S. concept, Japan still has a lower rate of unemployment (Elder & Sorrentino, 1993).

[9]Disadvantaged groups (older workers, people with disabilities, people of color, those with little education, and those with felony convictions) are over-represented among discouraged workers (Heslin, Bell & Fletcher, 2012). The Bureau of Labor Statistics has tracked the number of discouraged workers since 1994, identifying them as "marginally attached to the labor force." At the height of the Great Recession in 2010, BLS identified over 1.3 million discouraged workers, a number that was cut in half by 2015 Bureau of Labor Statistics (n.d.c).

he or she is "jobless, looking for jobs, *and* available for work." Actively looking for work is carefully defined to include activities in the previous four weeks such as contacting an employer about an interview, sending out résumés, and answering advertisements. Workers who are temporarily laid off are counted as unemployed (Bureau of Labor Statistics, 2001).

LO 15-8 Become Familiar with U.S. Policies That Affect Vulnerable Groups in the Workplace

EP 2a
EP 3a

We have explored conditions that affect all workers: the failure of wage-based employment to insulate workers from poverty, rising inequality, pressure for high productivity, and the escalating costs of employee benefits. Now we will consider contemporary realities that particularly affect women and people of color.

WOMEN AS WORKERS IN TODAY'S WORKFORCE

The labor force participation of massive numbers of women dates to the latter part of the 20th century. Prior to World War II, only 28 percent of all adult women were in the labor force; and by 2016, that figure had increased to 57 percent (Women's Bureau, n.d.). Today, most mothers with children under 18 (68 percent) are working, including those whose children are under 6 years of age (64 percent) (Bureau of Labor Statistics, 2016c). Several issues have arisen as a result of this trend, including gender differentials in earnings and retirement income, and employer responses to family responsibilities that generally fall to women.

Gender Differentials in Earnings

Women earn less than men. In 2016, on average, women who worked full-time earned about 80 cents for every dollar earned by men (Institute for Women's Policy Research, 2016). The gap has shrunk since the 1960s, but at the current rate of change the United States cannot expect to achieve pay equity until 2058. As the Institute for Women's Policy Research noted, "Most women working today will not see equal pay during their working lives" (Institute for Women's Policy Research, n.d., not paginated). Of course, as we see in Table 15.2, this ratio varies by occupation.

Many women, like Lilly Ledbetter, will simply run out of time. After working at the Goodyear Tire and Rubber Company for decades, Ms. Ledbetter learned that her wages were considerably lower than those paid to men in similar management positions. Upon retirement, she filed suit against the company for gender discrimination. Her case

TABLE 15.2 Median Weekly Earnings of Men and Women in Major Occupational Groups, 2015

Occupation	Men ($)	Women ($)	Women's Earnings as Percent of Men's (%)
Management/Professional	1,383	996	72
Service	585	463	79
Sales & Office	777	627	81
Natural Resources, Construction, & Maintenance	770	580	75
Production & Transportation	704	512	73
All Occupations	895	726	81

Source: Bureau of Labor Statistics, Household Data, Annual Averages, Median weekly earnings of full-time wage and salary workers by detailed occupation and sex (http://www.bls.gov/cps/cpsaat39.htm).

(*Ledbetter v. Goodyear Tire & Rubber Co.*) reached the Supreme Court, where a majority ruled against her because she had not filed suit within 180 days of receiving her first paycheck. Later, Congress passed the Lilly Ledbetter Fair Pay Act to change the timeliness requirements on federal discrimination suits.

Table 15.3 presents the distribution of American workers across major occupational groups. Although women have made inroads into traditionally male occupations such as law and medicine, most remain in sales and service jobs. There are also important occupational differences between white women and women of color. White and Asian women have greater access to managerial and professional occupations than African American and Hispanic women.

Proponents of human capital theory (discussed in Chapter 5) would argue that this difference, known as the "**gender wage gap**," occurs because women are less committed to their work, receive less education, have interrupted work histories, and fail to build up seniority on the job.

These human capital factors do not fully account for the gender difference in wages. As Senator Alan Cranston noted,

> Variables such as attachment to the workforce, level of experience, education, job commitment, and similar factors have been examined in various studies. These studies have attempted to explain the difference in earnings between male and female workers, but they have generally been able to account for less than one-fourth and never more than one-half of the earnings differentials on the basis of different labor force participation patterns of male and female workers. Virtually every research study has concluded that there remains a large gap which can be explained only by the existence of discriminatory employment practices. (*Congressional Record*, July 25, 1984, S9114)

The Equal Pay Act of 1963 required an employer to pay the same wage to employees holding the same job. Title VII of the Civil Rights Act of 1964 went one step further, prohibiting wage discrimination on the basis of race, sex, religion, or national origin. A 1981 Supreme Court decision on pay scales for female prison guards in Oregon held that Title VII prohibits wage discrimination even when the jobs are not identical (*Gunther v. County of Washington*).

During the early 1980s, events in the state of Washington brought the high cost of gender discrimination to the fore. In December 1983, U.S. District Court Judge Jack Tanner ordered the state of Washington to raise salaries for workers in fields dominated by women in an effort to correct "pervasive" discrimination among state employees. The state

TABLE 15.3   Occupational Distribution of American Workers (16 years and older), 2015

Occupation	African American		Hispanic or Latino		Asian American		White		Total	
	Men	Women	Men	Women	Men	Women	Men	Women	Men	Women
Management/ Professional	24.9	35.2	17.8	26.6	52.3	50.2	36.0	44.0	35.5	42.9
Service	21.6	27.7	19.9	31.8	12.7	20.0	13.1	19.8	14.2	21.1
Sales & Office	17.4	29.2	14.3	30.4	17.0	23.2	16.2	30.1	16.4	29.6
Natural Resources, Construction, & Maintenance	11.5	0.6	26.7	2.0	5.4	0.4	17.9	1.0	16.5	0.9
Production & Transportation	24.7	7.3	21.3	9.1	12.6	6.2	16.8	5.1	17.4	5.5

Source: Bureau of Labor Statistics, Household Data, Annual Averages, Employed Persons by Occupation, Race, Hispanic or Latino Ethnicity, and Sex (http://www.bls.gov/cps/cpsaat10.htm).

was further ordered to pay back wages to women dating to the time the discrimination was identified. The decision was appealed, and the case was settled out of court.

This case became a catalyst for action at the state level, and other states have since adopted "comparable worth" plans or conducted comparable worth studies. In these studies, jobs are evaluated on the basis of four categories: knowledge and skills, mental demands, accountability, and working conditions. Ratings are assigned within each category and a final score computed for each job. When wages in jobs with equal scores show consistent disparity, advocates argue that gender discrimination is the primary explanation. Rather than lowering the salaries of highly paid employees, remedies consist of increases to underpaid employees each year until their salaries approach parity.

Progress toward comparable worth reflects the long-standing American tradition of using public policy to remedy failures of the free market. Most progress toward pay equity has been made in the public sector, with cities such as Colorado Springs, Los Angeles, and San Jose and states such as Minnesota and Washington implementing corrected pay scales for public employees. The history of attempts to legislate comparable worth reveals profound resistance. At the heart of most objections is a belief that the free market, left unchecked, will eventually provide economic justice. As of this writing, federal legislation on comparable worth has been introduced, but nothing has passed. (For more information on comparable worth, contact the National Committee on Pay Equity listed in the Suggested Resources section at the end of this chapter.)

While legislative attempts to achieve pay equity for women may have stalled, some women are resorting to the courts. Betty Dukes, an employee at Wal-Mart, was at the heart of the largest gender bias lawsuit in the nation's history (*Dukes vs. Wal-Mart Stores)*. The suit alleged that the company pays women less and denies or delays their promotions. In 2004, a District Court judge granted the case class-action status, a decision that was confirmed in 2010. But in 2011 the Supreme Court ruled for Wal-Mart, holding that the plaintiffs did not constitute a class. In addition to seriously complicating the possibility of any class action suit in the United States, the court's unanimous decision denied Betty, along with over 1.6 million other women who had worked for Wal-Mart, their day in court.

Gender Differentials in Retirement

The gender gap in wages pales next to the gap in pension benefits. As Crystal and Shea (1990) pointed out, "A 'good' job may be distinguished from less 'good' jobs more sharply by its benefits, such as pension entitlement, than by its salary. The holder of such a 'good' job is more likely to be well-educated, to have a long-term attachment to the job and employer, to be male and to be white" (p. 438).

Women are less likely to be covered by a pension during their working years, and as a result, less likely to have their retirement income supplemented by pension benefits. This gender difference may be a key factor behind the greater incidence of poverty among elderly women (see Chapter 14). The post–World War II growth in private pensions led to higher retirement incomes for men who retired during the 1980s. As Radner (1991) noted, "Pension income was the only income type that was a substantial positive factor in the growth in mean total income of the aged" (from 1979 to 1989) (p. 11).

Some observers explain this gender gap by noting that the industries most likely to employ women (retail trade and nonprofessional services) are among those least likely to offer pension coverage. However, Korczyk (1993) argued that "[b]ased on all characteristics other than earnings, women are still less likely to be covered by pensions than similarly situated men" (p. 28). In her analysis, the gender gap persisted among men and women who were similarly situated with respect to job tenure, industry, union membership, age, occupation, and firm size. She suggested that "[w]omen's pension coverage lags behind that of men largely because the labor market treats women differently from men" (p. 32).

The gender gap in pension income should diminish for future cohorts of women. Korczyk (1993) reported that the gender gap tends to be less pronounced among younger workers. Most studies of trends in pensions note that growing numbers of working women do have coverage (Evan & Macpherson, 1994; Wiatrowski, 1993). Of course, the extent to which increased coverage translates into higher retirement income remains to be seen.

In what might now be considered a historical quirk, both contributions and benefits under a private pension plan were once computed based on gender, with women required to contribute more and/or to receive lower monthly benefits. As Gohmann and McClure (1987) note, the practice "seems economically logical," given women's greater life expectancy. Nevertheless, it is now illegal. In 1978, the Supreme Court used Title VII of the Civil Rights Act of 1964 to conclude that employers could not require women to make larger contributions to a pension plan in order to receive the same benefits a man in their situation would receive (*City of Los Angeles Department of Water and Power v. Mane Manhart*). A 1983 decision extended this ruling to preclude offering lower monthly benefits to women employees (*Arizona Governing Committee for Tax Deferred Annuity and Deferred Compensation Plans v. Nathalie Norm*).

Access to survivors' benefits is another significant pension issue for women. Prior to 1974, about one in five covered workers was in a plan with no provision for survivors. For wives of these workers, the death of a spouse meant complete loss of pension income, as well as a one-third reduction in Social Security benefits. Further, wives of workers whose plans did offer survivors' benefits could be divested of those benefits without their knowledge or consent.

With the 1974 passage of the Employee Retirement Income Security Act (ERISA), Congress accomplished the nation's first comprehensive pension reform. Three subsequent laws have expanded ERISA protections: the Tax Equity and Fiscal Responsibility Act of 1982 (TEFRA), the Retirement Equity Act of 1984 (REA), and the Tax Reform Act of 1986. (These policies were also discussed in Chapter 14.)

Under this legislation, defined benefit plans must offer employees the opportunity to elect a "joint and survivor option" in which payments are made to survivors following the death of the worker. This option must be provided at the time of retirement. Workers who select it opt for lower retirement income in exchange for coverage that extends for the life spans of their survivors. ERISA requires that a spouse give "knowing consent" when the worker elects to forgo the survivor annuity. The joint and survivor option is of limited value to low-wage workers who cannot afford to live on a reduced pension. The General Accounting Office reported that in 1989, only 45 percent of those with the lowest pension income elected survivor coverage (U.S. General Accounting Office, 1992). Of course, the growing number of workers who do not have a defined benefit plan do not have the option of electing joint and survivor coverage.

The gender gap in pay translates not only to lower pension income but also to limited ability to save for retirement. Women's median income from IRAs, Keogh, and 401K plans, as well as annuities and asset income, is lower than men's (U.S. Congress Joint Economic Committee, 2011). The one exception to this general rule of women receiving less income than men is public assistance.

Family Responsibilities

The vast majority of mothers in the United States with children under the age of 13 are employed. Their child care arrangements are, by and large, informal. Care by relatives is the most common type. The next most common form of child care is "family day care," in which a woman (usually a neighbor) looks after children in her own home. "Most family day care homes appear to operate in an underground market in which prices are relatively

BOX 15.7   Family Responsibility Discrimination

Also known as "caregiver discrimination," family responsibility discrimination (FRD) arises when employers discriminate against, or fail to accommodate, workers based on their family responsibilities. Those affected may include pregnant women, parents of young children, and individuals with sick or aging parents, partners, or spouses. Employers show this type of discrimination when they deny leaves of absence or when they make decisions regarding employment or promotion based on the assumption that a person's family responsibilities will interfere with his or her job performance.

Caregivers can file claims under a range of statutes, including the Family Medical Leave Act, the Americans with Disabilities Act, and the Employee Retirement Income Security Act of 1974 (ERISA). If gender or age are considerations, Title VII of the Civil Rights Act of 1964 or the Age Discrimination in Employment Act of 1967 may come into play.

AARP reported that about 2,207 lawsuits for FRD were filed in 2008. Employers' attention has been drawn to the largest FRD award to date: a $11.54 million verdict (*Schultz v. Advocate Health & Hospitals Corp.*) awarded to a hospital maintenance worker who was fired while caring for his severely compromised parents (Williams & Feinberg, 2012).

low" (p. 230), and an estimated 10 to 30 percent of these day care homes are licensed (Hayes, Palmer, & Zaslow, 1990). The widespread use of relatives and family day care in 1990 continues (Kilburn & Hao, 1996; Morrissey & Banghart, 2007).

The federal government supports child care through direct payments and through tax expenditures (introduced in Chapter 2). Where direct payments tend to focus on low-income families, tax expenditures are of greatest benefit to middle- and upper-class families who face the highest tax bills.

Direct payments to expand child care availability to low-income women have included programs funded through Temporary Assistance for Needy Families (TANF), Head Start, the Social Services Block Grants (SSBG), and other preschool programs. There is also limited federal funding for infrastructure subsidies that enhance the supply and quality of available child care by financing increased training and wages for caregivers, improved standards and regulations, and extended resource and referral services.

Tax subsidies have come to represent a growing proportion of federal child care expenditures. In 1972, 80 percent of federal child care dollars were paid for care of children from low-income families through provider subsidies such as Head Start and SSBG programs. By 1995, these combined programs accounted for about 69 percent of the total, while the child and dependent care tax credit accounted for 25 percent of federal expenditures in this area (Kilburn & Hao, 1996). Today, this tax credit represents the single largest federal expenditure for child care (Isaacs et al., 2012). Like any tax deduction, child care tax credits now offered by the federal government as well as many states have greatest value to those with the highest federal tax obligation—those who owe the most income tax.

"Flexible spending accounts" (FSAs) are another form of tax subsidy for child care. Established through the Economic Recovery Act of 1981, they permit employees to pay for their child care with "pretax dollars." Under these plans (regulated under Section 129 of the IRS code), employees specify their anticipated child care expenses up to $5,000 per year. The specified amount is withheld from gross salary on a regular basis and refunded upon presentation of receipts for child care expenses. Employers save Social Security and unemployment taxes on the portion of the salary allocated for child care, and employees are spared income and payroll taxes. Like the child care tax credit, FSAs are of greatest value to middle- and upper-income workers.

PEOPLE OF COLOR

In Chapter 10 we considered the roles of discrimination and oppression in limiting the resources and opportunities available to people of color in the United States. These twin forces operate in the labor market as well. African American and Hispanic workers in particular are subject to occupational segregation and elevated risk of unemployment.

African Americans

In Chapter 10 we saw that African Americans have lower household incomes than white Americans. Human capital explanations cannot fully account for this differential. At comparable levels of education, African Americans still receive lower incomes than white Americans. In 2014, the median weekly earnings of a non-Hispanic white American worker with a high school diploma or GED totaled $696, while those of an African American worker with the same level of education averaged $579, a difference of 17 percent. The same year, the median weekly income of a white worker with a bachelor's degree or more ($1,219) was 20 percent higher than that of African American workers with similar preparation ($970) (Bureau of Labor Statistics, 2015a).

Some of the difference is clearly associated with occupational segregation. Recent decades have seen significant gains in the occupational attainment of African Americans, who continue to be overrepresented in low-wage service occupations and production and transportation fields. This is illustrated in Table 15.2.

Unemployment rates provide another indication of labor force experiences. In 2014, the unemployment rate for African Americans was 11.3 percent—more than double the rate for non-Hispanic whites (5.3 percent) (Bureau of Labor Statistics, 2015b).

Latino or Hispanic Americans

Similar trends influence the earnings of Latino or Hispanic workers in the United States. A Latino or Hispanic worker with a high school diploma earned a median weekly income of $595 in 2014, 15 percent less than a white worker with the same education. Likewise, Latino or Hispanic workers with bachelor's degrees earned $937 per week, 23 percent less than their white counterparts (Bureau of Labor Statistics, 2015a).

Like African American workers, Latinos are overrepresented in the lower-paying service occupations and in production and transportation fields. They are also most likely to be employed in natural resources, construction, and maintenance occupations.

Latino or Hispanic Americans also tend to be overrepresented among the unemployed. In 2014 the unemployment rate for Latino or Hispanic Americans was 7.4 percent (Bureau of Labor Statistics, 2015b).

As we have seen, in the United States hard work does not guarantee economic security and for many it does not ensure a comfortable quality of life. Throughout this text we have identified some of the factors contributing to this insecurity: wage stagnation, unemployment, and rising pension insecurity. As we will see in the next section, U.S. labor policy offers limited protections to workers.

LO 15-9   Understand Key Provisions of U.S. Labor Policies

EP 3a, 4b
EP 5a

Like most U.S. social policies, labor policy involves the interaction of federal and state laws that have accumulated over decades. They reflect the thinking, not of a single mind, but of hundreds or even thousands of competing perspectives. The result is at times inconsistent, even irrational. A detailed consideration of labor law is clearly beyond the scope of this section, which will focus on policies that commonly apply once a person has been hired. These fit roughly into four categories: laws that govern wages and benefits, protective and antidiscrimination measures, health and safety policies, and laws that govern employee discharges. Finally, the earned income tax credit stands alone as a tax policy that enhances the well-being of low-income workers.

WAGES AND BENEFITS

The Minimum Wage

New Zealand was the first country to set a national **minimum wage** in 1894, and now most countries have either legislation or collective agreements that establish a floor for wages (Neumark & Wascher, 2008). The U.S. minimum wage was established in 1938 through the Fair Labor Standards Act. According to a Department of Labor historian, "When he felt the time was ripe, President Roosevelt asked Secretary of Labor Perkins, 'What happened to that nice unconstitutional bill you had tucked away?'" (Grossman, 1978). Evidently, Perkins's willingness to become Secretary of Labor was at least partly conditional on Roosevelt's agreement to promote a law that would "put a floor under wages." So, in 1938, despite vigorous industrial opposition, the minimum wage was set at 25 cents per hour.

Federal wage requirements are enforced by the Wage and Hour Division of the Department of Labor. The minimum wage does not apply to all workers. For example, youth (who are under 20 years of age) are subject to a subminimum wage during their first three months of employment. The minimum wage is not indexed to inflation, so any increase requires congressional and presidential approval. Most recently (as of this writing), the minimum wage was raised in 2009 to $7.25 per hour, but its purchasing power (its "real value") has not kept pace with inflation. According to the Department of Labor, the real value of the minimum wage peaked in 1978 at $9.51 (2013 dollars) per hour; by 2007, it had declined to a low of $6.60 (2013 dollars) per hour. (Please see Figure 15.1.) Of course, some states set minimum wages higher than the federal minimum, and a few set lower minimum wage rates. (See http://www.dol.gov/whd/minwage/america.htm for state minimum wage rates.)

The economic effects of the minimum wage are hotly debated. Opponents argue that raising it will increase unemployment among low-wage workers, but there is no clear evidence to support this claim. Supporters argue that increasing the minimum

---

BOX 15.8   The Living Wage

Living wage initiatives begin with the proposition that no one who works full time should have to live in poverty, and that work should be rewarded with wages that allow for a decent standard of living that provides for "the basics." The living wage movement has extended worldwide. In the United States it began in the mid-1990s when Baltimore, Maryland, adopted the nation's first living wage ordinance. Since then over 100 cities and counties have adopted ordinances that require employers who contract with them to pay a living wage. Some have raised concerns about "de-employment effects" of these ordinances.

That is, they predict that employers will simply not hire if they are required to pay a living wage. Studies have generated mixed results. Most recently, in 2008, Suzanne Clain looked at the impact of these ordinances on poverty rates. Using census data from 232 counties, she found "statistically significant evidence that living wage ordinances modestly reduce poverty rates ..." (Clain, 2008, p. 215). You should be able to find the estimated living wage for your community on the "living wage calculator" maintained by MIT (livingwage.mit.edu).

wage will reduce poverty and protect unskilled workers from exploitation in sweat-shops. Here, too, evidence appears to be equivocal (Neumark & Wascher, 2008). The antipoverty impact of the minimum wage is hard to predict because it is influenced by several factors, including the demand for labor, the ratio of minimum wage to poverty threshold, the extent to which a measure of poverty takes into account the depth of poverty, and the extent of income sharing among low-income households (Fields & Kanbur, 2005).

Benefits

Federal law distinguishes between two types of employee benefits: pension benefits and "welfare" benefits. Pension plans that qualify for favorable tax treatment are subject to nondiscrimination rules. This means that an employer cannot arbitrarily give pension coverage to a few favorite employees while neglecting the rest. Under the Employee Retirement Income Security Act (ERISA) of 1974, as amended, pension plans are also subject to "vesting" requirements. After these requirements have been met, workers have the legal right to receive a pension, even if they leave the job.

Welfare benefits, such as health insurance, life insurance, and disability coverage, are subject to fewer restrictions. Like pension plans, these benefits are also given favorable tax treatment. (They are deductible as a business expense.) But employers have wide discretion in determining how, when, and to whom these benefits will be offered.

Leave is also considered an employee benefit. Some countries stipulate the amount of leave employers must provide. In New Zealand, for example, workers are legally entitled to three weeks of paid leave and 11 paid public holidays each year. Apart from provisions governing family and medical leave, the United States does not mandate the provision of leave.

Family and Medical Leave

More than 80 percent of working women are in their prime childbearing years (between the ages of 18 and 44). Further, in 2003, 25.6 percent of all families with children were headed by single women, roughly double the 1970 proportion of 13 percent (Mulroy, 1995; U.S. Census Bureau, 2004b). Small wonder, then, that in the 1999 Report on the American Workforce, the U.S. Secretary of Labor, Alexis Herman, declared, "Since 80 percent of families now depend partly or fully on the paychecks of mothers … helping families deal with the competing needs of the home and the workplace must also be among our highest priorities" (Herman, 1999). Family and medical leave is designed to do just that.

In 1985, the first family and medical leave bill was introduced during the 99th Congress, which adjourned without voting on the bill. During the 100th Congress, the bill was reintroduced and amended several times. During the 101st Congress, the bill was amended and passed both the House and the Senate. It was vetoed by President George H. W. Bush on June 29, 1990. A House vote failed to override the veto. During the 102nd Congress, the bill was reintroduced and, after some amendment, passed both the House and the Senate. President Bush again vetoed the bill on September 22, 1992. The Senate voted to override the veto, but the House did not. The Family and Medical Leave Act (FMLA) was introduced on January 21, 1993, passed both houses, and was signed into law by President Clinton on February 5, 1993 (PL 103-3). Thus, debate about family and medical leave continued through eight years and two presidential vetoes before its passage in 1993.

Under current provisions, the Family and Medical Leave Act provides for up to 12 weeks of unpaid, job-protected leave per year—with uninterrupted health insurance coverage—for the birth or adoption of a child or the serious illness of the employee or an immediate family member. Businesses with fewer than 50 employees (a classification that includes most employers) are exempt. Employee eligibility is restricted to those who have worked 1,250 hours (25 hours per week) over the previous 12 months and who have worked at least 12 months. Employers may exempt key employees from coverage. Employees are required to provide 30 days' notice for foreseeable leaves and make a reasonable effort to schedule medical treatments to avoid unduly disrupting employers' operations. Employees must also provide medical certification justifying the need for the leave in the case of illness. Enforcement provisions parallel those of the Fair Labor Standards Act, with damages limited to double actual losses and a "good faith" exception granted to employers with reasonable grounds for believing they have not violated the act.

PROTECTIVE AND ANTIDISCRIMINATION STATUTES

In this section we will briefly review policies that have been developed to protect children in the workplace, as well as antidiscrimination statutes that target women, people with disabilities, and older workers. These laws interact closely with social norms governing what is and is not appropriate in employment. So even when enforcement may be problematic, they represent the nation's official view of what is and is not acceptable.

Child Labor Laws

Federal laws restrict the hours and types of jobs that children may work. Some states have additional, stricter provisions. Under federal law, restricted hours apply only to children aged 14 and 15, who may work from 7 a.m. to 7 p.m., except when school is in session. During the summer they may work until 9 p.m. They may work no more than 3 hours on a school day, 18 hours in a school week, 8 hours on a nonschool day, and 40 hours in a nonschool week. Children 16 or older are not subject to restrictions in working hours, and these restrictions do not apply to farm labor.

In the United States, children under the age of 13 may work in several positions. They may deliver newspapers, babysit, work as an actor or performer, work in a business solely owned or operated by their parents, and work on a farm owned or operated by their parents. Parents may not employ their children in manufacturing, mining, or any occupation declared hazardous by the Secretary of Labor. When they turn 14, children may work in offices, grocery stores, retail stores, restaurants, movie theaters, baseball parks, amusement parks, and gas stations. They may not work in several occupations, including construction, driving, manufacturing, and any occupation declared hazardous. When they turn 16, they may work in any occupation not declared hazardous. At 18 years of age, child labor laws no longer apply.

The Pregnancy Discrimination Act

Prior to the 1993 passage of the **Family and Medical Leave Act**, American women had only limited job protection when they became pregnant. What protection they did have dated to the Pregnancy Discrimination Act of 1978, which amended Title VII of the Civil Rights Act of 1964 to ensure that pregnant women would be treated the same as other employees. Essentially, the act required states and employers to extend temporary disability insurance policies to cover pregnant women. The Pregnancy Discrimination Act passed after heated debate, with opponents claiming it would substantially increase costs to business, create unfair economic burdens, and even lead to increased discrimination against women of childbearing age.

Americans with Disabilities Act (ADA)

As we saw in Chapter 8, the **Americans with Disabilities Act (ADA)** was enacted in 1990 to prohibit discrimination against people with disabilities. Public and private organizations are required to make "reasonable accommodation" to enable people with disabilities to perform job requirements, use transportation services, and access public venues. Accommodation might include making changes in existing facilities, restructuring jobs or modifying work schedules, acquiring devices or equipment, or providing readers or interpreters. Companies and organizations may forgo making accommodation if doing so would present them with "undue hardship," a term that is redefined based on the company's size, budget, and operations.

Determining what constitutes a disability is not solely a technical consideration. Politics and philosophy come to bear as well. Today, individuals who are disabled by virtue of addiction to alcohol or drugs are not protected under the ADA, but those who suffer from psychiatric diagnoses are. Those with contagious diseases such as HIV/AIDS and tuberculosis are covered by the ADA. People whose skills are limited by a learning disability are covered, while those who lack access to learning opportunities are not. Those experiencing stressful lives are not covered by the ADA, but those with a stress disorder that has been diagnosed by a psychiatrist are. Since 1994, the ADA has applied to employers with 12 or more employees. Its provisions are enforced by the Department of Justice.

Age Discrimination in Employment Act

Prior to passage of the **Age Discrimination in Employment Act (ADEA)** in 1967, help-wanted advertisements could, and did, list age as a basis for hiring. The notion that "older workers need not apply" was widespread and, as Schulz (1995) argues, may have been the cause of longer periods of unemployment experienced by older men. The 1964 Civil Rights Act did not prohibit discrimination on the basis of age, but Congress did direct the Department of Labor to conduct a study of age discrimination. The following year, a report submitted to Congress revealed "a persistent and widespread use of age limits in hiring that in a great many cases can be attributed to arbitrary discrimination against older workers on the basis of age and regardless of ability" (Rich & Baum, 1984, p. 179).

The ADEA prohibits discrimination on the basis of age in hiring, discharge, compensation, benefits, and other terms of employment. Its stated purpose is to "promote employment of older persons based on their ability rather than age; to prohibit arbitrary age discrimination in employment; and to help employers and workers find ways of meeting problems arising from the impact of age on employment" (U.S. Labor Code, Title 29, Chapter 14, Section 621, Congressional Statement of Findings and Purpose, http://www.law.cornell.edu/uscode/29/621.html).

ADEA protections originally extended only to workers between the ages of 40 and 65, but the act was amended in 1978 to cover workers up to age 69 and in 1986 to extend to workers of any age. The act applies only to employers with 20 or more employees and allows for discrimination when age is a "bona fide occupational requirement"—that is, when the employer can demonstrate a rational basis for the use of age-based decision making. Typically, such requirements have been applied to airplane pilots and air traffic controllers.

It is hard to gauge the effects of the statute on age discrimination in employment. On average, between 1991 and 1995, 17,000 complaints of age discrimination were filed each year with the Equal Employment Opportunity Commission (EEOC) (Administration on Aging, 1997). In 2012 the EEOC received 22,857 complaints, among which 770 were deemed to have reasonable cause to believe that discrimination had occurred (U.S. Equal

BOX 15.9   The Aging Workforce

The American workforce is aging. In part, this change reflects the reversal of a male trend toward early retirement. Women, on the other hand, have shown a steady increase in late-life employment over the decades. As if anticipating this trend, 80 percent of baby boomers report that they expect to work during their retirement years. Yet many workers—some say as many as one in three—must leave the workforce involuntarily due to ill health, a layoff, or a family problem (Munnell, 2006).

Employment Opportunity Commission, n.d.a). These complaints probably represent the tip of the iceberg, and it is fair to say that age-based discrimination remains an elusive social problem. Perhaps the ADEA's greatest impact is symbolic. The simple fact that age discrimination in employment is against the law of the land is, in itself, a statement of American values and expectations regarding the elderly.

HEALTH AND SAFETY POLICIES

OSHA

In 1970, Congress passed the **Occupational Safety and Health Act** to reduce workplace exposure to identified hazards, such as toxic chemicals, excessive noise, mechanical dangers, stressful heat or cold, and unsanitary conditions. The act establishes a "general duty" for employers to eliminate recognized hazards from the workplace. It also requires employers to comply with standards and guidelines issued by the U.S. Occupational Safety and Health Administration (OSHA).

Housed in the Department of Labor, OSHA oversees enforcement in the 50 states. OSHA issues detailed standards, such as "safety and health regulations for longshoring," as well as more general guidelines, such as the recent "ergonomic guidelines for the poultry processing industry." Federal and state OSHA officials conduct thousands of workplace inspections each year. These may be triggered by employee complaints, reports from other agencies, or accident reports. All employers are required to display an OSHA poster that informs employees of their safety and health rights. These posters are available in English and Spanish. Employers are encouraged to establish cooperative relationships with OSHA by seeking consultation about safety issues and accident prevention.

Sexual Harassment

In 1991, many Americans were glued to their televisions, watching Anita Hill, a young law professor, testify that she had experienced **sexual harassment** at the hands of President Reagan's nominee to the Supreme Court. The experience contributed to a growing awareness of the issue of sexual harassment in the workplace. Since then, thousands of women and some men have filed lawsuits claiming they were sexually harassed. The result has been a potpourri of (sometimes contradictory) judgments and a growing number of "backlash" lawsuits by alleged perpetrators against companies from which they were dismissed.

What is sexual harassment? Current law recognizes two forms of sexual harassment. In "quid pro quo harassment," sexual favors are demanded in exchange for favorable treatment or rebuffing sexual advances involves the risk of reprisal. Another form of harassment, recognized since a 1986 ruling by the Supreme Court (*Mentor Savings*

Bank v. Vinson), involves the creation of an "intimidating, hostile, or offensive" work environment. Both of these types of harassment are recognized by the EEOC as forms of sex-based discrimination. (See EEOC, "Guidelines on Discrimination Because of Sex," Title VII, Section 703, *Federal Register,* 45, April 11, 1980.)

Both forms of sexual harassment are prohibited by Title VII of the Equal Rights Act (Maypole & Skaine, 1983). Title IX of the Higher Education Amendments of 1972 prohibits sexual harassment on college and university campuses. State laws governing assault and battery or infliction of emotional distress have been applied to cases involving hostile work environments (Thomas, 1991). Finally, most large employers and public agencies have established policies that prohibit sexual harassment and establish procedures for victims to pursue. Often these are "zero tolerance" policies specifying that the slightest hint of sexual harassment will bring about disciplinary action.

In some cases, men who have been charged with sexual harassment have won large settlements against their former employers. Often these "backlash" cases charge that a man's First Amendment right to freedom of speech has been violated. In one 1993 case *(Silva v. University of New Hampshire)*, a court reinstated a professor who had been suspended for using sexual metaphors in his technical writing class. Other backlash cases have resulted in large settlements being awarded to men who were discharged on the basis of allegations of sexual harassment (e.g., *Mackenzie v. Miller Brewing Co.*).

Despite the array of policies and procedures designed to prevent and remedy sexual harassment, judicial practices and employment realities often prevent women from reporting incidents and pursuing legal remedies. In *Mentor Savings Bank v. Vinson,* the Supreme Court ruled that a victim's "sexually provocative" speech or dress was relevant to whether the conduct was offensive. This ruling opened the door to defenses that put women on trial for their relationships, behavior, and attire. Further, some courts have required that women demonstrate they resisted or complained about unwanted sexual demands. Thus, women who were in no position to refuse or complain may be denied access to legal remedies. In 1994, President Clinton signed the Violence Against Women Act, which restricts the extent to which a plaintiff's personal history can be brought in to defend against allegations of sexual harassment.

During the 1990s, the EEOC saw a substantial increase in sexual harassment complaints. Between 1991 and 1998, the number of claims filed annually with the EEOC increased from 7,000 to a high of nearly 16,000 (Henetz, 1998).[10] Since 2000, however, the number of complaints has steadily declined. In 2011, the EEOC reported receiving 11,364 complaints and found reasonable cause to believe harassment had occurred in 761 cases (U.S. Equal Employment Opportunity Commission, n.d.b). Resolving these cases often proves difficult: the body of case law regarding sexual harassment is contradictory, cases can degenerate into "he said/she said" allegations that are difficult to sort out, and there continues to be confusion regarding the distinction between harassment and discrimination.

As Yale University law professor Vicki Schultz noted, it is important to keep in mind that prohibition of sexual harassment does not prohibit sexuality per se, but gender

---

[10] Men, too, have been subjected to sexual harassment. In fact, a 1998 Supreme Court ruling (*Oncale v. Sundowner Offshore Services*) held that "[t]he prohibition of sexual harassment does not necessarily speak to an individual's gender, but forbids behavior so objectively offensive as to alter the conditions of the victim's employment." In this ruling the Court focused on the severity and persistence of the harassment. Roughly 12 percent of sexual harassment claims filed in 1997 involved male victims.

discrimination. The goal of this policy is to achieve equality in the workplace, not to prosecute people who tell off-color jokes (Schultz, 1998).

DISCHARGE POLICIES

Several policies are relevant when a worker leaves a job. These include notice requirements and measures governing health insurance.

Notice

Under the **Worker Adjustment and Retraining Notification of 1988 (WARN),** employers of more than 100 workers must provide at least 60 days' notice of plant closings and mass layoffs. Both terms are defined by the Department of Labor (see http://www .doleta.gov/programs/factsht/warn.htm). WARN provisions can also apply to the sale of a business. In addition to these federal provisions, state laws bear on the nature of notice required when an employee is laid off. Federal law does not require that employees be given advance notice of individual discharge decisions.

Health Coverage

When employees receive group health coverage, the employer is required to give them notice of their rights under the Consolidated Omnibus Budget Reconciliation Act (COBRA), passed in 1986. COBRA requires that "qualified beneficiaries" (employees with health coverage) be provided the opportunity to purchase membership in the group health plan when they lose group coverage due to loss of employment, retirement, divorce, death, or employer bankruptcy. Keep in mind that bankruptcy does not necessarily mean a company will go out of business. As we have seen with Kmart and other firms, a company can use bankruptcy protection to reorganize its debt and then continue to do business. COBRA applies to voluntary and involuntary departures but not to individuals who are fired for gross misconduct. COBRA restricts the cost of coverage to 102 percent of the actual cost to the employer for people who are similarly situated, and the coverage must be identical to that provided before the "qualifying event." Employees have up to 60 days to decide whether or not to "elect" coverage, and the first premium is due within 45 days of the election. The usual duration of coverage is 18 months, but this can be extended in a range of circumstances. (In cases of divorce or legal separation, COBRA coverage may be required for as many as 36 months.) Coverage may be terminated if an employer terminates all of its group health coverage. The federal COBRA law does not apply to health plans that cover fewer than 20 employees, although some states extend the law to smaller businesses.

Whereas COBRA was designed to help workers maintain their health coverage upon the loss of a job, the Health Insurance Portability and Accountability Act of 1996 (HIPAA) was designed to maintain coverage while employees move to different jobs by restricting the extent to which insurers can deny coverage. HIPAA does not specify the nature or cost of the coverage that is offered. It simply protects the employee from multiple periods without coverage for ongoing conditions.

HIPAA applies to virtually all employers with at least two employees. It prohibits insurers from denying coverage to a group based on the health status of an individual in this group. This was seen as a way to help small companies maintain group health coverage in the event an employee or employee's dependent developed a catastrophic health problem.

As we saw in Chapter 6, the Patient Protection and Affordable Care Act established additional protections against loss of health insurance, as well as incentives that encourage employers to provide health insurance.

EARNED INCOME TAX CREDIT

Established in 1974, the **earned income tax credit (EITC)** has become one of the nation's most effective and popular antipoverty initiatives. The EITC is also relatively unknown, to the extent that it could be considered a "hidden entitlement." Some view it as a way to offset the regressive effects of the payroll tax on low-income workers (see Chapter 4 for a discussion of the payroll tax). It also rewards work and supplements the earnings of low-income families with children (Hoffman & Seidman, 1990; Phillips, 2001).

The EITC, which is administered by the Internal Revenue Service (IRS), provides a refundable tax credit to eligible taxpayers. For low-income families, the EITC consistently exceeds their federal income tax obligation. In such cases, the IRS would first apply the credit to any taxes owed and then send the remaining amount directly to the family. In fiscal year 2000, the program distributed approximately $30.4 billion, an amount that exceeded federal expenditures on TANF and roughly equaled the combined federal expenditures for food stamps and SSI. In some states federal EITC benefits are supplemented by state earned income credits.

The EITC offers substantial gains to low- to moderate-income working families, with the greatest benefits going to families with children. In 2013, a qualifying family with one child could receive credit worth as much as $3,250. The EITC phases out with increased income and in 2013 a one-child, two-parent family went to zero at $43,210. Workers without children could receive up to $487 in 2013, with the credit phasing out for a couple at an income of $19,680 (Internal Revenue Service, n.d.b).

The EITC is a powerful antidote to poverty. Indeed, President Reagan called it the "best anti-poverty, best pro-family, best job creation measure to come out of Congress" (Gresham, 2008). In 2011, nearly 27 million taxpayers received $59.5 billion dollars in EITCs (Ellis, 2012). Further, in 2011 the credit lifted 9.4 million Americans out of poverty, among whom over half were children (Center on Budget and Policy Priorities, 2013).[11]

Despite its advantages, the EITC has encountered criticism. First, the IRS has reported a 21 percent error rate in EITC payments, which has led detractors to claim that it is simply another opportunity for poor people to "work the system." Second, because moderate-income workers experience a high rate of tax on earnings while the EITC is being phased out, opponents of the credit argue that the higher rates represent a disincentive to work; however, there is no evidence to support this view (Hoffman & Seidman, 1990).

LO 15-10   Understand the Impact of Globalization on Workers in the United States and Elsewhere

EP 4b
EP 5a

Globalization has had, and will continue to have, a significant impact on workers across the globe, increasing both profits and inequality while raising the specter of unemployment and declining wages for low-skilled workers.

Free market advocates generally argue that globalization supports economic growth, and the conditions of workers will not improve without economic growth. Their argument is not without merit. A report by the International Labour Organization (ILO, 2008)

---

[11]In 2005, at least four times as many individuals received the EITC as participated in the TANF program. Nearly 22.8 million tax returns claimed the EITC that year, while approximately 5.1 million individuals received TANF benefits. Note: The number of returns filed underestimates the number of individuals receiving EITC, as some married couples file jointly (Caputo, 2009).

examined global wage trends in recent years to estimate the extent to which workers have benefited from globalization through increased wages. The results suggest that on average, economic growth (measured as increases in per capita GDP) does translate into wage increases; however, the relationship is not perfect. That is, a 1 percent increase in GDP does not translate into a 1 percent increase in wages but rather a 0.75 percent increase in wages. On the other hand, during times of economic decline, such as the most recent recession, wages tend to fall faster than the GDP.

The net effect of these trends can be observed by considering the proportion of the total economic pie (the gross domestic product, or GDP) that is devoted to wages, or the "wage share." Generally, a declining wage share implies that more of the gains of economic growth are being distributed as profits. During the first years of the 21st century the proportion of the world's GDP committed to wages declined in most of the countries studied, including the United States (ILO, 2008).[12]

This trend toward a lower share for workers has been variously attributed to the weakening of unions (Rosenfeld, Denice, & Laird, 2016; Fichtenbaum, 2009), to technological progress (International Monetary Fund, 2007a, 2007b), and to globalization (ILO, 2008). By easing the flow of capital across borders and reducing barriers to international trade, globalization may intensify pressure toward a lower wage share. This impact varies by country, but international comparisons have identified some aggregate effects on the world's workers.

Growth in international trade may also exert a negative overall effect on wages, possibly because large low-wage exporters (such as Chinese manufacturers) drive wages down across the board. This process fuels a "race to the bottom," in which companies drive down wages for unskilled workers by relocating production facilities and outsourcing various functions. (Alex Gibney's 2010 documentary about lobbyist Jack Abramoff, *Casino Jack and the United States of Money,* tells the story of one such exporter.)

The same processes that lead to reduced wage share contribute to domestic wage inequality. In the United States, unskilled workers (particularly in manufacturing) were especially hard hit by the Great Recession, even as they are generally subject to greater risk of job loss. By contrast, skilled workers have been relatively insulated from job losses, with the highest-paid workers enjoying particularly strong wage growth in the wake of the Recession.

To some extent, globalization has reduced the power of national governments while increasing that of multinational corporations. In this competitive environment, U.S. labor policies, particularly those that address job loss and worker education, can buffer the disruptive effects of globalization, even as income supports, such as the minimum wage, and tax policies, such as the EITC, have the potential to reduce inequality. At the same time that social workers advocate for these policies in the United States, we may become involved in advocacy, organizing, and service delivery on behalf of workers around the world. Thus, we may find ourselves in a position akin to that of early labor organizers who sought to promote international worker solidarity.

---

[12]In 2009, the wage share of 38 countries increased; however, this was attributed to delayed wage adjustments in response to the economic crisis. Please see the ILO's Global Wage Report, 2009 Update, available online at http://www.ilo.org/wcmsp5/groups/public/---ed_protect/---protrav/---travail/documents/publication/wcms_116500.pdf

Closing Reflections

In *The End of Work,* Jeremy Rifkin (1995) argued that "the commodity value of human labor is becoming increasingly tangential and irrelevant." As technology advances and the world's productive processes are restructured, the overall demand for workers may diminish. While highly skilled and trained workers may be unaffected, those who have earned their living with physical or unskilled labor are increasingly vulnerable. Clearly, social workers must be at the forefront of efforts to protect these workers and their families.

Long-term employment trends could force us to rethink the way we value human beings. For centuries the dominant measure of a person's worth has been the market value of his, or more recently her, labor. Given our appreciation of the complex nature of individuals and communities, social workers are well positioned to encourage a cultural shift to a new perspective that values human beings as ends in themselves, rather than as means to achieve economic growth.

Think About It

1. We have considered two advocacy efforts on behalf of women: the failed attempt to pass the Equal Rights Amendment (Chapter 13) and the successful passage of Title VII of the Civil Rights Act (Chapter 15). How would you explain these different outcomes?

2. As professionals, social workers are expected to place client needs above self-interest. Yet, as workers, we may need to resort to strikes to improve working conditions and the quality of the services we provide. Under what circumstances would you be willing to go on strike? Would you ever cross a picket line to deliver services?

3. The movement of undocumented workers across the Mexican border has become a hot topic in recent years. How would you explain the current focus on this topic? What position does organized labor take on immigration reform? Does this make sense to you?

4. Apply the five-question social justice framework presented in Part I to a proposal to increase the minimum wage. Once you have finished with question 5, add a sixth question: "Why do I believe this is/is not fair?" Consider how your personal philosophy and experiences have influenced your answer to question 5.

5. Compare the antipoverty impact of the EITC with that of TANF. Which program more effectively moves families out of poverty? How would you explain this difference? Does your state provide an earned income tax credit for low-income workers? If not, is this an agenda item for local antipoverty advocates? Why or why not?

6. Does your state restrict the activities of public employee unions? Do any of these unions represent social workers?

Web-Based Exercises

For direct links to all the sites in these exercises, visit the *Foundations of Social Policy* Companion Site at www.cengagebrain.com and select the resources for Chapter 15.

1. Go to http://www.bls.gov/cps/#empstat, where the Bureau of Labor Statistics keeps a wealth of data. Find Unemployment in the left-hand menu. Under demographics you should be able to find answers to the following questions:
   a. What racial or ethnic group has the highest rate of unemployment?
   b. Does unemployment vary by marital status?
   c. What age group has the longest median duration of unemployment? Why do you think this is so?

2. Go to the website for the U.S. Equal Employment Opportunity Commission (www .EEOC.gov). Click on "Statistics" in the bottom menu under "About EEOC." Now click on "EEOC Enforcement and Litigation Statistics." Here you will find information on charges related to a large array of statutes. Select one of interest (i.e., Equal Pay Act Charges, Harassment Charges, Race-Based Charges) and look at the trend over the past 15 years.
   a. What proportion of complaints resulted in a finding of "no reasonable cause"?
   b. What proportion resulted in a finding of "reasonable cause"?
   c. How did the monetary benefits secured by the EEOC change?
   d. What conclusions can you draw from these figures about the role of the executive branch in implementing antidiscrimination policies?

Competency Notes

As mentioned in the preface to this text, the Council on Social Work Education has designated nine core competencies and related practice behaviors that must be addressed by accredited social work programs. In these notes, I will specify the way chapter content addresses these competencies and behaviors. (This is designed to assist with the accreditation process.) Please refer to the "helping hands" icons for the locations of specific content in this chapter. Here you will find a brief explanation of how the accompanying content relates to the specified competency or practice behaviors.

The following list indicates where EPAS competencies and practice behaviors are addressed in this chapter.

EP 2a   **Apply and communicate understanding of the importance of diversity and difference in shaping life experiences in practice at the micro, mezzo, and macro levels.** The chapter examines oppressive workplace dynamics and discrimination against vulnerable groups in the workplace, with a focus on U.S. immigration policies.

EP 3a   **Apply their understanding of social, economic, and environmental justice to advocate for human rights at the individual and system levels.** This chapter examines the impact of stereotyped gender roles and racist attitudes on policies affecting women and people of color in the workforce and discusses the role of social workers in unions and in advocacy and education efforts for workers. It also discusses the impact of affirmative action and the backlash against it.

EP 4b   **Apply critical thinking to engage in critical analysis of quantitative and qualitative research methods and research findings**. Research addressed in this chapter includes studies on the antipoverty effects of the minimum wage, the public health impacts of inequality, and the labor force impacts of affirmative action and globalization.

EP 5a   **Identify social policy at the local, state, and federal level that impacts well-being, service delivery, and access to social services**. The chapter addresses a range of labor policies and their relevance to the well-being of workers.

EP 5c   **Apply critical thinking to analyze, formulate, and advocate for policies that advance human rights and social, economic, and environmental justice**. *Trends and developments that have influenced labor policy from the 19th century to the present are discussed, along with the role of social workers in labor advocacy.*

Suggested Resources

Akabas, S. H., & Kurzman, P. A. (2005). *Work and the Workplace: Innovative Policy and Practice*. New York: Columbia University Press.

Economic Policy Institute. (2012). *The State of Working America, 2012*. Available at http://stateofworkingamerica.org/subjects/overview/.

Ehrenreich, B. (2001). *Nickel and Dimed: On (Not) Getting by in America*. New York: Metropolitan Books.

Massey, D. S., Durand, J., & Malone, N. J. (2003). *Beyond Smoke and Mirrors: Mexican Immigration in an Era of Economic Integration*. New York: Russell Sage Foundation.

Rifkin, J. (1995). *The End of Work: The Decline of the Global Labor Force and the Dawn of the Post-Market Era*. New York: G. P. Putnam's Sons.

Tichenor, D. J. (2002). *Dividing Lines: The Politics of Immigration Control in America*. Princeton: Princeton University Press.

Zweig, M. (2000). *The Working Class Majority: America's Best Kept Secret*. Ithaca, NY: Cornell University Press.

www.bls.gov. On this site the U.S. Bureau of Labor Statistics provides a gold mine of information, both current and historic, about labor in the United States.

www.eeoc.gov. This is the official site of the Equal Employment Opportunity Commission. It offers information on federal laws, background on the EEOC, instructions for filing a complaint, and news releases.

www.ufw.org. The United Farm Workers (UFW), now part of the AFL-CIO, continues their advocacy on behalf of migrant workers. At their site you will find action items, news releases, and inspiring quotes from UFW leaders.

Cycles of Liberation

If you have come to help me, you are wasting your time. But if you have come because your liberation is bound up with mine, then let us work together.

ABORIGINAL WOMAN, FAITHFUL FOOLS STREET MINISTRY

Liberation is integral to the pursuit of social justice. But the process of liberation is neither tidy nor linear; instead, we cycle from progress to retrenchment and back. We see this pattern across all three levels of practice: at the micro level, liberation stems from personal empowerment; at the mezzo level, it informs community development initiatives; and at the macro level, it results in cultural transformation. Sometimes it's hard to tell which level the impetus comes from. Individual change contributes to social movements, even as healthy communities nourish personal growth and empowerment.

Liberation flourishes on solidarity and love. Author bell hooks (2001) saw the roots of liberation in loving solidarity across sex, race, and class boundaries. She suggested, "As we work to be loving, to create a culture that celebrates life, that makes love possible, we move against dehumanization, against domination" (p. 608).

In his well-known work, *Pedagogy of the Oppressed,* Paulo Freire offered thoughts on how to overcome oppression. "Freedom," he explained, "is acquired by conquest, not by gift. It must be pursued constantly and responsibly" (2000, p. 47). Freire argued for a dialogue that supports liberation by disrupting the balance of power that sustains oppression.

In our anti-oppressive practices, social workers tap into cycles of liberation at various levels. We work at the interstices between individuals and communities, using empowerment strategies to transform lives and society. By contributing to dialogues, we make policies more responsive to the people they affect, and we battle against a tendency to use the power of government to oppress out-groups. In transformative practice we help clients understand and solve their problems with reference to the broad social context.

Andrea Ayvazian (2001) described the transformative potential of our profession well when she observed, "What does seem to create real and lasting change is highly motivated individuals—usually only a handful at first—who are so clear and consistent on an issue that they serve as a heartbeat in a community, steadily sending out waves that touch and change those in their paths" (p. 609). I hope this book will help prepare you to join the heartbeat of liberation.

A GLANCE TOWARD THE FUTURE

As our understanding of the physical and social environment becomes more sophisticated, the connections among people emerge in sharper relief. My liberation is inevitably bound up with yours, and with that of everyone who shares this planet. But this reality is not immediately apparent, and some continue to ignore it.If you are now entering the social work profession, you will be practicing well into the 21st century. Your work will be influenced by themes sourced deep in our history, many of which have been discussed in this book. As we turn to the future, our focus becomes speculative, taking into account emerging trends, ideas, and politics that will shape social welfare and social work practice in the years to come.

GLOBALIZATION AND GLOBAL GOVERNANCE

The term "globalization" refers to the flow of capital, labor, technology, and information across national borders. Taken to its theoretical extreme, globalization could make national boundaries and nation states irrelevant. At present, advanced communication and transportation technologies have enhanced the flow of people, information, and goods between countries, a process that challenges the sovereignty and authority of national governments. It is difficult for a nation to enforce environmental and labor laws within its borders when major corporations can evade them by relocating to another country.

In Chapter 2 we saw huge corporations holding local governments hostage — threatening to relocate unless they were granted special tax breaks or exemption from zoning ordinances. In Chapter 6 we explored the role of global governance in management of worldwide epidemics. In Chapter 15 we learned that globalization has increased corporate profits, sometimes at the expense of low-skilled workers. In an emerging global context, these issues assume new depth and complexity, challenging social workers' analytic skills and advocacy abilities. To work effectively in this context, social workers will need to be conversant with the organizations involved in transnational governance, including the United Nations, European Union, International Monetary Fund, World Bank, and World Trade Organization.

The United Nations

The most widely known of the major international organizations, the United Nations (U.N.), was founded during the aftermath of World War II on October 24, 1945. With an original membership of 51 countries, its stated purpose was "preserving peace through international cooperation and collective security."

Today, the U.N.'s 193 member nations include nearly every country in the world. The U.N. is made up of six main entities. Five are located at U.N. headquarters in New York: the General Assembly, the Security Council, the Economic and Social Council, the Trusteeship Council, and the Secretariat. The International Court of Justice is located at The Hague, Netherlands.

The General Assembly serves as a kind of parliament, with representatives from all member nations. Each nation has one vote, and decisions are made through either simple or two-thirds majority votes. Representatives have considered a wide range of topics, including globalization, nuclear disarmament, social and economic development, protection of the environment, and consolidation of new democracies. Assembly decisions are not binding, but they do carry the moral authority of the U.N.

The Security Council is primarily responsible for maintaining peace and security. It includes fifteen members: five permanent members (France, China, the Russian

Federation, the United Kingdom, and the United States) and ten elected by the General Assembly for two-year terms. Decisions made by the Security Council require nine affirmative votes and may be vetoed by any one of the five permanent members.

The Economic and Social Council is a natural home for social work practitioners. With 54 members elected from the General Assembly for three-year terms, the Council holds a major conference in July of each year. There, issues such as social development, the status of women, crime prevention, drug trafficking, and environmental protection are discussed. The Council carries out its humanitarian activities in cooperation with nongovernmental organizations (NGOs).

The Trusteeship Council meets rarely, as its work is mostly complete. It was established to provide international supervision to eleven trust territories administered by seven member states. By 1994, all the trust territories had become independent or self-governing. The last one to achieve independence was the Trust Territory of the Pacific Islands, administered by the United States.

The Secretariat is the executive body that directs the work of the United Nations. With a staff of approximately 8,900, its major office is in New York, with other locations in Geneva, Vienna, and Nairobi.

The International Court of Justice, also known as the World Court, arbitrates disputes between U.N. member nations. Nations are not obligated to participate in World Court proceedings, but those who do participate are obligated to comply with the Court's rulings.

The U.N. promotes social justice by encouraging political independence of former colonies. Through its Declaration on the Granting of Independence to Colonial Countries and Peoples, the U.N. has focused world opinion and attention on this issue. Since it was founded, nations with hundreds of millions of people have moved toward independence. In 1945, 750 million people lived in non-self-governing territories. Today, that number is approximately 1.3 million. The U.N. also led a 30-year campaign to end apartheid in South Africa and held a World Conference Against Racism, Racial Discrimination, Xenophobia, and Related Intolerance in South Africa in September 2001. The United States did not participate in conference deliberations, objecting to the inclusion of the Israeli-Palestinian conflict and reparations for the trans-Atlantic slave trade as agenda items.

To relieve suffering, the U.N. provides emergency assistance in the wake of natural disasters and environmental emergencies. Humanitarian aid is also provided through refugee programs and food assistance.

As a permanent member of the Security Council, the home country of most U.N. offices, and an important source of financial support, the United States plays a pivotal role in the U.N. Some Americans distrust the U.N., and congressional ambivalence has at times delayed payment of our country's dues.

The 9/11 attacks and subsequent invasion of Iraq raised Americans' awareness of the U.N. Many watched on February 5, 2003, as then-Secretary of State Colin Powell presented the case for invasion before the General Assembly in an attempt to gain international support and avoid condemnation by the U.N. Some resented the necessity of this presentation, feeling that the United States should not allow the U.N. to exert control over its military interventions. In March 2003, the United States, Spain, and the United Kingdom introduced a Security Council resolution authorizing the use of force to secure Iraqi compliance with prior resolutions concerning dismantling weapons programs. Faced with opposition from Germany, France, and Russia, the resolution was subsequently withdrawn.

The United States invaded Iraq on March 19, 2003. In May 2003 the Security Council approved Resolution 1483, which had been submitted by the United States and the United

Kingdom. This resolution recognized the United States and Great Britain as occupying powers, and called on them to improve security and stability in the country and provide opportunities for Iraqis to determine their political future.

The 2004 presidential debates saw both candidates agreeing that the United States did not need U.N. authorization to undertake military campaigns. At the same time, there was general agreement on the need for international cooperation in rebuilding Iraq. Resolution 1483 set the stage for this cooperation. This outcome illustrates the U.N.'s primary source of legitimacy and power. Without a standing military force, the U.N. cannot demand compliance with international law. Instead, it provides a forum for dialogue and collaboration.

U.N. sanctions are a powerful tool for maintaining the peace. Under the charter, the Security Council can call upon member nations to apply measures that do not involve armed force in order to maintain or restore international peace and security. These include asset freezes, travel and trade restrictions, and arms embargos. U.N. sanctions have been applied in 14 cases, involving Afghanistan, Angola, Ethiopia and Eritrea, Haiti, Iraq, Liberia, Libya, Rwanda, Sierra Leone, Somalia, South Africa, Southern Rhodesia, Sudan, and the former Yugoslavia. In most of these cases, sanctions were fully lifted. In 2006, the U.N. imposed sanctions on Iran that took a serious toll on the nation's economy and citizenry in order to discourage uranium enrichment. They were lifted in January 2016 in exchange for limits on Iran's nuclear program. Existing sanctions on North Korea were strengthened in 2009 as a response to that nation's nuclear and missile tests.

The European Union

In 2002 the euro became the common currency for member states of the European Union (EU) in the culmination of efforts toward unification that spanned 50 years. The EU traces its origins to the 1951 **Treaty of Paris**, which established a common market in coal and steel for six founding nations: Belgium, the Federal Republic of Germany, France, Italy, Luxembourg, and the Netherlands. The treaty was expanded to cover other goods with the 1957 **Treaty of Rome**. In later agreements these nations abolished customs duties and established common policies on trade and agriculture. The year 1979 saw the first elections to the European Parliament, elections that are now held every five years.

The EU was formally established under this name by the **Treaty on European Union**, signed at Maastricht in 1993. With this treaty, progress toward shared governance proceeded apace. In 1995 three new members were added: Austria, Finland, and Sweden; they were quickly followed by former Soviet nations. Today the EU includes 27 nations. Membership is open to all European countries that are prepared to follow EU law.

With over 300 million citizens and an annual budget in excess of 130 billion euros, the EU has become a significant global player, counterbalancing some of the economic and political might of the United States. EU governance is structured by treaties as well as policies approved by three bodies: the Council of the European Union (or Council of Ministers), the European Parliament (directly elected by citizens of the EU), and the European Commission (an independent executive body). The EU also operates a Court of Justice, Court of Auditors, the European Economic and Social Committee, the Committee of the Regions, the European Investment Bank, and the European Central Bank.

The euro has been an important unifying force for the EU, providing a measure of monetary stabilization to member nations. In addition, the Lisbon Treaty, ratified by all member nations in 2009, consolidated the legislative and budget authority of the European Parliament, established a Charter of Fundamental Rights to protect EU citizens, and created a new post of High Representative for the Union in Foreign Affairs and Security Policy.

Developments in the United Kingdom have underscored the tenuous nature of alliances within the EU. In 2014, Scotland held a national referendum that President Obama described as a "full and energetic exercise of democracy," asking whether it should become independent of Britain. Alongside economic considerations, one significant concern was whether an independent Scotland could become a full member of the EU. The referendum failed, as the "No" side secured 55 percent of the votes in September 2014.

Less than two years later, on June 23, 2016, voters in the United Kingdom elected to leave the EU in a referendum known as "Brexit." Their historic 52%–48% vote is not binding on the government. Nonetheless, Parliament immediately passed a motion that called on government to trigger "Article 50" and begin the two-year withdrawal process. As of this writing, the status of the UK vis à vis EU member states has yet to be decided; however, the voters of Scotland who overwhelmingly favored remaining in the EU may eventually have the opportunity to revisit their "No" vote on independence.

International Financial Organizations

Like the U.N., the International Monetary Fund (IMF) was established in the wake of World War II in 1946. Its purpose is "to promote international monetary cooperation, exchange stability, and orderly exchange arrangements; to foster economic growth and high levels of employment; and to provide temporary financial assistance to countries to help ease the balance of payments adjustment." Most of the world's nations belong to the IMF, which provides loans through the World Bank.

The IMF and the World Bank both have poverty reduction as a stated goal, and both have acknowledged that rising inequality has accompanied economic globalization. Critics, such as Global Exchange, argue that international financial organizations contribute to inequality by undermining public investment and increasing the wealth of global elites.

The World Bank provides development loans to third-world nations. These loans total approximately $16 billion each year and extend to over 100 nations and they usually finance major projects such as dams, roads, and power plants. These massive projects often, displace marginalized groups, even as they profit businessmen and other elites.

Also controversial are the Structural Adjustment Programs (SAPs) imposed as conditions for receiving loans. An SAP might, for example, require a nation to cut government spending and raise interest rates. Typically, SAPs take a **neoliberal** approach to economic development, liberalizing the markets and reducing the size of government in developing countries. Critics, even some within the IMF, argue that this approach could jeopardize long-term economic development by increasing inequality and decreasing public investment in social services, education, and health care (Ostry, Loungani, & Furceri, 2016).

The World Trade Organization

The World Trade Organization (WTO) came to public attention in December 1999 when demonstrations and violence rocked the streets of Seattle. The demonstrators' violence may have distracted observers from the substance of their critique.

The WTO was established in 1994 as a result of negotiations held in Uruguay under the General Agreement on Tariffs and Trade (GATT) as "the only international organization dealing with the global rules of trade between nations. Its main function is to ensure that trade flows as smoothly, predictably, and freely as possible." Representatives of member nations participate in trade negotiations under the auspices of the WTO, which are then submitted to domestic legislative processes for ratification.

In the United States, critics of trade agreements argue that ratification should require the two-thirds vote required to ratify international treaties. Instead, the U.S. Congress ratifies these agreements by a simple majority vote.

The WTO argues that it strengthens the international economy and breaks down international barriers by facilitating trade. It has been a fierce international advocate for the free market. Critics argue that the WTO is the agent of international corporations and that it undermines democratic processes. They suggest that the organization promotes a "race to the bottom" in labor and environmental protections.

The United States ran afoul of the WTO in March 2002 when President George W. Bush imposed tariffs on foreign steel. Designed to shore up the domestic steel industry, the measure drew the ire of the WTO, which ruled in November 2003 that the tariffs violated international trade rules. This decision gave other countries the right to impose retaliatory tariffs on U.S. exports, and the European Union (EU) announced that it would apply duties to American motorcycles, citrus fruit, farm equipment, and other goods. This response left Bush an unpleasant choice. If he rolled back the steel tariffs, he would anger voters in key steel states such as Pennsylvania and West Virginia. If he maintained the tariffs, he risked jeopardizing other industries. In December 2003 the Bush administration lifted the tariffs, and the EU immediately withdrew its threat of retaliatory tariffs. Relieved observers felt that a trade war had been averted.

Globalization has eased the flow of capital and information—but not labor—across national borders. The elites of some nations take advantage of this trend, consolidating their wealth and power at unprecedented levels. The resulting inequality may simply be an innocuous by-product of consolidation. But it can destabilize societies, creating a large underclass of disempowered workers and a tiny ruling class with only passing interest in their well-being. Multinational corporations may have become more powerful than nation states. Is this an inevitable consequence of the dominance of capitalist philosophy? In the following section we will consider the contrast between capitalist and socialist visions of social welfare.

CONTRASTING VISIONS OF SOCIAL WELFARE

In this book we have considered the recurring tension around the proper roles of public social welfare versus private markets. In the United States this tension has influenced social policies from welfare to labor law to health-care reform.

In Western industrialized nations, two dominant economic philosophies offer contrasting interpretations of the social welfare state and divergent approaches to inequality. The first, **welfare capitalism**, takes capitalism as given and places social welfare in a secondary role. In this view social policy functions as "the enabling state," facilitating individual contributions to economic productivity. An alternative view, **postindustrial socialism**, deemphasizes the market and treats the social sphere as more important. Under this view the role of social policy is to facilitate the expansion of the social sphere, liberating workers from economic pressures and demands.

THE ENABLING STATE

In their classic work, *The Enabling State*, Gilbert and Gilbert (1989) offered a cogent vision of welfare capitalism. Observing that public welfare expenditures leveled off in the 1970s and noting the expanded use of government lending and tax deductions to accomplish social policy goals, these authors argued that in the United States the welfare state "has been transformed into the enabling state." They suggested that in the enabling state, "social welfare transfers are interlaced throughout the fabric of modern capitalist society" (p. xii). According to this view, public resources should encourage and support private responsibility. A distinctively American approach, the enabling state would optimize the efficiencies and vitality of the private market while encouraging individual decisions that support social policy goals.

The risk, of course, is that vulnerable Americans will be left behind. Noting that "there is a tendency for this movement to dilute protection and aid for the weakest, most disadvantaged members of the community," the Gilberts argued that public policy must "temper the increasing concern for private responsibility with greater tolerance for public purpose" (pp. 185–186).

The enabling state is a capitalist view of the role and objectives of government. Government serves the purposes of the market, and social policy supports personal responsibility. Postindustrial socialists offer a sharply contrasting view.

THE BASIC INCOME

Baker (1987) offered a socialist critique of the welfare state, suggesting that "the present welfare state is a compromise which serves many interests. It helps people in need, but it also helps to keep them in their place. It is a system of support but also of control" (p. 10). Thus, the modern welfare state is seen as an agent of inequality—a device for sustaining an exploitative economic system. Socialist critiques extend to the free market, noting that it exploits workers, destroys the environment, and weakens social cohesion. The task of socialism, then, is to free the laborer from the market.

Postindustrial socialists advocate expansion of the social sphere of life. As Gorz (1994) explained, "The societal objective of productivity gains must be to bring about a contraction of the sphere governed by economic calculation and an expansion of the self-determined, self-organized spheres of activity in which human facilities can develop freely" (p. 20). According to this view, the technological developments of the 21st century could bring about "the end of work-based society" (Little, 1998, p. 19). Indeed, as a central tenet, postindustrial socialism rejects the link between work and survival.

We see a parallel argument about the impact of the market on the social life of Americans in Robert Putnam's book *Bowling Alone* (2000). In an exhaustive analysis, Putnam argued that recent decades have seen a decline in "civic engagement and social capital." Noting declining participation in a wide range of activities, including political, volunteer, religious, civic, and informal social events, Putnam traced these changes to the dominance of the economic market and to materialism. He went further, suggesting that these forces destroy neighborhoods and families and leave children in jeopardy. Putnam drew an analogy to the end of the 19th century, when the Gilded Age was marked by dramatic economic growth and weakened social ties. Calling for a return to "social capitalism," Putnam suggested that modern reformers draw inspiration from the early-20th-century Progressives who restored to the nation a measure of social commitment. His incremental approach fell short of postindustrial socialists' more far-reaching proposals to establish a "basic income."

The notion of a basic income, advanced by neo-Marxists, was actually introduced by Thomas Paine in his 1795 work, *Agrarian Justice*. The basic (or citizen's) income is a universal, unconditional benefit provided to all members of a society regardless of their work or household status. Supporters argue that the basic income would enhance productivity, in part by eliminating poverty and its attendant social and physical costs, but also by ensuring that those who choose to work (not to avoid poverty, but to increase their affluence and contribute to society) would be better qualified and more motivated. For example, Offe, Muckenberger, and Ostner (1996) argue that

> [i]t does not seem too far-fetched to assume that in wealthy industrial societies, citizens might be accorded the right to withdraw from paid work without penalty and at only the loss of income (but not poverty!) will as a result be better motivated, better qualified, and in a better physical and psychic condition to engage in it (for then they would be choosing it "voluntarily") than those from whom this choice is withheld, and who must consequently work knowing that non-engagement in paid work (or the failure of an attempted engagement in it) carries the threat of material need and social stigma. (p. 219)

Some, like Gorz (1985) and Atkinson (1996), have argued that a basic income is not enough to restore equity and community to postindustrial societies. Gorz suggested that, in addition to a more equitable distribution of income, society should provide an equitable distribution of the opportunity to contribute through work. In Gorz's view, an overall reduction in the number of hours worked should accompany the basic income to ensure that no one who is willing to work lacks the opportunity to do so. In another variation on the basic income proposal, Atkinson (1996) suggested that some kind of "social contribution" be required of those who receive the basic income. This contribution might entail being a good parent, a skilled artist, or an educated voter. Thus, rather than a basic income, the social welfare system would offer a "participation benefit."

Welfare capitalism and postindustrial socialism provide sharply contrasting visions. Certainly the enabling state was most compatible with the realities of 20th-century America. But the new century offers new opportunities, even as it demands new visions. Social workers may apply the notion of a basic income in their efforts to advance the cause of social justice. Of course, the practicality of any social welfare proposals will be determined by political realities.

CHANGING POLITICS

The end of the 20th century rekindled American enthusiasm for capitalism. The dissolution of the Soviet Union, the opening of Chinese markets, and the longest peacetime economic expansion in U.S. history all seemed to signal victory for the nation's dominant economic philosophy. This victory may have quieted the American Left, and it certainly gave impetus to what some describe as the "third wave" of American conservatism. With the 1994 election of a Republican majority in the House of Representatives, the nation seemed poised for a return to the laissez-faire politics of the 19th century. The Republican revolution was short-lived, however, and the "compassionate conservatism" of the George W. Bush administration came to sound remarkably like early-20th-century Progressivism. The president's rhetoric seemed to recognize the problems of the disadvantaged in his 2001 inaugural address:

> Where there is suffering, there is duty. Americans in need are not strangers, they are citizens; not problems, but priorities; and all of us are diminished when any are hopeless.

Although this rhetoric clearly did not foreshadow later developments, it did suggest that Bush recognized the power and attraction these ideas hold for the American electorate. Indeed, it may have indicated, as E.J. Dionne (1996) had argued five years earlier, that American Progressives "only look dead." Like Putnam, Dionne drew analogies between this turn of the century and the last. He suggested that during the economic transformation of the early 21st century Americans would look to a new Progressivism to restore a balance between the economic and the social spheres of life. Dionne articulated an agenda for New Progressives that might equally apply to social workers:

> [T]o succeed, a New Progressivism must be genuinely and not simply rhetorically new. Its task is to restore the legitimacy of public life by renewing the effectiveness of government and reforming the workings of politics.... The New Progressives are those who accept the need to make another large economic transition, but know that the transition will be successful only if government acts creatively, and with a strong concern for social justice. (pp. 16, 277)

As a presidential candidate Barack Obama took up this charge, galvanizing community activists in a campaign for change. It was hard to tell whether his landslide victory in 2008 signaled Americans' endorsement of a new progressive agenda or simply disgust with the failures of the previous administration. As president, Obama mobilized progressive activists and worked to increase public investment in health care, education, housing, and other domestic programs. Like Obama, President Trump entered the presidency with a strong mandate for change. Of course, as was true throughout the 2016 presidential campaign, the details of what, exactly, will change remain unclear.

Closing Reflections

Both policy practice and interpersonal practice of social work have been transformed by global developments. This illustrates an essential premise of chaos theory known as the "butterfly effect." Presented by MIT meteorologist Edward Lorenz in 1972, this premise holds that complex systems can be affected in unpredictable ways by small events. So the flap of a butterfly's wings in Brazil could set off a tornado in Texas. In the post-9/11 world we must see our social environment as a single complex system and recognize that simple acts of kindness or hatred have widespread consequences.

On September 11, 2001, American awareness of global issues was transformed by the murder of thousands of civilians. Terrorists attacked the citadels of U.S. economic and military power in a gesture of hatred unlike any this country had ever witnessed. Our nation's struggle to understand and respond to these attacks highlights many of the issues we have explored in this book.

Some attributed the violence to the "evil" tenets of Islamic fundamentalism. They labeled Muslims and Arabs "other" and used this as an excuse to persecute and harass them. But those who look beyond simple explanations found themselves reflecting on what social justice means in a global context, asking whether rich nations—out of enlightened self-interest, if nothing else—have an obligation to meet the basic needs of the world's disadvantaged. They asked whether the United States could responsibly withdraw from any international dialogue on oppression or social justice.

The terrorist attacks jarred us out of our complacency, awakening Americans to longstanding conditions in the Middle East. Isolated injustices such as the massive accumulation of wealth by elites in oil-rich nations became cause for concern. Then came the global recession, and in 2010, the regime of President Zine El Abidine Ben Ali of Tunisia fell to a massive campaign of civil resistance. This was the first of a series of protests that signaled the "Arab Spring." Governments in Egypt, Libya, and Yemen were forced from power, and uprisings erupted in other nations throughout the Middle East.

Then in 2011, **Occupy Wall Street** set up camp in Zuccotti Park, New York, and trumpeted its slogan, "We are the 99%." In the United States the movement raised public awareness about income inequality and corporate influence and, with it, the possibility of policy changes to address these problems. Through effective use of social and other media, the message echoed in protests around the world. Inequality, went from an obscure

Courtesy of Amanda Barusch

▶ Occupy Dunedin (New Zealand)

academic topic to a mainstay of political debates in the 2016 presidential election. And, with public awareness has come a growing call for change.

At the same time, the pursuit of environmental justice presents new opportunities and demands for social work advocates. Environmental risk—like many other risks—is disproportionately borne by poor people. This is true on both national and global scales. In the America, environmental contaminants (like lead, arsenic, and airborne pollutants) are concentrated in low-income, non-white communities. Global projections indicate that the effects of climate change will be particularly devastating in poor countries, whose governments lack the resources to insulate residents from extreme climate events, rising sea levels, and social disruption.

To respond to these changes and to stay relevant in the 21st century, social workers must be conversant not only with the traditional programs and policies of social welfare but also with environmental developments, tax law, labor regulations, global and domestic financial markets, and international debates about independence and democracy. We must look beyond labels and rhetoric to offer a vision of social welfare that takes into account environmental, economic, and political developments even as it advances the cause of social justice. We can draw inspiration from the Progressives of the past but must forge our own path, which will require unprecedented ingenuity. Our success will be measured on individual and global scales as we strive to eliminate the causes of hatred and build a world that offers liberty and justice for all.

Think About It

1. Noting that most of the poor in the United States have living space much larger than that of the average Japanese family, some would argue that America's poor are not disadvantaged. Do you agree or disagree with this statement? Why?

2. The 20th century was marked by rising inequality, yet life expectancies and, some would argue, the quality of life of the disadvantaged improved during this period. Does this improvement support the notion that inequality is the necessary price for expanding the economic pie? What are the implications of this observation for economic policies aimed at redistributing the nation's wealth?

3. Do you think the term "enabling state" accurately describes the role of the U.S. government in social welfare? Why or why not?

4. Dionne (1996) suggested that it is important for the New Progressives to "embrace the dual concepts of freedom and community." What does this mean to you? Are freedom and community compatible? Does community membership entail responsibilities and roles that limit individual freedom?

5. Do you think the WTO is more powerful than the U.N.? Consider the case of U.S. steel tariffs. Has the U.N. ever imposed sanctions on the United States? Has it ever declared a U.S. action in violation of international law?

6. Do you see any connections between Occupy America and the 2015 Sanders campaign?

Web-Based Exercises

For direct links to all the sites in these exercises, visit the *Foundations of Social Policy* Companion Site at www.cengagebrain.com and select the resources for Conclusion.

1. What's happening at the U.N.? Go to http://www.un.org/News and read the headlines from the U.N. News Centre. Select one of the stories to pursue in depth. What social justice implications do you see here? Anything of relevance to social workers and their clients?

2. What policy concerns are important to American manufacturers? Go to http://www .nam.org, the website of the National Association of Manufacturers (NAM). Under "Policy Issues" (and possibly in other locations as well), you will find material that gives a sense of the organization's priorities. How does the NAM feel about government regulations that protect worker safety? Environmental regulations? How about employee benefits? What do you see as the strengths and weaknesses of this organization's positions?

3. Visit www.ifsw.org and search the site for the definition of social work provided there by the International Federation of Social Workers. Is it congruent with your sense of the profession? Would you revise it in any way?

4. Will over-population become a social justice issue as humans compete for scarce natural resources, like water? Go to http://www.worldometers.info/world-population/ and watch the world's population grow. Scroll down to the top 20 largest countries by population, and see where that growth is concentrated.

Suggested Resources

Dominelli, L. (Ed). (2007). *Revitalising Communities in a Globalising World*. Hampshire, England: Ashgate.

Freire, P. (2000). *Pedagogy of the Oppressed* (Myra Bergman Ramos, Trans.). New York: Continuum. (Original work published in 1970).

International Social Work. This is the journal of three international social work organizations: the International Association of Schools of Social Work (IASSW), the International Council on Social Welfare (ICSW), and the International Federation of Social Workers (IFSW).

Koenig, M., & de Guchteneire, P. (Eds). (2007). *Democracy and Human Rights in Multicultural Societies*. Hampshire, England: Ashgate.

Loeb, P. R. (1999). *Soul of a Citizen: Living with Conviction in a Cynical Time*. New York: St. Martin's Griffin.

Mapp, S. C. (2008). *Human Rights and Social Justice in a Global Perspective: An Introduction to International Social Work*. New York: Oxford University Press.

Robertson, C. & Westerman, J. (Eds) (2015). *Working on Earth: Class and environmental justice*. University of Nevada Press.

Rothenberg, P. S. (2001). *Race, Class, and Gender in the United States: An Integrated Study*. New York: Worth Publishers. www.globalexchange.org. For a critical look at the activities of the IMF and the World Bank, visit this site, which is maintained by a human rights organization called Global Exchange. Founded in 1988 in San Francisco, Global Exchange is designed to increase global awareness in the United States.

www.imf.org. This site is maintained by the International Monetary Fund. In addition to a description of IMF activities, it provides research and statistics about economic issues and a link to the World Bank's site (www.worldbank.org).

www.un.org. The website of the United Nations offers a wealth of information about international issues as well as links to the websites of other international organizations.

www.wto.org. This site provides a fairly one-sided look at the mission and activities of the World Trade Organization.

References

Aarts, L. J. M., Burkhauser, R. V., & De Jong, P. R. (1996). *Curing the Dutch disease: An international perspective on disability policy reform* (International Studies on Social Security, Vol. 1). Farnham, Surrey, UK: Avebury Press.

Abraham Lincoln Online. (n.d.). Letter to Horace Greeley. Retrieved from http://www.abrahamlincolnonline.org/lincoln/speeches/greeley .htm (July 6, 2013).

Abramowitz, M. (1996). *Regulating the lives of women: Social welfare policy from colonial times to the present.* Boston: South End Press.

AbuDagga, A., Wolfe, S., Carome, M., Phatdouang, A., Torrey, E. F. (2016). *Individuals with serious mental illnesses in county jails: A survey of jail staff's perspectives.* (A joint effort of Public Citizen and the Treatment Advocacy Center.) Retrieved from http://www.citizen.org/documents/2330.pdf (September 15, 2016).

Achenbaum, W. A. (1978). *Old age in the new land: The American experience since 1790.* Baltimore: Johns Hopkins University Press.

Achenbaum, W. A. (1986). *Social Security: Visions and revisions.* Cambridge: Cambridge University Press.

Acierno, R., Hernandez, M., Amstadter, A., Resnick, H., Steve, K., Muzzy, W., & Kilpatrick, D. (2010). Prevalence and correlates of emotional, physical, sexual, and financial abuse and potential neglect in the United States: The National Elder Mistreatment Study. *American Journal of Public Health, 100,* 292–297.

Acs, G., & Loprest, P. (2007). *TANF Caseload Composition and Leavers Synthesis Report.* Retrieved from http://www.urban.org/UploadedPDF/411553_tanf_caseload.pdf (July 7, 2010).

Adams, M., Bell, L. A., & Griffin, P. (1997). *Teaching for diversity and social justice: A sourcebook.* New York: Routledge.

Administration for Children and Families. (2005). *Head Start impact study: First-year findings.* Retrieved from http://www.acf.hhs.gov/programs/opre/hs/impact_study/reports/first_yr_finds/firstyr_finds_title.html (December 30, 2007).

Administration for Children and Families. (2006). *AFCARS report #12: Final estimates for FY1998 through FY2002.* Retrieved from http://www.acf .hhs.gov/programs/cb/stats_research/afcars/tar/report12.htm (December 30, 2007).

Administration for Children and Families (2015). *The AFCARS Report, preliminary FY 2014 estimates as of July 2015.* Retrieved from http://www.acf.hhs.gov/sites/default/files/cb/afcarsreport22.pdf (December 6, 2016).

Administration on Aging. (1997). *Age discrimination: A pervasive and damaging influence.* Retrieved from http://www.aoa.gov/factsheets/ageism.html.

Administration on Aging. (2001). *Older Americans Act appropriation information.* Retrieved from http://www.aoa.gov/oaa/oaaapp.html.

Administration on Aging. (2011). *A profile of older Americans: 2011.* Retrieved from http://www.aoa .gov/Aging_Statistics/Profile/2011/docs/2011profile.pdf (November 8, 2013).

Administration on Aging. (2014). *A profile of older Americans: 2014.* Retrieved from http://www.aoa.acl.gov/aging_statistics/profile/2014/docs/2014-profile.pdf (November 8, 2016).

AFL-CIO. (2015). *The fight for better trade policy isn't over.* Retrieved from http://www.aflcio.org/About/Exec-Council/EC-Statements/The-Fight-for-Better-Trade-Policy-Isn-t-Over (November 13, 2016).

AIDS.gov. (n.d.) *Do you have to tell?* Retrieved from https://www.aids.gov/hiv-aids-basics/just-diagnosed-with-hiv-aids/talking-about-your-status/do-you-have-to-tell/index.html (October 30, 2016).

Albrecht, S. F., Skiba, R. J., Losen, D. J., Chung, C., & Middelberg, L. (2012). Federal policy on disproportionality in special education: Is it moving us forward? *Journal of Disability Policy Studies, 23*(1), 14–25.

Alexander, A. (2012). *The new Jim Crow: Mass incarceration in the age of colorblindness.* New York: The New Press.

Alexander, J. C., Eyerman, R., Giesen, B., Smelser, N. J., & Piotr, S. (2004). *Cultural trauma and collective identity.* Berkeley: University of California Press.

Alinsky, S. (1972). *Rules for radicals: A pragmatic primer for realistic radicals.* New York: Random House.

Allard, M. A., Albelda, R., Colten, M. E., & Cosenza, C. (1997). *In harm's way? Domestic violence, AFDC receipt, and welfare reform in Massachusetts*. A report from the University of Massachusetts, Boston.

Altman, D. (1999). Globalization, political economy, and HIV/AIDS. *Theory and Society, 28,* 559–584.

Altmeyer, A. J. (1966). The Formative Years of Social Security. Madison: University of Wisconsin Press.

American Academy of Matrimonial Lawyers. (2007). *Report of the American Academy of Matrimonial Lawyers on considerations when determining alimony spousal support, or maintenance.* Retrieved from http://www.aaml.org/library/articles/considerations-when-determining-alimony.

American City Bureau. (2009). *Giving USA 2009 – The annual report on philanthropy.* Retrieved from http://www.acb-inc.com/wp-content/uploads/Giving-USA-2009-Key-Findings.pdf (September 1, 2013).

American Civil Liberties Union (ACLU). (n.d.) *The prison crisis.* Retrieved from https://www.aclu.org/prison-crisis (November 27, 2016).

American Civil Liberties Union (ACLU). (1996). *English only: ACLU briefing paper.* Retrieved from http://www.aclu.org/library/pbp6.html.

American Civil Liberties Union. (ACLU). (2010). *Affirmative action.* Retrieved from http://www.aclu.org/womens-rights/affirmative-action (September 1, 2013).

American Civil Liberties Union. (ACLU). (2013). *As the drug testing dragnet widens, the poor continue to be swept in.* Retrieved from http://www.aclu.org/blog/criminal-law-reform-racial-justice/drug-testing-dragnet-widens-poor-continue-be-swept (May 21, 2013).

American Medical Association. (n.d.). *AMA policies on LGBT issues.* Retrieved from http://www.ama-assn.org//ama/pub/about-ama/our-people/member-groups-sections/glbt-advisory-committee/ama-policy-regarding-sexual-orientation.page (August 30, 2013).

American Psychiatric Association. (n.d.). *DSM-5 development.* Retrieved from http://www.dsm5.org/Pages/Default.aspx (June 9, 2013).

American Public Health Association. (n.d.). *Medicaid expansion.* Retrieved from http://www.apha.org/APHA/CMS_Templates/GeneralArticle.aspx? NRMODE=Published&NRNODEGUID={D5E1C04A-0438-4FD4-A423-CEFDA0D9878D}&NRORIGINALURL=%2fadvocacy%2fHealth%2bReform%2fACAbasics%2fmedicaid.htm&NRCACHEHINT=NoModifyGuest#Medi6 (May 6, 2013).

Americans for Tax Fairness. (2014). *Walmart on Tax Day: How taxpayers subsidize America's biggest employer and richest family.* Retrieved from http://www.americansfortaxfairness.org/files/Walmart-on-Tax-Day-Americans-for-Tax-Fairness-1.pdf (July 7, 2016).

Anderson, M. J. (2004). *Understanding rape shield laws.* National Alliance to End Sexual Violence. Retrieved from http://www.naesv.org/Resources/Articles/UnderstandingRapeShieldLaws.pdf (September 12, 2010).

Anderson, S., Cavanagh, J., Collins, C., Pizzigati, S., & Lapham, M. (2008). *Executive excess 2008: How average taxpayers subsidize runaway pay.* 15th Annual CEO Compensation Survey. Washington, DC: Institute for Policy Studies. Retrieved from http://www.faireconomy.org/files/executive_ excess_2008.pdf (May 3, 2009).

Appelbaum, N., Macpherson, A. S., & Rosemblatt, K. A. (Eds.). (2003). *Race and nation in modern Latin America.* Chapel Hill, NC: University of North Carolina Press.

Appelbaum, P. S. (1994). *Almost a revolution: Mental health law and the limits of change.* New York: Oxford University Press.

Aries, P. (1962). *Centuries of childhood: A social history of family life* (Robert Baldick, Trans.). New York: Vintage Books.

Aronowitz, S. (2012, January 1). Reflections on the Madison Uprising. *South Atlantic Quarterly, 111*(1), 214–222.

Atkinson, A. (1996, January–March). The case for a participation income. *Political Quarterly, 67,* 1.

Autor, D. (2011). *The unsustainable rise of the disability rolls in the United States: Causes, consequences, and policy options.* NBER Working Paper No. 17697. Retrieved from http://ssrn.com/abstract=1987244 (June 19, 2013).

Autor, D. (2014). Skills, education, and the rise of earnings inequality among the "other 99 percent." *Science, 344*(6186), 843–851.

Avalos, M., Affigne, A. D., & Travis, T. (1997, August). *Race, land, money and power: The persistence of racial stratification in Brazil and the U.S.* Paper presented at the Annual Meeting of the American Political Science Association, Washington, DC. Retrieved from http://www.providence.edu/polisci/affigne/pdf/brasil_u.s.pdf (December 11, 2007).

AVERT. (n.d.). *Worldwide HIV & AIDS statistics* (from UNAIDS). Retrieved from http://www.avert.org/worldstats.htm (July 13, 2010).

Ayers, E. (1984). *Vengeance and justice: Crime and punishment in the 19th century American South.* New York: Oxford University Press.

Ayvazian, A. S. (2001). Interrupting the cycle of oppression: The role of allies as agents of change. In P. S. Rothenberg (Ed.), *Race, class, and gender in the United States: An integrated study* (pp. 609–615). New York: Worth Publishers.

Badgett, M., Lee, V., Lau, H., Sears, B., & Ho, D. (2007). *Bias in the workplace: Consistent evidence of sexual orientation and gender identity discrimination.* Report, Williams Institute, University of California School of Law. Retrieved from http://williamsinstitute.law.ucla.edu/wp-content/uploads/Badgett-Sears-Lau-Ho-Bias-in-the-Workplace-Jun-2007.pdf (October 8, 2013).

Baily, M. N., & Bosworth, B. P. (2014). US manufacturing: Understanding its past and its potential future. *Journal of Economic Perspectives, 28*(1), 3–26. Retrieved from https://www.brookings.edu/wp-content/uploads/2016/06/us-manufacturing-past-and-potential-future-baily-bosworth.pdf (November 13, 2016).

Baker, J. (1987). *Arguing for equality.* London & New York: Verso.

Ball, H. (2000). *The Bakke case: Race, education and affirmative action.* Topeka: University Press of Kansas.

Ball, R. M. (1996). Medicare's roots: What Medicare's architects had in mind. *Generations, 20*(2), 13–18.

Barker, E. (Ed.). (1962). *The politics of Aristotle.* Cambridge, MA: Oxford University Press.

Barnett, W. (1973). *Sexual freedom and the Constitution.* Albuquerque: University of New Mexico Press.

Baronov, D. (2003). Colonial rule, AIDS, and social control in Puerto Rico. *Socialism and Democracy, 17*(34, No. 2), 171–189.

Barr, D. A. (2007). *Health disparities in the United States: Social class, race, ethnicity, and health.* Baltimore: Johns Hopkins University Press.

Barusch, A. S. (1995). Programming for family care: Mandates, incentives and rationing. *Social Work, 40*(3), 315–322.

Bass, S. A., Caro, F. G., & Chen, Y. (Eds.). (1993). *Achieving a productive aging society.* Westport, CT: Greenwood.

BBC News. (2015). *Bill Clinton regrets 'three strikes' bill.* Retrieved from http://www.bbc.com/news/world-us-canada-33545971 (November 28, 2016).

Bean, F., & Tienda, M. (1987). *The Hispanic population of the United States.* New York: Russell Sage.

Beard, J. H., Propst, R. N., & Malamud, T. J. (1982). The Fountain House model of psychiatric rehabilitation. *Psychosocial Rehabilitation Journal, 5,* 47–53.

Beck, D. L. (2004, January/February). Health, wealth and the Chinese Oedipus. *Society,* 64–67.

Beers, C. W. (1908). *A mind that found itself: An autobiography.* Garden City, NJ: Doubleday, Doran, & Co.

Bell, L. A. (1997). Theoretical foundations for social justice education. In M. Adams, L. A. Bell, & P. Griffin (Eds.), *Teaching for diversity and social justice: A sourcebook* (pp. 3–15). New York: Routledge.

Belle, D. (1984). Inequality and mental health: Low-income and minority women. In L. E. Walker (Ed.), *Women and mental health policy* (pp. 135–150). Beverly Hills: Sage.

Bentele, K. G., & Nicoli, L. T. (2012). Ending access as we know it: State welfare benefit coverage in the TANF era. *Social Service Review, 86*(2), 223–268.

Bergman-Evans, B. (2004). Beyond the basics: Effects of the Eden Alternative model on quality of life issues. *Journal of Gerontological Nursing, 30*(6), 27–34.

Berkowitz, E. D. (1987). *Disabled policy: America's programs for the handicapped.* Cambridge: Cambridge University Press.

Berkowitz, E. D. (2000, July 13). *Disability policy and history: Statement before the Subcommittee on Social Security of the Committee on Ways and Means.* Retrieved from http://www.ssa.gov/history/edberkdib.html.

Bernstein, J., McNichol, E., Mishel, L., & Zahradnik, R. (2000). *Pulling apart: A state-by-state analysis of income trends.* Washington, DC: Center on Budget and Policy Priorities. Economic Policy Institute. Retrieved from http://www.cbpp.org/l-18-00sfp-partl.pdf.

Beronio, K., Po, R., Skopec, L., & Glied, S. (2013). *ASPE Issue Brief: Affordable Care Act expands mental health and substance use disorder benefits and federal parity protections for 62 million Americans.* Retrieved from http://aspe.hhs.gov/health/reports/2013/mental/rb_mental.cfm (June 11, 2013).

Besharov, D. J., Myers, J. A., & Morrow, J. S. (2007). *Costs per child for early childhood education and care: Comparing Head Start, CCDF child care, and prekindergarten/preschool programs (2003/2004).* American Enterprise Institute for Public Policy Research. Retrieved from http://www.welfareacademy.org/pubs/childcare_edu/costperchild.pdf (August 5, 2010).

Betts, J. R., & Tang, Y. E. (2011). *The effect of charter schools on student achievement: A meta-analysis of the literature.* National Charter School Research Project. Retrieved from http://www.crpe.org/sites/default/files/pub_NCSRP_BettsTang_Oct11_0.pdf (September 8, 2013).

Biblarz, T. J., & Stacey, J. (2010). How does the gender of parents matter? *Journal of Marriage and Family, 72*(1), 3–22.

Bilder, S., & Mechanic, D. (2003). Navigating the disability process: Persons with mental disorders applying for and receiving disability benefits. *Milbank Quarterly, 81*(1), 75–106.

Bindman, A. B., Chattopadhyay, A., Osmund, D. G., Huen, W., & Bachetti, P. (2005). The impact of Medicaid managed care on hospitalizations for ambulatory care sensitive conditions. *Health Services Research, 40*(1), 19–38.

Binstock, R. H. (1983). The aged as scapegoat. *Gerontologist, 23,* 136–143.

Binstock, R. H. (1985). Perspectives on measuring hardship: Concepts, dimensions, and implications. *Gerontologist, 26,* 60–62.

Binstock, R. H., & Post, S. G. (Eds.). (1991). *Too old for health care? Controversies in medicine, law, and ethics.* Baltimore: Johns Hopkins University Press.

Blau, J. R., & Blau, P. M. (1982). The cost of inequality: Metropolitan structure and violent crime. *American Sociological Review, 47,* 114–129.

Blenkner, M., Bloom, M., & Nielson, M. (1971). A research and demonstration project of protective services. *Social Casework, 52,* 483–499.

Bluestone, B. (1994). The inequality express. *American Prospect, 20,* 81–93.

Blumberg, L. J. (2010). *How will the PPACA impact individual and small group premiums in the short and long term?* Urban Institute. Retrieved from http://www.urban.org/uploadedpdf/412128-PPACA-impact.pdf (July 15, 2010).

Blumberg, P. (1980). *Inequality in an age of decline.* New York: Oxford University Press.

Bonnie, R. J., Reinhard, J. S., Hamilton, P., & McGarvey, E. L. (2013). Mental health system transformation after the Virginia Tech tragedy. *Health Affairs, 32*(6), 793–804. doi:10.1377/hlthaff.28.3.93.

Bostock, D. (2000). *Aristotle's ethics.* New York: Oxford University Press.

Bouma, D. H., & Hoffman, J. (1968). *The dynamics of school integration: Problems and approaches in a northern city.* Grand Rapids, MI: Eardmans.

Boy Scouts of America. (2013). *Boy Scouts of America statement.* Retrieved from http://www.scouting.org/sitecore/content/MembershipStandards/Resolution/results.aspx (August 30, 2013).

Brace, C. L. (1872). *The dangerous classes of New York and twenty years' work among them.* New York: Wynkoop & Hallenbeck. (Reprinted in 1973 by NASW Press.).

Bremner, R. H. (Ed.). (1970). *Children and youth in America: A documentary history, 1600–1865* (Vol. 1). Cambridge, MA: Harvard University Press.

Brennan Center. (n.d.). *Right to vote: Key decisions in felony disenfranchisement litigation.* Retrieved from http://www.brennancenter.org/sites/default/files/legacy/d/download_file_36480.pdf (July 17, 2013).

Brody, E. M. (1971). Aging. In *The encyclopedia of social work* (pp. 55–77). New York: National Association of Social Workers Press.

Brown, D., Kowalski, A., & Lurie, I. (2015). *Medicaid as an investment in children: What is the long-term impact on tax receipts?* National Bureau of Economic Research, Working Paper 20835. Retrieved from http://www.nber.org/papers/w20835 (June 16, 2016).

Brown, E. J. (2009). Health care reform and disability rights. *Advance,* December. Retrieved from http://occupational-therapy.advanceweb.com/Article/Health-Care-Reform-andDisabilityRights.aspx (July 21, 2010).

Brown, R. S., Clement, D. G., Hill, J. W., Retchin, S. M., & Bergeron, J. W. (1993). Do health maintenance organizations work for Medicare? *Health Care Financing Review, 15*(1), 7–23.

Brown, T. J. (1998). *Dorothea Dix: New England reformer.* Cambridge, MA: Harvard University Press.

Bryan, P. (1994). Reclaiming professionalism: The lawyer's role in divorce mediation. *Family Law Quarterly, 2,* 177–222.

Buder, S. (2009). *Capitalizing on change: A social history of American business.* Chapel Hill, NC: University of North Carolina Press.

Bureau of Justice Assistance. (1994). *Understanding Community Policing: A framework for action.* Retrieved from https://www.ncjrs.gov/pdffiles/commp.pdf (November 28, 2016).

Bureau of Justice Statistics. (1987). *Violent crime trends: Special report.* Retrieved from https://www.bjs.gov/content/pub/pdf/vct.pdf (November 22, 2016).

Bureau of Labor Statistics. (n.d.c.). *Labor force statistics from the Current Population Survey/ Discouraged Workers/Historical Data Series.* Retrieved from http://www.bls.gov/cps/lfcharacteristics.htm#discouraged (December 11, 2016).

Bureau of Labor Statistics. (2001). *How the government measures unemployment.* Retrieved from http://www.bis.gov/cps/cps_htgm.htm (January 21, 2008).

Bureau of Labor Statistics. (2009a). *Employee benefits in the United States, March 2009.* Retrieved from http://www.bls.gov/news.release/pdf/ebs2.pdf (May 7, 2010).

Bureau of Labor Statistics. (2010, April). *Current employment statistics highlights.* Retrieved from http://www.bls.gov/web/empsit/ceshighlights.pdf (May 7, 2010).

Bureau of Labor Statistics. (2015a). *TED: The Economics Daily: Median weekly earnings by educational attainment in 2014.* Retrieved from http://www.bls.gov/opub/ted/2015/median-weekly-earnings-by-education-gender-race-and-ethnicity-in-2014.htm (November 13, 2016).

Bureau of Labor Statistics. (2015b). *BLS reports: Labor force characteristics by race and ethnicity, 2014.* Retrieved from http://www.bls.gov/opub/reports/race-and-ethnicity/archive/labor-force-characteristics-by-race-and-ethnicity-2014.pdf (November 13, 2016).

Bureau of Labor Statistics. (2015c). *Occupational employment and wages, May 2015* (21-1092: Probation Officers and Correctional Treatment Specialists). Retrieved from http://www.bls.gov/oes/current/oes211092.htm (November 28, 2016).

Bureau of Labor Statistics. (2016a). *Union members summary.* Retrieved from http://www.bls.gov/news.release/union2.nr0.htm (November 11, 2016).

Bureau of Labor Statistics. (2016b). *Characteristics of minimum wage workers, 2015.* Retrieved from http://www.bls.gov/opub/reports/minimum-wage/2015/home.htm (November 11, 2016).

Bureau of Labor Statistics. (2016c). *Employment characteristics of families summary* (Economic News Release). Retrieved from http://www.bls.gov/news.release/famee.nr0.htm (November 13, 2016).

Bureau of Prisons. (2015). Annual determination of average cost of incarceration. *Federal Register Notice.* Retrieved from https://www.federalregister.gov/documents/2015/03/09/2015-05437/annual-determination-of-average-cost-of-incarceration (November 28, 2016).

Burkhauser, R., & Daly, M. (2011). *The declining work and welfare of people with disabilities: What went wrong and a strategy for change.* Washington, DC: AEI Press.

Burton, C. E. (1992). *The poverty debate: Politics and the poor in America.* Westport, CT: Greenwood Press.

Butler, J. (2004). *Undoing gender.* Oxfordshire: Routledge.

Butler, J. D. (1896). British convicts shipped to American colonies. *The American Historical Review, 2*(1), 12–33. Retrieved from https://www.jstor.org/stable/pdf/1833611.pdf (November 19, 2016).

Butler, R. N., Oberlink, M. R., & Schechter, M. (Eds.). (1990). *Promise of productive aging: From biology to social policy.* New York: Springer.

Butler, S., Lave, J., & Reuschauer, R. D. (1998). *Medicare: Preparing for the challenges of the 21st century.* Washington, DC: National Academy of Social Insurance (distributed by Brookings Institution Press).

Byrom, B. (2001). A pupil and a patient: Hospital-schools in progressive America. In P. K. Longmore & L. Umansky (Eds.), *The new disability history: American perspectives* (pp. 133–156). New York: New York University Press.

Caffey, J. (1946). Multiple fractures in the long bones of infants suffering from chronic subdural hematoma. *American Journal of Roentgenology, 56,* 163–173.

Callahan, D. (1987). *Setting limits: Medical goals in an aging society.* New York: Simon & Schuster.

Callahan, D. (1990). *What kind of life: The limits of medical progress.* New York: Simon & Schuster.

Camejo, P. (1976). *Racism, revolution, reaction, 1861–1877: The rise and fall of radical reconstruction.* New York: Monad.

Caputo, R. K. (2009). EITC & TANF participation among young adult low-income families. *Northwestern Journal of Law and Social Policy, 4,* 136–149. Retrieved from http://www.law .northwestern.edu/journals/njlsp/v4/n1/8/8Caputo.pdf (November 10, 2010).

Carboni, J. L., & Milward, H. B. (2012). Governance, privatization, and systemic risk in the disarticulated state. *Public Administration Review, 72*(1), 36–44.

Cash, S. J., & Bridge, J. A. (2009). Epidemiology of youth suicide and suicidal behavior. *Current Opinion in Pediatrics, 21*(5), 613–619.

Castner, L., & Cody, S. (1999). *Trends in FSP participation rates: Focus on September 1999.* Retrieved from http://www.fns.usda.gov/oane/MENU/published/FSP/FILES/trends97.pdf.

Cavalieri, S. (2011). Between victim and agent: A third-wave feminist account of trafficking for sex work. *Indiana Law Journal, 86*(4), 1409–1458. Retrieved from http://ilj.law.indiana.edu/articles/86/86_4_cavalieri.pdf (May 16, 2013).

Center for Education Reform. (1999). *Just the FAQs— School choice.* Retrieved from http://www.edreform .com/faq/faqsc.htm.

Center for Health Care Strategies. (2010). *Medicaid by the numbers.* Retrieved from http://www.chcs.org/usr_doc/Medicaid_Fact_Sheet.pdf (October 21, 2010).

Center for Muslim-Jewish Engagement. (n.d.). *AL-TAWBA (Repentance, dispensation).* Retrieved from http://www.usc.edu/schools/college/crcc/engagement/resources/Stexts/muslim/quran/009 .qmt.html (July 19, 2010).

Center for Public Education. (n.d.). *Charter schools: Finding out the facts: At a glance.* Retrieved from http://www.centerforpubliceducation.org/Main-Menu/Organizing-a-school/Charter-schools-Finding-out-the-facts-At-a-glance (October 21, 2016).

Center for Responsible Lending. (n.d.). *Payday lending: How a short-term loan becomes long-term debt.* Retrieved from http://www .responsiblelending.org/payday-lending/.

Center on Budget and Policy Priorities. (2003). *Why are states' Medicaid expenditures rising?* Retrieved from http://www.cbpp. org/cms/index.cfm?fa=view&id=1409 (July 9, 2010).

Center on Budget and Policy Priorities. (2013). *Policy basics: The Earned Income Tax Credit.* Retrieved from http://www.cbpp.org/cms/?fa=view&id=2505 (October 27, 2013).

Center on Budget and Policy Priorities. (2015). *A quick guide to SNAP eligibility and benefits.* Retrieved from http://www.cbpp.org/research/a-quick-guide-to-snap-eligibility-and-benefits (July 7, 2016).

Center on Juvenile and Criminal Justice. (2007). *Race and juvenile justice system.* Retrieved from http://webmail.cjcj.org/jjic/race_jj.php (October 25, 2013).

Centers for Disease Control and Prevention (CDC). (n.d.a). *CDC fact sheet: New HIV infections in the United States.* Retrieved from http://www.cdc.gov/nchhstp/newsroom/docs/2012/HIV-Infections-2007-2010. pdf (June 1, 2013).

Centers for Disease Control and Prevention (CDC). (n.d.b.) Diabetes Data & Trends. Retrieved from http://www.cdc.gov/diabetes/statistics/prevalence_national.htm (June 1, 2013).

Centers for Disease Control and Prevention (CDC). (1999, August 27). Progress towards the elimination of tuberculosis, United States, 1999. *MMWR, 48*(33), 732–736. Retrieved from http://www.cdc.gov/epo/mmwr/preview/mmwrhtm Umm4833a2.htm.

Centers for Disease Control and Prevention (CDC). (2003). *Costs of intimate partner violence against women in the United States.* Retrieved from http://www.cdc.gov/violenceprevention/pdf/IPVBook-a.pdf (August 9, 2010).

Centers for Disease Control and Prevention (CDC). (2007). *American Indian and Alaska Native populations.* Retrieved from http://www.cdc.gov/omhd/Populations/AIAN/AIAN.htm (December 13, 2007).

Centers for Disease Control and Prevention (CDC). (2011). *QuickStats: Life expectancy at birth, by race and sex— United States, 2000–2009.* Retrieved from http://www.cdc.gov/mmwr/preview/mmwrhtml/mm6018a5.htm?s_cid=mm6018a5_w (June 2, 2013).

Centers for Disease Control and Prevention (CDC). (2015b). *National suicide statistics.* Retrieved from http://www.cdc.gov/violenceprevention/suicide/statistics (October 21, 2016).

Centers for Disease Control and Prevention (CDC). (2016). *HIV in the United States: At a glance.* Retrieved from http://www.cdc.gov/hiv/statistics/overview/ataglance.html (August 31, 2016).

Centers for Medicare & Medicaid Services. (n.d.b.). *Medicare and your mental health benefits.* Retrieved from https://www.medicare.gov/Pubs/pdf/10184-Medicare-Mental-Health-Bene.pdf (September 16, 2016).

Century Foundation. (2005). *Chile's privatization failures.* Retrieved from http://www.tcf.org/list.asp?type=NC&pubid=962 (June 30, 2010).

Cerne, F. (1995, March 20). Streetwise. *Hospitals and Health Networks,* 38–46.

Chalfant, H. P. (1985). *Sociology of poverty in the United States: An annotated bibliography.* Westport, CT: Greenwood.

Chalk, M. (1997). Privatizing public mental health and substance abuse services: Issues, opportunities, and challenges. *Quality Management in Health Care, 5*(2), 55–64.

Chamberlain, E. (1994, November/December). Blues for single-payer. *Humanist, 54*(6), 3–7.

Chambers, D. E. (1982). The U.S. poverty line: A time for change. *Social Work, 27*(4), 354–358.

Chambers, D. (2000). *Social policy and social programs: A method for the practical public policy analyst* (3rd ed.). New York: Macmillan.

Chandler, S., & Jones, J. (2003). Because a better world is possible: Women casino workers, union activism and the creation of a just workplace. *Journal of Sociology and Social Welfare, 30*(4), 57–78.

Chapin Hall Center for Children. (2009). *Racial and ethnic disparity and disproportionality in child welfare and juvenile justice: A compendium.* Chicago: University of Chicago Press. Retrieved from http://cjjr.georgetown.edu/pdfs/cjjr_ch_final.pdf (August 7, 2010).

Chapman, A. R., & van der Merwe, H. (2008). Assessing the South African transitional justice model. In A. R. Chapman & H. van der Merwe (Eds.), *Truth and reconciliation in South Africa: Did the TRC deliver?* (pp. 1–22). Philadelphia: University of Pennsylvania Press.

Chavez, L. (1991). *Out of the barrio: Toward a new politics of Hispanic assimilation.* New York: Basic Books.

Cherny, R. W., Issel, W., & Taylor, K. W. (2004). Introduction. In R. W. Cherny, W. Issel, & K. W. Taylor (Eds.), *American labor and the Cold War: Grassroots politics and postwar political culture* (pp. 1–7). Piscataway, NJ: Rutgers University Press.

Child Welfare League of America. (1997). *Breaking the link between child maltreatment and juvenile delinquency.* Washington, DC: CWLA.

Children's Bureau. (2015). *Foster care statistics.* Child Welfare Information Gateway. Retrieved from https://www.childwelfare.gov/pubPDFs/foster.pdf#page=9&view=Race and ethnicity (October 20, 2016).

Chinn, T., Lai, H. J., & Choy, P. (1969). *A history of the Chinese in California.* San Francisco: Chinese Historical Society of America.

Chipungu, S. S., & Bent-Goodley, T. B. (2004). Meeting the challenges of contemporary foster care. *Future of Children, 14*(1), 75–93. Retrieved from http://www.futureofchildren.org.

Cho, S. (2014). *3P Anti-trafficking Policy Index 2013 Report.* Retrieved from http://www.economics-human-trafficking.org/mediapool/99/998280/data/3P_Index_2013_Report_1_.pdf (June 7, 2016).

Christianson, S. (1998). *With liberty for some: 500 years of imprisonment in America.* Boston: Northeastern University Press.

Church, P., & Minter, S. (2000). *Transgender equality: A handbook for activists and policymakers.* Washington, DC: National Gay and Lesbian Task Force. Retrieved from http://www.thetaskforce.org.

Churchill, W. (1998). *A little matter of genocide: Holocaust and denial in the Americas, 1492 to the present.* San Francisco: City Lights Books.

Cingano, F. (2014). *Trends in income inequality and its impact on economic growth.* OECD Social, Employment, and Migration Working Papers, No. 163, OECD Publishing. Retrieved from http://dx.doi.org/10.1787/5jxrjncwxv6j-en.

Citrin, J., Reingold, B., Walters, E., & Green, D. P. (1990). The official English movement and the symbolic politics of language in the United States. *Western Political Quarterly, 43*(3), 553–560.

Clain, S. H. (2008). How living wage legislation affects U.S. poverty rates. *Journal of Labor Research, 29*(3), 205–218.

Clement, M. (1997). *The juvenile justice system: Law and process.* Boston, MA: Butterworth Heinemann.

Clines, F. (1997, May 31). Drill sergeant gets 6 months for sex abuse at army post. *The New York Times.* Retrieved from http://www.nytimes.com/1997/05/31/us/drill-sergeant-gets-6-months-for-sex-abuse-at-army-post.html (September 29, 2013).

Close Up Foundation. (1998). *U.S. immigration policy.* Retrieved from http://www.closeup.org/immigrat.htm.

Cohen, N. (2005, January 11). A bloody mess. *The American Prospect.* Retrieved from http://www .prospect.org/cs/articles?articleId=8997 (June 30, 2010).

Cohen, R. (2014). Does "Pay for Success" actually pay off? The ROI of social impact bonds. *Nonprofit Quarterly.* Retrieved from https://nonprofitquarterly.org/2014/10/17/does-pay-for-success-actually-pay-off-the-roi-of-social-impact-bonds/June 11, 2016.

Cohen, W. S. (1994). *Tax dollars aiding and abetting addiction: Social Security disability and SSI cash benefits to drug addicts and alcoholics.* Investigative Staff Report of the Minority Staff of the Senate Special Committee on Aging.

Cohn, N. (2016, November 9). Why Trump won: Working-class whites. *The New York Times.* Retrieved from http://www.nytimes.com/2016/11/10/upshot/why-trump-won-working-class-whites.html?_r=0 (November 13, 2016).

Coleman, M. T., Looney, S., O'Brien, J., Ziegler, C., Pastorino, C. A., & Turner, C. (2002). The Eden Alternative: Findings after one year of implementation. *Journal of Gerontology: Series A, Biological and Medical Sciences, 57*(7), M422–M427.

Commission of the European Communities. (1982). *Memorandum on the reduction and reorganization of working time.* Brussels: Author.

Common Core State Standards Initiative. (n.d.). *Implementing the Common Core State Standards.* Retrieved from http://www.corestandards.org/ (September 8, 2013).

Conger, R., Elder, G. H., Lorenz, F. O., Simons, R. L., & Whitbeck, L. B. (1994). *Families in troubled times: Adapting to change in rural America.* New York: Aldine De Gruyter.

Congressional Budget Office. (2010). *Health care: Cost estimates for health care legislation.* Retrieved from http://www.cbo.gov/publications/collections/health .cfm (July 14, 2010).

Congressional Budget Office (CBO). (2013). *S. 744, Border Security, Economic Opportunity, and Immigration Modernization Act.* Retrieved from https://www.cbo.gov/publication/44397 (January 1, 2017).

Congressional Research Service. (2002, April 18). *The USA PATRIOT Act: A sketch.* Order code RS21203. Retrieved from http://www.fas.org/irp/crs/RS21203.pdf.

Congressional Research Service. (2014). *Drug enforcement in the United States: History, policy, and trends.* By Lisa N. Sacco. Retrieved from https://www.fas.org/sgp/crs/misc/R43749.pdf (November 27, 2016).

Congressional Research Service. (2016). *FY2017 appropriations for the Department of Justice.* Nathan James, Analyst. Retrieved from https://www.fas.org/sgp/crs/misc/R44424.pdf (November 28, 2016).

Conrad, P. (1986, Summer). The social meaning of AIDS. *Social Policy, 17*(1), 51–56.

Consumer Financial Protection Bureau. (2013, April 24). *Payday loans and deposit advance products: A white paper of initial data findings.* Retrieved from http://files.consumerfinance.gov/f/201304_cfpb_payday-dap-whitepaper.pdf (May 21, 2013).

Cook, D. (1989). *Rich law, poor law.* Philadelphia, PA: Open University Press.

Cook, F. L. (1996). *Can public support for programs for older Americans survive?* Retrieved from http://www.northwestern.edu/IPR/publications/nupr/nuprvOlnl/cook.html.

Coplin, W. D., & O'Leary, M. K. (1998). *Public policy skills* (3rd ed.). Croton-on-Hudson, NY: Policy Studies Associates.

Corak, M. (2013a). Inequality from generation to generation: The United States in Comparison.

In R. Rycroft (Ed.), *The economics of inequality, poverty, and discrimination* (pp. 107–126). New York: Praeger.

Corak, M. (2013b). Income inequality, equality of opportunity, and intergenerational mobility. *Journal of Economic Perspectives, 27*(3), 79–102.

Costin, L. B. (1992). Cruelty to children: A dormant issue and its rediscovery, 1920–1960. *Social Service Review, 66,* 177–198.

Cotchett, J. W. (2004, July 11). Water wars: California's liquid gold shouldn't be entrusted to private conglomerates. *San Francisco Chronicle,* p. El.

Council on American-Islamic Relations (CAIR). (2004). *2004 Civil Rights Report: Unpatriotic Acts.* Retrieved from https://www.cair.com/civil-rights/civil-rights-reports/2004.html (December 6, 2016).

Courtney-Long, L. A., Carroll, D. D., Zhang, Q. C., Stevens, A. C., Griffin-Blake, S., Armour, B., & Campbell, V. (2015). *Prevalence of Disability and Disability Type Among Adults – United States, 2013.* Centers for Disease Control and Prevention (CDC). Retrieved from https://www.cdc.gov/mmwr/preview/mmwrhtml/mm6429a2.htm (September 20, 2016).

Cowell, A. J., Broner, N., & Dupont, R. (2004). The cost-effectiveness of criminal justice diversion programs for people with serious mental illness co-occurring with substance abuse: Four case studies. *Journal of Contemporary Criminal Justice, 20*(3), 292–314.

Cox, M. W. (1994). *Make adoption policies colorblind.* Retrieved from http://majorcox.com/columns/adoption.htm.

Cox, O. (1970). *Caste, class, and race: A study in social dynamics.* New York: Monthly Review Press.

Crain, R. L. (1968). *The politics of desegregation: Comparative case studies of community structure and policy-making.* Chicago: Aldine.

Crawford, J. (1992). *Language loyalties: A sourcebook on the official English controversy.* Chicago: University of Chicago Press.

Crawford, J. (1996). *Anatomy of the English-only movement: Social and ideological sources of language restrictionism in the United States.* Conference on Language Legislation and Linguistic Rights. University of Illinois at Urbana-Champaign. Retrieved from http://ourworld.compuserve.com/homepages/JWCRAWFORD/anatomy.htm.

Crimmins, E. M., Jung, K. K., & Sole-Auro, A. (2011). Gender differences in health: Results from SHARE, ELSA and HRS. *European Journal of Public Health, 21*(1), 81–91. Retrieved from http://ourworld .compuserve.com/homepages/JWCRAWFORD/anatomy.htm.

Cronqvist, H., & Thaler, R. H. (2004). Designer choices in privatized social-security systems: Learning from the Swedish experience. *The American Economic Review, 94*(2), 424–428.

Crumbley, J. (1999). *Transracial adoption and foster care: Practice issues for professionals.* Washington, DC: Child Welfare League of America.

Crystal, S., & Shea, D. (1990). Cumulative advantage, cumulative disadvantage, and inequality among elderly people. *Gerontologist, 30*, 437–443.

Cubanski, J., Casillas, G., & Damico, A. (2015). *Poverty among seniors: An updated analysis of national and state level poverty rates under the official and supplemental poverty measures*. Kaiser Family Foundation. Retrieved from http://kff.org/medicare/issue-brief/poverty-among-seniors-an-updated-analysis-of-national-and-state-level-poverty-rates-under-the-official-and-supplemental-poverty-measures/ (November 7, 2016).

Cuffel, B. J., Bloom, J. R., Wallace, N., Hausman, J. W., & Hu, T. (2002). Two-year outcomes of fee-for-service and capitated Medicaid programs for people with severe mental illness. *Health Services Research, 37*(2), 341–359.

Curcio, W. (1996). *The Passaic County study of AFDC recipients in a welfare-to-work program: A preliminary analysis*. Passaic County, NJ: Passaic County Board of Social Services.

Cutcher-Gershenfeld, J., Kochan, T., Ferguson, J., & Barrett, B. (2007). Collective bargaining in the twenty-first century: A negotiations institution at risk. *Negotiation Journal, 23*(3), 249–265.

Dakin, E., & Pearlmutter, S. (2009). Older women's perceptions of elder maltreatment and ethical dilemmas in Adult Protective Services: A cross-cultural exploratory study. *Journal of Elder Abuse & Neglect, 21*(1), 15–57.

Dalton, G. (Ed.). (1968). *Primitive, archaic and modern economies: Essays of Karl Polanyi*. New York: Anchor Books.

Dalton, H. (1925). *Some aspects of inequality of incomes in modern communities*. London: Routledge.

Daly, J., Jogerst, G., Brinig, M., & Dawson, J. (2003). Mandatory reporting: Relationship of APS statute language on state-reported elder abuse. *Journal of Elder Abuse & Neglect, 15*(2), 1–21.

Damerell, R. G. (1968). *Triumph in a white suburb: The dramatic story of Teaneck, NJ, the first town in the U.S. to vote for integrated schools*. New York: Morrow.

Daniel, P. (1972). *The shadow of slavery: Peonage in the south, 1901–1969*. Chicago: University of Illinois Press.

Daniels, H. (1988). *Am I my parents' keeper? An essay on justice between the young and the old*. New York: Oxford University Press.

Daniels, R., & Kitano, H. H. L. (1970). *American racism: Exploration of the nature of prejudice*. Englewood Cliffs, NJ: Prentice Hall.

Davey, M., & Zeleny, J. (2012, June 5). Walker survives Wisconsin recall vote. *The New York Times*. Retrieved from http://www.nytimes.com/2012/06/06/us/politics/walker-survives-wisconsin-recall-effort .html (October 27, 2013).

David, R., & Collins, J. (2007). Disparities in infant mortality: What's genetics got to do with it? *American Journal of Public Health, 97*(7), 1191–1197.

Davidson, L., & Linnoila, M. (Eds.). (2013). *Risk factors for youth suicide*. New York: Routledge.

Davies, P. S., Huynh, M., Newcomb, C., O'Leary, P., Rupp, K., & Sears, J. (2002, Summer). Modeling SSI financial eligibility and simulating the effect of policy options—Supplemental Security Income. *Social Security Bulletin, 64*(2), 16–45.

Davis, A. Y., & Rodriguez, D. (2000). The challenge of prison abolition: A conversation. *Social Justice, 27*(3), 212–218.

Davis, K. E., & Cloud-Two Dog, E. I. (2004). Oppression of indigenous tribal populations and Africans in America. In K. E. Davis & T. B. Bent-Goodley (Eds.), *The color of social policy* (pp. 3–20). Alexandria, VA: Council on Social Work Education.

Day, D. (1979). *The adoption of black children: Counteracting institutional discrimination*. Lexington: Lexington Books.

de Alth, S. (2011). ID at the Polls: Assessing the impact of recent state voter ID laws on voter turnout. *Harvard Law and Policy Review, 3*, 185–202. Retrieved from http://journalistsresource.org/wp-content/uploads/2011/09/Voter-ID-and-Turnout.pdf (July 17, 2013).

De Swaan, A. (1988). *In care of the state: Health care, education, and welfare in Europe and the USA in the modern era*. New York: Oxford University Press.

de Tocqueville, A. (1835). *Democracy in America* (Vols. 1–2). New York: Harper & Row. (Reprinted in 1996.).

Death Penalty Information Center. (2004). *Juvenile offenders who were on death row*. Retrieved from http://www.deathpenaltyinfo.org/article.php? did=204&scid=27 (January 1, 2008).

DeCoster, V. A. (2001). Challenges of type 2 diabetes and role of health care social work: A neglected area of practice. *Health and Social Work, 26*(1), 26–36.

Defense Logistics Agency. (n.d.). *1033 Program FAQs*. Retrieved from http://www.dla.mil/DispositionServices/Offers/Reutilization/LawEnforcement/ProgramFAQs.aspx (November 28, 2016).

Defense Task Force on Sexual Harassment and Violence at the Military Service Academies. (2005). *Report*. Retrieved from http://www.dtic.mil/dtfs/doc_recd/High_GPO_RRC_tx.pdf (September 29, 2013).

Deloria, V., & Lytle, C. M. (1983). *American Indians, American justice*. Austin, TX: University of Texas Press.

Denis, A. (2008). Intersectional analysis: A contribution of feminism to sociology. *International Sociology, 23*, 677–694.

Derlet, R. W., & Kinser, D. (1994, September 29). Access of Medicaid recipients to outpatient care. *New England Journal of Medicine, 331*(13), 877–878.

Diament, M. (2010, March 22). Health care vote ushers in big changes for people with disabilities. *Disability Scoop*. Retrieved from http://www.disabilityscoop.com/2010/03/22/health-care-vote/7388/ (July 21, 2010).

Diamond, D. (2010). Seeking answers on Medicaid expansion. *California Healthline.* Retrieved from http://www.californiahealthline.org/road-to-reform/2010/seeking-answers-on-medicaid-expansion.aspx (July 14, 2010).

DiFonzo, J. H. (1997). *Beneath the fault line: The popular and legal culture of divorce in twentieth-century America.* Charlottesville, VA: University Press of Virginia.

DiNitto, D. M. (1995). *Social welfare: Politics and public policy* (4th ed.). Needham Heights, MA: Allyn & Bacon.

Dionne, E. J. (1996). *They only look dead: Why progressives will dominate the next political era.* New York: Simon & Schuster.

Dobash, R. E., & Dobash, R. P. (1992). *Women, violence and social change.* London & New York: Routledge.

Dohrenwend, B. P. (1990). Socioeconomic status (SES) and psychiatric disorders: Are the issues still compelling? *Social Psychiatry and Psychiatric Epidemiology, 25,* 4–47.

Dolger, H., & Seeman, B. (1985). *How to live with diabetes* (5th ed.). New York: Norton.

Donovan, R., Kurzman, P. A., & Rotman, C. (1993). Improving the lives of home care workers: A partnership of social work and labor. *Social Work, 38*(5), 579–585.

Douglass, D. (1997). Taking the initiative: Anti-homosexual propaganda of the Oregon Citizens' Alliance. In S. L. Witt & S. McCorkle (Eds.), *Anti-gay rights: Assessing voter initiatives* (pp. 3–32). Westport, CT: Praeger.

Drug Enforcement Administration. (n.d.). *Global presence with a tradition of excellence.* Retrieved from https://web.archive.org/web/20080622214536/http://www.usdoj.gov/dea/pubs/history/1985-1990.html (November 27, 2016).

DuBois, J. M., Hine, A., Kennett, M., Kostelecky, K., Norris, J., Presti, R., … Ruggles, A. (2015). Anticipating HIV vaccines: Sketching an agenda for public health ethics and policy in the United States. *Saint Louis University Journal of Health Law & Policy, 8,* 225–258.

Duster, T. (1996). Individual fairness, group preferences, and the California strategy. *Representations, 55,* 41–58.

Dworak, R. J. (1980). *Taxpayers, taxes, and government spending: Perspectives on the taxpayer revolt.* New York: Praeger.

Dworsky, A., Dillman, K., Dion, M., Coffee-Borden, B., & Rosenau, M. (2012). *Housing for youth aging out of foster care: A review of the literature and program typology.* U.S. Department of Housing & Urban Development. Retrieved from http://papers.ssrn .com/sol3/papers.cfm?abstract_id=2112278 (September 11, 2013).

Dye, T. R., & Ziegler, L. H. (1996). *The irony of democracy: An uncommon introduction to American politics.* Belmont, CA: Wadsworth.

Eaton, W. W. (1985). *Epidemiologic field methods in psychiatry: The NIMH Epidemiological Catchment Area Program.* Orlando, FL: Academic Press.

Edman, I. (Ed.). (1956). *The works of Plato.* New York: Modern Library.

Education Commission of the States. (2016). *50-State Review.* Retrieved from http://www.ecs.org/ec-content/uploads/01252016_Prek-K_Funding_report-4.pdf (October 20, 2016).

Education Data Partnership. (2007). *The basics of California's school finance system.* Retrieved from http://www.edsource.org/pdf/QA_financefinal.pdf (December 30, 2007).

Egan, T. (2004, October 20). Towns hand out tax breaks, then cry foul as jobs leave. *Herald Tribune.* Retrieved from http://www.heraldtribune.com/apps/pbcs.dll/article?AID=/20041020/ZNYT02/410200700; http://www.ed-data.kl2.ca.us/Fmance/SFPnme2.asp.

Egloff, B., & Schmukle, S. C. (2002). Predictive validity of an Implicit Association Test for assessing anxiety. *Journal of Personality and Social Psychology, 83,* 1441–1445.

Ehrlichman, J. D. (1982). *Witness to power: The Nixon years.* New York: Simon & Schuster.

Eisenberg, J. (1995). Economics. *Journal of the American Medical Association, 273*(21), 1670–1671.

Elder, S., & Sorrentino, C. (1993, October). Japan's low unemployment: A BLS update and revision. United States Bureau of Labor Statistics. *Monthly Labor Review.* Retrieved from http://findarticles.com/p/articles/mi_mll53/is_nl0_v116/ai_14668379/pg_l (January 21, 2008).

Elder, T., & Powers, E. (2006). The incredible shrinking program: Trends in SSI participation of the aged. *Research on Aging, 28*(3), 341–358.

Elliott, C. (2008, January 7). Department of Medical Ethics: Guinea-pigging. *The New Yorker,* 36–41.

Ellis, B. (2012, April 12). Don't overlook this $6,000 tax credit. *CNN Money.* Retrieved from http://money.cnn.com/2012/04/12/pf/taxes/earned-income-tax-credit/ (October 27, 2012).

Engels, F. (1884/1972). *The origin of the family, private property, and the state.* New York: Pathfinder.

Erikson, K. (1976). *Everything in its path.* New York: Simon & Schuster.

Ernst, J. S., & Smith, C. A. (2011). Adult Protective Services clients confirmed for self-neglect: Characteristics and service use. *Journal of Elder Abuse and Neglect, 23*(4), 289–303.

Ertel, K. A., Rich-Edwards, J. W., & Koenen, K. C. (2011). Maternal depression in the United States: Nationally representative rates and risks. *Journal of Women's Health, 20*(11), 1609–1617.

Eskridge, W. N. (1999). *Gaylaw: Challenging the apartheid of the closet.* Cambridge, MA: Harvard University Press.

Estes, C. L., Swan, J. H., & Associates. (1993). *The long-term care crisis: Elders trapped in the no care zone.* Newbury Park, CA: Sage.

Eurostat. (2007). *Harmonized unemployment.* Retrieved from http://europa.eu.mt/estatref/mfo/sdds/en/une/une_sm.htm#concepts (January 21, 2008).

Euthanasia Research and Guidance Organization (ERGO). (1998). *Dr. Jack Kevorkian.* Retrieved from http://www.efn.org/-ergo/dr.k.html.

Evan, W. E., & Macpherson, D. (1994). *Trends in individual and household pension coverage. Final report submitted to Department of Labor.* Contract No 41USC252C3. Retrieved from http://www.sba .muohio.edu/evenwe/res%20papers/trends%20in% 20ind%20and%20hh.pdf.

Ezell, M. (2001). *Advocacy in the human services.* Belmont, CA: Brooks/Cole.

Ezorsky, G. (1991). *Racism and justice: The case for affirmative action.* Ithaca, NY: Cornell University Press.

Faillace, M. (2004). *Disability law deskbook: The Americans with Disabilities Act in the workplace.* New York: Practising Law Institute.

Fanshel, D. (1972). *Far from the reservation: The transracial adoption of American Indian children.* Metuchen, NJ: The Scarecrow Press.

Fanshel, D., & Shinn, E. B. (1978). *Children in foster care: A longitudinal investigation.* New York: Columbia University Press.

Farhang, S., & Katznelson, I. (2005). The Southern imposition: Congress and labor in the New Deal and Fair Deal. *Studies in American Political Development, 19,* 1–30.

Farmer, P. (1996). Social inequalities and emerging infectious diseases. *Emerging Infectious Diseases, 2*(4), 259–271.

Farrell, M., Rich, S., Turner, L., Seith, D., & Bloom, D. (2008). Welfare time limits: An update on state policies, implementation, and effects on families. (The Newin Group and MDRC). Retrieved from http://www.mdrc.org/sites/default/files/full_609.pdf (May 6, 2013).

Fazel, S., Khosla, V., Doll, H., & Geddes, J. (2008). The prevalence of mental disorders among the homeless in western countries: Systematic review and meta-regression analysis. *PLoS Medicine 5*(12), e225. doi:10.1371/journal.pmed.0050225.

Federal Bureau of Investigation (FBI). (2000, 2001). *Uniform Crime Reports for 2000, 2001.* Retrieved from http://www.fbi.gov/about-us/cjis/uc (November 6, 2010).

Federal Bureau of Investigation (FBI). (2008). *Uniform Crime Reports: Crime in the United States.* Expanded Homicide Data, Tables 2 and 10. Retrieved from http://www.fbi.gov/ucr/cius2008/offenses/expanded_information/homicide.html (November 10, 2010).

Federal Bureau of Investigation (FBI). (2009). *Hate crime statistics: 2008.* Retrieved from http://www.fbi.gov/ucr/hc2008/hcsummary.html (July 28, 2010).

Federal Bureau of Investigation (FBI). (2016). *Hate crime statistics: 2014.* Retrieved from https://ucr.fbi.gov/hate-crime/2014 (October 12, 2016).

Federal Communications Commission. (2013). *Office of Native Affairs and Policy: 2012 Annual Report.* Retrieved from https://transition.fcc.gov/cgb/onap/ONAP-AnnualReport03-19-2013.pdf (December 10, 2016).

Federal Deposit Insurance Corporation (FDIC). (2012). *2011 FDIC national survey of unbanked and underbanked households.* Retrieved from http://www.fdic.gov/householdsurvey/2012 _underbankedreport.pdf.

Fee, E., & Porter, D. (1991). Public health, preventive medicine, and professionalization: Britain and the United States in the nineteenth century. In E. B. Fee & R. M. Acheson (Eds.), *A history of education in public health: Health that mocks the doctors' rules* (pp. 15–43). Oxford, UK: Oxford University Press.

Feinson, M. C. (1991). Reexamining some common beliefs about mental health and aging. In B. B. Hess & E. W. Markson (Eds.), *Growing old in America* (4th ed., pp. 125–136). New Brunswick, NJ: Transaction.

Feld, B. C. (1999). *Bad kids: Race and the transformation of the juvenile court.* New York: Oxford University Press.

Ferguson, J. (2008). The eyes of the needles: A sequential model of union organizing drives, 1999–2004. *Industrial and Labor Relations Review, 3,* 3–21.

Fernandes, D. C. (2004). Race, socioeconomic development and the educational stratification process in Brazil. *Research in Social Stratification and Mobility, 22,* 365–422.

Fichtenbaum, R. (2009). The impact of unions on labor's share of income: A time-series analysis. *Review of Political Economy, 21*(4), 567–588. Retrieved from http://dx.doi.org/10.1080/09538250903214859.

Fields, B. (1982). Ideology and race in American history. In J. M. Kousser & J. M. McPherson (Eds.), *Region, race, and reconstruction: Essays in honor of C. Vann Woodward* (pp. 143–177). New York: Oxford University Press.

Fields, G. S., & Kanbur, R. (2005). *Minimum wages and poverty.* Retrieved from http://www.arts.cornell.edu/poverty/kanbur/FieldsKanburMinWage.pdf (August 23, 2010).

Fischer, D. H. (1977). *Growing old in America.* New York: Oxford University Press.

Fischer, L. R., & Eustis, N. N. (1989). Quicker and sicker: How changes in Medicare affect the elderly and their families. *Journal of Geriatric Psychiatry, 22*(2), 163–191.

Fisher, G. M. (1997, Spring). Setting American standards of poverty: A look back. *Focus, 19*(2), 47–52. Retrieved from http://www.ssc.wise.edu/irp/pubs/focl92.pdf.

Fisher, W. F. (1987). *Human communication as narration toward a philosophy of reason, value, and action.* Columbia, SC: University of South Carolina Press.

Fisher, W. H., & Drake, R. E. (2007). Forensic mental illness and other policy misadventures. Commentary on "Extending Assertive Community Treatment to criminal justice settings: Origins, current evidence, and future directions. *Community Mental Health Journal, 43*(5), 545–548.

Fix, M. E., & Passel, J. S. (2002). *The scope and impact of welfare reform's immigrant provisions.* Urban Institute New Federalism Discussion Paper No 02-03. Retrieved from http://www.urban.org/pubhcations/410412.html (February 5, 2008).

Flamm, M. (2016). *In the heat of the summer: The New York Riots of 1964 and the War on Crime.* Philadelphia: University of Pennsylvania Press.

Fleischer, D. Z., & Zames, F. (2001). *The disability rights movement from charity to confrontation.* Philadelphia: Temple University Press.

Fleury, R. E., Sullivan, C. M., Bybee, D. I., & Davidson, W. S. (1998). Why don't they just call the cops? Reasons for differential police contact among women with abusive partners. *Violence and Victims, 13*(4), 333–346.

Flora, P. (Ed.). (1983). *State, economy, and society in Western Europe, 1815–1975: A data handbook. Vol. 1, The growth of mass democracies and welfare states.* Frankfurt: Campus Verlag.

Flora, P., & Heidenheimer, A. J. (Eds.). (1981). *The development of welfare states in Europe and America.* New Brunswick and London: Transaction.

Foner, P. S. (1981). *Organized labor and the black worker: 1619–1981.* New York: International Publishers.

Fordyce, E. J. (1996, April–June). Urban mortality: Race or place? *Statistical Bulletin, 77*(2), 2–10.

Fox, M., & Passel, J. S. (1994). *Immigration and immigrants: Setting the records straight.* Washington, DC: Urban Institute. Retrieved from http://www.urban.org.

Fraikor, A. L. (1973). *An anthropological analysis of Tay-Sachs Disease: Genetic drift among the Ashkenazim Jews.* Boulder, CO: University of Colorado Press.

Frank, D. (2004). Where is the history of U.S. labor and international solidarity? Part I: A moveable feast. *Labor: Studies in Working Class History of the Americas, 1*(1), 95–119.

Frank, M. (2007). The evolution of male-male sexual behavior in humans: The alliance theory. *Journal of Psychology and Human Sexuality, 18*(A), 275–311.

Freeman, J. (1991). How "sex" got into Title VII: Persistent opportunism as a maker of public policy. *Law and Inequality: A Journal of Theory and Practice, 9*(2), 163–184.

Freire, P. (2000). *Pedagogy of the oppressed* (Myra Bergman Ramos, Trans.). New York: Continuum. (Original work published in 1970.)

Friedman, G. (2013). Funding HR 676: The Expanded and Improved Medicare for All Act: How we can afford a national single-payer health plan. Retrieved from http://www.pnhp.org/sites/default/files/Funding%20HR%20676_Friedman_7.31.13_proofed.pdf (December 22, 2016).

Friedman, M. (1955). The role of government in education. In R. A. Solo (Ed.), *Economics and the public interest.* Princeton, NJ: Trustees of Rutgers College.

Friedman, M. S. (1960). *Martin Buber: The life of dialogue.* New York: Harper Torchbook.

Friedman, M., & Friedman, R. (1979). *Free to choose.* New York: Harcourt Brace Jovanovich.

Friedman, R. C., & Downey, J. I. (2002). *Sexual orientation and psychoanalysis.* New York: Columbia University Press.

Friends Committee on National Legislation. (1987, August/September). With all due respect to the "founding fathers": Indian contributions to the U.S. Constitution. *Indian Report.* Retrieved from http://www.fcnl.org.

Frumkin, P., & Andre-Clark, A. (1999). The rise of the corporate social worker. *Society, 36*(6), 46–52.

Funiciello, T. (1993). *Tyranny of kindness: Dismantling the welfare system to end poverty in America.* New York: Atlantic Monthly Press.

Furber, G., Segal, L., Leach, M., Turnbull, C., Procter, N., Diamond, M., … & McGorry, P. (2015). Preventing mental illness: Closing the evidence-practice gap through workforce and services planning. *BMC Health Services Research, 15*: 283. **doi:** 10.1186/s12913-015-0954-5.

Galas, J. (1996). *Gay rights.* San Diego, CA: Lucent Books.

Galewitz, P. (2010, March 26). Consumer's guide to health reform. *Kaiser Health News.* Retrieved from http://www.kaiserhealthnews.org/Stories/2010/March/22/consumers-guide-health-reform.aspx (October 27, 2010).

Gans, H. (1971, July/August). The uses of poverty: The poor pay all. *Social Policy, 2*(2), 20–24.

Garces, E., Thomas, D., & Currie, J. (2000). *Longer term effects of Head Start.* RAND. Retrieved from http://www.rand.org/labor/DRU/DRU2439.pdf (August 5, 2010).

Garfinkel, I. (1992). *Assuring child support: An extension of Social Security.* New York: Russell Sage Foundation.

Garrett, A. B., & Glied, S. (1997). *The effect of U.S. Supreme Court ruling* Sullivan v. Zebley *on child SSI and AFDC enrollment.* Working Paper 6125. National Bureau of Economic Research. Retrieved from http://www.nber.org/papers/w6125.pdf?new_window=1 (June 20, 2013).

Gartrell, N. K., & Bos, H. M. W. (2010). U.S. National Longitudinal Lesbian Family Study: Psychological adjustment of 17-year-old adolescents. *Pediatrics, 126*(1), 1–11.

Gayle, H. (2000, September). An overview of the global HIV/AIDS epidemic, with a focus on the United States. *AIDS, 14*(Suppl. 2), s8–s17.

George, C. (2000). *Life under the Jim Crow laws.* San Diego, CA: Lucent Books.

George, R. M., & Lee, B. J. (1997). Abuse and neglect of children. In R. A. Maynard (Ed.), *Kids having kids: Economic costs and social consequences of teen pregnancy* (pp. 181–203). Washington, DC: Urban Institute Press.

Gerstein, J. (2010, March 29). Barack Obama struggles to capitalize in polls. *Politico.* Retrieved from http://www.politico.com/news/stories/0310/35162.html (July 14, 2010).

Geyman, J. (2010). *Hijacked! The road to single payer in the aftermath of stolen health care reform.* Monroe, ME: Common Courage Press.

Gibelman, M., & Schervish, P. H. (1995). Pay equity in social work: Not! *Social Work, 40*(5), 622–629.

Gil, D. G. (1992). *Unravelling social policy theory, analysis, and political action: Towards social equality* (5th ed.). Rochester, VT: Schenkman Books.

Gil, D. G. (1998). *Confronting injustice and oppression: Concepts and strategies for social workers.* New York: Columbia University Press.

Gilbert, N., & Gilbert, B. (1989). *The enabling state: Modern welfare capitalism in America.* New York: Oxford University Press.

Gilbert, N., & Terrell, P. (2002). *Dimensions of social welfare policy.* Boston: Allyn & Bacon.

Gilder, G. (1981). *Wealth and poverty.* New York: Basic Books.

Gill, C., Weisburd, D., Telep, C., Vitter, Z., & Bennett, T. (2014). Community-oriented policing to reduce crime, disorder, and fear and increase satisfaction and legitimacy among citizens: A systematic review. *Journal of Experimental Criminology, 10*(4), 399–428.

Gilman, S. E., Kawachi, I., Fitzmaurice, G. M., & Buka, S. L. (2002). Socioeconomic status in childhood and the lifetime risk of major depression. *International Journal of Epidemiology, 31*(2), 359–367.

Gilovich, T. (1991). *How we know what isn't so: The fallibility of human reason in everyday life.* New York: Free Press.

Global Commission on Drug Policy. (2011). *War on Drugs: Report of the Global Commission on Drug Policy.* Retrieved from http://www.globalcommissionondrugs.org/wp-content/themes/gcdp_v1/pdf/Global_Commission_Report_English.pdf (November 27, 2016).

Gohmann, S. F., & McClure, J. E. (1987). Supreme Court rulings on pension plans: The effect on retirement age and wealth of single people. *Gerontologist, 27,* 471–477.

Goldberg, A. E. Moyer, A. M., Black, K., & Henry, A. (2015). Lesbian and heterosexual adoptive mothers' experiences of relationship dissolution. *Sex Roles, 73*(3), 141–156.

Goldberg, D. T. (1993). *Racist culture philosophy and the politics of meaning.* Cambridge, MA: Blackwell.

Good, H. G. (1962). *A history of American education* (2nd ed.). New York: Macmillan.

Goozner, M. (2016). *Editorial: Drugs and insurance affordability will top the post-election agenda.* Retrieved from http://www.modernhealthcare.com/article/20161029/MAGAZINE/310299986/editorial-drugs-and-insurance-affordability-will-top-the-post (October 30, 2016).

Gordon, M. (1964). *Assimilation in American life: The role of race, religion, and national origins.* New York: Oxford University Press.

Gorz, A. (1985). *Paths to paradise: On the liberation from work.* London: Pluto Press.

Gorz, A. (1994). *Capitalism, socialism, ecology.* London: Verso.

Gossett, T. (1965). *Race: The history of an idea in America.* New York: Oxford University Press.

Gould-Werth, A., & Shaefer, H. (2012). Unemployment Insurance participation by education and by race and ethnicity. *Monthly Labor Review* (October), 28–41. Retrieved from http://www.bls.gov/opub/mlr/2012/10/art3full.pdf (June 14, 2016).

Grad, S. (2008, November 3). 70% of African Americans backed Prop. 8, exit poll finds. *Los Angeles Times,* L.A. Now. Retrieved from http://latimesblogs.latimes.com/lanow/2008/11/70-of-african-a.html (July 31, 2010).

Graetz, M. J., & Schenk, D. H. (1995). *Federal income taxation: Principles and policies.* Westbury, NY: Foundation Press.

Graham, H. D. (1990). *The civil rights era: Origins and development of national policy, 1960–1972.* New York: Oxford University Press.

Grambs, J. D. (1989). *Women over forty: Visions and realities.* Springer: New York.

Graves, E. J. (1995). 1993 Summary: National Hospital Discharge Survey. *Advance Data from Vital and Health Statistics,* No. 264. Hyattsville, MD: National Center for Health Statistics.

Gray, G. (1985). *National Commission on Unemployment and Mental Health. Resource Papers to the Report of the National Mental Health Association Commission on the Prevention of Mental and Emotional Disabilities.* Alexandria, VA: National Mental Health Association.

Gray, M., Dean, M., Agllias, K., Howard, A., & Schubert, L. (2015). Perspectives on neoliberalism for human service professionals. *Social Service Review, 89*(2), 368–392.

Green, A. R., Carney, D. R., Pallin, D. J., Ngo, L. H., Raymond, K. L., Iezzoni, L. I., & Banaji, M. R. (2007). Implicit bias among physicians and its prediction of thrombolysis decisions for black and white patients. *Journal of General Internal Medicine, 22*(9), 1231–1238. doi: 10.1007/s11606-007-0258-5.

Green, S. E. (2003). What do you mean, 'What's wrong with her?': Stigma and the lives of families of children with disabilities. *Social Science & Medicine, 57*(8), 1361–1374.

Greenberg, D. F. (1988). *The construction of homosexuality.* Chicago: University of Chicago Press.

Greenberg, G. (2013). The DSM and the nature of disease. *The New Yorker.* Retrieved from http://www.newyorker.com/online/blogs/elements/2013/04/the-dsm-and-the-nature-of-disease.html (June 9, 2013).

Greene, R. (1989). The growing need for social work services for the aged in 2020. In B. S. Vourlekis & C. G. Leukefeld (Eds.), *Making our case: A resource book of selected materials for social workers in health care* (pp. 11–17). Silver Spring, MD: National Association of Social Workers.

Greenstone, J. D. (1969). *Labor in American politics.* New York: Knopf.

Greenwald, A. G., Poehlman, T. A., Uhlmann, E. L., & Banaji, M. R. (2009). Understanding and using the Implicit Association Test: Meta-Analysis of Predictive Validity. *Journal of Personality and Social Psychology, 97*(1), 17–41.

Gregg, E. W., Mangione, C. M., Cauley, J. A., Thompson, T. J., Schwartz, A. V., Ensrud, K. E., … For the Study of Osteoporotic Fractures Research Group. (2002). Diabetes and incidence of functional disability in older women. *Diabetes Care, 25*(1), 61–67.

Gresenz, C. R., Watkins, K., & Podus, D. (1998). Supplemental Security Income (SSI), Disability Insurance (DI), and substance abusers. *Community Mental Health Journal, 34*(4), 337–350.

Gresham, G. (2008, July 14). EITC: To inform and protect. *New York Sun.* Retrieved from http://www .nysun.com/opinion/eitc-to-inform-and-protect/81797/ (October 27, 2013).

Grier, P. (2010, March 20). Health Care Reform Bill 101: What's a health "exchange"? *Christian Science Monitor.* Retrieved from http://www.csmonitor .com/USA/Politics/2010/0320/Health-care-reform-bill-101-What-s-a-health-exchange (July 14, 2010).

Grob, G. N. (1994). *The mad among us: A history of the care of America's mentally ill.* New York: Free Press.

Grossman, J. (1978, June). Fair Labor Standards Act of 1938: Maximum struggle for a minimum wage. *Monthly Labor Review,* 22–30.

Gudelunas, D. (2008). *Confidential to America: Newspaper advice columns and sexual education.* London: Transaction Publishers.

Gurr, T. R. (1989). The history of violent crime in America: An overview. In T. R. Gurr (Ed.), *Violence in America: The history of crime.* Newbury Park, CA: Sage.

Gutman, H. (1976). *The black family in slavery and freedom, 1750–1925.* New York: Pantheon Books.

Guttmacher Institute. (2002). *Teen pregnancy trends and lessons learned.* Retrieved from http://www.guttmacher.org/pubs/tgr/05/l/gr050107.html (December 31, 2007).

Guttmacher Institute. (2013a). *Facts on induced abortion in the United States: July 2013.* Retrieved from http://www.guttmacher.org/pubs/fb_induced_abortion.html (September 29, 2013).

Guttmacher Institute. (2013b). *State policies in brief: Parental involvement in minors' abortions.* Retrieved from http://www.guttmacher.org/statecenter/spibs/spib_PIMA.pdf (September 8, 2013).

Haber, C. (1983). *Beyond sixty-five: The dilemma of old age in America's past.* Cambridge, UK: Cambridge University Press.

Haber, C., & Gratton, B. (1994). *Old age and the search for security: An American social history.* Bloomington: Indiana University Press.

Haberman, M. (2013, September 30). Poll: Big support for anti-discrimination law. *Politico.* Retrieved from http://www.politico.com/story/2013/09/poll-big-support-for-anti-discrimination-law-97540.html? hp=r17 (October 8, 2013).

Haldeman, H. R. (1994). *The Haldeman diaries: Inside the Nixon White House.* New York: G. P. Putnam's Sons.

Hanlon, J. J., & Pickett, G. E. (1979). *Public health administration and practice.* St. Louis: Mosby.

Hardcastle, D. A., Wenocur, S., & Powers, P. R. (1996). *Community practice theories and skills for social workers.* New York: Oxford University Press.

Harrington, M. (1984). *The new American poverty.* New York: Holt, Rinehart & Winston.

Harris, A. J., Lobanov-Rostovsky, C., & Levenson, J. (2016). *Law enforcement perspectives on sex offender registration and notification: Summary report.* Retrieved from https://www.ncjrs.gov/pdffiles1/nij/grants/250181.pdf (December 9, 2016).

Harris, R. L. (1979). Early Black benevolent societies: 1780–1830. *The Massachusetts Review, 20*(30), 603–625. Retrieved from http://www.jstor.org/stable/25088988 (August 2012).

Harvey, S. (n.d.). *Rosie the Riveter: Real women workers in World War II.* Retrieved from http://www.loc.gov/rr/program/journey/rosie-transcript .html (January 18, 2007).

Hayashi, R. (2004). The environment of disability today. In G. May & M. Raske (Eds.), *Ending disability discrimination: Strategies for social workers* (pp. 45–70). Boston: Allyn & Bacon.

Hayashi, R. (2007). MiCASSA—My home. *Journal of Social Work in Disability and Rehabilitation, 6*(1–2), 35–52.

Hayes, C. D., Palmer, J. L., & Zaslow, M. J. (1990). *Who cares for America's children? Child care policy for the 1990s.* Washington, DC: National Academy Press.

Head, S. (1996, February 29). The new ruthless economy. *New York Review of Books,* 47–52.

Hefetz, A., & Warner, M. (2004). Privatization and its reverse: Explaining the dynamics of the government contracting process. *Journal of Public Administration Research and Theory, 14*(2), 171–190.

Henetz, P. (1998, March 15). Getting to the roots of gender discrimination. *Salt Lake Tribune,* p. Al.

Hening, W. W. (Ed.). (1809–1823). *The statutes at large: Being a collection of all the laws of Virginia from the first session of the legislature in the year 1619* (Vols. 1–13). Richmond, VA: Samuel Pleasants.

Heritage Foundation. (2010). Long overdue Head Start evaluation shows no lasting benefit for children. *The Foundry.* Retrieved from http://blog.heritage.org/2010/01/14/long-overdue-head-start-evaluation-shows-no-lasting-benefit-for-children/ (August 5, 2010).

Herman, A. (1999). *Report on the American workforce.* Secretary of Labor. Retrieved from http://stats.bls .gov/opub/rtaw/message.htm.

Herring, C. (Ed.). (1997). *African Americans and the public agenda: The paradoxes of public policy.* Thousand Oaks, CA: Sage.

Heslin, P. A., Bell, M. P., & Fletcher, P. O. (2012). The devil without and within: A conceptual model of social cognitive processes whereby discrimination leads stigmatized minorities to become discouraged workers. *Journal of Organizational Behavior, 33*(6), 840–862.

Hillary Clinton Campaign. (n.d.). *Criminal Justice Reform: Our criminal justice system is out of balance.* Retrieved from https://www.hillaryclinton.com/issues/criminal-justice-reform/ (December 6, 2016).

Himmelstein, D., & Woolhandler, S. (1995). Care denied: U.S. residents who are unable to obtain needed medical services. *American Journal of Public Health, 85*(3), 341–344.

Hinton, E. (2016). *From the War on Poverty to the War on Crime: The making of mass incarceration in America.* Cambridge, MA: Harvard University Press.

Hinton, E., Kohler-Hausmann, J., & Weaver, V. (2016, April 13). Did blacks really endorse the 1994 crime bill? *The New York Times.* Retrieved from http://www.nytimes.com/2016/04/13/opinion/did-blacks-really-endorse-the-1994-crime-bill.html (December 6, 2016).

Hirsch, A. (1992). *The rise of the penitentiary: Prisons and punishment in early America.* New Haven: Yale University Press.

Hoff, R. (1988). *I can see you naked: A fearless guide to making great presentations.* Kansas City: Andrews & McMeel.

Hoffman, C., & Paradise, J. (2008). Health insurance and access to health care in the United States. *Annals of the New York Academy of Sciences, 1136,* 149–160.

Hoffman, S. D., & Seidman, L. S. (1990). *The Earned Income Tax Credit: Antipoverty effectiveness and labor market effects.* Kalamazoo, MI: W. E. Upjohn Institute for Employment Research.

Hoffman, W. (2000). The trouble with Medicare HMOs: Health plans say money is the key, but critics see other problems. *ACP-ASIM Observer.* Retrieved from http://www.acponline.org/journals/news/dec00/medicarehmos.htm.

Holden, K., & Smeeding, T. (1990). The poor, the rich, and the insecure elderly caught in between. *Milbank Quarterly, 16,* 227–239.

Holinger, P. C., Offer, D., Barter, J. T., & Bell, C. C. (1994). *Suicide and homicide among adolescents.* New York: Guilford Press.

Holland, W. (2007). Negotiator for Steelworkers Union; Executive Director, Utah Democratic Party. Personal communication.

Holtzman, M. (2013). GLBT parents' rights during custody decision making: The influence of doctrine, statute, and societal factors in the United States. *Journal of GLBT Family Studies, 9*(4), 364–392. doi:10.1080/1550428X.2013.803346.

Holzer, C., Shea, B., Swanson, J., Leaf, P., Myers, J., George, L., ... & Bednarski, P. (1986). The increased risk for specific psychiatric disorders among persons of low socioeconomic status. *American Journal of Social Psychiatry, 6,* 259–271.

Holzer, H. J. (1996). *What employers want: Job prospects for less-educated workers.* Russell Sage Foundation. Retrieved from http://www.jstor.org/stable/10.7758/9781610442954.

hooks, B. (2001). Feminism: A transformational politic. In P. S. Rothenberg (Ed.), *Race, class, and gender in the United States: An integrated study* (pp. 601–608). New York: Worth Publishers.

Horne, G. (1997). *The fire this time: The Watts uprising and the 1960s.* Boston: De Capo Press.

Horsley, S. (2015). *U.S. communities called on to prevent homegrown terrorism.* National Security, KUER. Retrieved from http://www.npr.org/2015/02/18/387131815/communities-called-on-to-help-prevent-home-grown-terrorism (December 2, 2016).

Hosseini, M., Girgis, C., & Khan-Pastula, F. (2016). Was shooter's ex-wife right to call him "bipolar?" *CNN Opinion* (June 15). Retrieved from http://www.cnn.com/2016/06/15/opinions/is-bipolar-misnomer-in-florida-shooting-hossein-girgis-khan-pastula/ (September 19, 2016).

Human Rights Campaign. (n.d.). *Health insurance discrimination for transgender people.* Retrieved from http://www.hrc.org/resources/entry/health-insurance-discrimination-for-transgender-people (October 8, 2013).

Human Rights Watch. (2000). *Fingers to the bone: United States' failure to protect child farmworkers.* Retrieved from http://www.hrw.org/reports/2000/frmwrkr/ (January 21, 2008).

Iams, H. M., Reznik, G. L., & Tamborini, C. R. (2010). Earnings sharing in the U.S. Social Security System: A microsimulation analysis of future female retirees. *The Gerontologist, 50*(4), 495–508.

Indian Health Service. (2014). *HIS year 2014 profile.* Retrieved from https://www.ihs.gov/newsroom/factsheets/ihsyear2014profile/ (October 6, 2016).

Inhorn, M. C. (2006). Defining women's health: A dozen messages from more than 150 ethnographies. *Medical Anthropology Quarterly, 20*(3), 345–378.

Institute for Women's Policy Research. (n.d.). Pay equity & discrimination. Retrieved from http://www.iwpr.org/initiatives/pay-equity-and-discrimination (October 27, 2013).

Institute for Women's Policy Research. (2016). *The gender wage gap by occupation, 2015, and by race and ethnicity.* Retrieved from www.iwpr.org/publications/pubs/ (November 13, 2016).

Institute on Taxation and Economic Policy. (2013). *Who pays: A distributional analysis of the tax systems in all 50 states.* Retrieved from http://www .itep.org/whopays/ (February 6, 2013).

Internal Revenue Service. (n.d.a.). *SOI tax stats— Individual statistical tables by tax rate and income percentile. Table 3.5. Returns with modified taxable income [1]: Tax generated, by rate.* Data retrieved from http://www.irs.gov/taxstats/indtaxstats/article/0,,id=133521,00.html#_grp2 (May 14, 2010).

Internal Revenue Service. (n.d.b.). *Preview of 2013 EITC income limits, maximum credit amounts and tax law updates.* Retrieved from http://www.irs.gov/Individuals/Preview-of-2012-EITC-Income-Limits,-Maximum-Credit–Amounts-and-Tax-Law-Updates (October 27, 2013).

Internal Revenue Service. (2016). *The Tax Gap.* Retrieved https://www.irs.gov/uac/the-tax-gap (December 22, 2016).

International Institute for Strategic Studies (IISS) (2015). *Military balance, 2016.*Top 15 defense budgets 2015. Retrieved from https://www.iiss.org/-/media//images/publications/the%20military%20balance/milbal2016/mb%202016%20top%2015%20defence%20budgets%202015.jpg?la=en (June 10, 2016).

International Labour Organization (ILO). (n.d.). *Free trade agreements and labour rights.* Retrieved from http://www.ilo.org/global/standards/information-resources-and-publications/free-trade-agreements-and-labour-rights/lang--en/index.htm (November 13, 2016).

International Labour Organization (ILO). (2008). *Global wage report 2008/09: Minimum wages and collective bargaining, towards policy coherence.* Geneva: ILO. Retrieved from http://www.ilo.org/wcmsp5/groups/public/@dgreports/@dcomm/@publ/documents/publication/wcms_097013.pdf.

International Labour Organization (ILO). (2009). *World of work report 2009: The global jobs crisis and beyond.* Geneva: International Institute for Labour Studies. Retrieved from http://www.ilo.org (April 27, 2010).

International Monetary Fund (IMF). (2007a). Globalization and inequality: The globalization of labor. *World economic outlook.* Washington, DC: IMF.

International Monetary Fund (IMF). (2007b). Globalization and inequality. *World economic outlook: Spillovers and cycles in the global economy.* Washington, DC: IMF.

Isaacs, J., Toran, K., Hahn, H., Fortuny, K., & Steuerle, C. E. (2012). KIDS'SHARE2012: Report on federal expenditures on children through 2011. Retrieved from http://www.urban.org/UploadedPDF/412600-Kids-Share-2012.pdf (October 27, 2013).

Isaacs, J. (n.d.). *International comparisons of economic mobility: The social mobility project, Pew Charitable Trusts.* Retrieved from http://www.brookings.edu/~/media/Research/Files/Reports/2008/2/economic-mobility-sawhill/02_economic_mobility_sawhill_ch3.PDF (June 13, 2016).

Jackson, D. (2011, April 13). Obama: "I refuse to renew" Bush tax cuts for rich. *USA Today.* Retrieved from http://content,usatoday.com/communities/theoval/post/2011/04/obama-i-refuse-to-renew-bush-tax-cuts-for-rich/1#.URKpKPK8CSo (February 6, 2013).

Jacobson, P. H. (1959). *American marriage and divorce.* New York: Rinehart & Company.

Jacoby, R. (1975). *Social amnesia: A critique of conformist psychology from Adler to Laing.* Boston: Beach Press.

Jahnigen, D., & Binstock, R. H. (1991). Economic and clinical realities: Health care for older people.

In R. H. Binstock & S. G. Post (Eds.), *Too old for health care: Controversies in medicine, law, economics and ethics.* Baltimore: Johns Hopkins University Press.

Jamison, K. R. (1993). *Touched with fire: Manic-depressive illness and the artistic temperament.* New York: Macmillan.

Jansson, B. (1999). *Becoming an effective policy advocate: From policy practice to social justice* (3rd ed.). Pacific Grove: Brooks/Cole.

Jansson, B. (2002). *Becoming an effective policy advocate: From policy practice to social justice* (4th ed.). Belmont, CA: Wadsworth.

Jansson, B. S. (2008). *Becoming an effective policy advocate: From policy practice to social justice* (5th ed). Belmont, CA: Thomson Brooks/Cole.

Jeltsen, M. (2016). Wave goodbye to harsh Tennessee law targeting pregnant drug users. *The Huffington Post* (March 23, 2016). Retrieved from http://www.huffingtonpost.com/entry/tennessee-pregnant-women-drugs_us_56e862b3e4b065e2e3d79320 (September 17, 2016).

Johansen, B. (2002). Native Americans in the 2000 census: Far from the "vanishing race." *Native Americas, 19*(1/2), 42–45.

Johnson, J. C., & Smith, N. H. (2002, Fall). Health and social issues associated with racial, ethnic, and cultural disparities. *Generations,* 25–32.

Johnson, N., Nicholas, A., & Pennington, S. (2009). *Tax measures help balance state budgets: A common and reasonable response to shortfalls.* Center on Budget & Policy Priorities. Retrieved from http://www.cbpp.org/cms/index.cfm?fa=view&id=2815 (February 6, 2013).

Johnston, D. D. (1994). *The art and science of persuasion.* Boston: McGraw-Hill.

Joint Center for Housing Studies of Harvard University. (2010). *Long-term low income housing tax credit policy questions.* Retrieved from http://www.jchs.harvard.edu/sites/jchs.harvard.edu/files/long-term_low_income_housing_tax_credit_policy_questions.pdf (July 7, 2016).

Joint Center for Housing Studies of Harvard University. (2015). The State of the Nation's Housing: 2015. Retrieved from http://www.jchs.harvard.edu/sites/jchs.harvard.edu/files/jchs-sonhr-2015-full.pdf (July 7, 2016).

Jonas, S., & Kovner, A. (2002). *Health care delivery in the United States* (7th ed.). New York: Springer Publishing Company.

Jones, G. W. (Ed.). (1972). *Cotton Mather: The angel of Bethesda.* Bane, MA: American Antiquarian Society and Bane Publishers. Cited by Grob, 1994.

Jones, J. (n.d.). *Florida corrections—Centuries of progress. 1921.* Retrieved from http://www.dc.state.fl.us/oth/timeline/1921.html (November 20, 2016).

Joongbaeck, K. (2010). Neighborhood disadvantage and mental health: The role of neighborhood disorder and social relationships. *Social Science Research, 39*(2), 260–271.

Joslin, C. G. (2011). Searching for harm: Same-sex marriage and the well-being of children. *Harvard Civil Rights-Civil Liberties Law Review (CR-CL), 46*(81). Retrieved from http://papers.ssrn.com/sol3/papers.cfm?abstract_id=1800382 (August 25, 2013).

Joy, A. B., & Hudes, M. (2010). High risk of depression among low-income women raises awareness about treatment options. *California Agriculture, 64*(1), 22–25.

Jurik, N. J. (2004). Imagining justice: Challenging the privatization of public life. *Social Problems, 51*(1), 1–15.

Justice Advocacy Project. (n.d.). *Prop. 36 Progress Report*. Retrieved from https://law.stanford.edu/stanford-justice-advocacy-project/reports/ (November 27, 2016).

Kadushin, A. (1974). *Child welfare services* (2nd ed.). New York: Macmillan.

Kaiser Commission on Medicaid and the Uninsured. (2013a). *Enrollment-driven expenditure growth: Medicaid spending during the economic downturn, FY2007–2011*. Retrieved from http://www.kff.org/medicaid/upload/8309-02.pdf (April 25, 2013).

Kaiser Commission on Medicaid and the Uninsured. (2013b). *Where are states today? Medicaid and CHIP eligibility levels for children and non-disabled adults* (March 2013). Retrieved from http://kaiserfamilyfoundation.files.wordpress.com/2013/04/7993-03.pdf (September 1, 2013).

Kaiser Family Foundation. (n.d.). *Total Medicaid spending, FY 2006*. Retrieved from http://www.statehealthfacts.org/comparetablejsp?md=177&cat=4 (February 12, 2008).

Kaiser Family Foundation. (2006a). *Employee health benefits: 2006 annual survey*. Retrieved from http://www.kff.org/insurance/7315.cfm (January 21, 2008).

Kaiser Family Foundation. (2006b). *Race, ethnicity, and health care*. Retrieved from http://www.kff.org/minorityhealth/upload/7541.pdf (July 8, 2010).

Kaiser Family Foundation. (2007b). *Massachusetts health care reform plan: An update*. Retrieved from http://www.kff.org/uninsured/7494.cfm (November 4, 2007).

Kaiser Family Foundation. (2010a). *Medicaid and managed care: Key data, trends, and issues*. Commission on Medicaid and the Uninsured. Retrieved from http://www.kff.org/medicaid/8046 .cfm (July 9, 2010).

Kaiser Family Foundation. (2010b). *Focus on health reform: Summary of coverage provisions in the Patient Protection and Affordable Care Act*. Retrieved from http://www.kff.org/healthreform/upload/8023-R.pdf (July 13, 2010).

Kaiser Family Foundation. (2015a). *The facts on Medicare spending and financing*. Retrieved from http://kff.org/medicare/fact-sheet/medicare-spending-and-financing-fact-sheet/ (June 16, 2016)

Kaiser Family Foundation. (2015b). *Poverty among seniors: An updated analysis of national and state level poverty rates under the official and supplemental poverty measures*. Retrieved from http://kff.org/medicare/issue-brief/poverty-among-seniors-an-updated-analysis-of-national-and-state-level-poverty-rates-under-the-official-and-supplemental-poverty-measures/ (November 7, 2016).

Kaiser Family Foundation. (2010c). *Health care reform and the CLASS Act*. Retrieved from http://www.kff.org/healthreform/upload/8069.pdf (July 14, 2010).

Kaiser Family Foundation. (2013b). *U.S. federal funding for HIV/AIDS: The president's FY 2014 budget request*. Retrieved from http://kff.org/hivaids/fact-sheet/u-s-federal-funding-for-hivaids-the-presidents-fy-2014-budget-request/ (June 1, 2013).

Kaiser Family Foundation. (2016a). *HIV testing in the United States*. Retrieved from http://kff.org/hivaids/fact-sheet/hiv-testing-in-the-united-states/ (October 30, 2016).

Kaiser Family Foundation. (2016b). *Key facts about the uninsured population*. Retrieved from: http://kff.org/uninsured/fact-sheet/key-facts-about-the-uninsured-population/ (December 22, 2016).

Kanjilal, S., Gregg, E. W., Cheng, Y. J., Zhang, P. Nelson, D., Mensah, G., & Beckles, G. (2006). Socioeconomic status and trends in disparities in four major risk factors for cardiovascular disease among U.S. adults, 1971–2002. *Archives of Internal Medicine, 166*(21), 2348–2355.

Kanwar, V. (2001/2002). Capital punishment as "closure:" The limits of a victim-centered jurisprudence. *New York University Review of Law and Social Change, 27* (not paginated).

Karabanow, J. (2004). *Being young and homeless: Understanding how you enter and exit street life*. New York: Peter Lang.

Karatanycky, A. (2000). A century of progress. *Journal of Democracy, 11*(1), 187–200.

Karger, H. (1988). *Social workers and labor unions*. New York: Greenwood Press.

Karger, H. J., & Stoesz, D. (2002). *American social welfare policy: A pluralist approach*. Boston: Allyn & Bacon.

Karp, D. R., & Frank, O. (2016). Anxiously awaiting the future of restorative justice in the United States. *Victims and Offenders, 11*, 50–70.

Kasper, J., & O'Malley, M. (2007). *Changes in characteristics, needs, and payment for care of elderly nursing home residents: 1999 to 2004*. Kaiser Commission on Medicaid and the Uninsured. Retrieved from http://www.kff.org/medicaid/7663 .cfm (January 10, 2008).

Kates, B. (1985). *The murder of a shopping bag lady*. New York: Harcourt Brace Jovanovich.

Katz, H. J. (1994, February 19). *Statement before the subcommittees on Social Security and human resources of the House Committee on Ways and Means. Hearing on exploring means of achieving higher rates of treatment and rehabilitation among alcoholics and drug addicts receiving federal disability benefits*. 103rd Congress, 2nd Session.

Katznelson, I. (2005). *When welfare was white: The untold history of racial inequality in twentieth century America*. New York: W. W. Norton.

Kaushal, N., & Kaestner, R. (2005). Welfare reform and health insurance of immigrants. *Health Services Research, 40*(3), 697–722. Retrieved from http://www.ncbi.nlm.nih.gov/pmc/articles/PMC1361164/.

Kawa, S., & Giordano, J. (2012). A brief history of the *Diagnostic and Statistical Manual of Mental Disorders*: Issues and implications for the future of psychiatric canon and practice. *Philosophy, Ethics and Humanities in Medicine, 7,* 2. doi:10.1186/1747-5341-7-2.

Kaye, H. S. (Ed.). (2000). *Disability watch: The status of people with disabilities in the United States.* Retrieved from http://www.dralegal.org/publications/dw/.

Kaye, H. S., Kang, T., & LaPlante, M. P. (2002, May). Wheelchair use in the United States. *Disability Statistics Abstract, 23.* Retrieved from http://dsc .ucsf.edu/pub_listing.php?pub_typeabstract.

Kelley, M. (1999, April 28). *American Indian boarding schools: "That hurt never goes away."* CNEWS-Canada's Internet Network. Retrieved from http://www.canoe.ca/CNEWSFeatures9904/28_indians .html.

Kelly, M. A., Perloff, J. D., Morris, N. M., & Liu, W. (1993). Access to primary care among young African-American children in Chicago. *Journal of Health and Social Policy, 5*(2), 35–48.

Kempe, C. H., Silverman, F., Steele, B., Droegemueller, W., & Silver, H. (1962). The battered child syndrome. *Journal of the American Medical Association, 181,* 17–24.

Kenney, G. M., Zuckerman, S., Dubay, L., Huntress, M., Lynch, V., Haley, J., & Anderson, N. (2012). *Opting in to the Medicaid expansion under the ACA: Who are the uninsured adults who could gain health insurance coverage?* Urban Institute. Retrieved from http://www.urban.org/UploadedPDF/412630-opting-in-medicaid.pdf (May 6, 2013).

Kertesz, S. G., Crouch, K., Milby, J. B., Cusimano, R. E., & Schumacher, J. E. (2009). Housing first for homeless persons with active addiction: Are we overreaching? The *Milbank Quarterly, 87*(2), 495–534. doi:10.1111/j.1468-0009.2009.00565.

Kessler, R. C., Chiu, W. T., Demler, O., & Walters, E. E. (2005). Prevalence, severity, and comorbidity of twelve-month DSM-IV disorders in the National Comorbidity Survey Replication (NCS-R). *Archives of General Psychiatry, 62*(6), 617–627. doi:10.1001/archpsyc.62.6.617.

Kessler, R. C., McGonagle, K. A., Zhao, S., Nelson, C. B., Hughes, M., Eshleman, S., … , & Kendler, K. S. (1994). Lifetime and 12-month prevalence of DSM-III-R psychiatric disorders in the United States: Results from the National Comorbidity Survey. *Archives of General Psychiatry, 51,* 8–19.

Kessler-Harris, A. (1990). *A woman's wage: Historical meanings and social consequences.* Lexington: University of Kentucky Press.

Kilburn, M. R., & Hao, L. (1996). *The impact of federal and state policy changes on child care in California.* Rand Corporation Report. Retrieved from http://www.rand.org/publications/CF/CFI23/kilburn/.

Kilmer, B., Caulkins, J., Pacula, R., MacCoun, R., & Reuter, P. (2010). *Altered state? Assessing how marijuana legalization in California could influence marijuana consumption and public budgets.* RAND Corporation. Retrieved from http://www.rand.org/content/dam/rand/pubs/occasional_papers/2010/RAND_OP315.pdf (November 28, 2016).

Kim, K., Becker-Cohen, M., & Serakos M. (2015). *The processing and treatment of mentally ill persons in the criminal justice system: A scan of practice and background analysis.* Urban Institute. Retrieved from http://www.urban.org/sites/default/files/alfresco/publication-pdfs/2000173-The-Processing-and-Treatment-of-Mentally-Ill-Persons-in-the-Criminal-Justice-System.pdf (December 2, 2016).

Kingson, E. R., & Berkowitz, E. D. (1993). *Social Security and Medicare: A policy primer.* Westport, CT: Auburn House.

Kingson, E., & Quadagno, J. (1997). Social Security: Marketing radical reform. In R. B. Hudson (Ed.), *The future of age-based public policy* (pp. 117–133). Baltimore: Johns Hopkins University Press.

Kinsey, A. C., Pomeroy, W. B., & Martin, C. E. (1948). *Sexual behavior in the human male.* Philadelphia: W. B. Saunders.

Kinsey, A. C., Pomeroy, W. B., Martin, C. E., & Gebhard, P. H. (1953). *Sexual behavior in the human female.* Philadelphia: W. B. Saunders.

Klemm, J. D. (2000). Medicaid spending: A brief history. *Health Care Financing Review, 22*(1), 105–112. Retrieved from http://www.cms.gov/Research-Statistics-Data-and-Systems/Research/HealthCareFinancingReview/downloads/00fallpg105.pdf (April 26, 2013).

Kloss, H. (1998). *The American bilingual tradition* (2nd ed.). Washington, DC: ERIC, Clearinghouse on Language and Linguistics.

Koebel, C. T. (1998). Nonprofit housing: Theory, research, and policy. In C. T. Koebel (Ed.), *Shelter and society: Theory, research and policy for nonprofit housing* (pp. 3–20). New York: State University of New York Press.

Kogan, R. (2013). *To stabilize the debt, policymakers should seek another $1.4 trillion in deficit savings.* Center on Budget and Policy Priorities. Retrieved from http://www.cbpp.org/cms/index.cfm? fa=view&id=3885 (September 1, 2013).

Kopelman, L. M. (2005). Are the 21-year-old Baby Doe rules misunderstood or mistaken? *Pediatrics, 115*(3), 797–801. Retrieved from http://pediatrics.aappublications.org/cgi/content/full/115/3/797 (October 30, 2010).

Korczyk, S. M. (1993). *Why has women's pension coverage improved?* Paper presented at the 1993 meeting of the Eastern Economic Association.

Kozol, J. (1991). *Savage inequalities: Children in America's schools.* New York: Crown Publishers.

Kposowa, A. J. (2001). Unemployment and suicide: A short analysis of social factors predicting suicide in the U.S. National Longitudinal Mortality Study. *Psychological Medicine, 31*(1), 127–138.

Krause, N. (1986). Stress and sex differences in depressive symptoms among older adults. *Journal of Gerontology, 41,* 727–731.

Kreisher, K. (2002a). *Coming home: The lingering effects of the Indian Adoption Project. Children's Voice articles.* Child Welfare League of America. Retrieved from http://www.cwla.org/articles/cv0203indianadopt.htm (September 7, 2013).

Kreisher, K. (2002b). Gay adoption. *Children's Voice.* Child Welfare League of America. Retrieved from http://www.cwla.org/articles/cv0201gayadopt.htm (September 12, 2010).

Ku, L., & Broaddus, M. (2003). *Why are states' Medicaid expenditures rising?* Center on Budget and Policy Priorities. Retrieved from http://www.cbpp.org/1-13-03health.htm (February 12, 2008).

Ku, L., & Garrett, B. (2000). *How welfare reform and economic factors affected Medicaid participation.* Washington, DC: Urban Institute. Retrieved from http://www.urban.org/Template.cfm?NavMenuID24&template/TaggedContent/ViewPublication.cfm&PublicationID7369.

LaBruzza, A. L., & Mendez-Villarrubia, J. M. (1994). *Using DSM-IV: A clinician's guide to psychiatric diagnosis.* Northvale, NJ: Jason Aronson.

Langton, L., Planty, M., & Sandholtz, N. (2013). *Hate crime victimization, 2003–2011.* Bureau of Justice Statistics, Department of Justice. Retrieved from http://www.bjs.gov/index.cfm?ty=pbdetail&iid=4614 (December 13, 2013).

Lasch, C. (1979). *Haven in a heartless world: The family besieged.* New York: Basic Books.

Laufer-Ukeles, P. (2008). Selective recognition of gender difference in the law: Revaluing the caretaker role. *Harvard Journal of Law and Gender, 31*(1). Retrieved from http://www.thelizlibrary.org/liz/mother-caretaker.pdf (August 8, 2010).

Lee, K., & Dodgson, R. (2000). Globalization and cholera: Implications for global governance. *Global Governance, 6*(2), 213–236.

Leibowitz, A. H. (1969). English literacy: Legal sanction for discrimination. *Notre Dame Lawyer, 45*(7), 7–76.

Leiby, J. (1978). *A history of social welfare and social work in the United States.* New York: Columbia University Press.

Leighninger, L. (1990). Professionalism in British and American social work. *Current Research on Occupations and Professions, 5,* 29–42.

Lejano, R. (2006). *Frameworks for policy analysis: Merging text and context.* New York: Routledge.

Lemann, N. (1986). The origins of the underclass. *Atlantic Monthly* (June), 31–55; (July), 54–68.

Leonard, K. K., Pope, C. E., & Feyerherm, W. H. (Eds.). (1995). *Minorities in the juvenile justice system.* Thousand Oaks, CA: Sage.

Levine, D. (1997). The Constitution as rhetorical symbol in Western anti-gay-rights initiatives: The case of Idaho. In S. L. Witt & S. McCorkle (Eds.), *Anti-gay rights assessing voter initiatives* (pp. 33– 50). Westport, CT: Praeger.

Levine, M. J. (2003). *Children for hire: The perils of child labor in the United States.* Westwood, CT: Praeger Publishers.

Levinsky, N. G. (1993). The organization of medical care—Lessons from the Medicare end stage renal disease program. *New England Journal of Medicine, 329,* 1395–1399.

Levy, P. B. (2011). The dream deferred: The assassination of Martin Luther King, Jr., and the Holy Week Uprisings of 1968. In J. Elfenbain, T. Hollowak, & E. Nix (Eds.), *Baltimore '68: Riots and rebirth in an American city* (pp. 3–25). Philadelphia: Temple University Press.

Lewin Group. (1998). *Policy evaluation of the effect of legislation prohibiting the payment of disability benefits to individuals whose disability is based on drug addiction and alcoholism: Interim report, April 28, 1998.* Washington, DC: Social Security Administration.

Lewis, M. A., & Widerquist, K. (2002). *Economics for social workers: The application of economic theory to social policy and the human services.* New York: Columbia University Press.

Lewis, O. (1965). *La vida.* New York: Harper & Row.

Lichtenberg, F. S., & Sun, S. X. (2007, November/December). The impact of Medicare Part D on prescription drug use by the elderly. *Health Affairs,* 1735–1744.

Lichtenstein, A. (1996). *Twice the work of free labor: The political economy of convict labor in the new south.* New York: Verso.

Limerick, P. N. (1987). *The legacy of conquest: The unbroken past of the American West.* New York: Norton.

Liptak, A. (2004, November 12). Caution in the court for gay rights groups: Fearing backlash, legal challenges will focus on civil unions. *The New York Times,* p. A16.

Littell, J. (1995). Debates with authors: Evidence or assertions? The outcomes of family preservation services. *Social Service Review, 69,* 344–351.

Little, A. (1998). *Post-industrial socialism: Towards a new politics of welfare.* London: Routledge.

Loewen, J. (1995). *Lies my teacher told me.* New York: Simon & Schuster.

Longman, P. (1987). *Born to pay: The new politics of aging in America.* Boston: Houghton Mifflin.

Longmore, P. K., & Umansky, L. (2001). Disability history: From the margins to the mainstream. In P. K. Longmore & L. Umansky (Eds.), *The new disability history: American perspectives* (pp. 1–33). New York: New York University Press.

Loo, D.D., & Grimes, R. (2004). Polls, politics, and crime: The "law and order" issue of the 1960s. *Western Criminology Review, 5*(1), 50–67.

Lorwin, L. (1929). *Labor and internationalism.* New York: Macmillan.

Lubben, J. E., Damron-Rodriguez, J. A., & Beck, J. C. (1992). A national survey of aging curriculum in schools of social work. *Geriatric Social Work Education, 18,* 151–171.

Lubbers, J. S. (1998). *A guide to federal rulemaking.* Washington, DC: Government and Public Sector Lawyers Division of the American Bar Association.

Lyons-Padilla, S., & Gelfand, M. J. (2015). Want to stop Islamic terrorism? Be nicer to Muslims. *Washington Post,* November 24. Retrieved from https://www.washingtonpost.com/posteverything/wp/2015/11/24/want-to-stop-islamic-terrorism-be-nicer-to-muslims/?utm_term=.838dc0b37ef5 (December 2, 2016).

Maag, E. (2005). *Paying the price? Low-income parents and the use of paid tax preparers.* Urban Institute. Retrieved from http://webarchive.urban.org/publications/411145.html (June 12, 2016).

Maas, H. S., & Engler, R. E. (1959). *Children in need of parents.* New York: Columbia University Press.

MacAskill, E. (2007, August 13). U.S. tumbles down the world ratings list for life expectancy. *The Guardian.* Retrieved from http://www.guardian.co.uk/world/2007/aug/13/usaewenmacaskill (February 20, 2008).

MacCoun, R., & Reuter, P. (2001). Evaluating alternative cannabis regimes. *British Journal of Psychiatry, 178,* 123–128.

MacDonald, B. R., & O'Neil, M. (2006). *Being American: The way out of poverty: The discussion to transform Social Security, Medicare, and disability tax law.* World Institute on Disability, Oakland, CA. Retrieved from http://www.wid.org/publications/being-american-the-way-out-of-poverty-poverty-and-disability-in-the-u-s (June 20, 2013).

MacDonald, H. (2016). *The war on cops: How the new attack on law and order makes everyone less safe.* New York: Encounter Books.

Mandel, J. (1992). *Not slave, not free: The African American economic experience.* Durham, NC: Duke University Press.

Mangan, B. (2012). *Financial capability services for vulnerable populations: Inclusion of older adults* [panel discussion]. Presented at Conference on Financial Capability Across the Life Span, Center for Social Development, Washington University, St. Louis, MO.

Mark, T. L., Levit, K. R., Coffey, R. M., McKusick, D. R., Harwood, H. J., King, E. C., … , & Ryan, K. (2007). *National expenditures for mental health services and substance abuse treatment, 1993–2003.* SAMHSA Publication No. SMA 07-4227. Rockville, MD: Substance Abuse and Mental Health Services Administration. Retrieved from http://www.samhsa.gov.

Mark, T. L., Levit, K. R., Vandivort-Warren, R., Buck, J. A., & Coffey, R. A. (2011). Changes in U.S. spending on mental health and substance abuse treatment, 1986–2005, and implications for policy. *Health Affairs, 30*(2), 284–329. doi:10.1377/hlthaff.2010.0765.

Marmor, T. R., & Mashaw, J. L. (2006). Understanding social insurance: Fairness, affordability and the "modernization" of Social Security and Medicare. *Health Affairs, 25*(3), 114–134. Retrieved from http://www.healthaffairs.org.

Mason, M. (1994). *From father's property to children's rights.* New York: Cambridge University Press.

Mathematica. (2000). *Reaching those in need: Food stamp participation rates in the states.* Retrieved from http://www.mathematica-mpr.com/3rdLevel/fms2ndbrochure.hot.htm.

Mayfield, C. (Ed.). (1981). *Growing up Southern: Southern exposure looks at childhood, then and now.* New York: Pantheon Books.

Maynard, R. A. (Ed.). (1996). *Kids having kids: A Robin Hood Foundation special report on the costs of adolescent childbearing.* New York: Robin Hood Foundation.

Maypole, D. E., & Skaine, R. (1983, September/October). Sexual harassment in the workplace. *Social Work, 28*(5), 385–390.

McCahan, D. (1956). *Accident and sickness insurance.* S.S. Huebner Foundation for Insurance Education, University of Pennsylvania.

McCaslin, R. (1987). Substantive specialization in masters level social work curricula. *Journal of Social Work Education, 23*(2), 8–18.

McGee, M. (2007). *Self Help, Inc.: Makeover culture in American life.* New York: Oxford University Press.

McGuire, T. G., & Miranda, J. (2008). New evidence regarding racial and ethnic disparities in mental health: Policy implications, *Health Affairs, 27*(2), 393–403.

McHugh, R., & Kimball, W. (2015). *How low can we go? State unemployment insurance programs exclude record numbers of jobless workers.* Economic Policy Institute. Briefing Paper #392. Retrieved from http://www.epi.org/publication/how-low-can-we-go-state-unemployment-insurance-programs-exclude-record-numbers-of-jobless-workers/ (June 14, 2016).

McLaughlin, K. A., Xuan, Z., Subramanian, S. V., & Koenen, K. C. (2011). State-level women's status and psychiatric disorders among U.S. women. *Social Psychiatry and Psychiatric Epidemiology, 46,* 1161–1171.

McLoughlin, A. B., Gould, M. S., & Malone, K. M. (2015). Global trends in teenage suicide: 2003–2014. *QJM: An International Journal of Medicine, 108*(10), 765–780.

McLeod, H. R. (1995, Spring). The sale of a generation. *American Prospect.* Retrieved from http://www.prospect.org/web/page.ww?sectionroot&nameViewPrint&articleId5024.

McMurrer, D. P., & Chasanov, A. B. (1995, September). Trends in unemployment insurance benefits. *Monthly Labor Review,* 30–39.

McNeal, G. (2014). *Drones and aerial surveillance: Considerations for legislatures.* The Brookings Institute.

Retrieved from https://www.brookings.edu/research/drones-and-aerial-surveillance-considerations-for-legislatures/ (November 28, 2016).

McNulty, F. (1980). *The burning bed.* New York: Harcourt Brace Jovanovich.

McPhail, B. A. (2003). A feminist policy analysis framework: Through a gendered lens. *The Social Policy Journal, 2*(2/3), 39–61.

Mechanic, D. (1962). Some factors in identifying and defining mental illness. *Mental Hygiene, 46,* 66–14.

Mechanic, D. (1999). *Mental health and social policy: The emergence of managed care.* Needham Heights, MA: Allyn & Bacon.

Meranze, M. (1996). *Laboratories of virtue: Punishment, revolution, and authority in Philadelphia, 1760–1834.* Chapel Hill: University of North Carolina Press.

Merck Manual of Diagnosis and Therapy (16th ed.). (1992). Rahway, NJ: Merck.

MetLife. (2007). *Private and semi-private room nursing home rates increase 3% in 2001.* Retrieved from http://www.metlife.com/Applications/Corporate/WPS/CDA/PageGenerator/0,4773,P250% 5ES1010,00.html?FILTERNAME=@URL \&FILTERVALUE=/WPS\&IMAGE2.X=0 \&IMAGE2.Y=0 (January 9, 2008).

Michael, R. T., Gagnon, J. H., Laumann, E. O., & Kolata, G. (1994). *Sex in America: A definitive survey.* Boston: Little, Brown.

Micklethwaite, J., & Wooldridge, A. (2004). *The right nation: Conservative power in America.* New York: Penguin Press.

Mill, J. S. (1863). On the connection between justice and utility. In *Utilitarianism,* Chapter 5. (Originally published by London: Parker, Son, and Bourn.) Retrieved from http://www.utilitarianism.com/mill1.htm (September 1, 2013).

Miller, D. (1976). *Social justice.* Oxford, UK: Clarendon Press.

Miller, D. (1999). *Principles of social justice.* Cambridge, UK: Oxford University Press.

Miller, R., & Luft, H. (1994). Managed care plan performance since 1980: A literature analysis. *Journal of the American Medical Association, 271*(19), 1512–1516.

Mintz, S., & Kellogg, S. (1988). *Domestic revolutions: A social history of American family life.* New York: Free Press.

Miranda, L., Dixon, V., & Reyes, C. (2015). *How states handle drug use during pregnancy.* Pro Publica (September 30, 2015). Retrieved from https://projects.propublica.org/graphics/maternity-drug-policies-by-state (September 17, 2016).

Mishel, L. (2013). *Vast majority of wage earners are working harder, and not for much more.* Economic Policy Institute. Retrieved from http://www.epi.org/publication/ib348-trends-us-work-hours-wages-1979-2007/ (October 27, 2013).

Mishel, L., Bernstein, J., & Boushey, H. (2004). *The state of working America: 2002/2003.* Washington, DC: Economic Policy Institute.

Mishel, L., & Shierholz, M. (2013). *A decade of flat wages: The key barrier to shared prosperity and a rising middle class.* Economic Policy Institute. Retrieved from http://www.epi.org/publication/a-decade-of-flat-wages-the-key-barrier-to-shared-prosperity-and-a-rising-middle-class/ (October 27, 2013).

Mixson, P. (2010). Public policy, elder abuse, and Adult Protective Services: The struggle for coherence. *Journal of Elder Abuse and Neglect, 22*(1/2), 16–36.

Molloy, D., & Burmeister, L. (1990). Social workers in union-based programs. In S. L. A. Straussner (Ed.), *Occupational social work today* (pp. 37–51). Binghamton, NY: Haworth Press.

Morrissey, M. (2013). *Private-sector pension coverage fell by half over two decades.* Economic Policy Institute. Retrieved from http://www.epi.org/blog/private-sector-pension-coverage-decline/ (November 10, 2016).

Montgomery, A. E., Hill, L. L., Kane, V., & Culhane, D. P. (2013). Housing chronically homeless veterans: Evaluating the efficacy of a Housing First approach to HUD-VASH. *Journal of Community Psychology, 41*(4), 505–514.

Monti, D. J. (1994). *Wannabe: Gangs in suburbs and schools.* Cambridge, UK: Blackwell Publishers.

Moquin, W. (Ed.). (1972). *A documentary history of Mexican Americans.* New York: Bantam Books.

Morgan, E. (1975). *American slavery, American freedom: The ordeal of colonial Virginia.* New York: Norton.

Morris, A., & Maxwell, G. (1998). Restorative justice in New Zealand: Family group conferences as a case study. *Western Criminology Review, 1.* Retrieved from http://wcr.sonoma.edu/v1n1/morris.html.

Morrissey, J. P., & Goldman, H. H. (1986). Care and treatment of the mentally ill in the United States: Historical developments and reforms. *Annals of the American Academy of Political and Social Science, 484,* 12–27.

Morrissey, T. W., & Banghart, P. (2007). *Family child care in the United States.* Child Care Bureau, U.S. Department of Health and Human Services. Retrieved from http://www.childcareresearch.org/SendPdPresourceId=12036 (February 27, 2008).

Morrow-Howell, N., Hinterlong, J., & Sherraden, M. (Eds.). (2001). *Productive aging concepts and challenges.* Baltimore: Johns Hopkins University Press.

Movement Advancement Project. (n.d.). Non-discrimination laws. Retrieved from http://www.lgbtmap.org/equality-maps/non_discrimination_laws (October 12, 2016).

Moss, K. (1987). The "Baby Doe" legislation: Its rise and fall. *Policy Studies Journal, 15*(40), 629–651.

Mullaney, T. (2015). *Why corporate CEO pay is so high, and going higher.* Retrieved from http://www.cnbc.com/2015/05/18/why-corporate-ceo-pay-is-so-high-and-going-higher.html (November 11, 2016).

Muller, C. (2012). Northward migration and the rise of racial disparity in American incarceration, 1880–1950. *American Journal of Sociology, 118*(2). 281–326.

Mulroy, E. (1990). Single-parent families and the housing crisis. *Social Work, 35*, 542–546.

Mulroy, E. A. (1995). *The new uprooted single mothers in urban life*. Westport, CT: Auburn House.

Munch, S. (2006). The women's health movement: Making policy, 1970–1995. *Social Work in Health Care, 43*(1), 17–32.

Munnell, A. H. (2006). *Policies to promote labor force participation of older people*. Chestnut Hill, MA: Center for Retirement Research at Boston College. Retrieved from http://crr.bc.edu/working_papers/pohcies_to_promote_labor_force_participation_ of_older_people.html. (January 21, 2008).

Munoz, R. F., Mrazek, P. J., & Haggerty, R. J. (1996). Institute of Medicine report on prevention of mental disorders: Summary and Commentary. *American Psychologist, 51*(11), 1116–1122.

Muntaner, C., Eaton, W. W., Diala, C., Kessler, R. C., & Sorlie, P. D. (1998). Social class, assets, organizational control, and the prevalence of common groups of psychiatric disorders. *Social Science and Medicine, 47*(12), 2043–2053.

Murphy, T. F. (2005). The search for the gay gene. *British Medical Journal: International Edition, 330*(7498), 1033.

Murray, C. (1994). *Losing ground: American social policy, 1950–1980*. New York: Basic Books.

Musgrave, S., Meagher, T., & Dance, G. (2014). *The Pentagon finally details its Weapons-for-Cops giveaway*. The Marshall Project. Retrieved from https://www.themarshallproject.org/2014/12/03/the-pentagon-finally-details-its-weapons-for-cops-giveaway#.y9p5bam2V (November 28, 2016).

Nagourney, A. (2008, November 4). Obama wins election, McCain loses as Bush legacy is rejected. *The New York Times*, p. 1.

National Advisory Mental Health Council. (1991). *Building social work knowledge for effective services and policies: A plan for research development*. Washington, DC: NIMH. Available from IASWR, 750 First Street NE, Suite 700, Washington, DC 20002–4241.

National Alliance to End Homelessness. (2010). *Economy bytes: Doubled up in the United States*. Report May 18, 2010. Retrieved from http://www .endhomelessness.org/content/article/detail/3024 (July 7, 2010).

National Association for the Advancement of Colored People (NAACP). (1969). *Thirty years of lynching in the United States, 1889–1918*. New York: Arno Press.

National Association of Black Social Workers (NABSW). (1994). *Position statement: Preserving African American families*. Detroit: Author.

National Association of Social Workers (NASW). (n.d.). *Code of ethics*. (Approved 1996; Revised 2008). Retrieved from http://www.naswdc.org/pubs/code/default.asp (February 19, 2011).

National Association of Social Workers (NASW). (2011). *Social work salaries by gender: Occupational profile*. Retrieved from http://workforce. socialworkers.org/studies/profiles/Gender.pdf (September 29, 2013).

National Association of Social Workers (NASW). (2006). *Assuring the sufficiency of a frontline workforce: A national study of licensed social workers*. Retrieved from http://workforce.socialworkers.org/studies/nasw_06_execsummary.pdf (June 7, 2016).

National Association of Social Workers (NASW). (2010). *Criminal justice social work in the United States: Adapting to new challenges*. Washington, DC: NASW Center for Workforce Studies. Retrieved from http://workforce.socialworkers.org/studies/Criminal%20Justice%20in%20the%20United%20States.pdf (November 28, 2016).

National Association of State Units on Aging. (2005). *Quality in Medicaid waiver assisted living: The ombudsman program's role and perspective*. Retrieved from http://www.nasua.org/Medicaid_Assisted_Living_Waiver.pdf (January 9, 2007).

National Campaign to Prevent Teen Pregnancy. (2006). *The public costs of teen childbearing*. Retrieved from http://www.thenationalcampaign. org/costs/pdf/Science_Says_30.pdf (August 7, 2010).

National Center for Education Statistics (NCES). (2004). *Digest of education statistics, 2003*. Retrieved from http://nces.ed.gov/programs/digest/d03/.

National Center for Education Statistics (NCES). (2009). *Digest of education statistics, 2009,* Table 26: Expenditures of educational institutions related to the gross domestic product. Retrieved from http://nces.ed.gov/programs/digest/d09/tables/dt09_026 .asp?referrer=list (August 5, 2010).

National Center for Education Statistics. (2016). *Digest of education statistics*. Retrieved from https://nces.ed.gov/programs/digest/d15/tables/dt15_230.40.asp (October 21, 2016).

National Center for Health Statistics. (2012). Births: Final data for 2011. *National Vital Statistics Reports, 62*(11). Retrieved from http://www.cdc.gov/nchs/data/nvsr/nvsr62/nvsr62_01.pdf (September 8, 2013).

National Coalition for the Homeless. (1999). *The McKinney Act*. Fact sheet #19. Retrieved from http://www.nationalhomeless.org/mckmneyfacts .html.

National Coalition for the Homeless. (2009a). *Who is homeless?* Retrieved from http://www .nationalhomeless.org/factsheets/who.html.

National Coalition for the Homeless. (2009b). *Mental illness and homelessness*. Retrieved from http://www.nationalhomeless.org/factsheets/Mental_Illness.pdf (September 16, 2016).

National Conference of State Legislatures. (2007). *Managed behavioral health care carve-outs.* Health Chairs Project. Retrieved from http://www.ncsl.org/programs/health/forum/chairs/carveout.htm (December 3, 2007).

National Council on Crime and Delinquency. (2009). *Created equal: Racial and ethnic disparities in the US criminal justice system.* Retrieved from http://www.nccdglobal.org/sites/default/files/publication_pdf/created-equal.pdf (November 28, 2016).

National Education Association. (n.d.). *NEA offers plan to improve NCLB.* Retrieved from http://www.nea.org/esea/mdex.html (December 30, 2007).

National Education Association. (2007). *Truth in labeling: Disproportionality in special education.* Retrieved from http://www.nccrest.org/Exemplars/Disporportionality_Truth_In_Labeling.pdf (June 20, 2013).

National Health Care Anti-Fraud Association. (2008). *The problem of health care fraud.* Retrieved from http://www.nhcaa.org/eweb/DynamicPage.aspx?webcode=anti_fraud_resource_centr&wpscode=TheProblemOfHCFraud (July 8, 2010).

National Humanities Center Resource Toolbox. (n.d.). *Making the revolution: America, 1763–1791.* Retrieved from http://nationalhumanitiescenter.org/pds/makingrev/rebellion/text6/jeffersondraftdecindep.pdf (July 6, 2013).

National Indian Health Board. (2004). *Fiscal year 2005 AI/AN national budget perspective.* Retrieved from http://www.mhb.org.

National Institute of Mental Health. (n.d.). *Transforming the understanding and treatment of mental illness: Any Mental Illness (AMI) among US adults.* Retrieved from https://www.nimh.nih.gov/health/statistics/prevalence/any-mental-illness-ami-among-us-adults.shtml (December 2, 2016).

National Institute of Mental Health. (NIMH). (2000). *Insurance parity for mental health cost, access, and quality: Final report to Congress by the National Advisory Mental Health Council.* NIH Publication No. 00-4787. Retrieved from http://www.nimh.nih .gov/about/advisory-boards-and-groups/namhc/reports/nimh-parity.pdf.

National Institute on Aging (NIA), National Institutes of Health. (1987). *Personnel for health needs of the elderly through the year 2020.* DHHS-NIAH Pub. No. 87-2950. Washington, DC: U.S. Department of Health and Human Services.

National Institute on Drug Abuse (NIDA). (n.d.). Comorbidity: Why do drug use disorders often co-occur with other mental illnesses? Retrieved from https://www.drugabuse.gov/publications/research-reports/comorbidity-addiction-other-mental-illnesses/why-do-drug-use-disorders-often-co-occur-other-men (September 16, 2016).

National Institute on Drug Abuse (NIDA). (2011). *Drug facts: Comorbidity: Addiction and other mental disorders.* Retrieved from https://www.drugabuse.gov/publications/drugfacts/comorbidity-addiction-other-mental-disorders (September 16, 2016).

National Law Center on Homelessness and Poverty. (2007). *Homelessness in the United States and the human right to housing.* Retrieved from http://www.nlchp.org/content/pubs/HomelessnessintheUSandRightstoHousing.pdf.

National Policy and Resource Center on Women and Aging. (1996). A big decision for women: Should I buy long-term care insurance? *Women & Aging Letter, 1*(6). Retrieved from http://www.heller.brandeis.edu/national/ind.html.

National Public Radio. (2008). *"Stop snitching" movement confounding criminal justice: Special Series on Criminal Justice.* Retrieved from http://www.npr.org/templates/story/story.php?storyId=90280108 (November 22, 2016).

National Vital Statistics System. (2015). Infant mortality statistics from the 2013 period linked birth/infant death data set. *National Vital Statistics Reports, 64*(9). Retrieved from http://www.cdc.gov/nchs/data/nvsr/nvsr64/nvsr64_09.pdf (October 6, 2016).

National Youth Gang Center. (2009). *National youth gang survey analysis.* Retrieved from http://www.nationalgangcenter.gov/Survey-Analysis (November 10, 2010).

Navarro, V. (1991, September). Class and race: Life and death situations. *Monthly Review, 43*(4), 1–13.

Nelson, F. H., Rosenberg, B., & Van Meter, N. (2004). *Charter school achievement on the 2003 National Assessment of Educational Progress.* Retrieved from http://www.aft.org/pubs-reports/downloads/teachers/NAEPCharterSchoolReport.pdf.

Neumark, D., & Wascher, W. L. (2008). *Minimum wages.* Cambridge, MA: The MIT Press.

Nicholson-Crotty, S. (2004). The politics and administration of privatization contracting out for corrections management in the United States. *Policy Studies Journal, 32*(1), 41–57.

Nkansah-Amankra, S., Dhawain, A., Hussey, J., & Luchok, K. (2010). Maternal social support and neighborhood income inequality as predictors of low birth weight and preterm birth outcome disparities: Analysis of South Carolina Pregnancy Risk Assessment and Monitoring System Survey, 2000–2003. *Maternal & Child Health Journal, 14*(5), 774–785.

Noji, E. K. (2001). The global resurgence of infectious diseases. *Journal of Contingencies and Case Management, 9*(4), 223–232.

Nonprofit Finance Fund. (n.d.). *Pay for Success Learning Hub.* Retrieved from http://www.payforsuccess.org/provider-toolkit/pfs-projects (June 11, 2016).

North American Association of State and Provincial Lotteries (NASPL). (1999). *Lottery history.* Retrieved from http://www.naspl.org/history.html.

Northrup, H. R. (1970). *Negro employment in southern industry: A study of racial policies in five industries.* Philadelphia: Industrial Research Unit, Wharton School of Finance and Commerce, University of Pennsylvania.

Nozick, R. (1974). *Anarchy, state, and utopia*. New York: Basic Books.

Nussbaum, M. (2001). The costs of tragedy: Some moral limits of cost–benefit analysis. In M. D. Adler & E. A. Posner (Eds.), *Cost–benefit analysis: Legal, economic, and philosophical perspectives* (pp. 169–200). Chicago: University of Chicago Press.

Obama, B. (2016). United States health care reform: Progress to date and next steps. *Journal of the American Medical Association, 316*(5), 525–532.

O'Connor, M. K., & Netting, F. E. (2008). Teaching policy analysis as research: Consideration and extension of options. *Journal of Social Work Education. 44*(3), 159–172.

O'Connor, M. K., & Netting, F. E. (2011). *Analyzing social policy: Multiple perspectives for critically understanding and evaluating policy*. Hoboken, NJ: John Wiley & Sons.

Offe, C., Muckenberger, U., & Ostner, I. (1996). A basic income guaranteed by the state: A need of the moment in social policy. In C. Offe (Ed.), *Modernity and the state: East, west*. Cambridge: Polity Press.

Office of Juvenile Justice and Delinquency Prevention. (2014). *Disproportionate minority contact* (Literature Review). Washington, DC. Retrieved from https://www.ojjdp.gov/mpg/litreviews/Disproportionate_Minority_Contact.pdf (November 28, 2016).

Office of Management and Budget (OMB). (n.d.). *Unemployment Insurance (UI) program*. OMB Circular CFDA 11.225. Retrieved from http://www.whitehouse.gov/omb/circulars/al33_compliance/l7225.html (March 14, 2008).

Office of Management and Budget (OMB). (n.d.a.). *Chained CPI protections*. Retrieved from http://www .whitehouse.gov/omb/budget/factsheet/chained-cpi-protections (September 1, 2013).

Office of Management and Budget (OMB). (n.d.b.). *Historical tables*. Tables 3.1: Outlays by Superfunction and Function: 1940–2017 and 8.4: Outlays by Budget Enforcement Act Category as Percent of GDP: 1962–2017. Retrieved from https://www.whitehouse.gov/omb/budget/Historicals (June 10, 2016).

Office of Management and Budget (OMB). (2001). *A citizen's guide to the federal budget: Budget of the United States government, fiscal year 2001*. Retrieved from http://w3.access.gpo.gov/usbudget/FY2001/guidetoc.html.

Office of Management and Budget (OMB). (2013). *Fiscal year 2013: Analytical perspectives: Budget of the U.S. government*. Retrieved from http://www.whitehouse.gov/sites/default/files/omb/budget/fy2013/assets/spec.pdf (September 1, 2013).

Officer Down Memorial Page. (2015). Retrieved from https://www.odmp.org/search/year/2015 (October 4, 2016).

Offices of the United States Attorneys. (2016). *Crime Victims' Rights Act*. Retrieved from https://www.justice.gov/usao/resources/crime-victims-rights-ombudsman/victims-rights-act (December 6, 2016).

Ogunwole, S. U. (2002). *The American Indian and Alaska Native population: 2000*. Census 2000 Brief. Washington, DC: U.S. Census Bureau. Retrieved from http://www.census.gov/prod/2002pubs/c2kbr01-15.pdf (February 24, 2003).

O'Keefe, B. J., & Shepherd, G. J. (1987). The pursuit of multiple objectives in face-to-face persuasive interactions: Effects of construct differentiation on message organization. *Communication Monographs, 54*, 396–419.

O'Keefe, D. (1992). *Persuasion theory and research*. Newbury Park, CA: Sage.

Okin, S. (1989). *Justice, gender and the family*. New York: Basic Books.

Older Women's League. (2015). Women and Social Security. Retrieved from http://nwlc.org/resources/women-and-social-security/ (June 16, 2016).

Oliver, M. L., & Shapiro, T. (1990). Wealth of a nation: A reassessment of asset inequality in America shows at least one third of households are asset poor. *American Journal of Economics and Sociology, 49*(2), 129–152.

Omi, M., & Winaut, H. (1994). *Racial formation in the United States: From the 1960s to the 1990s* (2nd ed.). New York: Routledge.

Orenstein, M. (2008). *Privatizing pensions: The transnational campaign for Social Security reform*. Princeton, NJ: Princeton University Press.

Orentlicher, D. (1996, August 29). The legalization of physician-assisted suicide. *New England Journal of Medicine, 335*(9), 663–667.

Organisation for Economic Co-operation and Development (OECD). (n.d.a.). *Tax policy analysis: Revenue statistics tax ratios changes between 2007 and provisional 2011 data*. Table A. Retrieved from http://www.oecd.org/ctp/tax-policy/revenuestatisticstaxratioschangesbetween2007and2011.htm (September 1, 2013).

Organisation for Economic Co-operation and Development (OECD). (n.d.b.). *OECD.StatExtracts: Short-term labour market statistics, Harmonised Unemployment Rates (HURs)*. Retrieved from http://stats.oecd.org/index.aspx?queryid=36324 (October 27, 2103).

Organisation for Economic Co-operation and Development (OECD). (2009). *Comparative child well-being across the OECD*. Office of Economic Development. Retrieved from http://www.oecd.org/els/family/43570328.pdf (September 8, 2013).

Organisation for Economic Co-operation and Development (OECD). (2016). *OECD health statistics 2016: Frequently requested data*. Retrieved from http://stats.oecd.org/index.aspx?DataSetCode=HEALTH_STAT (September 14, 2016).

O'Rourke, S. P., & Dellinger, L. K. L. (1997). *Romer v. Evans*: The centerpiece of the American gay rights debate. In S. L. Witt & S. McCorkle (Eds.), *Anti-gay rights: Assessing voter initiatives* (pp. 133–140). Westport, CT: Praeger.

Orshansky, M. (1965). Counting the poor: Another look at the poverty profile. *Social Security Bulletin, 28*(1), 3–29.

Osborne, R. (1993). *Freud for beginners.* New York: Writer's and Reader's Publishing.

Osgood, D., Foster, E., & Courtney, M. (2010). Vulnerable populations and the transition to adulthood. *The Future of Children, 20*(1), 209–229.

Osipow, S. H., & Fitzgerald, L. F. (1993). Unemployment and mental health: A neglected relationship. *Applied and Preventive Psychology, 2,* 59–63.

Ostry, J. D., Loungani, P., & Furceri, D. (2016). Neoliberalism: Oversold? *Finance and Development, 53*(2). Retrieved from http://www.imf.org/external/pubs/ft/fandd/2016/06/ostry.htm#author (June 10, 2016).

Osumi, M. D. (1982). Asians and California's anti-miscegenation laws. In N. Tsuchida (Ed.), *Asian and Pacific American experiences: Women's perspectives.* Minneapolis: Asian/Pacific American Learning.

Owens, L. H. (1976). *This species of property: Slave life and culture in the old south.* New York: Oxford University Press.

Owens, M. J. (1999). Battered women and their children: A public policy response. *AFFILLIA: Journal of Women and Social Work, 14*(4), 439–459.

Paine, T. (1795). *Agrarian justice.* Retrieved from http://www.ssa.gov/history/paine4.html.

Park, R. (1974). *The collected papers of Robert Ezra Park.* New York: Arno.

Parker, A. C. (1916). *The constitution of the five nations, or the Iroquois book of the great law.* Albany, NY: A.C. Irocrafts, reprinted by Iroquois Reprints.

Patten, E., & Parker, K. (2011). *Women in the US Military: Growing share, distinctive profile.* Pew Research: Social & Demographic Trends. Retrieved from http://www.pewsocialtrends.org/2011/12/22/women-in-the-u-s-military-growing-share-distinctive-profile/ (September 29, 2013).

Pattillo-McCoy, M. (1999). *Black picket fences: Privilege and peril among the black middle class.* Chicago: University of Chicago Press.

Pavelka, S., & Leach, M. (2014). The political rise of restorative justice. *Huffington Post,* March 26. Retrieved from http://www.huffingtonpost.com/molly-rowan-leach/the-political-rise-of-res_b_5029413.html (November 28, 2016).

Pearson, J., & Griswold, E. A. (1997). Child support policies and domestic violence. *Public Welfare, 55*(1), 26–32.

Pearson, S. D., Sabin, J. E., & Emanuel, E. J. (1998). Ethical guidelines for physician compensation based on capitation. *New England Journal of Medicine: Sounding Board, 339,* 689–693.

Pecora, P., Fraser, M., Nelson, K., McCroskey, J., & Meezan, W. (Eds.). (1995). *Evaluating family-based services.* Hawthorne, NY: Aldine de Gruyter.

Pecora, P., Whittaker, J. K., Maluccio, A. N., & Barth, R. P. (2000). *The child welfare challenge: Policy, practice and research.* New York: Aldine de Gruyter.

Pedriana, N. (1999). The historical foundations of affirmative action, 1961–1971. *Research in Social Stratification and Mobility, 11,* 3–32.

Pension Benefit Guaranty Corporation (PBGC). (2001). *Pension Benefit Guarantee Corporation history.* Retrieved from http://www.pbgc.gov/about_pbgc/history/hptext.htm.

Perez, R. M. (2013). Paradise lost: Older Cuban-American exiles' ambiguous loss of leaving the homeland. *Journal of Gerontological Social Work, 56*(7), 596–622.

Perkins, J., Olson, K., & Rivera, L. (1996). *Making the consumers' voice heard in Medicaid managed care: Increasing participation, protection and satisfaction.* National Health Law Program. Retrieved from http://www.healthlaw.org/pubs/19970128consumersvoice.html.

Perlmutter, M. (Ed.). (1990). *Late life potential.* Washington, DC: Gerontological Society of America.

Perloff, J. D. (1996). Medicaid managed care and urban poor people: Implications for social work. *Health and Social Work, 21*(3), 189–195.

Perry, M. J. (1996). The relationship between social class and mental disorder. *Journal of Primary Prevention, 17*(1), 17–30.

Petchey, R. (1987). Health maintenance organizations: Just what the doctor ordered? *Journal of Social Policy, 16*(4), 489–507.

Petersen, D. A. (1988). *Personnel to serve the aging in the field of social work.* A report prepared by the Andrus Gerontology Center, University of Southern California, Los Angeles, CA, and the Association for Gerontology in Higher Education, Washington, DC.

Petersilia, J. (2000). When prisoners return to the community: Political, economic, and social consequences. *Sentencing & Corrections: Issues for the 21st Century* (November 2016). Washington, DC: U.S. Department of Justice. Retrieved from https://www.ncjrs.gov/pdffiles1/nij/184253.pdf (August 3, 2016).

Petr, C. G., & Johnson, I. C. (1999). Privatization of foster care in Kansas: A cautionary tale. *Social Work, 44*(3), 262–267.

PEW Economic Policy Group. (2010). *Financial reform project national poll: Major findings* (released March 25, 2010). Retrieved from http://www.pewfr.org/project_polls_detail?id=0006 (August 22, 2010).

Pfeffer, F. T., & Hallsten, M. (2012). *Mobility regimes and parental wealth: The United States, Germany, and Sweden in comparison.* Retrieved from http://www.psc.isr.umich.edu/pubs/pdf/rr12-766.pdf (April 30, 2013).

Philips, F. (2007, June 14). Legislators vote to defeat same-sex marriage ban. *Boston Globe.* Retrieved from http://www.boston.com/news/globe/city_region/breaking_news/2007/06/legislators_vot_1.html (December 27, 2007).

Phillips, K. R. (2001). *Who knows about the earned income tax credit?* Washington, DC: Urban Institute. Retrieved from http://newfederalism .urban.org/html/series_b/b27/b27.html.

Phillips, W. D., & Phillips, C. R. (1992). *The worlds of Christopher Columbus.* Cambridge, UK: Cambridge University Press.

Physician Payment Review Commission. (1991, April). *Annual report to Congress 1991.* Washington, DC: Author.

Pickard, H., & Fazel, S. (2013). Substance abuse as a risk factor for violence in mental illness: Some implications for forensic psychiatric practice and clinical ethics. *Current Opinion in Psychiatry, 26*(4), 349–354. doi:10.1097/YCO.0b013e328361e798.

Pirog, M. A., & Ziol-Guest, K. M. (2006). Child support enforcement: Programs and policies, impacts and questions. *Journal of Policy Analysis and Management, 25*(4), 943–990.

Piven, F. F., & Cloward, R. A. (1971). *Regulating the poor: The functions of public welfare.* New York: Pantheon Books.

Piven, F. F., & Cloward, R. A. (1997). *The breaking of the American social compact.* New York: New Press.

Pollard, L. J. (1980, September). Black beneficial societies and the Home for Aged and Infirm Colored Persons: A research note. *Phylon, 41*(3), 230–234.

Pomerleau, K., & Schuyler, M. (2016). *Details and analysis of Hillary Clinton's tax proposals.* Tax Foundation. Retrieved from http://taxfoundation.org/article/details-and-analysis-hillary-clinton-s-tax-proposals (June 12, 2016).

Population Reference Bureau. (1999). America's racial and ethnic minorities. *Population Bulletin, 54*(3). Retrieved from http://www.prb.org/Publications/PopulationBulletins/1999/AmericasRacialandEthnicMinoritiesPDF17MB.aspx (November 6, 2010).

Porter, E. (2015, July 28). Wall St. Money Meets Social Policy at Rikers Island. *The New York Times,* Retrieved from http://www.nytimes.com/2015/07/29/business/economy/wall-st-money-meets-social-policy-at-rikers-island.html?_r=0 (June 11, 2016).

Porter, K. H., Latin, K., & Primus, W. (1999). *Social Security and poverty among the elderly: A national and state perspective.* Washington, DC: Center on Budget and Policy Priorities. Retrieved from http://www.cbpp.org/4-8-99socsec.htm.

Preston, J. (2012, August 13). Young immigrants, in America illegally, line up for reprieve. *The New York Times.* Retrieved from http://www.nytimes.com/2012/08/14/us/young-immigrants-poised-for-deportation-deferral-program.html?_r=0 (October 25, 2013).

Price, K. (n.d.). Circular 3591 and why Dec. 12th is special in the fight against slavery. Retrieved from http://kennethdprice.com/2013/12/12/circular-3591/ (November 20, 2016).

Princeton Survey Research Associates. (1997). *National Omnibus Survey questions about teen pregnancy, for the* Association of Reproductive Health Professionals and the National Campaign to Prevent Teen Pregnancy. Washington, DC: Author.

Prison Policy Initiative. (2016). *Mass incarceration: The whole pie, 2016.* Retrieved from http://www.prisonpolicy.org/reports/pie2016.html (November 20, 2016).

Prospective Payment Assessment Commission. (1995). *PPRC annual report to Congress, 1995.* Washington, DC: U.S. Government Printing Office.

Public Citizen. (2003). *The other drug war 2003: Drug companies deploy an army of 675 lobbyists to protect profits.* Retrieved from http://www.citizen.org/_Drug_War2003.pdf.

Putnam, R. D. (2000). *Bowling alone: The collapse and revival of American community.* New York: Simon & Schuster.

Qazy, R. (2006). Biobehavioral science research on human sexual orientation. In D. Yip, *Psychology of gender identity: An international perspective* (pp. 1–34). Hauppauge, NY: NOVA Science Publishers.

Quadagno, J. (1989). Generational equity and the politics of the welfare state. *Politics and Society, 11,* 360–376.

Quadagno, J. (1994). *The color of welfare: How racism undermined the war on poverty.* New York: Oxford University Press.

Radner, D. B. (1991). Changes in the incomes of age groups, 1984–89. *Social Security Bulletin, 54,* 2–18.

Ramirez, J. D., Yuen, S. D., & Ramey, D. R. (1991). *Final report: Longitudinal study of structured English immersion strategy, early-exit, and late-exit transitional bilingual education programs for language-minority children.* San Mateo, CA: Aguirre International.

Raphael, J. (1996). *Prisoners of abuse: Domestic violence and welfare receipt.* A second report of the Women, Welfare and Abuse Project. Chicago: Taylor Institute.

Rappeport, A., & Sanger-Katz, M. (2016). Hillary Clinton takes a step to the left on health care. *The New York Times* (May 10). Retrieved from http://www.nytimes.com/2016/05/11/us/politics/hillary-clinton-health-care-public-option.html?_r=0 (June 9, 2016).

Rasell, E., & Weller, C. E. (2001). *Trust funds' rainy day postponed, again: Trustees' reports provide no justification for radical changes in Social Security and Medicare.* Washington, DC: Economic Policy Institute. Retrieved from http://www.epmet.org.

Rawls, J. (1971). *A theory of justice.* Cambridge, MA: Harvard University Press.

Reegan, L. J. (1997). *When abortion was a crime: Women, medicine and law in the United States, 1867–1973.* Berkeley: University of California Press.

Regan, J. J. (1985). *Adult Protective Services: Policy issue for the '80s.* Conference on Working with Victims of Abuse and Neglect, San Antonio, TX, November. (Cited by Mixson, 2010).

Regier, D. A., Narrow, W., Rae, D., Manderscheid, R., Locke, B., & Goodwin, F. (1993). The de facto

U.S. mental and addictive disorders service system: Epidemiological Catchment Area prospective one-year prevalence rates of disorders and services. *Archives of General Psychiatry, 50*, 85–94.

Regnerus, M. (2012). How different are the adult children of parents who have same-sex relationships? Findings from the New Family Structures Study. *Social Science Research, 41*(4), 752–770.

Reichmann, R. (1999). *Race in contemporary Brazil: From indifference to inequality.* University Park, PA: Pennsylvania State University Press.

Reisch, M. (1987). *The unique contribution of social work to the mental health professions.* Paper presented at the regional meeting of the California Council on Psychiatry, Social Work, and Nursing. San Francisco.

Reisch, M., & Gorin, S. H. (2001). Nature of work and future of the social work profession. *Social Work, 46*(1), 9–19.

Reischauer, R. D. (1999). *Investing Social Security reserves in private securities. Testimony before House Committee on Ways and Means, March 3.* Retrieved from http://www.brookings.edu/testimony/1999/0303saving_reischauer.aspx (June 30, 2010).

Reuters. (2011, March 10). *Factbox: Several states beyond Wisconsin mull union limits.* Retrieved from http://www.reuters.com/article/2011/03/11/us-usa-unions-states-idUSTRE7295QI20110311 (October 27, 2013).

Reynolds, B. C. (1963). *An uncharted journey: Fifty years of growth in social work.* New York: Citadel Press.

Reynolds, B. C. (1975). *Social work and social living.* Washington, DC: National Association of Social Workers. (Original work published 1951.)

Rhode, D. (1989). *Justice and gender: Sex discrimination and the law.* Cambridge, MA: Harvard University Press.

Rice, D. P. (1991). Ethics and equity in U.S. health care: The data. *International Journal of Health Services, 21*(4), 637–651.

Rich, B. M., & Baum, M. (1984). *The aging: A guide to public policy.* Pittsburgh: University of Pittsburgh Press.

Richards, D. A. J. (1999). *Identity and the case for gay rights: Race, gender, and religion as analogies.* Chicago: University of Chicago Press.

Richardson, T. R. (1989). *The century of the child: The mental hygiene movement and social policy in the United States and Canada.* Albany: State University of New York Press.

Richmond, M. (1917). *Social diagnosis.* New York: Russell Sage Foundation.

Rifkin, J. (1995). *The end of work: The decline of the global labor force and the dawn of the post-market era.* New York: G. P. Putnam's Sons.

Rimlinger, G. V. (1971). *Welfare policy and industrialization in Europe, America, and Russia.* New York: Wiley.

Rimmerman, C. A. (2000). A "friend" in the White House? Reflections on the Clinton presidency. In J. D'Emilio, W. B. Turner, & U. Vaid (Eds.), *Creating change: Sexuality,*

public policy, and civil rights (pp. 43–56). New York: St. Martin's Press.

Roberts, A., & Springer, D. (2007). *Social work in juvenile and criminal justice settings* (3rd ed). Springfield IL: Charles C. Thomas.

Roberts, A. R., & Kurtz, L. F. (1987). Historical perspectives on the care and treatment of the mentally ill. *Journal of Sociology and Social Welfare, 14*(4), 75–94.

Robertson, A. H., & Merrills, J. G. (1996). *Human rights in the world: An introduction to the study of the international protection of human rights.* Manchester, UK: Manchester University Press.

Robins, L. N., Helzer, J. E., Weissman, M. M., Orvaschel, H., Gruenberg, E., Burke, J. D., Jr., & Regier, D. A. (1984). Lifetime prevalence of specific psychiatric disorders in three sites. *Archives of General Psychiatry, 41*, 949–956.

Robins, L. N., & Regier, D. A. (Eds.). (1991). *Psychiatric disorders in America: The Epidemiological Catchment Area Study.* New York: Free Press.

Roemer, M. I. (1993). *National health systems of the world, Volume II: The issues.* New York: Oxford University Press.

Rolph, D. (n.d.). *The remarkable career of Sarah Wilson: Convict, princess, and marchioness of Colonial America.* Historical Society of Pennsylvania. Retrieved from https://hsp.org/blogs/history-hits/the-remarkable-career-of-sarah-wilson-convict-princess-and-marchioness-of-colonial-america (November 19, 2016).

Roscoe, M., & Morton, R. (1994). *Disproportionate minority confinement.* Office of Juvenile Justice and Delinquency Prevention (OJJDP). Retrieved from http://www.ncjrs.org/txtfiles/fe-9411.txt.

Rose, N. (1996). Psychiatry as a political science: Advanced liberalism and the administration of risk. *History of the Human Sciences, 9*(2), 1–23.

Rosen, G. (1993). *A history of public health* (expanded edition). Baltimore: Johns Hopkins University Press.

Rosenbaum, D. (2000). *Improving access to food stamps: New reporting options can reduce administrative burdens and error rates.* Washington, DC: Center on Budget and Policy Priorities. Retrieved from http://www.cbpp.org/9-l-00fs.htm.

Rosenbaum, S., Hughes, D., Butler, E., & Howard, D. (1988). Incantations in the dark: Medicaid, managed care, and maternity care. *Milbank Quarterly, 66*(4), 661–693.

Rosenbaum, S., & Teitelbaum, J. (2004). *Olmstead at five: Assessing the impact.* Kaiser Family Foundation. Retrieved from http://www.kff.org/medicaid/upload/Olmstead-at-Five-Assessing-the-Impact.pdf (July 21, 2010).

Rosenfeld, J., Denice, P., & Laird, J. (2016). *Union decline lowers wages of nonunion workers: The overlooked reason why wages are stuck and inequality is growing.* Economic Policy Institute. Retrieved from http://www.epi.org/publication/union-decline-lowers-wages-of-nonunion-workers-the-overlooked-reason-why-wages-are-stuck-and-inequality-is-growing/ (December 6, 2016).

Rosenthal, M. G. (2000). Public or private children's services? Privatization in retrospect. *Social Service Review, 74*(2), 281–305.

Rothman, D. (2002). *The discovery of the asylum.* New York: Aldine.

Roubideaux, Y. (2002). Perspectives on American Indian health. *American Journal of Public Health, 92*(9), 1401–1403.

Rowe, J. W., & Kahn, R. L. (1998). *Successful aging.* New York: Pantheon Books.

Rowland, D., & Salganicoff, A. (1994). Commentary: Lessons from Medicaid: Improving access to office-based physician care for the low-income population. *American Journal of Public Health, 84* (4), 550–552.

Rubenstein, W. B. (2002). Do gay rights laws matter? An empirical assessment. *Southern California Law Review, 75,* 65–119.

Rubin, A., & Babbie, E. (2001). *Research methods for social work* (4th ed). Belmont, CA: Wadsworth.

Rubin, I. S. (1998). *Class, tax, and power: Municipal budgeting in the United States.* Chatham, NJ: Chatham House Publishers.

Rubin, L. B. (1972). *Busing and backlash: White against white in a California school district.* Berkeley: University of California Press.

Ruggles, P. (1990). *Drawing the line: Alternative poverty measures and their implications for public policy.* Washington, DC: Urban Institute Press.

Russell, L. A. (1998). *Child maltreatment and psychological distress among urban homeless youth.* New York: Garland.

Sager, M. A., Easterline, D. V., Kindig, D. A., & Anderson, O. W. (1989). Changes in the location of death after passage of Medicare's prospective payment system: A national study. *New England Journal of Medicine, 320,* 433–439.

Saleebey, D. (1990). Philosophical disputes in social work: Social justice denied. *Journal of Sociology and Social Work, 17*(2), 29–40.

Salmon, J. (1995). A perspective on the corporate transformation of health care. *International Journal of Health Services, 25*(1), 11–42.

Sanders, M. L. (2010). *Should child custody awards be based on past caretaking? The effect of the approximation standard ten years after its adoption.* Retrieved from http://works.bepress.com/molly_sanders/1/ (September 29, 2013).

Sard, B. (2009). *Number of homeless families climbing due to recession: Recovery package should include new housing vouchers and other measures to prevent homelessness.* Center on Budget and Policy Priorities. Retrieved from http://www.cbpp.org/cms/index.cfm?fa=view&id=2228 (May 8, 2013).

Schaaf, G. (1990). *Wampum belts and peace trees: George Morgan, Native Americans and Revolutionary diplomacy.* Golden, CO: Fulcrum.

Schemo, D. (2003, September 23). Air Force ignored academy abuse. *The New York Times.* Retrieved from http://www.nytimes.com/2003/09/23/politics/23CADE.html?th (September 29, 2013).

Schmid, C. (1992). The English-only movement: Social bases of support and opposition among Anglos and Latinos. In J. Crawford (Ed.), *Language loyalties: A sourcebook on the official English controversy* (pp. 202–209). Chicago: University of Chicago Press.

Schneider, C. (1991). Discretion, rules, and law: Child custody and the UMDA's best-interest standard. *Michigan Law Review, 89,* 2215–2298.

Schott, L. (2009). *Policy basics: An introduction to TANF.* Center on Budget and Policy Priorities. Retrieved from http://www.cbpp.org/cms/?fa= view&id=936 (July 7, 2010).

Schott, L. (2010). *Using TANF emergency funds to help prevent and address family homelessness.* Center on Budget and Policy Priorities. Retrieved from http://www.cbpp.org/files/7-13-10tanf.pdf.

Schott, L. (2012). *Policy basics: An introduction to TANF.* Center on Budget and Policy Priorities. Retrieved from http://www.cbpp.org/cms/?fa= view&id=936 (April 26, 2013).

Schrecker, E. (Ed.). (2004). *Cold war triumphalism: Exposing the misuse of history after the fall of communism.* New York: New Press.

Schultz, V. (1998). Reconceptualizing sexual harassment. *Yale Law Review, 107,* 1683–1806.

Schulz, J. H. (1995). *The economics of aging* (6th ed.). Westport, CT: Auburn House.

Scotch, R. K. (2001). American disability policy in the twentieth century. In P. K. Longmore & L. Umansky (Eds.), *The new disability history: American perspectives* (pp. 375–397). New York: New York University Press.

Scott, E. S., & Emery, R. E. (2013). *Gender politics and child custody: The puzzling persistence of the Best Interest Standard.* Columbia Public Law & Legal Theory Working Papers. Paper 9200. Retrieved from http://lsr.nellco.org/columbia_pllt/9200 (September 29, 2013).

Scott, R. (2003). Five decades of federal initiatives concerning school desegregatory effects: What have we learned? *Journal of Social, Political, and Economic Studies, 28*(2), 177–215.

Scott, R. E. (2015). *The manufacturing footprint and the importance of U.S. manufacturing jobs.* Economic Policy Institute. Retrieved from http://www.epi.org/publication/the-manufacturing-footprint-and-the-importance-of-u-s-manufacturing-jobs/ (November 13, 2016).

Sedgh, G., Finer, L.B., Bankole, A., Eilers, M.A., & Singh, S. (2015). Adolescent pregnancy, birth, and abortion rates across countries: Levels and recent trends. *Journal of Adolescent Health, 56,* 223–230.

Segalman, R., & Basu, A. (1981). *Poverty in America: The welfare dilemma.* Westport, CT: Greenwood Press.

Selmi, P., & Hunter, R. (2001). Beyond the rank and file movement: Mary van Kleeck and social work radicalism in the Great Depression, 1931–1942. *Journal of Sociology and Social Welfare, 28*(2), 75–100.

Semuels, A. (2015, June 24). How housing policy is failing America's poor. *The Atlantic*. Retrieved from http://www.theatlantic.com/business/archive/2015/06/section-8-is-failing/396650/ (July 7, 2016).

Senate Committee on Aging. (1961). *The 1961 White House conference on aging: Basic policy statements and recommendations*. Retrieved from http://www.aging.senate.gov/reports/rpt261.pdf (October 5, 2013).

Senate Committee on Finance. (1995). *The Family Self-Sufficiency Act of 1995: Report together with additional views* (104th Congress, 1st Session). Retrieved from http://www.gpo.gov/fdsys/pkg/CRPT-104srpt96/html/CRPT-104srpt96.htm (October 30, 2010).

Senate Finance Committee. (2012). *Temporary Assistance for Needy Families: Update on program performance*. Statement of Kay E. Brown, Director Education, Workforce and Income Security Issues. (June 5, 2012). GAO-12-812T.

Sentencing Project. (2012). *State-level estimates of felon disenfranchisement in the United States, 2010*. Retrieved from http://sentencingproject.org/doc/publications/fd_State_Level_Estimates_of_ Felon_Disen_2010.pdf (July 17, 2013).

Sentencing Project. (2014). *Disproportionate minority contact in the juvenile justice system*. Retrieved from http://www.sentencingproject.org/wp-content/uploads/2015/11/Disproportionate-Minority-Contact-in-the-Juvenile-Justice-System.pdf (November 28, 2016).

Sentencing Project. (2015). *A lifetime of punishment: The impact of the felony drug ban on welfare benefits*. Retrieved from http://sentencingproject.org/wp-content/uploads/2015/12/A-Lifetime-of-Punishment.pdf (November 28, 2016).

Sentencing Project. (2016). *Felony disenfranchisement: A primer*. Retrieved from http://www.sentencingproject.org/publications/felony-disenfranchisement-a-primer/ (August 2, 2016).

Sewpaul, V., & Jones, D. (2004). *Global standards for the education and training of the social work profession*. (Adopted by the General Assemblies of IASSW and IFSW, Adelaide Australia, 2004. Retrieved from http://cdn.ifsw.org/assets/ ifsw_65044-3.pdf (November 28, 2013).

Seyfarth Shaw LLP. (2010). *Early retiree reinsurance program*. Retrieved from http://www.seyfarth.com/index.cfm/fuseaction/publications.publications_ detail/object_id/5af87e16 bf3a-45fe-b054-35c8da13ca65/EarlyRetiree ReinsuranceProgram.cfm (July 15, 2010).

Shanas, E. (1968). *Old people in three industrial societies*. New York: Atherton Press.

Shanas, E. (1980). Older people and their families: The new pioneers. *Journal of Marriage and the Family, 42*(1), 9–15.

Sharpe, E. (2013). The postindustrial city thesis and rival explanations of heightened order maintenance policing. *Urban Affairs Review, 50*(3), 340–365.

Shaw, L. A. (2010). Divorce mediation outcome research: A meta-analysis. *Conflict Resolution Quarterly, 27*(4), 447–467.

Sherk, J. (2007). *Analyzing economic mobility: Compensation is keeping pace with rising productivity*. Retrieved from http://www.heritage.org/Pvesearch/Labor/bg2040.cfm (January 20, 2008).

Shilts, R. (1993). *Conduct unbecoming: Gays and lesbians in the U.S. military*. New York: St. Martin's Press.

Short, J. F. (1997). *Poverty, ethnicity, and violent crime*. Boulder, CO: Westview Press.

Shorter, E. (2013, May 14). DSM-5 will be the last. *Oxford University Press Blog*. Retrieved from http://blog.oup.com/2013/05/dsm-5-will-be-the-last/ (September, 15, 2016).

Siemaszko, C. (2016). Kentucky clerk Kim Davis, who refused to issue marriage licenses to gays, seeks to end case. *NBC News*. Retrieved from http://www.nbcnews.com/news/us-news/kentucky-clerk-kim-davis-who-refused-issue-marriage-licenses-gays-n596476 (October 12, 2016).

Sierminska, E., Brandolini, A., & Smeeding, T. (2007). *Cross-national comparison of income and wealth status in retirement: First results from the Luxembourg Wealth Study (LWS) Center for Retirement Research at Boston College*. Retrieved from http://ideas.repec.org/p/crr/crrwps/wp2007-03.html (January 8, 2007).

Silva, M. (2007, October 3). Bush veto: Health care moving in wrong direction. *The swamp: Tribune's Washington Bureau*. Retrieved from http://www .swamppolitics.com/news/politics/blog/2007/10/bush_veto_health_care_moving_i.html (October 21, 2010).

Siminoff, I. (1986). Competition and primary care in the United States: Separating fact from fantasy. *International Journal of Health Studies, 16*(1), 57–69.

Simmons, L. W. (1945). *The role of the aged in primitive societies*. New Haven, CT: Yale University Press.

Simon, R. J. (1994). Transracial adoption: The American experience. In I. Gabor & A. J. Long (Eds.), *In the best interests of the child: Culture, identity and transracial adoption* (pp. 135–150). London: Free Association Books.

Simpson, P. (1985, October). If the wage system doesn't work, fix it. *Working Woman*, 118–159.

Singer, A., & Svajlenka, N. P. (2013). *Immigration facts: Deferred action for childhood arrivals*. Brookings Institute. Retrieved from http://www.brookings.edu/Research/Reports/2013/08/14-daca-immigration-singer (October 25, 2013).

Sisk, J. E., Gorman, S. A., Reisinger, A. L., Glied, S. A., DuMouchel, W. H., & Hynes, M. M. (1996, July 3). Evaluation of Medicaid managed care: Satisfaction, access, and use. *Journal of the American Medical Association, 276*(1), 50–55.

Skocpol, J. (1995). *Social policy in the United States: Future possibilities in historical perspective*. Princeton, NJ: Princeton University Press.

Slater, W. (1984, March 29). Latest Lamm remark angers the elderly. *Arizona Daily Star*, p. 1.

Slesnick, N. (2004). *Our runaway and homeless youth: A guide to understanding*. Westport, CT: Praeger.

Smil, V. (2013). *The rise and retreat of American manufacturing.* Cambridge: MIT Press.

Smith, R. (2010). *Reed Smith health care reform review.* Retrieved from http://www.ahcancal.org/advocacy/Documents/Reed%20Smith%20Health%20Care%20Reform%20Review.pdf (July 21, 2010).

Smith, S., & Grant, A. (2016). The corporate construction of psychosis and the rise of the psychosocial paradigm: Emerging implications for mental health nurse education. *Nurse Education Today, 39,* 22–25.

Snyder, H. N. (2011). *Arrest in the United States, 1980–2009.* Bureau of Justice Statistics. Retrieved from http://bjs.gov/content/pub/pdf/aus8009.pdf (November 27, 2016).

Social Security Administration. (n.d.a.). *Beneficiary data.* Retrieved from https://www.ssa.gov/oact/progdata/icp.html (June 16, 2016).

Social Security Administration. (n.d.b.). *Oral history collections.* Robert M. Ball. Retrieved from http://www.ssa.gov/history/orals/balloralhistory.html (July 10, 2010).

Social Security Administration. (n.d.c.). A *quarter-century of service to children: Katharine F. Lenroot.* Retrieved from http://www.socialsecurity.gov/history/kl25.html (March 14, 2008).

Social Security Administration. (1999). *Press release: Social Security begins issuing annual statements to 125 million workers.* Retrieved from http://www.ssa .gov/pressoffice/statement.html (June 30, 2010).

Social Security Administration. (2004). *Substantial gainful activity.* Retrieved from http://www.ssa.gov/OACT/COLA/SGA.html.

Social Security Administration. (2005). *Projected future course for SSA disability programs.* Retrieved from http://www.ssa.gov/policy/docs/chartbooks/disability_trends/sect06.html (July 1, 2010).

Social Security Administration. (2009). *Annual statistical report on the Social Security disability insurance program, 2008.* Retrieved from http://www.ssa.gov/policy/docs/statcomps/di_asr/ (July 21, 2010).

Social Security Administration. (2012). *The 2012 OASDI trustees report.* Retrieved from http://www.ssa.gov/oact/tr/2012/index.html (April 20, 2013).

Social Security Administration. (2015a). *The 2015 OASDI trustees report.* Retrieved from https://www.ssa.gov/oact/tr/2015/index.html (June 16, 2016).

Social Security Administration. (2015b). *Monthly statistical snapshot, April 2015.* Retrieved from https://www.ssa.gov/policy/docs/quickfacts/stat_snapshot/ (June 15, 2016).

Social Security Administration. (2015c). *Fast facts & figures about Social Security, 2015.* Retrieved from https://www.ssa.gov/policy/docs/chartbooks/fast_facts/2015/fast_facts15.pdf (June 16, 2016).

Social Security Administration. (2015d). *SSI Annual statistical report, 2014.* Retrieved from https://www.ssa.gov/policy/docs/statcomps/ssi_asr/2014/ssi_asr14.pdf (June 16, 2016).

Social Security Administration. (2016a). *Research, statistics, & policy analysis: Monthly Statistical Snapshot, May 2016.* Retrieved from https://www.ssa.gov/policy/docs/quickfacts/stat_snapshot/ (July 7, 2016).

Social Security Administration. (2016b). *2016 OASDI Trustees Report. II. Overview, A. Highlights.* Retrieved from https://www.ssa.gov/OACT/TR/2016/II_A_highlights.html#76460 (September 20, 2016).

Social Security Administration. (2016c). *Fast facts and figures about Social Security, 2016. Income of the aged population. Relative importance of Social Security, 2014.* https://www.ssa.gov/policy/docs/chartbooks/fast_facts/2016/fast_facts16.html (November 9, 2016).

Social Security Administration. (2016d). A Guide to Supplemental Security Income (SSI) for Groups and Organizations. Retrieved from https://www.ssa.gov/pubs/EN-05-11015.pdf (January 19, 2017).

Southern Poverty Law Center (SPLC). (1999, Spring). *Intelligence report. Hate crimes: Serious violence against gays said to rise.* Retrieved from http://www.splcenter.org/intelligenceproject/ip-4jl0.html.

Sowell, T. (1981). *Markets and minorities.* New York: Basic Books.

Sowers, W. E. (1998). Parallel process: Moral failure, addiction, and society. *Community Mental Health Journal, 34*(4), 331–336.

Specht, H., & Courtney, M. (1994). *Unfaithful angels: How social work has abandoned its mission.* New York: Free Press.

Stahl, A., Hyde, J., & Singh, H. (2016). *The effect of a 1999 rule change on obesity as a factor in Social Security disability determinations.* Mathematica Center for Studying Disability Policy. Working Paper Number: 2016-01. Retrieved from https://www.mathematica-mpr.com/our-publications-and-findings/publications/the-effect-of-a-1999-rule-change-on-obesity-as-a-factor-in-social-security-disability-determinations (September 20, 2016).

Stampp, K. M. (1956). *The peculiar institution: Slavery in the ante-bellum south.* New York: Vintage.

Stavis, P. F. (1995, July 21). *Civil commitment: Past, present, and future.* An address by Paul F. Stavis at the National Conference of the National Alliance for the Mentally Ill, Washington, DC. Retrieved from http://www.xqc.state.ny.us/cc64.htm.

Steadman, H. J., Osher, F. C., Robbins, P. C., Case, B., & Samuels, S. (2009). Prevalence of serious mental illness among jail inmates. *Psychiatric Services, 60*(6), 761–765.

Steele, E., & Redding, W. C. (1962). The American value system. *Western Speech, 26,* 83–91.

Stein, J. (2014). Supreme Court upholds Scott Walker's Act 10 Union Law. *Milwaukee-Wisconsin Journal Sentinel, Aug. 1, 2014.* Retrieved from http://archive.jsonline.com/news/statepolitics/supreme-court-to-rule-thursday-on-union-law-voter-id-b99321110z1-269292661.html (November 11, 2016).

Stein, T. (1995). Disability-based employment discrimination against individuals perceived to have AIDS and individuals infected with HIV or diagnosed with AIDS: Federal and New York statutes and case law. *AIDS & Public Policy Journal, 10*(3), 123–139.

Steinhauer, J. (2013, May 7). Sexual assaults in military raise alarm in Washington. *The New York Times.* Retrieved from http://www.nytimes.com/2013/05/08/us/politics/pentagon-study-sees-sharp-rise-in-sexual-assaults.html?_r=0 (September 29, 2013).

Sterba, J. P. (1980). *Justice: Alternative political perspectives.* Belmont, CA: Wadsworth.

Stiglitz, J.E. (2012) The Price of Inequality: How today's divided society endangers our future. New York: W.W. Norton & Company.

Stillwagon, E. (2000). HIV transmission in Latin America: Comparison with Africa and policy implications. *South African Journal of Economics, 68*(5), 985–1011.

Stone, C., Greenstein, R., & Coven, M. (2007). *Addressing longstanding gaps in unemployment insurance coverage.* Center on Budget and Policy Priorities. Retrieved from http://www.cbpp.org/cms/?fa=view&id=517 (July 19, 2010).

Stone, D. (2002). *Policy paradox: The art of political decision making* (rev. ed.). New York: Norton.

Strauss, V. (2012, March 30). Mega millions: Do lotteries really benefit public schools? *The Washington Post.* Retrieved from http://www .washingtonpost.com/blogs/answer-sheet/post/mega-millions-do-lotteries-really-benefit-public-schools/2012/03/30/gIQAbTUNlS_blog.html (September 8, 2013).

Strouse, J. (1998, November 23). The brilliant bailout. *New Yorker,* 62–77.

Stuart, P. (1997). Community care and the origins of psychiatric social work. *Social Work in Health Care, 25*(3), 25–36.

Stuntz, J. A. (2005). *Hers, his, and theirs: Community property law in Spain and early Texas.* Lubbock, TX: Texas Tech University Press.

Suarez-Orozco, M. M. (2006, July 17). Stranger anxieties: U.S. immigration and its discontents. *Harvard International Review.* Retrieved from http://hir.harvard.edu/articles/print.php? article=1447 (May 7, 2010).

Substance Abuse and Mental Health Services Administration (SAMHSA). (2014). *Projections of national expenditures for treatment of mental and substance use disorders: 2010–2020.* Substance Abuse & Mental Health Services Administration. Retrieved from http://store.samhsa.gov/shin/content/SMA14-4883/SMA14-4883.pdf (December 2, 2016).

Sullivan, J. (2016). *Percentage of employers still offering defined benefits is. . .* TIAA Global Asset Management, 401K Specialist. Retrieved from https://401kspecialistmag.com/percentage-of-employers-still-offering-defined-benefits-is/ (November 11, 2016).

Supreme Court of the United States. (1937). Opinion in *Helvering et al. v. Davis.*

Supreme Court of the United States. (1967). Decision in Loving v. Virginia. Retrieved from http://caselaw.findlaw.com/us-supreme-court/388/1.html (January 19, 2017).

Supreme Court of the United States. (2013a). *Syllabus. Hollingsworth et al. v. Perry et al.* Retrieved from http://www.supremecourt.gov/opinions/12pdf/12-144_8ok0.pdf (August 25, 2013).

Supreme Court of the United States. (2013b). *Syllabus. United States v. Windsor, Executor of the Estate of Spyer, et al.* Retrieved from http://www .supremecourt.gov/opinions/12pdf/12-307_6j37.pdf (August 25, 2013).

Supreme Court of the United States. (2013c). *Shelby County, Alabama v. Holder, Attorney General, et al.* Retrieved from http://www.supremecourt.gov/opinions/12pdf/12-96_6k47.pdf (July 17, 2013).

Surgeon General. (1999). *Mental health: A report of the surgeon general.* Retrieved from http://www .surgeongeneral.gov/library/mentalhealth.

Svihula, J., & Estes, C. L. (2008). Social Security privatization: An ideologically structured movement. *Journal of Sociology and Social Welfare, 35*(1), 75–104.

Swartz, M. S., & Swanson, J. W. (2004, September). Involuntary outpatient commitment, community treatment orders, and assisted outpatient treatment: What's in the data? *The Canadian Journal of Psychiatry.* Retrieved from http://www.cpa-apc.org/Publications/Archives/CJP/2004/september/swartz .asp.

Sweeney, E. P., & Fremstad, S. (2005). *Supplemental Security Income: Supporting people with disabilities and the elderly poor.* Center on Budget and Policy Priorities. Retrieved from http://www.cbpp.org/cms/?fa=view&id=512 (July 21, 2010).

Sweeney, J. (1999, June 24). *Statement by AFL-CIO President John Sweeney on the Employment Non-Discrimination Act.* Retrieved from http://igc.org/prideatwork/enda.html#2.

Szasz, T. (1960). The myth of mental illness. *American Psychologist, 15,* 113–118.

Taibbi, M. (2013, March 27). Cruel and unusual punishment: The shame of three strikes laws. *Rolling Stone.* Retrieved from http://www.rollingstone.com/politics/news/cruel-and-unusual-punishment-the-shame-of-three-strikes-laws-20130327 (November 28, 2016).

Takaki, R. (1993). *A different mirror: A history of multicultural America.* New York: Little, Brown.

Tasker, F. (2010). Same-sex parenting and child development: Reviewing the contribution of parental gender. *Journal of Marriage and Family, 72*(1), 35–40.

Tax Policy Center. (n.d.). *Key elements of the U.S. tax system.* Retrieved from http://www.taxpolicycenter.org/briefing-book/why-do-low-income-families-use-tax-preparers (June 12, 2016).

Tax Policy Center. (2012). *Average effective federal tax rates by cash income percentiles, 2010.* Retrieved from http://www.taxpolicycenter.org/numbers/displayatab.cfm?DocID=3279 (February 6, 2013).

Taylor, J. (2004). *The fundamentals of community health centers.* National Health Policy Forum. Retrieved from http://www.nhpf.org/library/background-papers/BP_CHC_08-31-04.pdf (July 14, 2010).

Taylor, M. J., & Barusch, A. S. (2004). Personal, family and multiple barriers of long-term welfare recipients. *Social Work, 49*(2), 175–183.

Tedeschi, J. T., & Rosenfeld, P. (1980). Communication in bargaining and negotiation. In M. E. Roloff & G. E. Miller (Eds.), *Persuasion: New directions in theory and research*. Beverly Hills: Sage.

Temkin-Greener, H., & Winchell, M. (1991). Medicaid beneficiaries under managed care: Provider choice and satisfaction. *Health Services Research, 26*(4), 509–529.

Temple-Raston, D. (2016). To stop kids from radicalizing, moms in Denmark call other moms. *NPR.* Retrieved from http://www.npr.org/sections/parallels/2016/05/08/476890795/to-stop-kids-from-radicalizing-moms-in-denmark-call-other-moms (September 19, 2016).

Tewksbury, R. (2005). Collateral consequences of sex offender registration. *Journal of Contemporary Criminal Justice, 21*(1), 67–81.

Thomas, C. S. (1991). *Sex discrimination in a nutshell* (2nd ed.). St. Paul: West.

Thomas, M. P. (1972). Child abuse and neglect: Part 1. Historical overview, legal matrix, and social perspectives. *North Carolina Law Review, 50,* 293–349.

Thomasson, M. (2002). From sickness to health: The twentieth-century development of U.S. health insurance. *Explorations in Economic History, 39,* 233–253. doi:10.1006/exeh.2002.0788.

Thornberry, T., & Burch, J. H., II. (1997). *Gang members and delinquent behavior.* Office of Juvenile Justice and Delinquency Prevention (OJJDP). Retrieved from http://www.ncirs.org/txtfiles/165154.txt.

Thornton, R. (1987). *American Indian holocaust and survival: A population history since 1492.* Norman, OK: University of Oklahoma Press.

Thornton, R. (1996). Tribal membership requirements and the demography of "old" and "new" Native Americans. In G. D. Sandefur, R. R. Rindfuss, & B. Cohen (Eds.), *Changing numbers, changing needs: American Indian demography and public health* (pp. 103–112). Washington, DC: National Academy Press.

Tilcsik, A. (2011). Pride and prejudice: Employment discrimination against openly gay men in the United States. *American Journal of Sociology, 117*(2), 586–626. Retrieved from http://www.jstor.org/stable/10.1086/661653 (August 30, 2013). doi:10.1086/661653.

Titmuss, R. (1971). *The gift relationship.* New York: Pantheon Books.

Tolle, S. W., Rosenfeld, A. G., Tilden, V. P., & Park, Y. (1999). Oregon's low in-hospital death rates: What determines where people die and satisfaction with decisions on place of death? *Annals of Internal Medicine, 130,* 681–685.

Toms, J. (2010). Mind the gap: MIND, the mental hygiene movement and the trapdoor in measures of intellect. *Journal of Intellectual Disability Research, 54*(1), 16–27.

Torrey, E. F. (1997). *Out of the shadows: Confronting America's mental illness crisis.* New York: John Wiley & Sons.

Torrey, E. F. (2011). Stigma and violence: Isn't it time to connect the dots? *Schizophrenia Bulletin, 37*(5), 892–896. doi:10.1093/schbul/sbr057.

Torrey, E. F., & Kaplan, R. J. (1995). A national survey of the use of outpatient commitment. *Psychiatric Services, 46,* 778–784.

Transnational Institute. (n.d.). *Drug law reform in Latin America.* Retrieved from http://druglawreform.info/en/country-information/latin-america/argentina/item/199-argentina (November 28, 2016).

Trattner, W. I. (1989). *From poor law to welfare state: A history of social welfare in America.* New York: Free Press.

Travis, J., Western, B., & Redburn, S. (Eds.). (2014). *The growth of incarceration in the United States: Exploring causes and consequences.* Washington, DC: National Academies Press.

Troy, D. E. (1998, October 19). Rule of law: Hate crime laws make some more equal than others. *Wall Street Journal.* Retrieved from http://www.aei.org/ra/ratroy3.htm.

Trupin, L., Sebesta, D. S., & Yelin, E. (2000). *Transitions in employment and disability among people ages 51 to 61.* University of California, San Francisco, Disability Statistics Center. Retrieved from http://dsc.ucsf.edu/publication.php? pub_id=3 (December 6, 2007).

Trupin, L., & Yelin, E. (2005). *Multiple jeopardies in the California labor market: The conjoint role of disability, race, gender, and age.* Final report to the Disability Research Institute, University of Illinois at Urbana-Champaign. Retrieved from http://www.dri.uiuc.edu/research/p05-08c/Yelin_Trupin_Final_Report.doc (December 6, 2007).

Tsemberis, S., Gulcur, L., Nakae, M. (2004). Housing first, consumer choice, and harm reduction for homeless individuals with a dual diagnosis. *American Journal of Public Health, 94*(4), 651–656.

Turnbull, H. R. (2005). Individuals with disabilities education act reauthorization: Accountability and personal responsibility. *Remedial & Special Education, 26*(6), 320–326.

Turner, J. (2005). *Social Security privatization around the world.* AARP Public Policy Institute. Working Paper #2005-15. Retrieved from http://assets.aarp.org/rgcenter/econ/2005_15_intl_ss.pdf (June 30, 2010).

United Nations. (2000). *Protocol to prevent, suppress and punish trafficking in persons, especially women and children, supplementing the United Nations Convention Against Transnational Organized Crime.* Retrieved from http://www.uncjin.org/Documents/Conventions/dcatoc/final_ documents_2/convention_%20traff_eng.pdf (May 16, 2013).

United Nations. (2010). *Rethinking poverty: Report on the world social situation.* Retrieved from http://www.un.org/esa/socdev/rwss/docs/2010/ (July 3, 2010).

United Nations General Assembly. (2016). Resolution: Our joint commitment to effectively addressing and countering the world drug problem. Retrieved from https://documents-dds-ny.un.org/doc/UNDOC/GEN/N16/110/24/PDF/N1611024.pdf?OpenElement (November 28, 2016).

Urban Dynamics. (1999). *Gangs 101.* Retrieved from http://www.lincolnnet.net/users/Irttrapp/block/gang101.htm.

Urban Institute. (2005). *Understanding the challenges of prisoner reentry: Research findings from the Urban Institute's prisoner reentry portfolio.* Retrieved from http://www.urban.org/sites/default/files/alfresco/publication-pdfs/411289-Understanding-the-Challenges-of-Prisoner-Reentry.PDF (December 6, 2016).

U.S. Census Bureau. (n.d.a.). *American community survey data on same sex households.* Retrieved from http://www.census.gov/hhes/samesex/data/acs.html (October 11, 2016).

U.S. Census Bureau. (n.d.b.). *History through the decades, index of questions.* Retrieved from http://www.census.gov/history/www/through_the_decades/index_of_questions/1790_1.html (July 27, 2010).

U.S. Census Bureau. (n.d.c.). *Quick facts.* Retrieved from http://quickfacts.census.gov/qfd/states/00000.html (October 25, 2013).

U.S. Census Bureau. (2001). *Overview of race and Hispanic origin 2000. Census 2000 brief.* Retrieved from http://www.census.gov/prod/2001pubs/c2kbr01-l.pdf.

U.S. Census Bureau. (2002a). *Demographic trends in the 20th century: Census 2000 special report.* Retrieved from http://www.census.gov/prod/2002pubs/censr-4.pdf (August 11, 2010).

U.S. Census Bureau. (2002b). *Statistical abstract of the United States* (116th ed.). Retrieved from http://www.census.gov/population/www/socdemo/race/indian.html (February 24, 2003).

U.S. Census Bureau. (2003). *Current population survey, 2003 annual social and economic supplement.* Retrieved from http://ferret.bls.census.gov/macro/032003/pov/new06_100_01.htm.

U.S. Census Bureau. (2004). *Evidence from census 2000 about earnings by detailed occupation for men and women. Census 2000 special reports.* Retrieved from http://www.census.gov (January 21, 2008).

U.S. Census Bureau. (2008). *Tables from the current population survey.* Retrieved from http://www.census.gov/hhes/www/cpstables/032009/pov/toc.htm (July 7, 2010).

U.S. Census Bureau. (2009) *Historic poverty tables – People, Table 3: Poverty status by age, race, and Hispanic origin.* Retrieved from http://www.census.gov/hhes/www/poverty/data/historical/people.html (October 23, 2013).

U.S. Census Bureau. (2010). *The next four decades: The older population in the United States: 2010 to 2050.* Retrieved from http://www.census.gov/prod/2010pubs/p25-1138.pdf (August 11, 2010).

U.S. Census Bureau. (2011a). *The Hispanic population: 2010. Census briefs.* Retrieved from http://www.census.gov/prod/cen2010/briefs/c2010br-04.pdf (July 17, 2013).

U.S. Census Bureau. (2011c). *Current population survey, Table PINC-04, Annual social and economic supplement.* Retrieved from http://www.census.gov/hhes/www/cpstables/032010/perinc/new04_000.htm (October 27, 2013).

U.S. Census Bureau. (2012a). *Americans with disabilities: 2010. Current population reports. P70-131.* Retrieved from http://www.census.gov/prod/2012pubs/p70-131.pdf (June 17, 2013).

U.S. Census Bureau. (2012b). *Current population survey (CPS) poverty tables, Table 3: People in poverty by selected characteristics: 2010 and 2011.* Retrieved from http://www.census.gov/hhes/www/poverty/data/incpovhlth/2011/table3.pdf (May 8, 2013).

U.S. Census Bureau. (2012c). *Current population survey (CPS) poverty tables. Pov01 and Pov02.* Retrieved from http://www.census.gov/hhes/www/cpstables/032012/pov/POV01_100.htm (May 8, 2013).

U.S. Census Bureau. (2012d). *Federal civilian employment by branch and agency: 1990 to 2010. Table 499.* Retrieved from http://www.census.gov/compendia/statab/2012/tables/12s0499.pdf (February 3, 2013).

U.S. Census Bureau. (2012e). *Health insurance, current population survey. Table HI01: Health insurance coverage status and type of coverage by selected characteristics: 2011, all races.* Retrieved from http://www.census.gov/hhes/www/cpstables/032012/health/h01_000.htm (June 1, 2013).

U.S. Census Bureau. (2014). *American community survey, 2014, 1 year estimates, Table B050031: Sex by age by nativity and citizenship status (Hispanic or Latino).* Retrieved from http://factfinder.census.gov/faces/tableservices/jsf/pages/productview.xhtml?pid=ACS_14_1YR_B05003I&prodType=table (October 6, 2016).

U.S. Census Bureau. (2015a). Income and poverty in the United States: 2014. *Current Population Reports (P60-252).* Retrieved from https://www.census.gov/content/dam/Census/library/publications/2015/demo/p60-252.pdf (August 21, 2016).

U.S. Census Bureau. (2015b). *Current population survey (CPS) poverty tables. Pov01 and Pov02.* Retrieved from https://www.census.gov/hhes/www/cpstables/032014/pov/pov01R_100.htm (August 21, 2016).

U.S. Census Bureau. (2015c). *America's families and living arrangements: 2014: Family households* (F table series, Table F1) Retrieved from http://www.census.gov/hhes/families/data/cps2014F.html (October 1, 2016).

U.S. Census Bureau. (2016). *Income and poverty in the United States: 2015*. Retrieved from http://www.census.gov/content/dam/Census/library/publications/2016/demo/p60-256.pdf (October 1, 2016).

U.S. Commission on Civil Rights. (1967). *Racial isolation in the public schools* Washington, DC: U.S. Government Printing Office.

U.S. Conference of Mayors. (2015). *Hunger and homelessness survey: A status report on hunger and homelessness in America's cities: 2014*. Retrieved from https://www.usmayors.org/pressreleases/uploads/2014/1211-report-hh.pdf (August 25, 2016).

U.S. Congress Joint Economic Committee. (2011). *The gender wage gap jeopardizes women's retirement security*. Retrieved from http://www.jec.senate.gov/public/?a=Files.Serve&File_id=f6fda396-2623-4e99-817e-bf9387360326 (October 27, 2013).

U.S. Congress, Office of Technology Assessment. (1994, September). *International comparisons of administrative costs in health care* (BP-H-135). Washington, DC: U.S. Government Printing Office. Retrieved from http://www.ota.nap.edu/pdf/data/1994/9417.pdf.

U.S. Department of Agriculture. (n.d.a.). *Supplemental Nutrition Assistance Program*. Retrieved from http://www.fns.usda.gov/snap/applicant_recipients/eligibility.htm#income (May 6, 2013).

U.S. Department of Agriculture. (n.d.b.). *Program data: Supplemental Nutrition Assistance Program*. Retrieved from http://www.fns.usda.gov/pd/snapmain.htm.

U.S. Department of Agriculture. (2012). *Building a healthy America: A profile of the Supplemental Nutrition Assistance Program*. Retrieved from http://www.fns.usda.gov/ORA/menu/Published/SNAP/FILES/Other/BuildingHealthyAmerica.pdf (May 6, 2013).

U.S. Department of Agriculture. (2013). *Supplemental Nutrition Assistance Program participation and costs*. Retrieved from http://www.fns.usda.gov/pd/SNAPsummary.htm.

U.S. Department of Agriculture. (2015). *Reaching those in need: Estimates of State Supplemental Nutrition Assistance program participation rates in 2012*. Retrieved from http://www.fns.usda.gov/reaching-those-need-estimates-state-supplemental-nutrition-assistance-program-participation-rates (July 7, 2016).

U.S. Department of Education. (n.d.a.). *The president's 2015 budget proposal for education*. Retrieved from http://www.ed.gov/budget15 (October 20, 2016).

U.S. Department of Education. (n.d.b.). *ESEA flexibility index*. Retrieved from http://www2.ed.gov/policy/elsec/guid/esea-flexibility/index.html (October 21, 2016).

U.S. Department of Education. (2010). *Dear colleague letter*. Office for Civil Rights. Retrieved from http://www2.ed.gov/about/offices/list/ocr/letters/colleague-201010.html (November 10, 2010).

U.S. Department of Education. (2014). *Dear colleague letter*. Office for Civil Rights. Retrieved from http://www2.ed.gov/about/offices/list/ocr/letters/colleague-bullying-201410.pdf (October 21, 2016).

U.S. Department of Education. (2015). *Fundamental change: Innovation in America's schools under Race to the Top*. Retrieved from http://www2.ed.gov/programs/racetothetop/rttfinalrptfull.pdf (October 21, 2016).

U.S. Department of Health and Human Services. (1994). Office of the Inspector General. *Requirements for Drug Addicts and Alcoholics on SSI*, OEI-01-94-00110.

U.S. Department of Health and Human Services, Centers for Medicare & Medicaid Services. (2005). *2005 CMS Statistics*. Retrieved from http://www.cms.gov/ResearchGenInfo/Downloads/2005CMSStats.pdf (July 10, 2010).

U.S. Department of Health and Human Services, Centers for Medicare & Medicaid Services. (2009). *2009 CMS statistics*. Retrieved from http://www.cms.gov/ResearchGenInfo/02_CMSStatistics.asp (July 10, 2010).

U.S. Department of Health and Human Services. (2013). *Administration issues final rules on contraception coverage and religious organization*. Retrieved from http://www.hhs.gov/news/press/2013pres/06/20130628a.html (September 29, 2013).

U.S. Department of Housing and Urban Development. (2007). *The applicability of housing first models to homeless persons with serious mental illness*. Retrieved from http://www.huduser.org/portal/publications/hsgfirst.pdf (June 10, 2013).

U.S. Department of Justice. (2006). *Mental health problems of prison and jail inmates*. Retrieved from http://www.ojp.usdoj.gov/bjs/pub/pdf/mhppji.pdf (February 12, 2008).

U.S. Department of Justice, Bureau of Justice Statistics. (2007a). *Prisoners in 2006*. Retrieved from http://www.ojp.usdoj.gov/bjs/pub/pdf/p06.pdf (December 13, 2007).

U.S. Department of Justice, Office of Juvenile Justice and Delinquency Prevention. (2007b). *Juvenile offenders and victims: 2006 national report*. Retrieved from http://ojjdp.ncjrs.org/ojstatbb/nr2006/index.html (December 31, 2007).

U.S. Department of Justice. (2011a). *Homicide trends in the United States, 1980–2008*. Retrieved from http://www.bjs.gov/content/pub/pdf/htus8008.pdf (September 8, 2013).

U.S. Department of Justice. (2011b). *Justice Department's new ADA rules go into effect on March 15, 2011*. Retrieved from http://www.justice.gov/opa/pr/2011/March/11-crt-324.html (June 19, 2013).

U.S. Department of Justice. (2012). *Crime in the United States: 2011*. Retrieved from http://www.fbi.gov/about-us/cjis/ucr/crime-in-the-u.s/2011/crime-in-the-u.s.-2011.

U.S. Department of Justice. (2014). *Special report: Rape and sexual assault victimization among college-age females,*

1995–2013. Retrieved from https://www.bjs.gov/content/pub/pdf/rsavcaf9513.pdf (October 31, 2016).

U.S. Department of Labor, Office of Disability Employment Policy. (n.d.a.). Home page. Retrieved from http://www.dol.gov/odep/ (June 20, 2013).

U.S. Department of Labor. (n.d.b.). *Unemployment insurance tax topic.* Retrieved from http://workforcesecurity.doleta.gov/unemploy/uitaxtopic. asp (April 17, 2013).

U.S. Department of State. (2015). *Immigrant visa statistics, Table XII: Significant source countries of international adoptions, fiscal years 2005–2014.* Retrieved from https://travel.state.gov/content/dam/visas/Statistics/AnnualReports/FY2014AnnualReport/FY14AnnualReport-TableXIII.pdf (October 20, 2016).

U.S. Department of Veterans Affairs. (n.d.). *A brief history of the VA.* Retrieved from http://www.va .gov/facmgt/historic/Brief_VA_History.asp (February 12, 2008).

U.S. Equal Employment Opportunity Commission. (n.d.a.). *Age Discrimination in Employment Act* (includes concurrent charges with Title VII, ADA and EPA) FY 1997–FY2015) Retrieved from http://www.eeoc.gov/eeoc/statistics/enforcement/adea.cfm (December 10, 2016).

U.S. Equal Employment Opportunity Commission. (n.d.b.). Sexual harassment charges, EEOC & FEPAs combined: FY 1997 – FY 2011. Retrieved from http://www.eeoc.gov/eeoc/statistics/enforcement/sexual_harassment.cfm (November 9, 2013).

U.S. General Accounting Office (GAO). (1980). *Section 8 subsidized housing: Some observations on its high rents, costs and inequities.* Report to Congress by the Comptroller General of the United States, CED-80-59. Washington, DC: U.S. Government Printing Office.

U.S. General Accounting Office (GAO). (1992, February). *Pension plans: Survivor benefit coverage for wives increased after 1984 pension law.* Report to the Chairman, Subcommittee on Retirement Income and Employment, Select Committee on Aging, House of Representatives, GAO/HRD-92-49. Washington, DC: U.S. Government Printing Office.

U.S. General Accounting Office (GAO). (1994a). *Social Security major changes needed for disability benefits for addicts.* GAO/HEHS-94-128. Washington, DC: U.S. Government Printing Office.

U.S. General Accounting Office (GAO). (1994b). *Tax gap: Many actions taken but a cohesive compliance strategy needed.* GGD 94-123. Retrieved from http://www.unclefed.com/GAOReports/gao94-123sum.html.

U.S. General Accounting Office (GAO). (2000). *Mental health community-based care increases for people with serious mental illness.* Report to the Committee on Finance, U.S. Senate GAO 01-224. Retrieved from http://www.gao.gov/newitems/d01224pdf.

U.S. General Accounting Office (GAO). (2004). *No Child Left Behind Act: Education needs to provide additional technical assistance and conduct implementation studies for school choice provision.* Report to the Secretary of Education. Retrieved from http://www.gao.gov/new.items/d057.pdf (December 30, 2007).

U.S. House of Representatives, Select Committee on Aging, Subcommittee on Human Services. (1988). *Older Americans Act: A staff summary.* Committee Publication No. 100-683. Washington, DC: U.S. Government Printing Office.

U.S. House of Representatives, Select Committee on Aging. (1990). *Medicare and Medicaid's 25th anniversary: Much promised, accomplished, and left unfinished.* Committee Publication No. 101-762. Washington, DC: U.S. Government Printing Office.

U.S. Interagency Council on Homelessness. (2010). *Opening doors: Federal strategic plan to prevent and end homelessness.* Retrieved from https://www.usich.gov/opening-doors (August 26, 2016).

U.S. National Archives and Records Administration. (2007). *Keating-Owen Child Labor Act of 1916.* Retrieved from http://www.ourdocuments.gov/doc.php?doc=59 (December 30, 2007).

U.S. Senate Special Committee on Aging. (1988, February 26). *Developments in aging* (Vol. 1). Washington, DC: U.S. Government Printing Office.

Van Ness, D. W. (1996). Restorative justice and international human rights. In B. Galaway & J. Hudson (Eds.), *Restorative justice: International perspectives.* St. Louis, MO: Willow Tree Press.

Van Soest, D., & Garcia, B. (2003). *Diversity education for social justice: Mastering teaching skills.* Alexandria, VA: Council on Social Work Education.

Van Tassel, E. F., Wirtz, B. H., & Wonders, P. (1993). *Why judges resign: Influences on federal judicial service, 1789 to 1992.* Federal Judicial History Office. Retrieved from http://ftp.resource.org/courts.gov/fjc/judgeres.pdf.

Van Wormer, K. (2004). *Confronting oppression, restoring justice: From policy analysis to social action.* Alexandria, VA: Council on Social Work Education.

Van Wormer, K., & McKinney, R. (2003). What schools can do to help gay/lesbian/bisexual youth: A harm reduction approach. *Adolescence, 38,* 409–420.

Vasak, K., & Alston, P. (Eds.). (1982). *The international dimensions of human rights.* Westport, CT: Greenwood Press.

Vaughan, C. P., Goode, P. S., Burgio, K. L., & Markland, A. (2011). Urinary incontinence in older adults. *Mount Sinai Journal of Medicine, 78,* 558–570.

Vos, B., Coates, R. B., Brown, K. A., & Umbreit, M. S. (2003). *Facing violence: The path of restorative justice and dialogue.* Monsey, NY: Criminal Justice Press.

Wadden, A. (1998). A liberal in wolf's clothing: Nixon's Family Assistance Plan in the light of 1990s welfare reform. *Journal of American Studies, 2,* 203–218.

Wade, P. (1997). *Race and ethnicity in Latin America*. London: Pluto Press.

Wagner, S. (2002). *How did the Taft-Hartley Act come about?* Retrieved from http://hnn.us/articles/1036 html (November 8, 2007).

Waid, M. D., & Barber, S. L. (2001). *Follow-up of former drug addict and alcoholic beneficiaries*. Social Security Administration, Office of Policy. Retrieved from http://www.ssa.gov/policy/docs/rsnotes/rsn2001-02.html (April 26, 2013).

Wakefield, J. (1988, June). Psychotherapy, distributive justice, and social work: Part 1. Distributive justice as a conceptual framework for social work. *Social Service Review,* 187–210.

Waldinger, R. (2006). Immigration reform: Too hot to handle. *New Labour Forum, 15*(2), 21–29.

Walker, F. A. (1874). *The Indian question*. Boston: J. R. Osgood.

Wallace, A. (2016). Where is weed legal? Map of US marijuana laws by state. *The Cannabist, Oct. 14*. Retrieved from: http://www.thecannabist.co/2016/10/14/legal-marijuana-laws-by-state-map-united-states/62772/ (December 6, 2016).

Walters, K. L. (1999). Urban American Indian identity attitudes and acculturation styles. *Journal of Human Behavior and the Social Environment, 2*(1/2), 163–178.

Wandersee, W. D. (1981). *Women's work and family values, 1920–1940*. Cambridge, MA: Harvard University Press.

Wang, P. S., Lane, M., Olfson, M., Pincus, H. A., Wells, K. B., & Kessler, R. C. (2005). Twelve-month use of mental health services in the United States: Results from the National Comorbidity Survey Replication. *JAMA Psychiatry, 62*(6), 629–640. doi:10.1001/archpsyc.62.6.629.

Ware, S. (1981). *Beyond suffrage: Women in the New Deal*. Cambridge, MA: Harvard University Press.

Washington Post. (2016). *Fatal force. 2015 police shootings*. Retrieved from https://www.washingtonpost.com/graphics/national/police-shootings/ (October 4, 2016).

Watkins, S. (1990). The Mary Ellen myth: Correcting child welfare history. *Social Work, 35*(6), 500–503.

Wayne, L., & Petersen, M. (2001). *A muscular lobby rolls up its sleeves. The New York Times*. Retrieved from http://query.nytimes.com/gst/fullpage.htmPres=9E02E5DF1639F937A35752-C1A9679C8B63 (February 12, 2008).

Weatherford, J. (1988). *Indian givers: How the Indians of the Americas transformed the world*. New York: Crown Publishers.

Weaver, H., & Brave Heart, M. Y. (1999). Examining two facets of American Indian identity: Exposure to other cultures and the influence of historical trauma. *Journal of Human Behavior and the Social Environment, 1*(1/2), 19–33.

Webster's Dictionary. (n.d.). Liberal. Retrieved from http://www.webster-dictionary.org/definition/Liberal (September 1, 2013).

Weickert, C. S., Weickert, T. W., Pillai, A., & Buckley, P. F. (2013). Biomarkers in Schizophrenia: A brief conceptual consideration. *Disease Markers, 35*(1), 3–9.

Weil, A. (1997). *The new Children's Health Insurance Program: Should states expand Medicaid?* New Federalism Series, Paper A-13. Washington, DC: Urban Institute. Retrieved from http://new federalism.urban.org/html/anfall3.htm.

Weiner, J. M. (1996). Managed care and long-term care: The integration of financing and services. *Generations, 20*(2), 47–52.

Weiner, L. Y. (1985). *From working girl to working mother: The female labor force in the United States, 1820–1980*. Chapel Hill: University of North Carolina Press.

Weitzman, L. J., & Maclean, M. (1992). *Economic consequences of divorce: The international perspective*. Oxford, UK: Clarendon Press.

Wells, K. (1995, September). *Proceedings of the NIMH Conference on Service Research*. Washington, DC.

Wexler, D. E., & Winnick, B. J. (1996). *Law in a therapeutic key: Developments in therapeutic jurisprudence*. Durham, NC: Carolina Academic Press.

Whitaker, T., & Arrington, P. (2008). *Social workers at work: NASW membership workforce study*. Washington, DC: NASW. Retrieved from http://workforce.socialworkers.org/studies/SWatWork.pdf (June 10, 2016).

Whitaker, T., Weismiller, T., & Clark, E. (2006). *Assuring the sufficiency of a frontline workforce: A national study of licensed social workers*. Washington, DC: National Association of Social Workers.

White House. (n.d.b.). *A drug policy for the 21st century*. Retrieved from https://www.whitehouse.gov/ondcp/drugpolicyreform (November 27, 2016).

White House. (2014). *Medicare trustees report shows significant improvements for seniors and taxpayers*. Retrieved from https://www.whitehouse.gov/blog/2014/07/28/medicare-trustees-report-shows-significant-improvements-seniors-and-taxpayers (June 15, 2016).

Whiteside, A. (2002). Poverty and HIV/AIDS in Africa. *Third World Quarterly, 23*(2), 313–332.

WHO World Mental Health Survey Consortium. (2004). Prevalence, severity, and unmet need for treatment of mental disorders in the World Health Organization World Mental Health Surveys. *Journal of the American Medical Association, 21*, 2581–2590.

Wiatrowski, W. J. (1993). Factors affecting retirement income. *Monthly Labor Review, 116*(3). Retrieved from http://stats.bls.gov/opub/mlr/1993/03/art2abs.htm.

Wiehe, V. R. (1998). *Understanding family violence: Treating and preventing partner, child, sibling, and elder abuse*. Thousand Oaks, CA: Sage Publications.

Wikander, U., Kessler-Harris, A., & Lewis, J. (1995). *Protecting women: Labor legislation in Europe, the United States, and Australia, 1880–1920.* Urbana: University of Illinois Press.

Willhelm, S. (1970). *Who needs the Negro.* Cambridge, MA: Schenkman.

Williams, D. D. (1993). Barriers to achieving health. *Child and Adolescent Social Work Journal, 10*(5), 355–363.

Williams, J. C., & Feinberg, L. (2012). *Protecting family caregivers from employment discrimination.* AARP Public Policy Institute. Retrieved from http://www.aarp.org/content/dam/aarp/research/public_policy_institute/health/protecting-caregivers-employment-discrimination-insight-AARP-ppi-ltc.pdf (October 27, 2013).

Wilson, C. A. (1996). *Racism: From slavery to advanced capitalism.* Thousand Oaks, CA: Sage.

Wilson, W. J. (1987). *The truly disadvantaged.* Chicago: University of Chicago Press.

Winicki, J. (2003). Children in homes below poverty: Changes in program participation since welfare reform. *Children and Youth Services Review, 25*(8), 651–668.

Wolf, R. S., & Pillemer, K. (1989). *Helping elderly victims: The reality of elder abuse.* New York: Columbia University Press.

Wolfe, B., & Perozek, M. (1997). Teen children's health and health care use. In R. A. Maynard (Ed.), *Kids having kids: Economic costs and social consequences of teen pregnancy* (pp. 181–203). Washington, DC: Urban Institute Press.

Wolfgang, B. (2016). Hillary Clinton's health plan to include a public option. *The Washington Times* (July 10, 2016). Retrieved from http://www.washingtontimes.com/news/2016/jul/10/hillary-clintons-health-plan-to-include-a-public-o/ (October 30, 2016).

Wolfson, Michael C., George A. Kaplan, John W. Lynch, Nancy A. Ross, and Eric Backlund, (1999). Relationship between income inequality and mortality: empirical demonstration. *British Medical Journal, 319*, 953 -55.

Women's Bureau, U.S. Department of Labor. (n.d.). *Facts over time: Women in the labor force.* Retrieved from https://www.dol.gov/wb/stats/facts_over_time.htm#labor (November 13, 2016).

Women's Legal Defense and Education Fund. (2009). *In the first nineteen months of the recession the national TANF caseload increased only 6.6%.* Retrieved from http://www.legalmomentum.org/assets/pdfs/slow-growth-in-tanf-rolls.pdf (July 7, 2010).

Wong, C. M. (2016, February 2). Sweet Cakes by Melissa violated Oregon law by turning away lesbian couple, officials rule. *The Huffington Post.* Retrieved from http://www.huffingtonpost.com/2015/02/03/sweet-cakes-by-melissa-violation-_n_6604526.html (December 6, 2016).

Wood, J. C., & Woods, R. N. (1990). *Milton Friedman critical assessments.* London: Routledge.

WordIQ.com. (n.d.). *Jeane Kirkpatrick.* Retrieved from http://www.wordiq.com/definition/Jeane_Kirkpatrick (July 15, 2010).

World Health Organization. (n.d.a.). *Global health observatory data.* Retrieved from http://www.who.int/gho/hiv/en/ (August 31, 2016).

World Health Organization. (WHO). (n.d.b.). *Safe and unsafe induced abortion: Global and regional levels in 2008 and trends during 1995–2008.* Retrieved from http://apps.who.int/iris/bitstream/10665/75174/1/WHO_RHR_12.02_eng.pdf (September 29, 2013).

World Health Organization. (2002). *World report on violence and health.* Retrieved from http://www .who.mt/violence_injury_prevention/en/ (December 31, 2007).

World Health Organization. (2005). *3 by 5 June 2005 Report.* Retrieved from http://www.who.mt/3by5/progressreport.June2005/en/ (February 12, 2008).

World Health Organization. (2010). *World health statistics: 2010.* Retrieved from http://www.who.int/whosis/whostat/EN_WHS10_Full.pdf (July 13, 2010).

World Health Organization. (2012). *World health statistics: 2012.* Retrieved from http://www.who.int/gho/publications/world_health_statistics/2012/en/ (June 3, 2013).

World Health Organization. (2016). *Global health observatory data repository.* Retrieved from http://apps.who.int/gho/data/node.imr (September 14, 2016).

Wright, M. H. (1928). The removal of the Choctaws to the Indian Territory 1830–1833. *Chronicles of Oklahoma, 6*(2), 103–128.

Yearby, R. (2011). Racial inequities in mortality and access to health care. *Journal of Legal Medicine, 32*(1), 77–91.

Yell, M. L., Rogers, D., & Lodge Rodgers, E. (1998). The legal history of special education. *Remedial and Special Education, 19*(4), 219–228.

Yellow Bird, M. J. (2001). Critical values and First Nations Peoples. In R. Fong & S. Furuto (Eds.), *Culturally competent social work practice: Practice skills, interventions, and evaluation* (pp. 61–74). Boston: Allyn & Bacon.

Youngers, C. A., & Walsh, J. M. (2009). Drug Decriminalization: A trend takes shape. *Americas Quarterly, The Environment (Fall).* Retrieved from http://www.americasquarterly.org/node/978 (November 28, 2016).

Zedlewski, S. R., & Meyer, J. A. (1987). *Toward ending poverty among the elderly and disabled: Policy and financing options.* Washington, DC: Urban Institute.

Zeleny, J., & Rutenberg, J. (2012, November 6). Divided U.S. gives Obama more time. *The New York Times.* Retrieved from http://www.nytimes.com/2012/11/07/us/politics/obama-romney-presidential-election-2012.html?pagewanted=all (January 30, 2013).

Zimmerman, J. (1995). *Tailspin.* New York: Doubleday Books.

Zuckerman, S., Evans, A., & Holahan, J. (1997). *Questions for states as they turn to Medicaid managed care* (Series A, No. A-11). Washington, DC: Urban Institute.

Zweig, M. (2000). *The working class majority: America's best kept secret.* Ithaca, NY: Cornell University Press.

Name Index

Subject Index